Recent Advances and Applications in Alternative Investments

Constantin Zopounidis
Technical University of Crete, Greece & Audencia Business School, France

Dimitris Kenourgios
National and Kapodistrian University of Athens, Greece

George Dotsis
National and Kapodistrian University of Athens, Greece

A volume in the Advances in Finance, Accounting, and Economics (AFAE) Book Series

IGI Global
DISSEMINATOR OF KNOWLEDGE

Published in the United States of America by
IGI Global
Business Science Reference (an imprint of IGI Global)
701 E. Chocolate Avenue
Hershey PA, USA 17033
Tel: 717-533-8845
Fax: 717-533-8661
E-mail: cust@igi-global.com
Web site: http://www.igi-global.com

Library of Congress Cataloging-in-Publication Data

Names: Zopounidis, Constantin, editor. | Kenourgios, Dimitris, 1973- editor. | Dotsis, George, 1976- editor.
Title: Recent advances and applications in alternative investments / Constantin Zopounidis, Dimitris Kenourgios, and George Dotsis, editors.
Description: Hershey : Business Science Reference, 2020. | Includes bibliographical references and index. | Summary: “”This book explores theoretical and empirical advances and applications in alternative investments”--Provided by publisher”-- Provided by publisher.
Identifiers: LCCN 2019039275 (print) | LCCN 2019039276 (ebook) | ISBN 9781799824367 (hardcover) | ISBN 9781799824374 (paperback) | ISBN 9781799824381 (ebook)
Subjects: LCSH: Investments. | Asset allocation. | Investment analysis.
Classification: LCC HG4521 .R364 2020 (print) | LCC HG4521 (ebook) | DDC 332.63--dc23
LC record available at https://lccn.loc.gov/2019039275
LC ebook record available at https://lccn.loc.gov/2019039276

This book is published in the IGI Global book series Advances in Finance, Accounting, and Economics (AFAE) (ISSN: 2327-5677; eISSN: 2327-5685)

British Cataloguing in Publication Data
A Cataloguing in Publication record for this book is available from the British Library.

For electronic access to this publication, please contact: eresources@igi-global.com.

Advances in Finance, Accounting, and Economics (AFAE) Book Series

ISSN:2327-5677
EISSN:2327-5685

Editor-in-Chief: Ahmed Driouchi, Al Akhawayn University, Morocco

MISSION

In our changing economic and business environment, it is important to consider the financial changes occurring internationally as well as within individual organizations and business environments. Understanding these changes as well as the factors that influence them is crucial in preparing for our financial future and ensuring economic sustainability and growth.

The **Advances in Finance, Accounting, and Economics (AFAE)** book series aims to publish comprehensive and informative titles in all areas of economics and economic theory, finance, and accounting to assist in advancing the available knowledge and providing for further research development in these dynamic fields.

COVERAGE

- Health Economics
- Macroeconomics
- Applied Finance
- Microfinance
- Economic Theory
- E-Accounting
- Economics of Agriculture and Biotechnology
- Internet Banking
- Economic Indices and Quantitative Economic Methods
- Wages and Employment

IGI Global is currently accepting manuscripts for publication within this series. To submit a proposal for a volume in this series, please contact our Acquisition Editors at Acquisitions@igi-global.com or visit: http://www.igi-global.com/publish/.

The Advances in Finance, Accounting, and Economics (AFAE) Book Series (ISSN 2327-5677) is published by IGI Global, 701 E. Chocolate Avenue, Hershey, PA 17033-1240, USA, www.igi-global.com. This series is composed of titles available for purchase individually; each title is edited to be contextually exclusive from any other title within the series. For pricing and ordering information please visit http://www.igi-global.com/book-series/advances-finance-accounting-economics/73685. Postmaster: Send all address changes to above address.

Titles in this Series

For a list of additional titles in this series, please visit:
http://www.igi-global.com/book-series/advances-finance-accounting-economics/73685

Mapping, Managing, and Crafting Sustainable Business Strategies for the Circular Economy
Susana Serrano Rodrigues (Polytechnic Institute of Leiria, Portugal) Paulo Jorge Almeida (Polytechnic Institute of Leiria, Portugal) and Nuno Miguel Castaheira Almeida (Polytechnic Institute of Leiria, Portugal)
Business Science Reference • © 2020 • 280pp • H/C (ISBN: 9781522598855) • US $195.00

Growth and Emerging Prospects of International Islamic Banking
Abdul Rafay (University of Management and Technology, Pakistan)
Business Science Reference • © 2020 • 500pp • H/C (ISBN: 9781799816119) • US $215.00

Economics, Business, and Islamic Finance in ASEAN Economics Community
Patricia Ordoñez de Pablos (The University of Oviedo, Spain) Mohammad Nabil Almunawar (Universiti Brunei Darussalam, Brunei) and Muhamad Abduh (Universiti Brunei Darussalam, Brunei)
Business Science Reference • © 2020 • 374pp • H/C (ISBN: 9781799822578) • US $215.00

Handbook of Research on Theory and Practice of Global Islamic Finance
Abdul Rafay (University of Management and Technology, Pakistan)
Business Science Reference • © 2020 • 888pp • H/C (ISBN: 9781799802181) • US $445.00

Challenges and Impacts of Religious Endowments on Global Economics and Finance
Buerhan Saiti (Istanbul Sabahattin Zaim University, Turkey) and Adel Sarea (Ahlia University, Bahrain)
Business Science Reference • © 2020 • 350pp • H/C (ISBN: 9781799812456) • US $225.00

Regional Trade and Development Strategies in the Era of Globalization
Akhilesh Chandra Prabhakar (Lovely Professional University, India) Gurpreet Kaur (Lovely Professional University, India) and Vasilii Erokhin (Harbin Engineering University, China)
Business Science Reference • © 2020 • 325pp • H/C (ISBN: 9781799817307) • US $225.00

For an entire list of titles in this series, please visit:
http://www.igi-global.com/book-series/advances-finance-accounting-economics/73685

IGI Global
DISSEMINATOR OF KNOWLEDGE

701 East Chocolate Avenue, Hershey, PA 17033, USA
Tel: 717-533-8845 x100 • Fax: 717-533-8661
E-Mail: cust@igi-global.com • www.igi-global.com

Table of Contents

Detailed Table of Contents

This chapter presents empirical evidence showing the impact of economic uncertainty and monetary policy on the volatility of commodity futures markets. The findings are in line with those of the relevant literature according to which rising uncertainty predicts rising volatility in commodity markets. The author shows that the unobservable economic uncertainty measures of Jurado et al. (2015) have a significant and long-lasting positive impact on the volatility of commodity prices. Hence, the OLS regression results show that commodity markets are significantly affected by the rising degree of unpredictability in the macroeconomy, while they are relatively immune to observable macroeconomic fluctuations. The expansionary monetary policy is followed by rising volatility in agricultural and energy markets, while it has much smaller effect on the volatility of metals markets. Financialization in commodity markets has increased the dynamic linkages between monetary policy shocks and commodity price volatility.

This chapter investigates the correlations between conventional and alternative investments during the quantitative easing (QE) programs launched by the U.S. Federal Reserve. Authors focus on different asset classes to examine the dynamics on their correlations and to highlight alternative investment options for rational investors and policy makers. Their analysis covers the period from January 3, 2005 to March

16, 2018. Research has significant policy implications and the empirical findings indicate a ripple effect of QE across conventional and alternative investments and suggest that their correlations differ by QE periods. Researchers also confirm the effectiveness of the portfolio rebalance channel pictured on specific assets' correlation sign, as well as the existence of specific patterns. UMP programs create portfolio rebalance since investors followed the required path set by the Fed.

This study describes the emergence and the structure of Real Estate Investment Trusts (REITs) and investigates whether European REITs provide higher risk-adjusted returns and portfolio diversification benefits relative to the market portfolio. The top public listed companies of five (5) established (Belgium, France, Germany, Netherlands, UK), three (3) emerging (Italy, Spain, Ireland) and one (1) nascent (Greece) European REIT markets, are considered over period 2007 – 2018. The empirical findings denote poor performance of most European REITS over the Global Financial Crisis period but strong risk adjusted returns, overall, outperforming the equivalent European stock market indices and bonds over the first years of post - GFC period. In the recent period (2015 – 2018), most European REITs continued to deliver positive but modest risk adjusted returns relative to the previous period. The analysis provides evidence of poor portfolio diversification benefits and weak cross country diversification benefits among the European REITs.

This chapter investigates the impact of the Global Financial Crisis and the European Sovereign Debt Crisis in ETFs across regions and segments. In particular, two tests are taking place, with the first one to examine if there is evidence of contagion effect and the second one to test the affection of risks in each pair of ETFs. The evidence across the stable period and the two crisis periods suggests the existence of the transmission of shocks from the Global Financial ETF to regional and sectoral

ETFs. However, there is evidence that some of the ETFs remain less unaffected during both crises and some of them are immune. Moreover, the authors examine the impact of several control variables, which represent various risks, to the correlation of each pair of ETFs and the results show the influence of the interest rate risk and interbank liquidity risk during the Global Financial Crisis and the European Sovereign Debt Crisis.

In this study, authors investigate the possibility of contagion/safe haven effects during the Global Financial Crisis (GFC) of 2007-2009 for two exotic assets: rare coins and wine lvx50. The data sample is monthly comprising a rare coins and wine lvx50 indices, as well as MSCI (Morgan Stanley Capital Index) World financial index as a benchmark for world financial sector, spanning from 2000 until 2016. According to Baur and Lucey (2010) an asset may be characterized as safe haven, by the following definition: "A safe haven is defined as an asset that is uncorrelated or negatively correlated with another asset or portfolio in times of market stress or turmoil". Employing a bivariate GARCH (1,1)-DCC model, authors uncover significant evidence of contagion effects among the MSCI World Financial and wine lvx50, while the pair MSCI World Financial and rare coins show a safe haven behaviour. These findings confirm a specific pattern of contagious and safe haven behaviors that provide important implications for international investors.

This chapter investigates the impact of central banks' unconventional monetary policies on sectors of unique and traditional alternative investments beyond the stock market. More specifically, authors examine how quantitative easing (QE) programs, imposed by the FED and the ECB during the financial crisis, affected the fine wine market and rare coins in comparison with real estate, commodities, and crude oil. The methodology used in this chapter includes multiple regression analysis. As dependent variables, the LVX 50 Index, the Rare Coin Values Index, the REIT Index, the CRB Commodity Index and the Crude Oil Futures Index, are used for each sector respectively. Our empirical analysis shows that the QE programs applied had different outcomes between our sample markets. Thus, investors should evaluate the signals associated with the announcements of prospective monetary policies in their attempt to achieve a sufficient portfolio diversification and to harvest superior returns at the same time.

Traditionally, the gold has been approved as a safe-haven investment after the collapse of Breton Woods. The global investors especially prefer to rebalance their portfolios by purchasing gold or its derivatives during financial crises. This research explores realized dynamic linkages between gold and the advanced stock market indices, after the end of the 2008 economic recession. This chapter used the fractionally co-integrated ECM by utilizing intraday data from 2013 and thereafter. The empirical outcomes support that there is a negative-realized dynamics between the advanced stock markets and the gold's price in the short and in the long run. Specifically, the short-term dynamics of gold's price seems to be higher on the French and Japanese stock market indices. Lastly, the long-term dynamics of gold's price seems to be higher on the Dow Jones and the FTSE100.

Regulators were the only institution who set the electricity prices, including costs of transmission, distribution, and generation. Nowadays, this has changed. Electricity prices are determined by the fundamental economic rule of supply and demand. The forthcoming work examines a potential relationship between electricity price and fuel mix. The authors use the Nordic System's electricity prices and generation. They conclude that hydropower and nuclear power plays a vital role in the futures energy mix and in the stability of electricity prices. A spillover effect is detected between electricity prices and fuel mix, but a need for further research is recommended.

"Algos" are algorithmic trading strategies that are meant to optimize the execution quality of the trades in terms of transaction costs and market-timing. This chapter presents the transaction costs taxonomy and popular algorithmic execution strategies. Authors empirically examine a dataset of hedge fund transactions. Our results suggest that implicit transaction costs are characterized by a significant buy-sell asymmetry. To get some insight about the possible determinants of Implicit Transaction Costs, authors investigate the algo type and stock characteristics such as market capitalization, relative volume, inverse prior close, price momentum, buy indicator and trade duration. Both in-sample and out-of-sample tests show that a significant portion of transaction costs can be anticipated before the trade execution. Results show that high-level execution strategies can be constructed to optimize the algo choice.

Over the past two decades, the diffusion of technological innovations introduced to the finance industry has been inconceivable. Internet, at the end of the 20th century, brought e-commerce, later e-payments, and more recently, e-money. Such innovations in digital world increase the impact on the business world, and so might do cryptocurrencies, currently spreading out across the globe. To this end, this chapter builds up an across-the-board synthesis of current investment trends and analysis, aiming to lead a way forward for research on this uncharted breed of alternative finance assets looming anew.

Crowdfunding is an innovative fin-tech mechanism for financing sustainable development. As this chapter demonstrates, crowdfunding can prove to be a powerful tool for financial inclusion, as it opens up funding possibilities for stakeholders, activities, and projects which would not be able to tap funding through the banking

a comprehensive and up-to-date review of the extant literature, useful for academics and practitioners with little or significant experience in the Islamic finance sector.

Preface

Assets under management in alternative investment vehicles have growth significantly during the last two decades. Alternative investments provide the opportunity to enhance portfolio diversification and harvest risk premiums that are not available in traditional asset classes like stocks, bonds and cash. There has been a surge of investment opportunities in alternative asset classes like commodities, real estate, cryptocurrencies, hedge funds, gold, rare coins, wine and a plethora of new financial products that offer to investors the opportunity to be exposed to alternative risk factors. Some of the alternative investments are not only available to institutional or specialized investors but are gradually becoming available to retail investors through various collective investment schemes.

The emergence of this new asset class is changing rapidly the investment field and has created the need to better understand the mechanics and risk-return tradeoffs of alternative investments. Alternative investments offer new opportunities to investors but also pose some significant challenges. The main objective of this book is to promote scientific research in the field of alternative investments and to help academics, finance professionals and policy makers to understand the recent developments in alternative asset classes, new products and investment strategies and new types of risk.

This handbook covers a wide spectrum of themes in alternative investments and we hope that the readers will find the material useful for understanding the underlying economics of various assets collectively known as alternative investments.

The scope of the chapter "Investing in Commodities in Times of Uncertainty and Lax Monetary Policy" is to present some stylized facts about commodity market volatility in times of uncertainty and expansionary monetary policy before and after the commodity financialization period. The author highlights some possible implications for investing in commodities in times of macroeconomic turbulence and lax monetary policy and addresses important questions like: is it optimal to invest in commodities in times of rising or falling uncertainty in the economy? Is the expansionary monetary policy followed by increasing or decreasing volatility in commodity futures markets? Has financialization increased or decreased the sensitivity of commodity markets to uncertainty and interest rate shocks?

The aim of the chapter "FED's Unconventional Monetary Policy and Correlation Dynamics Among Conventional and Alternative Investments" is to study the dynamics across conventional and alternative investment asset classes during the unconventional monetary policy programs implemented by the FED and to examine the existence of a portfolio rebalance channel. The authors use cross asset correlations to quantify the impact of central bank asset purchases on investors' portfolios and their empirical results provide a valuable guide to portfolio managers during times of unconventional monetary policy measures.

Real estate is a distinct asset class with its own idiosyncratic characteristics. The chapter "The Return Performance of Real Estate Investment Trusts (REITs) and Portfolio Diversification Benefits: Evidence From the European Market" investigates the return performance of real estate investment trusts (REITs) and their portfolio diversification benefits. The authors' empirical analysis concentrates in the European market and covers the time period 2007–2018.

Investments in exchange traded funds (ETFs) are constantly attracting huge amounts of capital, mainly from institutional investors. The purpose of the chapter "On Financial Contagion Through ETFs" is to shed light on contagion effects through ETFs, by investigating how a Global Financial ETF can transmit shocks to sectoral and regional ETFs during crisis periods. The authors discuss the implications of their empirical results with respect to portfolio management and investments in ETFs.

The chapter "Are Exotic Assets Contagious? Evidence From the Global Financial Crisis of 2007-2009" focuses on the impact of the global financial crisis (2007-2009) on rare coins and wine. The authors investigate empirically the time-varying conditional correlations of monthly changes in rare coins and wine indices and test for contagion effects in equity and currency markets.

The purpose of the chapter "The Impact of Unconventional Monetary Policies on Unique Alternative Investments: The Case of Fine Wine and Rare Coins" is to evaluate the effect of central banks' unconventional monetary policies on sectors of unique and traditional alternative investments beyond the stock market. In particular, the authors investigate the impact of QE, implemented by the FED and ECB during the financial crisis, on wine market, rare coins, real estate, commodities and crude oil. The aim of this chapter is to compare the effect of QE programs on unique alternative investments with the effect on traditional ones. Given the remarkable growth of alternative investing over the last decades, this comparison is essential in order to verify how unique alternative markets react in relation to traditional ones, especially in turbulent time periods when financial stability is at stake.

Gold is traditionally seen as a safe haven, especially during time of severe economic downturns. In the chapter "Gold's Price and Advanced Stock Markets: A

Post-Crisis Approach," the authors explores the realized dynamic linkages between gold's price and various international stock market indices and discuss how their relationship has evolved after the eruption of the global financial crisis in 2008.

The liberalization of energy markets has created a new asset class with come distinctive characteristics. The chapter "Spillover Volatility Between Fuel Mix and Electricity Prices" focuses on the relationship between the volatility of fuel mix and electricity prices. The authors use data from the Nordic Electricity System to examine the volatility of electricity prices and the relationship of electricity risk with various sources of electric power production. The results in this chapter are useful for managing electricity price risk.

Transaction costs are an important component of the performance of alternative investments. The chapter "Algorithmic Trading and Transaction Costs" presents a statistical-based framework for monitoring transaction costs. The authors present an overview of algorithmic trading and of the related transaction cost measures. They estimate the impact of transaction costs and propose heuristics that can be used for the improvement of trade execution strategies. As a case study, they empirically analyze the transaction costs of two long-short equity hedge funds and use regression-based models to investigate possible determinants of implicit trading costs.

Cryptocurrencies are becoming increasingly popular as an alternative asset class. Despite the rapid growth of cryptocurrency markets, investors still do not fully understand this new asset class. The chapter "Innovation Finance Beyond Bitcoin: Cryptocurrencies as Alternative Investments" addresses some fundamental questions regarding the nature, the use and the historical evolution of cryptocurrencies. The author provides an empirical analysis of cryptocurrencies' statistical behavior and discusses the use of cryptocurrencies in the construction of optimal portfolios.

Crowdfunding is an innovative fintech mechanism for raising capital and provides investors the opportunity to diversify portfolios and target higher returns. The chapter "Crowdfunding: An Innovative Instrument for Development Finance and Financial Inclusion" reviews crowdfunding and highlights its potential for credit provision to SMEs as opposed to traditional financing mechanism. The authors discuss the implications of crowdfunding for social ventures and financial inclusion and present a case study of a Greek crowdfunding platform.

The purpose of the chapter "A Bibliometric Analysis of Ethical Investments (EI) Research: Alternative Investments" is to present the evolution of academic research in Ethical Investments (EI) research between 1990 and 2019. The authors develop a general overview of the leading journals in EI research, which leads to the development of a future research agenda for bibliometric analysis. The survey covers all main areas of Social Sciences, Business, Management and Accounting, Economics, Econometrics and Finance as well as Decision Sciences and its connections with other analytical fields.

The distinct profile of Islamic banks, and Islamic finance in general, is of particular relevance to investors, as it enhances their diversification opportunities particularly during time of financial crises. The author of the chapter "Islamic Finance" provides an overview of the historical evolution of Islamic banking, provides a comprehensive review of Islamic financial instruments and discusses empirical studies that compare Islamic and conventional banks with respect to two major issues in banking, namely financial risk and efficiency.

Chapter 1
Investing in Commodities in Times of Uncertainty and Lax Monetary Policy

Athanasios Triantafyllou
https://orcid.org/0000-0002-0711-9851
University of Essex, UK

ABSTRACT

This chapter presents empirical evidence showing the impact of economic uncertainty and monetary policy on the volatility of commodity futures markets. The findings are in line with those of the relevant literature according to which rising uncertainty predicts rising volatility in commodity markets. The author shows that the unobservable economic uncertainty measures of Jurado et al. (2015) have a significant and long-lasting positive impact on the volatility of commodity prices. Hence, the OLS regression results show that commodity markets are significantly affected by the rising degree of unpredictability in the macroeconomy, while they are relatively immune to observable macroeconomic fluctuations. The expansionary monetary policy is followed by rising volatility in agricultural and energy markets, while it has much smaller effect on the volatility of metals markets. Financialization in commodity markets has increased the dynamic linkages between monetary policy shocks and commodity price volatility.

DOI: 10.4018/978-1-7998-2436-7.ch001

INTRODUCTION

Commodity markets are the the oldest kind of market and it is believed to have originated many centuries ago at around 4500BC. The reason for the ancient roots of the first commodity market, is that commodity markets were originally physical markets (a market in which people trade manufactured products such as wheat, sugar and gold). For this reason, commodity prices were primarily driven by the laws of sypply and demand (for commodities). As time went by, commodity markets, while being dominated by traditional market participants (commodity producers and commodity consumers), they have become more sophisticated. For example, the first well organized futures market was a market for copper futures contracts. Commodity futures and options markets were initially used for commodity producers and consumers as methods to hedge their price risk. For example, wheat producers could take a short position in wheat futures markets and hedge their price risk exposure they would otherwise have when trading at the wheat physical (spot) market (since via the futures market, they have an agreement to sell their commodity at a pre-specified price in a pre-specified date in the future (at maturity of the futures contract)).

Although commodity spot markets and commodity derivative markets have long worked as markets used solely by commodity producers and consumers, this is no longer the case for the majority of agricultural, metals and energy commodity markets. Since early 2000s, a large inflow of funds (like hedge funds and pension funds) has increased presence to commodity markets. Since early 2000s, a large inflow of funds (like hedge funds and pension funds) has increased presence to commodity markets, for example, according to Commodity Futures Trading Commission, the institutional holdings in commodity futures have increased from \$15 billion in 2003 to over \$200 billion in 2008. Hence, a large part of commodity markets is by now composed by institutional investors and not by traditional commodity market participants. The financialization of commodity markets has made structural changes in the nature and in the way commodity prices are determined. Since the early 2000s, the large inflow of funds and the increased presence of financial investors to commodity markets have transformed them into a separate asset class which has become more integrated to the rest of the financial markets (Basak & Pavlova, 2016; Cheng & Xiong, 2013; Irwin & Sanders, 2012; Silvennoinen & Thorp, 2015). The financialization and the further globalization of commodities has already given commodities a dual property: they an be a real asset (when held by commodity producers, investors and consumers) and a financial asset (when being part of the portfolio of investment banks, hedge funds, pension funds etc.). The effect of financialization on commodity prices and volatility is of crucial importance for traditional commodity market participants like commodity producers and investors. Moreover, volatility in commodity futures markets is singificant for non-conventional commodity market participants like hedge funds who use commodity derivatives for hedging or speculation purposes. For example, the key determinant of commodity option prices whose price is directly related to the volatility of the underlying commodity futures contracts[1].

The scope of this chapter is to present some stylized facts about commodity market volatility in times of uncertainty and expansionary monetary policy before and after the financialization (of commodities) period, and ultimately, to highlight some possible implications for investing in commodities in times of macroeconomic turbulence and lax monetary policy. For example, is it optimal to invest in commodities in times of rising or falling uncertainty in the economy? Is the expansionary monetary policy followed by increasing or decreasing volatility in commodity futures markets? Has financialization increased or decreased the sensitivity of commodity markets to uncertainty and interest rate shocks? The literature so far has identified an excess co-movement in agricultural, metals and energy commodity prices and has attributed this co-movement is correlated with macroeconomic fluctuations (Alquist et al., 2019; Byrne *et al.*, 2013; Delle Chiaie *et al.*, 2017; Pindyck & Rotemberg, 1990; Yin & Han, 2015; among others). Frankel and Rose (2010) claim that there are times when nearly all commodity prices move together towards the same direction, that it is difficult to ignore macroeconomic phenomena when searching for the determinants of commodity prices. Another strand of the literature has shown the significant role of monetary policy shocks and of interest rates on commodity prices (Frankel, 2008; Frankel & Rose, 2010; Frankel & Hardouvelis, 1985; Gordon & Rowenhorst, 2006; Gilbert, 2010; Gospodinov & Ng, 2013; Gubler & Hertweck, 2013; Triantafyllou & Dotsis, 2017; among others). For example, Frankel and Rose (2010) attribute the synchronous boom in commodity prices during the 2006-2008 period to the low interest rate environment and the lax monetary policy deployed by the Fed during this period[2].

While there is a vast amount in the literature showing the macroeconomic determinants of commodity prices, there is still limited empirical evidence showing the existence of common macroeconomic factors driving the time varying volatility in commodity markets. Some recent empirical studies have identified the role of macroeconomic factors, monetary policy and economic uncertainty as determinants of commodity price volatility in agricultural, metals and energy markets (Bakas & Triantafyllou, 2018; Karali & Power, 2013; Joets *et al.,* 2016; Prokopczuk *et al.,* 2019; Triantafyllou & Dotsis, 2017; Watugala, 2015; West & Wong, 2014; Van Robays, 2016)[3]. The primary implication of these studies is that investors must turn their attention to commodity option strategies (investing or betting on volatility by taking long positions in commodity option markets) in times of rising uncertainty in the macroeconomy. The recent empirical literature in the field has shown that the underlying macroeconomic conditions can act as early warning signals for investing (or disinvesting) in commodities.

This chapter, motivated by the recent empirical studies of the relevant literature on commodity price volatility, provides some preliminary empirical evidence showing that economic uncertainty has a positive impact on the volatility of agricultural (corn, cotton, soybeans, wheat), energy (crude oil, heating oil, petroleum, gasoline) and metals (copper, gold, silver, platinum) commodity futures markets. In more detail, in this chapter presents the findings of OLS forecasting regression models on commodity price volatility using various measures of economic uncertainty as explanatory variables.

Among all the different types of uncertainty shocks, the unobservable (latent) macroeconomic and financial uncertainty measures of Jurado *et al.* (2015) have the most significant effect and explain the largest part of time varying volatility in commodity markets. Jurado *et al.* (2015) estimate macroeconomic and financial uncertainty as the purely unforecastable (by economic agents) component of fluctuations in the US macroeconomy and financial markets respectively given all the available information the time the forecast is being made[4]. Hence, the findings of this chapter implicitly show that commodity market volatility is more heavily impacted by the rising degree of uncertainty (or unpredictability) regarding economic fluctuations and not by observable macroeconomic disturbances instead. In order for the effect of financialization (which occurred at early 2000s) on the economic uncertainty- commodity price volatility relationship to be examined, the OLS regression analysis is performed over the pore-2004 and the post-2004 period during which the financialization of commodity markets has been taken place. By this way, the subsample analysis tests whether the dynamic interactions between commodity market volatility and economic uncertainty have changed in magnitude during the post-financialization era period. The econometric results indicate that the impact of uncertainty shocks has exponentially increased during the post-financialization era. This shows that financialization of commodity markets, in addition of transforming the them into a separate financial asset class, it has increased the structural interconnections between uncertainty shocks and commodity market volatility.

Finally, the dynamic response of the volatility of agricultural, metals and energy market to monetary policy shocks is estimated. The VAR analysis shows that a one standard deviation negative shock in the Fed fund rate (expansionary monetary policy) increases the volatility in energy commodity markets. The positive impact of expansionary monetary policy shocks on energy price volatility is more than two times larger and more long-lasting when estimating the VAR models for the post-financialization (post-2004) period. Interestingly, the VAR analysis is the first evidence showing that for agricultural commodity markets, the impact of expansionary monetary policy shocks has turned from positive and insignificant during the pre-financialization period, to positive and significant during the post-financialization period. These results show that, for agricultural and energy commodity futures markets, financialization has resulted to tighter linkages between expansionary monetary policy shocks and commodity price volatility. Although the lax monetary policy results to falling stock-market volatility and risk aversion in the equity market (Bekaert et al., 2013; David & Veronesi, 2014), it has exactly opposite effects on agricultural and energy commodity markets. These results are a first preliminary indication that during periods of expansionary monetary policy, a profitable strategy for commodity investors is to go long in volatility in agricultural and energy futures markets (e.g. by taking long positions in straddles using commodity options in their portfolio) and short in equity volatility (e.g. by taking short positions in straddles composed by equity options). On the other hand, the VAR analysis shows a rather weak and transitory impact of monetary policy shocks on the volatility of metals commodity markets. These results are in line with those of the literature who still fails to identify whether the impact of expansionary monetary policy shocks on the volatility of metals commodity markets (like gold, copper and silver) is positive or negative (Hamoudeh & Yuan, 2008).

DATA AND METHODOLOGY

Commodity Futures and Macroeconomic Data

The time series dataset has monthly frequency and covers the period from January 1988 till December 2016. For the estimation of the monthly realized variance in commodity futures markets, the daily prices of the S&P GSCI indices on commodity futures have been used. More specifically, we use the daily prices of the broad commodity nearby futures index and the prices of agricultural, energy and metals commodity S&P GSCI commodity futures. The cross section of agricultural commodities includes corn, cotton, soybeans and wheat, the cross-section of energy commodities includes crude oil, heating oil, petroleum and unleaded gasoline and the cross-section of metals commodities includes gold, silver, copper and platinum. All the S&P GSCI daily commodity price series are downloaded from Datastream.

The unobserved (latent) measures of macroeconomic uncertainty (MU) and Financial Uncertainty (FU) are based on the methodology of Jurado *et al.* (2015). The measures of Jurado *et al.* (2015) are downloaded from: https://www.sydneyludvigson.com/data-and-appendixes. In the econometric analysis the 3-month ahead macroeconomic uncertainty (MU3) and financial uncertainty (FU3) measures have been utilized. Thus, the MU and FU time series correspond to the MU3 and FU3 estimated uncertainty series of Jurado et *al.* (2015)[5]. One alternative widely accepted measure of economic uncertainty is the Economic Policy Uncertainty (EPU) measure of Baker *et al.* (2016), according to which economic uncertainty is proxied by the uncertainty about economic policy which can be quantified by using the uncertainty related economic news of newspaper articles. The time series for the Economic Policy Uncertainty (EPU) (and its components which is fiscal policy uncertainty (EPUFISC), monetary policy uncertainty (EPUMON) and uncertainty about news about economic policy (EPUNEWS) are downloaded by the EPU website available at: http://www.policyuncertainty.com. The econometric models include some other widely accepted measures of economic uncertainty like the monthly time series of the VXO index, the Realized Variance of the daily returns of the S&P 500 stock-market index (SP500RV) and the level of Financial Regulation Uncertainty (FRU). The daily series of the S&P 500 index and the monthly FRU and VXO time series are downloaded from Datastream. Moreover, the multivariate regresion analysis includes US macroeconomic variables which are closely related with US economic activity like the US effective exchange rate, the US Industrial Production Index, the US Employment rate and the the slope of the term structure (TERM) which is the difference between the 10-year US government bond yield and the 3-month US-Treasury Bill rate[6].

Realized Variance in Commodity Markets

Volatility in commodity markets is estimated as the monthly Realized Variance (RV) of the daily returns of commodity futures. The monthly Realized Variance *(RV)* is estimated for the broad commodity market index and for the individual commodities as the variance of the daily returns of commodity futures for each monthly period. Following Ferderer (1996) and Wang *et al.* (2012), the monthly RV series for each commodity futures contract are constructed by computing for each monthly period the variance of the daily returns of GSCI commodity futures. The realized variance is calculated according to **Equation (1)** below:

$$RV_{t,T} = \frac{1}{T}\sum_{i=1}^{T}\left(\frac{F_{t+i}-F_{t+i-1}}{F_{t+i-1}} - \overline{\frac{F_{t+i}-F_{t+i-1}}{F_{t+i-1}}}\right)^2, \tag{1}$$

In Equation (1) F_t is the nearby commodity futures price on trading day *t*. $RV_{t,T}$ is the estimated realized variance for each monthly period *(t,T)*. The realized variance is then multiplied by 252 (the number of trading days for one calendar year) in order to be annualized ($COMRV = RV_{t,T} * 252$).

2.3 OLS Regression Models

For the estimation of the impact of latent financial and macroeconomic uncertainty shocks on commodity price volatility, we estimate a set of OLS regression models on commodity RV using different proxies of economic uncertainty as explanatory variables in the right-hand side of the regression equation. In order to measure the different impact of alternative measures of economic uncertainty, we estimate a bivariate regression model of the form given below:

$$COMRV_t = b_0 + b_1 MU_t + \varepsilon_t \tag{2}$$

Where COMRV is the realized variance of the GSCI commodity price index and MUS is the latent macroeconomic uncertainty factor of Jurado *et al.* (2015). In order to compare the impact of other alternative uncertainty measures on commodity price volatility, we estimate the same bivariate regression model using alternative measures of economic uncertainty in the right-hand side of the regression equation. More specifically, we use FU, EPU EPUMON, EPUFISC and EPUNEWS, FRU, SP500RV and VXO in the left hand side of the regression equation. In order to examine the predictive information content of alternative uncertainty measures, we estimate predictive regressions using lagged (instead of contemporaneous) time series in the right-hand side of the regression equation.

We finally estimate a multivariate regression model in which we control for various macroeconomic factors which are closely related with commodity price fluctuations like industrial production and the term spread (Karali & Power, 2013; Gordon *et al.*, 2012; among others). The multivariate OLS regression model is given in Equation (5) below:

$$COMRV_t = b_0 + b_1 SP500RET_t + b_2 TERM_t + b_3 EMPL_t + b_4 IPI_t + b_5 MU_t + \varepsilon_t \tag{3}$$

In equation (5) SP500RET is the monthly returns of S&P500 equity index, TERM is the slope (term spread) of the US Treasury yield curve (namely the difference between the 10-year US government bond yield and the 3-month maturity US Treasury bill rate), EMPL is the growth of the US employment rate, IPI is the growth of US Industrial production index, and MU is the latent uncertainty factor. We estimate the same set of multivariate regression models using alternative measures of economic uncertainty (instead of MU). Finally, in order to examine the effect of financialization on our relationship between uncertainty and commodity price volatility, we estimate the same set of bivariate and multivariate regression models for the post-financialization period (January 2004-December 2016 sample).

2.4 VAR Model

The literature on commodity prices and monetary policy utilized the standard VAR analysis to identify the significant role of monetary policy shocks on commodity prices (Frankel, 1984; Order & Fackler, 1989; among others). In this section we describe the respective VAR models used for the estimation of the impact of monetary policy shocks on commodity price volatility. Since a total of 12 commodities are included in the analysis, a respective number of 12 bivariate VARs is estimated using the Fed funds rate (FFR) and the monthly Realized Variance (RV) of commodity returns as endogenous variables in the VAR model. Following the approach of Bekaert *et al.* (2013), the Fed fund rate is the first endogenous variable and commodity RV (COMRV) is the second endogenous variable in the VAR ordering. The reduced form VAR model is given in **Equation (2)** below:

$$Y_t = A_0 + A_1 Y_{t-1} + \ldots + A_k Y_{t-k} + \varepsilon_t \tag{4}$$

Where A_0 is a vector of constants, A_1 to A_k are matrices of coefficients and ε_t is the vector of serially uncorrelated disturbances, with zero mean and variance-covariance matrix $E(\varepsilon_t, \varepsilon_t^{'}) = \sigma_\varepsilon^2 I$. The Schwartz optimal-lag length information criterion suggests 2 lags the bivariate VAR models (hence k=2)[7]. Y_t is the vector of endogenous variables given in **Equation (3)** below:

$$Y_t = [FFR_t\ COMRV_t] \tag{5}$$

Where FFR is the monthly level of the Fed funds rate and COMRV is the monthly realized variance of the daily returns of agricultural, metals and energy commodity futures analytically described in Subsection 2.2.

ECONOMETRIC ANALYSIS

3.1 Descriptive Statistics

This section presents the results on the relationship between macroeconomic and financial uncertainty and commodity price volatility. The **Figures 1** and **2** below show the synchronous movements of the time series of the monthly Realized Variance

Figure 1. Commodity price volatility and macroeconomic uncertainty

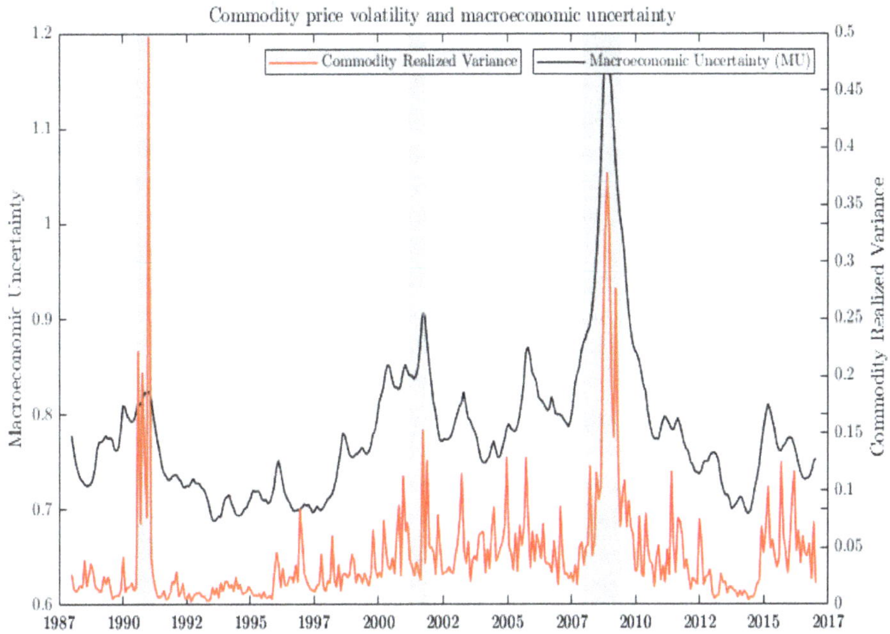

(RV) of the broad GSCI commodity futures price index and the Macroeconomic Uncertainty (MU) and Financial Uncertainty (FU).

This figure shows the monthly between macroeconomic uncertainty and the realized variance of the GSCI commodity futures index)

This figure shows the monthly between financial uncertainty and the realized variance of the GSCI commodity futures index).

Figures 1 and 2 show that the rapid rises in latent macroeconomic uncertainty (MU) are being followed by sudden spikes in the Realized Variance of the commodity price index and that the realizations of large shocks in the RV (e.g the 2008-2009 commodity volatility episode) coincides with heightened uncertainty in the US macroeconomy. In general, it can also be observed that spikes in commodity price volatility occur during US recessions during which uncertainty about future economic conditions reaches always a local maximum. **Figure 2** shows the respective contemporaneous time series movements of the Financial Uncertainty (FU) index and the RV in the commodity price index. The relationship between FU and commodity price RV is nearly the same with MU and RV, but there are some increases in the FU index which are not being followed by analogous jumps of the RV of commodity price

Figure 2. Commodity price volatility and financial uncertainty

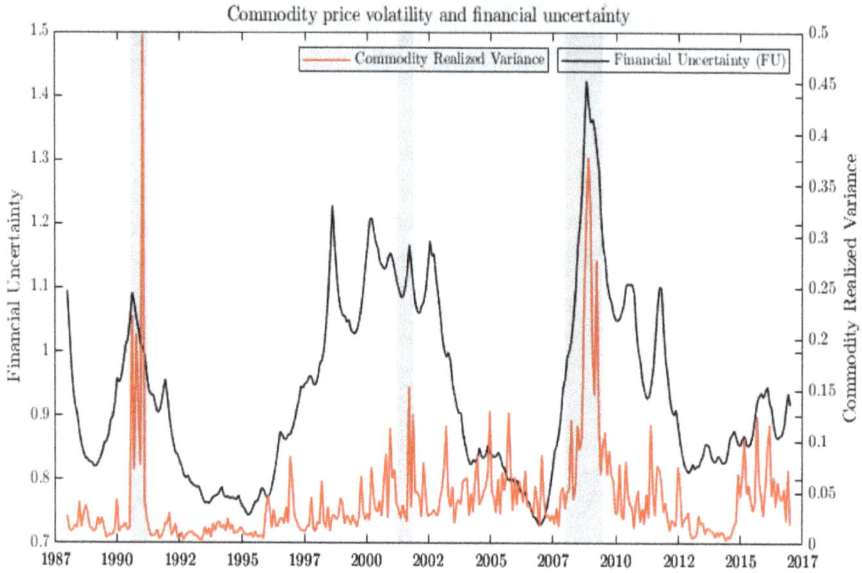

index. **Figure 3** shows the time series of individual commodity price volatility for agricultural, metals and energy markets.

This figure shows the monthly Realized Variance (RV) of the daily returns of agricultural, metals and energy commodity futures markets.

From **Figure 3** it can be observed that the co-movement and the increasing volatility in agricultural and energy markets increases significantly during recessionary periods which are characterized by heightened uncertainty in the macroeconomy (see Bloom, 2009; Baker *et al.*, 2016; Jurado *et al.*, 2015). In addition, **Figure 3** shows that the 2007-2008 Great Recession is associated with increasing volatility co-movement in seemingly unrelated commodity markets. Moreover, in **Table 1 and 2** we present some descriptive statistics for our commodity RV series for the pre-financialization (pre-2004) and for the post-financialization (post-2004) period respectively.

The descriptive statistics show that the mean values for agricultural, metals and energy volatility series are significantly increased during the post-financialization period. For example, while the mean value for the Realized Variance (RV) series of

Figure 3. Time-varying volatility in agricultural, energy and metals commodity futures markets

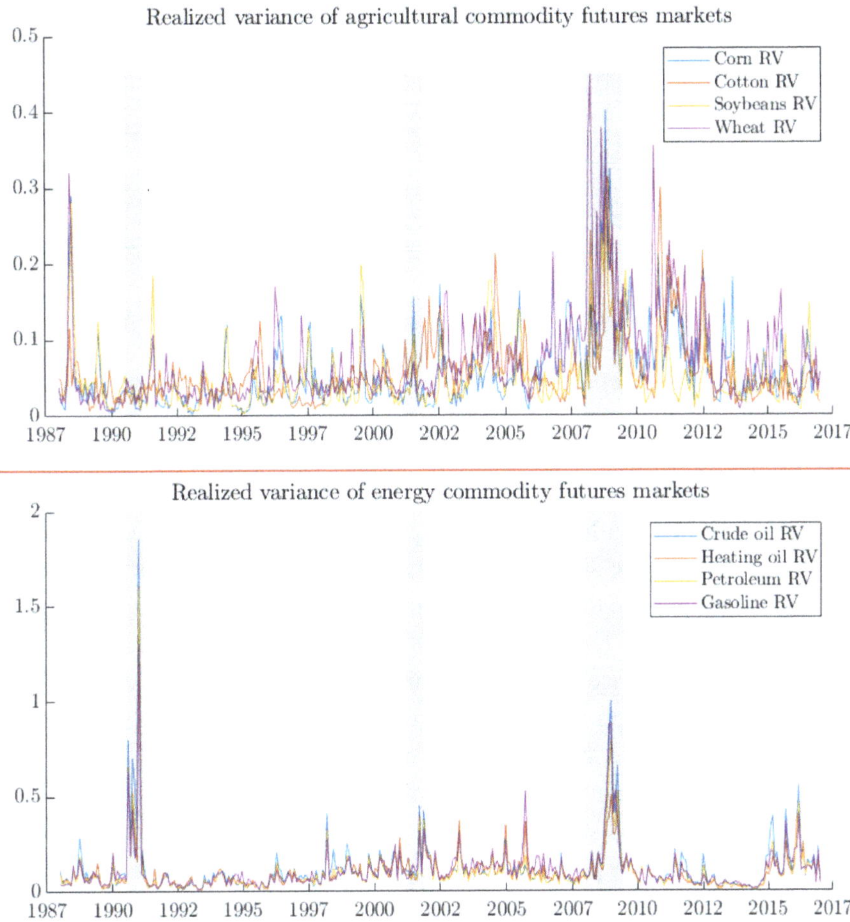

3.2 Economic Uncertainty and Commodity Price Volatility

In this section the econometric results showing the impact of uncertainty shocks before and after the financialization period are analytically presented. The estimated coefficients of these regression models provide an estimate of the impact of uncertainty shocks on the volatility in commodity markets. We measure the impact of uncertainty shocks by regressing the alternative uncertainty measures on the monthly realized variance of the commodity futures S&P GSCI market index. **Table 3** below reports the results of the univariate regression models (described in equation (2)) in which

Table 1. Descriptive statistics for commodity Realized Variance for the financialization (pre-2004) and for the post-financialization (post-2004) period

Panel A: Post-financialization (Jan 1988-Dec 2003)													
Commodity	**Corn**	**Cotton**	**Soybeans**	**Wheat**	**Crude oil**	**Heat oil**	**Gasoline**	**Petroleum**	**Copper**	**Gold**	**Silver**	**Platinum**	**Index**
Mean	0.039	0.046	0.040	0.047	0.114	0.104	0.099	0.095	0.049	0.017	0.047	0.038	0.032
St. dev.	0.039	0.027	0.037	0.038	0.164	0.135	0.115	0.135	0.053	0.019	0.040	0.035	0.046
Max	0.291	0.158	0.282	0.321	1.856	1.608	1.306	1.590	0.432	0.143	0.296	0.263	0.497
Min	0.002	0.007	0.003	0.007	0.010	0.012	0.010	0.010	0.004	0.001	0.007	0.002	0.003
Skewness	2.926	1.430	3.001	3.412	7.120	7.863	6.947	7.825	3.910	3.512	2.462	3.343	6.476
Kurtosis	14.648	5.555	15.497	20.100	69.556	83.496	68.142	81.469	23.820	19.558	12.282	19.311	60.012

we use all the widely accepted measures of Economic Uncertainty as explanatory variables.

The results presented in **Table 3** indicate that all the economic uncertainty measures have a positive and statistically significant impact on the realized variance of the commodity price index, with the only exemption being the fiscal policy uncertainty index. The insignificance of the fiscal policy uncertainty shocks is somewhat expected, since there is no empirical (or theoretical) evidence, linking commodity prices with fiscal policy. The coefficient of Macroeconomic uncertainty (MU) is strongly positively significant and many times larger compared to the estimated coefficients of the other proxies-measures of economic uncertainty. For example, the coefficient of the MU index is 0.359, while the estimated coefficients of the Economic Policy Uncertainty (EPU) and of the VXO index are 0.049 and 0.059 respectively. These results show the much stronger impact of MU on the realized variance of the commodity price index[8]. The OLS regression analysis clearly shows that the uncertainty shocks which matter most for commodity investors are the unpredictable ones. In addition, the adjusted R^2 value of the univariate regression

Table 2. Descriptive statistics for commodity Realized Variance for the financialization (pre-2004) and for the post-financialization (post-2004) period

Panel B: Pre-financialization (Jan 2004-Dec 2016)													
Commodity	**Corn**	**Cotton**	**Soybeans**	**Wheat**	**Crude oil**	**Heat oil**	**Gasoline**	**Petroleum**	**Copper**	**Gold**	**Silver**	**Platinum**	**Index**
mean	0.083	0.071	0.061	0.101	0.127	0.105	0.128	0.106	0.084	0.036	0.116	0.051	0.057
St. dev.	0.061	0.059	0.050	0.075	0.139	0.092	0.128	0.112	0.102	0.035	0.116	0.054	0.057
Max	0.402	0.314	0.350	0.449	1.002	0.527	0.883	0.794	0.898	0.243	0.728	0.430	0.378
Min	0.007	0.011	0.007	0.008	0.011	0.008	0.012	0.008	0.009	0.004	0.012	0.006	0.004
Skewness	1.859	1.960	2.222	1.966	3.238	2.221	3.386	3.176	4.366	2.823	2.860	3.732	3.230
Kurtosis	8.225	7.078	10.098	7.911	16.244	8.750	17.817	15.823	30.034	13.023	12.565	21.449	15.869

Table 3. Impact of economic uncertainty on commodity price volatility

	(1)	(2)	(3)	(4)	(5)	(6)	(7)	(8)	(9)
EPU	0.049**								
	(2.24)								
EPUNEWS		0.047**							
		(2.50)							
EPUMON			0.017*						
			(1.88)						
EPUFISC				0.016					
				(1.56)					
FRU					0.016**				
					(2.31)				
MU3						0.359***			
						(5.27)			
FU3							0.138**		
							(2.55)		
VXO								0.059**	
								(2.44)	
SP500RV									0.359*
									(1.86)
% R^2 adj.	7.4	9.4	3.3	3.0	9.7	39.8	15.4	16.7	21.7

Note: The estimated standard errors are corrected for autocorrelation and heteroskedasticity using the Newey-West (1987) estimator. t statistics in parentheses. * $p < 0.10$, ** $p < 0.05$, *** $p < 0.01$. For brevity, the estimated constant terms of the regression models are not reported in the table. All the variables have monthly frequency and cover the period from January 1988 till December 2016. All the explanatory variables are used in log-levels except VXO and SP500RV which are used in levels.

model in which we use the MU as the only determinant of RV of the commodity price index, reaches 39.9%, while the respective R^2 values for the rest univariate models in which we use the alternative economic uncertainty proxies are less than

22%. The results presented here provide an alternative explanation of the 'puzzle' of excess co-movement in commodity markets. Pindyck and Rotemberg (1990) were among the first to identify the "excess co-movement" of commodity prices. They show that this excess co-movement is well in excess of anything that can be explained by common macroeconomic factors like inflation, exchange rates or changes in aggregate demand. These empirical findings may provide an explanation to this "puzzling phenomenon" according to Pindyck and Rotemberg (1990), since we empirically verify that the macroeconomic uncertainty is a common macroeconomic factor which lies behind time-variation in commodity market price volatility. The results presented in this section do not contradict these empirical findings, but they may provide the macroeconomic 'explanation' of this inverse relationship between convience yields, inventory levels and volatility in commodity prices as implied by the 'Theory of Storage'. Rising macroeconomic uncertainty makes the path of future aggregate demand (and consequently of aggregate production) less predictable. For this reason, risk averse commodity producers prefer to hold physical inventory in order to face the uncertain aggregate demand conditions[9]. This rise in the convenience yield for holding physical inventory results to a rapid rise in the volatility of the commodity prices, as implied by the 'Theory of Storage' (Forg & See, 2001; Ng & Pirrong, 1994).

Moving further, we control for the major macroeconomic and stock-market variables and we show that the large positive impact of economic uncertainty on commodity price volatility remains robust to the inclusion of these variables on the left-hand side of our regression models. **Table 4** below shows the estimated coefficients of OLS regression models when controlling for macroeconomic and stock-market determinants of commodity market turbulence.

From **Table 4** it can be observed that the estimated coefficients of MU and FU remain positive and statistically significant, while the coefficients of the fiscal and monetary policy uncertainty become insignificant. Moreover, a forecasting exercise in using the EPU, MU and FU series as predictors of the volatility of the commodity price index is performed. The **Table 5, 6 and 7** below report the relevant results.

The OLS forecasting regression results indicate that the MU and FU series are statistically significant predictors of the commodity price volatility for both short and long-term forecasting horizons which range from one up to twelve months ahead. Unlike the FU and the MU, the EPU index gives statistically significant forecasts only for short-term (up to 3 month) forecasting horizons. These empirical findings are the first to show the predictive information content of economic uncertainty on the volatility of commodity prices. The results on the predictive power of the MU and FU series remain robust to the inclusion of some traditional determinants of commodity price volatility like the interest rates, the growth in Industrial Production Index and the volatility of the S&P 500 stock market index.

Table 4. Impact of economic uncertainty on commodity price volatility when controlling for macroeconomic factors

	(1)	(2)	(3)	(4)	(5)	(6)	(7)	(8)	(9)
SP500RET	-0.165**	-0.153*	-0.174**	-0.177**	-0.166**	-0.088	-0.138*	-0.116	-0.006
	(-1.98)	(-1.82)	(-1.97)	(-2.04)	(-2.00)	(-1.62)	(-1.81)	(-1.60)	(-0.12)
TERM	-0.296	-0.187	0.046	-0.074	-0.197	0.172	0.015	0.060	-0.049
	(-1.03)	(-0.69)	(0.18)	(-0.25)	(-0.72)	(0.84)	(0.06)	(0.23)	(-0.24)
EMPL	-4.517***	-4.341***	-4.557***	-4.557***	-4.426***	0.426	-3.165***	-2.906***	-3.596***
	(-4.61)	(-4.02)	(-4.14)	(-4.34)	(-4.48)	(0.44)	(-3.38)	(-2.84)	(-3.74)
IPI	-1.823**	-1.860**	-2.062**	-2.019**	-1.812**	-1.644***	-2.138***	-2.223***	-1.859***
	(-2.26)	(-2.30)	(-2.48)	(-2.43)	(-2.31)	(-3.10)	(-2.77)	(-2.82)	(-2.92)
EPU	0.033***								
	(2.66)								
EPUNEWS		0.027***							
		(2.62)							
EPUMON			0.004						
			(0.55)						
EPUFISC				0.006					
				(0.90)					
FRU					0.009**				
					(2.38)				
MU						0.304***			
						(5.61)			
FU							0.074***		
							(3.08)		
VXO								0.035***	
								(2.59)	
SP500RV									0.271*
									(1.96)
r2_a	0.311	0.312	0.286	0.289	0.312	0.431	0.319	0.332	0.377

Note: The estimated standard errors are corrected for autocorrelation and heteroskedasticity using the Newey-West (1987) estimator. t statistics in parentheses. * $p < 0.10$, ** $p < 0.05$, *** $p < 0.01$. For brevity, the estimated constant terms of the regression models are not reported in the table. All the variables have monthly frequency and cover the period from January 1988 till December 2016. All the explanatory variables are used in log-levels except VXO and SP500RV which are used in levels.

Table 5. Forecasting Commodity price volatility (RV) with the Macroeconomic Uncertainty (MU), Financial Uncertainty (FU) and Economic Policy Uncertainty (EPU) $RV_t = b_0 + b_1 MU_{t-k} + \varepsilon_t$

	(1)	(2)	(3)	(4)	(5)	(6)
MU_t	0.359***					
	(5.27)					
MU_{t-1}		0.351***				
		(4.97)				
MU_{t-2}			0.335***			
			(4.60)			
MU_{t-3}				0.312***		
				(4.25)		
MU_{t-6}					0.247***	
					(3.47)	
MU_{t-12}						0.151**
						(2.51)
% R^2 adj.	39.8	38.0	34.6	30.0	18.8	6.9

Lastly, bivariate regression models on the volatility of individual commodity prices are also estimated. By this way, we examine the different impact of uncertainty shocks to different agricultural, energy and metals markets. The tables below report the regression results when using the EPU index, the MU index and the FU index as explanatory variables of agricultural, energy and metals price volatility respectively.

From **Tables 8** through **15** we observe that the estimated regression coefficients of the MU and FU series are many times larger and significantly positive when compared to the regression coefficients of the EPU index. These results provide further empirical support to the initial VAR estimates and conclusions, according to which the unobservable MU and FU shocks are the ones which have the most significant macroeconomic impact in commodity markets. We additionally observe that the impact of macroeconomic shocks is larger on energy commodity volatility compared to the volatility of agricultural and mineral commodity markets.

Table 6. Forecasting Commodity price volatility (RV) with the Macroeconomic Uncertainty (MU), Financial Uncertainty (FU) and Economic Policy Uncertainty (EPU)

	(1)	(2)	(3)	(4)	(5)	(6)
FU_t	0.138**					
	(2.55)					
FU_{t-1}		0.137**				
		(2.56)				
FU_{t-2}			0.134***			
			(2.60)			
FU_{t-3}				0.126***		
				(2.65)		
FU_{t-6}					0.099***	
					(2.80)	
FU_{t-12}						0.036**
						(2.03)
% R^2 adj.	15.4	15.3	14.6	13.0	8.0	0.8

3.3. Uncertainty Shocks During the Financialization Era

In this section we conduct the empirical analysis for the more recent (post-2004 period) during which the large inflow of funds into the commodity asset class is known as financialization of commodity markets. The financialization of commodity markets has made structural changes in the nature and in their information content. Since the early 2000s, the large inflow of funds and the increased presence of financial investors to commodity markets have transformed them into a separate asset class which has become more integrated to the rest financial markets (Basak & Pavlova, 2016; Cheng & Xiong, 2013; Irwin & Sanders, 2012; Silvennoinen & Thorp, 2015). Tang and Xiong (2012) find that the financialization of commodity markets lies behind the increased post-2008 correlation of oil prices and non-energy commodity prices and for the increased volatility of non-energy commodities around 2008. Motivated by the empirical findings which show an increased interdependence between

Table 7. Forecasting Commodity price volatility (RV) with the Macroeconomic Uncertainty (MU), Financial Uncertainty (FU) and Economic Policy Uncertainty (EPU)

	(1)	(2)	(3)	(4)	(5)	(6)
EPU_t	0.049**					
	(2.24)					
EPU_{t-1}		0.039*				
		(1.85)				
EPU_{t-2}			0.035*			
			(1.77)			
EPU_{t-3}				0.020		
				(1.34)		
EPU_{t-6}					-0.000	
					(-0.02)	
EPU_{t-12}						-0.015*
						(-1.90)
% R^2 adj.	7.4	4.4	3.5	1.0	-0.3	0.4

Note: The estimated standard errors are corrected for autocorrelation and heteroskedasticity using the Newey-West (1987) estimator. t statistics in parentheses. * $p < 0.10$, ** $p < 0.05$, *** $p < 0.01$. The tables shows only the estimated beta coefficients for the bivariate regression models.

Table 8. Impact of Economic Policy Uncertainty (EPU) on the volatility of agricultural, energy and metals commodity futures markets

Agricultural Commodities				
	(2)	**(3)**	**(4)**	**(6)**
	Corn	**Cotton**	**Soybeans**	**Wheat**
EPU	0.032	0.047***	0.007	0.046**
	(1.59)	(2.73)	(0.46)	(2.46)
% R^2 adj.	2.7	7.9	-0.1	4.1

stock-market and commodity market returns (Adams & Gluck, 2015; Buyuksahin & Robe, 2014), we empirically examine whether the financialization process has increases the structural linkages between uncertainty shocks and commodity market

Table 9. Impact of Economic Policy Uncertainty (EPU) on the volatility of agricultural, energy and metals commodity futures markets

	Energy Commodities			
	(1)	**(2)**	**(3)**	**(4)**
	Crude oil	**Heat oil**	**Gasoline**	**Petroleum**
EPU	0.140**	0.097**	0.091*	0.127**
	(2.18)	(1.98)	(1.68)	(2.39)
% R^2 adj	6.7	4.5	4.3	7.1

Table 10. Impact of Economic Policy Uncertainty (EPU) on the volatility of agricultural, energy and metals commodity futures markets

	Metal Commodities			
	(1)	**(2)**	**(3)**	**(4)**
	Copper	**Gold**	**Silver**	**Platinum**
EPU	0.044	0.028**	0.079**	0.045***
	(1.24)	(2.49)	(2.21)	(2.61)
% R^2 adj	2.2	7.8	5.8	6.7

Note: The estimated standard errors are corrected for autocorrelation and heteroskedasticity using the Newey-West (1987) estimator. t statistics in parentheses. * $p < 0.10$, ** $p < 0.05$, *** $p < 0.01$. The table shows only the estimated beta coefficients for the bivariate regression models. All the variables have monthly frequency and cover the period from January 1988 till December 2016.

Table 11. Impact of Macroeconomic Uncertainty (MU) on the volatility of agricultural, energy and metals commodity futures markets

	Agricultural Commodities			
	(1)	**(2)**	**(3)**	**(4)**
	Corn	**Cotton**	**Soybeans**	**Wheat**
MU	0.241***	0.213***	0.168**	0.296***
	(2.94)	(4.46)	(2.57)	(4.29)
% R^2 adj.	16.0	16.3	11.5	17.9

turbulence. **Tables 16** and **17** below show the results of the OLS regression models for the post-2004 and the pre-2004 period.

Table 12. Impact of Macroeconomic Uncertainty (MU) on the volatility of agricultural, energy and metals commodity futures markets

Energy Commodities				
	(1)	(2)	(3)	(4)
	Crude oil	Heat oil	Gasoline	Petroleum
MU	0.732***	0.559***	0.717***	0.647***
	(4.17)	(6.82)	(4.46)	(4.99)
% R^2 adj.	19.1	15.3	29.6	18.6

Table 13. Impact of Macroeconomic Uncertainty (MU) on the volatility of agricultural, energy and metals commodity futures markets

Metal Commodities				
	(1)	(2)	(3)	(4)
	Copper	Gold	Silver	Platinum
MU	0.385***	0.158***	0.346**	0.278***
	(2.71)	(3.92)	(2.35)	(4.15)
% R^2 adj.	18.4	24.5	11.4	26.3

Note: The estimated standard errors are corrected for autocorrelation and heteroskedasticity using the Newey-West (1987) estimator. t statistics in parentheses. * $p < 0.10$, ** $p < 0.05$, *** $p < 0.01$. The table shows only the estimated beta coefficients for the bivariate regression models. All the variables have monthly frequency and cover the period from January 1988 till December 2016.

Table 14. Impact of Financial Uncertainty (FU) on the volatility of agricultural, energy and metals commodity futures markets

Agricultural Commodities				
	(1)	(2)	(3)	(4)
	Corn	Cotton	Soybeans	Wheat
FU	0.087*	0.103***	0.057	0.105**
	(1.68)	(3.06)	(1.43)	(2.05)
% R^2 adj.	5.4	10.1	3.3	5.8

Table 15. Impact of Financial Uncertainty (FU) on the volatility of agricultural, energy and metals commodity futures markets

	Energy Commodities			
	(1)	(2)	(3)	(4)
	Crude oil	**Heating oil**	**Gasoline**	**Petroleum**
FU	0.353***	0.246***	0.299***	0.297***
	(3.10)	(3.85)	(2.58)	(3.32)
% R^2 adj.	11.6	7.8	12.5	10.3

Table 15. Impact of Financial Uncertainty (FU) on the volatility of agricultural, energy and metals commodity futures markets

	Metals Commodities			
	(1)	(2)	(3)	(4)
	Copper	**Gold**	**Silver**	**Platinum**
FU	0.123	0.059**	0.121	0.139***
	(1.33)	(2.07)	(1.31)	(3.33)
% R^2 adj.	4.8	9.0	3.5	17.4

Note: The estimated standard errors are corrected for autocorrelation and heteroskedasticity using the Newey-West (1987) estimator. t statistics in parentheses. * $p < 0.10$, ** $p < 0.05$, *** $p < 0.01$. The table shows only the estimated beta coefficients for the bivariate regression models. All the variables have monthly frequency and cover the period from January 1988 till December 2016.

The empirical analysis indicates that the financialization in commodity markets has increased the interdependence and the sensitivity of commodity market volatility to uncertainty shocks. More specifically, from **Table 16** we see that the explanatory power and the significance of all the economic uncertainty measures has tremendously increased during the post-2000 period. The resutls contradict those of Karali and Power (2013) who find that the commodity specific factors dominated macroeconomic factors when used to explain the volatility during the recent 2006-2009 period in the US agricultural, energy and metals futures markets. On the contrary, the econometric analysis reveals that the common macroeconomic uncertainty factor explain a larger part of time variation of commodity price volatility in the post-financialization era, while this is not the case in the pre-2000 period[10]. On the other hand, the OLS regression results of **Table 17** for the pre-financialization period show that the explanatory power of all observable proxies is singificantly reduced during the pre-financialization period. This is another piece of empirical evidence

Table 16. Impact of economic uncertainty on commodity price volatility when controlling for macroeconomic factors during the post-financialization (post-2004) era

	(1)	(2)	(3)	(4)	(5)	(6)	(7)	(8)	(9)
SP500RET	-0.201*	-0.202*	-0.206*	-0.213*	-0.207*	-0.115	-0.175	-0.138	0.034
	(-1.68)	(-1.66)	(-1.69)	(-1.72)	(-1.76)	(-1.59)	(-1.53)	(-1.32)	(0.57)
TERM	0.163	0.324	0.434	0.440	0.187	0.575**	0.236	0.204	0.077
	(0.51)	(1.03)	(1.38)	(1.37)	(0.69)	(2.29)	(0.80)	(0.73)	(0.37)
EMPL	-4.324***	-4.228***	-4.134***	-4.251***	-4.174***	1.690	-3.154***	-2.470**	-2.306***
	(-4.17)	(-3.91)	(-3.79)	(-3.99)	(-4.02)	(1.24)	(-3.18)	(-2.16)	(-2.78)
IPI	-2.258**	-2.334**	-2.403**	-2.424**	-2.252**	-1.799***	-2.308**	-2.362**	-1.327**
	(-2.21)	(-2.25)	(-2.30)	(-2.34)	(-2.33)	(-3.00)	(-2.36)	(-2.44)	(-2.12)
EPU	0.021**								
	(2.34)								
EPUN		0.010							
		(1.43)							
EPUMON			0.003						
			(0.80)						
EPUFISC				0.000					
				(0.00)					
FRU					0.007				
					(1.42)				
MU						0.355***			
						(4.94)			
FU							0.059**		
							(2.10)		
VXO								0.033**	
								(2.02)	
SP500RV									0.463***
									(8.15)
% R^2 Adj.	40.6	39.7	39.4	39.3	40.2	59.6	41.1	42.8	62.9

Note: The estimated standard errors are corrected for autocorrelation and heteroskedasticity using the Newey-West (1987) estimator. t statistics in parentheses. * $p < 0.10$, ** $p < 0.05$, *** $p < 0.01$. For brevity, the estimated constant terms of the regression models are not reported in the table. All the variables have monthly frequency and cover the period from January 2004 till December 2016. All the explanatory variables are used in log-levels except VXO and SP500RV which are used in levels.

Table 17. Impact of economic uncertainty on commodity price volatility when controlling for macroeconomic factors during the pre-financialization (pre-2004) era

	(1)	(2)	(3)	(4)	(5)	(6)	(7)	(8)	(9)
SP500RET	-0.049	-0.036	-0.028	-0.053	-0.048	-0.056	-0.049	-0.025	-0.037
	(-0.66)	(-0.46)	(-0.34)	(-0.69)	(-0.62)	(-0.70)	(-0.61)	(-0.31)	(-0.38)
TERM	-0.942**	-0.800***	-0.730***	-0.918***	-0.678**	-0.401	-0.315	-0.153	-0.484**
	(-2.49)	(-2.65)	(-2.68)	(-2.59)	(-2.49)	(-1.59)	(-1.40)	(-0.53)	(-2.19)
EMPL	-1.303	-1.113	-1.975	-1.838	-2.243	-1.108	-1.759	-2.222	-2.599
	(-1.00)	(-0.88)	(-1.25)	(-1.20)	(-1.26)	(-0.79)	(-1.04)	(-1.25)	(-1.30)
IPI	-0.858	-1.002	-0.677	-0.655	-0.778	-1.141	-1.392	-1.366	-1.201
	(-1.18)	(-1.26)	(-1.00)	(-1.04)	(-1.10)	(-1.25)	(-1.36)	(-1.37)	(-1.22)
EPU	0.051								
	(1.49)								
EPUN		0.051							
		(1.52)							
EPUMON			0.019						
			(1.56)						
EPUFISC				0.022					
				(1.57)					
FRU					0.009				
					(1.48)				
MU						0.151			
						(1.51)			
FU							0.060**		
							(1.99)		
VXO								0.037*	
								(1.90)	
SP500RV									0.056
									(1.02)
% R^2 adj.	10.5	12.7	9.5	10.1	8.9	7.8	7.8	10.8	5.5

Note: The estimated standard errors are corrected for autocorrelation and heteroskedasticity using the Newey-West (1987) estimator. t statistics in parentheses. * $p < 0.10$, ** $p < 0.05$, *** $p < 0.01$. For brevity, the estimated constant terms of the regression models are not reported in the table. All the variables have monthly frequency and cover the period from January 1988 till December 2003. All the explanatory variables are used in log-levels except VXO and SP500RV which are used in levels.

Figure 4. Responses of volatility in agricultural markets to expansionary monetary policy shocks during the pre-financialization (pre-2004) period

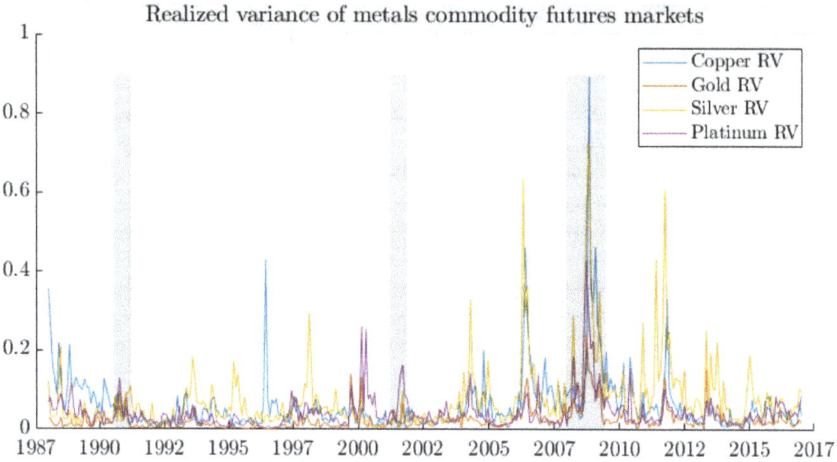

showing that financialization has increased the linkages between macroeconomic uncertainty and volatility in commodity markets.

3.4. Response of Commodity Price Volatility to Monetary Policy Shocks

This section reports the results of the bivariate VAR models in which we include monetary policy (Fed funds rate) and the commodity price volatility of agricultural, metals and energy commodity markets. Figures **4** to **9** show the estimated Orthogonalized Impulse Response Functions (OIRFs) of agricultural, metals and energy market volatility to expansionary monetary policy shock (a negative one standard deviation shock in the Fed funds rate).

This figure shows the Orthogonalized Impulse Response Functions (OIRFs) of the Realized Variance (RV) of agricultural futures markets to expansionary monetary policy shocks (negative one standard deviation shock in the Fed Funds rate). The estimated OIRFs are from bivariate VARs given in Equation (4) and (5) using data covering January 1988 till December 2003 (pre-financialization period). The estimated OIRFs are expressed in percentages (%).

This figure shows the Orthogonalized Impulse Response Functions (OIRFs) of the Realized Variance (RV) of agricultural futures markets to expansionary monetary policy shocks (negative one standard deviation shock in the Fed Funds rate). The estimated OIRFs are from bivariate VARs given in Equation (4) and (5)

Figure 5. Responses of volatility in agricultural markets to expansionary monetary policy shocks during the post-financialization (post-2004) period

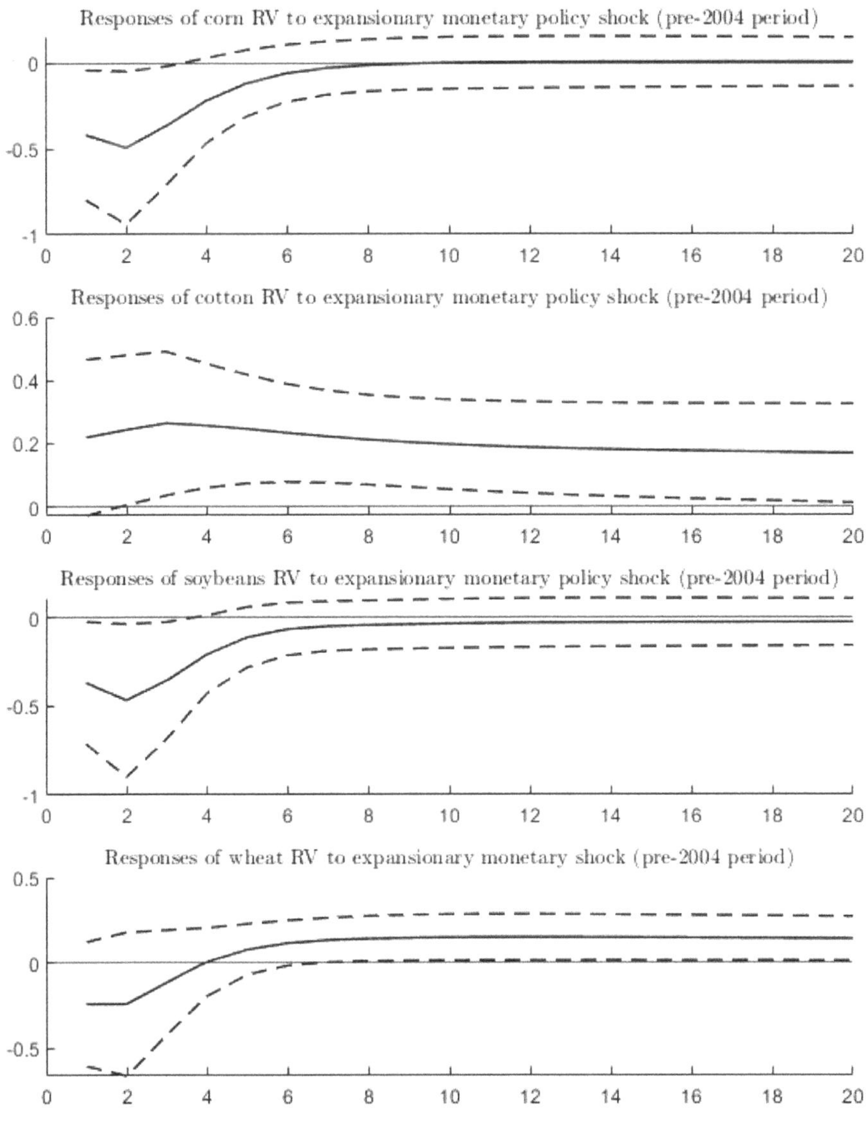

using data covering January 2004 till December 2016 (post-financialization period). The estimated OIRFs are expressed in percentages (%).

This figure shows the Orthogonalized Impulse Response Functions (OIRFs) of the Realized Variance (RV) of energy futures markets to expansionary monetary

Figure 6. Responses of volatility in energy markets to expansionary monetary policy shocks during the pre-financialization (pre-2004) period

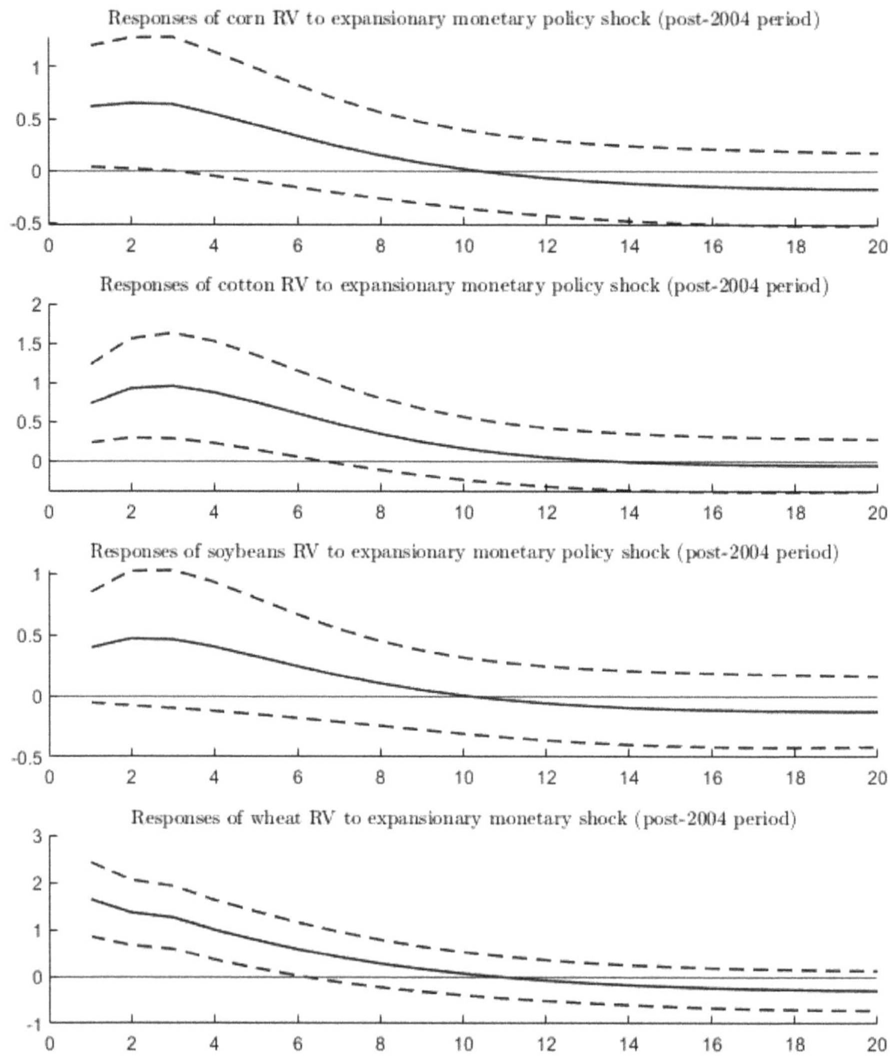

policy shocks (negative one standard deviation shock in the Fed Funds rate). The estimated OIRFs are from bivariate VARs given in Equation (4) and (5) using data covering January 1988 till December 2003 (pre-financialization period). The estimated OIRFs are expressed in percentages (%).

Figure 7. Responses of volatility in energy markets to expansionary monetary policy shocks during the post-financialization (post-2004) period

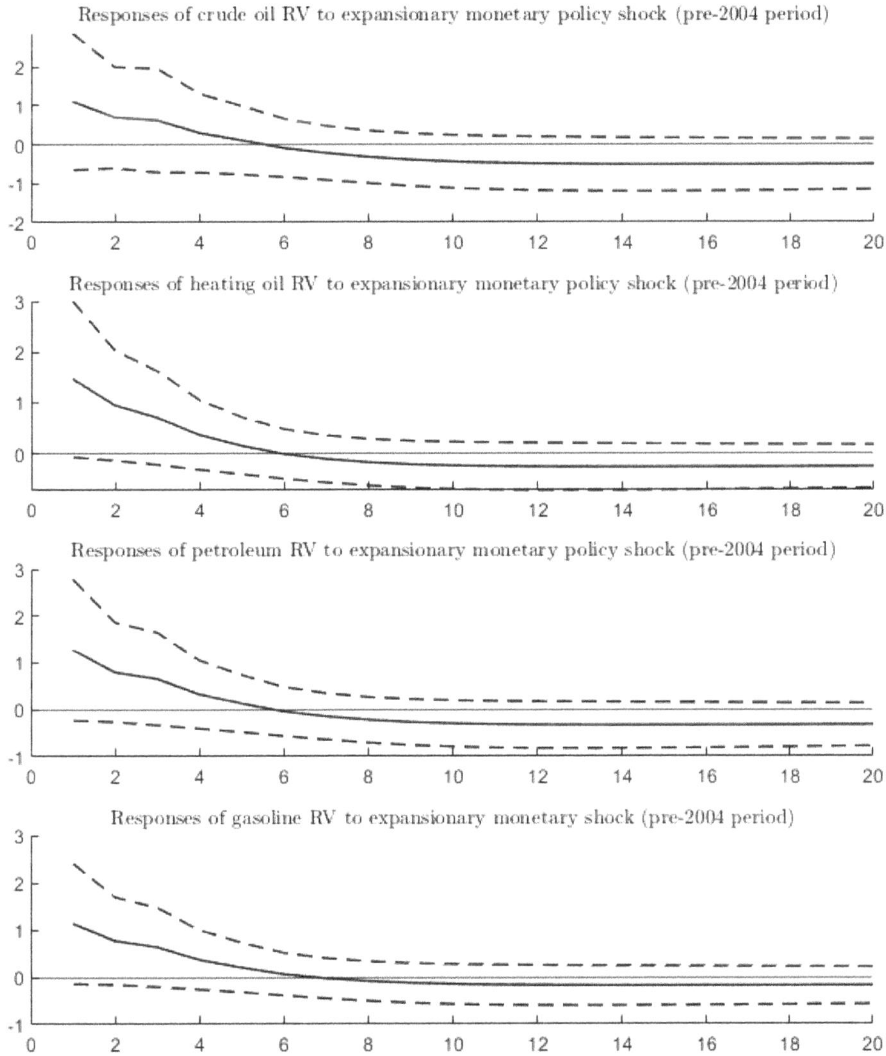

This figure shows the Orthogonalized Impulse Response Functions (OIRFs) of the Realized Variance (RV) of energy futures markets to expansionary monetary policy shocks (negative one standard deviation shock in the Fed Funds rate). The estimated OIRFs are from bivariate VARs given in Equation (4) and (5) using data

Figure 8. Responses of volatility in metals markets to expansionary monetary policy shocks during the pre-financialization (pre-2004) period

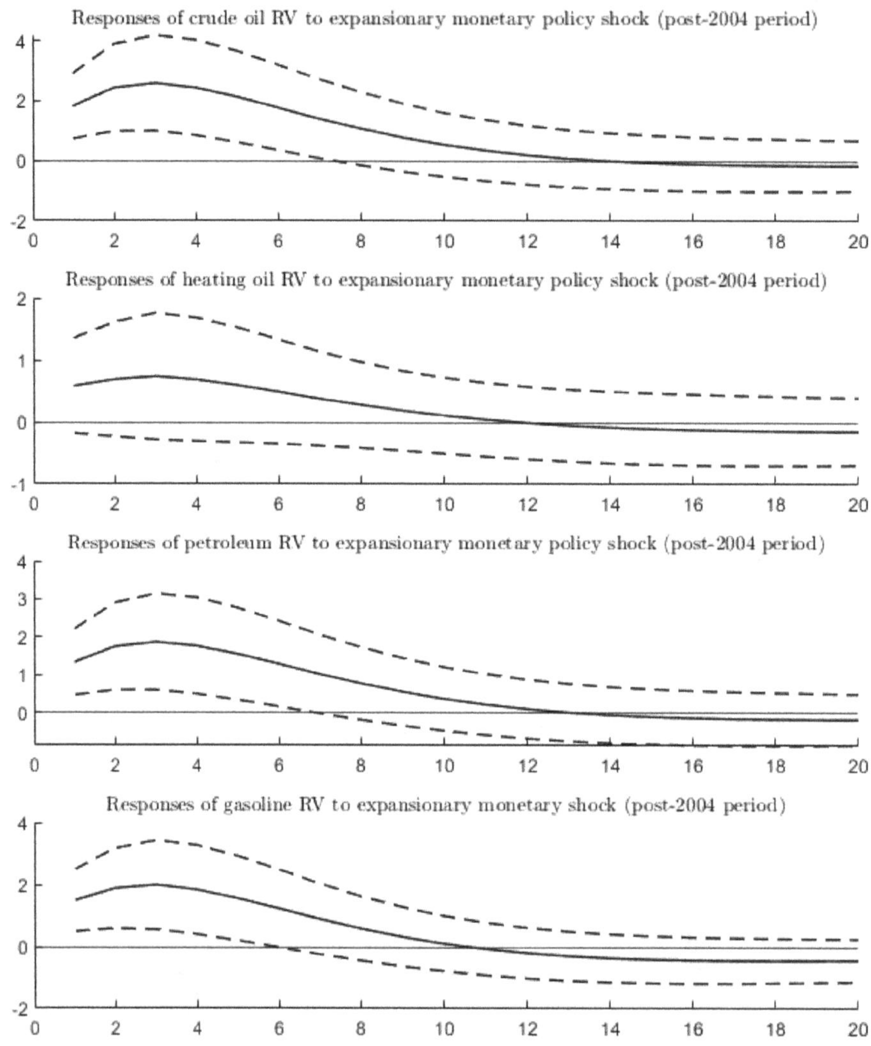

covering January 2004 till December 2016 (post-financialization period). The estimated OIRFs are expressed in percentages (%).

This figure shows the Orthogonalized Impulse Response Functions (OIRFs) of the Realized Variance (RV) of metals futures markets to expansionary monetary policy shocks (negative one standard deviation shock in the Fed Funds rate). The

Figure 9. Responses of volatility in metals markets to expansionary monetary policy shocks during the post-financialization (post-2004) period

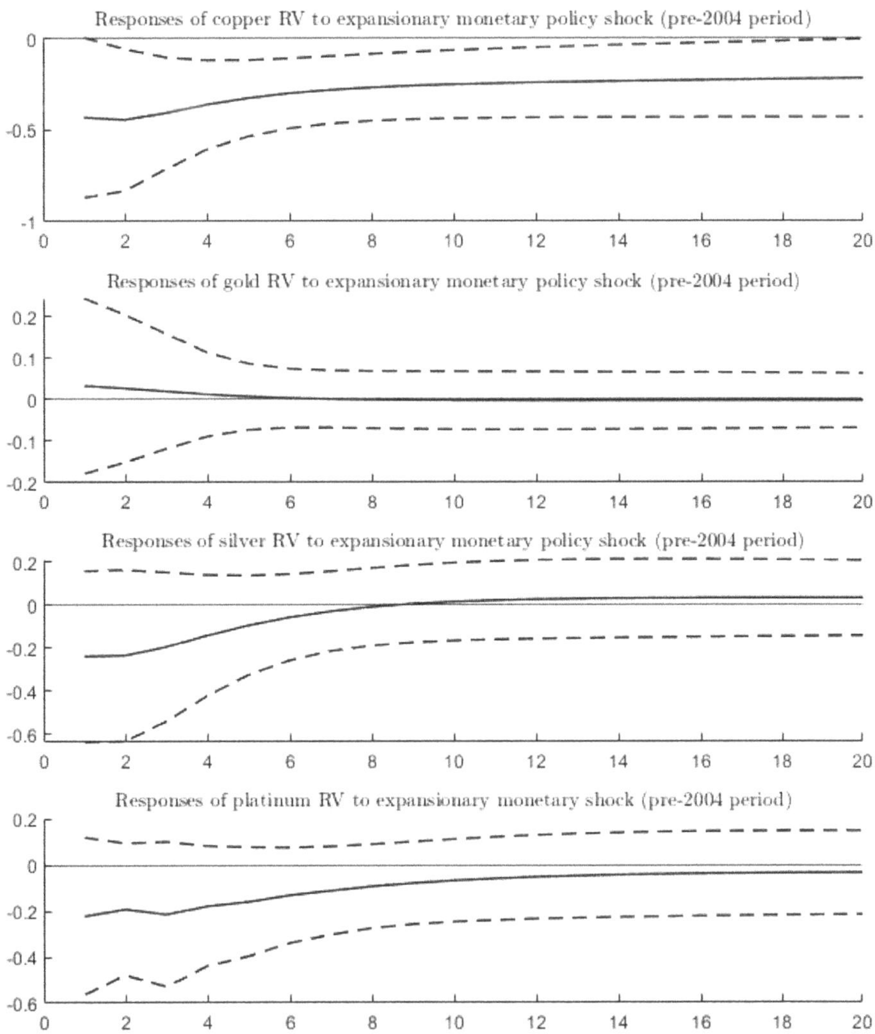

estimated OIRFs are from bivariate VARs given in Equation (4) and (5) using data covering January 1988 till December 2003 (pre-financialization period). The estimated OIRFs are expressed in percentages (%).

This figure shows the Orthogonalized Impulse Response Functions (OIRFs) of the Realized Variance (RV) of metals futures markets to expansionary monetary policy shocks (negative one standard deviation shock in the Fed Funds rate). The estimated OIRFs are from bivariate VARs given in Equation (4) and (5) using data covering January 2004 till December 2016 (post-financialization period). The estimated OIRFs are expressed in percentages (%).

From Figures **4** and **5** it can be observed that an expansionary monetary policy shock has an exactly opposite effect on the volatility of agricultural commodity futures markets. For example, while an expansionary monetary policy shock reduces volatility in the wheat market at about 50 basis points two months after the initial monetary policy shock during the pre-2004 period, it has the exactly opposite effect in the post-2004 period. Overall, the impact of monetary policy on the volatility of agricultural markets is negative during the post-financialization period and positive on the pre-financialization period. **Figures 6** and **7** show that the dynamic impact of monetary policy shocks on energy markets has tremendously increased during the post-financialization period. For example, while an expansionary monetary policy shock reduces volatility in crude oil markets at about 1% one month after the shock during the pre-financialization era, the same monetary policy shock reduces crude oil price volatility by more than 2% two months after the initial shock in the post-financialization era. On the other hand, the VAR analysis shown in **Figures 8** and **9** fails to reveal some robust econometric evidence regarding the impact of monetary policy shocks on the volatility of metals commodoty futures markets.

CONCLUSIONS

This chapter presents some stylized facts and some preliminary empirical evidence of the impact of uncertainty shocks and lax monetary policy on the volatility of commodity futures markets. Overal, this chapter shows that the rising macroeconomic uncertainty is associated with increasing volatility in commodity markets. The analysis indicates that the latent macroeconomic uncertainty shock which quantify the rising degree of unpredictability in the macroeconomy is the uncertainty shock which has the most significant and persistent impact on the volatility of commodity prices. On the other hand, the observable economic uncertainty measures have a rather transitory and less significant impact in the volatility of commodity prices. The results implicitly show that the more unpredictable the future state of the macroeconomy becomes, the more volatile the commodity prices. The policy implication behind these results might be the adoption of the appropriate monetary and fiscal policies, which will have as a result the reduction of the unpredictability of macroeconomic fluctuations. Commodity market turbulence does not seem to arise because of macroeconomic and/or stock-market fluctuations. On the contrary, it is affected by the rising degree of unpredictability of these fluctuations. Any macroeconomic policy which will result in reducing this unpredictability (e.g. an adoption of a highly transparent monetary policy), will implicitly reduce the fluctuations and the instability in commodity prices. Moreover, the econometric analysis reveals that the impact of uncertainty shocks on commodity market volatility is tremendously increased in the post-financialization (post-2004) period. These findings show that financialization of commodities has resulted to tighter interconnections between macroeconomic uncertainty and commodity market turbulence. Moreover, the VAR analysis indicates that the expansionary monetary policy is associated with rising volatility in agricultural and energy markets, especially for the post-financialization period. When examining the effect of monetary policy shocks to different commodity markets is examined, the VAR analysis shows that expansionary monetary policy shock has a more positive and long-lasting effect in the volatility of energy and agricultural futures markets. On the other hand, the reaction of metals market volatility to monetary policy shocks is sluggish and transitory. Overall, the analysis presented in this chapter shows that the uncertainty shocks and the expansionary monetary policy shocks increase commodity price instability and turbulence. These results implicitly reveal that commodity investors should go long on commodity market volatility in periods of expansionary monetary policy.

REFERENCES

Adams, Z., & Gluck, Z. (2015). Financialization in commodity markets: A passing trend or the new normal? *Journal of Banking & Finance*, *60*, 93–111. doi:10.1016/j.jbankfin.2015.07.008

Alquist, R., Bhattarai, S., & Coibion, O. (2019). Commodity-price comovement and global economic activity. Forthcoming at *Journal of Monetary Economics.*

Antonakakis, N., Chatziantoniou, I., & Filis, G. (2013). Dynamic co-movements of stock-market returns, implied volatility and policy uncertainty. *Economics Letters*, *120*(1), 87–92. doi:10.1016/j.econlet.2013.04.004

Anzuini, A., Lombardi, M. J., & Pagano, P. (2013). The Impact of Monetary Policy Shocks on Commodity Prices. *International Journal of Central Banking*, *9*(3), 125–150.

Bakas, D., & Triantafyllou, A. (2018). The impact of uncertainty shocks on the volatility of commodity prices. *Journal of International Money and Finance*, *87*, 96–111. doi:10.1016/j.jimonfin.2018.06.001

Baker, S. R., Bloom, N., & Davis, S. J. (2016). Measuring Economic Policy Uncertainty. *The Quarterly Journal of Economics*, *131*(4), 1593–1636. doi:10.1093/qje/qjw024

Basak, S., & Pavlova, A. (2016). A Model of Financialization of Commodities. *The Journal of Finance*, *71*(4), 1511–1556. doi:10.1111/jofi.12408

Batten, J. A., Ciner, C., & Lucey, B. M. (2010). The macroeconomic determinants of volatility in precious metals markets. *Resources Policy*, *35*(2), 65–71. doi:10.1016/j.resourpol.2009.12.002

Bekaert, G., Hoerova, M., & Lo Duca, M. (2013). Risk, Uncertainty and Monetary Policy. *Journal of Monetary Economics*, *60*(7), 771–788. doi:10.1016/j.jmoneco.2013.06.003

Bloom, N. (2009). The impact of uncertainty shocks. *Econometrica*, *77*(3), 623–685. doi:10.3982/ECTA6248

Buyuksahin, B., & Robe, M. A. (2014). Speculators, commodities and cross-market linkages. *Journal of International Money and Finance*, *42*, 38–70. doi:10.1016/j.jimonfin.2013.08.004

Byrne, J. P., Fazio, G., & Fiess, N. (2013). Primary commodity prices: Co-movements, common factors and fundamentals. *Journal of Development Economics*, *101*, 16–26. doi:10.1016/j.jdeveco.2012.09.002

Chen, Y. C., Rogoff, K. S., & Rossi, B. (2010). Can exchange rates forecast commodity prices? *The Quarterly Journal of Economics*, *125*(3), 1145–1194. doi:10.1162/qjec.2010.125.3.1145

Cheng, I.-H., & Xiong, W. (2013). The Financialization of Commodity Markets. NBER Working Paper No.19642

Daskalaki, C., Kostakis, A., & Skiadopoulos, G. (2014). Are there common factors in individual commodity futures returns? *Journal of Banking & Finance*, *40*, 346–363. doi:10.1016/j.jbankfin.2013.11.034

Delle Chiaie, S., Ferrara, L., & Giannone, D. (2017). Common factors of commodity prices. Bank of France Working Paper

Ferderer, J. P. (1996). Oil price volatility and the macroeconomy. *Journal of Macroeconomics*, *18*(1), 1–26. doi:10.1016/S0164-0704(96)80001-2

Frankel, J. A. (1984). Commodity prices and money: Lessons from international finance. *American Journal of Agricultural Economics*, *66*(5), 560–566. doi:10.2307/1240954

Frankel, J. A. (2008). *The Effect of Monetary Policy on Real Commodity Prices. In J. Y. Campbell: Asset Prices and Monetary Policy* (pp. 291–333). University of Chicago Press.

Frankel, J. A. (2013). *Effects of Speculation and Interest Rates in a 'Carry Trade' Model of Commodity Prices.* Written for Understanding International Commodity Price Fluctuations, an International Conference organized by the IMF and Oxford University 10.3386/w19463

Frankel, J. A., & Hardouvelis, G. A. (1985). Commodity Prices, Money Surprises and Fed Credibility. *Journal of Money, Credit, and Banking*, *17*(4), 425–438. doi:10.2307/1992439

Frankel, J. A., & Rose, A. K. (2010). Determinants of Agricultural and Mineral Commodity Prices. In *Inflation in an era of Relative Price Shocks.* Reserve Bank of Australia.

Gilbert, C. L. (1989). The impact of exchange rates and developing country debt on commodity prices. *Economic Journal (London)*, *99*(397), 773–784. doi:10.2307/2233770

Gilbert, C. L. (2010). How to Understand High Food Prices. *Journal of Agricultural Economics*, *61*(2), 398–425. doi:10.1111/j.1477-9552.2010.00248.x

Gordon, G., & Rouwenhorst, K. G. (2006). Facts and Fantasies about Commodity Futures. *Financial Analysts Journal*, *62*(2), 47–68. doi:10.2469/faj.v62.n2.4083

Gorton, G. B., Hayashi, F., & Rouwenhorst, K. G. (2012). The fundamentals of commodity futures returns. *Review of Finance*, *17*(1), 35–105. doi:10.1093/rof/rfs019

Gospodinov, N., & Ng, S. (2013). Commodity Prices, Convenience Yields and Inflation. *The Review of Economics and Statistics*, *95*(1), 206–219. doi:10.1162/REST_a_00242

Gubler, M., & Hertweck, M. S. (2013). Commodity price shocks and the business cycle: Structural evidence from the US. *Journal of International Money and Finance*, *37*, 324–352. doi:10.1016/j.jimonfin.2013.06.012

Hammoudeh, S., Nguyen, D. K., & Sousa, R. M. (2015). US Monetary Policy and Sectoral Commodity Prices. *Journal of International Money and Finance*, *57*, 61–85. doi:10.1016/j.jimonfin.2015.06.003

Irwin, S. H., & Sanders, D. R. (2012). Financialization and Structural Change in Commodity Futures Markets. *Journal of Agricultural and Applied Economics*, *44*(3), 371–396. doi:10.1017/S1074070800000481

Jurado, K., Ludvigson, S. C., & Ng, S. (2015). Measuring Uncertainty. *The American Economic Review*, *105*(3), 1177–1216. doi:10.1257/aer.20131193

Karali, B., & Power, G. J. (2013). Short-and long-run determinants of commodity price volatility. *American Journal of Agricultural Economics*, *95*(3), 724–738. doi:10.1093/ajae/aas122

Kelly, B., Pastor, L., & Veronesi, P. (2016). The Price of Political Uncertainty: Theory and Evidence from the Option Market. *The Journal of Finance*, *71*(5), 2417–2480. doi:10.1111/jofi.12406

Liu, L., & Zhang, T. (2015). Economic policy uncertainty and stock market volatility. *Finance Research Letters*, *15*, 99–105. doi:10.1016/j.frl.2015.08.009

Ng, V. K., & Pirrong, S. C. (1994). Fundamentals and Volatility: Storage, Spreads and the Dynamics of Metals Prices. *The Journal of Business*, *67*(2), 203–230. doi:10.1086/296630

Orden, D., & Fackler, P. L. (1989). Identifying monetary impacts on agricultural prices in VAR models. *American Journal of Agricultural Economics*, *71*(2), 495–502. doi:10.2307/1241620

Pindyck, R. S., & Rotemberg, J. J. (1990). Excess co-movement of commodity prices. *Economic Journal (London)*, *100*(403), 1173–1189. doi:10.2307/2233966

Prokopczuk, M., Stancu, A., & Symeonidis, L. (2019). The economic drivers of commodity market volatility. *Journal of International Money and Finance*, *98*, 102063. doi:10.1016/j.jimonfin.2019.102063

Shang, H., Yuan, P., & Huang, L. (2016). Macroeconomic factors and the cross-section of commodity futures returns. *International Review of Economics & Finance*, *45*, 316–332. doi:10.1016/j.iref.2016.06.008

Silvennoinen, A., & Thorp, S. (2015). Financialization, crisis and commodity correlation dynamics. *Journal of International Financial Markets, Institutions and Money*, *24*, 42–65. doi:10.1016/j.intfin.2012.11.007

Tang, K., & Xiong, W. (2012). Index investment and the financialization of commodities. *Financial Analysts Journal*, *68*(5), 54–74. doi:10.2469/faj.v68.n6.5

Triantafyllou, A., & Dotsis, G. (2017). Option-implied expectations in commodity markets and monetary policy. *Journal of International Money and Finance*, *77*, 1–17. doi:10.1016/j.jimonfin.2017.06.002

Van Robays, I. (2016). Macroeconomic uncertainty and oil price volatility. *Oxford Bulletin of Economics and Statistics*, *78*(5), 671–693. doi:10.1111/obes.12124

Wang, Z., Fausti, S. W., & Qasmi, B. A. (2012). Variance risk premiums and predictive power of alternative forward variances in the corn market. *Journal of Futures Markets*, *32*(6), 587–608. doi:10.1002/fut.20527

ENDNOTES

1 The vast majority of commodity option contracts are commodity futures options, which means that the underlying asset on which the option contract is written is the commodity futures with the same maturity date with the option.

2 It has to be stated at this point that the mainstream approach and findings in the literature on commodity markets falls under the province of microeconomics. More specifically, the price and volatility dynamics in commodity markets are mainly attributed to commodity market fundamentals which are based in the 'Theory of Storage' (see Kaldor, 1939; Brennan, 1958; Telser, 1958; Working, 1948, 1949; Fama & French, 1987). According to 'Theory of Storage', the commodity market turbulence and price spikes in commodity markets take place after the occurrence of rising convenience yields and subsequent commodity market fears about a stock-out in inventory levels.

3 There is still a lively debate in the literature regarding the existence (or not) of some common macro or monetary factors driving commodity futures returns and volatility. For example, Daskalaki *et al.* (2014) find that there are no common factors in the cross section of commodity futures returns. Batten *et al.* (2010) show that there are no common macroeconomic factors influencing the dynamics of the monthly volatility series of metals prices. According to their findings, while for example the monthly volatility of gold prices is affected by changes in monetary factors, the same is not true for silver. In further support of these empirical results and conclusions, Hamoudeh and Yuan (2008) find that while the monetary and oil price shocks reduce the volatility of precious metals (gold and silver), they do not have the same effect in the volatility of copper prices.

4 In more detail, the latent macroeconomic uncertainty measure of Jurado *et al.* (2015) is estimated as the squared forecast error of multivariate forecasting

regressions on US economic activity. According to the approach Jurado *et al.* (2015), time economic uncertainty does not necessarily coincide with the time variation of popular observable uncertainty proxies like stock-market volatility (see Bloom, 2009) or Economic Policy Uncertainty (Baker *et al.,* 2016). Jurado *et al.* (2015) argue that stock-market volatility "can change over time even if there is no change in uncertainty about economic fundamentals, if leverage changes, or if movements in risk aversion or sentiment are important drivers of economic fluctuations".

5 For robustness purposes, the same OLS regression analysis is conducted using the MU1, MU12, FU1, FU12 measures of economic uncertainty and our results remain unaltered. These results can be available upon request.

6 All the explanatory variables which are used in the empirical analysis are stationary (the ADF and the PP unit roots tests reject the hypothesis of a unit root for the variables used in the right-hand side of our forecasting regression models). The results of the unit root tests can be provided upon request.

7 The results remain unaltered if alternative lag-length criteria are used. These additional results can be available upon request.

8 We have to state here that the significantly larger coefficients of the MU index do not result from a different scale in the measurement of uncertainty. In order to have comparable results, we have multiplied the MU and the FU indices with 100 in order to be comparable and in line with the other economic uncertainty measures. Our time series plots of the various uncertainty measures which are presented in the Appendix verify this claim.

9 More recent empirical findings (Gospodinov & Ng, 2013) show that the convenience yields of commodity markets are significant indicators of future inflation. Specifically, they attribute the forecasting power of the convenience yields on their ability to indicate future economic conditions.

10 In order to provide robustness to my claims regarding the significance of the financialization period, I run the same regression results for the pre-financialization (pre-2004) period. Our results for the pre-2004 period provide robustness to my conclusions, since I find that the most economic uncertainty series turn from significant to insignificant during the pre-2000 period.

Chapter 2
FED's Unconventional Monetary Policy and Correlation Dynamics Among Conventional and Alternative Investments

Ioannis Tsakalos
University of the Aegean, Greece & Hellenic Open University, Greece

Efthymios Roumpis
Hellenic Open University, Greece

ABSTRACT

This chapter investigates the correlations between conventional and alternative investments during the quantitative easing (QE) programs launched by the U.S. Federal Reserve. Authors focus on different asset classes to examine the dynamics on their correlations and to highlight alternative investment options for rational investors and policy makers. Their analysis covers the period from January 3, 2005 to March 16, 2018. Research has significant policy implications and the empirical findings indicate a ripple effect of QE across conventional and alternative investments and suggest that their correlations differ by QE periods. Researchers also confirm the effectiveness of the portfolio rebalance channel pictured on specific assets' correlation sign, as well as the existence of specific patterns. UMP programs create portfolio rebalance since investors followed the required path set by the Fed.

DOI: 10.4018/978-1-7998-2436-7.ch002

INTRODUCTION

Global economic environment is changing rapidly and recent developments require more flexible investment strategies as well as different monetary policies. Firms tend to operate and trade internationally while investors are more keen to fund firms and governments in new markets. The main reason, besides their will to increase their earnings, is portfolio diversification to minimize the market risk. On the other hand, governments try to secure a sustain economic environment by adjusting money supply as well as changing basic interest rate. In other words, governments invoke the appropriate monetary policy under the current circumstances.

There is a large body of literature focusing on monetary policy as well as the Central Banks' means by which they manipulate the economic activity, production, financial markets and investment strategies. Investors mainly aim to maximize their profit and receive positive returns. Even though markets seem to act independently, there are many different parameters which impact above economic aspects. However, markets' correlation differs during the economic cycle. When markets' volatility is rising and firms' fundamental economic ratios become weaker, stability is more vulnerable and recession needs to be treated centralized, by Central Banks and Governments.

Governments may employ lower tax policies, create a better economic environment for investors and try to attract foreign investors to rekindle economy. However, those actions' results may not be seen as soon as they expected and further actions need to be taken. These actions refer to monetary instruments which have a direct impact on economic decisions. Central Banks first lower the interest rates to motivate investors change their strategy, but this is not effective always. When interest rates reach almost zero levels, the basic monetary instrument - the interest rate - becomes inefficient to fire the economy. Thus, unconventional monetary policies are employed to minimize the impact of recession and sustain markets to recent high levels.

The most common unconventional monetary policy is the quantitative easing (QE) which was first applied in Japan in the end of 20th century when Japanese market stagnated after continuous interest rate decreases. Japan's unique monetary decision was also applied by Fed in United States during the recent global financial crisis. Even though quantitative easing had significant impact on economy's rebound, markets' development continued till the beginning of 2019. After a decade of QE policy, Fed rose interest rate increase in December 2018, but market reaction was not that optimistic. In contrary with Japan in the late '90s, U.S. economy may need more time to be characterized sustainable. Thus, another UMP period needs to be implemented to sustain economy. In line with the Fed UMP, European Central Bank (ECB) and Bank of England (BoE) also applied a similar monetary policy in order to force investors rebalance their portfolios.

Generally, Joyce et al. (2012) concluded that there are a number of channels through which QE might be expected to affect the behavior of investment community, including policy signaling, portfolio rebalancing, and liquidity effects, authors attempt to quantify the effects of these QE programs by focusing on the changes on conventional and alternative investments' correlations.

These effects are well described by Kryzanowski et al. (2017) and Steeley (2017). In this chapter, authors provide new insights into the impact of Fed's UMP regimes on the cross-assets correlation dynamics of alternative financial assets by applying the dynamic conditional correlation model to investigate the correlation dynamics across QE and unconventional periods of programs across a range of assets. Furthermore, they examine whether cross-assets correlations differ across the implementation periods of Fed UMP, as well as the effectiveness of the portfolio rebalance channel and the existence of a ripple effect among specific asset classes. Results provide evidence regarding the ripple effect across conventional and alternative investments which is pictured on specific assets' correlation sign. They also highlight the portfolio rebalance among different assets.

The motivation of this research is to study the effectiveness of the UMP followed by Fed and the existence of the portfolio rebalance channel. Should the portfolio rebalance channel works effectively, the UMP followed by Fed succeeded to shift investors behavior.

The aim of this chapter is to capture the dynamics across conventional and alternative investment options during the UMP programs applied by Fed by employing the dynamic conditional correlation model following a large number of researchers who capture correlation dynamics between different asset classes.

This chapter extends the literature on unconventional monetary policy decisions by identifying investments options and investors' behavior. Similar to the traditional monetary policy decisions, this study may be helpful to portfolio managers during UMP programs.

BACKGROUND

Last decade global financial markets came across a challenging environment. Banking sector trustworthiness was criticized by global financial organizations, credit rating agencies, investors, regulatory authorities and supervisory agencies. Market recession followed a series of financial bankruptcies and global economy needed large financial aid and significant time to rebound and shift the investment climate. Within this framework, Federal Reserve Bank (Fed) proceeded to unique monetary policy decisions by implementing unconventional monetary policies. Table 1 presents in brief Fed's UMP programs and their period of implementation.

Table 1. Fed's Unconventional Monetary Programs

Program	Description	Period of Implementation
QE1	Fed purchased $1.5 trillion in Bonds, including $1.2 trillion in US Agency Debt and $300 billion in US Treasuries.	25 Nov 2008 – 10 Aug 2010
QE2	QE2 consists of the purchase of $827 billion US Treasuries and matured securities declined US Agency debt and MBS to $247 billion.	27 Aug 2010 – 20 Jun 2012
QE3	Treasury bond purchasing program to replace Operation Twist	22 Aug 2012 – 12 Dec 2012
Tapering	Fed reduces the pace of its asset purchases	19 Jun 2013 – 29 Oct 2014
Federal Fund Rate Increase		17 Dec 2015 – 19 Mar 2018

According to literature review, global financial crisis affected the global economic activity and led many economies to a continuous recession (Samitas & Tsakalos, 2013; Dimitriou et al., 2013). Real Economy and firms' financial ratios were affected significantly. Increasing unemployment rate and challenging economic environment created an unstable field for firms. Global financial crisis affected almost all sectors across different regions worldwide. Kenourgios and Dimitriou (2015) examined the effect of global financial crisis on ten sectors in developed and emerging regions during different phases of the financial crisis. They found evidence that there were contagion effects across regional stock markets and regional financial and non-financial sectors. Contagion created spread to many financial markets as a consequence of their direct or indirect connection with US economy, or later with the European Union markets, through various contagion channels (Shikimi & Yamada, 2019; Baur, 2012; Kalbaska & Gatkowski, 2012; Bekaert et al., 2014), which are well described by Kaminsky et al. (2003). Many other researchers investigated the impact that global financial crisis had on various stock markets, commodities etc. (Apergis et al., 2019; BenMim & BenSaida, 2019; Wang et al., 2019; Luchtenberg & Vu, 2015).

Following the devastation that financial crisis caused to global economy, governments and authorities had to react. Despite the adverse circumstances, they had to prepare the breeding ground to rekindle economy and manipulate firms' and investors' behavior. The main path to shift their investment strategies is to decrease the interest rates. When this is inefficient though, they have to proceed to unconventional means, such as the quantitative easing.

Central banks' role is crucial and define the success of the intended monetary policy. Following Governments' monetary policy decision, Central Banks - in coordination with the concerned authorities - use miscellaneous transmission channels to implement the required policies. There is a significant number of researchers which extended the literature regarding the transmission channels (Borrallo Egea & Hierro 2019; Buch et al., 2019; Serati & Venegoni, 2019; Falagiarda et al., 2015; Joyce et al., 2012).

Borrallo Egea and Hierro (2019) used a VAR model to examine the effectiveness of the monetary policy both before and after the 2007 subprime crisis in US, as well as the sovereign debt crisis in Eurozone. Findings emphasize on the risk channel in US and the credit channel in Eurozone, stating though that UMP was effective in the first phase of the implementation only. Additionally, Serati and Venegoni (2019), who also examined both crises in US and the Eurozone, concluded that there was a clear effect on the credit and interest rate channel after the policy transmission tampering.

On the other hand, there is a number of researchers who provided evidence that the main transmission channel during the implementation of the ECB UMPs was the portfolio rebalancing channel. Varghese and Zhang (2018) highlighted the importance of the traditional signaling channel, however the portfolio rebalancing channel had a larger impact in the new phase. In regards to the portfolio rebalancing channel, Bernanke (2010, 2012) highlighted the increasing need for investors to rebalance their portfolios by replacing assets and changing the correlations among them. However, Falagiarda et al. (2015) argue that the portfolio rebalancing and signaling channels were effective during the SMP period.

Despite the required channel or the effectiveness of the transmission channels, Central Banks' expectations diverge and their main concern is to bring the economy back to normal, even by employing nonconventional monetary policies. Some researchers doubt about the effectiveness of UMP programs (Galesi, 2018; Sheedy, 2017), while others provide evidence that quantitative easing had a positive effect on GDP and inflation for small banks (Matousek et al., 2019)

The spillovers impact of UMP, on various financial assets and different economies, has been examined and analyzed by several researchers in the post crisis period (Hohberger et al., 2019; Todorov, 2019; Apostolou & Beirne, 2018; Churm et al., 2018; Mamaysky, 2018; Thornton & Di Tomasso, 2018; Fassas & Papadamou, 2018; Shogbuyi & Steeley, 2017; Steeley, 2017; Kryzanowski et al., 2017; Bernhard & Ebner, 2017; Mamatzakis & Bermpei, 2016).

Regarding the correlation dynamics among asset classes though, some researchers focused on the relation between assets during crises and UMP periods. Steeley (2017) employed a multivariate DCC-GARCH model and provided evidence that volatility rises during the financial crash which remains only during the first QE phase. Furthermore, Kryzanowski et al. (2017) concluded that correlations among asset classes (bonds, equities and currency forwards) - during the US Federal Reserve UMP programs - diverge by QE period across developed and emerging countries and, also, there is a spillover effect on the international financial markets. Despite the importance of the aforementioned studies and their useful findings, authors try to extend literature review by investigating the correlation dynamics among alternative assets during the UMP periods of implementation and quantifying the variation on assets' correlation.

MAIN FOCUS OF THE CHAPTER

Data and Methodology

Data

In order to capture the dynamics among alternative investment options, we have selected a set of indices which include the following indices: the Morgan Stanley MSCI World Equity Index, the earlier Goldman Sachs and currently S&P Commodity Weighted Index, representing unleveraged, log-only investments in commodity futures (S&PGSC), the spot gold prices (Gold), the Brent Crude Oil prices (Brent), the Natural Gas prices (NG), the Shipping, Baltic Dry Index (BDI) and the Morgan Stanley MSCI World Real Estate Index (MSCIRE) for the Global Real Estate Industry. The data are derived from Bloomberg

Table 2 summarizes a range of key statistics of the performance of the selected assets. One can easily spot a significant variation in the statistic values across the different asset classes. Mean returns are positive for the MSCI World Equity Index (0.018), as well as the Morgan Stanley Real Estate Index (0.010), Gold (0.033) and Brent (0.014), while we observe negative figures for the S&P Commodity Weighted Index (-0.020), the Natural Gas (-0.022) and the Shipping Baltic Dry Index (-0.040). Equity indices (MSCIWO and MSCIRE) indicate the highest risk-standard deviations while the Natural Gas, BDI, S&P Commodity index and Brent Crude Oil have the lowest values of risk. The gold exhibits the most rewarding performance (0.033) associated with the highest volatility (0.047). Also, there is evidence of fat tails and asymmetry in the excess returns when compared to the normal distribution. More specifically, equity markets returns showed negative skewness and large kurtosis (13.243 for the MSCI World Equity and 11.753 for the Real Estate Indices). On the other hand, Brent, Natural Gas and BDI returns have positive skewness and an excess kurtosis. In terms of kurtosis, S&P Commodity Index and Gold have also excess kurtosis, while their skewness is negative (-0.199 & -0.225, respectively).

This table reports summary statistics for the daily returns of the asset classes over the period 3 January 2005 to 16 March 2018, a total of 3445 daily observations. 'Skew' and 'Kurt' denote the skewness and Kurtosis of the series, respectively.

Table 2. Summary statistics for the asset returns

	Mean	Std. Deviation	Median	Min	Max	Skew	Kurt
MSCIWO	0.018	0.060	1.008	-7.325	9.096	-0.525	13.243
S&PGSC	-0.020	0.000	1.449	-8.649	7.215	-0.199	6.161
Gold	0.033	0.047	1.147	-7.800	7.386	-0.225	7.805
Brent	0.014	0.009	2.091	-10.946	12.707	0.019	6.423
NG	-0.022	0.000	3.090	-14.893	26.771	0.620	7.808
BDI	-0.040	0.000	2.200	-12.072	13.658	0.077	6.629
MSCIRE	0.010	0.051	1.131	-8.255	7.585	-0.424	11.753

MSCIWO: Morgan Stanley MSCI world equity index; S&PGSC: S&P commodity weighted index; GOLD: gold; BRENT: Brent crude oil; NG: natural gas; BDI: Baltic dry index; MSCIRE: MSCI World Real Estate index.

Methodology

In order to examine the dynamics in the correlation of returns between conventional and alternative investments, we use the Dynamic Conditional Correlation (DCC) model. The DCC model enables us to confirm the existence of a ripple effect on assets' interdependence. Even though, there are already some studies which examined the unconventional monetary policies and they present empirical analyses regarding the unconventional monetary policy programs, there is limited evidence on the impact of non-conventional monetary policy interventions on the conventional and alternative investments' correlations.

Let r_t denote the (N × 1) vector time series of assets returns. Following the conventional approach, we assume a first-order autoregressive process, *AR*(1), for asset classes returns in the mean equation. Specifically, we specify the return equation (equation 1) as:

$$r_t = \phi_0 + \phi_1 \cdot r_{t-1} + \varepsilon_t \tag{1}$$

where $\varepsilon_t \mid \mathcal{F}_{t-1} \sim N\left(0, H_t\right)$, $\mathcal{F}_t$ pictures the information up to and including time *t* and H_t refers to the covariance matrix.

The DCC model estimator of conditional variances and correlations functions in two phases: initially, authors estimate a univariate GARCH model for all assets and then, the univariate variance estimations are introduced as inputs to obtain dynamic correlations. The DCC model captures the dynamics of time-varying conditional correlations, with the covariance matrix, H_t, specified as in equation (2):

$$H_t = D_t R_t D_t \tag{2}$$

where $D_t = diag\left\{\sqrt{h_{i,t}}\right\}$ is a m x m diagonal matrix with the square roots of the conditional variances in the diagonal; and, $R_t \equiv \left\{\rho_{ij}\right\}_t$ is the time-varying conditional correlations matrix. Both D_t and R_t and, as a consequence, H_t are assumed to be positive defined. The first order univariate GARCH process is indicated in equation (3):

$$h_{i,t} = \omega_i + \alpha_i \cdot \varepsilon_{i,t-1}^2 + \beta \cdot h_{i,t-1} \tag{3}$$

where $i = 1, 2, \ldots, m$, indicates the i-th equation in the vector autoregressive (VAR) model and $h_{i,t}$ is the conditional variance of the error term, $\varepsilon_{i,t}$, of the i-th equation, obtained from the first estimation step. In the next step, the standardized residuals' vector is employed to develop the DCC correlation specification as in the following equations:

$$Q_t = \left(1 - \theta_1 - \theta_2\right)\bar{Q} + \theta_1 \eta_{t-1} \eta_{t-1}^{'} + \theta_2 Q_{t-1} \tag{4}$$

and

$$R_t = Q_t^{*-1} Q_t Q_t^{*-1} \tag{5}$$

where $\bar{Q} = E\left[\eta_t \eta_t^{'}\right]$, the unconditional covariance of the standardized residuals, is obtained from the initial estimation step and

$$Q_t^* = \left(diag\left(Q_t\right)\right)^{-1/2} = diag\left(\frac{1}{\sqrt{q_{11,t}}}, \ldots, \frac{1}{\sqrt{q_{mm,t}}}\right)$$

is a diagonal matrix composed of the square root of the diagonal elements of Q_t. In equation (3), θ_1 and θ_2 are scalar parameters, $\eta_t \left(\eta_t = D_t^{-1} \varepsilon_t\right)$ is the standardized residual matrix and Q_t is the covariance matrix of η_t. The parameters θ_1 and θ_2 capture the impact of previous shocks and previous dynamic conditional correlations on current dynamic conditional correlations. The DCC (1,1) parameters, θ_1 and

θ_2, are positive and their sum is lower than 1 ($\theta_1 + \theta_2 < 1$), which ensures that Q_t is positive and mean-reverting. This means that, following a shock, the correlation among the underlying assets returns to long-term unconditional level. The correlation estimators of equation (4) are as follows (equation 6):

$$\rho_{ij,t} = \frac{q_{ij,t}}{\sqrt{q_{ii,t} q_{jj,t}}} \text{ for } i, j = 1, 2, \ldots, n \text{ and } i \neq j.$$

The DCC model is estimated by the maximization of the log-likelihood function in equation (7):

$$L = -\frac{1}{2}\sum_{t=1}^{T}\left(mlog\left(2\pi\right)\right) + 2log\left|D_t\right| + log\left|R_t\right| + \eta_t' R_t^{-1} \eta_t$$

Empirical Results

Table 3 presents the DCC model parameters' estimation, the alpha and beta coefficients. Both parameters a and b found to be positive and a+b<1, supporting the presence of dynamic correlations. The estimates of the DCC parameter b typically reflect high persistence.

Following figures present the dynamic conditional correlations among the selected alternative assets. Figures portray the interdependence among different investment options which helps authors to capture the dynamics during the recent global financial crisis. Additionally, Fed's unconventional monetary policy effect is clearly seen in some pairs which confirms the significant role that UMP have. Quantitative Easing employed to rekindle economy mainly via the portfolio rebalancing channel. The ripple effect, created by the implementation of the new monetary policy, led investors and firms to alter their portfolio structure by selecting alternative assets instead of safe heavens such as bonds which changed their correlation among them.

More specifically, Figure 1 presents the dynamic conditional correlations between MSCI World Equity Index and commodity alternative assets, namely S&P Commodity Index, Gold & Brent Crude Oil. The implementation of the QE shifted the dynamic correlations among above assets making their relation more vulnerable to monetary decisions. In Figure 1, the relation among Brent Crude Oil and Gold with the MSCI World Equity Index becomes negative during some periods around and after the QE period.

Table 3. Estimation of the DCC model parameters

Panel A. Alpha Parameter Estimates of the DCC Model							
	MSCIWO	**S&PGSC**	**Gold**	**Brent**	**NG**	**BDI**	**MSCIRE**
MSCIWO	1	0.039	0.036	0.037	0.012	0.040	0.085
S&PGSC	(4.457)	1	0.028	0.079	0.014	0.023	0.026
Gold	(3.584)	(2.658)	1	0.022	0.006	0.009	0.035
Brent	(3.224)	(2.287)	(2.256)	1	0.007	0.000	0.030
NG	(0.330)	(2.451)	(1.320)	(2.566)	1	0.006	0.009
BDI	(0.529)	(0.572)	(0.526)	(0.000)	(1.178)	1	0.010
MSCIRE	(7.295)	(3.087)	(1.56)	(4.465)	(0.529)	(2.322)	1
Panel B. Beta Parameter Estimates of the DCC Model							
	MSCIWO	S&PGSC	Gold	Brent	NG	BDI	MSCIRE
MSCIWO	1	0.956	0.942	0.956	0.967	0.316	0.915
S&PGSC	(106.3)	1	0.953	0.871	0.986	0.557	0.968
Gold	(46.64)	(43.04)	1	0.964	0.978	0.837	0.907
Brent	(82.99)	(7.360)	(42.27)	1	0.992	0.979	0.960
NG	(8.292)	(175.4)	(56.55)	(302.12)	1	0.759	0.973
BDI	(1.993)	(0.233)	(6.559)	(9.406)	(4.815)	1	0.941
MSCIRE	(70.10)	(92.40)	(13.29)	(97.77)	(23.23)	(15.99)	1

Notes: The table presents the estimated alpha parameters (Panel A) and beta parameters (Panel B) of the DCC model. The upper diagonal figures are the estimated parameters and the lower diagonal figures denote the t-statistics.

Figure 2 portrays the noncorrelated relation among the MSCI World Equity Index and the alternative markets (shipping and real estate), which allows firms and investors to waive high volatile periods as well as invest in alternative options. Also, its positive dynamic correlation with natural gas decreases the years following the UMP periods. However, energy market - which is represented by Brent Crude Oil (Figure 1) and Natural Gas (Figure 2) - came across a turbulent period in which geopolitical facts impacted its interdependence with the financial markets.

Figure 3 refers to the high dynamic correlation between S&P Commodity Index and Brent Crude Oil almost during the whole sample period, confirming that Oil market leads the commodity industry and its fluctuation depends mainly on the behavior of traditional energy products. In regard to the correlation among S&P Commodity Index with Gold and Natural Gas, authors show that QE decreased their dynamic correlation over the years.

Figure 1. Dynamic conditional correlation among MSCI world equity index Vs S&P commodity index, Gold & Brent

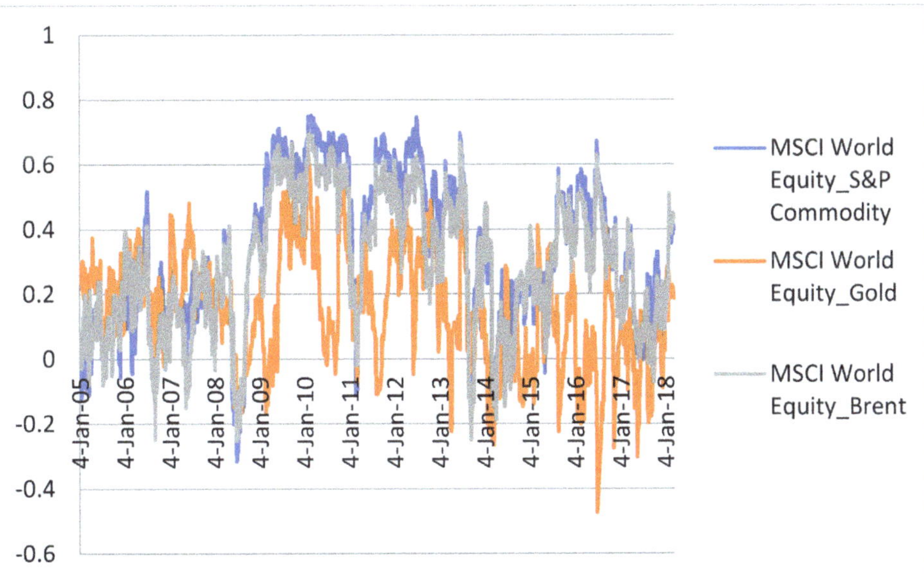

Figure 2. Dynamic conditional correlation among MSCI world equity index Vs natural gas, BDI & MSCI world real estate index

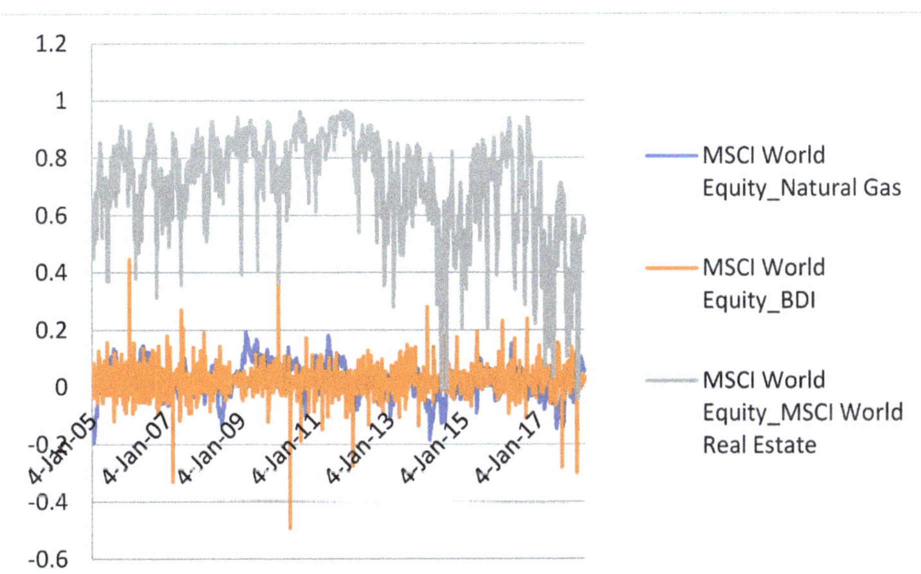

Figure 3. Dynamic conditional correlation among S&P commodity index Vs Gold, Brent & natural gas

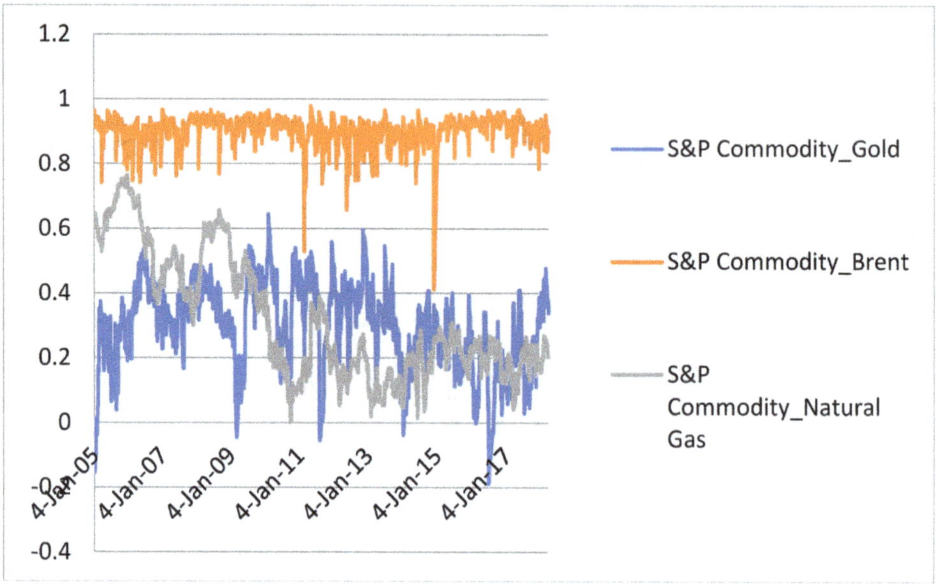

Similar with the MSCI World Equity Index, S&P Commodity Index seems to be non correlated with the Shipping Index (BDI), while its positive relation with the MSCI World Real Estate Index - during the UMP periods - receives higher values. Additionally, the interdependence between Gold and Brent Crude Oil is positive correlated and volatile, but - during the post UMP period - their dynamic correlation decreases.

Concerning the dynamic correlation between Gold and the Baltic Dry Index, authors confirm the important role that shipping has during the QE implementation period since their correlation fluctuates to very low levels. Similar, but slightly higher, is the relation among Gold and Natural Gas during the UMP period, while the post QE period authors captured also negative values. Furthermore, Gold's correlation with Natural Gas is volatile during both the QE period and the post UMP one.

Referring to Brent Crude Oil, its dynamic correlation with the MSCI World Real Estate Index increases the years 2009-2012, but the post QE period returns to previous range (Figure 6). On the other hand, Brent and Natural Gas interdependence is lowering mainly due to the Shale Gas industry which changed the global energy map. BDI and Brent is also non correlated.

Finally, Figure 7 presents the low dynamic correlation among BDI and Natural Gas (slightly negative), as well as the volatile relation among MSCI World Real Estate Index and BDI, and MSCI World Real Estate Index and Natural Gas.

Figure 4. Dynamic conditional correlation among S&P commodity index Vs BDI & MSCI world real estate index, and Gold Vs Brent

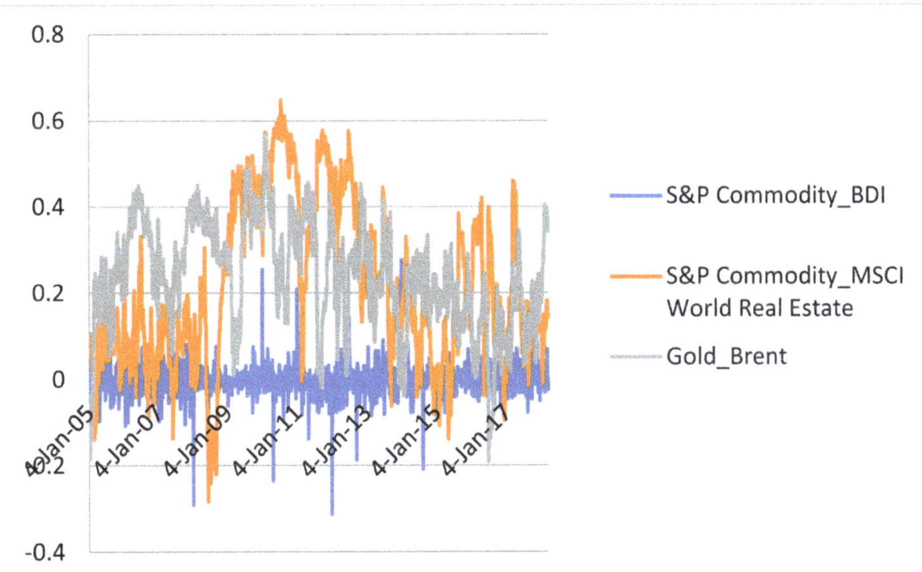

Figure 5. Dynamic conditional correlation among Gold Vs natural gas, BDI & MSCI world real estate index

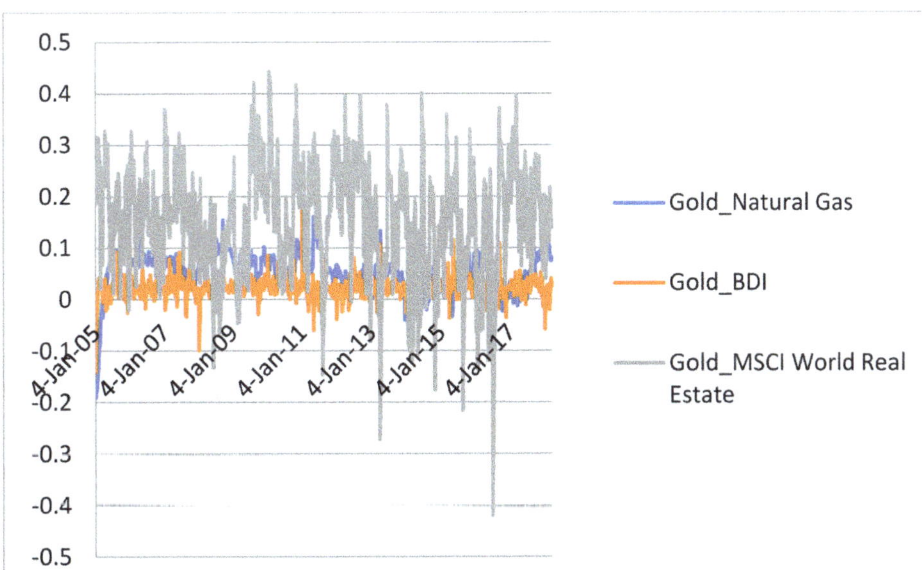

Figure 6. Dynamic conditional correlation among Brent Vs natural gas, BDI & MSCI world real estate index

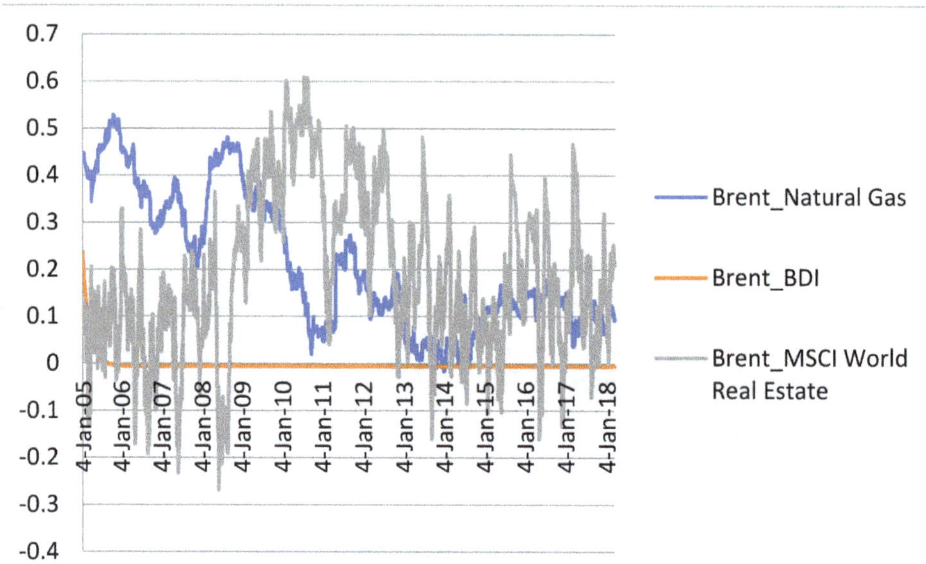

Figure 7. Dynamic conditional correlation among natural gas Vs BDI and MSCI world real estate index and BDI Vs MSCI world real estate index

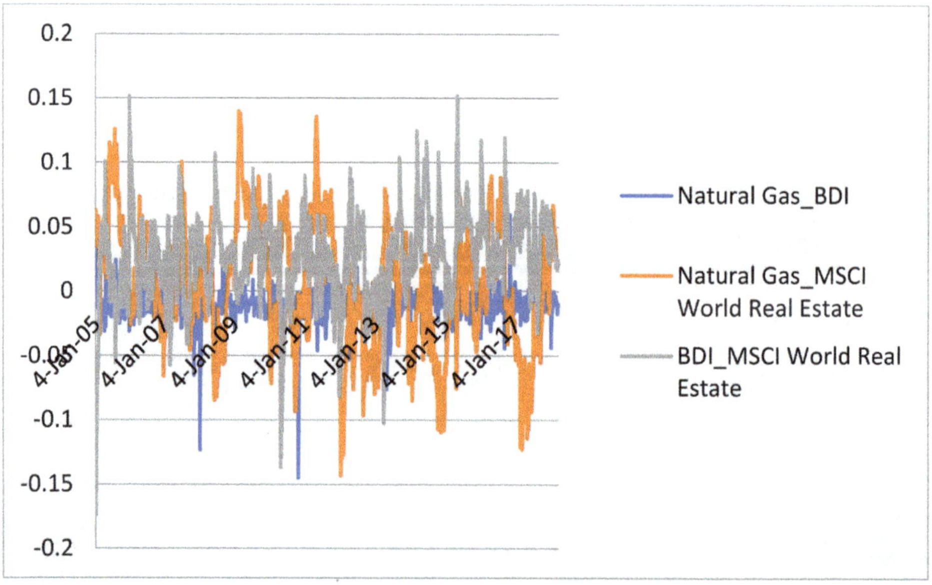

Empirical findings support that Fed QE programs impacted positively the cross correlations among between Equities with commodities and real estate. Tapering led - in most of the pairs - to a lower impact and supports the effectiveness of the portfolio rebalance channel. Shipping is not significantly correlated with the rest alternative investment options. In conclusion, we confirm that there is a ripple effect which is clearly seen and the effectiveness of the portfolio rebalance channel is pictured on alternative assets correlation sign.

CONCLUSION

In this chapter, authors examined the correlation dynamics among alternative investment options. The period under investigation ranges from 2005 till the beginning of 2018. Study focuses on the unconventional monetary means by which Central Banks try to manipulate investors behavior. Authors capture the dynamics among equity indices, Commodities and Shipping index during a long period around the UMP programs.

Researchers investigate the change on alternative assets correlations during the sample period, trying to conclude whether there is a shift on investors' portfolios. Cross-assets correlations - during the three UMP periods in the U.S. - support that investors changed their portfolios' structure by shifting funds to different investment options. This is in line with the findings of Kryzanowski et al. (2017) and confirm that portfolio rebalance channel works effectively. Additionally, authors highlight the importance of the UMP and their significant effects on economy during economic crises, in contrary with the conventional monetary policies.

However, authors acknowledge some limitations to their analysis. First, UMP effect is not the only parameter which defines investors' behavior. There is a number of factors which also forces investors to alter their portfolio structure by selecting unconventional investment options. Also, depreciation of specific assets may be investment opportunities such as real estate or shipping.

Authors provide evidence that the portfolio rebalance channel works effectively regarding the transmission of the UMPs. Albeit results support that there is an effect of UMPs on most of the asset pairs, the extend of the dynamics among asset classes differ. Findings highlight that Fed's UMPs seem to be effective in terms of the portfolio rebalance channel for alternative options such as energy, real estate and equity market. The results are useful for global investors, traders and portfolio managers in terms of whether UMP programs force them to alternative investments options.

REFERENCES

Afonso, A., Argyrou, M., Gadea, M. D., & Kontonikas, A. (2018). "Whatever it takes" to resolve the European sovereign debt crisis? Bond pricing regime switches and monetary policy effects. *Journal of International Money and Finance*, *86*, 1–30. doi:10.1016/j.jimonfin.2018.04.005

Apergis, N., Christou, C., & Kynigakis, I. (2019). Contagion across US and European financial markets: Evidence from the CDS markets. *Journal of International Money and Finance*, *96*, 1–12. doi:10.1016/j.jimonfin.2019.04.006

Apostolou, A., & Beirne, J. (2018). Volatility spillovers of unconventional monetary policy to emerging market economies. *Economic Modelling*, *79*(c), 118–129.

Baur, D. G. (2012). Financial contagion and the real economy. *Journal of Banking & Finance*, *36*(10), 2680–2692. doi:10.1016/j.jbankfin.2011.05.019

Bekaert, G., Ehrmann, M., Fratzscher, M., & Mehl, A. (2014). Global crises and equity market contagion. *The Journal of Finance*, *69*(6), 2597–2649. doi:10.1111/jofi.12203

BenMim, I., & BenSaida, A. (2019). Financial contagion across major stock markets: A study during crisis episodes. *The North American Journal of Economics and Finance*, *48*, 187–201. doi:10.1016/j.najef.2019.02.005

Bernanke, B. S. (2010). What the Fed did and why: supporting the recovery and sustaining price stability. *The Washington Post,* November 4.

Bernanke, B. S. (2012). Monetary policy since the onset of the crisis. Federal Reserve Bank of Kansas City Economic Symposium, Jackson Hole, Wyoming.

Bernhard, S., & Ebner, T. (2017). Cross-border spillover effects of *unconventional monetary policies* on Swiss asset prices. *Journal of International Money and Finance*, *75*, 109–127. doi:10.1016/j.jimonfin.2017.04.001

Borrallo Egea, F., & Hierro, L. A. (2019). Transmission of Monetary Policy in the US and EU in times of expansion and crisis. *Journal of Policy Modeling*, *41*(4), 763–783. doi:10.1016/j.jpolmod.2019.02.012

Bowman, D., Londono, J. M., & Sapriza, H. (2015). U.S. unconventional monetary policy and transmission to emerging market economies. *Journal of International Money and Finance*, *55*, 27–59. doi:10.1016/j.jimonfin.2015.02.016

Buch, C. M., Bussiere, M., Goldberg, L., & Hills, R. (2019). The International Transmission of Monetary Policy. *Journal of International Money and Finance, 91*, 29–48. doi:10.1016/j.jimonfin.2018.08.005

Burriel, P., & Galesi, A. (2018). Uncovering the heterogeneous effects of ECB unconventional monetary policies across euro area countries. *European Economic Review, 101*, 210–229. doi:10.1016/j.euroecorev.2017.10.007

Chen, Q., Filardo, A., He, D., & Zhu, F. (2015). Financial crisis, US unconventional monetary policy and international spillovers. *Journal of International Money and Finance, 67*, 62–81. doi:10.1016/j.jimonfin.2015.06.011

Chiang, T. C., Jeon, B. N., & Li, H. (2007). Dynamic correlation analysis of financial contagion: Evidence from Asian markets. *Journal of International Money and Finance, 26*(7), 1206–1228. doi:10.1016/j.jimonfin.2007.06.005

Cho, J. W., Choi, J. H., Kim, T., & Kim, W. (2016). Flight-to-quality and correlation between currency and stock returns. *Journal of Banking & Finance, 62*, 191–212. doi:10.1016/j.jbankfin.2014.09.003

Churm, R., Joyce, M., Kapetanios, G., & Theodoridis, K. (in press). Unconventional monetary policies and the macroeconomy: The impact of the UK's QE2 and funding for lending scheme. *The Quarterly Review of Economics and Finance.*

Dimitriou, D., Kenourgios, D., & Simos, T. (2013). Global financial crisis and emerging stock market contagion: A multivariate FIAPARCH-DCC approach. *International Review of Financial Analysis, 30*, 46–56. doi:10.1016/j.irfa.2013.05.008

Falagiarda, M., McQuade, P., & Tirpák, M. (2015). *Spillovers from the ECB's non-standard monetary policies on non-euro area EU countries: evidence from an event-study analysis*. European Central Bank.

Fratzscher, M., Lo Duca, M., & Straub, R. (2013). On the international spillovers of US quantitative easing, *DIW Discussion Papers, no. 1304*.

Fratzscher, M., Lo Duca, M., & Straub, R. (2016). ECB Unconventional Monetary Policy: Market Impact and International Spillovers. *IMF Economic Review, 64*(1), 36–74. doi:10.1057/imfer.2016.5

Gospodinov, N., & Jamali, I. (2012). The Effects of Federal Funds Rate Surprises on S&P 500 Volatility and Volatility Risk Premium. *Journal of Empirical Finance, 19*(4), 497–510. doi:10.1016/j.jempfin.2012.04.009

Hohberger, S., Priftis, R., & Vogel, L. (in press). The distributional effects of conventional monetary policy and quantitative easing: Evidence from an estimated DSGE model. *Journal of Banking & Finance*.

Joyce, M., Miles, D., Scott, A., & Vayanos, D. (2012). Quantitative easing and unconventional monetary policy – an introduction. *Economic Journal (London)*, *122*(564), F271–F288. doi:10.1111/j.1468-0297.2012.02551.x

Kalbaska, A., & Gatkowski, M. (2012). Eurozone sovereign contagion: Evidence from the CDS market (2005-2010). *Journal of Economic Behavior & Organization*, *83*(3), 657–673. doi:10.1016/j.jebo.2012.05.010

Kaminsky, G. L., Reinhart, C. M., & Vegh, C. A. (2003). The Unholy Trinity of Financial Contagion. *The Journal of Economic Perspectives*, *17*(4), 51–74. doi:10.1257/089533003772034899

Kenourgios, D., & Dimitriou, D. (2015). Contagion of the Global Financial Crisis and the real economy: A regional analysis. *Economic Modelling*, *44*, 283–293. doi:10.1016/j.econmod.2014.10.048

Kenourgios, D., Papadamou, S., & Dimitriou, D. (2015a). Intraday Exchange Rate Volatility Transmissions Across QE Announcements. *Finance Research Letters*, *14*, 128–134. doi:10.1016/j.frl.2015.05.007

Kenourgios, D., Papadamou, S., & Dimitriou, D. (2015b). On Quantitative Easing and High Frequency Exchange Rate Dynamics. *Research in International Business and Finance*, *34*, 110–125. doi:10.1016/j.ribaf.2015.01.003

Luchtenberg, K. F., & Vu, Q. V. (2015). The 2008 financial crisis: Stock market contagion and its determinants. *Research in International Business and Finance*, *33*, 178–203. doi:10.1016/j.ribaf.2014.09.007

Lyonnet, V., & Werner, R. (2012). Lessons from the Bank of England on "Quantitative Easing" and Other "Unconventional" Monetary Policies. *International Review of Financial Analysis*, *25*, 94–105. doi:10.1016/j.irfa.2012.08.001

MacDonald, M. (2017). International capital market frictions and spillovers from quantitative easing. *Journal of International Money and Finance*, *70*, 135–156. doi:10.1016/j.jimonfin.2016.08.003

Maggio, M., Kermani, A., & Palmer, C. (2016). How quantitative easing works: Evidence on the refinancing channel, Working Paper 22638, National Bureau of Economic Research.

Mamatzakis, E., & Bermpei, T. (2016). What is the effect of unconventional monetary policy on bank performance? *Journal of International Money and Finance*, *67*, 239–263. doi:10.1016/j.jimonfin.2016.05.005

Mamaysky, H. (2018). The time horizon of price responses to quantitative easing. *Journal of Banking & Finance*, *90*, 32–49. doi:10.1016/j.jbankfin.2018.02.016

Matousek, R., Papadamou, S., Sevic, A., & Tzeremes, N. (In press). The effectiveness of quantitative easing: Evidence from Japan. *Journal of International Money and Finance, 99*

Meinusch, A., & Tillmann, P. (2016). The macroeconomic impact of unconventional monetary policy shocks. *Journal of Macroeconomics*, *47*, 58–67. doi:10.1016/j.jmacro.2015.11.002

Neely, C. J. (2015). Unconventional Monetary Policy Had Large International Effects. *Journal of Banking & Finance*, *52*, 101–111. doi:10.1016/j.jbankfin.2014.11.019

Rosa, C. (2011). The High-Frequency Response of Exchange Rates to Monetary Policy Actions and Statements. *Journal of Banking & Finance*, *35*(2), 478–489. doi:10.1016/j.jbankfin.2010.09.008

Samitas, A., & Tsakalos, I. (2013). How can a small country affect the European economy? the Greek contagion phenomenon. *Journal of International Financial Markets, Institutions and Money*, *25*, 18–32. doi:10.1016/j.intfin.2013.01.005

Serati, M., & Venegoni, A. (2019). The cross-country impact of ECB *policies*: Asymmetries in – Asymmetries out? *Journal of International Money and Finance*, *90*, 118–141. doi:10.1016/j.jimonfin.2018.09.008

Sheedy, K. (2017). Conventional and unconventional monetary policy rules. *Journal of Macroeconomics 54*(A), 127-147.

Shikimi, M., & Yamada, K. (2019). Trade and financial channels as the transmission mechanism of the financial crisis. *International Review of Economics & Finance*, *63*, 364–381. doi:10.1016/j.iref.2019.04.008

Shogbuyi, A., & Steeley, J. M. (2017). The effect of quantitative easing on the variance and covariance of the UK and US equity markets. *International Review of Financial Analysis*, *52*, 281–291. doi:10.1016/j.irfa.2017.07.009

Song, Z., & Zhu, H. (2018). Quantitative easing auctions of Treasury bonds. *Journal of Financial Economics*, *128*(1), 103–124. doi:10.1016/j.jfineco.2018.02.004

Thorton, J., & Di Tomasso, C. (2018). Unconventional monetary policy and the 'currency wars'. *Finance Research Letters, 26*, 250–254. doi:10.1016/j.frl.2018.02.010

Tillmann, P. (2016). Unconventional monetary policy and the spillovers to emerging markets. *Journal of International Money and Finance, 66*, 136–156. doi:10.1016/j.jimonfin.2015.12.010

Timmer, Y. (2018). Emerging market corporate bond yields and monetary policy. *Emerging Markets Review, 36*, 130–143. doi:10.1016/j.ememar.2018.04.001

Todorov, K. (2019). (accepted for publication). Quantify the quantitative easing: Impact on bonds and corporate debt issuance. *Journal of Financial Economics*. doi:10.1016/j.jfineco.2019.08.003

Varghese, R., & Zhang, Y. S. (2018). A new wave of ECB's unconventional monetary policies: domestic impact and spillovers. *IMF Working Paper, WP/18/11*.

Wang, X., Liu, H., Huang, S., & Lucey, B. (2019). Identifying the multiscale financial contagion in precious metal markets. *International Review of Financial Analysis, 63*, 209–219. doi:10.1016/j.irfa.2019.04.003

Chapter 3
The Return Performance of Real Estate Investment Trusts (REITs) and Portfolio Diversification Benefits:
Evidence From the European Market

Panagiotis Petris
National and Kapodistrian University of Athens, Greece

Panayotis Alexakis
National and Kapodistrian University of Athens, Greece

ABSTRACT

This study describes the emergence and the structure of Real Estate Investment Trusts (REITs) and investigates whether European REITs provide higher risk-adjusted returns and portfolio diversification benefits relative to the market portfolio. The top public listed companies of five (5) established (Belgium, France, Germany, Netherlands, UK), three (3) emerging (Italy, Spain, Ireland) and one (1) nascent (Greece) European REIT markets, are considered over period 2007 – 2018. The empirical findings denote poor performance of most European REITS over the Global Financial Crisis period but strong risk adjusted returns, overall, outperforming the equivalent European stock market indices and bonds over the first years of post - GFC period. In the recent period (2015 – 2018), most European REITs continued to deliver positive but modest risk adjusted returns relative to the previous period. The analysis provides evidence of poor portfolio diversification benefits and weak cross country diversification benefits among the European REITs.

DOI: 10.4018/978-1-7998-2436-7.ch003

INTRODUCTION

Real estate assets due to their tangible nature are considered to be secure and value – appreciating investments. An investor benefits, in the long – run, from the capital appreciation gains of the real estate asset and, in the short – run, from the monthly fixed income that the property produces through rent. However, real estate markets are considered highly decentralized and illiquid. Property investments necessitate the disposal of large amounts of capital, on the part of the investor, restraining access to small-scale investors. Also, the requirement of sizeable investments and large capital injections makes it difficult for the private investors to diversify their portfolios, remaining prone against asset specific risk. Portfolio diversification is a process of capital allocation on different asset classes. The significance of portfolio diversification is that it reduces the exposure on one particular asset and hence against the overall investment risk, by spreading capital across different asset classes, provided the risks of these assets are not directly related (Markowitz, 1952).

The above-mentioned drawbacks were first concerned by the US congress with the establishment of the Real Estate Investment Trusts (hereinafter called REIT(s)) regime in the 1960s (Cigar Exercise Tax Extension). REITs are mainly close – ended funds (public listed)[1] traded on the major stock exchanges, which invest in income - producing real estate assets and distribute that income as dividends to the shareholders. The potential benefits of the REIT regime are summarized in three main sources. First, the REIT regime allows investors to immediate access (even) large scale property investments. Second, (public listed) REITs are tradable in the Stock Exchange, thusly benchmarked against an index and easily liquidated at par value. Third, the REITs investments provide portfolio diversification benefits and low correlation with other stocks and bonds.

The high growth of the US REITs, took place in the 1980s, especially after the Tax Reform Act of 1986. Today, roughly 60 years after the US REITs establishment the sector, in US only, is estimated at more than one (1) trillion $ market capitalization, occupying approximately 65% of the FTSE EPRA/NAREIT global real estate index (ERPA, 2018). In Europe, REITs were first introduced in Netherlands (1969), followed by France (2003), UK and Germany (2007). According to the European Public Real Association (ERPA) research (2018), the total listed real estate sector in Europe is valued at 490 bn $, with Germany being the dominant player (107 bn $), followed by the UK (100 bn $) and France (94 bn $). Today, the REIT regime exists in nearly forty (40) countries, and according to each country's stage of (REIT regime) maturity, are grouped into four different classes[2]: nascent, emerging, established and mature (Ernest & Young, 2018).

To this end, this study investigates the return performance of real estate investment trusts (REITs) and portfolio diversification benefits. The study concentrates in the

European market considering the top public listed companies of five (5) established (Belgium, France, Germany, Netherlands, UK), three (3) emerging (Italy, Spain, Ireland) and one (1) nascent (Greece) European REIT markets. The examining period is 2007 – 2018. The full period is broken down into three sub- periods[3], in order to capture the effect of the GFC (Global Financial Crisis) on the European REITs. The three standard measurement methods are used, namely, the Sharpe ratio (Sharpe, 1966), the Treynor index (Treynor, 1965) and the Jensen Alpha index (Jensen, 1968), to analyze whether European REITs provide higher risk-adjusted returns relative to the market portfolio. Correlation analysis is also used to assess the REIT portfolio diversification benefits. Also, Johansen cointegration (Johansen, 1988; Johansen, 1991) and Granger causality tests (Granger, 1969; Granger, 1986) are conducted to investigate whether there are (international) long – run linkages and short run interactions among the European REITs.

The extant literature provides numerous alternative measures to assess market performance, such as: the modified sharpe ratio (Israelsen, 2005), the adjusted sharpe ratio (Pezier and White, 2008) the Sortino ratio (Sortino and Van der Meer, 1991), the Omega ratio (Shadwick and Keating, 2002), the appraisal ratio (Treynor and Black, 1973), the Treynor and Mazuy measure (1966) and the risk adjusted performance (RAP) (Modigliani – Modigliani, 1997). Other measures used, are the market risk adjusted performance (MRAP) (Scholtz & Willkens, 2005), the Burke ratio (Burke, 1994), the Calmar ratio (Young, 1991), the upside potential ratio (Sortino et al., 1999), the Value – at – Risk (Var) (Le Sourd, 2007). The literature, also, provides several methodologies to examine long run linkages between the financial markets such as: the Engle – Granger cointegration test (Engle – Granger, 1987), the Augmented Least Squares (Bewley, 1979), the Spectral Regression test (Phillips, 1988). Additionally, to investigate short run dynamics: the variance decomposition analysis (Cholesky factorization, Structural VAR decomposition) and the impulse response functions (IRF) and for correlation analysis generalized autoregressive conditionally heteroskedasticity models are also used (Bollerslev, 1986) (i.e. Dynamic Conditional Correlation GARCH).

The extant studies which concentrate on evaluating, the risk adjusted performance and diversification benefits of the US, Asian and international REITs[4] are extensive. However, the empirical literature which deals with European REITs is limited and provides mixed results. Newell et al. (2016) study in the UK, suggests that the UK REITs delivered low risk adjusted returns relative to UK stocks, over period 2007 – 2014, and since the global financial crisis started to deliver stronger risk adjusted returns but with limited portfolio diversification benefits. In the same direction, Newell and Marzuki (2018) study in the German market, denotes that German REITs underperformed relative to German stock over 2007 – 2015, but since the global financial crisis delivered enhanced risk adjusted returns but with limited portfolio diversification benefits. Contrary, French REITs (SIICs), delivered greater risk adjusted returns relative to stocks over period 2003 – 2012 with even stronger in the post global financial crisis period. In the same way, as for the UK and German REITs, the portfolio diversification benefits for the SIICs/French REITs were limited with stocks (Newell et al., 2013). Another study by Marzuki and Newell (2018) indicates that Spanish Real Estate Investment Trusts (SOCIMIs) delivered strong risk adjusted returns compared to stock over period 2014 – 2018, but once again with limited portfolio diversification benefits. An empirical research by Coskun et al. (2017) denotes that the Turkish REIT portfolio provides higher level of risk diversification benefits than banks but lower than investment trusts.

This work supplements the limited extant empirical literature of the European REIT market in at least the following ways. First, the study assesses the impact of Global Financial Crisis on the market performance of the European REITs, within a cross country framework. Second, it is the first work to assess international long run and short-term linkages among European REITs. Thusly, this article also aims to shed light on whether the European REIT market delivers cross - border diversification benefits.

The outcomes of the study suggest poor performance of almost all European REITS in the GFC period (2007 – 2009). In the first years of the post – GFC period (2010 – 2014) most European REITs delivered strong risk adjusted returns and overall outperformed the equivalent European stock market indices and bonds. In the recent period (2015 – 2018), most REITs continued to deliver positive risk adjusted returns but overall underperformed relative to the previous period (2010 – 2014). Over the full investigating period, the empirical results display strong correlation of a similar degree of all European REITs with the equivalent stock market indices suggesting weak portfolio diversification benefits. The empirical findings also denote cross border long run linkages and short run interactions among the REITs, implying reduced cross-country diversification benefits of the European REIT market. The highest long run linkages are found in the SOCIMIs (Spanish REITs) and the FBIs (Dutch REITs) and the strongest short run interdependences are evident in the SIICs (French REITs) and the BE – REITs (Belgian REITs). The most influential are the G- REITs (Germany), the SOCIMIs/Spain and the SIIQs/Italy, displaying strong effects on other European REITs. Higher cross - border diversification benefits, both in the long and the short run, are evident in the UK REITs.

The remainder of the paper proceeds as follows. Section 2 describes the European REIT structure, Section 3 includes the methodology, Section 4 the data description and Section 5 discusses the empirical results. The last Section concludes the analysis and makes suggestions for future research.

European REIT Structure

This section provides a brief discussion of the European REIT structure which is significant diverge in terms of financial requirements and activity rules. The BE – REITs (Belgium) are either public limited liability companies, or Belgian limited partnerships with shares. For the BE – REITs the required minimum share capital is 1.20 million € and their main activity is real estate. Portfolio risk diversification is regulated and allows a maximum of 20% of the total assets of the BE – REITs, to be invested in one real estate project. The BE-REITs are required to distribute on an annual basis the positive difference between 80% of their net operational result and the net decrease of their indebtedness. Capital gains are not included in the distribution obligation.

The SIICs (French REITs) are either corporations or companies whose capital is divided into stocks that can be listed. For the SIICs, the required minimum share capital is 15 million € and their main activity is property acquisition or/and construction with the aim of renting out the property. The SIICs are not subjected to asset level restrictions. At least 95% of the tax-exempt profits and 60% of the capital gains must be distributed.

The G-REITs (Germany) are joint stock companies that must have a share capital of at least 15 million €. At least 75% of the total assets of the G-REITs must be comprised of immovable properties, and at least 75% of their gross earnings must be from rental business, (leasing, letting) and disposal of immovable properties. G-REITs have to distribute at least 90% of their net income.

The FBIs (Dutch REITs) are either a private/ public limited liability companies or open – ended mutual investment funds or any comparable foreign legal entities liable to Dutch corporate income tax. For the FBIs there is no specific minimum share capital but follow the capital requirements from the Dutch company law. FBIs are only permitted to invest in passive, portfolio investments and are allowed to invest abroad. FBIs distribute all profits to their shareholders and capital gains are allocated to a tax-free reserve.

The UK REITs are close ended listed companies, following the normal listing requirements in respect of share capital (at least £ 700,000). UK REITs must derive at least 75% of their profits from renting and 75% of their assets must be used for renting. UK REITs must hold at least three separate property assets and each property asset shall not exceed 40% of the total assets (diversification). For UK REITs, 90% of the rental income shall be distributed whereas capital gains are not included on the distribution obligation.

The Irish REITS are (Irish) incorporated companies listed on the main market of a recognized stock exchange in an EU member state and must have a nominal value of share capital of not less than 25,000 €. Similar to UK REITs regime, the

Irish REITs must also derive at least 75% of aggregate income from renting and 75% of their assets must be used for renting. Also, must hold at least three separate property assets and each property asset shall not exceed 40% of the total assets (diversification). For the Irish REITs, 85% of the rental income shall be distributed whereas capital gains are not included on the distribution obligation.

The SIIQs (Italian REITs), are joint stock companies listed on a regulated market and the ordinary listing requirements are applicable in relation to share capital. The SIIQs portfolio must be at least 80% in real estate assets and 80% of the income must come from real estate activities. The SIIQs shall distribute 75% of the net profits and 50% of the capital gains shall be derived from leasing activities.

The SOCIMIs (Spanish REITs) are listed joint stock corporations with a minimum share capital of 5 million €. The SOCIMIs portfolio must contain at least 80% of "qualified assets" (real estate rentals/investments, foreign REITS) and at least 80% of the revenue must be derived from these qualifying assets. These assets are also subject to minimum three-year holding period by the SOCIMIs. The SOCIMIs shall distribute 80% of the profits derived from rental income and 50% of the profit derived from transfer of the real estate and qualifying assets

The Greek REICs have the legal form of the companies listed in the Athens stock Exchange and have a required minimum capital share of 25 million €. Greek REICs are subjected to several activity restrictions e.g. at least 80% of the total REIC assets must consist of real estate, REIC shall not invest in a single property exceeding 25% of its total assets. The Greek REICs shall distribute at least 50% of their annual net profits to its shareholders and capital gains are not included on the distribution obligation.

METHODOLOGY

The empirical strategy involves a two stage analysis. In the first stage the three standard measurement methods, namely the Sharpe ratio, the Treynor index and the Jensen Alpha index, are used to examine whether REITs provide higher risk-adjusted returns and portfolio diversification benefits relative to the market portfolio.

The Sharpe index gives how much an investment return exceeds the risk-free return, which is set as the benchmark, for a given standard deviation. The standard deviation includes both market (systematic) and investment specific risk (non-systematic).

The Sharpe ratio is given by:

$$Sharpe\,ratio = \frac{R_{REITs} - R_{risk\,free}}{\sigma} \tag{1}$$

Where,

R_{REITs} = the average return on REITs.

$R_{risk\ free}$ = the risk-free rate.

σ = the standard deviation of the returns on REITs.

The Treynor ratio is another risk adjusted performance measurement index used to give the excess investment return over the risk-free rate. The Treynor ratio accounts only for the market risk (systematic risk), considering that asset (investment) specific risk (non-systematic) is eliminated by portfolio diversification.

The Treynor ratio is given by:

$$Treynor\ ratio = \frac{R_{REITs} - R_{risk\ free}}{\beta} \tag{2}$$

Where,

R_{REITs} = the average return on REITs.

$R_{risk\ free}$ = the risk-free rate.

β = beta of REITs in relation to the overall market.

Additionally, the Jensen alpha index is used to measure the investment risk-adjusted return above or below that provided in the Capital Asset Pricing Model, and is given by:

$$alpha = R_{REITs} - \left[R_{risk\ free} + \beta \left(R_{market} - R_{risk\ free} \right) \right] \tag{3}$$

where

R_{REITs} = the average return on REITs.

$R_{risk\ free}$ = the risk-free rate.

R_{market} = the average return on the overall market.

β = beta of REITs in relation to the overall market.

In the second stage of the empirical analysis, co integration test is implemented to investigate whether there are long run relationships between the REITs. Hence, the Johansen test (Johansen, 1988; Johansen, 1991) is conducted and the following equation is specified:

$$\Delta X_t = \mu + \sum_{i-1}^{k-1} \Gamma \Delta X_{t-i} + \prod X_{t-k} + \varepsilon_t \tag{4}$$

The variables which are included in X_t, are the stock adjusting closing prices of each of the REITs, considered in the analysis. The term Π is matrix which is expressed by $\Pi = \alpha\beta'$, (a is the matrix of adjustment parameters and β' the matrix of cointegrating vectors). If all rows in matrix Π are filled with zeros (rank(Π) = 0) there will be no cointegration among the variables (stock adjusting closing prices of the REITs) and the model reduces to VAR in first differences (no long run relationship, whereas If $\Pi \neq 0, (0 < rank(\Pi) = r < n)$, there will be r cointegration relationships.

To investigate short run dynamics and whether there is causal interaction among the REITs, Granger causality test (Granger, 1969; Granger, 1986) is conducted. Granger causality is suggestive in the sense that the lagged values of X should contain better information for Y than the information included in the lagged value of Y alone.

$$\Delta Y_t = a + \sum_{i=1}^{m} \beta_\iota \left(\Delta Y_{t-i}\right) + \sum_{j=1}^{n} \tau_j \left(\Delta X_{t-j}\right) + \mu_t \tag{5}$$

$$\Delta X_t = \theta + \sum_{i=1}^{p} \varphi_\iota \left(\Delta X_{t-i}\right) + \sum_{j=1}^{k} \psi_j \left(\Delta Y_{t-j}\right) + \eta_t$$

Where Y represents the monthly returns of one European REIT and X represents the monthly returns of the next European REIT, considered in the causality test. The terms $\beta_\iota, \tau_j, \varphi_\iota, \psi_j$ are the regression coefficients, a and θ are the constant terms, μ_t, η_t are the error terms and m, p, n, k represent the number of lagged terms.

DATA

The data considered in the analysis are the monthly returns, of a total of twenty – three (23) Real Estate Investment Trusts, which are the top public listed European REITs of five (5) established (Belgium, France, Germany, Netherlands, UK), three (3) emerging (Italy, Spain, Ireland) and one (1) nascent (Greece) European REIT markets. The sample data spans over period 01 January 2007 – 31 December 2018, but is broken down into three sub- periods: (a) the GFC period (01 Jan 2007 – 31 Dec 2009), (b) the first years of post - GFC period (01 Jan 2010 – 31 Dec 2014) and

(c) the most recent period (01 Jan 2015 – 31 Dec 2018), to better assess the effect of the GFC on the European REIT market. To evaluate the market performance, the equivalent major stock market indices are used: FTSE 100 (UK), DAX (Germany), AEX (Netherlands), CAC 40 (France), BEL 20 (Belgium), FTSE MIB (Italy), IBEX 35 (Spain), ISEQ (Ireland), AGC (Greece). Also, the equivalent 10 year government bond yields are used to account for the risk free rate. The stock adjusting closing prices and government bond yields are derived from *Yahoo!* Finance and Investing.com web sites, respectively.

EMPIRICAL RESULTS

Diversification Benefits

Table 1, contains the REIT correlation analysis over the full investigating period (January 2007 – December 2018). Overall the European REITs considered in the analysis are strongly correlated (average r=0.49) to a similar degree with the equivalent stock market indices, hence implying weak portfolio diversification benefits. Higher correlation with stocks is slightly evident over the first years of post GFC period (r=0.52) and (slightly) lower in the most recent period (r=0.45). The REITs considered present portfolio diversification benefits with bonds, especially in the most recent period (r= 0.06).

Risk Adjusted Returns

Tables 3 - 8, summarize the outcomes of the European REIT performance analysis and the risk adjustment measures. During the GFC period (2007 – 2009) all European REITs considered (apart from Retail Estates, Vastned Retail, Westfield and Derwent London) display negative average annual returns. The highest negative is found in the SOCIMI/Spanish REIT, UK REITs and the SIIQ/Italian REIT. From table 2, it is obvious that overall stock market indices (except UK/FTSE 100, DAX, IBEX 35, FTSE MIB index), over this period, delivered even worse (higher negative) annual returns but with lower overall risk level. Ireland (-21,40%), Greece (-17.20%) and Italy (-14.80%) were the worst performing stock markets among the nine (9). On a risk adjusted basis, most European REITs delivered poor performance (negative Sharpe - Treynor and Jensen alpha indices), but less negative (apart from UK - REITs and SOCIMI/Spanish REIT) than the overall stock market performance (higher negative Sharpe ratio). The Jensen alpha of the three SIICs (French REITs) considered in the analysis, namely Gecina, Klépierre and Covivio, for which evident the (only) positive but low alphas (a=0.197%, a=0.076%, a=0,044%), further justify

Table 1. Correlation analysis

	01 Jan 2007 - 31 Dec 2009		01 Jan 2010 - 31 Dec 2014		01 Jan 2015- 31 Dec 2018	
Belgium	**BEL 20 index**	**Bonds**	**BEL 20 index**	**Bonds**	**BEL 20 index**	**Bonds**
Warehouses De Pauw	0,471	-0,203	0,492	-0,188	0,368	0,173
Cofinimmo	0,562	-0,107	0,558	-0,307	0,461	0,206
Aedifica	0,500	-0,154	-0,007	-0,086	0,355	0,204
Benifimmo	0,397	0,072	0,500	-0,321	0,513	0,086
Retail Estates	0,498	-0,288	0,183	-0,125	-0,012	0,209
BEL 20 index	1,000	-0,312	1,000	-0,232	1,000	-0,100
BE - REIT Average	0,485	-0,136	0,345	-0,205	0,337	0,176
France	CAC 40 index	Bonds	CAC 40 index	Bonds	CAC 40 index	Bonds
Gecina	0,677	-0,349	0,649	-0,085	0,594	-0,090
Klépierre	0,545	-0,459	0,619	-0,162	0,559	0,076
Covivio	0,516	-0,361	0,679	-0,223	0,433	0,078
Icade	0,439	-0,403	0,615	-0,078	0,529	-0,033
CAC 40 index	1,000	-0,366	1,000	-0,194	1,000	-0,109
SIIC Average	0,635	-0,393	0,712	-0,137	0,623	0,008
Germany	DAX index	Bonds	DAX index	Bonds	DAX index	Bonds
Alstria Office REIT AG	0,446	-0,373	0,414	-0,082	0,444	-0,005
Hamborner REIT AG	0,646	-0,534	0,390	-0,289	0,544	-0,052
DAX index	1,000	-0,253	1,000	-0,160	1,000	-0,289
G REIT Average	0,546	-0,454	0,601	-0,186	0,663	-0,028
Netherlands	AEX index	Bonds	AEX index	Bonds	AEX index	Bonds
Westfield	0,464	-0,469	0,586	-0,193	0,642	0,054
Eurocommercial Properties NV	0,451	-0,426	0,558	-0,143	0,439	0,055
Wereldhave	0,438	-0,276	0,436	-0,178	0,435	0,028
Vastned Retail	0,372	-0,431	0,586	-0,224	0,524	0,106
AEX index	1,000	-0,453	1,000	-0,086	1,000	-0,172
FBI Average	0,545	-0,400	0,633	-0,184	0,608	0,061
UK	FTSE 100 index	Bonds	FTSE 100 index	Bonds	FTSE 100 index	Bonds
SEGRO plc	0,592	-0,054	0,683	-0,158	0,472	-0,049
British Land Co plc	0,469	-0,249	0,662	0,020	0,325	-0,029
Hammerson plc	0,391	-0,162	0,686	-0,082	0,435	-0,051
Derwent London	0,491	-0,332	0,720	-0,080	0,223	0,045
FTSE 100 index	1,000	-0,216	1,000	-0,090	1,000	-0,287
UK - REIT Average	0,588	-0,199	0,750	-0,075	0,491	-0,021
Italy	FTSE MIB index	Bonds	FTSE MIB index	Bonds	FTSE MIB index	Bonds
Immobiliare Grande Distribuzione SIIQ	0,450	-0,387	0,505	-0,062	0,750	0,015
FTSE MIB index	1,000	-0,401	1,000	0,020	1,000	0,012

	01 Jan 2007 - 31 Dec 2009		01 Jan 2010 - 31 Dec 2014		01 Jan 2015- 31 Dec 2018	
Spain	IBEX 35 index	Bonds	IBEX 35 index	IBEX 35 index	IBEX 35 index	Bonds
Inmobiliaria Colonial SA	0,426	-0,398	0,308	-0,089	0,607	0,172
IBEX 35 index	1,000	0,007	1,000	0,045	1,000	-0,107
Ireland	ISEQ index	Bonds	ISEQ index	Bonds	ISEQ index	Bonds
Hibernia REIT plc	n/a	n/a	n/a	n/a	-0,049	-0,023
Irish Residential Properties plc	n/a	n/a	n/a	n/a	0,441	-0,122
ISEQ index	n/a	n/a	n/a	n/a	1,000	0,085
Irish - REIT Average	n/a	n/a	n/a	n/a	0,441	-0,122
Greece	AGC index	Bonds	AGC index	Bonds	AGC index	Bonds
Grivalia Properties REIC	0,507	0,250	0,599	0,134	0,400	0,098
AGC index	1,000	0,011	1,000	0,143	1,000	0,080
All REIT Average	**0,488**	**-0,277**	**0,519**	**-0,136**	**0,454**	**0,059**

Notes: Table 2 includes the results of the correlation test among the European REITs, the equivalent major stock markets and government bonds.

the period's weak REIT performance. The three REITs were still poor compensated, over this period, despite undertaking an additional market risk (higher betas, b>1) relative to the other REITs (with b<1).

Over the first years of the post GFC period (2010 – 2014), almost all European REITs, apart from the two emerging market REITs, namely the SIIQ/Italy, and the SOCIMI/Spain, delivered high returns, exceeding stocks and bonds and also reduced their overall risk (standard deviation less than 7% in average). At the same time, the majority of the European markets provided strong average annual returns with the strongest found in the DAX/Germany (14.50%), whereas the Southern European markets still remained negative performing markets (Greece (-13.54%), Italy (-0.08%) and Spain (-0.16%). All three risk adjusted performance measures, indicate that almost all REITs (except G – REITs/Germany, SIIQ/Italy, SOCIMI/Spain) outperformed the market. It is notable that the Greek REIC (nascent market), despite the country's excessive bond yield rate (risk free rate>over 13%) that is considered in this analysis, outperformed the overall market, delivering remarkable risk adjusted returns.

In the most recent period (2015 – 2018) most of the established market REITs (except the FBIs/Dutch REITs and Klépierre, British Land Co plc, Hammerson) delivered positive risk adjusted returns but underperformed relative to the previous period. Additionally, it is the period that the emerging market REITs, namely the

SOCIMI/Spain and the SIIQ/Italy, started to deliver positive returns. It is also a period of a reduced overall risk for all European REITs with an average standard deviation of 5%. For the nascent market, the period's poor risk adjusted performance of the Greek REIC is attributed to its reduced returns relative to the country's (long run excessive) bond yield rates. The results also show that both stocks and bonds provided modest returns relative to the previous period, whereas the Southern European stock markets (except for Spain (-2.69%)) seem to recover after a long - run period of recession. It is also notable that most European REITs reduced their systematic risk (lower volatility relative to the market) displaying a lower beta over the most recent period.

Long – Term Relationships

Cointegration test is conducted to investigate whether there are long run relationships among the twenty – one[5] (21) European REITs. The cointegration relationship is examined for the full period of the study (Jan 2009 – Dec 2018). All twenty – one (21) REITs are categorized by geographical area in eight (8) groups and the test is conducted, using pair wise groups, in order to trace cross border linkages among the REITS.

The Augmented Dickey – Fuller test (Dickey and Fuller, 1979), called ADF test hereinafter, t- statistic indicates that all series are non stationary in levels (log normalized stock adjusting closing prices) but in their first differences (stock returns) are integrated of order one (1).

Thusly, the multivariate Johansen trace statistic test is conducted to the non-stationary series to determine the number of cointegrating vectors in the data. The test is applied assuming an intercept (no trend) in the cointegrating equation and the VAR part. The lag length is chosen by applying the Akaike information criterion (Akaike, 1973).

Table 10 includes the multivariate co integration results between the examined REIT groups in a two-dimensional matrix. Overall the test displays cross border linkages between the REITs, implying reduced long - run international diversification benefits in the European REIT market. The SOCIMI (Spanish REIT) and the FBIs (Dutch REITs) have the most long run relationships, each REIT group holding six (6) cointegration relationships. The SIICs (French REITs) and the BE – REITs follow with five (5) and four (4) cointegration relationships, respectively, whereas the least are evident in the UK REITs.

Table 3. Performance analysis (Sub - Period: 01 Jan 2007 - 31 Dec 2009)

Established Markets						
Company name						
	Average Annual Return (%)	Std. Dev (%)	sharpe ratio	Treynor ratio	Jensen alpha (%)	beta
Belgium (BE – REITs)						
Warehouses De Pauw	-4,270	6,510	-1,304	-0,202	-0,021	0,419
Cofinimmo	-11,630	5,530	-2,866	-0,373	-0,094	0,425
Befimmo	-3,810	8,540	-0,940	-0,173	-0,010	0,464
Retail Estates	5,490	5,860	0,217	0,032	0,074	0,398
BEL 20 index	-11,050	7,111	-2,147	-	-	-
Bonds	4,219	-	-	-	-	-
France (SIICs)						
Gecina	-1,310	18,310	-0,293	-0,028	0,197	1,951
Klépierre	-1,840	12,230	-0,482	-0,056	0,076	1,050
Covivio	-4,570	12,460	-0,692	-0,085	0,044	1,013
Icade	-5,990	9,920	-1,013	-0,147	-0,012	0,685
CAC 40 index	-8,786	6,174	-2,080	-	-	-
Bonds	4,056	-	-	-	-	-
Germany (G - REITs)						
Alstria Office REIT AG	-8,860	16,470	-0,770	-0,065	-0,010	1,951
Hamborner REIT AG	-5,770	7,220	-1,328	-0,147	-0,057	0,653
DAX index	-2,159	6,936	-0,862	-	-	-
Bonds	3,821	-	-	-	-	-
Netherlands (FBIs)						
Westfield	2,900	7,190	-0,164	-0,027	0,040	0,433
Eurocommercial Properties NV	-4,710	7,470	-1,176	-0,201	-0,036	0,437
Wereldhave	-4,740	9,000	-0,980	-0,172	-0,027	0,511
Vastned Retail	4,250	9,950	0,017	0,004	0,059	0,480
AEX INDEX	-7,824	7,489	-1,589	-	-	-
Bonds	4,077	-	-	-	-	-
UK REITs						
SEGRO plc	-32,360	13,440	-2,732	-0,250	-0,256	1,468
British Land Co plc	-19,900	8,670	-2,797	-0,323	-0,186	0,750
Hammerson plc	-10,540	11,890	-1,253	-0,174	-0,084	0,857
Derwent London	13,470	10,490	0,869	0,096	0,163	0,950
FTSE 100 index	-3,201	5,268	-1,434	-	-	-
Bonds	4,352	-	-	-	-	-

Emerging Markets						
Company name						
	Average Annual Return (%)	Std. Dev (%)	sharpe ratio	Treynor ratio	Jensen alpha (%)	beta
Italy (SIIQs/SIINQs)						
Immobiliare Grande Distribuzione SIIQ	-19,290	11,640	-2,043	-0,339	-0,102	0,702
FTSE MIB index	-14,798	7,244	-2,664	-	-	-
Bonds	4,496	-	-	-	-	-
Spain (SOCIMIs)						
Inmobiliaria Colonial SA	-51,750	15,700	-3,566	-0,565	-0,466	0,990
IBEX 35 index	-5,223	6,560	-1,442	-	-	-
Bonds	4,234	-	-	-	-	-
Ireland (Irish REITs)						
Hibernia REIT plc	n/a	n/a	n/a	n/a	n/a	n/a
Irish Residential Properties plc	n/a	n/a	n/a	n/a	n/a	n/a
ISEQ index	-21,385	8,427	-3,094	-	-	-
Bonds	4,685	-	-	-	-	-
Nascent Markets						
Greece (REICs)						
Grivalia Properties REIC	-9,110	8,590	-1,625	-0,310	-0,041	0,450
GC AT index	-17,160	9,417	-2,337	-	-	-
Bonds	4,850	-	-	-	-	-

Notes: Table 4, summarizes the risk – adjusted performance of the European REITs, during the GFC period. Also contains the performance of the equivalent stock market indices and bonds over the same period.

Causal Interactions

The cointegration test suggests that there is a long run relationship between the series but not which series causes the other. To investigate causality among the REITs, Granger Causality test is applied. The test requires all variables to be stationary. Hence, the first differences (REIT returns) are considered and a lag length using the Akaike information criterion. Figure 1, graphically illustrates the causality network among the REITs. Overall, the G- REITs (Germany) and the two REITs of the emerging markets (SOCIMI/Spain, SIIQ/Italy) deliver the strongest effect on the other European REITs. Namely, immobiliare Grande Distribuzione SIIQ (Italian REIT), Alstria Office REIT AG (German REIT), and Immobiliaria Colonial SA

Table 5. Performance analysis (Sub - Period: 01 Jan 2010 - 31 Dec 2014)

Established Markets						
Company name	Average Annual Return (%)	Std. Dev (%)	sharpe ratio	Treynor ratio	Jensen alpha (%)	beta
Belgium (BE – REITs)						
Warehouses De Pauw	22,130	3,950	4,858	0,362	0,165	0,530
Cofinimmo	6,130	3,760	0,849	0,056	0,003	0,572
Befimmo	12,450	4,540	2,095	0,154	0,064	0,619
Retail Estates	17,800	3,690	4,027	0,808	0,139	0,184
BEL 20 index	7,998	3,603	1,404	-	-	-
Bonds	2,940	-	-	-	-	-
France (SIICs)						
Gecina	17,370	7,020	2,113	0,150	0,1245	0,987
Klépierre	16,120	7,000	1,941	0,145	0,113	0,939
Covivio	14,900	7,380	1,675	0,114	0,097	1,085
Icade	9,630	6,580	1,078	0,081	0,050	0,877
CAC 40 index	4,951	4,538	0,532	-	-	-
Bonds	2,535	-	-	-	-	-
Germany (G - REITs)						
Alstria Office REIT AG	12,900	5,490	1,997	0,236	0,0513	0,465
Hamborner REIT AG	8,610	3,930	1,698	0,213	0,0274	0,314
DAX index	14,486	4,803	2,613	-	-	-
Bonds	1,935	-	-	-	-	-
Netherlands (FBIs)						
Westfield	19,090	6,340	2,599	0,183	0,138	0,901
Eurocommercial Properties NV	14,960	6,420	1,923	0,142	0,098	0,869
Wereldhave	11,990	6,240	1,502	0,142	0,074	0,660
Vastned Retail	6,250	6,820	0,533	0,038	0,008	0,967
AEX INDEX	7,032	4,058	1,089	-	-	-
Bonds	2,236	-	-	-	-	-
UK REITs						
SEGRO plc	13,980	6,300	1,752	0,094	0,080	1,181
British Land Co plc	19,840	5,240	3,224	0,177	0,144	0,952
Hammerson plc	18,350	5,560	2,774	0,147	0,127	1,046
Derwent London	22,310	5,350	3,621	0,183	0,166	1,056
FTSE 100 index	5,555	3,584	0,820	-	-	-
Bonds	2,615	-	-	-	-	-

Emerging Markets						
Company name	Average Annual Return (%)	Std. Dev (%)	sharpe ratio	Treynor ratio	Jensen alpha (%)	beta
Italy (SIIQs/SIINQs)						
Immobiliare Grande Distribuzione SIIQ	-2,790	10,030	-0,718	-0,091	-0,037	0,789
FTSE MIB index	-0,080	6,324	-0,710	-	-	-
Bonds	4,411	-	-	-	-	-
Spain (SOCIMIs)						
Inmobiliaria Colonial SA	-20,640	16,140	-1,562	-0,314	-0,214	0,802
IBEX 35 index	-0,155	6,084	-0,776	-	-	-
Bonds	4,564	-	-	-	-	-
Ireland (Irish REITs)						
Hibernia REIT plc	n/a	n/a	n/a	n/a	n/a	n/a
Irish Residential Properties plc	n/a	n/a	n/a	n/a	n/a	n/a
ISEQ index	13,597	4,550	1,759	-	-	-
Bonds	5,594	-	-	-	-	-
Nascent Markets						
Greece (REICs)						
Grivalia Properties REIC	18,030	12,010	0,342	0,059	0,233	0,700
GC AT index	-13,536	10,112	-2,715	-	-	-
Bonds	13,920	-	-	-	-	-

Notes: Table 6, summarizes the risk – adjusted performance of the European REITs, during the first years of the post GFC period. Also contains the performance of the equivalent stock market indices and bonds over the same period.

(Spanish REITs) are the most influential REITs, each granger causing 10 (ten), nine (9) and seven (7) other REITs. Thusly, the test implies weak cross border diversification opportunities in the short run. The most dense causal network is found in the SIICs (French REITs) and in the BE – REITs (Belgian REITs), denoting the strongest short run interdependence. The least causal relationships are found in the UK REITs, implying weakest short linkage and stronger diversification benefits relative to the other REITs.

Comparing the outcomes of the first stage (REIT performance) analysis and the findings of the cointegration and causality tests, it is obvious that the interdependence between European REITS, can also be seen by an identical co-movement in the risk adjustment return of the REITS. It appears that European REITs are interrelated both in the short and the long run, with (almost) all REITs revealing negative

Table 7. Performance analysis (Sub - Period: 01 Jan 2015 - 31 Dec 2018)

Established Markets						
Company name	Average Annual Return (%)	Std. Dev (%)	sharpe ratio	Treynor ratio	Jensen alpha (%)	beta
Belgium (BE – REITs)						
Warehouses De Pauw	23,230	4,810	4,687	0,496	0,227	0,455
Cofinimmo	8,110	3,510	2,116	0,179	0,076	0,414
Befimmo	2,000	4,440	0,296	0,023	0,015	0,585
Retail Estates	7,040	3,560	1,786	-5,941	0,064	-0,011
BEL 20 index	0,338	3,811	-0,091	-	-	-
Bonds	0,684	-	-	-	-	-
France (SIICs)						
Gecina	9,500	5,530	1,591	0,112	0,0739	0,785
Klépierre	-3,110	4,780	-0,798	-0,060	-0,050	0,639
Covivio	4,520	4,540	0,840	0,081	0,030	0,470
Icade	6,190	5,350	1,025	0,081	0,043	0,676
CAC 40 index	2,490	4,098	0,436	-	-	-
Bonds	0,704	-	-	-	-	-
Germany (G - REITs)						
Alstria Office REIT AG	8,630	4,530	1,826	0,195	0,0753	0,425
Hamborner REIT AG	6,690	4,240	1,493	0,130	0,0548	0,488
DAX index	2,100	4,631	0,376	-	-	-
Bonds	0,358	-	-	-	-	-
Netherlands (FBIs)						
Westfield	-6,400	5,380	-1,282	-0,080	-0,101	0,865
Eurocommercial Properties NV	-1,540	5,810	-0,350	-0,032	-0,044	0,639
Wereldhave	-11,620	5,960	-2,033	-0,187	-0,145	0,649
Vastned Retail	-0,200	5,050	-0,138	-0,010	-0,031	0,662
AEX INDEX	4,189	3,909	0,945	-	-	-
Bonds	0,495	-	-	-	-	-
UK REITs						
SEGRO plc	17,620	4,990	3,251	0,209	0,162	0,777
British Land Co plc	-3,800	5,730	-0,907	-0,085	-0,052	0,613
Hammerson plc	-10,200	6,220	-1,865	-0,130	-0,116	0,893
Derwent London	2,970	6,800	0,231	0,031	0,016	0,199
FTSE 100 index	1,363	2,973	-0,012	-	-	-
Bonds	1,399	-	-	-	-	-

Emerging Markets						
Company name						
	Average Annual Return (%)	Std. Dev (%)	sharpe ratio	Treynor ratio	Jensen alpha (%)	beta
Italy (SIIQs/SIINQs)						
Immobiliare Grande Distribuzione SIIQ	1,110	8,270	-0,103	-0,008	0,010	1,103
FTSE MIB index	0,255	5,498	-0,310	-	-	-
Bonds	1,958	-	-	-	-	-
Spain (SOCIMIs)						
Inmobiliaria Colonial SA	12,440	4,900	2,233	0,177	0,135	0,618
IBEX 35 index	-2,685	4,707	-0,889	-	-	-
Bonds	1,499	-	-	-	-	-
Ireland (Irish REITs)						
Hibernia REIT plc	6,460	4,960	1,122	-0,984	0,056	-0,057
Irish Residential Properties plc	13,230	3,810	3,238	0,313	0,119	0,394
ISEQ index	2,115	4,177	0,293	-	-	-
Bonds	0,893	-	-	-	-	-
Nascent Markets						
Greece (REICs)						
Grivalia Properties REIC	5,310	6,160	-0,306	-0,063	0,0004	0,300
GC AT index	0,777	8,033	-0,799	-	-	-
Bonds	7,193	-	-	-	-	-

Notes: Table 4, summarizes the risk – adjusted performance of the European REITs, over the most recent period. Also contains the performance of the equivalent stock market indices and bonds over the same period.

risk adjusted performance over the GFC period and positive (of the same pattern) performance over the post – GFC period. The findings reveal that European REITs are also cross border tightly integrated and deliver reduced diversification benefits, over the examining period.

CONCLUSION

By using the three risk adjusted performance measures (Sharpe ratio, Treynor ratio and Jensen alpha index), the study reveals negative risk adjusted performance of most European REITS over the Global Financial Crisis period (2007 – 2009) but strong performance of the majority of REITs outperforming the stocks and bonds,

Table 9. ADF unit toot test results

Full Period (Jan 2007 - Dec 2018)	ADF - Unit Root Tests (Level)	ADF - Unit Root Tests (1st Difference)
BE - REITs (Belgian REITs)		
Warehouses De Pauw	1,197	-13,681***
Cofinimmo	-0,784	-12,058***
Befimmo	-0,398	-10,839***
Retail Estates	0,166	-11,563***
SIICs (French REITs)		
Gecina	-1,182	-11,289***
Klépierre	-1,310	-11,273***
Covivio	-1,327	-10,576***
Icade	-1,601	-11,504***
FBIs (Dutch REITs)		
Westfield	-0,999	-11,823***
Eurocommercial Properties NV	-0,937	-14,411***
Wereldhave	-1,880	-14,863***
Vastned Retail	-2,294	-11,947***
Greek REIc		
Grivalia Properties REIC	-0.865	-15,711***
UK REITs		
SEGRO plc	-1,901	-5,239***
British Land Co plc	-1,586	-13,046***
Hammerson plc	-1,825	-11,444***
Derwent London	-0,488	-13,279***
SIIQ (Italian REIT)		
Immobiliare Grande Distribuzione SIIQ	-0,573	-11,397***
SOCIMI (Spanish REIT)		
Inmobiliaria Colonial SA	-1.648	-10.509***
G - REITs (German REITs)		
Alstria Office REIT AG	-1.034	-10.775***
Hamborner REIT AG	-0,351	-11.348***

***Notes*:** Table 9 includes the ADF - Unit Toot Test results of the twenty - one (21) variables, included in the empirical analysis. The ADF critical values -3.476, -2.881, -2.577 correspond to 1%, 5% and 10% significance level, respectively.

Table 10. Johansen multivariate cointegration test results

	BE-REITs	SIICs (French REITs)	FBIs (Dutch REITs)	Greek REIC	UK REITs	SIIQ (Italian REIT)	SOCIMI (Spanish REIT)	G – REITs (German REITs)
BE-REITs	YES	NO	YES	YES	NO	NO	YES	NO
SIICs (French REITs)	NO	NO	YES	NO	YES	YES	YES	YES
FBIs (Dutch REITs)	YES	YES	NO	YES	YES	NO	YES	YES
Greek REIC	YES	NO	YES	-	NO	NO	YES	NO
UK REITs	NO	YES	YES	NO	YES	NO	NO	NO
SIIQ (Italian REIT)	NO	YES	NO	NO	NO	-	YES	YES
SOCIMI (Spanish REIT)	YES	YES	YES	YES	NO	YES	-	YES
G – REITs (German REITs)	NO	YES	YES	NO	NO	YES	YES	NO

Notes: Table 10, is a two-dimensional matrix that shows the cointegrating relationships for every pair of the eight (8) European REIT groups over the full period of investigation (Jan 2009 – Dec 2018). Due to missing data, Irish REITs are not included in the (full period) co integration test.

in the first years of the post – GFC period (2010 – 2014). In the recent period, most European REITs continued to deliver positive risk adjusted returns but underperformed relative to the previous period (2010 – 2014). The empirical findings also suggest high correlation of the REITs with the equivalent stock market indices and hence weak diversification benefits. By implementing Johansen multivariate cointegration test, the study reveals international long run relationships between the REITs with the highest found in the SOCIMI (Spanish REIT) and the FBIs (Dutch REITs). By implementing Granger causality test, short run interaction among the REITs is revealed, implying reduced short run cross country diversification benefits in the European REIT market. Overall, the weakest short run diversification benefits are evident in the SIICs/French REITs and BE – REITs/Belgian REITs. The strongest effect is delivered by the G – REITs (Germany) and the SOCIMIs/Spain, SIIQs/

Figure 1. Granger causality test results

***Notes:** Figure 1, includes the results of the granger causality test between the twenty - one (21) REITs. Due to missing data, Irish REITs are not included in the (full period) Granger Causality Test.*

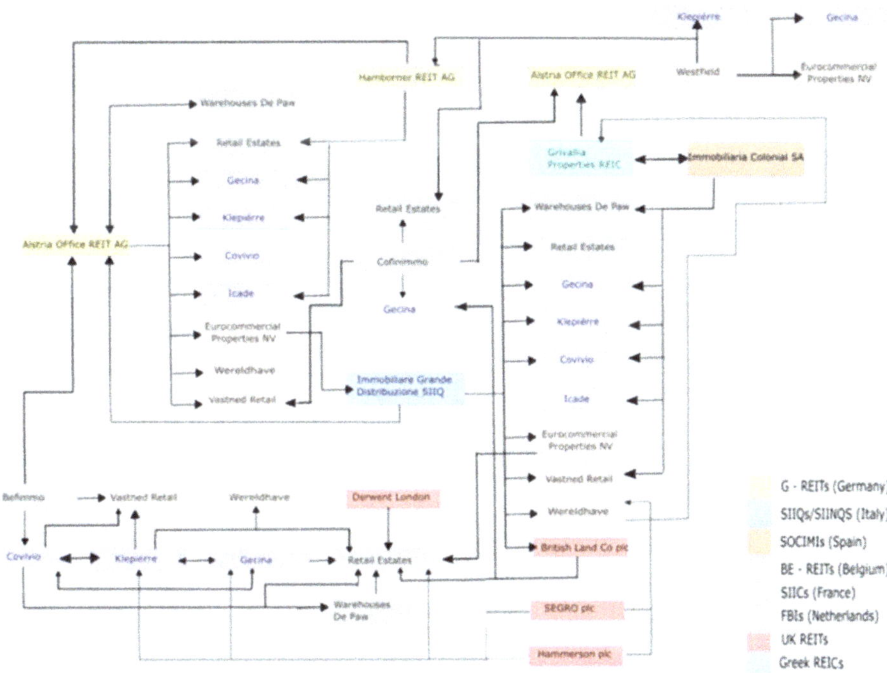

Italy, whereas the UK REITs delivered higher cross country diversification benefits relative to the other European REITs.

Future studies could expand this work, by implementing variance decomposition and impulse response function tests in order to assess the percentage contribution and (positive or negative) response of each European REIT on the other.

REFERENCES

Akaike, H. (1973). Information Theory and an Extension of the Maximum Likelihood Principle. In B. N. Petrov, & F. Csaki (Eds.), *Proceedings of the 2nd International Symposium on Information Theory*, Budapest: Akademiai Kiado, pp. 267-281.

Bewley, R. A. (1979). The Direct Estimation of the Equilibrium Response in a Linear Model. *Economics Letters*, *3*(4), 357–361. doi:10.1016/0165-1765(79)90011-9

Bollerslev, T. (1986). Generalized autoregressive conditional heteroskedasticity. *Journal of Econometrics*, *31*(3), 307–327. doi:10.1016/0304-4076(86)90063-1

Burke, G. (1994). A Sharper Sharpe Ratio. *Futures*, 56–57.

Corgel, J., McIntosh, W., & Ott, S. (1995). Real estate investment trusts: A review of the financial economics literature. *Journal of Real Estate Literature*, *3*, 13–43.

Coskun, Y., Selcuk-Kestel, A. S., & Yilmaz, B. (2017). Diversification benefit and return performance of REITs using CAPM and FAMA – French: Evidence from Turkey. *Borsa Istanbul Review*, *17*(4), 199–215. doi:10.1016/j.bir.2017.08.003

Dickey, D. A., & Fuller, W. A. (1979). Distribution of the Estimators for Autoregressive Time Series with a Unit Root. *Journal of the American Statistical Association*, *74*, 427–431.

Engle, F., & Granger, C. W. J. (1987). Co-Integration and Error Correction: Representation, Estimation, and Testing. *Econometrica*, *55*(2), 251–276. doi:10.2307/1913236

Ernest & Young. (2018). *Global Perspectives: 2018 REIT report,* EY.

European Public Real Estate Association. (2018). *Global REIT Survey 2018.* ERPA.

Feng, Z., Price, S., & Sirmans, C. (2011). An overview of equity REITs: 1993 - 2009. *Journal of Real Estate Literature*, *19*, 307–334.

Granger, C. W. J. (1969). Investigating causal relations by econometric models and cross - spectral methods. *Econometrica*, *3*(3), 424–438. doi:10.2307/1912791

Granger, C. W. J. (1986). Developments in the study of cointegrated economic variables. *Oxford Bulletin of Economics and Statistics*, *48*(3), 213–228. doi:10.1111/j.1468-0084.1986.mp48003002.x

Israelsen, C. (2005). A Refinement to the Sharpe Ratio and Information Ratio. *Journal of Asset Management*, *5*(6), 423–427. doi:10.1057/palgrave.jam.2240158

Jensen, M. C. (1968). The Performance of Mutual Funds in the period 1945 –1964. *The Journal of Finance*, *23*(2), 389–416. doi:10.1111/j.1540-6261.1968.tb00815.x

Johansen, S. (1988). Statistical analysis of cointegration vectors. *Journal of Economic Dynamics & Control*, *12*(2-3), 231–254. doi:10.1016/0165-1889(88)90041-3

Johansen, S. (1991). Estimation and hypothesis testing of cointegrating vectors in Gaussian vector autoregressive models. *Econometrica*, *59*(6), 1551–1580. doi:10.2307/2938278

Kim, B. S. (2009). The impact of the Global Financial Crisis on Asia – Pacific real estate markets: Evidence from Korea, Japan, Australia and US REITs. *Pacific Rim Property Research Journal, 15*(4), 398–416. doi:10.1080/14445921.2009.11104288

Le Sourd, V. (2007). *Performance Measurement for Traditional Investment*. EDHEC Risk and Asset Management Research Centre.

Lin, C. Y. (2018). *The Significance of Residential REITs in Japan as an Institutionalised property sector*. Department of Economic Finance and Property, Western Sydney University.

Loo, W. K., Anuar, M. A., & Ramakrishnan, S. (2015). The dynamic linkage among the Asian REITS market. *Pacific Rim Property Research Journal, 21*(2), 115–126. doi:10.1080/14445921.2015.1058036

Markowitz, H. (1952). Portfolio Selection. *The Journal of Finance, 7*, 77–91.

Marzuki, M., & Newell, G. (2018). The emergence of Spanish REITs. *Journal of Property Investment & Finance, 36*(5), 495–508. doi:10.1108/JPIF-05-2018-0032

Modigliani, F., & Modigliani, L. (1997). Risk-Adjusted Performance. *Journal of Portfolio Management, 23*(2), 45–54. doi:10.3905/jpm.23.2.45

Newell, G., Adair, A., & Nguyen, K. (2013). The significance and performance of French REITs (SIICs) in a mixed-asset portfolio. *Journal of Property Investment & Finance, 31*(6), 575–588. doi:10.1108/JPIF-01-2011-0004

Newell, G., & Marzuki, M. (2016). The significance and performance of UK - REITs in a mixed-asset portfolio. *Journal of European Real Estate Research, 9*(2), 171–182. doi:10.1108/JERER-08-2015-0032

Newell, G., & Marzuki, M. (2018). The emergence and performance of German REITs. *Journal of Property Investment & Finance, 36*(1), 91–103. doi:10.1108/JPIF-01-2017-0001

Newell, G., & Osmadi, A. (2009). The development and preliminary performance analysis of Islamic REITs in Malaysia. *Journal of Property Research, 26*(4), 329–247. doi:10.1080/09599916.2009.485417

Newell, G., & Peng, H. W. (2009). The impact of the global financial crisis on A - REIT risk. *Pacific Rim Property Research Journal, 15*(4), 453–470. doi:10.1080/14445921.2009.11104291

Newell, G., & Peng, H. W. (2012). The significance and performance of Japan REITs in a mixed-asset portfolio. *Pacific Rim Property Research Journal, 18*(1), 21–34. doi:10.1080/14445921.2012.11104348

Newell, G., Pham, A. K., & Ooi, J. (2015). The significance and performance of Singapore REITs in a mixed-asset portfolio. *Journal of Property Investment & Finance, 33*(1), 45–65. doi:10.1108/JPIF-12-2010-0027

Newell, G., Wu, Y., Chau, K. W., & Wong, S. K. (2010). The development and performance of REITs in Hong Kong. *Pacific Rim Property Research Journal, 16*(2), 190–206. doi:10.1080/14445921.2010.11104301

Peng, H. W., & Newell, G. (2012). The role of Taiwan REITs in investment Portfolios. *Pacific Rim Property Research Journal, 18*(1), 67–80. doi:10.1080/14445921.2012.11104351

Pezier, J., & White, A. (2008). The relative Merits of Alternative Investments in Passive Portfolios. *Journal of Alternative Investments, 10*(4), 37–49. doi:10.3905/jai.2008.705531

Pham, A. K. (2011). The performance of Thai-REITs in a mixed-asset portfolio. *Pacific Rim Property Research Journal, 17*(2), 197–214. doi:10.1080/14445921.2011.11104324

Pham, A. K. (2011). The significance and performance of South Korean REITs in a mixed-asset portfolio. *Journal of Real Estate Literature, 19*, 373–390.

Phillips, P. C. B. (1988). *Spectral Regression for Cointegrated Time Series, Cowles Foundation Discussion papers 872, Cowles Foundation for Research in Economics*. Yale University.

Scholtz, H., & Wilkens, M. (2005). A Jigsaw Puzzle of Basic Risk-adjusted Performance Measures. *Journal of Performance Measurement*, 57–64.

Shadwick, W., & Keating, C. (2002). A universal performance measure. *Journal of Performance Measurement*, 55–84.

Sharpe, W. F. (1966). Mutual Fund Performance. *The Journal of Business, 39*(S1), 119–138. doi:10.1086/294846

Sortino, F. A., & Van der Meer, R. (1991). Downside Risk. *Journal of Portfolio Management, 17*(4), 27–32. doi:10.3905/jpm.1991.409343

Sortino, F. A., Van der Meer, R., & Plantinga, A. (1999). The Dutch Triangle. *Journal of Portfolio Management, 26*(1), 50–59. doi:10.3905/jpm.1999.319775

Treynor, J. (1965). How to Rate Management of Mutual Funds. *Harvard Business Review*, *8*, 63–75.

Treynor, J., & Black, F. (1973). How to Use Security Analysis to Improve Portfolio Selection. *The Journal of Business*, 61–86.

Treynor, J., & Mazuy, K. (1966). Can Mutual Funds Outguess the Market? *Harvard Business Review*, 131–136.

Young, T. W. (1991). Calmar Ratio: A Smoother Tool, Futures magazine, pp. 40.

Zietz, E., Sirmans, S., & Friday, S. (2003). The environment and performance of Real Estate Investment Trusts. *Journal of Real Estate Portfolio Management*, *9*, 127–165.

ENDNOTES

1 There are also public non – listed and private REITs but these are not considered in the analysis of this study.

2 **Nascent REIT Markets:** Bahrain, Brazil, Costa Rica, Bulgaria, Greece, Hungary, India, Israel, Kenya, Pakistan, Philippines, Saudi Arabia, Taiwan, Thailand, Vietnam. **Emerging Markets:** Finland, Ireland, Italy, Malaysia, Mexico, South Africa, South Korea, Spain, Turkey, UAE. **Established REIT Markets:** Australia, Belgium, Canada, France, Germany, Hong Kong, Japan, Netherlands, New Zealand, Singapore, UK. **Mature REIT Markets:** United States.

3 (a) the GFC period (01 Jan 2007 – 31 Dec 2009), (b) the first years of the post GFC period (01 Jan 2010 – 31 Dec 2014) and (c) the most recent period (01 Jan 2015 – 31 Dec 2018).

4 US - REITs (Corgel et al., 1995; Feng et al., 2011; Zietz et al., 2003), Australian – REITs (Newell & Peng, 2009), Japan – REITs (Lin, 2018; Newell & Peng, 2012), Hong Kong - REITs (Newell et al, 2010), Thai – REITs (Pham, 2011), Singapore - REITs (Newell et al., 2015), Malaysian - REITs (Newell & Osmadi, 2009), South Korean – REITs (Pham, 2011), Taiwan – REITs (Peng & Newell, 2012), Asian - REITs (Loo et al., 2015), Asia – Pacific REITs (Kim, 2009).

5 Irish REITs are not included in the full period test due to lack of data over the first two (2) investigating sub periods of the study.

Chapter 4
On Financial Contagion Through ETFs

Alexia Thomaidou
Department of Economics, National and Kapodistrian University of Athens, Greece

Dimitris Kenourgios
https://orcid.org/0000-0003-2676-2524
Department of Economics, UoA Center for Financial Studies, National and Kapodistrian University of Athens, Greece

ABSTRACT

This chapter investigates the impact of the Global Financial Crisis and the European Sovereign Debt Crisis in ETFs across regions and segments. In particular, two tests are taking place, with the first one to examine if there is evidence of contagion effect and the second one to test the affection of risks in each pair of ETFs. The evidence across the stable period and the two crisis periods suggests the existence of the transmission of shocks from the Global Financial ETF to regional and sectoral ETFs. However, there is evidence that some of the ETFs remain less unaffected during both crises and some of them are immune. Moreover, the authors examine the impact of several control variables, which represent various risks, to the correlation of each pair of ETFs and the results show the influence of the interest rate risk and interbank liquidity risk during the Global Financial Crisis and the European Sovereign Debt Crisis.

DOI: 10.4018/978-1-7998-2436-7.ch004

INTRODUCTION

During the past decades, exchange-traded funds (ETFs, hereafter) were launched to provide an investment tool for investors who are seeking rapid and low cost exposure to equity market indices, industry sector indices and other asset classes. An ETF is a type of security that involves a collection of securities, such as stocks, that often tracks an underlying index, although they can invest in any number of industry sectors or use various strategies. Although ETFs are in many ways similar to mutual funds, they are listed on exchanges and ETF shares trade throughout the day just like ordinary stock. Choosing ETF as an investment strategy can provide a diversified portfolio without an extended investment planning. Since ETFs provide a large amount of information about the equity markets or any other market (Itzhak et al., 2012; Chang et al., 2017), this offers the opportunity to investigate the transmission of shocks among markets, segments, regions or sectors.

The purpose of this paper is to shed light on contagion effects through ETFs, by investigating how a Global Financial ETF can transmit shocks to sectoral and regional ETFs during crisis periods and providing implications for portfolio management and investments in ETFs. Taking into consideration studies about volatility and return spillovers among ETFs, the authors conduct an analysis of the transmission of shocks during two turbulent periods; the Global Financial Crisis and the European Sovereign Debt Crisis (GFC and ESDC, hereafter) using ETF daily returns, as an extension of the existing literature on the contagion effects. Forbes and Rigobon (2002) have defined the contagion as "*the propagation of shocks among markets in excess of the transmission explained by fundamentals*". They support the existence of two types of contagions: pure contagion and shift contagion. The pure contagion is defined as the contagion of shocks which are not transmitted through financial, economic and market fundamentals. The shift contagion is defined as the change in the strength of the propagation of shocks between a crisis period and a normal period (Forbes & Rigobon, 2002; Pericoli & Sbracia, 2003).

Defining contagion as the excess correlation of economic and financial assets (Bekaert et. al., 2003), contagion is the outcome of optimal portfolio diversification as investors tend to choose assets without being optimal informed about them (Calvo & Mendoza, 2000). Contagion effects might also be strengthening by financial globalization. Baur (2012) found that crisis contagion is a global issue and there is no immunity to shocks even between financial sectors stocks and real economy stocks. The issue of contagion comes up in the recent literature as a result of the GFC and the ESDC. Many studies examine the contagion effects among different types of assets such as stocks, bonds, commodities, sector stock indices, hedge funds, foreign exchange markets, futures, etc. (Chiang et al., 2007; Dungey et al.,

2006; Jorion & Zhang, 2007; Aloui et al., 2011, Ye et al., 2012; Brière & Szafarz., 2012; Philippas & Siriopoulos, 2013; Kenourgios, 2014).

As far as the authors know, there is a small number of studies which examine the contagion effects through ETFs. Itzhak et al. (2012) show that actions of arbitrage within ETFs and their underlying asset can stimulate liquidity shocks and therefore ETFs have the potential to create contagion across asset classes. Broman (2012) shows that one channel of contagion might be the commonality in mispricing due to the systematic risk exposure within country ETFs and the underlying assets. Bouaziz et al. (2012) examine the potential existence of contagion between ETFs during the GFC, triggered by the U.S. subprime crisis, for a group of developed and emerging countries and deduce the existence of contagion effects among developed and emerging countries, but also across different markets. This paper contributes to the existent literature by testing for equity ETF contagion on regions and sectors, on a crisis level. By using daily data on various ETFs from July 31, 2007 to December 29, 2017, the authors estimate a Dynamic Conditional Correlation (DCC) GARCH model introduced by Engle (2002). The particular model is used as it allows showing the time-varying conditional correlations among ETF's returns during both crisis and after those.

There are several questions to be answered by this research. *(1) Is there a contagion through ETFs across regions and sectors?* Following several studies (Bekaert et al., 2005; Hortal et al., 2010; Phylaktis & Xia, 2009; Baur, 2011; Kenourgios & Dimitriou, 2015), which separate their data collection and analysis into two ways, aggregate stock indices and sector stock indices, the authors will adopt the same approach as their aim is to investigate the transmission channels of contagion through this particular alternative asset class. Phylaktis & Xia (2009) find that there are sectors which are channels of contagion and others which are not and the last ones can be a useful tool of portfolio diversification during turmoil periods. Baur (2011) shows that even if no country and sector was unspoiled to harsh times and the effectiveness of portfolio diversification was limited, there are some sectors, such as healthcare, telecommunications and technology which were less touched by the GFC. *(2) In which crisis period a contagion effect is mostly noticed?* Each crisis period had specific characteristics which are identified, and so the results will show which period is the most pathogenic. In this way, it will be easy to identify the reason of this pathogen and to understand the characteristics of the period, which affect the market through ETFs. (3) *Which risk mostly affects ETFs during the crisis periods?* Many efforts have been given to understand which factors affect a market or a segment or an investor decision. The answer of this kind of question will be an indicator to analysts who want a diversified and hedged portfolio.

The empirical results show that almost all sectoral and regional ETFs are affected during the GFC and the ESDC. The second part of the analysis shows that risks exist and affect ETFs during the crisis periods, but during the stable periods it is proved that there is no statistical significant evidence of affection. The rest of this paper is organized as follows. Section 2 presents the methodology, while section 3 the data sample and a preliminary analysis. Section 4 displays the empirical findings and section 5 concludes.

METHODOLOGY

Benchmark Model

A robust empirical analysis of financial contagion requires overcoming a heteroskedasticity problem when measuring correlations and the lack of a dynamic increment in the regressions (Forbes & Rigobon, 2002; Pesaran & Pick, 2007). Otherwise, «*continued market correlation at high levels is considered to be «no contagion, only interdependence*» (Forbes & Rigobon, 2002). To avoid the above restrictions, the authors utilize the DCC (Engle, 2002) derived from the multivariate GARCH model to test for increased co-movement among a portfolio of ETFs in crisis period compared to tranquil period.[1]

The dynamic conditional correlation DCC-GARCH model developed by Engle (2002) investigates the second order moments dynamics of financial time-series and overcomes the heteroskedasticity problem raised by Forbes and Rigobon (2002). The estimation of DCC-GARCH model is composed of two steps: the first step is about the estimation of a univariate GARCH model and the second step estimates the conditional correlations which vary through time.

The DCC-GARCH model is defined as follows;

$$X_t = \mu_t + h_t^{1/2} * \varepsilon_t \quad (1)$$

$$\mathrm{H_t = H_t{*}R_t{*}D_t} \quad (2)$$

$$\mathrm{R_t} = \left(\mathrm{diag}\left(\mathrm{Q_t}\right)\right)^{-1/2} {*}\mathrm{Q_t}{*}\left(\mathrm{diag}\left(\mathrm{Q_t}\right)\right)^{-1/2} \quad (3)$$

$$\mathrm{H_t} = \mathrm{diag}\left(\sqrt{\mathrm{h_{ii,t}}}\right) \quad (4)$$

where, $X_t = (X_1, X_2, ..., X_N)$ is the vector of the past observations,

H_t are the multivariate conditional variances,

$\mu_t = (\mu_1, \mu_{2,...,} \mu_N)$ is the vector of conditional returns,

$\varepsilon_t = (\varepsilon_1, \varepsilon_{2,...,} \varepsilon_N)$is the vector of the standardized residuals,

R_t is a N×N symmetric dynamic correlations matrix

D_t is a diagonal matrix of conditional standard deviations for return series, obtained from estimating a univariate GARCH model with $\sqrt{h_{ii,t}}$ on the ith diagonal, i=1, 2,...,N.

The DCC specification is defined as follows;

$$Q_t = (1 - \psi - \zeta) * \bar{Q} + \zeta * Q_{t-1} + c * \delta_{i,t-1} * \delta_{j,t-1} \tag{5}$$

$$\mathrm{H}_t = H_t^{*-1} * \mathrm{Q}_t * H_t^{*-1} \tag{6}$$

where,

$(Q_t) = \lfloor q_{ij,t} \rfloor$ is (N×N) time varying covariance matrix of standardized residuals $(\delta_{i,t} = \frac{\varepsilon_{i,t}}{\sqrt{h_{i.t}}})$,

$\bar{Q}$ is the unconditional correlations of $\delta_{i,t}, \delta_{j,t}$ and ψ and ζ are nonnegative scalar parameters that satisfies $\psi + \zeta \lessdot 1. Q_t^* = \left[q_{ii,t}^*\right] = \sqrt{q_{ii.t}}$ is a diagonal matrix with the square root of the ith diagonal element of Q_t on its ith diagonal position.

Dynamic Conditional Correlations across the Phases of the Crises

In this part of the analysis, the authors create dummy variables which are equal to one for each of the three periods and zero otherwise. This procedure would allow testing whether the magnitude of the contagion coefficients changes across the three periods and whether it differs across regions and sectors. The latter would indicate the existence of ETF-specific contagion on the regional level and the sectoral level, on a crisis level. Further, the authors took into the analysis six control variables which represent specific risk factors (volatility risk, interest rate risk, interbank liquidity risk and market risk) in order to examine if each of them influences the estimated time-varying conditional correlation. To avoid endogeneity problems, the authors use lags to the control variables. In this set up, the authors investigate the dynamic patterns of correlation changes across the two crises by estimating regressions for ETFs of the form:

$$\widehat{\rho}_{ij,t} = \sum_{k=1}^{3} \beta_k * DM_{k,t} + \sum_{v=1}^{6}\sum_{k=1}^{3} \beta_{v,k} * DM_{k,t} * X_{v,t-1} + e_t \qquad (7)$$

where $\hat{\rho}_{ij,t}$ is the pairwise conditional correlation between each ETF and a Global Financial ETF, k *counts the three different periods (GFC, ESDC, stable); v counts the six control variables; t counts the three periods, while* $DM_{k,t}$ is the dummy variable and $X_{v,t-1}$ is the control variable with a lag.

Testable Hypotheses

By estimating the DCC-GARCH model and the conditional variance equation (7), the authors will test if there is a contagion from the Global Financial ETF (considered as a source of contagion) to equity ETFs, taking into account six different control variables. To conclude if such an event occurs, the authors will apply several different tests, regarding the three dummies and the control variables.

Under the null hypothesis, if the coefficients of the dummy β_k in equation 7 are zero or/and negative across the turmoil periods, this indicates the absence of contagion effects. Alternatively, a positive and statistically significant dummy coefficient β_k across the two crisis periods implies the spread of a crisis from the global financial ETF to the examined ETF. Specifically, the null hypothesis (H_0) is tested against the one-sided alternative (H_1) that the turmoil conditional correlations are greater at the 10%, 5% and 1% significance levels.

The first test refers to the examination of the existence of contagion effect during the two crisis periods. $H_0 : \beta_k \leq 0$ (no contagion) $H_1 : \beta_k > 0$ (contagion)

The second test refers to the examination of the potential influence of the control variables to the estimated time-varying conditional correlations of each ETF pair.

$H_0 : \beta_{v,k} = 0$ (no influence) $H_1 : \beta_{v,k} \neq 0$ (influence)

DATA AND PRELIMINARY ANALYSIS

Data Set

The data comprises daily closing prices of fifteen sectoral ETFs from global and US regions, five regional ETFs[2] and a global financial ETF, which is considered as source of contagion, taking into account that the crises started from the financial sector. The sectors are the following: Basic Materials, Financial, Real Estate, Mortgages, US Banks, Financial Services, Broker Deals & Services Exchange, Consumer Cyclical, Industrials, Utilities, Private Equity, Energy, Technology and Gold Miners.

The sectorial ETFs are the following. MXI-iShares Global Materials ETF tracks global materials companies and its tracked index is S&P Global 1200 Materials Sector Index. RXI- iShares Global Consumer Discretionary ETF is a compact market-cap-weighted index of global consumer discretionary stocks and its tracked index is S&P Global 1200 Consumer Discretionary Sector Index. EXI - iShares Global Industrials ETF represents global industrial stocks and the index of tracking is S&P Global 1200 Industrials Sector Index. JXI- iShares Global Utilities ETF tracks an index of companies in the utilities industry worldwide, ex-US utility segment. IXC- iShares Global Energy ETF follows global energy companies and its underlying index is S&P Global 1200 Energy Sector Index. IXN- iShares Global Tech ETF is the only ETF which tracks global technology companies worldwide. GDX- VanEck Vectors Gold Miners ETF is a gold-mining ETF, tracking global gold-mining companies. PSP- Invesco Global Listed Private Equity ETF focused in private equity firms and the benchmark index is the Red Rocks Global Listed Private Equity Index. IAI- iShares U.S. Broker-Dealers & Securities Exchanges ETF focuses on investment service providers as well as securities and commodities exchanges. IYG- iShares U.S. Financial Services ETF represents a wide variety of US stocks in financial sector. On the other hand, IYF- iShares U.S. Financials ETF is a market-cap-weighted index of US financial companies. IYR- iShares U.S. Real Estate ETF deals on the US real estate equities listed on the major US exchanges and REM- iShares Mortgage Real Estate ETF is a portfolio of residential and commercial mortgage REITs. KBE-SPDR S&P Bank ETF represents an equal weighted index of US banking firms. The last one of the sectoral ETFs is VAW- Vanguard Materials ETF which is a very broad index of US materials companies.

The five regional ETFs are the following. EZU-iShares MSCI Eurozone ETF representing large and midcap companies from Eurozone. ADRA- Invesco BLDRS Asia 50 ADR Index Fund is an ETF which tracks a wide variety of Asian companies. ITOT- iShares Core S&P Total U.S. Stock Market ETF tracks American companies listed on the MYSE and the NASDAQ. ILF- iShares Latin America 40 ETF represents the 40 biggest companies in Latin America market. Finally, IOO- iShares Global 100 ETF is an index of 100 large- cap multinational companies across the world. The benchmark ETF, which is using as the independent variable and source of contagion is IXG- iShares Global Financials ETF, a high beta ETF tracking large- and midcap global financial stocks.

The control variables are the following; VIX, DJIA, EU interest rate term spread, US interest rate term spread, the change in the TED spread and the change in the

European counterpart of the TED spread. The data collected from Bloomberg and Yahoo.Finance covering the period of 08/01/2007 until 12/29/2017, leading to a sample size of 2624 observation. For each ETF and control variable, the return is estimated as $r_t = \frac{(p_t - p_{t-1})}{p_{t-1}}$, where p_t is the price on day t. Table 1 shows the ticker name of each ETF and the name the authors give for the purpose of the empirical analysis [r_i with i = (1, 2, …, 20)].

As regards to the control variables, first differences of the returns are taken. To investigate if there are other variables which influence the correlation of the pairs of ETFs, the authors take into account four risks; volatility risk (VIX), interest rate risk (USIR, EUIR), interbank liquidity risk (TED, EUTED) and market risk (DJIA). The interest rate term spread, otherwise known as the change in the yield slope, is used as a prognosticator of real economic activity. It is computed as the difference between 10-year government bond yield and 3-month bond yield of the respective government bond. The change in the TED spread counts the funding liquidity (Brunnermeir, 2009; Pelizzon et al., 2016). It is computed as the difference between the three-month EURIBOR (Euro Interbank Offered Rate)[3] (in the case of the European counterpart of TED spread) or the LIBOR (London Interbank Offered Rate) expressed in US dollars and the 3-month respective government bond rate.[4] VIX is a volatility index created by the Chicago Board options Exchange (CBOE), which represents the expected level of fear by investors. VIX collects all of the closet at-the-money call and put S&P500 index option premium prices to obtain the weighted average of the implied volatility series (Chang et al., 2017). DJIA (Dow Jones Industrial Average) is a price-weighted average index of 30 significant stocks traded on the New York Stock Exchange (NYSE) and the NASDAQ.

Descriptive statistics for each ETF and the six control variables are presented in Tables 2, 3 and 4. Table 2 refers to sectoral ETFs and shows high value of kurtosis and in some cases negative and positive skewness. In our dataset, the authors observe that approximately the standard deviation is the same, indicating the same risk. Table 3 presents the descriptive statistics for the regional ETFs across the period of our analysis, while Table 4 the descriptive statistics of the first differences of the six control variables. Among the six control variables, VIX has the highest standard deviation, which is logical as VIX measures the volatility in the market. Variables expressed in € are denominated in USD.

Identification of the Crisis Periods

The identification of the turmoil period and the stable period is determined by three different approaches according to the existing contagion literature. The first approach

Table 1. ETF's name and its ticker

Sectoral ETF	
MXI	iShares Global Materials ETF
RXI	iShares Global Consumer Discretionary ETF
EXI	iShares Global Industrials ETF
JXI	iShares Global Utilities ETF
IXC	iShares Global Energy ETF
IXN	iShares Global Tech ETF
GDX	VanEck Vectors Gold Miners ETF
PSP	PowerShares Global Listed Private Equity Portfolio ETF
IAI	iShares U.S. Broker-Dealers & Securities Exchanges ETF
IYG	iShares US Financial Services ETF
IYF	iShares U.S. Financials ETF
IYR	iShares U.S. Real Estate ETF
REM	iShares Mortgage Real Estate Capped ETF
KBE	SPDR S&P Bank ETF
VAW	Vanguard Materials ETF
Regional ETF	
EZU	iShares MSCI Eurozone ETF
ADRA	BLDRS Asia 50 ADR ETF
ITOT	iShares Core S&P Total U.S. Stock Market ETF
ILF	iShares Latin America 40 ETF
IOO	iShares Global 100 ETF
Source of Contagion ETF	
IXG	iShares Global Financials ETF

is introduced by Forbes and Rigobon (2002) and is based on major economic and financial events, the second is a statistical approach of endogenously identification of turmoil periods (Boyer et al., 2006; Rodriquez, 2007) and the third approach is a combination of the first two approaches (Baur, 2012; Dimitriou et al., 2013; Kenourgios, 2014).

For the purpose of this study, the authors will use the first method. The Bank of International Settlements (BIS, 2009) and the Federal Reserve Board of St. Louis (FED, 2009) provide a timeline of the GFC.[5] It spans from 1st August 2007 until 31st March 2009. Based on the provided timeline by the European Commission[6], the ESDC started on the 5th November 2009 and we consider the exit of Cyprus from

Table 2. Descriptive statistics for the regional ETFs from 8/1/2007 until 12/29/2017

	EUROPE	ASIA-PASIFIC	USA	LATIN AMERICA	GLOBAL
	EZU	ADRA	ITOT	ILF	IOO
MEAN	0.000186	0.000236	4.25E-05	0.000259	0.000267
MEDIAN	0.000737	0	0.000731	0.000817	0.000626
MAX.	0.146064	0.179105	0.107828	0.262458	0.120479
MIN.	-0.11512	-0.115929	-1,000,000	-0.194667	-0.103536
Std. Dev.	0.018126	0.016421	0.023287	0.022314	0.01335
Skewness	0.049098	0.301179	-3,020,854	0.339878	-0.014503
Kurtosis	10.815400	13.640570	1,298.179000	17.391300	13.714470
Prob.	0.000000	0.000000	0.000000	0.000000	0.000000
J-Berra	6679.179	12418.570	1.84E+08	22694.51	12551.54
Obs.	2624	2624	2624	2624	2624

the economic adjustment program on March 31, 2016 as the ending point. After those crisis periods, the authors assume that there is a stabilization period.

Empirical Analysis

This section presents the empirical findings which are derived into the following framework. First, the authors separate the period from 08/01/2007 to 29/12/2017 into three sub-periods: the GFC from 08/01/2007 until 03/31/2009, the ESDC from 11/05/2009 until 03/31/2016 and a stable period from 04/01/2017 until 12/29/2017. Second, the authors estimate the DCC-GARCH model to derive the time-varying conditional correlations among a particular ETF (IXG) and each ETF, respectively. By extracting the results, as a third stage the authors estimate an OLS regression using the three different periods, six control variables and the results from the DCC-GARCH model.

The diagrammatical depiction of the DCC results is shown in Figure 1.[7] It can be observed from the graphs that, as regards the sectoral ETFs, there is a potential contagion effect as the correlation is above zero. The regional ETFs graphs depict that all of them, except the US region ETF (ITOT), are influenced by the Global Financial ETF, which is a sign of contagion.

Table 5 shows the extracted results from the first part of equation 7, indicating the correlation among the Global Financial ETF and each ETF across the three periods. The results show that the financial sector influence every sector and region in stable and turmoil periods. As regard the sectoral ETFs, only the Gold Miners

Table 3. Descriptive statistics for the sectoral ETFs from 8/1/2007 until 12/29/2017

	GLOBAL							
	MXI	**RXI**	**EXI**	**JXI**	**IXC**	**IXN**	**GDX**	**PSP**
MEAN	0.00024	0.000392	0.000318	0.000159	0.000192	0.000471	0.000214	0.000199
MEDIAN	0.000487	0.000786	0.000824	0.000664	0.000648	0.000924	-0.000277	0.000949
MAX.	0.163693	0.112909	0.107132	0.157058	0.154173	0.112311	0.265384	0.18383
MIN.	-0.130898	-0.108517	-0.091795	-0.090061	-0.131509	-0.08445	-0.155322	-0.131973
Std. Dev.	0.018332	0.013668	0.014365	0.012646	0.017582	0.013412	0.02808	0.019595
Skewness	-0.0729	-0.31885	-0.223286	0.314117	-0.017914	-0.146267	0.367974	-0.033895
Kurtosis	11.842710	10.769690	9.814838	21.495150	12.782410	9.275454	8.645362	14.811500
Prob.	0.000000	0.000000	0.000000	0.000000	0.000000	0.000000	0.000000	0.000000
J-Berra	8,551.477	6,644.707	5,099.465	37,442.880	10,462.850	4,315.048	3,543.683	15,253.760
Obs.	2624	2624	2624	2624	2624	2624	2624	2624
	USA							
	IAI	IYG	IYF	IYR	REM	KBE	VAW	IAI
MEAN	0.000351	0.000344	0.000316	0.000444	0.001334	0.000346	0.000416	0.000351
MEDIAN	0.000823	0.000246	0.000498	0.000793	0.0008	0.000381	0.000906	0.000823
MAX.	0.151288	0.171007	0.156634	0.163253	3,028,763	0.202143	0.108868	0.151288
MIN.	-0.155959	-0.172414	-0.156959	-0.206112	-0.16103	-0.196304	-0.123041	-0.155959
Std. Dev.	0.020598	0.022425	0.019923	0.021178	0.061534	0.02456	0.016512	0.020598
Skewness	0.159003	0.413123	0.256296	0.052565	4,540,249	0.466197	-0.427161	0.159003
Kurtosis	12.296820	14.938550	14.802670	17.136140	2,234.662000	15.510420	9.548755	12.296820
Prob.	0.000000	0.000000	0.000000	0.000000	0.000000	0.000000	0.000000	0.000000
J-Berra	9,460.835	15,657.800	15,259.190	21,849.340	5.45E+08	17206.880	4768.689	9,460.835
Obs.	2624	2624	2624	2624	2624	2624	2624	2624

ETF is not influenced during the stable period and under the first test, and regarding the regional ETFs, there is no evidence of contagion between the Global Financial ETF and the American ETF during both crises.

The results from Table 5 also show similarities between ETFs and the Global Financial ETF. There is a significant decrease of the level of coefficients between the GFC and the stable period and between the ESDC and the stable period. About the global sectoral ETFs, a positive and significant coefficient implies contagion for each of the two crisis periods. The results show that all the global sectoral ETFs are affected during the GFC and the ESDC. From the eight global ETFs, the seven are affected during the crisis periods, indicating contagion effect as the coefficient level is decreased in the stable period. The gold miners' ETF is not affected during the stable period and also the correlation with the global financial ETF is weak during the crisis periods, indicating independency from the financial sector.

The seven US sectoral ETFs are all affected across all the crisis periods. The results show a significant decrease of the coefficients from the GFC period to the stable period and from the ESDC to the stable period. The most affected during the GFC are the Financial Services ETF, Financials ETF, U.S Banks ETF and Broker Deals & Services Exchanges ETF with a coefficient that approximately equals to

Table 4. Descriptive statistics for the control variables from 8/1/2007 until 12/29/2017

	D(VIX)	D(DJIA)	D(EUIR)	D(EUTED)	D(TED)	D(USIR)
MEAN	2.98E-05	-5.68E-06	0.000413	0.000416	-3.05E-05	0.000387
MEDIAN	0.004184	-0.000292	-0.001918	0.001	0	-0.0009
MAX.	0.678501	0.127585	0.638967	0.7989	0.99	0.628
MIN.	-0.769583	-0.115294	-0.602155	-0.6726	-0.8	-0.5461
Std. Dev.	0.112221	0.017826	0.085312	0.054437	0.060349	0.073679
Skewness	-0.353901	0.417223	0.16621	-1.05142	0.773742	0.243309
Kurtosis	7.311616	11.5187	12.01181	65.18757	72.64302	13.04916
J-Berra	2086.489	8007.203	8887.954	423146.3	530342.7	11062.76
Prob.	0	0	0	0	0	0
Obs.	2624	2624	2624	2624	2624	2624

Notes: First differences of the returns of each variable are taken. The control variables are the following: Volatility risk (VIX), interest rate risk for USA and Europe (USIR, EUIR), interbank liquidity risk (TED, EUTED) and market risk (DJIA)

Figure 1. Dynamic conditional correlations. Notes: Fig. 1 shows the DCCs between the Global Financial ETF and each other ETF during the period August 2007-December 2017

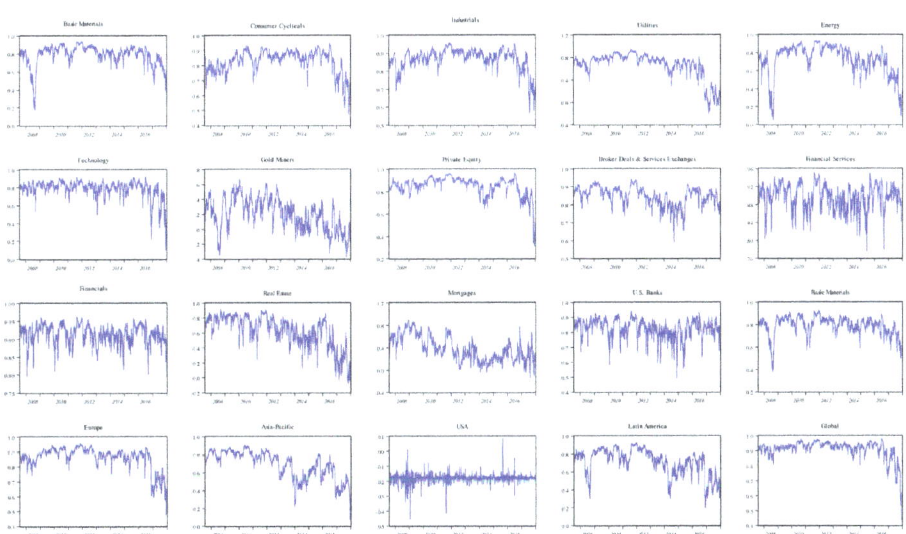

Table 5. Estimation results for sectoral, US and regional ETFs (Test 1)

Sectoral ETFs																	
Global Region																	
	Basic Materials		**Consumer Cyclicals**		**Industrials**		**Utilities**		**Energy**		**Technology**		**Gold Miners**		**Private Equity**		
GFC	0.684	C***	0.775	C***	0.843	C***	0.701	C***	0.608	C***	0.809	C***	0.192	C***	0.847	C***	
ESDC	0.832	C***	0.865	C***	0.894	C***	0.756	C***	0.791	C***	0.814	C***	0.252	C***	0.876	C***	
STABLE	0.701	↓***	0.749	↓***	0.803	↓***	0.265	↓***	0.555	↓***	0.676	↓***	-0.034	-	0.754	↓***	
U.S. Region																	
	Broker Deals & Services Exchanges		Financial Services		Financials		Real Estate		Mortgages		U.S. Banks		Basic Materials				
GFC	0.882	C***	0.903	C***	0.917	C***	0.785	C***	0.655	C***	0.852	C***	0.750	C***			
ESDC	0.838	C***	0.894	C***	0.914	C***	0.658	C***	0.328	C***	0.814	C***	0.814	C***			
STABLE	0.835	↓***	0.896	↓***	0.906	↓***	0.306	↓***	0.237	↓***	0.828	↓***	0.724	↓***			
Regional ETFs																	
	Europe		Asia-Pacific		USA		Latin America		Global								
GFC	0.854	C***	0.813	C***	-0.018***	-	0.729	C***	0.907	C***							
ESDC	0.891	C***	0.690	C***	-0.018***	-	0.741	C***	0.934	C***							
STABLE	0.75	↓***	0.507	↓***	-0.018***	-	0.547	↓***	0.821	↓***							

Notes: This table presents the results from the eq.7 during the GFC (August 2007–March 2009), the ESDC (November 2009-March 2016) and stable (April 2016–December 2017) periods. The rejection of the null hypothesis against the one-sided alternative that the correlation is greater than zero, at the 10%, 5%, and 1% significance levels, is denoted by *, **, and ***, respectively. A positive and statistically significant coefficient during the crisis period provides evidence on contagion (C). In the stable period, the authors use the symbol (↓) which depicts a decrease of the statistically significant coefficient relative to the crisis periods and the symbol (-) if there is a rejection of the alternative hypothesis or no statistically significant results.

0.89. During the ESDC, the most affected ETFs are Financials ETF and Financial Services ETF. During the stable period, the ETFs which display a statistically significant reduced coefficient are the Real Estate ETF and the Mortgages ETF.

Regarding the regional ETFs, the results show a positive and statistically significant correlation during the crisis periods, suggesting a contagion effect. Among the five regional ETFs, only the USA ETF is not affected by the Global Financial ETF, showing no contagion, as the null hypothesis from the test 1 is not rejected. During GFC, the coefficient of the global region ETF is the largest among the other three and the least affected is the Latin America ETF. During the ESDC, the most affected is the Global ETF and the least affected is the Asia- Pacific with a coefficient that equals to 0.0690. Regarding the stable period, the results show a decrease in the coefficient level from the crisis period, with the most infected -even declined- to be the Global ETF.

Moving forward, there is evidence indicating that all sectors and regions have been influenced differently during the two crisis periods by the different control variables. Tables 6 and 7 display the estimation results from the second part of the equation 7, using OLS estimation with Newey-West estimated variance-covariance metrics (Newey & West, 1987) to test the potential influence of the control variables to the estimated time-varying conditional correlation (test 2) The linkages between the estimated correlations and the control variables are different in each case, indicating that if an investor wants to include an ETF in his/her portfolio, he/she has to take into account different factors to achieve a diversified portfolio, such as the region, sector, the exposure of the ETF in interest rate risk, the volatility and the composition of the ETF.

Table 6 shows that during the GFC, the control variable VIX affects only the correlation between Mortgages ETF and the Global Financial ETF, while no other ETF is affected by the volatility risk. TED affects the correlation between the Global Financial ETF and the following ETFs: Technology ETF, Financial Services ETF, Financials ETF and U.S. Banks ETF. EUTED affects the correlation between the Global Financial ETF and the following ETFs: Utilities ETF, Broker Deals & Services Exchanges ETF and Mortgages ETF. USIR affects only the Broker Deals & Services Exchanges ETF. The EUIR affects the correlation between the Global Financial ETF and the following ETFs: Private Equity ETF, Financial Services ETF, Financials ETF, Mortgages ETF and U.S. Banks ETF. The linkages between the control variables and the correlation between the Global Financial ETF and each ETF in every case do not exist for the 40% of the sectoral ETFs during the GFC period.

During the ESDC, the only control variable which is positive and statistical significant is the EUTED. The least affects the Industrials ETF's correlation with the Global Financial ETF and the Basic Materials ETF's correlation with the Global Financial ETF. Regarding the stable period, the results show that only USIR control variable positively affects the correlation of the Global Financial ETF with the Mortgages ETF, implying the connection of the composition of the particular ETF with the US interest rates. Across all the periods, the control variable DJIA does not affect any correlation between the Global Financial ETF and each ETF.

Table 7 presents the estimations results for regional ETFs, extracted from the second part of equation 7 and tests if the control variables affect the estimated correlation derived from the DCC model. The control variables VIX and DJIA do not affect any pair of ETFs' correlation, indicating that the volatility risk and the market risk do not influence the regional ETFs' correlation with the Global Financial ETF. During the GFC, the correlation of the Global ETF with the Global Financial ETF is affected by the TED and the EUIR and Latin America ETF is affected by the EUTED during the ESDC. It is notable that even if the USA ETF has no sign of contagion, the control variable EUIR affects it during both crisis periods. This can be due to the composition of an ETF and perhaps to other variables which have to be taken under consideration.

The overall pattern of contagion based on Tables 6 and 7 depicts that the most affected sectors from the control variables are: Broker Deals & Services Exchanges, Financial Services, Financials, Mortgages and U.S. Banks. The least affected are Industrials, Utilities, Technology, Private Equity and Basic Materials. Across every

Table 6. Statistically significant effects of the control variables on the conditional correlations of global sectoral and US ETFs (Test 2)

Sectoral ETFs																		
GLOBAL REGION																		
	VIX			TED			DJIA			EUTED			USIR			EUIR		
	GFC	ESDC	STABLE	GFC	ESDC	STABLE	GFC	ESDC	STABLE	GFC	ESDC	STABLE	GFC	ESDC	STABLE	GFC	ESDC	STABLE
Basic Materials														↓**				
Consumer Cyclicals										↓**			↓**					
Industrials											↑*							
Utilities										↑**	↓*							
Energy																		
Technology				↑**										↓**				
Gold Miners					↓***													
Private Equity										↓*			↓*			↑***		
U.S. Region																		
Broker Deals & Services Exchanges										↑**			↑***					
Financial Services				↑**										↓**		↑**		
Financials				↑**										↓**		↑**		
Real Estate												↓**						
Mortgages	↑*									↑***				↓*	↑**	↑***		
U.S. Banks				↑**										↓*		↑**		
Basic Materials											↑***							

Notes: This table presents the results from the second part of eq.7 during the GFC (August 2007–March 2009), the ESDC (November 2009-March 2016) and stable (April 2016–December 2017) periods. The control variables are: Volatility risk (VIX), interest rate risk (USIR, EUIR), interbank liquidity risk (TED, EUTED) and market risk (DJIA). The estimates of the dummy coefficients are reported here. For the test 2, the rejection of the null hypothesis against the two-sided alternative that the coefficient is different than zero, at the 10%, 5%, and 1% significance levels, is denoted by *, **, and ***, respectively. A positive and statistically significant coefficient shows positive influence (↑). A negative and statistically significant coefficient shows negative influence (↓). This note also applies in Table 7.

Table 7. Statistically significant effects of the control variables on the conditional correlations of regional ETFs (Test 2)

Regional ETFs																		
	VIX			TED			DJIA			EUTED			USIR			EUIR		
	GFC	ESDC	STABLE	GFC	ESDC	STABLE	GFC	ESDC	STABLE	GFC	ESDC	STABLE	GFC	ESDC	STABLE	GFC	ESDC	STABLE
Europe														↓**				
Asia-Pacific																		
USA																↓*	↑**	
Latin America											↑**							
Global				↑**												↑**		

period, the only unaffected sectors are Basic Materials, Consumer Cyclicals, Energy, Gold Miners and Real Estate.[8]

CONCLUSIONS

This paper investigates the financial crisis contagion across a sample of ETFs and a set of control variables, which indicate specific risks, on regional and sectoral level, using daily returns from August 2007 to December 2017. The dynamic conditional correlation (DCC) analysis across GFC, ESDC and a stable period indicates that the Global Financial ETF (which is considered as source of contagion taking into account that the crises started from the financial sector) affects all the sectoral and regional ETFs, only the regional USA ETF is unaffected during all periods, but is vulnerable to the European interest rate risk during the ESDC period.

In line with previous studies (Itzhan et al., 2012; Bouaziz et al., 2012), the results show that all sectors are affected during the GFC and ESDC, but during the stable period the Gold Miners ETF has not been affected by the Global Financial ETF. Gold Miners ETF is the only sector which has the lowest correlation with the Global Financial ETF, indicating the independency from the Financial Sector during all periods. It is noticeable that the correlation between the Global Financial ETF and any ETF is declined from the GFC period to the stable period and the same is occurring between the ESDC period and the stable period, as well. This implies that the previous crises do not affect any more the sectoral ETFs and indeed there was contagion in the ETF market. About the regional ETFs, only the US region ETF is not affected by the Global Financial ETF and the least affected is the Latin America ETF during the GFC, while during the ESDC the least affected is the Asia-Pacific ETF.

By regressing the estimated correlations with the three dummies (GFC, ESDC and stable) and the control variables to examine potential influence of the control variables to the estimated time-varying conditional correlation, the authors conclude that the volatility risk (expressed by VIX) and the market risk (expressed by DJIA) do not affect any of the regional and sectoral ETFs, except Mortgages ETF, which is influenced by the volatility in the market. This implies that the volatility and the tense in the market do not enhance the contagion effect among ETFs. The interest rate risk and the interbank liquidity risk do affect every sectoral ETF, showing the existence of a shift contagion during the GFC and ESDC. There is no evidence of influence in the sectoral ETFs during the stable period, except from U.S. Energy ETF, which is affected by the European interest rate risk, indicating the dependence of this particular ETF with the European interest rates. Regarding the regional ETFs, the correlation of Europe ETF and Asia-Pacific ETF with the Global Financial ETF is not affected by any control variable, depicting the immunity in any risk.

Concluding, it is highly important for an investor, who wants to include ETFs to his/her portfolio, to take into account all the risks, classify them in terms of the desired exposure to each one and search the composition of the ETF, the benchmark index and the invested sectors. Finally, future research can investigate how the particular ETFs are affected by the crisis by analyzing ETFs' underlying assets and how any particular component of an ETF is affected, as well as the role of specific country fundamentals in affecting the ETFs market.

REFERENCES

Aloui, R., Ben Aossa, M. S., & Nguyen, D. K. (2011). Global financial crisis, extreme interdependences, and contagion effects: The role of economic structure? *Journal of Banking & Finance*, *35*(1), 130–141. doi:10.1016/j.jbankfin.2010.07.021

Baur, G. (2012). Financial contagion and the real economy. *Journal of Banking & Finance*, *36*(10), 2680–2698. doi:10.1016/j.jbankfin.2011.05.019

Bekaert, G., Harvey, C., & Ng, A. (2005). Market integration and contagion. *The Journal of Business*, *78*(1), 39–70. doi:10.1086/426519

BIS. (2009). *The international financial crisis: Timeline, impact and policy responses in Asia and the Pacific*. Bank for International Settlements.

Bouaziz, M., Selmi, N., & Boujelbene, Y. (2012). Contagion effect of the subprime financial crisis: Evidence of DCC multivariate GARCH models. *European Journal of Economics, Finance, and Administrative Sciences*, *44*, 66–76.

Boyer, B. H., Kumagai, T., & Yuan, K. (2006). How do crises spread? Evidence from accessible and inaccessible stock indices. *The Journal of Finance*, *61*(2), 957–1003. doi:10.1111/j.1540-6261.2006.00860.x

Brière, M. A. C., & Szafarz, A. (2012). No contagion, only globalization and flight to quality. *Journal of International Money and Finance*, *31*(6), 1729–1744. doi:10.1016/j.jimonfin.2012.03.010

Broman, M. (2012). Commonality in ETF Mispricing and Contagion. Available at https://www.semanticscholar.org/paper/Commonality-in-ETF-Mispricing-and-Contagion-Broman/a5716a1b908f2e626cccb86723a673803eb46867

Brunnermeier, K. (2009). Deciphering the liquidity and credit crunch 2007-2008. *The Journal of Economic Perspectives*, *23*(1), 77–100. doi:10.1257/jep.23.1.77 PMID:20052301

Calvo, S., & Mendoza, E. (2000). Rational contagion and the globalization of securities markets. *Journal of International Economics*, *51*(1), 79–113. doi:10.1016/S0022-1996(99)00038-0

Chang, C., Hsieh, T., & McAleer, M. (2017). Connecting VIX and Stock Index ETF. *Tinbergen Institute Discussion Paper*.

Chiang, T., Jeon, B., & Li, H. (2007). Dynamic correlation analysis of financial contagion: Evidence from Asian markets. *Journal of International Money and Finance*, *26*(7), 1026–1228. doi:10.1016/j.jimonfin.2007.06.005

Dimitriou, D., Kenourgios, D., & Simos, T. (2013). Global financial crisis and emerging stock market contagion: A multivariate FIAPARCH-DCC approach. *International Review of Financial Analysis*, *30*, 46–56. doi:10.1016/j.irfa.2013.05.008

Dungey, M., Fry, R., González-Hermosillo, B., & Martin, V. (2006). Contagion in international bond markets during the Russian and LTCM crises. *Journal of Financial Stability*, *2*(1), 1–27. doi:10.1016/j.jfs.2005.01.001

Engle, R. (2002). Dynamic conditional correlation: A simple class of multivariate generalized autoregressive conditional heteroskedasticity models. *Journal of Business & Economic Statistics*, *20*(3), 339–350. doi:10.1198/073500102288618487

FED. (2009). The financial crisis: A timeline of events and policy actions.

Forbes, K., & Rigobon, R. (2002). No contagion, only interdependence: Measuring stock market co-movements. *The Journal of Finance*, *57*(5), 2223–2261. doi:10.1111/0022-1082.00494

Horta, P., Mendes, C., & Vieira, I. (2010). Contagion effects of the subprime crisis in the European NYSE Euronext markets. *Portuguese Economic Journal*, *9*(2), 115–140. doi:10.100710258-010-0056-6

Itzhak, B., Franzoni, A., & Moussawi, R. (2017). Exchange Traded Funds (ETFs). *Annual Review of Financial Economics*, *9*(1), 169–189. doi:10.1146/annurev-financial-110716-032538

Jorion, P., & Zhang, G. (2007). Good and bad credit contagion: Evidence from credit default swap. *Journal of Financial Economics*, *84*(3), 860–883. doi:10.1016/j.jfineco.2006.06.001

Kenourgios, D. (2014). On financial contagion and implied market volatility. *International Review of Financial Analysis, 34*, 21–30. doi:10.1016/j.irfa.2014.05.001

Kenourgios, D., & Dimitriou, D. (2015). Contagion of the Global Financial Crisis and the real economy: A regional analysis. *Economic Modelling, 44*, 283–293. doi:10.1016/j.econmod.2014.10.048

Newey, W. K., & West, K. D. (1987). Hypothesis Testing with Efficient Method of Moments Estimation. *International Economic Review, 28*(3), 777–787. doi:10.2307/2526578

Pelizzon, L., Subrahmanyam, G. M., Tomio, D., & Uno, J. (2016). Sovereign credit risk, liquidity, and European central bank intervention: Deus ex machina? *Journal of Financial Economics, 122*(1), 86–115. doi:10.1016/j.jfineco.2016.06.001

Pericoli, M., & Sbracia, M. (2003). A primer on financial contagion. *Journal of Economic Surveys, 17*(4), 571–608. doi:10.1111/1467-6419.00205

Pesaran, M. H., & Pick, A. (2007). Econometric issues in the analysis of contagion. *Journal of Economic Dynamics & Control, 31*(4), 1245–1277. doi:10.1016/j.jedc.2006.03.008

Philippas, D., & Siriopoulos, C. (2013). Putting the "C" into crisis: Contagion, correlations and copulas on EMU bond markets. *Journal of International Financial Markets, Institutions and Money, 27*, 161–176. doi:10.1016/j.intfin.2013.09.008

Phylaktis, K., & Xia, L. (2009). Equity Market Comovement and Contagion: A Sectoral Perspective. *Financial Management, 38*(2), 381–409. doi:10.1111/j.1755-053X.2009.01040.x

Rodriquez, J. (2007). Measuring financial contagion: A copula approach. *Journal of Empirical Finance, 14*(3), 401–423. doi:10.1016/j.jempfin.2006.07.002

Ye, W., Liu, X., & Miao, M. (2012). Measuring the subprime crisis contagion: Evidence of change point analysis of copula functions. *European Journal of Operational Research, 222*(1), 96–103. doi:10.1016/j.ejor.2012.04.004

ENDNOTES

1 There are also alternative methods to estimate dynamic correlations (dynamic copulas with and without regime-switching, wavelets, etc.). We choose a DCC framework because it allows us to maintain comparability with much of the

existing contagion literature. Moreover, relative to the other models, DCC models are easier to implement and interpret.

2 Europe (Total Market), USA (Total Market), Latin America (Large Cap), Asia-Pacific (Large Cap), Global (Large Cap).

3 EURIBOR is transformed to US dollars.

4 In our analysis, we use as government bonds the German Government Bund (expressed to US dollars) and the US Treasury Bill.

5 This methodology has been also followed by Kenourgios (2014).

6 http://europa.eu/rapid/press-release_IP-17-2401_en.htm

7 The ARCH and GARCH parameters of DCC model are statistically significant and non-negative, while multivariate autocorrelation tests show that there is no evidence of statistical misspecification (results not reported here but are available upon request).

8 In order to check the robustness of our results, the sensitivity of the crisis period definition and the stable period is analyzed. The results, not presented here, show that the crisis/stable period definition does not affect the central results.

Chapter 5
Are Exotic Assets Contagious?
Evidence From the Global Financial Crisis of 2007-2009

Dimitrios Dimitriou
National and Kapodistrian University of Athens, Greece

Theodore Simos
University of Ioannina, Greece

ABSTRACT

In this study, authors investigate the possibility of contagion/safe haven effects during the Global Financial Crisis (GFC) of 2007-2009 for two exotic assets: rare coins and wine lvx50. The data sample is monthly comprising a rare coins and wine lvx50 indices, as well as MSCI (Morgan Stanley Capital Index) World financial index as a benchmark for world financial sector, spanning from 2000 until 2016. According to Baur and Lucey (2010) an asset may be characterized as safe haven, by the following definition: "A safe haven is defined as an asset that is uncorrelated or negatively correlated with another asset or portfolio in times of market stress or turmoil". Employing a bivariate GARCH (1,1)-DCC model, authors uncover significant evidence of contagion effects among the MSCI World Financial and wine lvx50, while the pair MSCI World Financial and rare coins show a safe haven behaviour. These findings confirm a specific pattern of contagious and safe haven behaviors that provide important implications for international investors.

DOI: 10.4018/978-1-7998-2436-7.ch005

INTRODUCTION

Such turmoil conditions were affected the world economy during the last decade. Thus, it seems an interesting idea for researchers to examine the behaviour of unorthodox assets for portfolio diversification reasons, namely "exotic assets". To the best of our knowledge it is the first study that on two unorthodox exotic assets: rare coins and wine. The so-called "exotics", used to be non-traditional financial investments that hedge funds choose for diversification, hedging and return-enhancement reasons. Money managers have begun to look exotic assets as way to diversify risk while searching for assets that may provide a safe haven during turmoil period. Critics, however, call them too risky and opaque. Some examples of "exotic" assets are artist rare instruments, expensive French wine, rare coins and rare collectables in general. Exotic assets and unorthodox investments in general are a high priority issue during crises, since as Bernanke quotes:

I think one of the lessons of the Depression - and this is something that Franklin Roosevelt demonstrated - was that when orthodoxy fails, then you need to try new things. And he was very willing to try unorthodox approaches when the orthodox approach had shown that it was not adequate.

According to Baur and McDermott (2010):

A haven is defined as a place of safety or refuge. In times of stormy weather, ships seek out the safe haven of a port or harbour to ride out the storm. A safe haven asset must therefore be some asset that holds its value in 'stormy weather' or adverse market conditions. Such an asset offers investors the opportunity to protect wealth in the event of negative market conditions.

The exotic assets considered by many investors as not only a shield against financial crises but also as a high return investment. The authors are going to investigate this "wish" in depth throughout this chapter.

This work focuses on the impact of the Global Financial Crisis (2007-2009) on rare coins and wine, which made the world stock markets to tremble. The authors empirically investigate the time-varying conditional correlations of monthly Morgan Stanley Capital Index (MSCI, hereinafter) World Financial, Rare coins and Wine indices. In order to empirically investigate contagion among equity and currency markets, the authors model simultaneously the dynamic conditional correlations (DCC, hereinafter) for the pairs: i) MSCI World Financial-Rare coins and ii) MSCI World Financial-wine via two bivariate Generalized Autoregressive Conditional Heteroskedasticity (GARCH, hereinafter) GARCH (1,1)-DCC models. The authors also test for a level shift increase of DCCs during the crisis period by incorporating a dummy variable in an Ordinary Least Squares (OLS, hereinafter) equation. Based on previous literature (Dimitriou et al., 2013; Dimitriou & Kenourgios, 2013; Bank of International Settlements –BIS-, 2009) the authors define the Global Financial Crisis (GFC, hereinafter), the period setting the starting date at 1st August 2007 and the end date the 31st March 2009.

This paper contributes to international finance literature in at least two ways. Firstly, the authors provide a robust analysis of time-varying correlations among markets that goes beyond a simple analysis of correlation breakdowns. By employing a DCC model the authors investigate the second order moments dynamics of financial time-series, overcoming the heteroskedasticity problem raised by Forbes and Rigobon (2002). Secondly, the authors focus on rare coins and wine, two unique exotic assets. The authors are not aware of any study testing various "exotic" assets, such as wine and rare coins, as most safe haven literature focus mainly on precious metals (such as gold, silver etc.). Although many studies mainly support the safe haven attitude of gold (see, e.g., Bredin et al., 2017; Baur & Lucey, 2010; Baur & McDermott, 2010), its price has been skyrocketed after 2008.[1] Thus, it seems that investors have to pay a high price for the feeling of security. In parallel to continuous uncertainty in financial markets (i.e., the ongoing Brexit procedure and the overall increase of global geopolitical risk), the need for safe haven assets is more imminent than ever. This evidence is enhance the examination of wine and rare coins as alternative safe haven assets.

In a nutshell, the empirical results supporting the evidence of safe haven behaviour for Rare coins, while the Wine lvx50 shows evidence of contagion during the GFC. An understanding of contagion/safe haven pattern on these exotic assets is an essential part of investors' information set. From the investors' point of view, knowledge of exotic asset behaviour under turmoil periods is important in determining hedging and diversification of their international investment. The purpose of this work is to shed light of possible contagion or safe haven behaviour through exotic assets, investigating how the Global Financial Crisis can transmit shocks to them and may contribute to the portfolio management and investments in exotic assets.

The chapter proceeds as follows. The literature review presented at Section 2. The econometric methodology is presented in Section 3. Then the details of the data sets utilized throughout the study, as well as the crisis period identification are presented in Section 4. The empirical results of DCC dynamics and the behavior of OLS parameters analytically explained in Section 5. Finally, conclusions are presented in Section 6.

LITERATURE REVIEW

Thus, during the GFC, many investors start to search for safer assets to put their money, in order to protect from contagion. Forbes and Rigobon (2002) have defined the contagion as "contagion is the propagation of shocks among markets in excess of the transmission explained by fundamentals". The authors will accept the complexity of the notion and also will adopt the theory by Rigobon, who separates the notion into two categories: pure contagion and shift contagion. The pure contagion is defined as the contagion of shocks which are not transmitted through financial, economic and market fundamentals. The shift contagion is defined as the change in the strength of the propagation of shocks between a crisis period and a normal period (Forbes & Rigobon, 2002; Flavin et al., 2008; Flavin & Panopoulou, 2010; Pericoli & Sbracia, 2003). Defining contagion as the excess correlation of economic and financial assets (Bekaert et al., 2003), contagion is the outcome of optimal portfolio diversification as investors tend to choose assets without being optimal informed about them (Calvo & Mendoza, 2000)[2]. Contagion effects might be strength by financial globalization. Baur (2012) found that crisis contagion is a global issue and there is no immunity to shocks even between financial sectors stocks and real economy stocks.

Furthermore, there is vast prior literature that apply DCC-GARCH models, in order to empirically investigate possible contagion effects (through excess correlation) and how the GFC affected the exotic assets. The seminal paper of Engle (2002) proposed a new class of multivariate models called dynamic conditional correlation (DCC) models is proposed. These have the flexibility of univariate GARCH models coupled with parsimonious parametric models for the correlations. Furthermore, they are not linear but can often be estimated very simply with univariate or two-step methods based on the likelihood function. According to Engle (2002) they perform well and provide sensible empirical results in many cases. The DCC approach is very popular to financial analysis and used widely at to financial contagion literature.

A highly cited paper of Dimitriou et al. (2013) examines the contagion effects of the global financial crisis via a multivariate Fractionally Integrated Asymmetric Power ARCH (FIAPARCH) dynamic conditional correlation (DCC) for the period 1997–2012. They authors examine five most important emerging equity markets, namely Brazil, Russia, India, China and South Africa (BRICS, hereinafter), as well as US during different phases of the crisis. The findings do not show a pattern of contagion for all BRICSs' markets that could be attributed to their common trade and financial characteristics.

Another interesting research of Dimitriou and Kenourgios (2013) investigates the interdependence of US dollar exchange rates expressed in other major currencies. Focusing on different phases of the Global financial crisis (GFC) and the Eurozone Sovereign Debt Crisis (ESDC) supporting a decrease of exchange rates correlations during the turmoil periods. Dimitriou et al. (2017) examine the dynamic linkages among major exchange rates during the Global Financial Crisis and Eurozone Sovereign Debt Crisis. The results indicate i) that the Canadian Dollar and Great British Pound were affected mainly by the US Dollar across the two crises due to strong financial and economic ties among the three economies, ii) while the Japanese Yen shows evidence of a safe-haven currency.

Kenourgios et al. (2018) investigate the spread of the Global Financial Crisis (GFC) and the Eurozone Sovereign Debt Crisis (ESDC) to different market capitalization segments across countries and regions, concluding to mixed results. Alexakis et al. (2016) provide new evidence on emerging stock market contagion during the Global Financial Crisis (GFC) and the Euro zone Sovereign Debt Crisis (ESDC). Examining the three emerging Baltic markets and developed European markets, proxied by the EUROSTOXX50 stock index indicate a diverse contagion pattern for the Baltic region across the two crises. Kenourgios et al. (2016) investigate the contagion effects of the Global Financial Crisis (GFC) and Eurozone sovereign debt crisis (ESDC) on Islamic equity and bond markets. Using a sample of Islamic stock indices from various developed and emerging markets and the global Islamic stock and bond (sukuk) indices, the results fail to provide strong contagion evidence between conventional and Islamic equity and bond indices, supporting the decoupling hypothesis of the Islamic securities.

Kenourgios and Dimitriou (2014) investigate the contagion effects of the Global Financial Crisis (2007–2009) by examining ten sectors in six developed and emerging regions during different phases of the crisis. Evidence shows that the GFC can be characterized by contagion effects across regional stock markets and regional financial and non-financial sectors. Also, Kenourgios (2014) investigates volatility contagion across U.S. and European stock markets during the Global Financial Crisis (GFC) and the Eurozone Sovereign Debt Crisis (ESDC). Empirical evidence indicates the existence of contagion in cross-market volatilities and a different pattern of infection is observed across the crises.

Dimitriou and Simos (2014) investigate the contagion effects of stock and FX markets for the USA and European monetary union (EMU) during the US subprime crisis of 2007-2009 via a DCC-GARCH(1,1). Their findings suggest the presence of contagion for the US stock market and Uncovered Interest rate Parity (UIP). Kenourgios et al. (2013) investigate the contagion effects of the 2007-2009 global financial crisis across multiple asset markets and different regions. Results provide evidence on the existence of a correlated-information channel as a contagion mechanism among the i) U.S. stocks, ii) real estate, iii) commodities and iv) emerging Brazilian bond index. Kenourgios and Padhi (2012) investigate financial contagion of three emerging market crises of the late 1990s, as well as the US subprime crisis of 2007, focusing on financial markets of emerging economies, US and global indices.

Furthermore, Argyrou and Kontonikas (2012) offer a detailed empirical investigation of the EMU sovereign-debt crisis as they find a marked shift in market pricing behaviour from a 'convergence-trade' model before August 2007 to one driven by macro-fundamentals and international risk thereafter. Kenourgios et al. (2011) investigate financial contagion in a multivariate time-varying asymmetric framework, focusing on four emerging equity markets, namely Brazil, Russia, India, China (BRIC) and two developed markets (U.S. and U.K.), during five recent financial crises. The results suggest that emerging BRIC markets are more prone to financial contagion, while the industry-specific turmoil has a larger impact than country-specific crises.

Baur (2011) analyzes the incidences of sector-specific contagion during the Global Financial Crisis of 2007-2009. The empirical analysis comprising ten sectors in 25 major developed and emerging stock markets shows that the crisis led to an increased co-movement of returns and thus contagion among financial sector stocks across countries. Chiang et al. (2007) apply a dynamic conditional-correlation model to nine Asian daily stock-return data series from 1990 to 2003. The empirical evidence confirms a contagion effect.

Some memorable works concerning financial contagion are Bekaert et al. (2003), Hortal et al. (2010) and Phylaktis and Xia (2009), which separate their data collection and analysis into two ways, aggregate stock indices and sector stock indices, in order to investigate the transmission channels of contagion. A notable work of Baur and Lucey (2010) examines constant and time-varying relations between US, UK and German stock and bond returns and gold returns to investigate gold as a hedge and a safe haven concluding that gold is a hedge against stocks on average.

A wavelet approach by Conlon et al. (2017) demonstrates that hedging properties are not limited to a single historical cohort and gold is shown to comove unexpectedly with inflation. Another innovative paper of Baur and McDermott (2017) test the hypothesis that gold represents a safe haven against stocks of major emerging and developing countries and they find that gold was a strong safe haven for most developed markets during the recent financial crisis. Also, Joy (2011) using a model of dynamic conditional correlations covering 23 years of weekly data for 16 major dollar-paired exchange rates finds that during the past 23 years gold has behaved as a hedge against the US dollar.

ECONOMETRIC METHODOLOGY

A robust empirical analysis of financial contagion requires overcoming a heteroskedasticity problem when measuring correlations and the lack of a dynamic increment in the regressions (Forbes & Rigobon, 2002). Otherwise, a continued market correlation at high levels is considered to be «no contagion, only interdependence» (Forbes & Rigobon, 2002). To avoid the above restrictions, the authors utilize the DCC (Engle, 2002) derived from the multivariate GARCH model to test for increased or decreased co-movement among the exotic assets in crisis period compared to tranquil period. The dynamic conditional correlation DCC-GARCH model investigates the second order moments dynamics of financial time-series and overcomes the heteroskedasticity problem raised by Forbes and Rigobon (2002). The estimation of DCC-GARCH model is composed of two steps: the first step is about the estimation of a univariate GARCH model and the second step estimates the conditional correlations which vary through time. The DCC-GARCH model is specified as follows

$$H_t = D_t C_t D_t \tag{1}$$

where $D_t = diag\ (h_{11t}^{1/2} ......h_{NNt}^{1/2})$. The estimates of time-varying standard deviations are obtained from univariate GARCH(1,1) models with $\sqrt{h_{ii,t}}$ on the ith diagonal. The C_t is a $n \times n$ time-varying conditional correlation matrix. The authors assume that the elements of D_t are generated by the following univariate GARCH(1,1) process

$$h_{\ i,t} = \omega_i + \alpha_i u_{i,t-1}^2 + \beta_i h_{i,t-1} \tag{2}$$

where ω_i is the constant term, α_i captures the ARCH effect and β_i measures the persistence of the volatility. The evolution of correlation in the DCC model is given by:

$$Q_t = (1 - \alpha - \beta)\overline{Q} + \alpha u_{t-1} u_{t-1}^{'} + \beta Q_{t-1} \tag{3}$$

where $Q_t = (q_{ij,t})$ is the $n \times n$ time-varying covariance matrix of residuals, $\overline{Q} = E[u_t u_t^{'}]$ is the $n \times n$ time-invariant variance matrix of u_t, while α and β are nonnegative scalar parameters satisfying $\alpha + \beta < 1$. Because Q_t does not have unit elements on the diagonal, the correlation matrix C_t is obtained by scaling it as follows:

$$C_t = (diag(Q_t))^{-1/2} Q_t (diag(Q_t))^{-1/2} \tag{4}$$

A typical element of C_t has the form:

$$\rho_{ij,t} = q_{ij,t} / \sqrt{q_{ii,t} q_{jj,t}}, \quad i, j = 1, 2.....n, \text{ and } i \neq j \tag{5}$$

Thus, the correlation coefficient at time t is defined as follows:

$$\rho_{ijt} = \frac{(1-\alpha-\beta)\overline{q}_{ij} + \alpha u_{it-1} u_{jt-1} + \beta q_{ijt-1}}{\sqrt{(1-\alpha-\beta)\overline{q}_{ii} + \alpha u_{it-1}^2 + \beta q_{it-1}} \sqrt{(1-\alpha-\beta)\overline{q}_{jj} + \alpha u_{jt-1}^2 + \beta q_{jt-1}}} \tag{6}$$

The correlation coefficients are of key importance in this study, as they provide important information on the behaviour of the MSCI World Financial, Rare coins and Wine lvx50 return series over time.

DATA SET DESCRIPTION AND CRISIS PERIOD IDENTIFICATION

The data set employed is monthly, comprising 199 observations for each market, spanning from 1st January 2000 until 31th August 2016. The Morgan Stanley Capital Index (MSCI) World Financial Index, Rare coins index and Wine lvx50 index index are used in this study. The monthly stock log-returns are evaluated by $r_{i,t} = \ln(p_{i,t} / p_{i,t-1})$, where $p_{i,t}$ is the index of index i at time t. Figure 1 shows that MSCI World Financial Index have a significant downturn during the period of the crisis, while the exotic assets seem that are not severely affected. In all plots of Figure 2 the authors observe that returns exhibit volatility clustering, revealing the presence of heteroskedasticity and justifying the use of the GARCH family of models.

The World Financial data are gathered from MSCI. Instead of using specific stock market index (A possible example would be the US market) the authors prefer the use of the MSCI index for several reasons. First, these indices are constructed on a consistent basis by MSCI making cross-country comparison meaningful. Second, these indices are value-weighted reflecting a substantial percentage of total market capitalization. In addition the serial correlation in returns due to non-synchronous trading is minimized. MSCI indices are widely employed in the literature due to comparability reasons and exclusion of dual listing (see Maghyereh, 2004 for more details on MSCI indices). Thus, the MSCI World Financial index seems to be a nice proxy for world financial stock market.

Figure 1. MSCI world financial index

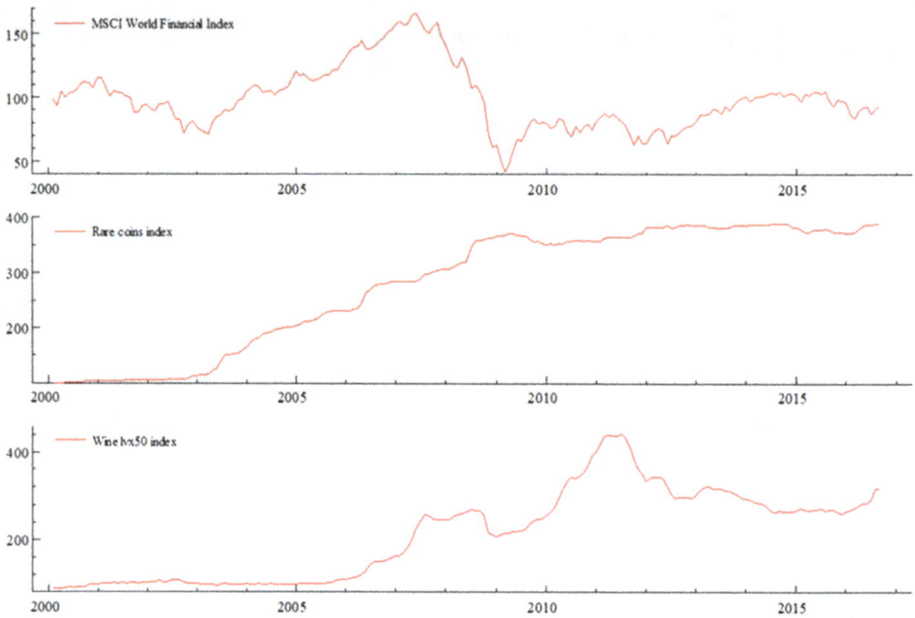

Figure 2. MSCI world financial index (returns)

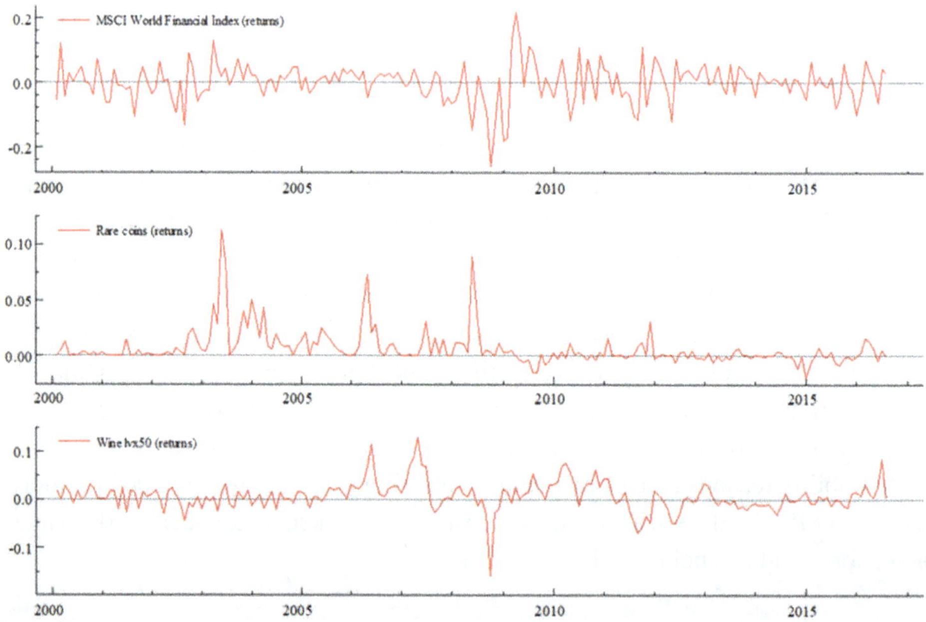

Table 1. Descriptive statistics for MSCI world financial index, rare coins and wine lvx50 returns

	MSCI World Financial	Rare coins	Wine lvx50
Panel A: Descriptive Statistics			
Mean	0.0015	0.0069	0.0070
Std. Dev.	0.0593	0.0160	0.0301
Skewness	-0.4502	3.4684	-0.0431
Exc. Kurtosis	2.6460	15.703	6.0932
Jarque-Bera	32.469***	611.41***	130.81***
ADF unit root test (levels)	-11.34	-7.940	-7.102

Note: *** denote statistical significance at 1% level. For the ADF test, the choice of lag length is based on Schwarz Information Criterion. The critical values at 1% and 5% significant levels are −3.47 and −2.88, respectively.

Descriptive statistics of the dataset used in this study are presented in Table 1. Analyzed data have asymmetric distributions with fat tail. Results of the Augmented Dickey-Fuller test show that all data series are stationary. Based on the Jarque-Bera test the authors can reject the null hypothesis of normality distribution at a significance level 0.01.

The identification of the turmoil period and the stable period is determined by three different approaches according to the existing contagion literature. The first approach is introduced by Forbes and Rigobon (2002) and is based on the analysis of major economic and financial events, the second is a statistical approach of endogenously identification of turmoil periods (Boyer et al., 2006; Rodriquez, 2007) and the third approach is about a combination of the first two approaches (Baur, 2012; Dimitriou et al., 2013). For the purpose of this study, the authors will use the first method, introduced by Forbes and Rigobon (2002). Regarding the GFC, the Bank of International Settlements (BIS,2009) and the FED -Federal Reserve Board of St. Louis- (2009) provides a timeline starting at 1st August 2007 and overs the 31st March 2009. After those periods, the authors assume that there is stabilization.

In Figure 3 the authors plot the conditional volatility behaviour of the series over time and identify the states of excess volatility. These states of excess volatility are all located mainly within the crisis period based on economic and financial news events identified above.

Figure 3. Conditional volatility (MSCI world financial index)

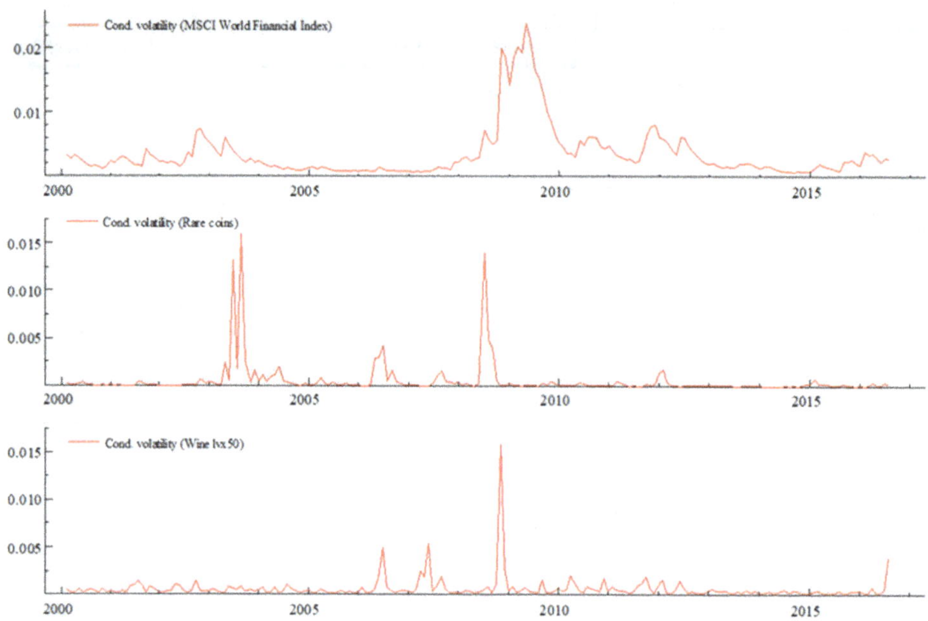

EMPIRICAL RESULTS

The Bivariate GARCH(1,1)-DCC

The estimation results of the bivariate GARCH (1,1)-DCC model are stated in Table 2. Panel A presents the estimation results of the univariate GARCH (1,1) model. Lag length is selected by the Akaike (AIC) and Schwarz (SIC) information criteria. The ARCH and GARCH parameters are statistically significant and non-negative, justifying the appropriateness of the GARCH(1,1) specification.

In the second stage of estimations, presented in Panel B, the authors employ the dynamic conditional correlation (DCC) model of Engle (2002). This specification guarantee the conditional correlation matrices to be positive definite at every time point. The ARCH and GARCH parameters (alpha and beta) are statistically significant and non-negative, justifying the robustness of our results. The sum of the estimated ARCH and GARCH coefficients in the variance equation are close to unity, implying that the volatility exhibits a high degree of persistence. The evolution of the estimated conditional correlations dynamics (DCCs) are plotted in Figure 4. The DCCs display fluctuations over the entire sample period, suggesting that the assumption of constant correlations are not appropriate.

Table 2. The bivariate GARCH(1,1)-DCC model estimation results

	MSCI World Fin.	Rare Coins	MSCI World Fin.	Wine lvx50
Panel A: GARCH Equation				
Const. (M)	0.0072**	0.0055***	0.0072**	0.0042*
t-stat.	(2.445)	(3.319)	(2.445)	(1.754)
Const. (V)	1.1836*	1.8641***	1.1836*	2.4475***
t-stat.	(1.667)	(3.837)	(1.667)	(4.714)
Arch	0.2228***	0.1765***	0.2228***	0.2229**
t-stat.	(3.056)	(4.237)	(3.056)	(1.981)
Garch	0.7583***	0.8192***	0.7583***	0.7508**
t-stat.	(14.170)	(5.697)	(14.170)	(2.426)
Panel B: Bivariate DCC Equation				
alpha	0.0384**		0.2413***	
t-stat.	(2.157)		(5.975)	
beta	0.9376***		0.7345***	
t-stat.	(49.22)		(2.609)	

Note: The lag length is determined by the AIC and SIC criterion. ***, ** and * denote statistical significance at 1%, 5% and 10% levels, respectively.

The Analysis of DCCs Behavior During the US Subprime Crisis

In this part of our analysis, following Chiang et al. (2007) methodology, the authors construct a dummy variable dum which is equal to unity for the period of the GFC (i.e., 1st August 2007 to 31st March 2009) and zero otherwise. The authors employ an ordinary least squares (OLS) technique to describe the conditional correlation dynamics. In order to model the level shift of DCCs the authors include the dummy variable (dum), corresponding to the US subprime crisis period, in the following simple equation:

$$\rho_{ij,t} = c_0 + b_1 dum + \eta_{ij,t} \tag{7}$$

where c_0 is a constant term and $\rho_{ij,t}$ are the pairwise conditional correlations.

At this point, it is useful to proceed to some definitions about the types of assets. According to Baur and Lucey (2010) an asset may be characterized as **safe haven**;

Figure 4. Conditional correlation (MSCI world financial index- rare coins)

A safe haven is defined as an asset that is uncorrelated or negatively correlated with another asset or portfolio in times of market stress or turmoil.

The specific property of a safe haven asset is the nonpositive correlation with a portfolio in extreme market conditions. This property does not force the correlation to be positive or negative on average but only to be zero or negative in specific periods. Hence, in normal times or bullish market conditions the correlation can be positive or negative. If the haven asset is negatively correlated with the other asset or portfolio in extreme adverse market conditions, it is compensating the investor for losses since the price of the haven asset rises when the price of the other asset or portfolio falls.

The definition of a safe haven proposed above is consistent with the definitions provided by Webster's dictionary. The word "haven" is defined as a harbor or port, a place of safety and a place offering favorable opportunities or conditions haven is thus a place of safety that offers investors shelter (i.e., nonnegative returns) in extreme market conditions.

Table 3. Tests of changes in dynamic correlations during the GFC (2007-2009)

OLS Eq.(7)	Corr (World-Rare Coins)	Corr (World – Wine lvx50)
c_0	0.0187**	0.0223***
t-stat.	(7.139)	(3.693)
b_1	-1.3841***	0.1523***
t-stat.	(-5.590)	(9.561)

Note: ***, **, and * represent statistical significance at 1%, 5% and 10% levels, respectively.

A positive and statistically significant dummy coefficient (b_1) in the OLS equation indicates that the correlation during the crisis has increased compared to that of the control period, supporting the presence of contagion effects. A positive and statistically significant dummy coefficient in the conditional variance equation indicates higher volatility of the correlation coefficients.

5.2.1 Estimation and Interpretation of Results

Estimates of Eq. (7) are displayed in Table 3. Estimates of the mean equation (7) identify evidence of safe haven or contagion effects, during the GFC, among the pairs of MSCI World Financial – Rare coins and MSCI World Financial – Wine lvx50. Specifically, for the MSCI World Financial and Rare coins, the dummy coefficient (b_1) is negative and statistically significant. This fact reinforces the view that the shock is felt on the conditional correlation, which confirm a regime shift in the market integration. Not only an absence of contagion effects, during the US subprime crisis, exists for rare coins, but there is strong evidence of safe haven behaviour. The authors can assume that rare coins can be act as safe haven asset against world financial movements. It is obvious that when the crisis hit the financial markets the rare coins have a completely different path. With a fluctuating economy and the devaluation of the US dollar, investing in rare coins seems to be one of the best ways to ensure wealth protection during monetary, economic and social crisis. This fact is very useful for investors since they can succeed the best diversification policy for their portfolios during crises period. Among other advantages over traditional investing, the rare coin market is the most private and thinly traded of all financial markets. Rare coins provide numerous financial benefits to investors that seems to be work as a shield against the GFC. Consider the following:

1. There are no forms to fill out when you buy or sell investment rare coins

2. They can be easily traded and gifted.
3. There is no annual dividend tax to pay because coins do not pay dividends.
4. The capital gains on your rare coins can only be taxed at time of liquidation.

On the other hand, wine lvx50 shows a contagious behaviour since the b_1 coefficient is positive and statistically significant. As a more efficient market, it seems that wine is not a good idea for a well-balanced portfolio against crises.

CONCLUSIONS

This article has explored the possible contagion/safe haven effects, during the 2007-2009 Global Financial Crisis for the exotic assets: rare coins and wine. By employing a robust GARCH(1,1)-DCC model, our results suggest the presence of contagion for the wine, while the rare coins seems to have a safe haven behavior. These results indicate that possibilities for portfolio diversification exist even in periods of severe financial turmoil. Our study haven an important contribution to the study of wine and rare coins hedging properties. As investors tend to diversify their investment across different assets, results of our analysis would be crucial input for investors in portfolio diversification and hedging their stock positions in traditional financial assets by investing in the aforementioned exotic assets.

REFERENCES

Alexakis, P., Kenourgios, D., & Dimitriou, D. (2016). On emerging stock market contagion: The Baltic region. *Research in International Business and Finance*, *36*, 312–321. doi:10.1016/j.ribaf.2015.09.035

Arghyrou, M. G., & Kontonikas, A. (2012). The EMU sovereign-debt crisis: Fundamentals, expectations and contagion. *Journal of International Financial Markets, Institutions and Money*, *22*(4), 658–677. doi:10.1016/j.intfin.2012.03.003

Bank for International Settlements (BIS). (2009). The international financial crisis: timeline, impact and policy responses in Asia and the Pacific. Bank for International Settlements (August).

Baur, D. G. (2012). Financial contagion and the real economy. *Journal of Banking & Finance*, *36*(10), 2680–2692. doi:10.1016/j.jbankfin.2011.05.019

Baur, D. G. (2012). Financial contagion and the real economy. *Journal of Banking & Finance*, *36*(10), 2680–2698. doi:10.1016/j.jbankfin.2011.05.019

Baur, D. G., & Lucey, B. M. (2010). Is Gold a Hedge or a Safe Haven? An Analysis of Stocks, Bonds and Gold. *Financial Review*, *45*(2), 217–229. doi:10.1111/j.1540-6288.2010.00244.x

Baur, D. G., & McDermott, T. K. (2010). Is gold a safe haven? International evidence. *Journal of Banking & Finance*, *34*(8), 1886–1898. doi:10.1016/j.jbankfin.2009.12.008

Bekaert, G., Harvey, C., & Ng, A. (2003). Market integration and contagion. *The Journal of Business*, *78*(1), 39–70. doi:10.1086/426519

Boyer, B. H., Kumagai, T., & Yuan, K. (2006). How do crises spread? Evidence from accessible and inaccessible stock indices. *The Journal of Finance*, *61*(2), 957–1003. doi:10.1111/j.1540-6261.2006.00860.x

Bredin, D., Conlon, T., & Potì, V. (2017). The price of shelter - Downside risk reduction with precious metals. *International Review of Financial Analysis*, *49*, 48–58. doi:10.1016/j.irfa.2016.12.005

Calvo, S., & Mendoza, E. (2000). Rational contagion and the globalization of securities markets. *Journal of International Economics*, *51*(1), 79–113. doi:10.1016/S0022-1996(99)00038-0

Chiang, T. C., Jeon, B. N., & Li, H. (2007). Dynamic correlation analysis of financial contagion: Evidence from Asian markets. *Journal of International Money and Finance*, *26*(7), 1206–1228. doi:10.1016/j.jimonfin.2007.06.005

Conlon, T., Lucey, B. M., & Uddin, G. S. (2018). Is gold a hedge against inflation? A wavelet time-scale perspective. *Review of Quantitative Finance and Accounting*, *51*(2), 317–345. doi:10.100711156-017-0672-7

Dimitriou, D., & Kenourgios, D. (2013). Financial crises and dynamic linkages among international currencies. *Journal of International Financial Markets, Institutions and Money*, *26*, 319–332. doi:10.1016/j.intfin.2013.07.008

Dimitriou, D., Kenourgios, D., & Simos, T. (2013). Financial crises and dynamic linkages among international currencies. *Journal of International Financial Markets, Institutions and Money*, *26*, 319–332. doi:10.1016/j.intfin.2013.07.008

Dimitriou, D., Kenourgios, D., & Simos, T. (2013). Global financial crisis and emerging stock market contagion: A multivariate FIAPARCH-DCC approach. *International Review of Financial Analysis*, *30*, 46 56. doi:10.1016/j.irfa.2013.05.008

Dimitriou, D., Kenourgios, D., & Simos, T. (2017). Financial crises, exchange rate linkages and uncovered interest parity: Evidence from G7 markets. *Economic Modelling*, *66*, 112–120. doi:10.1016/j.econmod.2017.06.003

Dimitriou, D., & Simos, T. (2013). Contagion channels of the U.S. subprime crisis: Empirical evidence from USA, EMU, China and Japan equity markets. *Journal of Financial Economic Policy*, *5*(1), 61–71. doi:10.1108/17576381311317781

Dimitriou, D., & Simos, T. (2014). Contagion effects on stock and FX markets A DCC analysis among USA and EMU. *Studies in Economics and Finance*, *31*, 246–254. doi:10.1108/SEF-07-2012-0075

Engle, R. F. (2002). Dynamic conditional correlation—A simple class of multivariate GARCH models. *Journal of Business & Economic Statistics*, *20*(3), 339–350. doi:10.1198/073500102288618487

FED. (2009). The financial crisis: A timeline of events and policy actions.

Flavin, T., & Panopoulou, E. (2010). Detecting shift and pure contagion in East Asian equity markets: A Unified Approach. *Pacific Economic Review*, *15*(3), 401–421. doi:10.1111/j.1468-0106.2010.00510.x

Flavin, T., Panopoulou, E., & Unalmis, D. (2008). On the stability of domestic financial market linkages in the presence of time-varying volatility. *Emerging Markets Review*, *9*(4), 280–301. doi:10.1016/j.ememar.2008.10.002

Forbes, K., & Rigobon, R. (2002). No contagion, only interdependence: Measuring stock market co-movements. *The Journal of Finance*, *57*(5), 2223–2261. doi:10.1111/0022-1082.00494

Horta, P., Mendes, C., & Vieira, I. (2010). Contagion effects of the subprime crisis in the European NYSE Euronext markets. *Portuguese Economic Journal*, *9*(2), 115–140. doi:10.100710258-010-0056-6

Joy, M. (2011). Gold and the US dollar: Hedge or haven? *Finance Research Letters*, *8*(3), 120–131. doi:10.1016/j.frl.2011.01.001

Kenourgios, D. (2014). On financial contagion and implied market volatility. *International Review of Financial Analysis*, *34*, 21–30. doi:10.1016/j.irfa.2014.05.001

Kenourgios, D., & Dimitriou, D. (2015). Contagion of the Global Financial Crisis and the real economy: A regional analysis. *Economic Modelling*, *44*, 283–293. doi:10.1016/j.econmod.2014.10.048

Kenourgios, D., Nader, N., & Dimitriou, D. (2016). Islamic financial markets and global crises: Contagion or decoupling? *Economic Modelling*, *57*, 36–46. doi:10.1016/j.econmod.2016.04.014

Kenourgios, D., & Padhi, P. (2012). Emerging markets and financial crises: Regional, global or isolated shocks? *Journal of Multinational Financial Management*, *22*(1-2), 24–38. doi:10.1016/j.mulfin.2012.01.002

Kenourgios, D., Samitas, A., & Paltalidis, N. (2011). Financial crises and stock market contagion in a multivariate time-varying asymmetric framework. *Journal of International Financial Markets, Institutions and Money*, *21*(1), 92–106. doi:10.1016/j.intfin.2010.08.005

Maghyereh, A. (2004). Oil price shocks and emerging stock markets. *International Journal of Applied Econometrics and Quantitative Studies*, *1-2*, 27–40.

Pericoli, M., & Sbracia, M. (2003). A primer on financial contagion. *Journal of Economic Surveys*, *19*(4), 571–608. doi:10.1111/1467-6419.00205

Phylaktis, K., & Xia, L. (2009). Equity Market Comovement and Contagion: A Sectoral Perspective. *Financial Management*, *38*(2), 381–409. doi:10.1111/j.1755-053X.2009.01040.x

Rodriquez, J. (2007). Meausuring financial contagion: A copula approach. *Journal of Empirical Finance*, *14*(3), 401–423. doi:10.1016/j.jempfin.2006.07.002

ENDNOTES

1 See the following link: https://goldprice.org/gold-price-chart.html

2 As Dimitriou et al. (2013) state: "The contagion literature summarizes several types of transmission channels: the correlated information channel or the wake-up call hypothesis, the liquidity channel, the cross-market hedging channel and the wealth effect channel (see Chiang, Jeon, & Li, 2007; Pericoli & Sbracia, 2003 for a survey of the literature on each contagion channel). Although testing directly for a specific contagion channel may be more useful, many difficulties (e.g., the lack of availability of consistent financial and microstructure data and prior identification of the relevant fundamental variables) exacerbate problems related to the implementation. Thus, most of the recent papers focus on the investigation of asset-return co-movements, using various types of correlation analyses. Following these studies, the authors define financial contagion as a significant increase in correlation between stock returns in different markets".

Chapter 6
The Impact of Unconventional Monetary Policies on Unique Alternative Investments:
The Case of Fine Wine and Rare Coins

Spyros Papathanasiou
National and Kapodistrian University of Athens, Greece

Andreas Papanastasopoulos
National and Kapodistrian University of Athens, Greece

Drosos Koutsokostas
Hellenic Open University, Greece

ABSTRACT

This chapter investigates the impact of central banks' unconventional monetary policies on sectors of unique and traditional alternative investments beyond the stock market. More specifically, authors examine how quantitative easing (QE) programs, imposed by the FED and the ECB during the financial crisis, affected the fine wine market and rare coins in comparison with real estate, commodities, and crude oil. The methodology used in this chapter includes multiple regression analysis. As dependent variables, the LVX 50 Index, the Rare Coin Values Index, the REIT Index, the CRB Commodity Index and the Crude Oil Futures Index, are used for each sector respectively. Our empirical analysis shows that the QE programs applied had different outcomes between our sample markets. Thus, investors should evaluate the signals associated with the announcements of prospective monetary policies in their attempt to achieve a sufficient portfolio diversification and to harvest superior returns at the same time.

DOI: 10.4018/978-1-7998-2436-7.ch006

INTRODUCTION

Since the outbreak of the global economic crisis in 2008, many economies have been forced at different times to adopt new policy measures in order to maintain currency and financial market stability. A low interest rate environment encourages households and companies to borrow, consume and invest, which boosts domestic demand and should therefore have a positive effect on Gross Domestic Product growth. Central banks aim to strengthen business sentiment, which is a necessary condition for future investments. The Federal Reserve (FED) and the European Central Bank (ECB) have been key players in trying to provide added value to their citizens-monetary policy actions to support growth in employment, investment and consumption. Moreover, they have undoubtedly protected their currency from further exogenous shocks and the financial system from disturbances.

Central banks' policy measures include enhanced credit support, credit easing, quantitive easing, interventions in foreign exchange and securities markets, and the provision of liquidity in foreign currency. These tools have been used to support the functioning of the financial sector and to protect the real economy from the fallout of the financial crisis. Announcements related to the FED's three rounds of the Large-Scale Asset Purchase Program (LSAP), Securities Market Program (SMP), Outright Monetary Transactions (OMT), Covered Bond Purchase Program (CBPP), Public Sector Purchase Program (PSPP), also known as quantitative easing (QE) programs, consisted of suggestions of possible future purchases, firm statements of planned purchases, including time-frames and quantities, and announcements of purchase slowdowns (Neely, 2011). These announcements changed market expectations of future asset purchases by the FED or the ECB and, in consistency with the efficient market hypothesis, immediately affected asset prices, as well as real estate, purchases of goods, crude oil, wine market and rare currency values.

The purpose of this chapter is to evaluate the effect of central banks' unconventional monetary policies on sectors of unique and traditional alternative investments beyond the stock market. In particular, we investigate the impact of QE, implemented by the FED and ECB during the financial crisis, on wine market, rare coins, real estate, commodities and crude oil. The aim of our study is to compare the effect of QE programs on unique alternative investments with the effect on traditional ones. Given the remarkable growth of alternative investing over the last decades, this comparison is essential in order to verify how unique alternative markets react in relation to traditional ones, especially in turbulent time periods when financial stability is at stake.

The methodology used in our analysis encompasses multiple regression analysis. As dependent variables, the LVX 50 Index (Fine Wine), the Rare Coin Values Index, the REIT Index (Real Estate), the CRB Commodity Index and the Crude Oil Futures

Index, are taken into account for each sector respectively. As independent ones, dummy variables, representing the impact of several QE programs are formed. In the case of programs imposed in the Euro zone, two periods are taken into consideration. The first period entails the Securities Market Program (05/10/2010-09/06/2012) and the Outright Monetary Transactions (07/26/2012-09/06/2012). The second period consists of the Covered Bond Purchase Program (10/20/2014-Dec.2018) and the Public Sector Purchase Program (03/09/2015-Dec.2018). Regarding the programs initiated in the U.S., four phases (2008-2010, 2010-2012, 2012-end of 2012, 2013-2014) associated with the LSAP, undertaken by the FED, are constructed.

Our analysis shows that the QE programs implemented by the EBC had mainly a negative but statistically insignificant impact on the various sectors, irrespective of the period covered. On the other hand, the programs executed by the FED had a mixed effect on the returns of the indexes and several statistically significant coefficients were found for the dummy variables representing the phases of the programs' implementation. More specifically, as regards the traditional alternative investments, a negative and statistically significant coefficient was found for the first period of the LSAP for the REIT and CRB Commodity Index. As far as the unique alternative investments are concerned, a negative and statistically significant coefficient was found for the first and second phase concerning the Fine Wine sector, whilst the impact on Rare Coin Values Index was insignificant.

This chapter contributes to the existing literature by providing evidence of performance evaluation of unique alternative investments like Fine Wine and Rare Coins (Papathanasiou et al, 2019a). To the best of our knowledge, this is the first research attempting to incorporate these unique investment instruments. Furthermore, another uniqueness of our analysis is based on the data employed, which covers many sectors and a prolonged period of study. Our empirical results will be of great interest to investors who choose to incorporate alternative assets into their portfolios, as they indicate that the latter should evaluate the signals associated with the announcements made by the central banks', relating to monetary policies, in their attempt to achieve a sufficient portfolio diversification and to harvest superior returns simultaneously. Furthermore, our findings will draw the attention of fund companies, as they suggest potential alterations in the synthesis of their portfolios concurrently with unconventional monetary policy announcements. Moreover, our empirical results will appeal to policy-makers, as the latter can be informed of the potential effects of the monetary policy actions on various sectors of the economy.

The rest of this chapter is organized as follows. First, we describe the aim of conventional and unconventional monetary policy. Consequently, the literature review on unconventional monetary policy is cited. The next section describes the data and the models used in the study. Afterwards, the findings of our analysis are presented and discussed and finally we conclude.

BACKGROUND

The aim of monetary policy is to achieve a low and stable inflation through a short-term interest rate at which a central bank provides funds to banks or the interbank market and the impact of this policy on the wider economy is reliably quantified. Within this framework, the setting of interest rates is done judgmentally using a wide variety of macroeconomic signals, but in a manner that could be approximated with reference to so-called Taylor rules, whereby interest rates respond more than one for one to changes in inflation and also respond to fluctuations in the output gap. This effectively summarizes what constituted conventional monetary policy amongst the mature economies. Its operation led to an effective and predictable use of monetary policy and a largely successful pursuit of low inflation.

The financial crisis and its aftermath of the worst global recession since the 1930s, poses a number of challenges for monetary policy and central banks. While conventional monetary policy achieved a low and stable inflation, it did not prevent asset market bubbles from occurring (Koutsokostas & Papathanasiou, 2017; Kenourgios et al., 2019b; Koutsokostas et al., 2018; 2019). Before the crisis, a significant literature examined the role of monetary policy in containing asset market bubbles. Joyce et al (2012) argues that the main aim of monetary policy should be to contain inflation, that ex ante it is far from clear that bubbles can be identified or dealt with by monetary policy and that it may be more effective to use monetary policy to mop up the aftermath of a burst bubble than use it to tackle its build-up.

This view has been widely challenged since the financial crisis. Central banks now have a much greater focus on financial stability in addition to targeting inflation. Central banks augmented their arsenal of policy instruments with macroprudential tools (see for instance in the UK, the creation of a Financial Policy Committee to run macroprudential policy alongside with the Monetary Policy Committee) and strengthened capital adequacy and liquidity rules through Basel III. The aim of these policies was to achieve financial stability and prevent or at least moderate asset market bubbles.

The other main challenge has been the ability of conventional monetary policy to mop up the aftermath of the crisis and stimulate the economy into sustainable recovery. The result was that conventional monetary policy proved ineffective, as it did not impact market rates as expected and problems with financial intermediation meant that the usual monetary transmission mechanism was not working (Joyce et al., 2012).

The aforementioned challenges central banks were faced with, resulted in the application of unconventional monetary policy actions. Unconventional monetary policy can take many forms, as it could be defined by what it is not rather than what it is. In some cases (for instance Denmark), it involves the usage of negative interest rates. The more common forms of unconventional monetary policy deal with the massive expansion of central banks' balance sheets and their attempts to influence interest rates other than the usual short-term official rates. For example, the FED implemented policies known as "credit easing", when mortgage-backed securities were purchased. With the purchase of these securities more assets were held and FED's balance sheet was expanded. The purchase of these assets also resulted in the provision of liquidity to a market that had dried up in the wake of the financial crisis and in lowering mortgage interest rates promptly, providing credit lines to a prominent part of the economy. The FED has also carried out "Operation Twist". In this case, the size of the balance sheet is not affected, but a central bank aims to influence non-standard interest rates. In Operation Twist, the FED uses the proceeds of its sales from short-term Treasury bills to buy long-term Treasury notes. As the amount of sales is equal to the amount of purchases, the central bank's balance sheet remains stable, but through the purchase of long-term bonds, their prices rise and long-term interest rates fall.

The most prominent form of unconventional monetary policy has been quantitative easing (QE). Japan was the first to apply QE trying to deal with the bursting of a real estate bubble and the deflationary pressures during the 1990s. Conventional monetary policy aims to affect short-term interest rates through open market operations. By buying and selling government securities in the open market, central banks aim to expand or contract the amount of money in the banking system. These fluctuations in banks' reserves are the means so that the desired changes in interest rates are achieved. With QE, a shift in focus towards targeting quantity variables takes place. When short-term interest rates are at or approaching zero and normal open market operations are no longer effective, central banks target at purchasing specified amounts of government securities from the banking sector and therefore boost the level of cash reserves the banks hold in the system. The goal is that by aiming a relatively high level of reserves, this eventually will spill over into lending into the broader economy, helping drive asset prices up and remove deflationary forces (Joyce et al., 2012).

Implementing monetary policy with non-traditional tools though is challenging, as the experience of this policy remains limited. Therefore, the benefits and costs of the proposed policy actions should be carefully compared. The potential benefit of such implementation could lie on the possibility of better economic outcomes, since non-traditional policy tools can be effective in providing financial accommodation. On the other hand, the potential costs must be taken into consideration alongside with the potential benefits. The first possible cost of conducting non-traditional monetary policy is the possibility that the functioning of securities markets could be impaired in an event of a central bank's dominant presence in these markets. In this case, trading among private agents could dry up, leading to liquidity's degradation and price discovery (Bernanke, 2012a). One second potential cost is that large expansions in banks' balance sheets may shake public confidence in a central bank's ability to withdraw from its accommodative policies at the proper time, resulting in financial turbulence. Moreover, by reducing long-term yields, non-traditional policies could provoke an imprudent yield for investors, threatening financial stability. Lastly, further extensions on the balance sheets could cause financial losses should interest rates rise to an unexpected level (Papathanasiou et al., 2019b).

The unconventional policy actions taken by central banks in a number of major economies led to a burgeoning literature regarding their effectiveness. A number of recent studies center in on the effects of U.S. unconventional monetary policy measures and the spillovers to advanced and emerging markets around the world. For instance, Moore et al. (2013) investigate whether LSAPs by the FED influenced capital flows out of the U.S. and into emerging market economies (EMEs) and also analyze the degree of pass-through from long-term U.S. government bond yields to long-term EME bond yields. They conclude that decreases in the 10-year U.S. Treasury yield attributable to LSAPs, increased foreign capital to flow into many EMEs and, consequently, lowered their government bond yields.

Christensen and Gillan (2018) examine whether QE programs affect market liquidity. They argue that central banks' LSAPs can reduce priced frictions to trading through a liquidity channel that operates by temporarily increasing the bargaining power of sellers in the market for the targeted securities. In their research, they analyze how the FED's second QE program, that incorporated purchases of Treasury inflation-protected securities (TIPS), affected a measure of liquidity premiums in TIPS yields and inflation swap rates. Their conclusions show that, depending on the duration of the program, the liquidity premium measure averaged about 10 basis points lower than expected, which in turn implies that QE can improve market liquidity. This persistent presence of the central banks that can increase the bargaining power of sellers relative to buyers and, eventually, lower securities' liquidity premiums had also been denoted by Duffie et al. (2007). In the same way, liquidity premiums of securities not targeted by a QE program are unlikely to be affected by the liquidity channel, as no modification in the bargaining power occurs in this case.

Bauer and Neely (2013) use term structure models to evaluate the relative importance of LSAP channels in mediating the impact of the FED's asset purchases on international bond yields. In addition to U.S. yields, they study the effects on interest rates in Canada, Germany, Australia and Japan, and take into account announcements associated with the three LSAP programs during the period from 2008 to 2012. Their empirical results show a decline in yields in most countries attributable to the signaling channel and the portfolio balance channel. They find the strongest evidence of signaling effects for the U.S. and Canada and these results are consistent to all three LSAP programs considered. For Germany and Australia they also find presence of signaling effects, but likely more moderate, while for Japan the effects were negligible. Overall, they find that the international effects of the FED's LSAP programs on foreign yields are in accordance with past sensitivity to conventional U.S. monetary policy surprises and with the covariance of foreign and U.S. bond returns.

Kenourgios et al. (2015) investigate the effects of QE announcements by the ECB, the Bank of England and the Bank of Japan on intraday volatility transmissions among the corresponding currencies. Their empirical results on the effect of the QE announcements by each central bank show that the volatility of EUR and JPY is increased over the periods of QE announcements by the corresponding banks. In addition, the volatility of EUR is reduced before the Bank of Japan's announcements, while GBP's volatility is also decreased around the ECB's QE announcements.

Chen et al. (2015) study the impact of U.S. QE programs on both the emerging and advanced economies, using a global vector error-correction model and carrying out counterfactual analyses. They analyze the effects of reduction in the U.S. term and corporate spreads. Their empirical results show that the U.S. QE measures reduce the U.S. corporate spreads in a higher degree than they lower the U.S. term spread. In addition, U.S. QE measures might have prevented the appearance of recession and deflation in advanced economies. Finally, they document diverse effects on the emerging economies and in many instances larger in extent, compared to those highlighted in the U.S. and other advanced economies.

Macdonald (2017) investigates the impact of large-scale, unconventional asset purchases by central banks of advanced countries on emerging market economies for the period 2008-2014. His results show that these large-scale programs were associated with statistically significant currency appreciations, decreases in long-term local-currency sovereign yields and increases in equity market prices across a large sample of EMEs. However, a significant heterogeneity in the way these programs affected EMEs asset prices is denoted. Macdonald (2017) indicates the degree of capital market frictions as an explanatory factor for the observed heterogeneity in how asset prices were affected. His results are robust even after controlling for the domestic exchange rate regime and capital control policies in EMEs. Furthermore, Macdonald (2017) highlights as determinants for the size and direction of asset price movements in EMEs the type of assets purchased and the presence of advanced country central banks involved in the purchases.

Bowman et al. (2015) investigate the effects of U.S. unconventional monetary policies on sovereign yields, foreign exchange rates and stock prices in emerging market economies (EMEs) and analyze the relevancy between these effects and country-specific characteristics. Their findings show that EMEs asset prices responded to unconventional monetary policy announcements, but these responses were not large relating to a model that takes into consideration each country's time-varying vulnerability to U.S. interest rates affected by monetary policy shocks.

Kenourgios et al. (2019a) examine the effects of unconventional monetary policy executed by the ECB on the cross-market correlations between bond, stock and currency forward markets. Using a dynamic conditional correlation analysis, they investigate differences on the correlation dynamics across four unconventional monetary policy periods and a range of developed and emerging economies. Their empirical results show a spillover effect on both developed and emerging markets, even though this impact is not similar across assets and countries. They also find that the latest phase, launched in 2014, has a more distinct effect in comparison to earlier unconventional monetary policy programs.

Inoue and Rossi (2019) study the effects of conventional and unconventional monetary policy on exchange rates. They take into account periods in the U.S. by using a novel identification procedure that defines monetary policy shocks as changes in the whole yield curve due to unanticipated monetary policy moves and allows shocks to differ depending on the way they affect agents' expectations about the future direction of interest rates, as well as their perceived on the uncertainty of the economy. Their findings show that: i) quantitative easing leads to a depreciation of the country's spot nominal exchange rate in both conventional and unconventional periods, ii) there is an essential heterogeneity in monetary policy shocks over time and their impact depend on the way they affect agents' expectations, iii) changes in expected real interest rates contribute to the transmission of monetary policy shocks.

Ambler and Rumler (2019) measure the effects of unconventional monetary policy announcements on ex-ante real interest rates across the euro area. Their results show evidence of statistically significant effects of announcements due to increases in inflation expectations. Moreover, their empirical results illustrate that these announcement effects depend on the degree to which they have been anticipated by the markets.

MAIN FOCUS OF THE CHAPTER

The methodology used in this study includes multiple regression analysis. As dependent variables, the returns of S&P U.S. REIT Index, Commodity Research Bureau Index, Crude Oil WTI Futures, Rare Coin Values Index and Liv-ex Fine Wine 50 Index are used for each sector respectively. The monthly prices of Liv-ex Fine Wine 50 Index are obtained from Liv-ex Ltd, while those for Rare Coin Values Index from US Coin Values Advisor. The rest of the data is acquired from Bloomberg.

The S&P U.S. REIT Index defines and measures the investable universe of publicly traded real estate investment trusts domiciled in the United States. The

Commodity Research Bureau (CRB) Index comprises a basket of various commodities concerning energy contracts, agriculture, precious and industrial metals. The CRB Index is a representative indicator of the global commodity markets, as it is designed to provide the directional movement of prices in overall commodity trades. The West Texas Intermediate (WTI) is a grade of crude oil used as a benchmark in oil pricing. It is described as medium crude oil due to its relatively low density and sweet due to its low sulfur content. It is the underlying commodity of New York Mercantile Exchange's oil futures contracts. The Rare Coins Value Index follows the percent change movements of 87 selected U.S. coins. The purpose of the index is to estimate the overall direction of the U.S. rare coin market. The index is calculated on a monthly basis and its current value is compared to the previous month's estimated value. Each coin participates in the index with an equal weight and, therefore, an average percent difference of all 87 coins is monthly computed. Finally, the Liv-ex Fine Wine 50 Index tracks the daily price movement of the most heavily traded commodities in the fine wine market-the Bordeaux First Growths. It includes only the ten most recent vintages (excluding En Primeur, currently 2006-2015), with no other qualifying criteria applied.

As independent variables, dummy variables representing the impact of several QE programs are created. These dummy variables take the value zero either one to indicate the absence or presence of some effect that may be expected to alter the outcome. In the case of programs implemented by the ECB, two periods are taken into account. The first period incorporates the Securities Market Program (SMP) and the Outright Monetary Transactions (OMT). The second period includes the Covered Bond Purchase Program (CBPP) and the Public Sector Purchase Program (PSPP). Details regarding the implementation of the above-mentioned programs are given in Appendix 1. Regarding the programs launched by the FED, four phases associated with the LSAP are taken into consideration, as shown in Appendix 2.

As control variable, the Volatility Index (VIX) is used which measures the market's expectation of a 30-day forward looking volatility. The VIX Index is calculated on a real time basis by the Chicago Board Options Exchange (CBOE) and is also known as «Fear Gauge» or «Fear Index», as it represents the investors' fear of a market crash. The index is constructed using the implied volatilities on S&P 500 index options and represents the market's sentiment of 30-day future volatility of the S&P 500 Index which is regarded to be the leading indicator of the U.S. stock market.

Thus, the regression model applied to investigate the impact of QE programs executed by the ECB on alternative investments is described by the following equation:

$$Q_i = a \times DT0_{\_ECB} + b \times DT1_{\_ECB\_SMP\_OMT} + c \times DT2_{\_ECB\_CBPP\_PSPP} + g \times VIX \quad (1)$$

Table 1. The impact of ECB's QE on real estate REIT

Dependant variable:		REAL ESTATE REIT		
Method:		Least squares		
Sample:		1/2000-7/2016		
Observations:		199		
VARIABLE	COEFFICIENT	Std. Error	T-statistic	Probability
DT0_ECB	-1.3860	0.4676	-2.9643	0.0034
DT1_ECB_SMP_OMT	-1.3899	1.0578	-1.3139	0.1904
DT2_ECB_CBPP_PSPP	-1.5244	1.2466	-1.2228	0.2229
VOLUME_VIX	-12.1324	1.8651	-6.5048	0

Source: Bloomberg

where Q_i represents the return for each index of the various sectors, $DT0_{\_ECB}$, $DT1_{\_ECB\_SMP\_OMT}$, $DT2_{\_ECB\_CBPP\_PSPP}$ the dummy variables for the period when none QE was implemented, the first and second period of implementation respectively, *VIX* the return of the Volatility index and *a*, *b*, *c* and *g* are regression's parameters.

Regarding the QE programs carried out by the FED, the regression model used is given as follows:

$$Q_i = a \times DT0_{\_FED} + b \times DT1_{\_FED} + c \times DT2_{\_FED} + d \times DT3_{\_FED} + e \times DT4_{\_FED} + g \times VIX \quad (2)$$

where $DT0_{\_FED}$, $DT1_{\_FED}$, $DT2_{\_FED}$, $DT3_{\_FED}$, $DT4_{\_FED}$ stands for the dummy variable for the period when none QE program was implemented, the first, second, third and fourth period of implementation respectively and Q_i, *VIX*, *a*, *b*, *c*, *d*, *e* and *g* are defined as above.

Finally, in order to overcome any problems associated with heteroskedasticity and serial correlation during regression analysis, the Newey and West (1987) method is employed.

SOLUTIONS AND RECOMMENDATIONS

The results of the regression model (1) to estimate the impact of ECB's QE programs on real estate index are presented in Table 1.

As shown, the Securities Market Program (SMP) and the Outright Monetary Transactions (OMT) have a negative impact on real estate REIT index, as the coefficient is equal to -1.3899, but statistically insignificant (probability > 5%). Similarly, the

Table 2. The impact of FED's QE on real estate REIT

Dependant variable:		REAL ESTATE REIT		
Method:		Least squares		
Sample:		1/2000-7/2016		
Observations:		199		
VARIABLE	COEFFICIENT	Std. Error	T-statistic	Probability
DT0_FED	-1.1452	0.5036	-2.2740	0.0241
DT1_FED	-2.4870	1.2456	-1.9966	0.0473
DT2_FED	-2.1138	1.8055	-1.1708	0.2431
DT3_FED	-1.2799	1.1659	-1.0979	0.2736
DT4_FED	-1.8222	1.5255	-1.1945	0.2338
VOLUME_VIX	-12.0251	1.8733	-6.4192	0.0000

Source: Bloomberg

Covered Bond Purchase Program (CBPP) and the Public Sector Purchase Program (PSPP) influence the REIT index negatively, as the coefficient equals -1.5244, but similarly the coefficient is not statistically significant (probability > 5%).

As regards the impact of FED's QE programs on real estate, results show that the variables $DT2_{\_FED}$, $DT3_{\_FED}$ and $DT4_{\_FED}$ have a negative impact on real estate REIT index, but in all cases the coefficients are statistically insignificant, as it is observed from Table 2. On the other hand, the coefficient of the first period of implementation, represented by the variable $DT1_{\_FED}$, is negative (-2.4870) and statistically significant (probability = 0.0473).

We proceed our research investigating the effect of QE programs on Commodity Research Bureau index. As it can be seen from Table 3, SMP and OMT programs have a negative impact on CRB index (coefficient = -0.4570), while CBPP and PSPP programs a positive one (coefficient = 0.3811), but in both cases this impact is not statistically significant (probability > 5%).

On the other hand, as shown in Table 4, a negative effect on CRB index is found for the two first periods of the programs initiated by the FED, as both coefficients are negative (-2.1179 and -1.4233 respectively), and for the first period this effect is statistically significant (probability = 0.0010). For the remaining periods, a positive, but statistically insignificant, impact is found in each case.

Regarding the impact of QE programs on Crude Oil Futures index, a negative effect for the first period of the programs implemented by the ECB is observed (coefficient = -0.8447) and a positive one (coefficient = 0.7880) for the second respectively, but none of them is statistically significant (probability > 5%), as it can be seen from Table 5.

Table 3. The impact of ECB's QE on commodity research bureau index

Dependant variable		CRB COMMODITY		
Method:		Least squares		
Sample:		1/2000-7/2016		
Observations:		199		
VARIABLE	COEFFICIENT	Std. Error	T-statistic	Probability
DT0_ECB	-0.4957	0.2423	-2.0459	0.0410
DT1_ECB_SMP_OMT	-0.4570	0.5481	-0.8337	0.4054
DT2_ECB_CBPP_PSPP	0.3811	0.6459	0.5900	0.5559
VOLUME_VIX	-3.3782	0.9665	-3.4954	0.0006

Source: Bloomberg

On the other hand, the FED's QE programs have a negative impact on Crude Oil Futures index for the first (coefficient = -3.1135), second (coefficient = -1.1411) and fourth (coefficient = -7.7490) period, but in all cases this impact is statistically insignificant (probability > 5%), with the exception of the case for the fourth period (tapering), where a statistically significant coefficient is found (probability = 0.0116) as it is observed from Table 6. The third's period coefficient is positive and equals 2.8088, but it is not statistically significant.

We proceed our analysis investigating the impact of QE programs on unique alternative investments. In Table 7, we examine the correlation between the Rare Coin Values index and the programs executed by the ECB. As shown, both programs

Table 4. The impact of FED's QE on commodity research bureau index

Dependant variable:		CRB COMMODITY		
Method:		Least squares		
Sample:		1/2000-7/2016		
Observations:		199		
VARIABLE	COEFFICIENT	Std. Error	T-statistic	Probability
DT0_FED	-0.2424	0.2556	-0.9485	0.3441
DT1_FED	-2.1179	0.6321	-3.3504	0.0010
DT2_FED	-1.4233	0.9162	-1.5534	0.1220
DT3_FED	0.3672	0.5916	0.6206	0.5356
DT4_FED	0.1574	0.7741	0.2033	0.8391
VOLUME_VIX	-3.4073	0.9507	-3.5842	0.0004

Source: Bloomberg

Table 5. The impact of ECB's QE on crude oil futures index

Dependant variable:		CRUDE OIL FUTURES		
Method:		Least squares		
Sample:		1/2000-7/2016		
Observations:		199		
VARIABLE	COEFFICIENT	Std. Error	T-statistic	Probability
DT0_ECB	-1.0476	0.7638	-1.3716	0.1718
DT1_ECB_SMP_OMT	-0.8447	1.7279	-0.4888	0.6255
DT2_ECB_CBPP_PSPP	0.7880	2.0362	0.3870	0.6992
VOLUME_VIX	-7.8045	3.0400	-2.5618	0.0112

Source: Bloomberg

have a negative impact on the underlying index, as denoted by the negative values of the coefficients, but statistically not significant (probability > 5%).

With respect to the programs carried out by the FED, the first and fourth period have a positive effect on the Rare Coin Values index (coefficient is equal to 0.1115 and 0.0187 respectively), whilst the second and third period a negative one (coefficient equals -0.1784 and -0.2052 respectively), as it can be seen from Table 8. Notwithstanding, in each case the probability is higher than 5%.

Finally, we explore the impact of QE programs on fine wine sector. In Table 9, the programs implemented by the ECB are taken into account. As shown, the first program has a positive impact on Liv-ex Fine Wine 50 index (coefficient = 0.3361),

Table 6. The impact of FED's QE on crude oil futures index

Dependant variable:		CRUDE OIL FUTURES		
Method:		Least squares		
Sample:		1/2000-7/2016		
Observations:		199		
VARIABLE	COEFFICIENT	Std. Error	T-statistic	Probability
DT0_FED	-0.6810	0.8181	-0.8325	0.4062
DT1_FED	-3.1135	2.0233	-1.5388	0.1255
DT2_FED	-1.1411	1.8937	-0.6026	0.5475
DT3_FED	2.8088	2.4779	1.1335	0.2584
DT4_FED	-7.7490	3.0419	-2.5474	0.0116
VOLUME_VIX	-0.6810	0.8181	-0.8325	0.4062

Source: Bloomberg

Table 7. The impact of ECB's QE on rare coin values index

Dependant variable:		RARE COINS		
Method:		Least squares		
Sample:		1/2000-7/2016		
Observations:		199		
VARIABLE	COEFFICIENT	Std. Error	T-statistic	Probability
DT0_ECB	-0.8645	0.1301	-6.6450	0.0000
DT1_ECB_SMP_OMT	-0.2749	0.2943	-0.9339	0.3515
DT2_ECB_CBPP_PSPP	-0.0480	0.3468	-0.1384	0.8900
VOLUME_VIX	0.2996	0.5189	0.5773	0.5644

Source: US Coin Values Advisor

while the second program a negative one (coefficient = -0.9525). However, none of the coefficients is statistically significant (probability > 5%).

Regarding the programs implemented by the FED, the first two periods have a negative impact on the underlying index (coefficient is equal to -2.6197 and -2.0697 respectively) and this impact is statistically significant, as the probability in both cases is less than 5% as shown in Table 10. As concerns the remaining two periods, results denote that they have a positive effect on the wine sector (coefficient equals 0.9238 and 1.0780 respectively) but not statistically significant, as the probability in each case is higher than 5%.

Table 8. The impact of FED's QE on rare coin values index

Dependant variable:		RARE COINS		
Method:		Least squares		
Sample:		1/2000-7/2016		
Observations:		199		
VARIABLE	COEFFICIENT	Std. Error	T-statistic	Probability
DT0_FED	-1.0335	0.1368	-7.5524	0.0000
DT1_FED	0.1115	0.3385	0.3294	0.7422
DT2_FED	-0.1784	0.4906	-0.3637	0.7165
DT3_FED	-0.2052	0.3168	-0.6476	0.5180
DT4_FED	0.0187	0.4145	0.0452	0.9640
VOLUME_VIX	0.1040	0.5090	0.2043	0.8383

Source: US Coin Values Advisor

Table 9. The impact of ECB's QE on liv-ex fine wine 50 index

Dependant variable:		WINE LVX		
Method:		Least squares		
Sample:		1/2000-7/2016		
Observations:		199		
VARIABLE	COEFFICIENT	Std. Error	T-statistic	Probability
DT0_ECB	-0.8853	0.2460	-3.599	0.0004
DT1_ECB_SMP_OMT	0.3361	0.5565	0.6040	0.5465
DT2_ECB_CBPP_PSPP	-0.9525	0.6558	-1.4524	0.1480
VOLUME_VIX	-0.8139	0.9812	-0.8296	0.4078

Source: Liv-ex Ltd

Summarizing, our empirical results show that the QE programs implemented by the ECB had primarily a negative, but statistically insignificant, impact on the various sectors, irrespective of the period covered. On the other hand, the programs executed by the FED had a mixed effect on the returns of the indexes and several statistically significant coefficients were found for the dummy variables representing the phases of the programs' implementation. In particular, regarding traditional alternative investments, a negative and statistically significant coefficient was received for the first period of the LSAP program for the REIT and CRB Commodity Index. As far as the unique alternative investments are concerned, a negative and statistically significant coefficient was found for the first and second period concerning the

Table 10. The impact of FED's QE on liv-ex fine wine 50 index

Dependant variable:		WINE LVX		
Method:		Least squares		
Sample:		1/2000-7/2016		
Observations:		199		
VARIABLE	COEFFICIENT	Std. Error	T-statistic	Probability
DT0_FED	-0.7992	0.2528	-3.1614	0.0018
DT1_FED	-2.6197	0.6252	-4.1900	0.0000
DT2_FED	-2.0681	0.9062	-2.2821	0.0236
DT3_FED	0.9238	0.5852	1.5787	0.1161
DT4_FED	1.0780	0.7657	1.4079	0.1608
VOLUME_VIX	-0.8594	0.9403	-0.9140	0.3618

Source: Liv-ex Ltd

Fine Wine sector, whilst the impact on Rare Coin Values index was not statistically significant.

FUTURE RESEARCH DIRECTIONS

This chapter examined thoroughly the case of unconventional monetary policies on sectors of traditional and unique alternative investments, using a remarkable dataset. The results presented in our study may serve as a basis for future research, provided that more countries that will have put in practice QE will be taken into account, in order to extract more comprehensive conclusions.

CONCLUSION

In this chapter the impact of unconventional monetary policies on unique and traditional alternative investments is investigated. In particular, the effect of QE programs, executed by the FED and the ECB, on unique alternative investments (fine wine, rare coins) is compared with the effect on traditional alternative investments (real estate, commodities and crude oil). For the purpose of our study, multiple regression analysis is used. As dependent variables, representative indexes of each sector are selected (LVX 50 Index, Rare Coin Values Index, REIT Index, CRB Commodity Index and Crude Oil Futures Index). As independent ones, dummy variables, representing the impact of QE programs are formed. In the case of programs executed in the Euro area, two dummy variables are constructed. The first one represents the impact of the Securities Market Program (05/10/2010-09/06/2012) and the Outright Monetary Transactions (07/26/2012-09/06/2012), while the second the Covered Bond Purchase Program (10/20/2014-Dec.2018) and the Public Sector Purchase Program (03/09/2015-Dec.2018). In reference to the programs implemented by the FED, four dummy variables, related to the Large-Scale Asset Purchase Program, are created correspondingly. Our empirical results reveal that QE programs on the Euro zone had mainly a negative, though statistically insignificant impact on all sectors, irrespective of the period studied. On the other hand, the programs launched by the FED, had a mixed impact and several statistically significant coefficients were detected. More specifically, as concerns the traditional alternative investments, a negative and statistically significant coefficient was found for the first period of the LSAP Program, with the exception of the case when Crude Oil Futures index is concerned. Regarding the unique alternative investments, a negative and statistically significant coefficient was found for the first and second phase of the program for the Fine Wine sector, whereas the impact on Rare Coin Values index was statistically insignificant.

Our analysis reaches the following conclusions. First, our empirical results question the possibility of policy-makers to drive up demand on the observed markets, a fact that could spur transactions and give a boost to economic growth. Therefore, different mixture of monetary policy actions, in order for the desired goals to be achieved, should be taken into consideration. Second, as markets interconnect, investors should evaluate the signals, associated with the announcements of QE programs declared by central banks, in their attempt to diverse their portfolios efficiently and gain superior returns at the same time. Third, the generally negative impact of unconventional monetary policy actions on sectors of alternative investments indicates the necessity of fund companies to restructure the synthesis of their offered portfolios prior to the implementation of such measures. Thus, lessening the proportion of alternative assets simultaneously with unconventional monetary policy announcements could contribute to the formation of more effective investment portfolios. Lastly, the Fine Wine market seems more "vulnerable" to the effects of QE programs. This should draw the attention of policy makers regarding monetary policy measures, as the Fine Wine market is a promising sector, contributing high value to nationals Gross Domestic Product.

RESTRICTIONS

The data is provided and may be used solely for the purpose of inclusion in an educational project or research. Liv-ex grants the authors permission to publish the data solely as an integrated part of the project or research paper. The data may not be used for commercial purposes (either sale or use for commercial gain). Any publication of the data, or inclusion of the data in the research, must contain a reference to Liv-ex as the source and include the restriction that "the data is not to be used for commercial purposes".

ACKNOWLEDGMENT

We would like to express our deep gratitude to Mr. Daniel Goevert (US Coin Values Advisor), Mr. Greg Smart (Liv-ex Ltd) and to Mr. Neil Taylor (Liv-ex Ltd) for their advice, assistance and useful critiques of this research work. Our special thanks are extended to the staff of Liv-ex Ltd and US Coin Values Advisor for their assistance with the collection of the data.

REFERENCES

Ambler, S., & Rumler, F. (2019). The effectiveness of unconventional monetary policy announcements in the euro area: An event and econometric study. *Journal of International Money and Finance*, *94*, 48–61. doi:10.1016/j.jimonfin.2019.02.007

Bauer, M. D., & Neely, C. J. (2013). International channels of the Fed's unconventional monetary policy. *Federal Reserve Bank of San Francisco, Working Paper Series*, 1-32.

Bernanke, B. S. (2012a). Monetary policy since the onset of the crisis. *Speech at the Federal Reserve Bank of Kansas city economic symposium*, Jackson Hole, 31 August.

Bowman, D., Londono, J. M., & Sapriza, H. (2015). U.S. unconventional monetary policy and transmission to emerging market economies. *Journal of International Money and Finance*, *55*, 27–59. doi:10.1016/j.jimonfin.2015.02.016

Chen, Q., Filardo, A., He, D., & Zhu, F. (2015). Financial crisis, US unconventional monetary policy and international spillovers. *IMF, Working Paper*, 1-31.

Christensen, J. H. E., & Gillan, J. M. (2018). Does quantitative easing affect market liquidity? *Federal Reserve Bank of San Francisco, Working Paper Series*, 1-35.

Duffie, D., Garleanu, N., & Pedersen, L. H. (2007). Valuation in over-the counter markets. *Review of Financial Studies*, *20*(5), 1865–1900. doi:10.1093/rfs/hhm037

Inoue, A., & Rossi, B. (2019). The effects of conventional and unconventional monetary policy on exchange rates. *Journal of International Economics*, *118*, 419–447. doi:10.1016/j.jinteco.2019.01.015

Joyce, M., Miles, D., Scott, A., & Vayanos, D. (2012). Quantitative easing and unconventional monetary policy-an introduction. *Economic Journal (London)*, *122*(564), 271–288. doi:10.1111/j.1468-0297.2012.02551.x

Kenourgios, D., Drakonaki, E., & Dimitriou, D. (2019a). ECB's unconventional monetary policy and cross-financial-market correlation dynamics. *The North American Journal of Economics and Finance*, *50*, 101045. doi:10.1016/j.najef.2019.101045

Kenourgios, D., Kagiana, N., & Katevatis, A. (2019b). ECB's unconventional monetary policy and European bank stock returns. *International Journal of Financial Engineering and Risk Management*, *3*(2), 180–199. doi:10.1504/IJFERM.2019.101301

Kenourgios, D., Papadamou, S., & Dimitriou, D. (2015). On quantitative easing and high frequency exchange rate dynamics. *Research in International Business and Finance*, *34*, 110–125. doi:10.1016/j.ribaf.2015.01.003

Koutsokostas, D., & Papathanasiou, S. (2017). Mutual funds in Greece: Case study of domestic equity mutual funds during a financial crisis. *Managerial Finance, 43*(7), 812–827. doi:10.1108/MF-10-2016-0293

Koutsokostas, D., Papathanasiou, S., & Balios, D. (2019). Adjusting for risk factors in mutual fund performance and performance persistence: Evidence from the Greek market during the debt crisis. *The Journal of Risk Finance, 20*(4), 352–369. doi:10.1108/JRF-07-2018-0108

Koutsokostas, D., Papathanasiou, S., & Eriotis, N. (2018). Can mutual fund managers predict security prices to beat the market? The case of Greece during the debt crisis. *The Journal of Prediction Markets, 12*(3), 40–62.

Macdonald, M. (2017). International capital market frictions and spillovers from quantitative easing. *Journal of International Money and Finance, 70*, 135–156. doi:10.1016/j.jimonfin.2016.08.003

Moore, J., Nam, S., Suh, M., & Tepper, A. (2013). Estimating the impacts of US LSAPs on emerging market economies' local currency bond markets. *Federal Reserve Bank of New York, Staff Reports,* 1-43.

Neely, C. J. (2011). The large-scale asset purchases had large international effects. *Federal Reserve Bank of St. Louis, Working Paper Series*, 1-43.

Newey, W. K., & West, K. D. (1987). A simple, positive semi-definite, heteroskedasticity and autocorrelation consistent covariance matrix. *Econometrica, 55*(3), 703–708. doi:10.2307/1913610

Papathanasiou, S., Koutsokostas, D., Balios, D., & Eriotis, N. (2019a). Winemaking sector in Greece. An accounting-based approach. *International Journal of Corporate Finance and Accounting, 6*(2), 1–17. doi:10.4018/IJCFA.2019070101

Papathanasiou, S., Papamatthaiou, N., & Balios, D. (2019b). Bitcoin as an alternative digital currency. Exploring the publics' perception vs experts. *International Journal of Financial Engineering and Risk Management, 3*(2), 146–171. doi:10.1504/IJFERM.2019.101296

ADDITIONAL READING

Eo, Y., & Kang, K. H. (in press). The effects of conventional and unconventional monetary policy on forecasting the yield curve. *Journal of Economic Dynamics & Control.*

Evgenidis, A., & Salachas, E. (2019). Unconventional monetary policy and credit channel in the euro area. *Economics Letters*, *185*, 108695. doi:10.1016/j.econlet.2019.108695

Puonti, P. (2019). Data-driven structural BVAR analysis of unconventional monetary policy. *Journal of Macroeconomics*, *61*, 103131. doi:10.1016/j.jmacro.2019.103131

Rosenberg, S. (2019). The effects of conventional and unconventional monetary policy on house prices in the Scandinavian countries. *Journal of Housing Economics*, *46*, 101659. doi:10.1016/j.jhe.2019.101659

Sheedy, K. D. (2017). Conventional and unconventional monetary policy rules. *Journal of Macroeconomics*, *54*, 127–147. doi:10.1016/j.jmacro.2017.07.007

Wang, L. (2019). Measuring the effects of unconventional monetary policy on MBS spreads: A comparative study. *The North American Journal of Economics and Finance*, *49*, 235–251. doi:10.1016/j.najef.2019.03.020

Wang, L. (in press). Unconventional monetary policy and stock repurchases: Firm-level evidence from a comparison between the United States and Japan. *Research in International Business and Finance*.

Wu, J. C., & Zhang, J. (2019). Global effective lower bound and unconventional monetary policy. *Journal of International Economics*, *118*, 200–216. doi:10.1016/j.jinteco.2019.01.016

KEY TERMS AND DEFINITIONS

Commodity: A commodity is a basic good used in commerce that is interchangeable with other commodities of the same type. Commodities are most often used as inputs in the production of other goods or services. The quality of a given commodity may differ slightly, but it is essentially uniform across producers.

Crude Oil: Crude oil is a naturally occurring, unrefined petroleum product composed of hydrocarbon deposits and other organic materials. A type of fossil fuel, crude oil can be refined to produce usable products such as gasoline, diesel and various forms of petrochemicals. It is a nonrenewable resource, which means that it can't be replaced naturally at the rate we consume it and is, therefore, a limited resource.

Fine Wine Market: The fine wine market is overwhelmingly made up of red wines with only a very small percentage of exceptions to this rule.

Quantitative Easing: A form of unconventional monetary policy.

Rare Coins Value Index: Follows the percent change movements of 87 selected U.S. coins.

Real Estate: Real estate is property made up of land and the buildings on it, as well as the natural resources of the land including uncultivated flora and fauna, farmed crops and livestock, water, and any additional mineral deposits.

Unconventional Monetary Policy: A monetary policy which directly targets the cost and availability of external financing to banks, households and non-financial companies.

APPENDIX 1

Table 11. The implementation of QE programs by the ECB

Period	Program	Period of implementation
DT0	None QE Program	
DT1 period of first QE program	Securities Market Program (SMP)	10th of May 2010 - 6th of September 2012
	Outright Monetary Transactions (OMT)	26th of July 2012 - 6th of September 2012
DT2 period of second QE program	Covered Bond Purchase Program (CBPP3)	20th of October 2014 –Dec.2018
	Public Sector Purchase Program (PSPP)	9th of March 2015 –Dec.2018

APPENDIX 2

Table 12. The implementation of QE programs by the FED and relevant important announcements

Period	Date	Program	Event	Brief description
Dt0_fed	1/1/2000-11/25/2008	None QE	No event	
Dt1_fed	11/25/2008	QE1	FOMC statement	LSAPs announced: Fed will purchase $100 bil. in GSE debt and $500 bil. in MBS.
	12/01/2008	QE1	Bernankespeech	First suggestion of extending QE to Treasuries.
	12/16/2008	QE1	FOMC statement	First suggestion of extending QE to Treasuries by FOMC.
	01/28/2009	QE1	FOMC statement	Fed stands ready to expand QE and buy Treasuries.
	03/18/2009	QE1	FOMC statement	LSAPs expanded: Fed will purchase $300 billion in long-term Treasuries and an additional $750 and $100 bil. in MBS and GSE debt, respectively.
	08/12/2009	QE1	FOMC statement	LSAPs slowed: All purchases will finish by the end of October, not mid-September.
	09/23/2009	QE1	FOMC statement	LSAPs slowed: Agency debt and MBS purchases will finish at the end of the 2010:Q1.
	11/04/2009	QE1	FOMC statement	LSAPs downsized: Agency debt purchases will finish at $175 bil.
	08/10/2010	QE1	FOMC statement	Balance sheet maintained: The Fed will reinvest principal payments from LSAPs in Treasuries.
Dt2_fed	08/27/2010	QE2	Bernankespeech	Bernanke suggests role for additional QE "should further action prove necessary".
	09/21/2010	QE2	FOMC statement	FOMC emphasizes low inflation which "is likely to remain subdued for some time before rising to levels the Committee considers consistent with its mandate".
	10/12/2010	QE2	FOMC minutes released	FOMC members "sense" is that "[additional] accommodation may be appropriate before long".
	10/15/2010	QE2	Bernankespeech	Bernanke reiterates that Fed stands ready to further ease policy.
	11/03/2010	QE2	FOMC statement	QE2 announced: Fed will purchase $600 bil. in Treasuries.
	06/22/2011	QE2	FOMC statement	QE2 finishes: Treasury purchases will wrap up at the end of month, as scheduled; principal payments will continue to be reinvested.
	09/21/2011	Maturity Extension Program	FOMC statement	Maturity Extension Program ("Operation Twist") announced: The Fed will purchase $400 bil. of Treasuries with remaining maturities of 6 to 30 years and sell an equal amount with remaining maturities of 3 years or less; MBS and agency debt principal payments will no longer be reinvested in Treasuries, but instead in MBS.
	06/20/2012	Maturity ExtensionProgram	FOMC statement	Maturity Extension Program extended: The Fed will continue to purchase long-term securities through the end of 2012. Purchases/ sales will continue at the current pace, about $ 45 bil./month.
Dt3_fed	08/22/2012	QE3	FOMC minutes released	FOMC members "judged that additional monetary accommodation would likely be warranted fairly soon…"
	09/13/2012	QE3	FOMC statement	QE3 announcement: The Fed will purchase $40 bil. of MBS per month as long as "the outlook for the labor market does not improve substantially…in the context of price stability".
	12/12/2012	QE3	FOMC statement	QE3 expanded: The Fed will continue to purchase $45 bil. of long-term Treasuries per month but will no longer sterilize purchases through the sale of short-term Treasuries.
Dt4_fed	06/19/2013	Tapering		Ben Bernanke announced a "tapering" of some of the Fed's QE policies contingent upon continued positive economic data. Specifically, he said that the Fed could scale back its bond purchases from $85 billion to $65 billion a month during the upcoming September 2013 policy meeting. He also suggested that the bond-buying program could wrap up by mid-2014.
	09/18/2013	Tapering		The Fed decided to hold off on scaling back its bond-buying program.
	02/2014	Tapering		Begantaperingpurchases.
	10/29/2014	Tapering		Purchases were halted on 29 October 2014 after accumulating $4.5 trillion in assets.
Dt0_fed	10/29/2014-2016	None QE		

Chapter 7
Gold's Price and Advanced Stock Markets:
A Post-Crisis Approach

Nikolaos Stoupos
https://orcid.org/0000-0002-9914-0761
University of Macedonia, Greece & University of Patras, Greece

Apostolos Kiohos
University of Macedonia, Greece

ABSTRACT

Traditionally, the gold has been approved as a safe-haven investment after the collapse of Breton Woods. The global investors especially prefer to rebalance their portfolios by purchasing gold or its derivatives during financial crises. This research explores realized dynamic linkages between gold and the advanced stock market indices, after the end of the 2008 economic recession. This chapter used the fractionally co-integrated ECM by utilizing intraday data from 2013 and thereafter. The empirical outcomes support that there is a negative-realized dynamics between the advanced stock markets and the gold's price in the short and in the long run. Specifically, the short-term dynamics of gold's price seems to be higher on the French and Japanese stock market indices. Lastly, the long-term dynamics of gold's price seems to be higher on the Dow Jones and the FTSE100.

DOI: 10.4018/978-1-7998-2436-7.ch007

INTRODUCTION

Gold has been traditionally selected as a safe-haven investment across the globe due to rarity and the high value of this metal. Historically, the gold is characterized as an alternative investment against the high volatility on stock, capital and money markets (Junttila *et al.,* 2018). The financial crises, that occurred after the collapse of Bretton Woods, show revealed that the investors, individuals and financial institutions tend to invest their capital on gold, as a strategy in order to hedge their funds against the abnormal volatility during the financial crises. For instance, the 1979 oil crisis boomed the gold's price and on the other hand the value of stock markets diminished as the majority of investors turned into gold in order to safeguard their money. Additionally, similar trends observed at the early 2000s recession where a decline in economic activity mainly occurred in developed countries. The recession affected the European Union during 2000 and 2001 and the United States in 2002 and 2003. Lastly, the global financial crisis of 2008-2009 was the apogee, where each stock market in developed economies crushed and the investors attempted to protect their funds by investing on energy commodities, precious metals and high rating government bonds, such as Germany's. Nevertheless, in spite of the end of global financial crisis 2008 the value of gold remained in higher prices instead of the pre-crisis era. In particular, the gold's price remained in the range of 1100 $/ ounce (lower bound) to 1.400 $/ounce (higher bound) after the end of 2010. On the other hand, the stock market indices in the modern economies have been increasing continuously during the post-crisis era. For instance, Dow Jones and DAX have increased by 164% and 11%, respectively, from the beginning of 2010 to nowadays (April 2019).

The aim of this letter is to explore the realized dynamic linkages between the gold's price and the stock market indices in modern economies. Specifically, we attempt to explore if gold and stock markets are used by the investors and the financial bodies as alternative investments in the modern era, despite the end of global financial crisis. We used the fractionally co-integrated error correction model (FCECM) (Johansen, 2008) in order to discover the realized dynamic linkages in the short and in the long run. We believe that the outcomes of this research are important for private investors, risk analysts, investment banks and funds. There are individuals and institutions that have become more skeptical about potential investments in currencies, stocks and energy commodities, such as Crude or Brent oil. Also, IMF reports warn investors, official and private bodies that the world economy is at risk of a new financial crisis. For instance, a dramatic raise in lending by the so-called shadow banks in China and the failure to impose tough restrictions on insurance companies and asset managers, that handle trillions of dollars of funds, are highlighted by the IMF as causes for concern (IMF, 2018). Therefore, plenty of investors have decided to hold safe-haven investments (gold or silver and their derivatives) and in their portfolios due to the unstable and uncertain economic conditions through the globe.

LITERATURE REVIEW

Singhal *et al.* (2019) investigated the dynamic relationship among international oil prices, international gold prices, exchange rate and stock market index in Mexico. Their findings suggest that international gold prices positively affect the stock price of Mexico while oil price affects them negatively. Boako *et al.* (2018) found out evidence of a significant co-jump of gold and stock market returns. This is in sharp contrast to the safe-haven and diversification attributes of gold. According to Huang and Kilic (2018) The ratio of gold to platinum prices (GP) reveals persistent variation in risk and proxies for an important economic state variable. In specific GP ratio predicts future stock returns in the time series, explains stock return variation in the cross-section, and is significantly correlated with option-implied tail risk measures. Irandust (2017) examined the causal linkage between metal prices and share values for 10 European countries over the period of January 2011 to September 2016. His result show that the metal price index and stock price index are not causally related. Bouri *et al.* (2017) utilized implied volatility indices and examine short-term and long-term causality dynamics between gold and the Chinese and Indian stock markets. They discovered significant bi-directional effects between gold and the Chinese and Indian stock markets in both high and low frequencies, suggesting that the safe-haven property of gold is not stable.

According to Bams *et al.* (2017), an independent increase in the stock, oil or gold markets uncertainty coincides with negative returns in different industries. Gold price uncertainty is an asset-specific factor that is neither priced across nor within industries. Nguyen *et al.* (2016) explored the role of gold as a safe haven in international stock markets using various copula techniques to capture complex dependencies between stock markets and gold prices. The results show that gold may be a safe haven asset during market crashes. In addition, Choudhry *et al.* (2015) investigated the nonlinear dynamic co-movements between gold returns, stock market returns and stock market volatility during the recent global financial crisis for the UK (FTSE 100), the US (S&P 500) and Japan (Nikkei 225). Their evidence implies that gold may not perform well as a safe haven during the financial crisis period due to the bidirectional interdependence between gold returns and, stock returns as well as stock market volatility. Also, Apergis *et al.* (2014) investigated the nature of spillovers between precious metal prices, i.e. gold and silver, stock markets and a number of macroeconomic variables for the G7 countries. Their findings display that the price transmission across precious metal markets, stock markets and the macroeconomy is substantial. Chen and Lin (2014) studied the relation between gold and stocks for the four severe bear markets since 1960s. Their findings show that gold was a good instrument for hedging stock market risk. Lastly, Baur and Lucey (2010) examined constant and time-varying relations between U.S., U.K. and German stock and bond returns and gold returns to investigate gold as a hedge and a safe haven. They discovered that gold is a hedge against stocks on average and a safe haven in extreme stock market conditions.

DATASET ANALYSIS

The present research uses the units of the eight most advanced stock markets (S&P500, CAC-40, FTSE-100, NASDAQ, NIKKEI-225, Dow Jones, DAX-30 and HSI-40), as dependent variables. Which represent the 75% of the total stock market capitalization in modern economies through the globe (March 2019). Additionally, we utilized the price of gold as independent variable in order to examine its dynamic impacts on the advanced stock markets. In order to safeguard the fit and stability of our model, we used the natural logarithmic values of stock market indices and gold' price. We chose 15 minutes' frequency intraday data from 00:00 GMT 01 January 2013 to 31 March 2019. We decided to select high frequency data in order to examine the pragmatic trading condition among the gold's price and the stock markets.

Important milestones for the construction of the intra-day time series are the following:

1) **Non-trading Hours**: We excluded any trading from the dataset that took place from Friday 21:00:01 GMT until Sunday 20:59:59 GMT.
2) **Holidays**: We do not include any bank holidays in our dataset where the trading activity is extremely low. In particular, we removed the following bank holidays: Christmas, Boxing Day, New Years' Eve, Catholic Good Friday, Catholic Easter Monday, International Workers' Day and Thanksgiving Day.
3) **Common Sample**: We chose the trading days when the stock markets and gold's price are traded in order to have a common sample across each time series.
4) **Time Zone**: We decided to use the Greenwich Mean Time (GMT) as our time-zone in order to construct and weight our dataset.
5) **Calendar Sampling**: We selected the calendar sampling as it is most commonly used in the global literature and hence, permits the comparability of the results.
6) **Open Stock Markets**: We used only the operating hours of every stock market (S&P500, Dow Jones and NASDAQ: 14:30-21.00 GMT, NIKKEI225: 00:00-

Table 1. Data presentation

Country	Stock Index	Acronym	Trading Measure	Frequency GMT
France	CAC-40	PX1	EUR	15 mins
UK	FTSE-100	UKX	GBP	15 mins
Japan	NIKKEI-225	NI225	JPY	15 mins
US	S&P-500	INX	USD	15 mins
US	NASDAQ	IXIC	USD	15 mins
US	DJI-30	DJI	USD	15 mins
Germany	DAX-30	DAX	EUR	15 mins
Hong Kong	HSI-40	HSI	HKD	15 mins
Global	Gold	XAU	USD	15 mins

Source: DataStream ®

06.00 GMT, HSI40: 01:15-08.00 GMT, CAC40 and FTSE-100: 08:00-16:30 GMT, DAX30: 07:00-21.00 GMT).

Table 1 presents the features of each variable by indicating the nature, the acronym and the official symbol at the international markets.

Figure 1 shows the historical evolution of the advanced stock indices and the gold's price from 3012 to first trimester 2019. The timelines reveal that there is a clear negative long-term relationship between the stock market indices and the gold's price after the end of the financial crisis 2008.

METHODOLOGY

We produced our empirical results by using two diagnostics tests (Ng & Perron, 2001, unit root test) and the fractionally co-integrated Error Correction model (Johansen, 2008)

Ng and Perron Unit Root Test

Ng and Perron (2001) combines GLS detrending with SD to design new test. The proposed testconsists of a suite of four tests, namely MZa, MZt, MSB and MPT. The four test statistics proposed by Ng-Perron are:

Figure 1. Timeline analysis of Gold's price and stock indices
Note: The figures report the movement of stock indices and gold's price from 01/01/2013 to 31/03/2019. The data was extracted from the official database of the Datastream®.

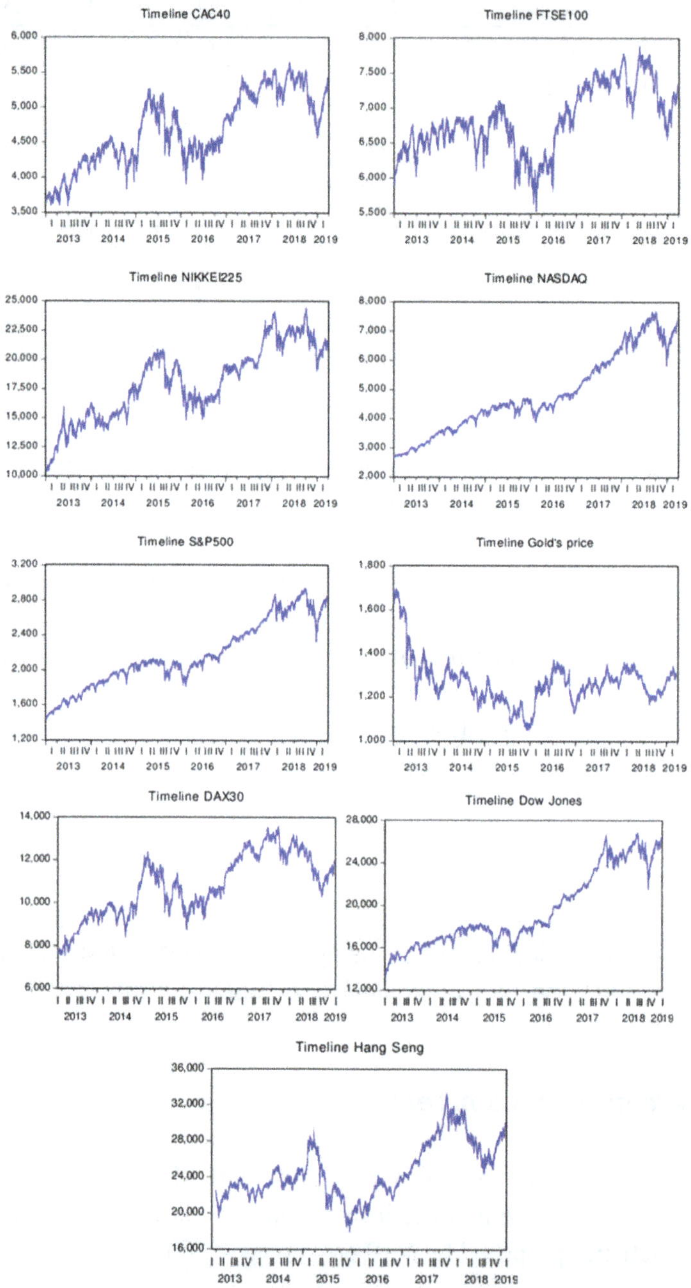

$$MZ_a = \left(\frac{T^{-1}\widetilde{y}_t - \hat{f}(0)}{2k} \right) \tag{1}$$

$$MZ_t = MZ_a * MSB \tag{2}$$

$$MSB = \left(\frac{k}{\hat{f}(0)} \right)^{\frac{1}{2}} \tag{3}$$

$$MPT = \frac{\bar{c}^2 k - \bar{c}T^{-1}\left(\tilde{y}_t\right)^2}{\hat{f}(0)}, when\ d_t^0 \tag{4}$$

$$MPT = \frac{\bar{c}^2 k + \left(1-\bar{c}\right)T^{-1}\left(\tilde{y}_t\right)^2}{\hat{f}(0)}, when\ d_t^1 \tag{5}$$

Where d_t^0 represent drift and d_t^1 drift and trend in DGP, and $k = \sum_{t=1}^{T} \frac{\left(\tilde{y}_{t-1}\right)^2}{T^2}$. The symbol $\hat{f}(0)$ indicates the estimate of spectral density at frequency zero.

Fractionally Cointegrated Vector Autoregression (FCVAR) or Fractionally Cointegrated Error Correction Model (FCECM)

The Fractionally Cointegrated Vector Autoregression (FCVAR) model is proposed in Johansen (2008), and first applied in Johansen and Nielsen (2010; 2012; 2016); its advantages are highlighted by Caporin *et al.* (2013). The FCVAR model allows for long memory (fractional integration) in the equilibrium errors (Johansen 1995), and, following Figuerola-Ferretti and Gonzalo (2010), it is allowed for the existence of long-run backwardation or contango in the equilibrium as well, i.e. a non-unit cointegration coefficient. According to Johansen (2008), the initia; formula of the fractionally co integrated error correction model is:

$$\Delta^d x_t = \alpha\beta'\Delta^{d-b}L_b x_t + \sum_{i=1}^{k}\gamma_i \Delta^d L_b^i x_t + \varepsilon_t \tag{6}$$

Where Δ^d the fractional operator, and L_b is the fractional lag operator defined is the fractional lag operator defined as above. The elements of $\beta' x_t$ are the cointegrating relationships in the system, where r represents the number of long-run equilibrium relationships, i.e. the cointegration or co-fractional rank. $\gamma = \gamma_i, \ldots, \gamma_k$ govern the short-run dynamics. The coefficients in matrix α represent the speed of adjustment towards equilibrium for each of the variables in response to shocks. The fractional parameter d is the order of integration of the individual time series and d - b (with $b < 0$) is the degree of fractional cointegration, the fractional integration order of $\beta' x_t$ which is lower compared to that of itself. In other words, fractional cointegration assumes the existence of a common stochastic trend which is integrated of order d, and the short-term departures from the long-run equilibrium being integrated of order d-b (Johansen and Nielsen 2012).

The model describes cointegration and adjustment towards equilibrium, but it is more general, as it incorporates fractional integration and cointegration. X_t are integrated of d order, and b is the strength of the cointegrating relations (a higher means less persistence in the cointegrating relations; can also be called the cointegration gap).

Our Fractionally Co-Integrated Error Correction Model (FCECM)

The following formula represents the Fractionally Co-Integrated Error Correction Model that we used in our research.

$$\Delta^d index_t = \alpha\beta' L_b gold_{t-1} + \sum_{i=1}^{k} \gamma_i \Delta^d L_b^i index_{t-1} + \varepsilon_t \tag{7}$$

Where, $index_t$ is the dependent variable (natural logarithmic value of stock market indices), $gold_t$ represents the natural logarithmic price of gold, γ is the coefficient of short-term dynamics, β' is the coefficient of long-term dynamics and α represent the speed of adjustment towards equilibrium for each of the variables in response to shocks.

EMPIRICAL EVIDENCE

Table 2 provides evidence about the stationarity of the time series (first differences) by using the unit root test of Ng and Perron (2001). We observe that both examined variables are non-stationary (unit root) at 1% level of significance.

Table 2. Estimation Results of Ng and Perron unit root test

Variables	MZa	MZt	MSB	MPT
Δ(lnDJI)	-16.966 (-13.80)*	-16.97 (-2.58)*	0.084 (0.17)*	0.491 (1.78)*
Δ(lnSP500)	-19.547 (-13.80)	-98.86 (-2.58)	0.005 (0.17)	0.002 (1.78)
Δ(lnNasdaq)	-19.545 (-13.80)	-98.85 (-2.58)	0.005 (0.17)	0.002 (1.78)
Δ(lnNikkei)	-19.533 (-13.80)	-98.83 (-2.58)	0.005 (0.17)	0.001 (1.78)
Δ(lnCAC40)	-19.543 (-13.80)	-98.85 (-2.58)	0.005 (0.17)	0.001 (1.78)
Δ(lnFTSE100)	-19.534 (-13.80)	-98.82 (-2.58)	0.005 (0.17)	0.002 (1.78)
Δ(lnDAX30)	-18.598 (-13.80)	-96.43 (-2.58)	0.005 (0.17)	0.001 (1.78)
Δ(lnHSI40)	-17.768 (-13.80)	-56.51 (-2.58)	0.044 (0.17)	0.25 (1.78)
Δ(lnGold price)	-19.545 (-13.80)	-98.86 (-2.58)	0.005 (0.17)	0.001 (1.78)

Note: *critical values of Ng-Perron test statistics in parentheses, a=0.01

When, RANK=0 the likelihood ratio (LR) statistic is significantly larger than the corresponding critical value, meaning that we reject the null hypothesis of zero cointegrating relations. When RANK=1 the LR statistic is significantly smaller than the corresponding critical value and thus we do not reject the null of one cointegrating relation. Our results, at Table 3, show that there is one significant cointegration relationship for all examined variables. This means that there are dynamics in the long-run for each variable.

According to Johansen and Nielsen (2012), when there are co-integration relationships at the examined variables, we are able to proceed to the estimation of a fractional co-integrated error correction model in order to discover the dynamic short- and long-term linkages.

The following Tables (4 and 5) present the empirical findings of the FCECM model by using no restrictions in constant. We used the natural logarithmic values of the stock markets indices, as dependent variables, based on the specific characteristics that we described in section 3. Also, the control variables are the natural logarithmic value of gold. The gold's price was measured in US dollars, according to their official pricing in the global financial markets.

The adjustment speed back to equilibrium (ECT) is negative and statistically significant for every examined currencies indicating the there is a co-integration

Table 3. Cointegration rank test by Johansen and Nielsen

Variables	Rank=0				Rank=1				Rank=2	
	d	b	LR	$CV_{5\%}$	d	b	LR	$CV_{5\%}$	d	b
Ln(DJI)	0.692	0.351	23.82	9.49	**0.985**	**0.295**	0.059	3.84	1.05	0.287
Ln(SP500)	0.708	0.334	24.50	9.49	**0.974**	**0.321**	1.68	3.84	1.02	0.248
Ln(Nasdaq)	0.666	0.389	22.35	9.49	**0.972**	**0.348**	2.34	3.84	0.984	0.366
Ln(Nikkei)	0.542	0.487	22.79	9.36	**0.999**	**0.452**	0.33	3.84	1.04	0.488
Ln(CAC40)	0.525	0.498	19.82	9.36	**1.03**	**0.598**	0.01	3.59	1.01	0.615
Ln(FTSE100)	0.687	0.352	17.66	9.49	**0.989**	**0.458**	1.09	3.84	0.971	0.491
Ln(DAX30)	0.583	0.502	16.39	9.36	**1.00**	**0.484**	0.35	3.84	0.988	0.648
Ln(HSI40)	0.678	0.345	20.91	9.49	**0.976**	**0.378**	2.51	3.84	1.02	0.444
Ln(gold)	0.601	0.486	19.41	9.49	**0.986**	**0.438**	1.09	3.84	0.991	0.528

Note: maximum k is set at 3 and this gives the order of the error correction mechanism in the FCVAR system. The LR is the Likelihood Ratio statistics, computed for rank r = 0 and 1. This is not available for rank 2 since we are not rejecting any more rank.

relationship and stability at the model. The negative sign of ECT reveals a convergence from short run to long run and shows a causal relationship of the explanatory variables with the dependent variable. For instance, the ECT is equal to -0.0040 for Nasdaq and then the -0.40% of a deviation from the error correction mechanism is corrected within 15 minutes due to gold price movements. The short-term coefficient presents negative dynamics for every examined currency. We observe the largest short-term impact of gold price happens on Nikkei225 and CAC40. In particular, an increase of gold price will lead to a fall of the French and Japanese stock market index, and vice versa. This means that a rise of gold price affects negatively the value of the stock market indices in the short-run.

Table 4. FCECM estimation results (no restrictions and constant term) Gold price

Parameters	CAC40	FTSE100	DAX30	HSI40
d	1.03	0.989	1.00	0.976
b	0.598	0.458	0.484	0.378
Long-term dynamics (β)	-1.191 (-95.59)*	-2.239 (-226.27)*	-1.474 (-2.10)*	-1.407 (-2.61)*
Short-term dynamics (γ)	-0.146 (-12.63)*	-0.087 (-8.76)*	-0.001 (-2.13)*	-0.002 (-2.87)*
ECT (α)	-0.00013 (-18.72)*	-0.0002 (-3.36)*	-0.0003 (-2.05)*	-0.0002 (-2.61)*

*statistically significant at 0.05 level

Table 5. FCECM estimation results (no restrictions and constant term) Gold price

Parameters	DJI	S&P500	NASDAQ	NIKKEI225
d	0.985	0.974	0.972	0.999
b	0.295	0.321	0.348	0.452
Long-term dynamics (β)	-6.173 (-3.08)*	-1.105 (-7.16)*	-1.267 (-16.86)*	-1.387 (-7.19)*
Short-term dynamics (γ)	-0.003 (-2.99)*	-0.067 (-7.16)*	-0.079 (-6.81)*	-0.172 (-101.03)*
ECT (α)	-0.0009 (-2.20)*	-0.0008 (-2.28)*	-0.0004 (-2.41)*	-0.00014 (-2.47)*

*statistically significant at 0.05 level

Moreover, we observe that the long-term dynamics are negative for every examined currency. The long-term coefficient is strongly negative for Dow Jones and FTSE100 index. In specific, an increase of gold price will lead to a significant decrease of value of these indices in the long-run, and vice versa. This means that a rise of gold price will drive to a reduction of these indices in the long run. However, we should point out that the price of gold influence negatively every advanced stock market index.

CONCLUSION

Traditionally, the gold was used by the investors and the financial institutions as safe-haven investment in order be protected against the volatility risk of stock markets, currencies and bonds, especially during the zenith of a financial crisis. The price gold has significantly increased from 2008 on, as side effect of the global financial crisis of that time. Alas, the financial stability has returned to capital, money and stock markets from 2012 on, the investors are still skeptical regarding to the sustainability of the new certainty conditions in the global economy. Additionally, the IMF reports warn investors, official and private bodies that the world economy is at risk of a new financial crisis (IMF, 2018). Although, the stock market indices in developed countries have reached the highest historical points (e.g. Dow Jones at 26.700 units), the gold's price remained in a higher price instead of the pre-crisis era.

The empirical outcomes of this letter support that there is a negative-realized dynamics between the advanced stock markets and the gold's price in the short and in the long-run. The short-term dynamics of gold's price seems to be higher on the French and Japanese stock market indices. This may happen because the gold may also be used as a portfolio diversifier or a safe haven against the Nikkei 225 and CAC40 in the short run. Also, the short-term portfolio rebalancing on the stock indices play an important role to these negative dynamics. Furthermore, we found out that the long-term dynamics of gold's price seems to be higher on the Dow Jones and the FTSE100. We believe that it occurs due to the expectations of the investors for the long-term sustainability of these indices increase. In particular, plenty of investors and financial bodies believe that the Dow Jones is overpriced and they expect a sharp adjustment in the long-run. Also, the investors and the shareholders of the UK stock market index are anxious about the potential outcome of the BREXIT negotiations. Therefore, it is reasonable to choose the gold as a safe-haven investment in order to be safeguarded against the potential vast fall of FTSE-100 in the long future.

Our results are aligned with the evidence of Irandust (2017), Bouri *et al.* (2017) and Choudhry et al. (2015). Lastly, we believe that it would be academically interesting to examine if the short- and long-term relationship between gold and advanced stock market indices takes, also, place for the developing stock markets. However, this is a proposal for the potential research who will explore this research topic.

REFERENCES

Apergis, N., Christou, C., & Payne, J. (2014). Precious metal markets, stock markets and the macroeconomic environment: A FAVAR model approach. *Applied Financial Economics*, *24*(10), 691–703. doi:10.1080/09603107.2014.899668

Bams, D., Blanchard, G., Honarvar, I., & Lehnert, T. (2017). Does oil and gold price uncertainty matter for the stock market? *Journal of Empirical Evidence*, *44*, 270–285. doi:10.1016/j.jempfin.2017.07.003

Baur, D., & Lucey, B. (2010). Is Gold a Hedge or a Safe Haven? An Analysis of Stocks, Bonds and Gold. *Financial Review*, *45*(2), 217–229. doi:10.1111/j.1540-6288.2010.00244.x

Boako, G., Tiwari, A. K., Ibrahim, M., & Qiang, J. (2018). (in press). Analysing dynamic dependence between gold and stock returns: Evidence using stochastic and full-range tail dependence copula models. *Finance Research Letters.*

Bouri, E., Roubaud, D., Jammazi, R., & Assaf, A. (2017). Uncovering frequency domain causality between gold and the stock markets of China and India: Evidence from implied volatility indices. *Finance Research Letters*, *23*, 23–30. doi:10.1016/j.frl.2017.06.010

Caporin, M., Ranaldo, A., & Santucci de Magistris, P. (2013). On the predictability of stock prices: A case for high and low prices. *Journal of Banking & Finance*, *37*(12), 5132–5146. doi:10.1016/j.jbankfin.2013.05.024

Chen, A. S., & Lin, J. W. (2014). The relation between gold and stocks: An analysis of severe bear markets. *Applied Economics Letters*, *21*(3), 158–170. doi:10.1080/13504851.2013.844321

Figuerola-Ferretti, I., & Gonzalo, J. (2010). Modelling and measuring price discovery in commodity markets. *Journal of Econometrics*, *158*(1), 95–107. doi:10.1016/j.jeconom.2010.03.013

Huang, D., & Kilic, M. (2018). (in press). Gold, platinum, and expected stock returns. *Journal of Financial Economics*.

International Monetary Fund. (2018). A Decade after the Global Financial Crisis: Are We Safer?. *Global Financial Stability Report*, 1-99.

Irandoust, M. (2017). Metal prices and stock market performance: Is there an empirical link? *Resources Policy*, *52*, 389–392. doi:10.1016/j.resourpol.2017.05.001

Johansen, S. (1995). *Likelihood-Based Inference in Cointegrated Vector Autoregressive Models*. New York: Oxford University Press. doi:10.1093/0198774508.001.0001

Johansen, S. (2008). A representation theory for a class of vector autoregressive models for fractional processes. *Econometric Theory*, *24*(3), 651–676. doi:10.1017/S0266466608080274

Johansen, S., & Nielsen, M. O. (2010). Likelihood inference for a nonstationary fractional autoregressive model. *Journal of Econometrics*, *158*(1), 51–66. doi:10.1016/j.jeconom.2010.03.006

Johansen, S., & Nielsen, M. O. (2012). Likelihood inference for a fractionally cointegrated vector autoregressive model. *Econometrica*, *80*(6), 2667–2732. doi:10.3982/ECTA9299

Johansen, S., & Nielsen, M. O. (2016). The role of initial values in conditional sum-of-squares estimation of nonstationary fractional time series models. *Econometric Theory*, *32*(5), 1095–1139. doi:10.1017/S0266466615000110

Junttila, J., Pesonen, J., & Raatikainen, J. (2018). Commodity market-based hedging against stock market risk in times of financial crisis: The case of crude oil and gold. *Journal of International Financial Markets, Institutions and Money*, *56*, 255–280. doi:10.1016/j.intfin.2018.01.002

Ng, S., & Perron, P. (2001). Lag-length selection and the construction of unit root tests with good size and power. *Econometrica*, *69*(6), 1519–1554. doi:10.1111/1468-0262.00256

Nguyen, C., Bhatti, M. I., Komornikova, M., & Komornik, J. (2016). Gold price and stock markets nexus under mixed-copulas. *Economic Modelling*, *58*, 283–292. doi:10.1016/j.econmod.2016.05.024

Singhal, S., Choudhary, S., & Biswal, P. C. (2019). Return and volatility linkages among International crude oil price, gold price, exchange rate and stock markets: Evidence from Mexico. *Resources Policy*, *60*, 255–261. doi:10.1016/j.resourpol.2019.01.004

Chapter 8
Spillover Volatility Between Fuel Mix and Electricity Prices

Konstantinos Kakouris
University of Piraeus, Greece

Dimitrios Psychoyios
University of Piraeus, Greece

ABSTRACT

Regulators were the only institution who set the electricity prices, including costs of transmission, distribution, and generation. Nowadays, this has changed. Electricity prices are determined by the fundamental economic rule of supply and demand. The forthcoming work examines a potential relationship between electricity price and fuel mix. The authors use the Nordic System's electricity prices and generation. They conclude that hydropower and nuclear power plays a vital role in the futures energy mix and in the stability of electricity prices. A spillover effect is detected between electricity prices and fuel mix, but a need for further research is recommended.

INTRODUCTION

The last decades, energy markets have been liberalized starting from the fuel markets and continued with electricity markets in mid – 1990s. The distinction between energy markets is a necessity in order to facilitate research and decision making. The energy markets are categorized in three market groups: the fuel market (oil, gas, coal etc.), the electricity market and the market of emissions and insurances for sudden outages. Nowadays, electricity is exchanged in competitive markets, like other commodities, abandoning the regulated market structure. Nevertheless,

DOI: 10.4018/978-1-7998-2436-7.ch008

electricity could be described as an unusual commodity, in a sense that, it is a non-storable product and the demand must be covered immediately. Hence, electricity is characterized as a "flow commodity" with limited storage and transportation.

Concerning the calculation of electricity prices, there are some other features, like temperature and weather conditions, season and day duration, unpredictable outages and grid congestion which accelerates the randomness of the process. The scientific community believes that, not only these features are responsible for the phenomenon of high volatility in electricity prices but also there is another opinion that fossil fuels can affect electricity prices through CO_2 emissions, as well. It is based in the environmental policies of low – carbon technologies, which introduce further uncertainty in energy markets. These uncertainties in correlation with some random movements of carbon credits and fossil fuels' prices are factors that increase the already high volatility in electricity prices. To analyze, the cost of generating electricity is sensitive to fossil fuels' prices and fuels' costs. To be more precise, coal plants affect electricity generation more than 35%. In other words, fossil fuels' market prices affect electricity prices in a sense that the unpredictable prices in fossil fuels and their variability make electricity prices highly volatile (Mari, 2014). As a ramification, the forecast of the price are quite difficult and uncertain; the researchers don't know in which extend volatility is spanned. Nonetheless, a solution was proposed in order to hedge and control the high volatility. Nuclear power is a carbon – free technology, thus, volatility becomes more sustainable and more predictable because it offers a possibility of risk hedging (Mari, 2014).

There are seven groups of electricity prices; price of high demand, price of low demand, price of different periods (seasons), price of weekends, price of working days, price of vacations and price of business activities. Taking into account the natural features of electricity and the aforementioned categories, the reader understands that, in order to calculate the precise future price of electricity is more than complex. The cause of the complexity is hidden behind the factors, affecting the prices' volatility in electricity, which is difficult to observe and determine. The unobserved components can be named as "Unspanned Stochastic Volatility" components. These components have no information about assessments in future changes; that plays a vital role in decision making of investors, and electricity generators, as well as it provides explanations about volatility risk and hedging. The index, R^2 (R – squared), can be consider as a measure of unexplained volatility or as an estimation of the amount of explained volatility. For instance, a very low price of R – squared means the existence of highly unexplained volatility (Collin – Dufresne & Goldstein, 2002).

Into this framework, electricity needs must meet four elements: cover, safety, efficiency and reasonable prices. Taking, all the above, into consideration, researchers decide to make models and develop methodologies in order to deal with these problems. Certainly, these models' analysis demands parameters such as time period, price variances and trends. The analysis of the data and the results occur through the development of GARCH, ARCH, ARIMA, Demand Elasticity, Levelized Cost of Electricity (LCOE) and Weighted Average Cost of Capital (WACC) models. In general, the dominate opinion in literature suggests that the electricity price must be examined seasonal (seasonality) and has the trend to return in its mean price (mean reversion) by the "Invisible hand of the market", as Adam Smith stated in his book "The Wealth of Nations", in 1776 (Smith, 1776).

It's largely known that other forms of energy are needed for the production of electric power[1]; conventional energy (fossil fuels), renewable energy (solar, wind, tidal, hydropower etc.) and nuclear energy, to name but a few. Naturally, factors like political instability in regions with enormous fossil resources – natural inventories, the misbelief of these regions' energy policy and the expansion of the renewable energy, are likely the most significant components to keep energy markets highly volatile. A dominant theory suggests that, there is an appropriate fuel mix which can hedge the volatility risk in electricity prices. Nevertheless, it is worth mentioned that nuclear energy and hydropower play crucial role smoothing the uncertainty and stabilizing the volatility risk in electricity prices. Yet, there is another parameter which indirect affects electricity prices additionally of the fuel cost. The CO_2 prices[2] lead the electricity ones to sudden fluctuations; make them sensitive to insignificant changes in emissions' prices. CO_2 emissions are a countable element in generation cost and have an influence in energy markets due to the application of more intensive and strict climate policy (Garcia – Martos, Rodriguez & Sanchez, 2011). Generally speaking, when choosing energy fuels, it is essential to take into account economic, social and environmental consequences (Köne & Büke, 2007).

The Figure 1 illustrates the fuels is needed for electricity generation. The figure on the left notes the main fuels for electricity production (coal, nuclear, renewables and natural gas) from 2010 until 2018. Furthermore, it gives information for the near future mix of sources. The figure on the right provides historical trends and projections as well, focusing in the forms of different renewables. Solar, wind and hydroelectric power seems to hold the biggest share according to US Energy Information Administration.

Energy markets will be suffer from extreme volatility for decades because of the continuous changes in policies, globalization, growing energy demand, increasing intensity of climate change, geopolitical strategies and tensions, as well as deregulation of electricity markets (Efimova & Serletis, 2014). It is important to mention that electricity demand is predicted to rise with lower rates over the next few years. This trend can be confirmed by the Figure 2. Electricity demand seems to follow lower rates of growth especially after 2020 with an average rate of 0.9%. The Figure 2 illustrates a comparison between the growth of electricity demand and

Figure 1. Historical data and projections for the fuel mix in the US
Source: EIA, Annual Energy Outlook 2019

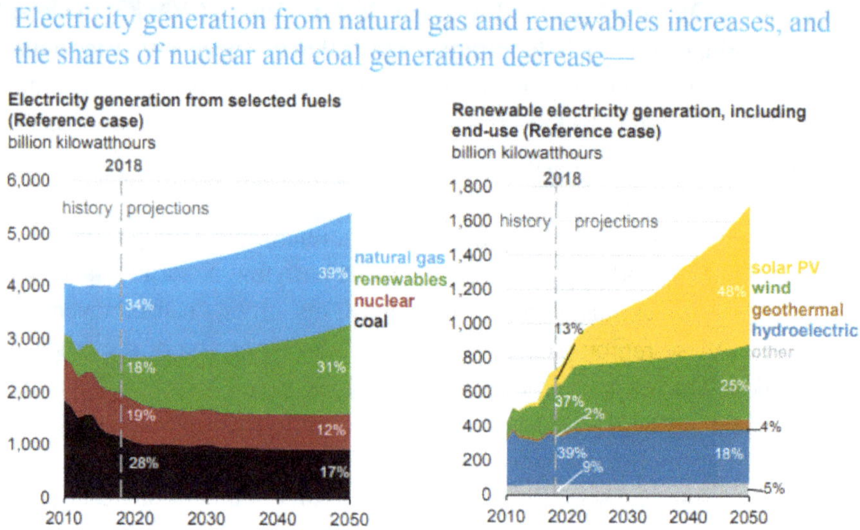

GDP. The point after mid – 80s considers as a benchmark, where the GDP growth rate overcomes the growth rate of electricity use. This graph corresponds in the US.

Nevertheless, to the best of our knowledge, there is no published paper that examines relationship between the volatility of fuel mix and electricity prices. In this work, the authors try to contribute in order to fill this gap.

A common opinion supports diversification of fuel mix in electricity generation to stabilize electricity prices' volatility. Over the years, a growing number of countries attempt to find the appropriate proportions of fuels in order to forecast changes in energy prices. Nevertheless, the impact of limited transmission is quite significant as well. Limitations were originated by restricted capacity of the grid lines and by the losses in the transmission line. These two features make electricity distribution more expensive and sometimes impossible in plenty areas. As a result, prices begin to behave locally and are dependent by local business activities, weather conditions, climate, energy generation plants etc.

To give more attention in international electricity prices, divergence in global framework is due to divergence in commodity prices, in regulation, in technologies and in international trade of electricity. International grids are an extension of local and national grids. Nordic Power System is one of transnational developed system grids. The participants in the system are countries such as Norway, Sweden, Finland, Denmark and Iceland. The system works as follows: when the capacity limits are

Figure 2. Electricity use and GDP growth rate
Source: EIA, Annual Energy Outlook 2013

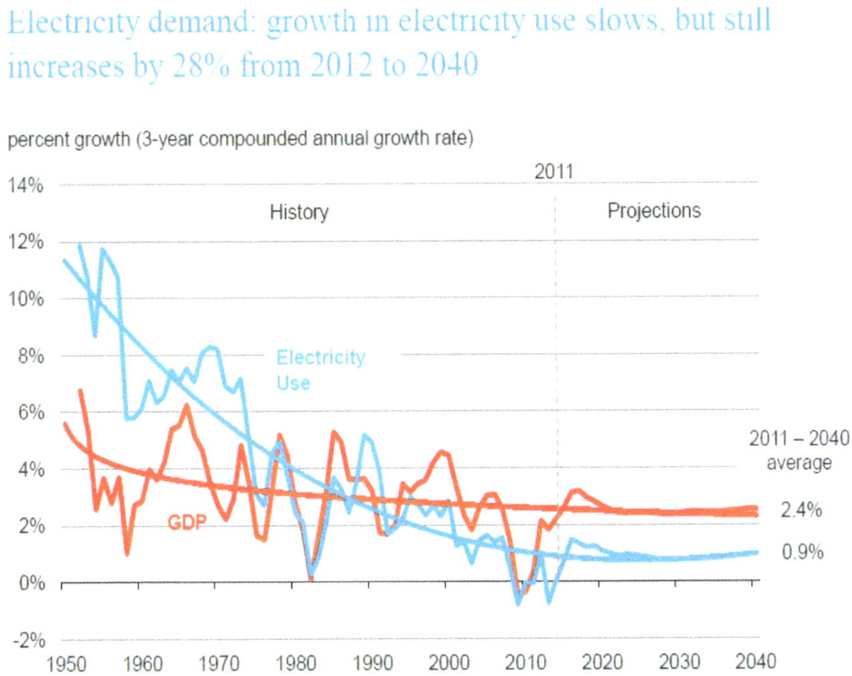

overpassed, the spot prices are adjusted in wider region. If electricity congestion takes place in a country, system operators act immediately in order to hedge and manage the situation. Statistical results from this market comes to the conclusion that in the warm seasons the price average level is less than cold seasons by 22%. Electricity prices are extremely unstable; variation reaches around 189%. A big part of the variation is explained by spikes which are created by shocks, like announcements about change in temperature (Lucia & Schwartz, 2002). Generally, the proportion of explained variance is around 75% in electricity market, where in other markets reaches 95% (Koekebakker & Ollmar, 2005). Even though, electricity demands follow a standard framework throughout the week.

Figure 3 provides information about each country's monthly energy generation and consumption. In general, energy generation and energy consumption are clearly in the same level except for Norway which seems to be an export country, while Finland an import country. Hydropower dominates in the generation procedure in Norway and Iceland, where in Finland and Sweden nuclear power plays a counterpart role. Iceland is supported not only by hydropower but also by wind power and

Figure 3. Monthly generation and total consumption of electricity in Nordic power system 2007 – 2008, GWh
Source: European Network of Transmission System Operators for Electricity (entsoe)

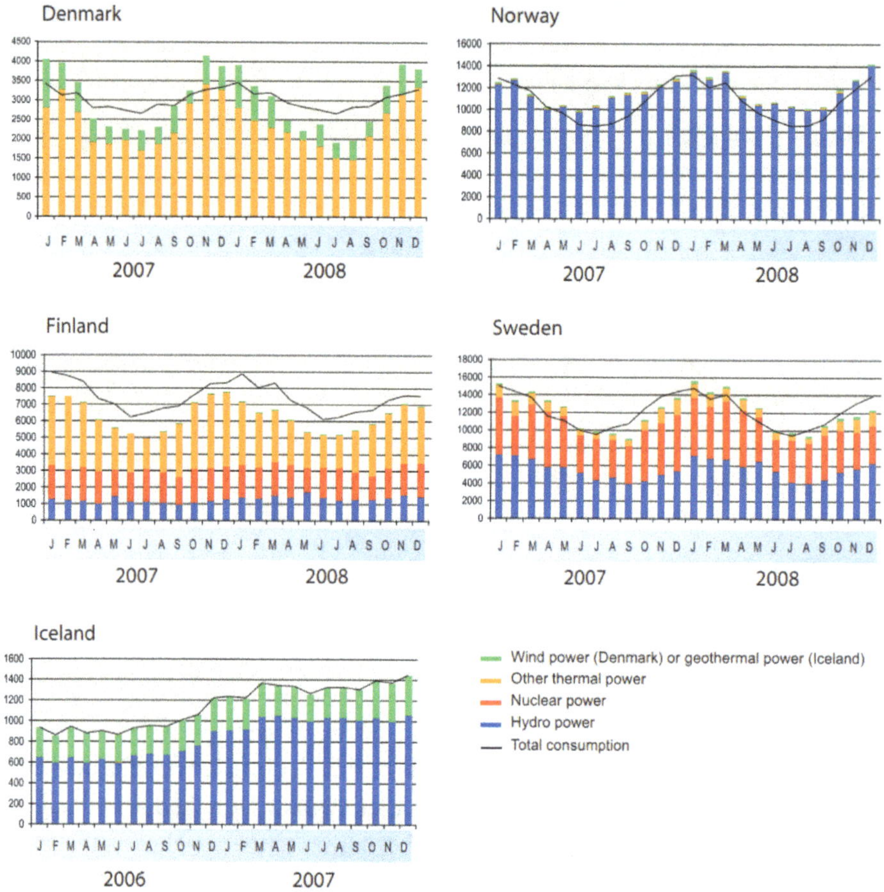

geothermal power. In the following paragraphs, the case of fuel mix is discussed for electricity generation in the US and worldwide.

Figure 4 describes the fuel participation in electricity production proportionally (on the right figure) and quantitatively (on the left figure) in the US, in a time period of thirteen years, from 2006 until 2019. From the specific figure, some interesting results come to light. Coal slowly has lost its share through the years from natural gas and non – hydro renewables. Nevertheless, coal still plays a central role in the US. In other energy forms, hydro power and nuclear power seems to follow more stable paths over the years (US Energy Information Administration, 2018).

Figure 4. Fuel shares of total electricity generation in the US
Source: U.S. Energy Information Administration

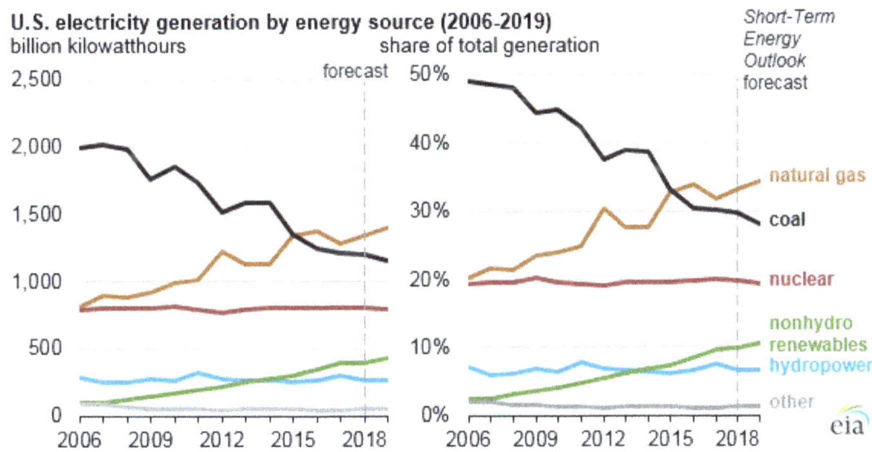

Globally, the main natural contributors in electricity generation are coal, natural gas and renewables (Figure 5 and Figure 6). More precisely, coal holds approximately the 40% of the world's electricity generation. It's the most preferable fuel because it is cheap, accessible, abundant, and easily distributed, stored and used. Even though, coal combustion is characterized by a significant drawback; air pollution through Greenhouse Gas Emissions (GHG). Natural gas holds the second place with share of around 20% and has an upward trend. It is more clean technology (fuel) than coal concerning air pollution. Two main disadvantages of natural gas are the higher price and volatility. Long – distance transportation and increasing global market demand are what affecting natural gas use. Another energy form is renewable energy. Renewables are sustainable and naturally replenished due to non – creation of air pollution, during the energy generation process, and infinite inventories. Naturally, disadvantages exist in the case of renewables. Electricity generation takes place locally and it is not portray as reliable as fossil fuels and nuclear power. Last but not least, nuclear power plays a crucial role, especially in developed economies. It is more reliable source than renewables and it is characterized by more clear electricity production process than coal and natural gas. Nonetheless, nuclear accidents have led the governments in these countries to turn in alternative choices (Environmental Bureau, Government of Hong Kong, 2014).

Figure 5. Electricity generation by fuel and stated policies scenario, 2018-2040

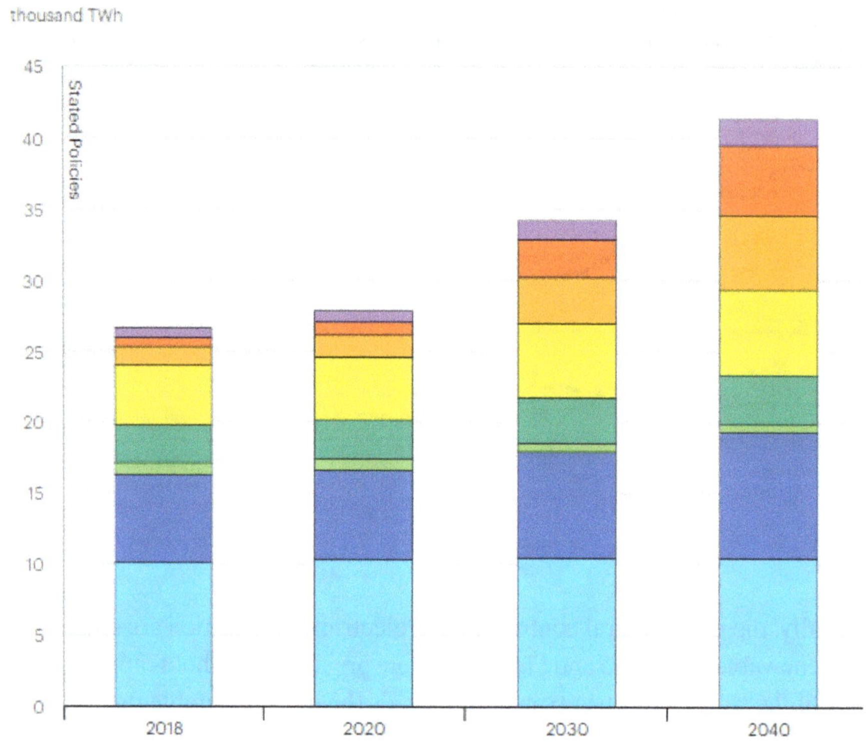

LITERATURE REVIEW

Recent years a lot of literature research has been made in the field of commodities, where the research focuses in storable commodities. There is not much research in non – storable commodities, like electricity, as a consequence plenty methods have been developed in order to forecast and calculate electricity prices.

According to a study (Liu & Shi, 2013), there are three categories of methodology. First of all, the game theory; it includes equilibrium models such as "Nash equilibrium", "Cournot model" and "Bertrand model". The method proceeds to strategies and finds optimal solutions. Secondly, stimulation models; even if the method includes the physical characteristics of electricity and operating systems, it has two severe drawbacks. Simulations must take into account the complexity of the models and the various parameters affecting it, as well as the high computational cost. Thirdly, time series forecasting methods; it examines the behavior of electricity prices in the

Figure 6. Electricity generation by fuel and sustainable development scenario, 2018-2040
Source: World Energy Outlook 2019, International Energy Agency (IEA)

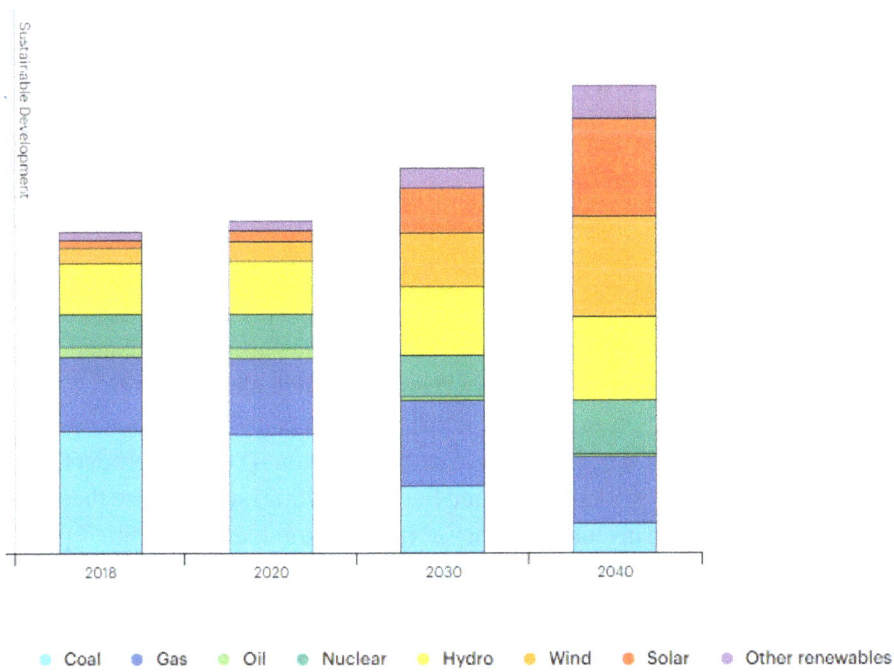

past in order to forecast future electricity prices. Naturally, the electricity prices are not a linear function of time, as a result time series techniques is tend to fall within some problems in the accuracy of the electricity forecasts. In order to deal with this problem, some researchers suggest models based in neural networks (Lago et al., 2018; Cerjanet al., 2019). Nevertheless, there are two types of models in time series forecasting; the artificial intelligence techniques and statistical models (ex. AR, ARMA, MA, ARIMA etc.). Through their literature research, Liu and Shi (2013) found that the most popular models for volatility prediction in electricity prices are GARCH and ARCH models. For their empirical analysis two models are used; the first is the Generalized Autoregressive Conditional Heteroskedastic (GARCH) model and the second is the Autoregressive Integrated Moving Average (ARIMA) model. These models are largely used to estimate volatility and the mean value of electricity prices. They examined data (18960 observations) from hourly prices (LMP)[3] in ISO New England[4] from January 1st of 2008 to February 28th 2010. To clarify, the data from the first two years are used for different models and the remaining data (1416) are used in order to test the accurate predictions of the models. The outcome of their research indicates the road of privatization through the continuous deregulated markets. This conclusion makes more urgent the accurate predictions of electricity prices. To this extend, they stated that "An accurate hourly ahead price forecasting can help power suppliers to adjust their bidding strategies to achieve the maximal revenue, and meanwhile consumers can derive a plan to minimize their cost and to predict themselves against high prices" (Liu & Shi, 2013, p. 166).

Certainly, the authors believe that the characteristics of electricity prices should be examined in order to understand the volatility of electricity prices and the spillover effects with the volatility of fuel mix. Geman and Roncoroni (2006) refer some of them starting from the prices' trends. Prices tend to return in the average value (constant or periodic), which presents marginal cost. Secondly, there are some random moves around the average trend. These random moves can be explained by imbalances in supply and demand. Moreover, spikes[5] are very common in electricity prices. They are created by imbalances in supply and demand which cannot be smoothed away through the use of inventories, because electricity is a non – storable product.

On the other hand, the work of Lucia and Schwartz (2002) supports the theory of hedging the price, through inventories. They notice that storable commodities' prices are determined not only by supply and demand mechanism, but also by the level of inventories. As a result, imbalances in supply and demand do not necessarily translate in imbalances of electricity prices at the same level. Broadly speaking, studies are in favor of negative correlation between inventories and future spot price volatility.

Nevertheless, after the deregulation of energy markets, Geman and Roncoroni (2006) were interested to model electricity spot prices and they consider the convenience yield[6] is insignificant, in contrast with the other commodities; meaning that there is no reason to exist in the context of electricity because it is a non – storable product. Going a bit further, there is no benefit from holding the commodity because it cannot be stored and there is not cost of storage. They studied the data from Megawatt – Daily of three major US power markets: COB (California Oregon Border), PJM (Pennsylvania – New Jersey – Maryland) and ECAR (East Center Area Reliability Coordination Agreement). In terms of price behavior, the previous markets represents "low – pressure", "medium – pressure" and "high – pressure" markets, respectively. Data selection includes 750 daily average prices. These markets are taken into account as representative of the US power markets because they are distributed in various locations and are used different mix of generation. Furthermore, they introduced some indices that explain power prices like temperature, fuel mix and types of grid. A clear conclusion comes to light; difference was discovered between the markets in terms of daily variation extend. A significant observation was that the spikes can be smoothed easily if there is hydroelectric power.

A work focusing in extreme jumps in electricity prices is conducted by Huisman and Mahieu (2003). They mainly studied extreme jumps and modelling electricity prices. According to their survey, participants in energy markets face more risk than the participants in other markets, due to higher daily volatility of energy prices compared to stock prices, which reaches around 29% and 20%, respectively. They noticed that, after a period of spikes, the force which the price reverts to the long – term price trend, is stronger than in normal periods. To summarize their conclusions, they found that electricity prices are characterized by high volatility, mean – reversion[7], seasonality and frequent extreme jumps.

Roques, Newbery and Nuttall (2008) examined the correlation between electricity, fuel and CO_2 in liberalized electricity markets. They used a two-step simulation approach. The first step was the Monte – Carlo simulation and the second step was the Mean – Variance Portfolio theory in order to diversify the risk of fuel, CO_2 and electricity prices. The latter gives incentives to investors to risk money on liberalized electricity markets even if the risk is higher in energy markets (Huisman & Mahieu, 2003). Three case studies were examined from Britain (2001 – 2005) and a correlation between electricity, fuel and CO_2 revealed. The correlation between fuel and electricity prices is affected by plenty factors as the type of fuel used by power plant, fuel contracts, operational strategies of electricity power plants, and the behavior of traders in electricity and fuel markets. For instance, in Britain, the correlation between natural gas prices and electricity prices is significantly high and increases over the years – from 40% in 2001 to 90% in 2005.

Energy prices seem to follow a continuous growing path over the next few years according to Efimova and Serletis (2014). It is expected that natural gas price will increase by 60%, the electricity price by 7%, and the price of crude oil by 62%, until 2035. Their work tries to fill the gap on energy price volatility modelling by using and expanding the univariate GARCH model, trivariate BEKK & DCC model and multivariate GARCH. Univariate GARCH model considers more accurate in prices' forecast. The collected data refer to oil, natural gas and electricity wholesale daily prices in time period of twelve years, from January 2nd 2001 to April 26th 2013. Figure 7 shows the Log of the Spot Oil Price, the Log of the Gas Price and the Log of the Electricity Price with the blue line and the daily growth rate with the black line for each component. The technic of using logarithms can be lead to smoothing away the large fluctuations of prices. From their empirical research, they discovered that a 10% increase in the S&P 500 Index is causing a 1.2% increase in oil price. Furthermore, electricity price volatility seems to be more abnormal than natural gas price volatility. According to Efimova and Serletis (2014), crude oil price volatility is of great interest to energy participants and policymakers. It is sometimes used as a macroeconomic indicator. Concerning the natural gas, the proportion of 31.2% is used to generate electricity in the US. The rest is used for residential consumers'

Figure 7. Daily growth rate of oil, gas and electricity prices
Source: Efimova and Serletis, Energy Economics 43, (2014), 264 - 273

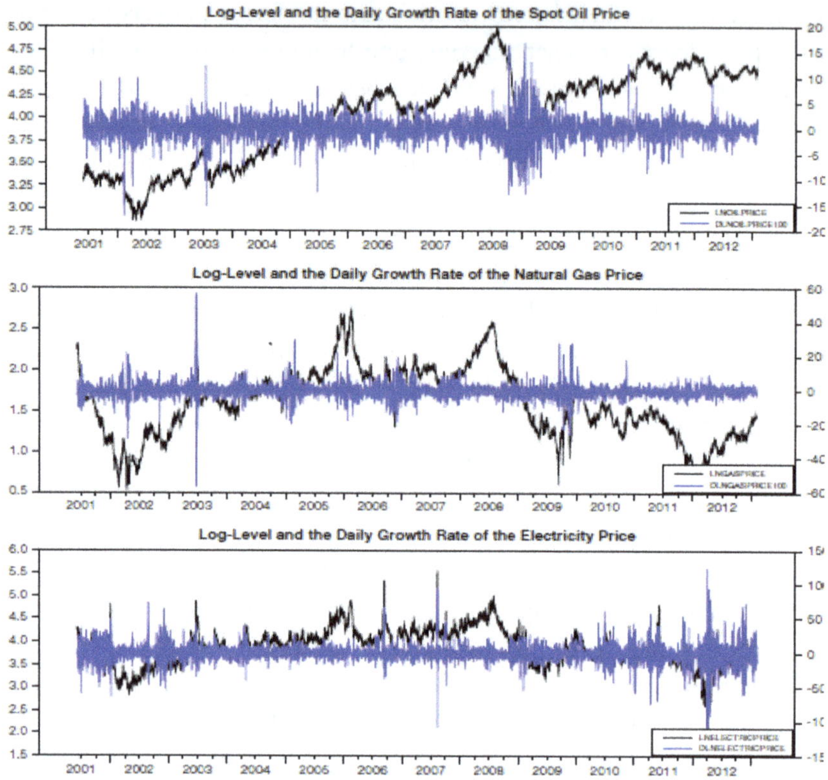

purposes and for the industrial sector, in proportion of 32.4% and 27.8%, respectively. They were underlying the significant spillover effect, affecting natural gas and electricity markets, but not the oil markets. More precisely, an increase in crude oil price by 10% will give an increase in electricity price by 0.28% and a decrease in natural gas next period's price by 1.3%. On the other hand, 10% increase in natural gas will increase next period's electricity price by 1.3% - 1.4%. These findings of spillover effect suggest that there is a hierarchy of influence from oil to gas and electricity markets. Generally, correlation between oil and gas as well as oil and electricity decreases over time of recession and time of slow economic growth. At the same time, correlation between gas and electricity increases.

To summarize, as many studies agree with each other, volatility in prices is explained by the growing demand in electricity and by the fact that electricity is a "flow commodity" and cannot be stored. Naturally, not only the nature of the electricity affects its prices but also the raw materials which contributes in electricity generation. As raw materials considers fossil fuels, nuclear power and renewable resources. Some aforementioned studies find out that the volatility in fuel mix affects the electricity prices. To clarify, as generation production supported by fuels, like natural gas, which are volatile from their nature, electricity prices are condemned because of their dependence in such fuels. Certainly, there are some theoretical solutions in this problem. Hydropower and nuclear energy comes to solve the problem of volatility. Electricity from hydro power can be considered as storable commodity. Therefore, electricity price volatility can be smoothed and hedged by "inventories". This issue needs further research in order to examine the structure and operation of a hydroelectric power station in conjunction with the benefits from the environmental, economic and energy aspect. The same purpose should follow the research in nuclear power plants.

Broadly speaking, spillovers are in foreground in economics and finance. Thus, researchers developed a lot of econometric models to calculate and measure spillovers between markets. The most popular model is a multivariate GARCH model or BEKK – GARCH model (Aboura & Chevallier, 2014). With the right methodology, fuel mix volatility and its correlation with electricity prices can estimate spillover volatility between them. Because of the literature research scarcity in spillover effects between fuel mix and electricity prices, it is recommended the application of the methodology from other cases, such as spillovers between stock markets and energy markets. General ideas are limited in factors that can hedge volatility and lower the spikes. Namely, hydroelectric power should be hold a bigger share in electricity generation and fuel mix with rich transmission networks must be included to stabilize the highly fluctuated prices.

The question which needs further research is separated in two parts. The first part should answer the question, if these factors are the only ones which affect electricity prices' volatility and the second part should answer, if these factors are actually the only factors which affect the volatility of prices. Afterwards, the extension of influence in electricity prices' volatility should be examined. In other words, in which proportion each component is responsible for this spillover effect.

AUTHORS' RESEARCH

Data Selection

Data selection for the Nordic Electricity System was occurred by different institutions and organizations. Specifically, electricity prices and production were selected by the Nord Pool Spot. Electricity price is represented by the system price. The daily data[8] sample included the dates between 01/01/2012 and 19/12/2014, without taking into consideration the weekends. Data adjustments were made in order to examine the Nordic System as a whole. In authors' empirical analysis, electricity price (system price) will be considered as the dependent variable (PRICE___MWH_). With the word "production", the authors mean that there are four deferent sources for electricity production; non – hydroelectric renewables (wind, tidal, solar, geothermal, biomass) (RES__MWH_), nuclear power (NUCLEAR__MWH_), fossil fuels, (oil, coal, natural gas) (FOSSIL__MWH_) and hydropower plants (HYDRO__MWH_). Data was selected from World Bank Database and US Energy Information Administration – Independent Statistics & Analysis as well. Oil and Gas price units are converted in €/MWh in order to make the research more reliable and correct. The exchange rate ($ to €) is selected by OANDA Corporation[9].

Seasonality

Seasonality is one of the most critical factors in economic time series variables, especially in case of commodity prices. The deseasonalization process removes the short – term fluctuations from the data. As a consequence, long – term components can be clearly identified and mistakes can be avoided. Table 4 in Appendix A indicates that Monday is the only day which has a p – value less than 5%, which means that Monday is statistically significant. In other words, Monday prices must be deseasonalized. In addition, Figure 8 illustrates that the deseasonalization process smooth away the prices[10].

Deseasonalization process includes the following steps:

- **Centered Moving Average (CMA):** CMA was calculated by the average of the average from the first seven days, and the average from the next day and by 7 days. To clarify, the first average is calculated by the values of electricity prices from Sunday 1/1/2012 to Saturday 7/1/2012 and the second average is calculated from Monday 2/1/2012 to Sunday 8/1/2012. Using these two averages and find their average gives the result of the CMA. This process continues further in the next weeks.
- **Ratio**: The ration is calculated by the system price divided by the CMA.
- *Unadjusted Factor*. The unadjusted factor is the average of the ration value from each day separately, and is repeated every week.
- **Sum of Unadjusted and Sum of Adjusted Factors**: The adjusted factor's sum takes the number of 7 because there are 7 days per week. The unadjusted factor's sum takes the number of the sum of the unadjusted factors every week. The latter is equal to 6.993158.

Figure 8. Graph for system price and centered moving average

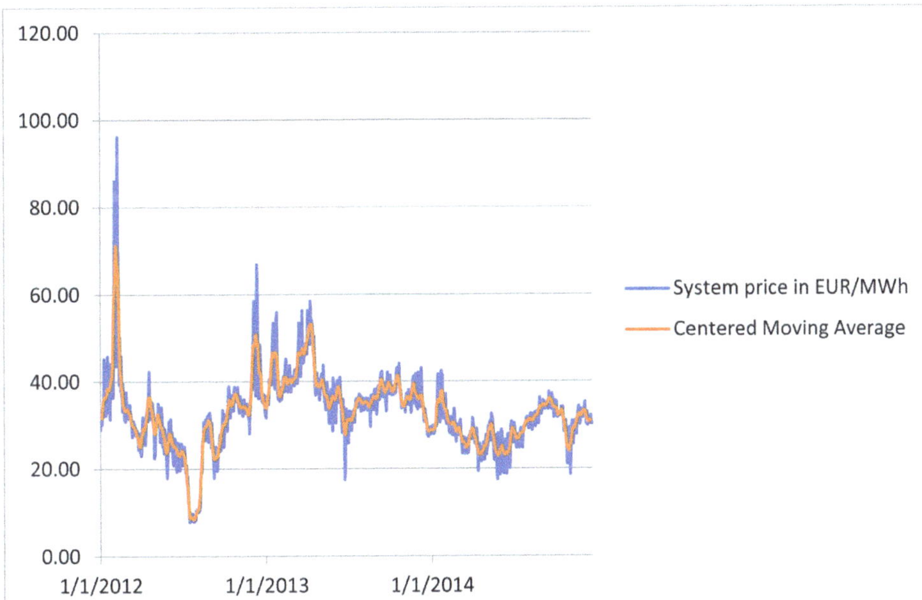

- **The Adjusted Factor**: The adjusted factors are calculated by the corresponding unadjusted factor multiplied with the following fraction $\frac{Sum\ Adjusted}{Sum\ Unadjusted}$.
- **Deseasonalized Price**: The deseasonalized price is originated by the system price divided by the adjusted factor for each day separately. The outcome of this process gives the prices that are significant because there are not any short term fluctuations.

Electricity Prices

Electricity prices follow a downward trend until the beginning of the third quarter of 2012; after that an increase takes place until the first quarter of 2013 and continue with a less fluctuated path from the second quarter of 2013 and afterwards. The observation of the data indicates two main phases; the price is rocketed from around 41 to 96 euros per MWh in the first quarter of 2012 and the price reaches its minimum value of the whole sample, approximately 7.92 €/MWh in July of 23rd. The aforementioned trends are illustrated by Figure 9.

Figure 9. Daily electricity prices (except weekends) in Nordic system from 2012–2014

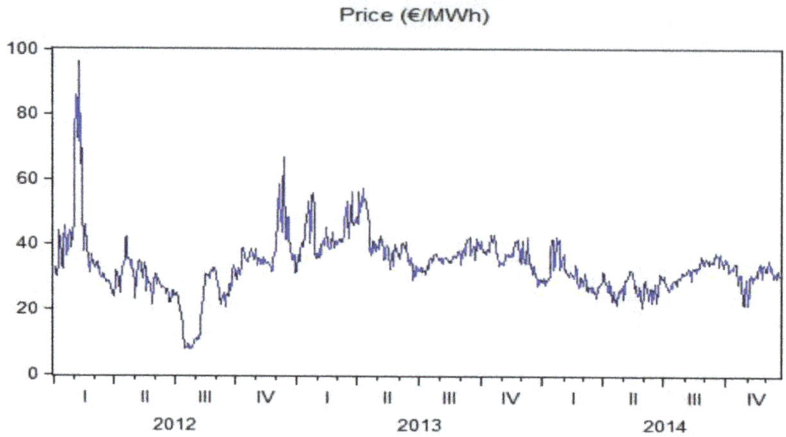

Methodology

GARCH (1, 1) model and Principal Component Analysis (PCA) used by the authors. The GARCH (1, 1) model is originated by the GARCH (p, q) model, where p is the ARCH terms and the q is the GARCH terms. The general form of a GARCH equation is represented in Appendix B, equation (2). If we consider the equation (2) and try to put values in p and q term then we can have the desirable model. For GARCH (1, 1) model the following values is determined and the GARCH equation takes the form of equation (3) below:

$$p = q = 1, GARCH\left(p, q\right) \rightarrow GARCH\left(1,1\right)$$

$$\sigma_t^2 = a_0 + a_1 u_{t-1}^2 + \gamma_1 \sigma_{t-1}^2 \quad (3)$$

The GARCH (1, 1) model's outcomes are represented in Table 5 Appendix C. Briefly, the results, represented in Table 5 in Appendix C, are the following two equations,

Mean Equation 1 1

$$Y_t = b_0 + b_1 X_{1t} + b_2 X_{2t} + b_3 X_{3t} + b_4 X_{4t} + u_t \quad (4)$$

(4)→PRICE___M_=20.78639 + 5.70E-05HYDRO__MWH_ + 0.000188FOSSIL__MWH_-2.96E-05RES__MWH_-0.000156NUCLEAR__MWH_ (5)

Variance Equation 12

$$\sigma_t^2 = a_0 + a_1 u_{t-1}^2 + \gamma_1 \sigma_{t-1}^2 + \delta_1 X_5 + \delta_2 X_6 \quad (6)$$

→GARCH = 20.91070 + 0.570621RESID (-1) ^2 + 0.358414GARCH (-1) - 0.121197OIL_PRICES___MWH_- (6)

0.264251GAS_PRICES___MWH_ (7)

Equations (5) and (7) are the estimations of the GARCH (1, 1) model. The variables in "Mean Equation" are defined in subsection "Data Selection". On the other hand, the variables in "Variance Equation" are defined as follows:

Where, OIL_PRICES___MWH_: price of oil, calculated in ¬/ *MWh*

GAS_PRICES___MWH_: price of natural gas, calculated in ¬/ *MWh*

GARCH (-1): GARCH term or previous days volatility of electricity prices

RESID (-1) ^2: ARCH term or previous period square residuals

GARCH: Variance of the residuals derived from equation (5) or volatility of electricity price

The p – value of all variables is considered less than 5%. As a result, all the variables, except GAS_PRICES___MWH_, are considered as statistically significant. Furthermore, it is important to mention that OIL_PRICES___MWH_ and GAS_PRICES___MWH_ are considered as exogenous variables or predetermined variables.

Principal Component Analysis

Principal Component Analysis (PCA) is a very useful tool when someone wants to reduce the number of the variables and make linear combinations of the data. Every linear combination is accorded to a principal component. The first principal component (F1) is the linear combination that has maximum variance, so it accounts for as much variation in the data as possible. The second principal component (F2) is the linear combination that accounts for as much of the remaining variation as possible, with the constraint that the correlation between the first and second component is 0. The number of principal components is diversified by research due to different data. As a result, the nth principal component (Fn) must be uncorrelated with all the previous defined components. In conclusion, all principal components are uncorrelated with each other. Naturally, the extraction and use of the right factors are determined after the application of some criteria. According to Hair, Andersen, Tatham and Black (1995), there are three criteria:

- **Kaiser's Criteria or Eigenvalue Criterion**: The only factors considered significant are these with eigenvalues greater to 1 (eigenvalue > 1) (Table 1).
- **Scree Test Criterion**: Scree plot has one axis to the left where the eigenvalues are placed. The right axis represents the cumulative variability and the horizontal axis indicates the 7 principal components. The shape of the curve is used to evaluate the point where the break is occurred. The point below to this break indicates the number of factors should be taken into account (Table 1).
- **The Cumulative Percent of Variance Criterion**: Even if there is no predetermined fixed threshold, the measure depends on the research topic and scientific field (Table 1).

The analysis of the criteria results a total of 2 factors out of 7. More specifically, eigenvalues of component 1 and 2 is more than 1 (F1 = 3.723 > 1, F2 = 1.702 > 1), so they are considered significant. From the cumulative percentage, the first two factors are explaining around 77.5% of the total data's variation. Finally from the scree plot, the break point seems to be the F4, as a result the data should be analyzed with 3 components. The first three components have a cumulative percentage of 87.946% which is more preferable than 77.5%, but the third factor (F3) is insignificant. In conclusion, for the purpose of this research, the first two factors (F1 and F2) will be used for further analysis as 77.5% is considered as an acceptable number, which describes the data quite well. In this manner, the variables are decreasing from 7 to 2, which were the first purpose of a PCA. Further to the aforementioned criteria, successive differences between the eigenvalues should be examined. A sharp drop from one eigenvalue to the next may serve as another indicator of how many eigenvalues should be considered. The result of first differences are 2.021, 0.970, 0.224, 0.291, 0.147 and 0.020, for F2 – F1, F3 – F2, F3 – F4, F4 – F5, F5 – F6 and F6 – F7, respectively.

Table 2 notes the coefficients of the factors (F1 and F2). The calculation of each new factor is presented in equations (8) and (9) using the eigenvectors from Table 2.

For the first component:

$$F1 = 0.310PRICE + 0.473FOSSIL + 0.478HYDRO + 0.491NUCLEAR + 0.456RES + 0.049OIL_{PRICES} - 0.002GAS_{PRICES} \quad (8)$$

Table 1a. Scree plot

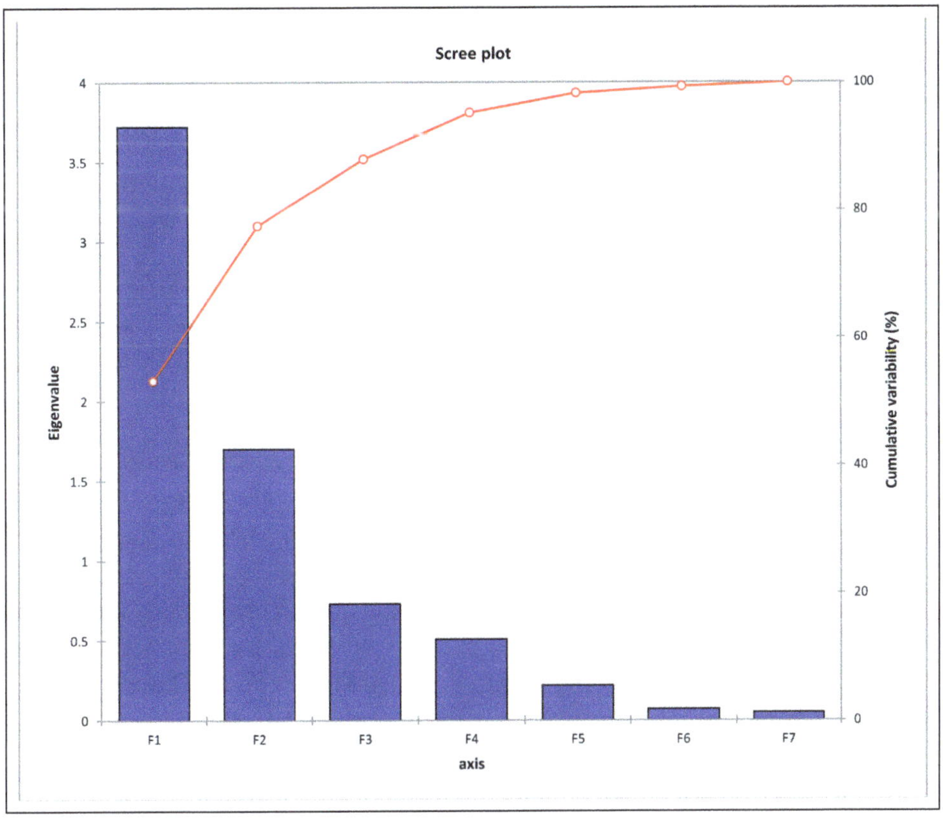

Table 1b. Eigenvalue

	F1	F2	F3	F4	F5	F6	F7
Eigenvalue	3.723	1.702	0.732	0.508	0.217	0.070	0.050
Variability (%)	53.180	24.311	10.454	7.250	3.098	0.997	0.709
Cumulative %	53.180	77.491	87.946	95.196	98.294	99.291	100.000

and for the second component:

$$F2 = -0.091PRICE - 0.205FOSSIL - 0.007HYDRO + 0.058NUCLEAR + 0.290RES - 0.641OIL_{PRICES} + 0.671GAS_{PRICES} \quad (9)$$

Table 2. Coefficients of F1 and F2 factors

Eigenvectors		
	F1	F2
Price (€/MWh)	0.310	-0.091
FOSSIL (MWh)	0.473	-0.205
HYDRO (MWh)	0.478	-0.007
NUCLEAR (MWh)	0.491	0.058
RES (MWh)	0.456	0.290
Oil Prices (€/MWh)	0.049	-0.641
Gas Prices (€/MWh)	-0.002	0.671

Hence, PCA introduces new combination of the variables. Nevertheless, in order to interpret the components, the calculation of the correlation between each component and each variable is necessary. The correlations between the principal components and the original variables are presented in the Table 3.

From Table 3, we are looking for these variables which are strongly correlated with each component. In other words, our purpose is to find which number is large in magnitude or far from zero in either negative or positive direction[13]. The correlations in blue are the most significant ones; they are above of 0.5 in absolute values. The first principle component is strongly correlated with five out of seven variables (Price, Fossil, Hydro, Nuclear and Renewables (RES)). The outcome indicates that these five variables vary together; when one increases the others increases as well. Furthermore, if the first principle component increases then the five variables which are strongly correlated with this component increases as well. F1 is mainly a measure of nuclear, hydro and fossil as it is appeared to be more strongly correlated with

Table 3. Correlations between the principal components and the original variables

Factor Loadings or Correlation Between Variables and Factors		
	F1	F2
Price (€/MWh)	0.599	-0.119
FOSSIL (MWh)	0.912	-0.267
HYDRO (MWh)	0.923	-0.009
NUCLEAR (MWh)	0.948	0.075
RES (MWh)	0.880	0.379
Oil Prices (€/MWh)	0.095	-0.837
Gas Prices (€/MWh)	-0.003	0.876

these variables than Price and RES. Moreover, if there is an increase in production from nuclear power, then an increase will be observed in the production from fossil fuels, hydropower and renewables, but also the price will be increased as well. The results from the Table 3 can be confirmed by Figure 10.

For the F1 component, Oil and Gas prices are almost zero, which means zero correlation between these two variables and the F1. On the other hand, F2 is strongly correlated with oil and gas prices and is not correlated with the other five variables. More specifically, gas price is positively correlated (0.876) and oil price is negatively correlated (-0.837) with the F2. This means that, when F2 increases then gas prices increases and oil prices decreases. This component suggests that if there is an increase in gas prices the oil prices will be decreased. The latter seems quite reasonable, because these two products are considered as substitutes with each other.

Finally, in order to complete the PCA is needed a scatter plot of the components scores (Figure 11). Each of these points represents a day. Taking into account the place of each point in the scatter plot, we understand the followings:

- The points close to the right line of the graph have very high values of F1. As a result, we expect these days to have high values for Price, Nuclear, Fossil, RES and Hydro. In other words these days, electricity prices will be high. In contrast, if we are looking for the points near to the left line, we should expect that these days the 5 variables will have low values.

- The points exactly below of the top line have high values of F2. So, we should expect that these days would have high values in gas prices and low values in oil prices. On the other hand, if we look the points near above the bottom line, we should expect low values in gas prices and high values in oil prices.

AUTHORS' RESULTS

GARCH (1, 1) model reveals that natural gas prices have no effect on electricity prices' volatility. This outcome verified from the p – value which is more than 0.05; more precisely the p – value = 0.1098 > 0.05, which means that it is not statistically significant. PCA indicate that F2 component is strongly correlated with oil prices. Hence, on the one hand, an increase in gas prices causes a decrease in oil prices and leaving the electricity prices untouched and on the other hand, increase in oil prices gives a decrease in gas prices and a slightly decrease in electricity prices. As a consequence, gas prices can affect oil prices but not the electricity prices. In contrast, oil prices can affect gas prices and electricity prices. This spillover effect

Figure 10. Correlation between the variables and the first and second principal component

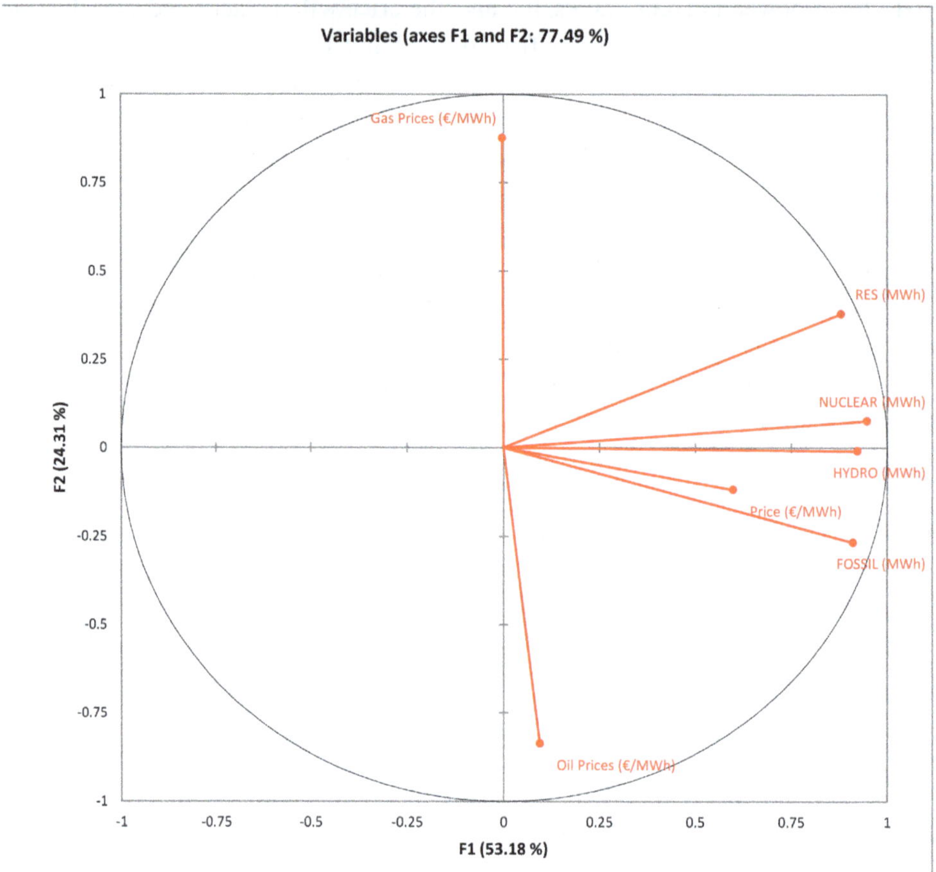

comes to an agreement with Efimova and Serletis (2014) study which they found a spillover effect, proposing the existence of oil influence into gas and electricity markets. Furthermore, the researchers found that the variance of electricity prices reaches 80.5%[14] from 01/01/2012 to 19/12/2014, in the Nordic System. There is a popular opinion that supports the higher share of nuclear and hydropower in the fuel mix in order to produce electricity. These two types of energy are considered very significant for the stabilization of the electricity prices and for the spikes' control. They smoothed away these frequent abnormalities in electricity prices.

Hydropower considers as a storable product. Geman and Roncoroni (2006) as well as Lucia and Schwartz (2002), support the theory of inventories[15], and believe that the electricity prices can be controlled and hedged by inventories. In authors' research, electricity generation from hydro power is statistically significant; it can

Figure 11. Results for F1 and F2

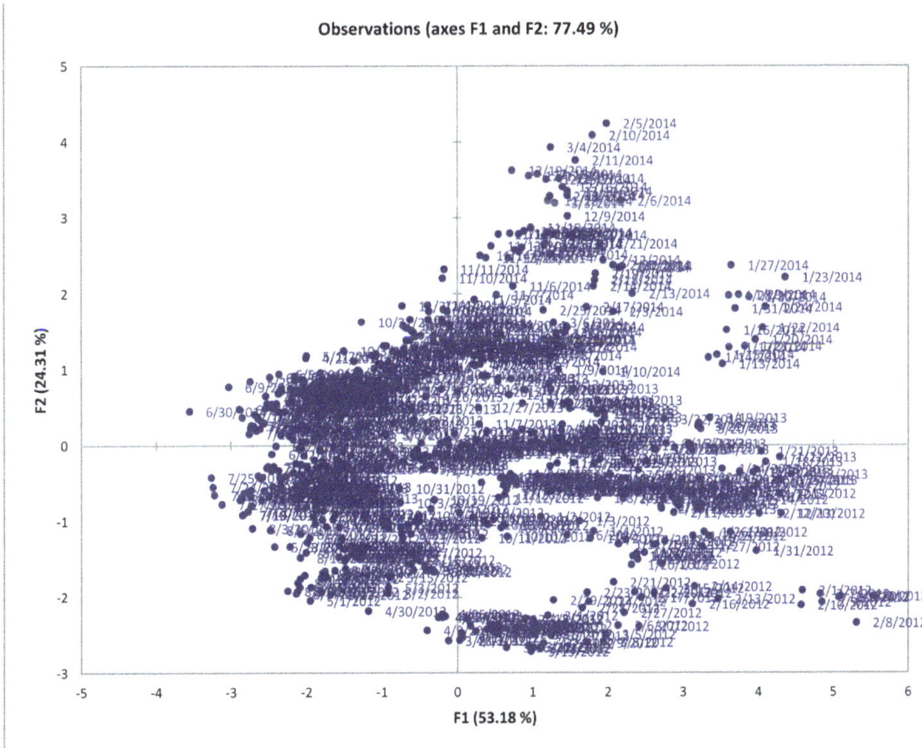

affect electricity prices. Theoretically speaking, if the proportion of electricity production from hydropower increased then a positive impact in electricity prices' volatility will occur. Thus, the nature of electricity, as a non – storable product becomes lower and more insignificant.

Mari's (2014) study indicates that CO_2 emissions affect electricity prices through the extended use of fossil fuels. Nuclear power seems to be the answer to this problem because it is a carbon – free technology. The substitution of fossil fuels becomes mandatory because of the following chain-like mechanism. Fossil fuels prices affect electricity prices, but fossil fuels prices are volatile from their nature. The result is that electricity prices become volatile as well. As a consequence, nuclear power seems to be a valuable solution in order to stop this dead – end. According to the authors' analysis, nuclear power significantly affects electricity prices. Taking all the above into consideration, it is discovered that electricity production from fossil fuels affects electricity prices by both factors; the emissions and fossil fuels volatility prices.

To this extend, the authors agree with Mari's (2014) work and idea[16] and they suggest that production from hydropower and nuclear power plants should hold a bigger share in future. These two forms of energy, can transform electricity from non – storable product to a storable product and from "pollutant" to a free – carbon product. The last two forms introduce new ideas fighting prices' extreme volatility. Garcia–Martos, Rodriguez and Sanchez (2011), support this theory of CO_2 emissions. They believe that climate policy has become stricter, thus the emissions add more operational costs in the industries, and as a consequence costs jump to the energy market, making it more vulnerable and more unstable.

Finally, an interesting result come out from Roques, Newbry and Nuttall (2008) research, where they support that the correlation between electricity prices and gas prices reach the level of 90% in the region of Britain in 2005. In current work, the results are quite different. There is no statistically significant correlation between electricity prices and natural gas prices, which indicates that gas prices do not affect volatility in electricity prices. On the other hand, decreasing oil prices increases the variation of electricity prices.

CONCLUSIONS AND SUGGESTIONS

To estimate the variance in commodities' prices, researchers prefer to use GARCH models. Due to the fact that there is not much literature in this specific topic, the authors decided to choose the same model in order to explain volatility in electricity prices. Volatility of electricity prices cannot be avoided due to its nature and the fuel vulnerable prices. The inevitable volatility can be hedged and fought by more electricity production from hydro power and nuclear power and by suitable fuel mix with rich transmission networks.

From the analysis of this chapter, we suggest that the share of hydropower should be increased in order to stabilize the electricity prices, through the storability. Secondly, the share of nuclear power in electricity generation should be increase as well, but not forget the risk of nuclear accidents. It could control and affect positively the electricity prices through the carbon – free technology criterion. Last, the share of fossil fuels, considering the volatility of their prices and the greenhouse gas emissions, should be minimized.

Finally, there is a lot of room to extend the investigation of this topic and further research is essential in order to come with more reliable results. There is poor data selection and literature, related to this topic. Thus, it may drive us to the wrong way. If there is a larger amount of data and literature, the results could be more reliable, and thus, the likelihood of wrong conclusions is minimized. So further research may be wise to be occurred, in the near future, in order to find and cross the existing and the future results. That will lead to more trustful and valuable outcomes and suggestions which will deem significant for policy making. Suitable policies can be created, but only if policy makers and other interested parties have in mind the right results concerning energy and fuel mix.

REFERENCES

Aboura, S., & Chevallier, J. (2014). Cross – market spillovers with "volatility surprise". *Review of Financial Economics*, *23*(4), 194–207. doi:10.1016/j.rfe.2014.08.002

Brooks, C. (2008). *Introductory Econometrics for Finance* (2nd ed.). Cambridge University Press. doi:10.1017/CBO9780511841644

Cerjan, M., Petricic, A., Delimer, M. (2019). HIRA model for short – term electricity price forecasting.

Christou, G. K. (2008). *Introduction in Econometrics*. Gutenberg Publications.

Collin – Dufresne, P., & Goldstein, R. S. (2002). Do bonds span the fixed income markets? Theory and Evidence for Unspanned Stochastic Volatility. *The Journal of Finance*, *LVII*(4).

Efimova, O., & Serletis, A. (2014). Energy markets volatility modelling using GARCH. *Energy Economics*, *43*, 264–273. doi:10.1016/j.eneco.2014.02.018

Garcia, C. R., Contreras, J., Akkeren, M., & Garcia, J. B. C. (2005). A GARCH forecasting model to predict day – ahead electricity prices. *IEEE Transactions on Power Systems*, *20*(2), 867–874. doi:10.1109/TPWRS.2005.846044

García-Martos, C., Rodríguez, J., & Sánchez, M. J. (2011). Forecasting electricity prices and their volatility using Unobserved Components. *Energy Economics*, *33*(6), 1227–1239. doi:10.1016/j.eneco.2011.07.005

Geman, H., & Roncoroni, A. (2006). Understanding the fine structure of electricity prices. *The Journal of Business*, *79*(3), 1225–1261. doi:10.1086/500675

Government of Hong Kong. (2014). *Future fuel mix for electricity generation*. Environmental Bureau.

Hair, J. F., Andersen, R. E., Tatham, R. L., & Black, W. C. (1995). *Multivariate data analysis* (4th ed.). Englewood Cliffs, NJ: Prentice Hall.

Huisman, R., & Mahieu, R. (2003). Regime jumps in electricity prices. *Energy Economics*, *25*(5), 425–434. doi:10.1016/S0140-9883(03)00041-0

Kirschen, D. S., Strbac, G., Cumperayot, P., & Mendes, D. (2000). Factoring the elasticity of demand in electricity prices. *IEEE Transactions on Power Systems*, *15*(2), 612–617. doi:10.1109/59.867149

Koekebakker, S., & Ollmar, F. 2005. Forward curve dynamics in the Nordic electricity market. Managerial Finance, 31(6), 73-94. doi:10.1108/03074350510769703

Köne, A. C., & Büke, T. (2007). An Analytical Network Process (ANP) evaluation of alternative fuels for electricity generation in Turkey. *Energy Policy*, *35*(10), 5220–5228. doi:10.1016/j.enpol.2007.05.014

Lago, J., Ridder, F. D., Vrancx, P., & Schutter, B. D. (2018). Forecasting day – ahead electricity prices in Europe: The importance of considering market integration. *Applied Energy*, *211*, 890–903. doi:10.1016/j.apenergy.2017.11.098

Lie, H., & Shi, J. (2013). Applying ARMA – GARCH approaches to forecasting short – term electricity prices. *Energy Economics*, *37*, 152–166. doi:10.1016/j.eneco.2013.02.006

Lucia, J. J., & Schwartz, E. S. (2002). Electricity prices and power derivatives: Evidence from Nordic Power Exchange. *Review of Derivatives Research*, *5*(1), 5–50. doi:10.1023/A:1013846631785

Mari, C. (2014). Hedging electricity price volatility using nuclear power. *Applied Energy*, *113*, 615–621. doi:10.1016/j.apenergy.2013.08.016

Nogales, F. J., Contreras, J., Conejo, A. J., & Espinola, R. (2002). Forecasting next – day electricity prices by time series models. *IEEE Transactions on Power Systems*, *17*(2), 342–348. doi:10.1109/TPWRS.2002.1007902

Roques, F. A., Newbery, D. M., & Nuttell, W. J. (2008). Fuel mix diversification incentives in liberalized electricity markets: A mean – variance portfolio theory approach. *Energy Economics*, *30*(4), 1831–1849. doi:10.1016/j.eneco.2007.11.008

Smith, A. (1776). *An inquiry into the nature and causes of the wealth of nations*. London, UK: W. Straham and T. Cadell.

Syriopoulos, K., & Filippas, D. T. (2010). *Econometric Models and Applications in EViews*. Anikoula Publications.

Wooldridge, M. J. (2006). *Introduction in Econometrics* (Vol. A). Papaziti Publications.

ENDNOTES

1 See Figure 1

2 There is international emissions trade systems, like EU ETS, where putting a price on carbon dioxide emissions. That gives motivation in companies to follow "clean" investments and develop low – carbon technologies

3 Real time location – based marginal prices

4 ISO New England manages a few electric power markets in the United States. These power markets allow generators to sell their electricity to marketers, who sell the electricity to end users (businesses, households).

5 Spikes are considered to be created by sudden disruptions in the transmission grid, extreme weather conditions and generation outages

6 First introduced for agricultural commodities (Kaldor, 1939)

7 The electricity prices are forced to fall back to a normal level after a shock or jump

8 The data was selected in MWh and the price in €/MWh.

9 Unfortunately, the exchange rates were not daily, so the authors decided to choose weekly exchange rates

10 Some additional graphs are represented in Appendix C

11 Mean Equation values are taking from the first part of the Table 5 of Appendix C

12 Variance Equation values are taking from the second part of the Table 5 of Appendix C

13 The significant numbers will be more than 0.5 in absolute values

14 The variance was estimated by squared standard deviation of electricity prices

15 Inventories can hedge the risk of volatility

16 Diversification in electricity generation is very optimistic

17 Explanation of Dummy Variable Trap is beyond this research. See Christou (2004), p. 165.

Appendix A

Table 4. Seasonality examination

Dependent Variable: PRICE_IN_EUR_MWH				
Method: Least Squares				
Date: 12/22/14 Time: 13:21				
Sample: 1/02/2012 12/19/2014				
Included observations: 775				
Variable	Coefficient	Std. Error	t-Statistic	Prob.
C	33.68032	0.723904	46.52594	0.0000
TUESDAY	0.535484	1.023755	0.523059	0.6011
WEDNESDAY	0.938839	1.023755	0.917054	0.3594
THURSDAY	0.555355	1.023755	0.542468	0.5877
FRIDAY	-0.167032	1.023755	-0.163156	0.8704
R-squared	0.002005	Mean dependent var		34.05285
Adjusted R-squared	-0.003180	S.D. dependent var		8.998241
S.E. of regression	9.012535	Akaike info criterion		7.241541
Sum squared resid	62543.86	Schwarz criterion		7.271559
Log likelihood	-2801.097	Hannan-Quinn criter.		7.253090
F-statistic	0.386705	Durbin-Watson stat		0.129970
Prob(F-statistic)	0.818236			

Monday denoted as C, because C is the constant term in the above table, and takes a $p - \text{value} = 0.0000 < 0.05$; it is statistically significant variable. The authors did not use five dummy variables (MONDAY, THUESDAY, WEDNESDAY, THURSDAY, FRIDAY) but they used four dummy variables (TUESDAY, WEDNESDAY, THURSDAY, FRIDAY) in order to avoid dummy variable trap[17].

Appendix B

ARCH & GARCH Model

ARCH model is described from the following equation:

$$\sigma_t^2 = a_o + a_1 u_{t-1}^2 + a_2 u_{t-2}^2 + \ldots + a_p u_{t-p}^2 \quad (1)$$

Where, σ_τ^2 : *variation of disruption term*

u_t : *disruption term*

a_0 : *constant coefficient*

u_{t-1}^2 : *squared price of disruption term of previous period*

It is denoted as follows: **ARCH (p)**.

GARCH model is a Generalized ARCH model and it has the following formation:

$$\sigma_t^2 = a_0 + a_1 u_{t-1}^2 + \ldots + a_p u_{t-p}^2 + \gamma_1 \sigma_{t-1}^2 + \ldots + \gamma_q \sigma_{t-q}^2 \quad (2)$$

Where, γ : *weighted coefficient*

It is denotes: **GARCH (p, q)**.

Table 5. GARCH (1, 1) outcomes

Dependent Variable: PRICE____MWH_				
Method: ML - ARCH (Marquardt) - Normal distribution				
Date: 01/21/15 Time: 15:59				
Sample: 1/02/2012 12/19/2014				
Included observations: 775				
Convergence achieved after 48 iterations				
Presample variance: backcast (parameter = 0.7)				
GARCH = C(6) + C(7)*RESID(-1)^2 + C(8)*GARCH(-1) + C(9)				
*OIL_PRICES____MWH_ + C(10)*GAS_PRICES____MWH_				
Variable	Coefficient	Std. Error	z-Statistic	Prob.
C	20.78639	0.932904	22.28139	0.0000
HYDRO__MWH_	5.70E-05	3.18E-06	17.88933	0.0000
FOSSIL__MWH_	0.000188	8.65E-06	21.71380	0.0000
RES__MWH_	-2.96E-05	9.73E-06	-3.039629	0.0024
NUCLEAR__MWH_	-0.000156	1.06E-05	-14.72540	0.0000
	Variance Equation			
C	20.91070	3.866048	5.408804	0.0000
RESID(-1)^2	0.570621	0.093590	6.097040	0.0000
GARCH(-1)	0.358414	0.060422	5.931874	0.0000
OIL_PRICES____MWH_	-0.121197	0.016404	-7.388176	0.0000
GAS_PRICES____MWH_	-0.264251	0.165258	-1.599015	0.1098
R-squared	0.290674	Mean dependent var		33.90574
Adjusted R-squared	0.286989	S.D. dependent var		8.977161
S.E. of regression	7.580314	Akaike info criterion		5.990033
Sum squared resid	44245.09	Schwarz criterion		6.050070
Log likelihood	-2311.138	Hannan-Quinn criter.		6.013131
Durbin-Watson stat	0.178477			

Appendix C

From Table 6, electricity prices seem to correlate significantly with the electricity generation from fossil fuels, hydropower, nuclear power, RES and oil prices. Gas prices are not significantly correlated with electricity prices in significance level of 5%.

In Table 7, some interesting statistics are observed. Minimum and maximum corresponds in the minimum and maximum price of each variable. The authors would like to insist in electricity price and take a more careful glance. With the mean value equals to 33.906, the maximum price seems to take outliers. This is a mark that extreme volatility exists in electricity prices.

Table 6. Correlation matrix between the variables

Correlation Matrix (Pearson (n))							
Variables	**Price (€/ MWh)**	**FOSSIL (MWh)**	**HYDRO (MWh)**	**NUCLEAR (MWh)**	**RES (MWh)**	**Oil Prices (€/MWh)**	**Gas Prices (€/ MWh)**
Price (€/ MWh)	**1**	**0.553**	**0.445**	**0.382**	**0.393**	**0.072**	-0.056
FOSSIL (MWh)	**0.553**	**1**	**0.776**	**0.814**	**0.724**	**0.282**	**-0.245**
HYDRO (MWh)	**0.445**	**0.776**	**1**	**0.912**	**0.758**	0.070	-0.051
NUCLEAR (MWh)	**0.382**	**0.814**	**0.912**	**1**	**0.866**	0.066	0.058
RES (MWh)	**0.393**	**0.724**	**0.758**	**0.866**	**1**	**-0.194**	**0.325**
Oil Prices (€/ MWh)	**0.072**	**0.282**	0.070	0.066	**-0.194**	**1**	**-0.496**
Gas Prices (€/MWh)	-0.056	**-0.245**	-0.051	0.058	**0.325**	**-0.496**	**1**
**Values in bold are different from 0 with a significance level alpha=0.05*							

Table 7. Statistics from the data

Summary Statistics							
Variable	**Observations**	**Obs. with missing data**	**Obs. without missing data**	**Minimum**	**Maximum**	**Mean**	**Std. deviation**
Price (€/ MWh)	775	0	775	7.920	96.150	33.906	8.977
FOSSIL (MWh)	775	0	775	35591.568	148645.284	88583.716	21897.515
HYDRO (MWh)	775	0	775	436577.623	882035.427	627757.137	103359.702
NUCLEAR (MWh)	775	0	775	150151.539	311750.256	227555.183	38088.019
RES (MWh)	775	0	775	81514.335	223171.351	133508.112	28880.398
Oil Prices (€/MWh)	775	0	775	76.199	159.149	132.263	12.132
Gas Prices (€/MWh)	775	0	775	4.730	20.459	9.379	2.096

Chapter 9
Algorithmic Trading and Transaction Costs

George Chalamandaris
https://orcid.org/0000-0003-1388-0249
Athens University of Economics and Business, Greece

Dimitrios Antonopoulos
Athens University of Economics and Business, Greece

ABSTRACT

"Algos" are algorithmic trading strategies that are meant to optimize the execution quality of the trades in terms of transaction costs and market-timing. This chapter presents the transaction costs taxonomy and popular algorithmic execution strategies. Authors empirically examine a dataset of hedge fund transactions. Our results suggest that implicit transaction costs are characterized by a significant buy-sell asymmetry. To get some insight about the possible determinants of Implicit Transaction Costs, authors investigate the algo type and stock characteristics such as market capitalization, relative volume, inverse prior close, price momentum, buy indicator and trade duration. Both in-sample and out-of-sample tests show that a significant portion of transaction costs can be anticipated before the trade execution. Results show that high-level execution strategies can be constructed to optimize the algo choice.

INTRODUCTION

Superior investment performance is the result of a meticulously planned process that involves the concurrent pursuance of multiple objectives. Although some among

DOI: 10.4018/978-1-7998-2436-7.ch009

these objectives are purely financial (e.g. estimating expected returns, quantifying market/credit risks and extreme losses, etc.), other – no less important - are operational in nature. Efficient trade execution belongs to the latter category and constitutes an undisputed key factor of success; one that can effectively "make or break" a successful investment process. For, it is common knowledge in the world of practitioners - especially in the quant investment fund business - that transaction costs can easily erode portfolio returns and destroy strategies, that looked – at least in theory – very promising and innovative.

This chapter presents a statistical-based framework for monitoring transaction costs. Specifically, we present an overview of algorithmic trading and of the related transaction cost measures. We estimate their impact on investment performance and propose heuristics that can be used for the improvement of trade execution strategies.

As case study, we empirically analyze the transaction costs of two - relatively small, yet very active in the global markets - long-short equity hedge fund businesses. We measure implicit trading costs using different types of measures and examine their distributional properties. We then investigate possible determinants of implicit trading costs, using regression-based models. Finally, we test the out-of-sample predictive power of the explanatory models.

The rest of this chapter is organized as follows. Section 2 defines transaction costs and their components. In section 3 we discuss issues related to algorithmic trading including popular strategies. Section 4 provides a brief review of the literature on transaction costs. Section 5 describes the data and section 6 presents the empirical results. Finally, section 7 summarizes and concludes.

TRANSACTION COSTS

In market microstructure, liquidity is commonly defined as the ease with which market-users can trade (buy/sell) the asset of exchange, once they decide to do so. For that reason, market-users are typically called the "buy side" of the market – since they "buy" liquidity services, whereas the providers of such services (brokers/dealers/market-makers/standing limit orders) are known as the "Sell side". Within this context, transaction costs are the premia paid by the "buy side" to the "sell side" as compensation for the liquidity the latter provide.

Transaction costs are divided into two broad categories: Explicit and Implicit costs. Explicit costs are pre-determined, often fixed, and relatively easy to calculate. These include commissions, fees, taxes and bid-ask spreads. Implicit costs, on the other hand are more subtle, and as such they need to be inferred from the observed prices only after making specific assumptions. Implicit costs include investment delay, market impact costs, opportunity costs and market timing costs.

Explicit Transaction Costs

Fixed explicit costs include commissions, fees and tax costs.

Commissions are charged by brokers and are commonly expressed per share or as a percentage of the total transaction value. They are negotiable and vary by broker, fund, trading type or trading difficulty.

Fees are categorized into *custodial* fees that investors pay to institutions to hold the securities in safekeeping, and *transfer* fees, which arise when the ownership over a stock is transferred. The latter include clearing and settlement costs, exchange fees, ticket charges and SEC transaction fees.

Tax law commonly stipulates two types of transaction-related taxes. Taxes on short-term and long-term capital gains and taxes on dividends. Generally, tax rates vary by country, investment and type of earnings. Consequently, tax planning is an important concern that must be addressed in investment strategies.

Bid-ask spread is a direct, variable transaction cost and is defined as the difference between the quoted sell and buy price. In theory, the bid-ask spread compensates market-makers for the risks (e.g., funding, adverse selection, counterparty risk) arising from the management of their inventory. Typically, a state of abundant liquidity is associated with small bid-ask spreads.

Implicit Transaction Costs

The time interval between the decision of a portfolio manager to buy or sell a security and the execution of the actual trade is referred to as the *Investment Delay*. Investment delay cost is the price change that occurs during that interval. Evidently, the severity of this cost depends mostly on the validity of the decision to wait for better terms, rather than ask for immediate execution.

Conversely, the price of immediacy is mostly related to the *market impact cost*. This is defined as the difference between the next and previous transaction prices. There are two types of market impact costs, temporary and permanent. *Temporary* market impact cost is typically caused by short-lived gaps between order flow and liquidity supply. If supply is scarce, market-users will have to pay a premium (discount) to entice liquidity providers and thus execute their trades immediately. Instances of "price reversals" are often indicative of such gaps. On the other hand, *permanent* market impact cost is caused by trades with significant information content.

The *half spread* is often used (e.g. Torre & Ferrari, 1999) as a prior estimate of the market impact. The main idea is that any small-sized roundtrip-trade (a market "buy", followed by a market "sell") will entail a transaction cost equal to the market's bid-ask spread, or equivalently, a cost equal to the half of the bid-ask spread per trade. In that sense, any difference between the observed market impact and the half-spread (its prior) represents additional transaction cost. Having said that, it is also possible that the actual market impact is smaller than its prior level if the trader decides to forego immediate liquidity in exchange for price concessions from the liquidity providers. For instance, when a trader uses tick-sensitive orders (buy downtick/sell-uptick) or breaks a parent order into smaller ones, he effectively extends the trading horizon in the hope that this will dampen the temporary market impact.

Market timing costs occur when the price of the security changes at the time of the transaction and can be attributed to other market participants or market volatility. It is empirically estimated that market timing costs are higher for larger trades when they are broken into small portions and traded over a long period of time. Also, they are proportional to the standard deviation of the security returns multiplied by the square root of the time until the completion of the trade.

Opportunity cost is defined as the cost of not transacting at all. In that case, the portfolio manager misses an investment opportunity because the trade fails to execute. It is often estimated as the deviation of the desired investment from the actual investment after transaction costs. Given that this quantity depends on price volatility, it follows that the longer the trading horizon, the greater the risk of facing high opportunity costs.

Order Types and Liquidity

Market orders are unconditional instructions for immediate execution of the entire order size at the best possible price. *Limit orders* can be executed only at the specified- or-better price. Otherwise, they remain as "*standing*" in the limit order book until their eventual execution or cancellation.

Generally speaking, a highly liquid market is characterized by the combinations of large traded volumes, immediate execution and low market impact. "Buy side" participants with the intent to buy or sell securities provide *depth* in the market. A large portion of these participants reveal their intent and place limit orders. Others, with real-time access to the market, wait for the right circumstances before they submit their orders. It is exactly for this reason that the limit order book represents the observable component of the current demand (limit buy orders) and supply (limit sell orders) in the market. Unsurprisingly, a "full" order book is indicative of market depth, whereas a "half-empty" book alludes to high transaction costs. Given that a "deep" market can absorb the execution of large-sized orders without significant market impact costs ("*price resilience*"), depth is regarded as the more permanent component of liquidity.

"Sell-side" participants (Brokers and dealers), on the other hand, provide only short-term liquidity as they intermediate between "Buy-side" agents to execute the orders that have been delegated to them. Indeed, a market-maker will operate within the aggregate bid-ask spread of market-users, just to top-up liquidity on that already present in the market. In that context, standing limit-orders serve as an insurance for the dealer, in the sense, that when he doesn't manage to balance his inventory with incoming customer order flows, he has the opportunity to do so by resorting to the standing limit orders. If the aggregate volume of these orders is large and aggressively priced, then the dealer will pay a very small cost to get rid of his excess inventory. By contrast, if the liquidity provided by the order book is not sufficient to cover the excess inventory, the market-maker will be forced to charge his customers large bid-ask spreads to compensate himself for the risks he is taking on.

Thus, liquidity, transaction size and transaction costs are interrelated.

Measures of Implicit Transaction Costs

To measure the true implicit transaction costs, we need to estimate the difference between the "true" price of the security - which is, of course, not observable - and the execution price. As the execution price depends on the current state of available liquidity relative to the order terms (size, immediacy, direction), it becomes obvious that implicit transaction costs can be very volatile.

There are many different measures of transaction costs. In general, they are estimated as the difference between the execution price and a market benchmark. The difference between these measures lies in the benchmark that is used for the calculation.

$$* \frac{Execution \Pr ice - Benchmark \Pr ice}{Execution \Pr ice} \tag{1}$$

where side is equal to 1 for buys and -1 for sells. Benchmark price can be any of

- The *closing* price on the day *prior* to the trade (Perold, 1988).
- The *opening* price on the *same day* (pre-trade measure).
- The volume-weighted average price of all market transactions during the trading horizon (*VWAP* - Berkowitz et al., 1988).
- The closing price of the trading horizon.
- The opening / closing price on the next day (post-trade measure - Beebower & Priest, 1980).

It is also common to control for market-wide movement by subtracting the market index return over the trading horizon. Clearly, different benchmarks result in different measurements of the ITC.

ALGORITHMIC TRADING

A Review of Popular Execution Strategies

Automated processes have been expanding rapidly over the last decade, effectively supplanting humans in many aspects of the investment business. For instance, quant funds are the largest source of institutional trading, accounting for 36% of the institutional trading volume of shares in 2019, up from just 18% in 2010 (source TABB group). At the same time, computer-managed portfolios (index funds, quant and ETFs) manage 35% of the total value of US public equities, whereas human-managed funds run only 24% of the total (source: "March of the machines", The Economist, October 5th 2019).

Nevertheless, it is in the field of trade execution where automated processes dominate entirely their human counterparts. According to Deutsche Bank, 80% of cash-equity and 90% of futures-equity trades are executed by algorithms without human intervention. Order execution in equity derivative markets is also dominated by automated processes according to TABB group.

Execution algorithms, in general, determine the time, size and terms of trade schedule with the goal of minimizing the risk-adjusted costs according to the customer's broad objectives. Specifically, based on the trader's utility function, the *order placement engine* (also known as the "micro-trader") plans a sequence of orders ("*trajectory*") to the aim of executing optimally a target quantity of shares. Within this framework, human inputs determine only the parameters of the optimization problem, such as the utility/loss function and size/price restrictions.

There are a few execution strategies offered by institutional brokers/dealers to their customers, known as "algos".

Most algos submit order through the primary markets, while other algos use in addition alternative venues such as *Electronic Crossing Networks*. The main advantage of ECNs is the absence of information leakage from the submitted orders. Indeed, ECN orders are not publicly displayed, nor cause any market impact when executed. On the contrary, standing limit orders in open market books can be exploited by "parasitic" traders (e.g. front-runners). However, these algos can only be used for trading small sizes, as it is almost impossible to get significant depth in the ECN market.

The main algos used in our analysis are:

- *VWAP* (*Volume-Weighted Average Price*) is one of the most popular algos as it aims to match the order execution schedule with the daily trading volume (DTV) pattern. The intuition behind this strategy is that if the intensity of the order submission schedule is synchronized with the period of highest liquidity in the market, then it is likely that transaction costs will be lower on aggregate. Because the DTV pattern is usually U-shaped, this algo spawns the majority of trades within the first and last few hours of the day. Of course, this strategy makes sense only if the order size is large, with precarious market impact. Typically, trades larger than 10% of the average daily traded volume (ADTV) are executed through this algo. If, on the contrary, the order size is small (below 5%) relative to the usual traded volume, then shorter execution horizons are much more reasonable to adopt. A VWAP model typically uses a simple historical average of the fractional volume to forecast the daily trading volume. As this estimate can be very noisy, especially in the case of illiquid stocks, the actual volume pattern of the day may substantially differ from it. Most importantly, this algo cannot be used on trades motivated by public information (e.g. news releases, earnings surprises, etc.), as in that case the immediacy of execution is of paramount importance for market participants. By contrast, it is widely utilized by traders with private information and passive fund managers.

- The objective of the *Time-Weighted Average Price* (*TWAP*) strategy is to minimize market impact costs preserving a constant rate of trading over the execution period. It is the simplest strategy to implement and, in its basic form, it only breaks a large (market) parent order into smaller ones, executing them at a constant rate throughout the execution period. Sometimes, to further improve execution quality, this strategy places limit instead of market orders to obtain more favorable prices.
- The *Participation* strategy is based on maintaining a trading rate as a constant fraction of the market's total trading rate during the execution period. However, this strategy is unable to guarantee a target fill quantity, as it does not use a trading schedule. Effectively, this algo submits market orders proportional to the observed trading volume. The main advantage of this strategy is that it can closely track and follow the actual trading volume pattern, unlike a VWAP strategy which only uses an estimate. However, *Participation* algos cause on average higher market impact costs as they end up placing fewer and larger market orders.
- *Market-on-Close* attracts traders or portfolio managers, who minimize risk-adjusted costs relative to the closing price of the day. Often, these traders try to manipulate (game) the close price to make their execution seem good. For instance, they may choose to trade aggressively near the close of the day in their effort to make the closing price to equal to their trade print[1]. In general this algo is not very efficient in terms of market impact.
- The *Implementation Shortfall* strategy minimizes risk-adjusted costs based on the arrival price as a benchmark. According to the IS strategy, a risk-

averse trader would execute all the target quantity the moment he arrives in the market, if the market impact (implementation shortfall) was zero. Otherwise, he will have to consider different market/limit order trajectories. The algo assesses alternative trading schedules and chooses the one that appears to optimize the loss-function. The feasible region of solutions usually incorporates both front-weighted and back-weighted order schedules. (IS) strategy adjusts its aggressiveness based on real-time market movement, that is it increases or decreases the rate of execution depending on the short-term movement of the stock price,

- *At Open* strategy aims to achieve the opening price. If the required liquidity exceeds the volume traded in the opening call market, the remaining order size is executed through a sequence of limit orders set at the opening price. This means that the execution of the entire order size is not guaranteed.
- *Tap* algo seeks optimal execution in both displayed and non-displayed venues simultaneously, including ECNs and alternative platforms . It generates a sequence of market, limit and tick-sensitive orders gauging the currently available liquidity of the market at around the bid-ask quotes of the market.
- *Tap Now* strategy is the most aggressive variant of Tap and aims to opportunistically draw liquidity from all possible sources, while optimizing and adjusting the rate of execution, based on price and market impact. This strategy targets completion over minimizing price impact and has no volume limit. It posts in all accessible non-displayed venues and always requires a price limit.
- *Perimeter* strategy enables trading outside of regular US market hours by controlling the urgency of the order.

LITERATURE REVIEW

The literature about the measurement of transaction costs predated the explosion of algorithmic trading by almost a decade, setting up the optimization problem that automated strategies were devised to solve.

On Transaction Cost Metrics

In one of the earliest attempts in the field, Collins and Fabozzi (1991) review the definition of trading costs and introduce a framework for evaluating the transaction process in depth. Specifically, they define different categories of costs (execution, opportunity, implementation, market timing and implied execution costs, market impact) and different methodologies for measuring them (pre-trade, post-trade and intra-day) using the appropriate price benchmarks. As case study, the authors present a total cost comparison between the actual portfolio and an investor's desired portfolio, as well as a stock summary report that can help a portfolio manager identify stocks that are difficult to trade. Overall, the authors emphasize the importance of analyzing the trade execution costs when assessing the transaction process.

To further strengthen this point, Keim (2003) incorporate transaction costs into the implementation of momentum, size and value strategies. Analyzing the costs of the three investment styles, he finds that the momentum strategy costs are conditional on prior price movements. Most importantly, he indicates that conditional costs can be orders-of-magnitude higher than the unconditional ones. As a result, the reported average returns of simulated strategies may not be sufficient to cover the costs of their implementation in most cases.

On the Asymmetry of Transaction Costs

Another popular theme in the transaction cost literature is the asymmetry of transaction costs within the same market. Chan and Lakonishok (1993) in their paper, examine the effect of stock trading on prices and show that the magnitude of this effect is small on average. Among all other determinants of price impact, Chan and Lakonishok (1993) argue that the identity of the money manager and of his investment style is the most influential. The authors attribute price pressure to mostly institutional trading and document a significant buy/sell asymmetry in the implicit transaction cost of market orders. In their analysis of the post-trade behavior of prices, they conclude that sell orders reflect short-run liquidity, whereas buy orders reflect either information effects or inelastic excess demand curves. Specifically, they show that the price impact of sell orders is usually indicative of a temporary discount, whereas buy-orders have a distinctly more permanent effect on price levels.

Chiyachantana et al. (2004) examine the same asymmetry using international data that span both a bullish (January 1997 to March 1998) and a bearish (January to September 2001) periods. In contrast to previous papers, they suggest that the buy-sell asymmetry in transaction costs is not necessarily caused by the superior information content of buy orders but is rather a product of the causal relationship between liquidity and transaction costs. Indeed, they find that in rising markets buys tend have higher market impact than sells, simply because these orders demand even more liquidity from the side that is lacking. In falling markets, the opposite holds further corroborating the short-term liquidity explanation. In addition, they state that this buy-sell asymmetry depends also on order characteristics, firm-specific factors and cross-country differences. For instance, they find that price impact is negatively correlated with prices and market capitalization. Trading costs are relatively higher for emerging and non-liberalized markets or for markets with poor shareholder rights.

Hu (2009) also reconciles the two perspectives by focusing on the benchmark used for measuring the market impact. He finds that when a trader uses pre-trade measures, buy orders seem to have higher implicit trading costs during rising markets. By contrast, post-trade measures show the opposite, that is sell-orders as having the higher implicit trading costs during rising markets. Given that both types of measures are highly influenced by market movements, the author suggests the use of during-trade measures, such as VWAP, which are neutral to market movements.

On Strategies to Optimize Execution

Keim and Madhavan (1995) analyze the behavior of institutional traders by examining their motives, determinants of trade duration and the choice of order type. In particular, they found a link between the buy-or-sell decision and past excess returns. For instance, they indicate that as order size and market liquidity increase, trade duration increases too, while they also confirm the buy-sell asymmetry, in that buy orders tend to have higher duration than sell. Finally, they also show that institutions with different investment strategies tend to choose different order types, e.g. index trackers use more often than not market orders.

In a follow-up paper, (Keim & Madhavan, 1997), the same researchers analyze the determinants and magnitude of transaction costs. Using data that include distinct investment styles (technical, index, value) they find that costs vary with trader-specific factors, reflecting differences in trading ability, trade difficulty and market liquidity. In their sample, Value Traders mainly use limit orders and have negative implicit costs when they sell exchange-listed stocks, while technical traders have the greatest demand for liquidity and rely on market orders. In addition, market impact appears to be low in liquid stocks with large market capitalization and relatively stable. By contrast, total costs tend to rise with trade size for small-cap stocks in a nonlinear fashion. Finally, the paper notes that trade initiation and exchange listing affect trading costs.

Bikker et al. (2007) make a similar analysis examining the market impact costs of one of the largest pension funds in the world. Their results show that market impact costs depend on momentum, volatility, trade type (agency/single or principal), trading strategy, trading venue, sector and timing. Intuitively enough, longer-duration trades appear to have lower market impact costs despite exhibiting higher volatility. Also, trades that demand immediate liquidity have higher costs, but less uncertainty.

Transaction Costs and Trade Facilitators

Conrad et al. (2001) focus on brokers and divide trades into two categories. The first category consists of orders that are directed to "soft-dollar" brokers, that is, brokers that execute trades and provide other, non-execution-related services. The second, is comprised only of execution-only orders. The paper shows that institutional customers base their choice of broker type on trade difficulty and investment style. Furthermore, it estimates the shadow price for soft dollar payments to be approximately equal to 23 basis points, although these costs vary across traders.

Domowitz et al. (2001) study the interaction between cost, liquidity and volatility. Specifically, they analyze a panel data from 47 countries finding significant variation across countries. The paper highlights a trend according to which, risk-averse traders shift their trading forum preferences towards crossing networks, automated limit order book systems and guaranteed principal bids, so as to make the market impact of their trade more predictable. Most importantly, they show that the composition of globally efficient portfolios changes substantially, once transaction costs and turnover are included in the optimization problem.

Finally, Conrad et al. (2003) focus on the use of alternative trading systems. The authors classify orders into those directed to crossing systems, electronic communication networks and traditional brokers. Unsurprisingly, they find evidence that transaction costs are higher when orders are executed by traditional brokers. In their sample, crossing systems have the lowest fill rate, but have also the lowest transaction costs, after ECNs. Finally, they note that both the 1997 order handling rules and the change in tick sizes played a crucial role in the reduction ECNs' advantages.

DATA

The data sample used in this study contains information on the equity transactions of two long/short hedge fund for the period 05/02/2014 – 12/09/2017. It includes records of 372,930 trades such as order identifiers, security name, sector, trade date, duration, strategy, region, order quantity, arrival and execution price, excluding limit orders and OTC trades. Also, additional data about prices, market capitalization, volume, shares outstanding, exchange rates and market indices etc. for the respective period have been obtained from Capital IQ and Bloomberg. The dataset spans transactions from 16 countries including USA, UK, Greece, Switzerland, Australia, Japan, Singapore, Hong Kong, France etc. Following the hedge-funds' practice, we divide the sample into 6 regions: Europe, Australia, Japan, U.K., the USA and Asia excluding Japan (i.e. Hong Kong and Singapore). For each of these regions, we use the respective market indices[2]. The fund used during that period two different prime brokers. Both of them are regarded as among the largest in the market of algorithmic trading

EMPIRICAL RESULTS AND DISCUSSION

Measurement of Implicit Transaction Costs and Summary Statistics

For each trade in our dataset we estimate Prior Close cost, VWAP cost, Close cost as well as Average cost. The latter is an intraday measure that captures volatility, and is defined as the average of High, Low, Open and Close prices for each security on a given day.

Following Hu (2009), we decompose Prior Close cost and Close cost into two common components: a VWAP cost component and a Market Movement cost component.

$$\text{Prior Close Cost} = \text{VWAP Cost} + \text{Market Movement Cost Prior Close to VWAP} \langle = \rangle \left(\text{Side}*\frac{P_E - \text{Prior Close}}{P_E}\right) = \left(\text{Side}*\frac{P_E - \text{VWAP}}{P_E}\right) + \left(\text{Side}*\frac{\text{VWAP} - \text{Prior Close}}{P_E}\right) \quad (2)$$

$$\text{Close Cost} = \text{VWAP Cost} - \text{Market Movement Cost VWAP to Close} \langle = \rangle \left(\text{Side}*\frac{P_E - \text{Close}}{P_E}\right) = \left(\text{Side}*\frac{P_E - \text{VWAP}}{P_E}\right) - \left(\text{Side}*\frac{\text{Close} - \text{VWAP}}{P_E}\right) \quad (3)$$

As equations (2) and (3) show, prior close cost is equal to VWAP cost plus market movement cost prior close to VWAP and close cost is equal to VWAP cost minus market movement cost VWAP to close.

We also define Prior Close cost Net of Market Index Movement (PCNMIM)

$$\text{PCNMIM} = \text{Prior Close Cost} - \text{Market Index Movement} \Leftrightarrow$$

$$= \left(\text{Side}*\frac{P_E - \text{Prior Close}}{P_E}\right) - \left(\text{Side}*\frac{\text{Close} - \text{Prior Close}}{\text{Prior Close}}\right) \quad (3)$$

In Table 1, we present descriptive statistics of the implicit trading cost measures and of their components. We can see that all measures are fairly symmetric around their medians with significantly fat tails. As expected, the Prior Close cost is much higher in magnitude than VWAP cost, as the latter constitutes only one of the former's constituents. For instance, the median (mean) of prior close cost is equal to 15.08 bps (44.82 bps), while the median (mean) of VWAP cost equals 6.73 bps (39.15 bps). The Close cost metric provides the lowest-in-magnitude measurement

Table 1. Descriptive statistics of measures of implicit transaction costs and market index movement

Percentile	Prior Close Cost (bps)	VWAP Cost (bps)	Close cost (bps)	Average Cost (bps)	Prior close cost net of market index movement (bps)	Market Movement Cost Prior close to VWAP (bps)	Market Movement Cost VWAP to Close (bps)	Market Index Movement (bps)
Mean	44.82	39.15	32.19	0.68	44.89	7.40	6.33	-4.045
Std Deviation	116.29	34.72	46.07	177.43	107.11	47.22	82.10	64.76
10th	-222.78	-60.18	-95.60	-466.17	-226.65	-95.20	-206.23	-147.53
25th	-79.45	-17.07	-31.01	-199.47	-92.21	-38.37	-80.7657	-65.19
Median	15.08	6.73	0	8.19	5.79	1.98	17.084	-3.73
75th	122.07	37.85	42.10	218.28	109.65	46.59	120.69	50.27
90th	277.90	92.96	116.49	451.39	249.87	109.66	261.95	142.92

with a median (mean) equal to 0 bps (32.19 bps). Also, the median (mean) of the Market Index Movement is equal to -4.04 bps (-3.74 bps).

This table presents the percentiles as well as the mean and the standard deviation of implicit trading cost measures and their components, all measured in basis points. All trading costs are measure in basis points.

Our dataset includes orders from 6 different algorithmic trading strategies: VWAP (48% of total), At Open (21%), Implementation Shortfall (11%), TWAP (8%), Tap/ Tap Now (7%) and Perimeter (5%). The trading horizon is defined in all cases to be equal to one day. In other words, all the orders we consider in our sample were executed within the same day that they were submitted to the broker.

In Table 2, we present a few summary statistics of transaction orders such as the number of transactions, the principal and the shares traded as well as the average magnitude of explicit (i.e. commissions) and implicit trading cost measures and their components. These statistics describe all the transactions of our sample and are distinguished into buy and sell orders. The whole sample includes 372,930 orders (192,479 buys and 180,451 sells), 479.96 million shares traded (241.33 million shares bought, and 238.67 million shares sold). These correspond to a dollar value of $2,229.8 million traded ($1,188.3 million in buy and $1,041.7 million in sell orders) in 11,831 different equities.

Consistent with Hu (2009), we observe that commissions do not exhibit a significant buy-sell asymmetry, being on average around 5.15 bps. Also in line with previous studies, our findings show that the implicit trading costs for sell orders are higher than for buy orders, in all cases. For example, implicit costs range from 32.19 bps (-83.05 bps for buys and 147.24 bps for sells) for close cost to 44.82 bps (-86.49 bps for buys and 175.85 bps for sells) for prior close cost, on average, while

Table 2. Descriptive statistics

Side	N	$ Principal Traded (M)	Shares Traded (M)	Commissions (bps)	Prior Close Cost (bps)	VWAP Cost (bps)	Close cost (bps)	Average Cost (bps)	Prior close cost net of market index movement (bps)	Market Movement Cost Prior close to VWAP (bps)	Market Movement Cost VWAP to Close (bps)	Market Index Movement (bps)
All	372,930	2,229.8	479.96	5.15	44.82	39.15	32.19	0.68	44.89	7.40	6.33	-4.04
Buys	192,479	1,188.1	241.33	5.06	-86.49	-72.38	-83.05	1296.74	-82.40	-13.91	11.19	-4.11
Sells	180,451	1,041.7	238.66	5.21	175.85	147.20	147.24	-1295.66	171.89	28.07	0.90	-3.97

VWAP cost ranges in between, with an average of 39.15 bps (-72.38 bps for buys and 147.20 bps for sells). In addition, the prior close cost that is net of market index movement has an average of 44.89 bps (-82.40 bps or buys and 171.89 bps for sells).

This table presents a few summary statistics of transaction orders as well as of trading costs and their components. The principal traded is expressed in millions of US dollars and the shares traded in millions. The transaction costs are measured in basis points.

In Table 3, we further decompose the above statistics into two segments of stock return magnitude (high/low), as that was recorded on the trade date. Following Hu (2009) again, we set the cutoff points at -2% and 2%. The first segment includes high return stocks ($Ri \leq -2\%$ or $Ri > 2\%$) and the second includes low return stocks ($Ri > -2\%$ or $Ri \leq 2\%$). We observe almost the same pattern as in the case of using all the sample. Commissions do exhibit buy-sell asymmetry in either case and sell orders have higher implicit trading costs than buy orders in all cases. What is intriguing is the fact that commissions of high movement stocks are lower by about 0.77 bps on average, whereas implicit trading costs are lower in low movement stocks. VWAP cost for instance is equal to 47.67 bps for low movement stocks and 15.93 bps for high movement stocks.

This table presents a few summary statistics of transaction orders as well as of trading costs and their components, like in the previous table (2), but each measure is divided into two categories: a high movement category which includes stocks with return $Ri \leq -2\%$ or $Ri > 2\%$ and a low movement category which includes stocks with return $R_i > -2\%$ or $Ri \leq 2\%$ during the trading horizon. It is defined that the trading horizon is always one day. The principal traded is expressed in millions of US dollars and the shares traded in millions. The transaction costs are measured in basis points.

Table 3. Descriptive statistics with stocks' return segmentation

Specific Return During the Trading Horizon	Side	N	$ Principal Traded (M)	Shares Traded (M)	Commissions (bps)	Prior Close Cost (bps)	VWAP Cost (bps)	Close cost (bps)	Average Cost (bps)	Prior close cost net of market index movement (bps)	Market Movement Cost Prior close to VWAP (bps)	Market Movement Cost VWAP to Close (bps)	Market Index Movement (bps)
High Movement	All	72,763	570.02	109.81	4.61	32.70	15.93	3.24	-25.38	29.233	17.01	12.53	6.31
Ri ≤ -2%	Buys	36,229	284.34	55.60	4.59	-254.67	-225.56	-242.34	1332.97	-253.96	-26.49	17.16	4.43
or Ri > 2%	Sells	36,534	285.67	54.20	4.63	316.78	254.65	246.01	-1368.12	309.17	60.02	7.95	2.58
Low Movement	All	300,167	1,658.93	170.18	5.38	50.39	47.67	45.88	13.16	52.15	2.31	2.94	1.06
R_i > -2%	Buys	155,250	773.94	85.72	5.28	-6.64	0.32	-7.44	1279.53	-0.96	-7.94	8.35	0.41
or Ri ≤ 2%	Sells	144,917	885.88	84.46	5.49	107.78	95.29	99.53	-1260.66	105.58	12.64	-2.50	0.79

Panel Decomposition Regressions of Implicit Transaction Costs with Fixed Effects

In Table 4, we perform decomposition regressions of implicit trading costs, where each cost measure is regressed separately on each of its components.

At first, we run unbalanced panel regressions using all the sample and then divide the sample into two segments: the first segment, like in the previous section, includes high-return stocks and the second one includes the low-return ones. We use different equities as cross-section identifiers and allow each equity to have its own intercept (fixed effects). Also, all standard errors are robust to heteroskedasticity and autocorrelation being clustered by stock. We focus only in the R-squares in order to capture the importance of each component. In contrast to Hu (2009), who showed that the dominant is the market movement cost component and thus prior close cost can be approximated without knowing the execution price, in our sample we observe that dominant is the VWAP cost component. Specifically, we show that prior close cost and close cost depend mostly on VWAP cost (R^2 = 98.88% and R^2 = 99.87% respectively) with the slope coefficient being close to one. In addition, the findings, when we divide the sample into high and low movement, reinforce the previous results. Thus, we conclude that prior close and close cost can be approximated with high accuracy by VWAP cost.

This table presents panel decomposition regressions of implicit trading costs with fixed effects, where each cost measure is regressed separately on each of its components. First, we run regressions using all the sample. At the second stage, we divide the sample into two segments: the first segment, includes stocks with high movement and the second one includes stocks with low movement during the

Table 4. Panel decomposition regressions of implicit transaction costs with fixed effects

	Dependent Variables	Intercept	Market Movement Cost Prior close to VWAP (bps)	Market Movement Cost VWAP to Close (bps)	VWAP Cost (bps)	R^2
All	Prior Close Cost (bps)	5.81*** (0.19)	-	-	1.019*** (0.00)	0.98
		25.69*** (8.91)	2.70** (1.20)	-	-	0.07
	Close Cost (bps)	-5.03*** (0.13)			0.98*** (0.00)	0.99
		18.26 (17.95)		-3.31 (3.86)		0.03
High Movement	Prior Close Cost (bps)	15.93*** (0.16)	-	-	1.026*** (0.01)	0.98
$R_i \leq -2\%$ or $R_i > 2\%$		2.07 (7.66)	1.74*** (0.43)			0.16
	Close Cost (bps)	-11.66*** (0.04)	-	-	0.99*** (0.00)	0.99
		6.88 (10.51)	-	0.19 (1.00)	-	0.09
Low Movement	Prior Close Cost (bps)	2.19*** (0.14)			0.99*** (0.00)	0.99
$R_i > -2\%$ or $R_i \leq 2\%$		50.75*** (0.76)	0.47 (0.31)			0.07
	Close Cost (bps)	-2.16*** (0.12)			0.99*** (0.00)	0.99
		48.65*** (0.45)		0.54** (0.24)		0.06

trading horizon. The dependent variables are prior close cost and close cost and the independent variable is either VWAP cost or one of the two market movement costs. Trading costs are expressed in basis points and standard errors are clustered by equity and are presented in parentheses below each coefficient. We allow each equity to have its own intercept (fixed effects). R-squares are also presented for each regression. Statistical significance is indicated by *** for the 1% level, ** for the 5% level and * for the 10% level.

Panel Regression Analysis of Implicit Transaction Costs with Fixed Effects

We analyze how various factors can affect trading costs. Specifically, we run multiple unbalanced panel regressions using Prior Close cost, VWAP cost and Close cost as dependent variables and, as independent variables, factors that have been identified affecting trading costs. As in 6.2, we use stock-fixed effects. All standard errors are again clustered by equity.

Follow previous studies (e.g. Keim & Madhavan, 1995, 1997, 1998, 2003; Domowitz et al., 1999, 2001; Conrad et al., 2001, 2003; Bikker et al., 2007; Chiyachantana et al., 2007; Hu, 2009) we use the following variables as possible determinants of the implicit transaction cost:

- *Buy indicator* (1 for buy orders and 0 for sell orders).
- The natural logarithm of *market capitalization*.
- The natural logarithm of *relative volume*. The latter is measured as the executed quantity divided by the average trading volume over the 5 previous trading days.
- *Inverse prior close price*.
- *Return volatility* of stock returns over the 10 previous trading days (bps).
- *Price momentum* measured as the volume-weighted average daily stock return over the last 5 trading days prior to the trade (%) to examine if there is a buying or selling trend for a specific equity.
- *Sided market index return*. This is the market index return during the trading horizon (multiplied by -1 for sell orders), which aims to control for the market movement during the trade.
- *Duration* of the trade, from the start time of each trade until the end time, measured in seconds.

In addition, we include a dummy variable for each region (Europe, USA, UK, Australia and Japan, excluding AEXJP because intercept is included), as well as a dummy variable for each algorithmic trading strategy (VWAP, TWAP, Tap, At-Open, IS, excluding Perimeter). In table 5, we present the results of the above-mentioned regressions.

This table presents an analysis of how various factors affect transaction costs using multiple unbalanced panel regressions with fixed effects. The dependent variables are prior close cost, VWAP cost and close cost, all expressed in basis points. As independent variables we use the following: buy indicator, log(market capitalization), log(relative volume), inverse prior close, return volatility expressed in basis points, price momentum, VWAP strategy dummy, tap strategy dummy, at open strategy dummy, perimeter strategy dummy, IS strategy dummy, sided market

Table 5. Panel regression analysis of implicit transaction costs with fixed effects

	Prior Close Cost (bps)	VWAP Cost (bps)	Close Cost (bps)
Intercept	-4,236.2* (2,263.4)	-4,077.9* (2,203.0)	-4,077.9* (2,203.0)
Buy indicator	-250.8*** (93.3)	-227.4** (95.5)	-226.3** (95.5)
Log (market capitalization)	612.6* (321.0)	581.1* (312.0)	549.3* (312.0)
Log (relative volume)	0.9*** (0.0)	0.9*** (0.0)	0.9*** (0.0)
Inverse Prior Close	296.7* (156.1)	267.2* (149.5)	267.2* (149.5)
Return Volatility (bps)	0.0 (0.0)	0.1 (0.1)	0.1 (0.1)
Price momentum	1,202.1* (719.3)	1,164.8 (736.5)	1,164.8 (736.5)
VWAP Strategy Dummy	132.1** (66.0)	184.5*** (70.3)	174.3*** (66.5)
Tap Strategy Dummy	79.1 (54.0)	121.1** (58.1)	121.0** (58.1)
At Open Strategy Dummy	39.4 (41.4)	66.1 (46.7)	66.1 (46.7)
Perimeter Strategy Dummy	90.5 (55.1)	134.2** (59.2)	134.2** (59.2)
IS Strategy Dummy	68.4 (50.3)	110.0** (55.0)	110.0** (55.0)
Sided Market Index Return	3,320.2 (2,866.4)	-3,569.1 (3,012.6)	-3,569.1 (3,012.6)
Duration (seconds)	-0.0** (0.0)	-0.0** (0.0)	-0.0** (0.0)
R^2 (overall)	0.11	0.09	0.07
Number of Observations	372,930	372,930	372,930
Number of Clusters	11,763	11,763	11,763

index return during the trading horizon expressed in basis points (multiplied by -1 for sell orders) and duration in seconds. The regional dummy variables were omitted because of multicollinearity. Standard errors are clustered by equity and are presented in parentheses below each coefficient. We allow each equity to have its own intercept (fixed effects). Overall R-squares, the number of observations and the number of clusters are also presented for each regression. Statistical significance is indicated by *** for the 1% level, ** for the 5% level and * for the 10% level. The exact definition of each variable is presented in section 5.3.

As shown in the above table, the common factors that are statistically significant are the following: buy indicator, market capitalization, relative volume, inverse prior close, VWAP and duration. In addition, Tap, TWAP and IS strategies are statistically significant in VWAP cost and close cost regressions, while price momentum is only in prior close cost regression. As expected, the signs of the variables are the same among the 3 regressions, while only the buy indicator and the duration are negatively related to transaction costs. Thus, an increase in market capitalization, relative volume and inverse prior close increases transaction costs, whereas an increase in duration decreases costs. The buy indicator shows that sell orders present higher transaction costs, that is buy orders indicate lower mean transaction costs than sell orders by 250.8 bps, 227.4 bps and 226.3 bps respectively for each of the 3 regressions. Also, by examining the algorithmic trading strategies used, we observe that the use of VWAP, Tap, TWAP and IS strategies increase transaction costs with VWAP presenting the highest increment (for instance 184.57 bps more than the other strategies in VWAP cost regression). What is unexpected is the fact that return volatility and market index return do not affect transaction costs, while the region dummies are omitted because of multi-collinearity.

Our findings are consistent with previous research. For instance, Keim and Madhavan (1997) showed positive relation of transaction costs with trade size and inverse price and negative relation with market capitalization. Conrad et al. (2001) reported positive slope coefficients of trade size and inverse price, and negative for the buy indicator. Chiyachantana et al. (2004) found a negative relation of transaction costs the trade direction (buy indicator) when market was bearish, and a positive relation one when the market was bullish with the inverse stock price, the complexity of decision and volatility. Hu (2009) found that costs are negatively related to buy and to sided market index return and sided stock return, while they are positively related to market capitalization, relative volume, inverse prior close and return volatility.

Out-of-Sample Forecast of Implicit Transaction Costs

In the last section of our empirical analysis, we perform a forecasting exercise to assess the robustness of our in-sample findings. Specifically, we test the predictive power of the 3 models, without including duration and market index movement, since these two variables are not known before the trade has taken place.

We start by running stepwise regressions (via the forward entry method) using the two thirds of the sample, that is until 09/05/2016, as shown in Table 6. We end up with a model that includes only the slope coefficients that are statistically significant at the 1% level. Using the estimated model, we forecast the transaction costs of the next trade batch (set of trades that were executed within a single day).

The clock is reset. We re-estimate our model moving our sample forward to include the last batch of trades, that is, the one that was not included in the sample during the previous iteration. We perform the forecasting step for the next trade batch, and we repeat this procedure until we reach the end of our dataset along the time dimension (12/09/2017).

Table 6. Out-of-sample forecast of implicit transaction costs

	Prior Close Cost (bps)	VWAP Cost (bps)	Close Cost (bps)
Intercept	182.7*** (22.2)	162.3*** (22.6)	154.0*** (21.5)
Buy indicator	-263.7*** (31.5)	-234.7 *** (32.1)	-231.4*** (30.4)
Log (market capitalization)	-	-	-
Log (relative volume)	1.0*** (0.1)	1.0*** (0.1)	1.0*** (0.1)
Inverse Prior Close	-	-	-
Return Volatility (bps)	-	-	-
Price momentum	-	-	-
Europe dummy	-	-	-
USA dummy	-	-	-
UK dummy	-	-	-
Australia dummy	-	-	-
Japan dummy	-	-	-
VWAP Dummy	-	-	-
Tap/Tap Now Dummy	-	-	-
At Open Dummy	-	-	-
TWAP Dummy	-	-	-
IS Dummy	-	-	-
Sided Market Index Return	-	-	-
Duration (seconds)	-	-	-
R^2 (overall)	0.018	0.018	0.018
Number of Observations	172,930	172,930	172,930
Mean Squared Errors (MSE)	45.26	41.71	42.65
Forecast of the Respective Naïve Models (Mean of Transaction Costs)	48.8	44.4	36.5
Mean Squared Errors (MSE) of the Respective Naïve Models	45.72	42.11	42.99

We also use three naïve models as benchmarks - one for each type of cost measure (prior cost, VWAP cost, close cost). These models assume that transaction costs are always equal to the mean value up to that point. We calculate the mean squared errors (MSE) to compare the realized with the forecasted values.

In Table 6, we present the forecasting models as these were estimated on the first step of the iterative procedure. Overall, we see that in terms of MSE, the forecasting models outperform their naïve benchmarks, even though their R^2s are not particularly high. Among the three regressions, VWAP cost has the lowest MSE, and thus the better accuracy.

This table presents an analysis the first batch of models we used for forecasting ITCs. In this case, we employ stepwise regressions with the forward entry method on the 2/3s of the sample in order to forecast the next batch of trades that took place within the same day. The dependent variables are prior close cost, VWAP cost and close cost, all expressed in basis points. Independent variables were picked from the following set: buy indicator, log(market capitalization), log(relative volume), inverse prior close, return volatility expressed in basis points, price momentum, Europe dummy, USA dummy, UK dummy, Australia dummy, Japan dummy, VWAP strategy dummy, tap strategy dummy, at open strategy dummy, perimeter strategy dummy and IS strategy dummy. In the forecasting model, we use only the coefficients that are statistically significant in the 1% level. Then, we estimate the mean squared errors of each prediction to gauge its quality. Standard errors are presented in parentheses below each coefficient. R-squares and the number of observations are also presented for each regression. Statistical significance is indicated by *** for the 1% level, ** for the 5% level and * for the 10% level. The exact definition of each variable is presented in section 5.3.

To provide further insight into the distributional properties of the all forecasting errors for all the out-of-sample trade batches, we report the descriptive statistics of their absolute values in Table 7. It is easy to see, that in all three cases the forecasting model stochastically-dominates its naïve benchmark in the first-order sense.

This table presents the mean, the standard deviation and 5 percentiles of the absolute forecast errors of the 6 previously mentioned prediction models.

In addition, in Table 8, we present the descriptive statistics of the forecasted and of the realized transaction costs. We see that the mean and variance of the forecasted ITCs are in general lower than the respective moments of the realized ITCs. However, the comparison of the forecasting models with their naïve benchmarks shows that the former have significant predictive power that can be exploited for constructing optimal execution strategies at a higher than the algo level.

This table presents the mean, the standard deviation and 5 percentiles of the forecasted and the realized transaction costs, except for the three naïve models

Table 7. Descriptive statistics of absolute forecast errors

	Absolute Forecast Errors of Prior Close Cost (bps)	Absolute Forecast Errors of VWAP Cost (bps)	Absolute Forecast Errors of Close Cost (bps)	Absolute Forecast Errors of Prior Close Cost (bps) (naïve model)	Absolute Forecast Errors of VWAP Cost (bps) (naïve model)	Absolute Forecast Errors of Close Cost (bps) (naïve model)
Mean	154.2	69.5	89.9	160.6	77.1	100.8
Standard Deviation	646.4	634.0	638.4	656.8	644.3	647.8
10th Percentile	15.6	12.0	9.9	16.5	12.9	11.7
25th Percentile	40.8	25.7	28.3	42.1	27.8	28.8
Median	88.5	44.2	45.3	89.3	44.4	49.4
75th Percentile	165.6	58.4	91.0	178.7	61.2	97.7
90th Percentile	301.1	108.9	184.4	316.8	102.5	176.6

Table 8. Descriptive statistics of forecasted and realized implicit transaction costs

	Forecasted Prior Close Cost (bps)	Forecasted VWAP Cost (bps)	Forecasted Close Cost (bps)	Prior Close Cost (bps)	VWAP Cost (bps)	Close Cost (bps)
Mean	16.3	20.2	13.5	28.8	17.9	15.0
Standard Deviation	61.9	27.4	75.7	76.2	35.0	85.7
10th Percentile	-89.4	-30.9	-85.9	-180.1	-42.5	-99.9
25th Percentile	-47.2	-8.7	-23.7	-64.1	-11.2	-34.5
Median	7.0	5.5	2.2	13.5	6.2	0
75th Percentile	76.5	26.0	47.7	103.6	29.4	48.0
90th Percentile	178.8	58.4	150.1	233.0	72.0	117.8

according to which transaction costs are always equal to the mean value of the realized transaction costs, for the period 09/05/2016 - 28/07/2017.

CONCLUSION

In this paper, we presented an overview of the transaction costs taxonomy and of the most popular algorithmic trading strategies.

We empirically examined the transaction of two small-sized hedge funds active in long-short equity trading. Our in-sample results showed that sell orders have higher transaction costs than buy orders, as Hu (2008) and other previous studies have documented before us. Breaking the sample into trades coinciding with high/low stock return magnitude we corroborated the presence of this buy-sell asymmetry.

Being in line with previous literature, we searched for the determinants of Implicit Transaction Costs (ITCs) among variables, such as market capitalization, relative volume, return volatility, inverse prior close, duration as well as the choice of the chosen execution strategy (algo).

Finally, we tested out-of-sample the predictive power of the regression models, by running one-step ahead stepwise forecasting regressions on the 1/3 of the sample. Comparison of the three more models with their respective naïve benchmarks showed that a significant part of ITCs can be predicted a priori. This finding is very significant because it implies that execution strategies can be constructed at a level higher than the level of the algo. In other words, one can optimize the choice of the appropriate algo using the forecasted ITCs.

Future research may seek to confirm our evidence in larger datasets of transactions. At the same time, it is possible that non-linear specifications (with the possible use of machine learning models) could better forecast ITCs to use for the construction of efficient execution strategies.

ACKNOWLEDGMENTS

We would like to thank Mr. Nikolaos Mamakos, the CEO of SilentSeas Group, Mr. Dimitrios Dimakos and Mr. Nikolaos Rentoumis from the Operations and Risk Management Department of SilentSeas S.A. for their support.

REFERENCES

Beebower, G., & Priest, W. (1980). The tricks of the trade. *Journal of Portfolio Management*, *6*(2), 36–42. doi:10.3905/jpm.1980.408739

Berkowitz, S. A., Logue, D. E., & Noser, E. A. Jr. (1988). The total costs of transacting on the NYSE. *The Journal of Finance*, *43*(1), 97–112. doi:10.1111/j.1540-6261.1988.tb02591.x

Bikker, J. A., Spierdijk, L., & van der Sluis, P. J. (2007). Market Impact Costs of Institutional Equity Trades. *Journal of International Money and Finance*, *26*(6), 974–1000. doi:10.1016/j.jimonfin.2007.01.007

Bodie, Z., Kane, A., & Marcus, A. (2014). *Investments*. New York: McGraw-Hill Education.

Chan, L. K. C., & Lakonishok, J. (1993). Institutional Trades and Intraday Stock Price Behavior. *Journal of Financial Economics*, *33*(2), 173–199. doi:10.1016/0304-405X(93)90003-T

Chiyachantana, C. N., Jain, P. K., Jiang, C., & Wood, R. A. (2004). International evidence on institutional trading behavior and price impact. *The Journal of Finance*, *59*(2), 869–898. doi:10.1111/j.1540-6261.2004.00651.x

Collins, B. M., & Fabozzi, F. J. (1991). A Methodology for Measuring Transaction Costs. *Financial Analysts Journal*, *47*(2), 27–36. doi:10.2469/faj.v47.n2.27

Conrad, J. S., Johnson, K. M., & Wahal, S. (2001). Institutional trading and soft dollars. *The Journal of Finance*, *56*(1), 397–416. doi:10.1111/0022-1082.00331

Conrad, J. S., Johnson, K. M., & Wahal, S. (2003). Institutional trading and alternative trading systems. *Journal of Financial Economics*, *70*(1), 99–134. doi:10.1016/S0304-405X(03)00143-0

Domowitz, I., Glen, J., & Madhavan, A. (1999). *International Equity Trading Costs: A Cross-Sectional and Time-Series Analysis. Technical Report*. Pennsylvania State University, International Finance Corp., University of Southern California.

Domowitz, I., Glen, J., & Madhavan, A. (2001). Liquidity, volatility and equity trading costs across countries and over time. *International Finance*, *4*(2), 221–255. doi:10.1111/1468-2362.00072

Fabozzi, F. J., Focardi, S. M., & Kolm, P. N. (2010). *Quantitative Equity Investing: Techniques and Strategies*. Hoboken, NJ: John Wiley & Sons.

Fabozzi, F. J., & Markowitz, H. M. (2011). *The Theory and Practice of Investment Management*. Hoboken, NJ: John Wiley & Sons. doi:10.1002/9781118267028

Gang, H. (2009). Measures of Implicit Trading Costs and Buy-Sell Asymmetry. *Journal of Financial Markets*, *12*(3), 418–437. doi:10.1016/j.finmar.2009.03.002

Gujarati, D. N., & Porter, D. C. (2009). *Basic Econometrics*. Irwin, NY: McGraw-Hill.

Harris, L. (2015). *Trading and Electronic Markets: What Investment Professionals Need to Know*. CFA Institute Research Foundation Publications.

Keim, D. B. (2003). *The cost of trend chasing and the illusion of momentum profits*. Unpublished Working Paper, University of Pennsylvania.

Keim, D. B., & Madhavan, A. (1995). Anatomy of the trading process: Empirical evidence on the behavior of institutional traders. *Journal of Financial Economics*, *37*(3), 371–398. doi:10.1016/0304-405X(94)00799-7

Keim, D. B., & Madhavan, A. (1996). The upstairs market for large-block transactions: Analysis and measurement of price effects. *Review of Financial Studies*, *9*(1), 1–36. doi:10.1093/rfs/9.1.1

Keim, D. B., & Madhavan, A. (1997). Transaction costs and investment style: An inter-exchange analysis of institutional equity trades. *Journal of Financial Economics*, *46*(3), 265–292. doi:10.1016/S0304-405X(97)00031-7

Keim, D. B., & Madhavan, A. (1998). The Cost of Institutional Equity Trades. *Financial Analysts Journal*, *54*(4), 50–69. doi:10.2469/faj.v54.n4.2198

Kissell, R. (2014). *The Science of Algorithmic Trading*. USA: Elsevier.

Perold, A. F. (1988). The implementation shortfall: Paper versus reality. *Journal of Portfolio Management*, *14*(3), 4–9. doi:10.3905/jpm.1988.409150

Rachev, S. T., Mittnik, S., Fabozzi, F. J., Focardi, S. M., & Jašić, T. (2007). *Financial Econometrics: From Basics to Advanced Modeling Techniques*. Hoboken, NJ: John Wiley & Sons.

Torre, N. G., Mark, J., & Ferrari, M. J. (1999). *The Market Impact Model.* Barra Research Insights.

ENDNOTES

1 Trade print is defined as the price at which the trade takes place.

2 S&P 500 for USA, Topix 100 for Japan, ASX 300 for Australia, Hang Seng for AEXJP, FTSE 100 for UK, STOXX 600 for Europe.

APPENDIX: TABLES

Table 9 presents the percentiles as well as the mean and the standard deviation of implicit trading cost measures and their components, all measured in basis points. All trading costs are measure in basis points.

Table 10 presents a few summary statistics of transaction orders as well as of trading costs and their components. The principal traded is expressed in millions of US dollars and the shares traded in millions. The transaction costs are measured in basis points.

Table 11 presents a few summary statistics of transaction orders as well as of trading costs and their components, like in the previous table (2), but each measure is divided into two categories: a high movement category which includes stocks with return Ri ≤ -2% or Ri > 2% and a low movement category which includes stocks

Table 9. Descriptive Statistics of Measures of Implicit Transaction Costs and Market Index Movement

Percentile	Prior Close Cost (bps)	VWAP Cost (bps)	Close cost (bps)	Average Cost (bps)	Prior close cost net of market index movement (bps)	Market Movement Cost Prior close to VWAP (bps)	Market Movement Cost VWAP to Close (bps)	Market Index Movement (bps)
Mean	44.82	39.15	32.19	0.68	44.89	7.40	6.33	-4.045
Std Deviation	116.29	34.72	46.07	177.43	107.11	47.22	82.10	64.76
10th	-222.78	-60.18	-95.60	-466.17	-226.65	-95.20	-206.23	-147.53
25th	-79.45	-17.07	-31.01	-199.47	-92.21	-38.37	-80.7657	-65.19
Median	15.08	6.73	0	8.19	5.79	1.98	17.084	-3.73
75th	122.07	37.85	42.10	218.28	109.65	46.59	120.69	50.27
90th	277.90	92.96	116.49	451.39	249.87	109.66	261.95	142.92

Table 10. Descriptive Statistics

Side	N	$ Principal Traded (M)	Shares Traded (M)	Commissions (bps)	Prior Close Cost (bps)	VWAP Cost (bps)	Close cost (bps)	Average Cost (bps)	Prior close cost net of market index movement (bps)	Market Movement Cost Prior close to VWAP (bps)	Market Movement Cost VWAP to Close (bps)	Market Index Movement (bps)
All	372,930	2,229.8	479.96	5.15	44.82	39.15	32.19	0.68	44.89	7.40	6.33	-4.04
Buys	192,479	1,188.1	241.33	5.06	-86.49	-72.38	-83.05	1296.74	-82.40	-13.91	11.19	-4.11
Sells	180,451	1,041.7	238.66	5.21	175.85	147.20	147.24	-1295.66	171.89	28.07	0.90	-3.97

Table 11. Descriptive Statistics with Stocks' Return Segmentation

Specific Return During the Trading Horizon	Side	N	$ Principal Traded (M)	Shares Traded (M)	Commissions (bps)	Prior Close Cost (bps)	VWAP Cost (bps)	Close cost (bps)	Average Cost (bps)	Prior close cost net of market index movement (bps)	Market Movement Cost Prior close to VWAP (bps)	Market Movement Cost VWAP to Close (bps)	Market Index Movement (bps)
High Movement	All	72,763	570.02	109.81	4.61	32.70	15.93	3.24	-25.38	29.233	17.01	12.53	6.31
Ri ≤ -2%	Buys	36,229	284.34	55.60	4.59	-254.67	-225.56	-242.34	1332.97	-253.96	-26.49	17.16	4.43
or Ri > 2%	Sells	36,534	285.67	54.20	4.63	316.78	254.65	246.01	-1368.12	309.17	60.02	7.95	2.58
Low Movement	All	300,167	1,658.93	170.18	5.38	50.39	47.67	45.88	13.16	52.15	2.31	2.94	1.06
R_i > -2%	Buys	155,250	773.94	85.72	5.28	-6.64	0.32	-7.44	1279.53	-0.96	-7.94	8.35	0.41
or Ri ≤ 2%	Sells	144,917	885.88	84.46	5.49	107.78	95.29	99.53	-1260.66	105.58	12.64	-2.50	0.79

Table 12. Panel Decomposition Regressions of Implicit Transaction Costs with Fixed Effects

	Dependent Variables	Intercept	Market Movement Cost Prior close to VWAP (bps)	Market Movement Cost VWAP to Close (bps)	VWAP Cost (bps)	R^2
All	Prior Close Cost (bps)	5.81*** (0.19)	-	-	1.019*** (0.00)	0.98
		25.69*** (8.91)	2.70** (1.20)	-	-	0.07
	Close Cost (bps)	-5.03*** (0.13)			0.98*** (0.00)	0.99
		18.26 (17.95)		-3.31 (3.86)		0.03
High Movement	Prior Close Cost (bps)	15.93*** (0.16)	-	-	1.026*** (0.01)	0.98
R_i ≤ -2% or R_i > 2%		2.07 (7.66)	1.74*** (0.43)			0.16
	Close Cost (bps)	-11.66*** (0.04)	-	-	0.99*** (0.00)	0.99
		6.88 (10.51)	-	0.19 (1.00)	-	0.09
Low Movement	Prior Close Cost (bps)	2.19*** (0.14)			0.99*** (0.00)	0.99
R_i > -2% or R_i ≤ 2%		50.75*** (0.76)	0.47 (0.31)			0.07
	Close Cost (bps)	-2.16*** (0.12)			0.99*** (0.00)	0.99
		48.65*** (0.45)		0.54** (0.24)		0.06

with return $R_i > -2\%$ or $Ri \leq 2\%$ during the trading horizon. It is defined that the trading horizon is always one day. The principal traded is expressed in millions of US dollars and the shares traded in millions. The transaction costs are measured in basis points.

Table 12 presents panel decomposition regressions of implicit trading costs with fixed effects, where each cost measure is regressed separately on each of its components. First, we run regressions using all the sample. At the second stage, we divide the sample into two segments: the first segment, includes stocks with high movement and the second one includes stocks with low movement during the trading horizon. The dependent variables are prior close cost and close cost and the independent variable is either VWAP cost or one of the two market movement costs. Trading costs are expressed in basis points and standard errors are clustered by equity and are presented in parentheses below each coefficient. We allow each equity to have its own intercept (fixed effects). R-squares are also presented for each regression. Statistical significance is indicated by *** for the 1% level, ** for the 5% level and * for the 10% level.

Table 13 presents an analysis of how various factors affect transaction costs using multiple unbalanced panel regressions with fixed effects. The dependent variables are prior close cost, VWAP cost and close cost, all expressed in basis points. As independent variables we use the following: buy indicator, log(market capitalization), log(relative volume), inverse prior close, return volatility expressed in basis points, price momentum, VWAP strategy dummy, tap strategy dummy, at open strategy dummy, perimeter strategy dummy, IS strategy dummy, sided market index return during the trading horizon expressed in basis points (multiplied by -1 for sell orders) and duration in seconds. The regional dummy variables were omitted because of multicollinearity. Standard errors are clustered by equity and are presented in parentheses below each coefficient. We allow each equity to have its own intercept (fixed effects). Overall R-squares, the number of observations and the number of clusters are also presented for each regression. Statistical significance is indicated by *** for the 1% level, ** for the 5% level and * for the 10% level. The exact definition of each variable is presented in section 5.3.

Table 14 presents an analysis the first batch of models we used for forecasting ITCs. In this case, we employ stepwise regressions with the forward entry method on the 2/3s of the sample in order to forecast the next batch of trades that took place within the same day. The dependent variables are prior close cost, VWAP cost and close cost, all expressed in basis points. Independent variables were picked from the following set: buy indicator, log(market capitalization), log(relative volume), inverse prior close, return volatility expressed in basis points, price momentum, Europe dummy, USA dummy, UK dummy, Australia dummy, Japan dummy, VWAP strategy dummy, tap strategy dummy, at open strategy dummy, perimeter strategy dummy and

Table 13. Panel Regression Analysis of Implicit Transaction Costs with Fixed Effects

	Prior Close Cost (bps)	VWAP Cost (bps)	Close Cost (bps)
Intercept	-4,236.2* (2,263.4)	-4,077.9* (2,203.0)	-4,077.9* (2,203.0)
Buy indicator	-250.8*** (93.3)	-227.4** (95.5)	-226.3** (95.5)
Log (market capitalization)	612.6* (321.0)	581.1* (312.0)	549.3* (312.0)
Log (relative volume)	0.9*** (0.0)	0.9*** (0.0)	0.9*** (0.0)
Inverse Prior Close	296.7* (156.1)	267.2* (149.5)	267.2* (149.5)
Return Volatility (bps)	0.0 (0.0)	0.1 (0.1)	0.1 (0.1)
Price momentum	1,202.1* (719.3)	1,164.8 (736.5)	1,164.8 (736.5)
VWAP Strategy Dummy	132.1** (66.0)	184.5*** (70.3)	174.3*** (66.5)
Tap Strategy Dummy	79.1 (54.0)	121.1** (58.1)	121.0** (58.1)
At Open Strategy Dummy	39.4 (41.4)	66.1 (46.7)	66.1 (46.7)
Perimeter Strategy Dummy	90.5 (55.1)	134.2** (59.2)	134.2** (59.2)
IS Strategy Dummy	68.4 (50.3)	110.0** (55.0)	110.0** (55.0)
Sided Market Index Return	3,320.2 (2,866.4)	-3,569.1 (3,012.6)	-3,569.1 (3,012.6)
Duration (seconds)	-0.0** (0.0)	-0.0** (0.0)	-0.0** (0.0)
R^2 (overall)	0.11	0.09	0.07
Number of Observations	372,930	372,930	372,930
Number of Clusters	11,763	11,763	11,763

IS strategy dummy. In the forecasting model, we use only the coefficients that are statistically significant in the 1% level. Then, we estimate the mean squared errors of each prediction to gauge its quality. Standard errors are presented in parentheses below each coefficient. R-squares and the number of observations are also presented for each regression. Statistical significance is indicated by *** for the 1% level, ** for the 5% level and * for the 10% level. The exact definition of each variable is presented in section 5.3.

Table 14. Out-of-Sample Forecast of Implicit Transaction Costs

	Prior Close Cost (bps)	VWAP Cost (bps)	Close Cost (bps)
Intercept	182.7*** (22.2)	162.3*** (22.6)	154.0*** (21.5)
Buy indicator	-263.7*** (31.5)	-234.7 *** (32.1)	-231.4*** (30.4)
Log (market capitalization)	-	-	-
Log (relative volume)	1.0*** (0.1)	1.0*** (0.1)	1.0*** (0.1)
Inverse Prior Close	-	-	-
Return Volatility (bps)	-	-	-
Price momentum	-	-	-
Europe dummy	-	-	-
USA dummy	-	-	-
UK dummy	-	-	-
Australia dummy	-	-	-
Japan dummy	-	-	-
VWAP Dummy	-	-	-
Tap/Tap Now Dummy	-	-	-
At Open Dummy	-	-	-
TWAP Dummy	-	-	-
IS Dummy	-	-	-
Sided Market Index Return	-	-	-
Duration (seconds)	-	-	-
R^2 (overall)	0.018	0.018	0.018
Number of Observations	172,930	172,930	172,930
Mean Squared Errors (MSE)	45.26	41.71	42.65
Forecast of the Respective Naïve Models (Mean of Transaction Costs)	48.8	44.4	36.5
Mean Squared Errors (MSE) of the Respective Naïve Models	45.72	42.11	42.99

Table 15 presents the mean, the standard deviation and 5 percentiles of the absolute forecast errors of the 6 previously mentioned prediction models.

Table 16 presents the mean, the standard deviation and 5 percentiles of the forecasted and the realized transaction costs, except for the three naïve models according to which transaction costs are always equal to the mean value of the realized transaction costs, for the period 09/05/2016 - 28/07/2017.

Table 15. Descriptive Statistics of Absolute Forecast Errors

	Absolute Forecast Errors of Prior Close Cost (bps)	**Absolute Forecast Errors of VWAP Cost (bps)**	**Absolute Forecast Errors of Close Cost (bps)**	**Absolute Forecast Errors of Prior Close Cost (bps) (naïve model)**	**Absolute Forecast Errors of VWAP Cost (bps) (naïve model)**	**Absolute Forecast Errors of Close Cost (bps) (naïve model)**
Mean	154.2	69.5	89.9	160.6	77.1	100.8
Standard Deviation	646.4	634.0	638.4	656.8	644.3	647.8
10th Percentile	15.6	12.0	9.9	16.5	12.9	11.7
25th Percentile	40.8	25.7	28.3	42.1	27.8	28.8
Median	88.5	44.2	45.3	89.3	44.4	49.4
75th Percentile	165.6	58.4	91.0	178.7	61.2	97.7
90th Percentile	301.1	108.9	184.4	316.8	102.5	176.6

Table 16. Descriptive Statistics of Forecasted and Realized Implicit Transaction Costs

	Forecasted Prior Close Cost (bps)	**Forecasted VWAP Cost (bps)**	**Forecasted Close Cost (bps)**	**Prior Close Cost (bps)**	**VWAP Cost (bps)**	**Close Cost (bps)**
Mean	16.3	20.2	13.5	28.8	17.9	15.0
Standard Deviation	61.9	27.4	75.7	76.2	35.0	85.7
10th Percentile	-89.4	-30.9	-85.9	-180.1	-42.5	-99.9
25th Percentile	-47.2	-8.7	-23.7	-64.1	-11.2	-34.5
Median	7.0	5.5	2.2	13.5	6.2	0
75th Percentile	76.5	26.0	47.7	103.6	29.4	48.0
90th Percentile	178.8	58.4	150.1	233.0	72.0	117.8

Chapter 10
Innovation Finance Beyond Bitcoin:
Cryptocurrencies as Alternative Investments

Dimitrios Koutsoupakis
National and Kapodistrian University of Athens, Greece

ABSTRACT

Over the past two decades, the diffusion of technological innovations introduced to the finance industry has been inconceivable. Internet, at the end of the 20th century, brought e-commerce, later e-payments, and more recently, e-money. Such innovations in digital world increase the impact on the business world, and so might do cryptocurrencies, currently spreading out across the globe. To this end, this chapter builds up an across-the-board synthesis of current investment trends and analysis, aiming to lead a way forward for research on this uncharted breed of alternative finance assets looming anew.

INTRODUCTION

When reflecting upon the recent developments in alternative finance, there is nothing more, no doubt, that has intrigued academics, investment professionals, institutions and the general public than the next brand new asset class that did not exist a decade ago namely "cryptocurrency". But why is it called this way? More importantly why is it an investment and in particular an alternative one? And, be that as it may, then what kind of alternative investment? It is broadly established that alternative investments

DOI: 10.4018/978-1-7998-2436-7.ch010

are linked to "non-traditional" approaches contrary to the "traditional" ones which academia and industry usually associate with investments in (a) securities and (b) cash. These fundamental questions will be approached by this chapter.

The first ever cryptocurrency was proposed by the pseudonymous Satoshi Nakamoto back in 2008 in a paper made publicly available on an internet forum. Note that the term "cryptocurrency" never appears in the original paper. It is not a term coined by the creator of Bitcoin rather it emerged later on by community members. It is argued that Satoshi Nakamoto interest was to invent the first payment system without intermediary (the Blockchain) rather than a revolutionary currency *per se* (the Bitcoin). Interesting enough, note that the title of his work underlines the "*cash system*" rather the "asset" wherein he decided to name it after the latter (*Bitcoin: A peer-to-peer electronic cash system*). Until today, the identity of the author whose 9-page work spawned an (alternative) asset market of USD 813 bil. market cap and of USD 44 bil. daily (24h) volume (peaked on January 7th, 2018) remains an enduring mystery. Bitcoin v.01 open-source software was uploaded on January 9th, 2009. Such cash systems operating via peer-to-peer (open) networks epitomize the new concept branded as socialization of Finance.

In principle, the centerpiece of this sophisticated breakthrough allows the record, validation and storage of information of unique value to be securely and transparently distributed but not copied (thus retaining the property of uniqueness of the asset) across network's participants (peers) making the need for a third party (middleman) acting as custodian/gatekeeper to ensure trust obsolete. The last part spells out very simply what exactly Bitcoin's innovation has resolved. Marc Andreessen, the computer scientist who co-authored Mosaic, that is the first widely used Web browser has argued that Bitcoin in 2008 may have fueled the next technological revolution following Personal Computers in 1975 and the Internet in 1993 for its potential to "*be programmed to record virtually everything of value and importance to humankind*" (Tapscott & Tapscott, 2016).

The remaining of this chapter is organized as follows. The next section offers broad definitions and historical events of the topic as well as delivers a useful literature review into the discussion. Then, the investments opportunities in cryptocurrency asset markets and ecosystems are presented and analyzed accordingly. Last sections sum up limitations, challenges, research the way forward and conclude.

BACKGROUND & TERMINOLOGY

Broad Definitions & the Bitcoin

This technological breakthrough has introduced many new terms. Amidst the mass divergent usages of these, this section collects, draws the following methodological framework and exemplifies. To begin with, the term distributed ledgers technology (DLT) is the wider and more accurate that engulfs the two other more popular terms namely cryptocurrency and blockchain. Altogether, distributed ledger makes up an open-source software that virtualizes two outputs which include:

1. **A native Unit of Account:** This is created and circulates within a shared database (see below) and acts effectively as the unit of account. Broadly called cryptocurrency[1]. It is created either (a) as a reward for that a distributed network with no central authority needs economic incentives to govern participants' motives or (b) as a right for the exchange of traditional currency with a newly launched cryptocurrency that would offer benefits usually in the form of acceptance as a means of payment for goods and services within this specific network.
2. **A Shared Database:** This lists all past transactions (which all peers constantly update and achieve consensus on the true state of nature) and is called blockchain. Its operation is based on a selected type of algorithm. This determines how the peers of the system reach consensus on the true state of nature of the blockchain, thus which transactions of the block are valid. There are (a) permissionless Blockchains like Bitcoin where anyone can contribute in validating transactions, thus even malicious actors and (b) permissioned that only by invitation can someone validate transactions.

By way of example, in Bitcoin's network, the software delivers the next two outputs:

- **Bitcoins** (with lowercase)**:** are the native assets divided down to 8 decimal places with the smallest unit named satoshi in homage to the original creator, Satoshi Nakamoto. Hence, 1 bitcoin equals to 10^8 satoshi. In the protocol that regulates the supply schedule of bitcoins, the main rules are as follows:
    - Total supply capped at 21 mil units.
    - New units come out every 10min which is approximately the time required to settle a block. A block is like a page of a ledger where the

newly validated transactions are recorded and added to the previous block creating a chain of blocks, thus the blockchain.

  - New units are created at a rate which is increasing at a decreasing rate every 210.000 blocks, thus approximately every four years is cut in half. Note that the first block issued 50 bitcoins and today (as per July 2019) is 12,5.

Uses of Cryptocurrencies

It is curious thing, worthy of mention, that cryptocurrencies play a dual role i.e. payment within their own payment system (the Blockchain) and investment.

- **Payment:** Agents can cryptocurrencies for payments of goods. Hileman & Rauchs (2017) distinguish between two categories of such payments.
  - "Payment Rail" whereby cryptocurrencies stand for a channel for that they simply "*play the role of a means to an end*" (money exit the crypto finance ecosystem) taking benefit from faster, cheaper and anonymous transfer of sovereign currencies.
  - "Cryptocurrency Payments" whereby they are used to pay for a service or a good delivered (money stays in the ecosystem).
- **Investment:** Agents enter into investment transactions by storing cryptocurrency value with the purpose of gaining benefit in the form of realized/unrealized capital gain in the future. This chapter focuses on this role.

But if cryptocurrencies are currencies, why then are not part of traditional investments and cash? An easy argument would be that currencies are only supplied by sovereign authorities. But this is not persuasive enough. The next section supplies this chapter with an explanation of the different asset classes of cryptocurrencies which is allows the reader to understand that cryptocurrencies include various categories some of which are far from characterized as cash but some other may in the future qualify as cash supplied by "Blockhain community platforms".

The Finance Innovation Nexus After Bitcoin

Having now defined the fundamental principles, the introduction of the innovation nexus after Bitcoin naturally is asked for. Back in 2009, Bitcoin was the first but not the only cryptocurrency. To this end, a basic classification of the numerous cryptocurrencies that have been issued in the last ten years so that the reader can gain a solid understanding of their significant differences. In literature, a common classification is the following:

- **Altcoins Running on Built-in "First Wave of Innovation" Blockchain:** Called altcoins, thus alternative to Bitcoin for that they are very similar to the original blueprint and display little innovation. They are either created (a) from scratch by replicating the open-source code of Bitcoin or (b) as spin-offs (called hard forks)[2] from the original Bitcoin network. Altcoins have been openly regarded as clones of Bitcoin only to feature different parameter values in the protocol i.e. different block time for clearing transactions, supply function, and issuance scheme).
- **dAppcoins (Coin Stacks or Application Coins[3]) Running on Built-in "Second Wave of Innovation" Blockchain (can be also referred to as altchains for that they offer an alternative type of blockchain):** These cryptocurrencies are also altcoins but in addition come about with a new kind of Blockchain technology called second wave which focus on becoming a platform for the development and execution of various smart contract (called dApps) on top of their network or applications more generally (Ripple is included here). So, on these blockchains except from the native asset, more assets can be issued and circulated by anyone.
- **Utilitycoins (also referred to as tokens when running without built-in Blockchain, thus on top of second wave Blockchain innovation):** Called utility for that they are created to serve a particular business cause where there is an underlying asset in the real economy to which are either redeemed or converted. Thus, the cryptocurrency derives utility from this asset. Some of them offer discount for any future fees if paid by cryptocurrency and other additional features. Such cryptocurrency case usually incorporates the characteristics of investment for that traditional currency is exchanged today for future (thus uncertain) economics benefits. From the issuer perspective, the traditional currency accumulated finances the project.
- **Stablecoins (also referred to as tokens when running without built-in Blockchain, thus on top of second wave Blockchain innovation):** The price of these cryptocurrencies is targeted not to vary for that it is pegged against another traditional currency or commodity or even a synthetic composite of assets. They are usually developed on top of a Blockchain Platform.

Altogether, figure 1 below collects and classifies on the basis of the above taxonomy 50 selected cryptocurrencies throughout the last ten-year trading history (the trading ticker in parenthesis). Today, there are approximately 900 coins and 1.400 tokens. The higher number of tokens demonstrate the rapid growth in this

Figure 1. Evolution of the cryptocurrency universe over the last ten years
Source: Authors, 2019

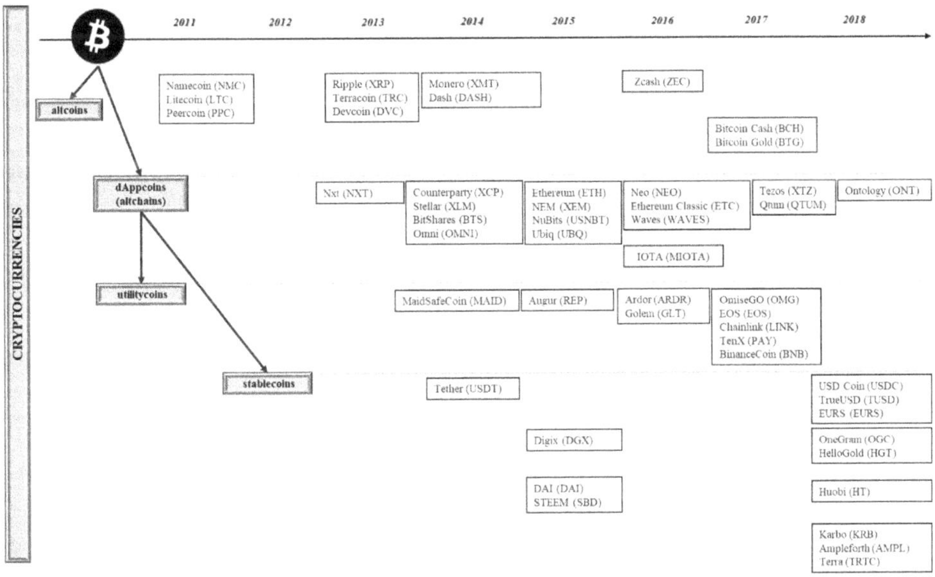

class due to the easiness of developing tokes for that they use another Blockchain in initial offering and subsequent recording of transactions.

History & Institutional Watchdogs

It is apparent from the historical standpoint of view, there have been quite a lot significant events after the release of Bitcoin in 2009. These are summarized as follows:

- **2008:** The domain name bitcoin.org is registered by Satoshi Nakamoto.
- **2009:** Bitcoin network is uploaded. Bitcoin price is effectively close to zero.
- **2010:** The first private digital exchange listing Bitcoin goes live. Its name Bitcoinmarket.com
- **2011:** The first transaction with bitcoins as a means of payment for the purchase of a real good in the economy takes place. According to Yermack (2014) who actually quotes Wallace (2011) the object of acquisition was two pizza procured at a cost of 10,000 bitcoins in 2009:

the pizza parlor did not accept bitcoins directly, and instead a third-party broker was enlisted who agreed to procure the pizza using a credit card (based on a real currency) and accept the bitcoins, worth almost $5 million at recent prices, as consideration. (Yermack, 2014)

- **2011:** Namecoin becomes the second cryptocurrency and first altcoin. That year and for the first time after two years of trading, Bitcoin takes parity with US Dollar.
- **2014:** Three key events occur as 1 bitcoin trades between USD 300 and USD 800.
    - Nxt becomes the first altchain (and dAppcoin) to allow other assets to be issued and circulated on its blockchain.
    - A new and controversial procedure to raise capital named Initial Coin Offerings (abbreviated ICO) and Initial Token Offerings (abbreviated ITO) enters the crypto-scene. The first ever that took place was by the cryptocurrency labeled "Counteryparty" on February, 3 in 2014 (close date of the ICO) whereby USD 1,79 mil were raised in exchange for the crowd-sale of specific units of this cryptocurrency.
    - MaidSafeCoin becomes the first token running on another surrogate blockchain.
- **2015:** Tether becomes the first stable cryptocurrency issued by a private company enabling the concept of IOU obligation of the cryptocurrency issuer. That year 1 bitcoin continues to trade less than USD 1.000.
- **2017:** In late 2017, Bitcoin reaches the all-time peak (USD 20.000). In December of that year, two US based Exchanges namely the Chicago Mercantile Exchange (CME) and the Chicago Board Options Exchange (CBOE) launch the first Bitcoin futures contracts opening the market to institutional investors.
- **2018:** End of December that year, the creators of the "Basis" project, a new Blockchain wherein three cryptocurrencies co-exist i.e. Basis stablecoin, Basis Shares and Basis Bonds issue an emotional statement announcing that they are obliged to cease their operations. The reason is that US authorities characterized the two latter assets as "unregistered securities" and that the team would have to apply US securities regulation to the system which among others does not permit the sale of these assets for at least one year. Eighteen months earlier, Basis project had raised USD 133m. The team announced that they will return what is left to investors[4].

Bitcoin's increasing hype had regulators on the toes. It was only a matter of time for institutional authorities to show interest in formally examining cryptocurrencies and in some cases even take actions. In Europe, the European Central Bank (ECB)[5] was the first institution to be concerned with. In October 2012, ECB issues a 55-page report on virtual currencies schemes, only to deduce that they pose no risk to price stability in the real economy due to (a) their low volume traded, (b) lack of wide acceptance and (c) limited connection to real assets. Of course, as expected ECB underscores the hazard of illegal transactions through crypto-currencies and for that reason accolades the role of centralized real currency and payment systems.

In early 2013 in the United States, the Financial Crimes Enforcement Network (FinCEN) and the Stock-Exchange Commission (SEC) openly acknowledged Bitcoin as 'convertible virtual currency'. On the contrary, the Chinese Government declared that Bitcoin "is not even a currency" and in effect banned its commercial use. It is not peculiar that countries in which Bitcoin has been officially banned are mostly centralized in one way or another i.e. Vietnam, Thailand, Bangladesh, Sweden, Russia, Iceland, Bolivia, India, Ecuador and China as said.

During the same period, SEC issued a public statement for investors being preoccupied that crypto-currencies 'may lure investors to fabricated transactions' (released on 23/07/2013). By that time, US agencies complete in-depth investigations leading virtual currencies to seizure and even corporate executives to sentence. Major examples that raised *polemic* were 'Liberty Reserve' and 'e-gold'. In late 2014, a federal judge in the United States sentenced a Bitcoin entrepreneur for easing illegal transactions (drugs) via Silk Road, an online black market where products are denominated and paid in bitcoins.

In the United Kingdom in September 2014, Bank of England released a study on the potential risks and benefits of crypto-currencies.[6] The findings bears a resemblance to ECB's i.e. (i) they do act as money though to a limited extent for relatively few people, (ii) the economics of the scheme both at micro and macro level pose challenges and (iii) they do not pose a material risk to monetary or financial stability in the UK.

In 2015, the Euro Banking Association (EBA) launched an exhaustive study on crypto-technologies recognizing four major manifestations namely currencies, asset registries, application stacks and asset-centric technologies.

In late 2015[7], The Court of Justice of the European Union has ruled that the services of a Bitcoin exchange in exchanging Bitcoin for a traditional currency is exempt from value added tax on the basis of the 'currency' exemption.

In 2017, in the United States of America, SEC announces that tokens are securities whether are purchased using U.S. dollars or virtual currencies and thus now subject to federal securities laws. Later that year, Bitcoin derivatives are launched but trading volume is considerably, though regulators still explore the approval of listing Exchange

Traded Funds and exchange products in general holding cryptocurrencies. Another concern for regulators is Initial Coin Offering procedures and so far only some guidelines in the form of questions have been submitted to the investment public.

Current Research Trends on Cryptocurrencies

Current research is interested in the legal, technological and finance/economics aspects of cryptocurrencies. In the micro-financial economics firmament, the main strand of literature revolves around the demand-side of cryptocurrencies and the main puzzles are price formation, volatility and possible empirical anomalies. In other words, research examines cryptocurrencies' behavior as an investment asset.

Under this frame, preliminary studies probe into the profile of cryptocurrencies' investors. For Grinberg (2012) the holders of bitcoins vary including early adopters, enthusiasts, criminals, speculators, online merchants such as web hosts, casinos, illicit drug marketplaces, auction sites, NPOs and adult media.

The area that receives the greatest attention examines the underlying users' demand motives, thus whether demand cryptocurrencies for speculation (store of value) or for facilitating transactions (medium of exchange). First research studies in this field (Barber, Boyen, Shi & Uzun, 2012; Vejačka, 2014) had very early identified volatility, legislation influence, anonymity, availability (number of subjects accepting payments) and awareness (media impact) to be notable demand factors. Buchholz, Delaney, and Warren (2012) and Glaser et al. (2014) empirically test the relationship between Bitcoin price and queries on search engines to find that attractiveness for investors is a key factor for price formation.

In the last years, the leading strand of literature probes into identifying trading patterns. It is worth adding that, given their generally observed inclination to high volatility, cryptocurrencies' have been lately excessively examined to be uncorrelated with all other financial classes (Kajtazi & Moro, 2019; Corbet, Meegan, Larkin, Lucey & Yarovaya, 2019) making them suitable for portfolio diversification purposes but not for hedging as Bouri, Molnár, Azzi, Roubaud & Hagfors (2017) conclude in their empirical work. Dyhrberg (2016) argues that bitcoin may be "*useful in risk management and ideal for risk averse investors in anticipation of negative shocks to the market*". Finally, Griffin & Shams (2018) stretches the point that in the case of Bitcoin, bearish prices may be associated with blur trading strategies involving privately controlled digital currency exchanges and "related" cryptocurrencies such as Tether (USDT). Since 2018, the cryptocurrency Tether which is 1:1 pegged to the US dollar has replaced the US dollar as the most tradable pair with Bitcoin leader. This means that such stablecoins offer the advantage of crypto-for-crypto trading while a traditional currency exists as an anchor. Lately this new strand of literature is growing as more stable cryptocurrencies pop up for that their absence of volatility gives a ground for considering possible integration with the traditional monetary system. This means that stablecoins do not have any investment interest for that they only mimic the variation of traditional currencies.

On the other hand, the macro-monetary firmament still lacks a clear methodological context. Schilling, L., & Uhlig, H. (2019) model an economy with two competing currencies with no intrinsic value (dollar and Bitcoin) and offer a pricing equation for the digital currency which does not invalidate its role as means of payment.

CRYPTOCURRENCIES IN INVESTMENT PRACTICE

This part accumulates the scattered pieces the new constellation of alternative finance, spurred by the Bitcoin blueprint over the last ten years, causing alternative finance borders to fade. Thus far, this includes numerous (a) ecosystems and (b) assets to invest in making Bitcoin just the tip of the iceberg. This section analysis how investments funds flow to this market both indirectly (in the ecosystem) and directly (in the asset).

Investing in the Ecosystem: The Cryptocurrency Industry

The Bitcoin hype has been so intense that the "cryptocurrency / blockchain project" was allegedly on the way to outpace in fundraising the entire 1995 internet project[8] as more and more crypto-finance startups have been clinching seed capital to craft innovative technological market products and services in this new ecosystem. So, from the industry perspective, investments to set up and finance firms operating in this ecosystem fall into the manufacturing and services sectors. Hileman & Rauchs (2017) present estimated levels of employment and turnover operating in each sector. It goes without saying that the industry holds a role of imperative importance as it facilitates the operation of the asset markets (cryptocurrencies).

- **Manufacturing Firms**: Develop two types of cryptocurrency products categorized as follows:
    - Hardware equipment including:
        - Machinery for efficient mining.
        - ATMs for cryptocurrency exchanges.
        - Hardware wallets.
    - Software equipment for cryptocurrencies including:
        - Online, offline digital wallets sold on wholesale (to primary and tertiary sector) and on retail (thus, directly to end-consumers). Note

that digital wallets are data files that store recorded transactions, outstanding balances and private keys.

- Specialized platforms for exchanges, payment firms and digital banks and of course Blockchains. It is underscored that software platforms are also developed and sold outside the p2p finance ecosystem e.g. banking institutions, firms that test the adoption of Blockchain/shared-ledger technology.

Here, investment strategy is substantial for that requires production of goods. The revenue model includes sale of products and subscription fees for services.

- **Financial Services Firms:** These act as market makers and bring close buyers and sellers:

  - (a) Bureaux de change (Digital Cryptoccurrency Exchanges), where cryptocurrencies interact with other cryptocurrencies and with the well-established Foreign Exchange market. Cryptocurrencies are traded in pairs where even margin trading is available. Legislation and compliance AML (Anti-Money laundering) / KYC (Know-Your-Customer). varies by country. Usually such institutions are supervised by the respective central bank which originally grants this type of license.

Here, investment is more substantial for that requires significant set-up, legal and marketing costs. Even some cryptocurrencies take part in this sector and use Initial Coin Offering process to raise investment funds and develop the project. An example is Binance which claims to be a pure decentralized exchange platform directly connecting buyers and sellers.

Investing in the Asset: The Cryptocurrency Markets

But what are the possible ways for an investor to enter into the cryptocurrency markets? It is certain that investment requires an initial outlay of capital. Investment placements to obtain the asset may take the next forms.

- **Exchanged:**
  - Purchased during an ICO process over the internet. For the period 2013-2018, studies (Boreiko, D., & Sahdev, N. K.,2018) indicate that more than 1.524 ICOs were recorded. Accumulated ICO funds should be around USD 9 bil through this controversial open-finance procedure to invest in acquiring units of cryptocurrencies sold. The most successful

ICO so far took place in June 2018 when "EOS" token completed a crowd-sale of USD 4,2 bil. A few months earlier "Telegram Open Network" token raised USD 1,7bil. In the 3rd place is "Tezos" token with USD 230 mil.

    - Purchased from a currency exchange that act as market-makers by offering liquidity or over-the-counter.

- **Airdropped:**
    - Mined, thus earned after the ICO process via a lottery competition. Miners are natural and legal persons acting as peers/full-nodes facilitating in validation of transactions that in turn enlarge supply and fall into two broad categories namely:
        - Self-mining, thus performed by individuals who "work" independently.
        - Pool-mining, thus performed by a group of individuals by analogy with a co-operative scheme (usually a company is behind) where participants contribute collectively their CPU and rewards are distributed analogously. The downside of this is that decentralization (pure competition) is replaced by centralization (oligopoly) as concentration of computation power or hashrate in crypto terminology in a few mining-pools may enable manipulation of the blockchain.
    - Accrued, assumed holding a long position in the asset this receives an "interest" (like a saving deposit) on the cryptocurrency in the future as long as the investor does not dispose it. By way of example this is the case with Steem Power (SP), an internal non-tradable cryptocurrency created within the Steem-Blockchain that derives value from the Steem, tradable cryptocurrency. The pros of the SP asset is that it offers influence in participating in the Blockchain operations just like voting rights in shares. The cons of this SP is that it is illiquid in the sense that a holder for a specific period of time does not have the right to convert it to another Steem cryptocurrency which is tradable with sovereign currencies. This has the features of an equity.

Note that most mining activity takes place in China followed by Iceland, India, Georgia and Venezuela. There are two reasons for this concentration i.e. cheap electricity and lax environmental policies. All the same, in this case investment is not substantial, thus opened even to natural persons as only requires to spend money in capital expenditures to acquire the appropriate technical equipment for mining while incur operating expenses during mining (e.g. electricity cost). Note that investments in CapEx serves as a key indicator that reflects future expectations on profitability and expansion of mining business. The revenue model is related to winning the mining-competition and receive the new units of the cryptocurrency or/and receive transaction fees by the participants for transacting via the blockchain.

Understanding the Cryptocurrency Trading Metrics

Trading cryptocurrencies embroils comprehension of particular metrics in this new market. Below, the most relevant that readers may find when look at platforms that trade cryptocurrencies:

Ticker: Every cryptocurrency has a ticker symbol just like equities. Bitcoin's is BTC.

Launch Date: It is an indicative measure of how long the asset has been traded.

Price: The price for each unit of cryptocurrency (which is further divided into decimals accordingly) expressed in another currency.

Max Supply: It is the amount of all units to be issued. There are two cases, thus capped (like Bitcoin and Ripple) and uncapped cryptocurrencies (like Tether). The former category is further distinguished between mineable and non-mineable supply.

Mineable Supply: Mineable cryptocurrencies are based on a consensus algorithm that governs the pre-determined change in supply. Non-mineable (or pre-mined) cryptocurrencies have all units of supply released. This is the case with Ripple and most of utilitycoins.

Circulating Supply: For cases like Bitcoin this is straightforward and it is always known how many units of the cryptocurrency has already been issued so far. However, in cases like Ripple this is open to debate. In this case, many of Ripple cryptocurrencies that were pre-mined are deposited in an escrow account that Ripple Incorporation (the company that develops Ripple Blockchain) controls. It goes without saying that in such cases, supply and in its aftermath price can be manipulated.

Volume: This is estimated in another currency and measured within a specified time frame (day, month). It represents how liquid the market is in terms of investment activity.

Transaction Count: In relation to volume, this metric states the number of transactions occurred within a specified time frame.

Markets: Number of pairs of this cryptocurrency listed in digital currency exchanges. This number is a liquidity indicator of the cryptocurrency.

Transaction Fee: A key metric expressed in a sovereign currency that reveals the cost for transacting within the Blockchain. Effectively, compares which Blockchain is cheaper. Today, in most Blockchain's the average transaction cost is close to USD 0.005.

Market Capitalization (Market Cap) or Network Value (NV): It is the product of price and circulating supply. Historically, market cap (capitalization) denotes the total market value of a publicly traded firm and equals the share price times the number of shares outstanding. Note that this financial term and not a monetary one such as monetary base is widely used in cryptocurrency language because the amount of digital assets (units) in circulation is always and precisely known. Cryptocurrencies are an unprecedented asset case for that they incorporate financial characteristics from both securities and currencies.

White-paper: This is a not quantitative metric but probably the most essential one for investment appraisal in this market. It is a prerequisite for each team prior to an initial offering to make available on the internet the so-called white-paper usually written in academic format just like Satoshi Nakamoto did in 2008 whereby the proposed cryptocurrency is explained as well as how the funds, if crowd-sale takes place are going to be allotted.

General Market Information

Today, 10 years after Bitcoin the crypto-finance ecosystem features over 2.300 crypto-currencies traded over nearly 20.000 markets (pairs listed in exchanges) amounting to a total market capitalization of close to USD 300 bil and daily volume of approximately USD 60 mil. Table 1 provides a market overview of the top-15 traded assets.

In the first rank for ten consecutive years is Bitcoin but accompanied with two more hard forks of Bitcoin. This highlights the trust of the investment community on the Bitcoin blueprint. The last column on the right shows how liquid the pair is, this in how many exchange markets is listed.

Bitcoin (Declining) Dominance and (Increasing) Prominence

Bitcoin is the first and remains the most popular case among cryptocurrencies. This popularity is measured by the market capitalization, that is the product of price per one unit of cryptocurrency and the supply of available units in circulation. While in currencies the monetary base (the supply) can only be estimated, in cryptocurrencies this number of how many units have been issued is always known in precise and resemble to how stocks' market cap index. Very interestingly, scholars have shrewdly embraced 'networks effects' literature to relate substitution effect and reinforcement effect with Bitcoin demand for store of value and medium of exchange use respectively. In fact, Gandal and Halaburda (2014), anticipate that convergence (reinforcement effect) towards one dominant-player in (intra)competition within cryptocurrencies, thus Bitcoin is most likely. However, empirical data suggest that cryptocurrency

Table 1. Cryptocurrency data (in USD, as per July 30, 2019)

Name (Launch Year)	Coin Type	Market Cap in USD	Price in USD	Volume (24h) in USD	Circulating Supply & Ticker Symbol	Markets Traded
Bitcoin (2009)	Bitcoin	$169.610.819.668	$9.504,21	$15.705.735.089	17.845.862 BTC	>400
Ethereum (2015)	dAppcoin	$22.469.791.941	$209,80	$6.147.308.086	107.103.401 ETH	>400
Ripple (2012)	dAppcoin*	$13.281.261.477	$0,310073	$935.656.506	42.832.704.971 XRP	>400
Litecoin (2011)	Altcoin	$5.685.981.076	$90,43	$2.778.330.817	62.878.343 LTC	>400
Bitcoin Cash (2017)	Altcoin	$5.494.789.807	$306,65	$1.453.443.707	17.918.563 BCH	360
BinanceCoin (2017)	Utilitycoin*	$4.238.189.114	$27,25	$156.142.012	155.536.713 BNB	214
Tether (2014)	Stablecoin**	$4.020.260.813	$0,998187	$17.778.926.209	4.027.564.415 USDT	>400
EOS (2018)	dAppcoin*	$3.849.595.240	$4,16	$1.919.570.068	925.266.655 EOS	328
BitcoinSV (2018)	Altcoin	$2.599.240.107	$145,58	$385.040.700	17.854.986 BSV	135
Stellar (2014)	dAppcoin*	$1.632.042.646	$0,083196	$89.018.251	19.616.918.913 XLM	268
Cardano (2017)	Altcoin	$1.579.285.245	$0,060913	$46.097.742	25.927.070.538 ADA	92
TRON (2018)	dAppcoin*	$1.462.619.944	$0,021934	$447.513.228	66.682.072.191 TRX	245
Unis Sed Leo (2019)	Utilitycoin*	$1.338.006.381	$1,34	$6.831.275	999.498.893 LEO	17
Monero (2014)	Altcoin	$1.332.262.111	$77,79	$88.113.637	17.125.814 XMR	128
Dash (2014)	Altcoin	$941.289.336	$105,20	$346.464.445	8.947.392 DASH	251

(Data Source: coinmarketcap, 2017-2019)

Additional notes: *indicate that the asset is not mineable, thus the total supply equals circulating supply. **indicates that the asset is not mineable but the supply varies as the issuer controls the quantity.

competition within the ecosystem features also substitution effects for that as Bitcoin market value surge so do the rest of cryptocurrencies. Therefore, Bitcoin maintains a prominent rather dominant role in the market.

In figure 2, Bitcoin market cap (which follows the same path as its market price since supply is pre-determined) is combined with Bitcoin market share or Bitcoin dominance-index as commonly said. It is self-evident that Bitcoin and cryptocurrency ecosystem as a whole increased their value from 2017 onwards as soon competition entered and Bitcoin's share started to plunge. Bitcoin's dominance from 100% back in early 2009 has now fallen to approximately 50%.

Figure 2. Bitcoin market capitalization (top) & market share (bottom) for the period 2013-2019
Source: coinmarketcap, 2019

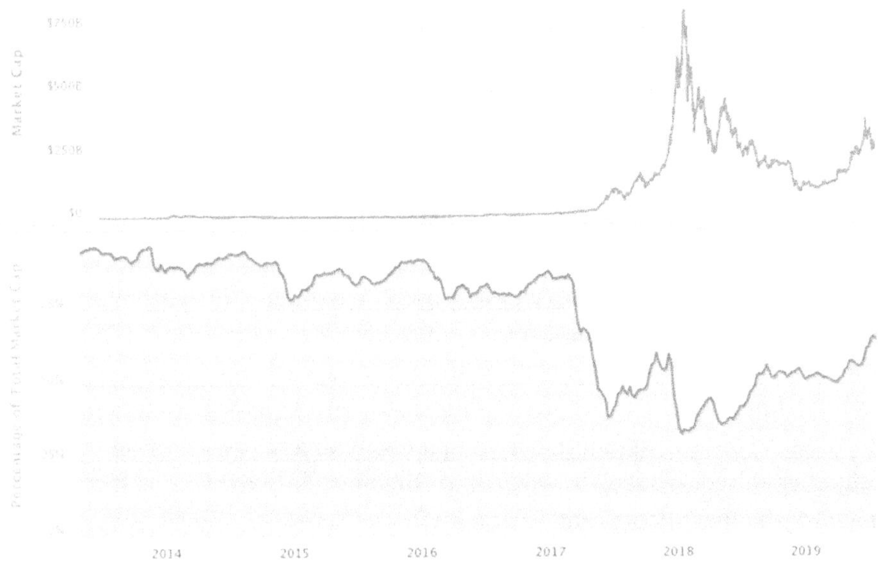

Cryptocurrency Analysis by Asset Class

This empirical analysis uses a representative sample and provide evidence of the general trading characteristics of these assets. In literature, still there is no consensus on whether cryptocurrencies constitute an individual asset class mainly due to the heterogenous characteristics among cryptocurrencies. For that reason, this analysis focus on the asset classes within this market. Dataset used was retrieved from coinmarketcap. This website collects data from several exchanges and calculates daily weighted averages for prices and trading volumes.

Risk-return Profile by Asset Class Leaders 2017-2019

The selected time window for this analysis is 26th July 2017 – 26th July 2019. Thus, a complete two-year period when all following assets were traded. The five selected assets namely Bitcoin, Ethereum, Litecoin, BinanceCoin, USDTether represent the market leader of each asset class namely Bitcon, dAppcoins, Altcoins, Utilitycoins, Stablecoins respectively as per July 2019.

It is observed that the distribution of daily returns of all assets look leptokurtic and Utilitycoin exhibit the highest degree of kurtosis and standard deviation. As a result, the distribution of the Utilitycoin is right-skewed. This is reasonable as such cryptocurrencies are the closest to resemble equities. Average daily returns are close to zero within the range (0,1%-0,3%) while Altcoin exhibit the highest. As expected, Stablecoin return is zero, but price is not always 1 USD as it is originally pegged probably due to market inefficiencies that are quickly restored. Yet, the price range stablecoin is the narrowest as anticipated.

In Figure 3, distribution and volatility of the selected assets are illustrated.

In appendix 1, Table 4 calculates for the top15 cryptocurrencies from a dataset of 9.714 observations in total of daily-close returns the average mean and standard deviation for the two-year period as well as the Sharpe ratio (given by the fraction of return of asset i over standard deviation of asset i) assuming that risk free return is equal to zero. The results are depicted in figure 4 where on the y axis is the average daily return for the period examined and the bubble specify the volatility of return. Utilitycoins high mean returns are accompanied with high risk as anticipated. In contrast, stablecoin's zero return is accompanied with a minor variation as trading opportunities raised. Notice, however, that Bitcoin's daily return was less volatile compared with other altcoins and Ethereum for the period examined. But, the latter had also lower daily return. Altcoin (Litecoin) has a daily return close to Bitcoin's but exhibit higher risk.

Analysis by Market Cap / Network Value and Volume

As per June 30, 2019, the total size of the cryptocurrency market as measured by the market cap or network value (NV) indicator stands at about USD 325 bil and 24 daily volume USD 74 bil. As such, the five asset class leaders account for 74% of total network value and 81% of total daily volume respectively. This indicates that cryptocurrency asset class categorization is an important filter for analysis. Investors in cryptocurrencies tend to follow the leader in each category as reinforcement effects become fiercer and substitution effects to raise when a new kind of cryptocurrency emerge and attract investment interest for each innovative character. Innovation is a critical factor in this full of sentiment market. Very interesting data arrive from stablecoins. While Tether accounts for only 1% of total cryptocurrency market cap, trading volume is equal to Bitcoin's, the most valuable asset. This highlights the fact that stablecoins mandate is exactly this, high volume due to price stability they offer. On the other hand, utilitycoins have very poor trading volume (close to 0%) because their investment profile is long alike in equities. Table 2, accumulates the relevant data from table 1.

Additionally, figure 5 offers a graphical representation of the above table.

Figure 3. Daily returns 2017-2019 of selected market leaders
Source: Authors, 2019

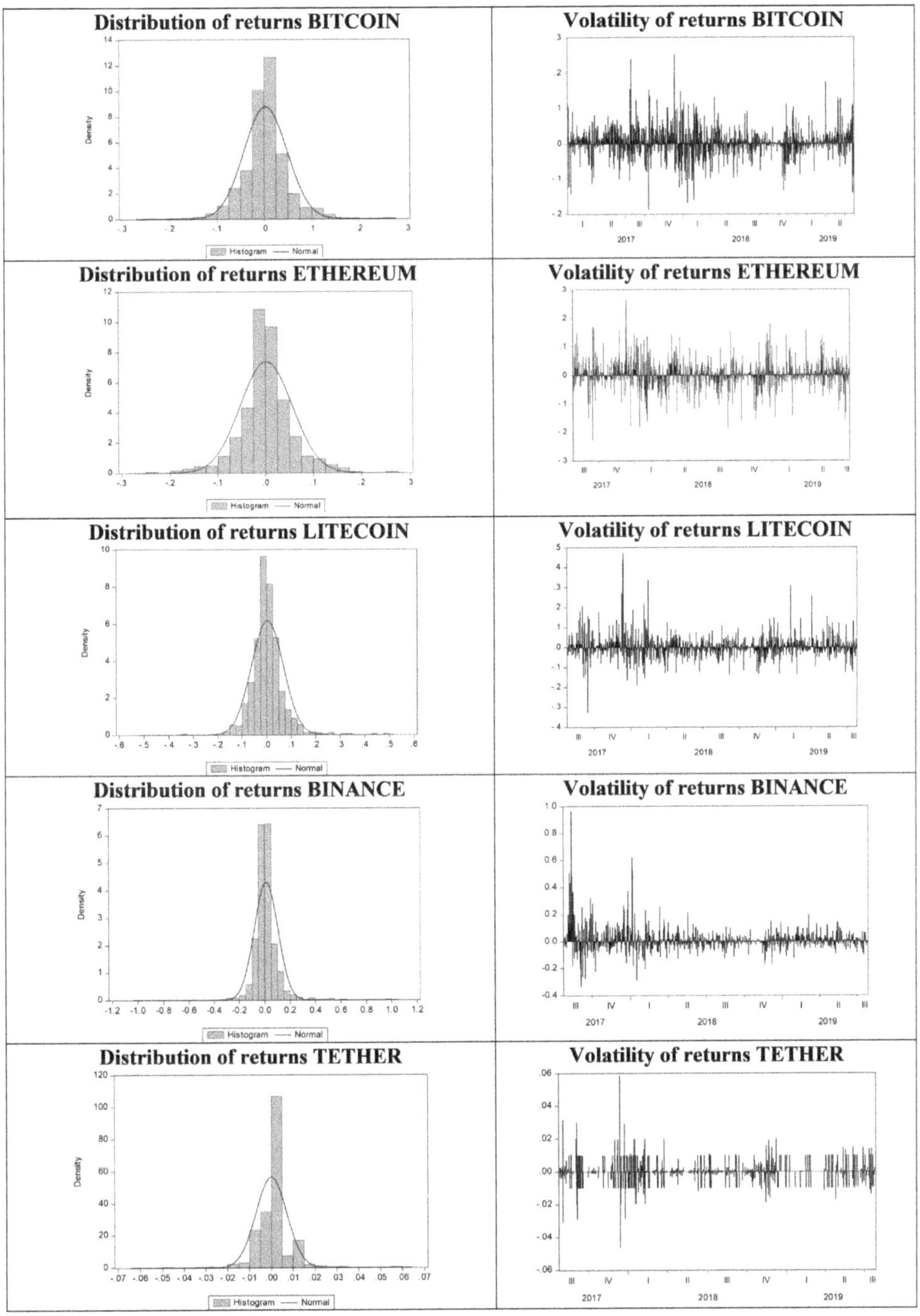

Figure 4. Relative comparison by risk-return indicators
Source: Authors, 2019

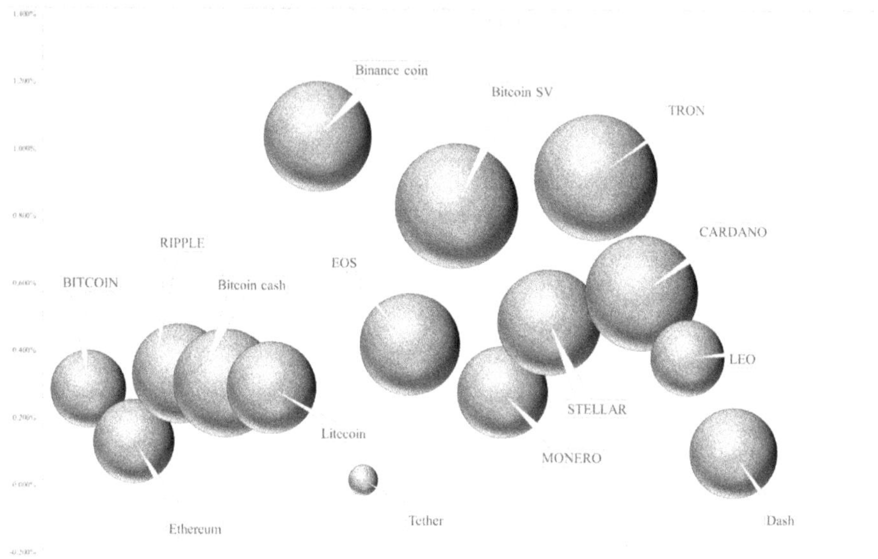

Table 2. Market value and 24h volume of top15 cryptocurrencies (as per July, 30 2019)

	Bitcoin	Altcoins	dAppcoins	Utilitycoins	Stablecoins
Assets	1	6	5	2	1
Market cap	169,610,819,668	17,632,847,682	42,695,311,248	5,576,195,495	4,020,260,813
% in total	52%	5%	13%	2%	1%
Volume	15,705,735,089	5,097,491,048	9,539,066,139	162,973,287	17,778,926,209
% in total	18%	6%	11%	0%	20%

(Data Source: coinmarketcap, 2017-2019)

Competition Within the Cryptocurrency Market

This section is interested in understanding the relative movements within this market on the basis of the classification this chapter offered in advance. In appendix 2, Table 5 shows the correlation coefficient for the five asset class leaders against a common sovereign currency, that is the US Dollar. As expected, all cryptocurrencies move to the same direction for that they are positive correlate with the exception of Tether.

Figure 5. Market cap and 24h volume for top15 cryptocurrencies
Source: Authors, 2019

This happens because this stablecoins follows the movement of an asset outside the cryptocurrency market, that is the US Dollar. Bitcoin is in strong relation with its altcoin (Litecoin) while the strongest positive correlation exhibit Ethereum with Litecoin (0,90) and the weakest Binancecoin and Ethereum (zero).

As a second step, this empirical analysis divides in quarters the two-year period (2017-2019) under examination. In appendix 3, table 6 shows the figures for each pair whereas figure 6 graphically presents the outcome. All figures are normalized to the unit at the beginning. The movement of the utilitycoin (Binanceoin) bears resemblance to a security. Notice the hype in the first quarter which happens just after its initial coin offering in 2017. The initial great trading interest in the utilitycoin then smooths as Bitcoin ends up in the period examined (July 2019) with the higher appreciation compared with the previous quarter (April 2019). For the whole period examined, Binancecoin experienced extreme movements as well as the highest appreciation in percentage terms (from USD 0,11 to 27,89) followed by Bitcoin (250%), Litecoin (116%) but Ethereum's was only 1%. Stablecoin's price change was of course 0%.

Next, figure 7 brings an alternative perspective to the above considerations and appendix 4 shows the relevant table 7. Under this consideration, the figure shows how the other cryptocurrencies moved in relation to the market leader (Bitcoin), again divided in quarters throughout the two-year period examined. It is self-

Figure 6. Selected crypto-currencies price evolution against USD (2017-2019)
Source: Authors, 2019

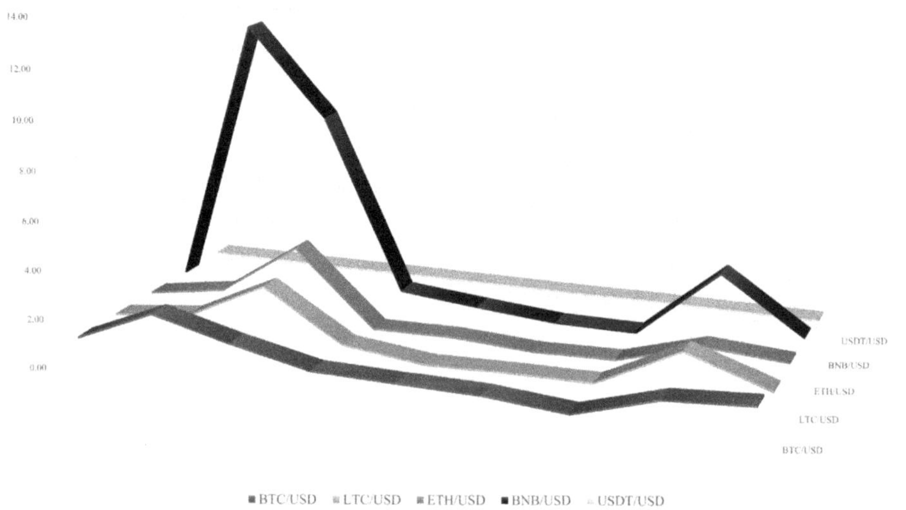

evident that all pairs ended up higher, thus Bitcoin strengthens its dominant value. Nonetheless, quarterly analysis suggests that Bitcoin had moments of decline in relative value as indicated by the lines below the unit level. In more detail, in the end of the second quarter (January 2018) all cryptocurrencies outperform Bitcoin which bounces back later on.

Competition Across Traditional and Other Alternative Investments

As a next step in this empirical inquiry, market leader Bitcoin is compared to other traditional and alternative investments in terms of basic risk-return profile aiming to display differences in fundamental concepts. But, which asset classes should be chosen and based on which economic rationale? In the first place, cryptocurrencies have been inquired whether the fit in the following institutional forms:

- **Are they bank deposits?** Today, only Bitcoin value stands at more than 20 times the whole banking sector of an EU country (Greece).
- **Are They low cost wealth transporters equities?** Today, only Bitcoin value stands at 20 times the market value of one of leading money transfer firms worldwide (The Western Union Company).

Figure 7. Selected crypto-currencies price evolution against BTC (2017-2019)
Source: Authors, 2019

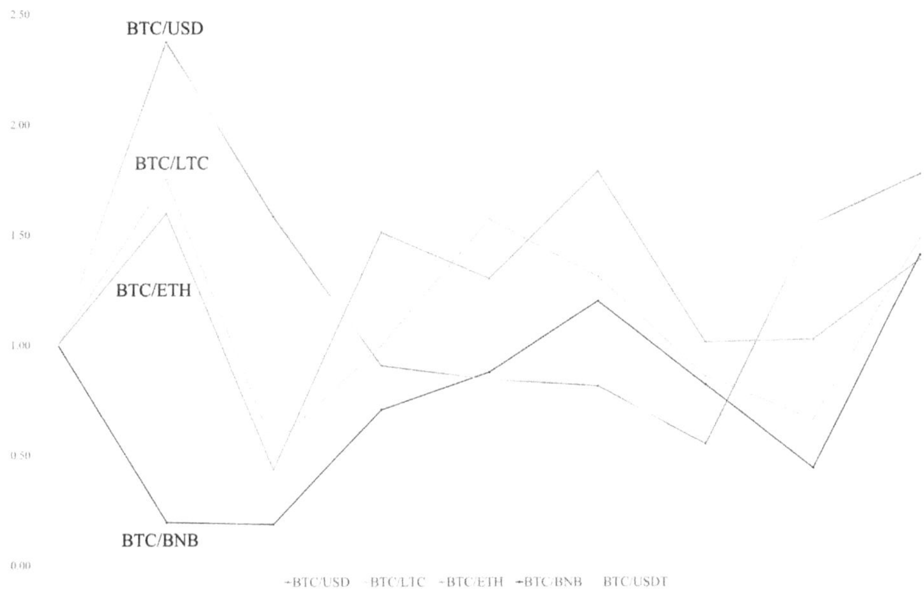

- **Are they digital-financial commodities?** Today, Gold value stands at 2 times the value of Bitcoin (assuming 5.482 billion ounces of gold in the entire world according to Reuters.
- **Are they cash controlled by central banks?** Today, Bitcoin value stands at 20 times the whole monetary base (M0) of an EU country (Denmark). Note that the monetary base of the biggest economy worldwide is USD 3,8 trillion (USA). Recall that there are central banks (e.g. Belgium, Japan, Greece, Switzerland, and South Africa) that are publicly-traded.

Ankenbrand & Bieri (2018) compare the aggregate cryptocurrency market and established asset classes (using proxy indexes) for the period 2013-2018. As anticipated, cryptocurrencies' index average return is 13 times higher and standard deviation 8 times higher compared with stocks but correlation is significantly poor. Comparison of Bitcoin with traditional and alternative investments is shown in table 8 for a wider period of 5 years. Bitcoin's extreme volatility and negative daily return on average may be attributed to a newly established market as selection of data window is important. Danish Korona.

Table 3. Descriptive statistics between Bitcoin and selected traditional investments and alternative investments rate of return performance (2014-2019)

	Cryptocurrency BTC/USD	**sovereign currency Danish Korona/USD**	**Commodity Gold/USD**	**Equity Western Union**
Mean	-27,31%	0,02%	0,01%	0,02%
Standard Error	0,0073	0,0001	0,0348%	0,0368%
Median	-8,068%	0,007%	-0,0327%	0,0000%
Mode	-75,497%	0,000%	0,0000%	0,0000%
Standard Deviation	0,3105	0,0052	0,0126	0,0130
Sample Variance	0,0964	0,0000	0,0001	0,0001
Kurtosis	-1,5352	2,5769	5,7962	2,5635
Skewness	-0,3856	-0,0933	0,3526	0,0225
Range	1,0676	0,0533	0,1437	0,1328
Minimum daily return	-81,52%	-2,95%	-6,99%	-6,87%
Maximum daily return	25,25%	2,38%	7,38%	6,41%
Number of observations	1825	1367	1328	1260
Confidence Level(95,0%)	0,014256881	0,000273896	0,000682176	0,00072257

(Data Source: investing.com, 2014-2019)

Cryptocurrencies in Modern Portfolio Theory and Practice

In the early cryptocurrency years, investing in cryptocurrencies was characterized by a single and quite straight-forward strategy; "put money in Bitcoin and wait". But, as the market started to grow in the advent of other cryptocurrencies that showed strong market capitalization and volume, then new strategies arise. As a result, researchers started to construct Markowitz mean-variance models derived from classic finance literature applied to traditional and alternative investments as well in an attempt to examine portfolio diversification issues. Recall that under such models,

Expected return: $E\left(R_p\right)=\sum_i w_i E\left(R_i\right)$

Portfolio return variance: $\sigma_p^2=\sum_i w_i^2\sigma_i^2+\sum_i\sum_j w_i w_j \sigma_i \sigma_j \rho_{ij}$ Where (i) is the asset, (w_i) the weight of each asset in the portfolio, (σ_i) the standard deviation of asset i and (ρ_{ij}) the correlation coefficient of assets i and j. Under this frame, Brauneis & Mestel (2019) test for various portfolios and their out-of-sample analysis support

Figure 8. Efficient frontier and portfolio strategies across cryptocurrencies
Source: Authors, 2019

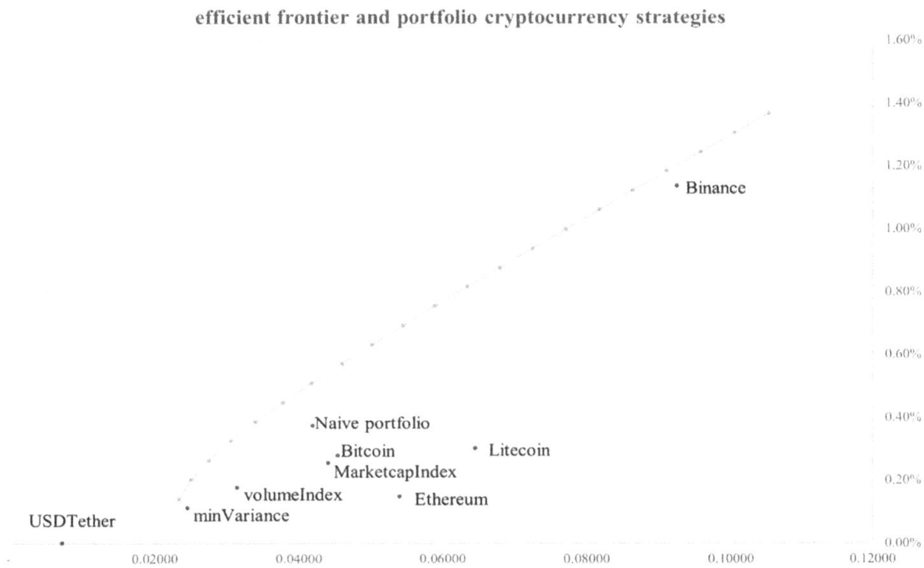

that blending cryptocurrencies yield better combinations of mean-variance. Liu 2019) use less number of cryptocurrencies, yet end up to the same conclusion. Later on, research shifted attention to investment strategies mixing traditional and alternative investment assets with cryptocurrencies. Baumöhl (2019) examine connections with the Foreign Exchange market and Kurka (2019) extend to include other traditional asset classes such as commodities and securities. In the same spirit, though focusing only on the market leader (Bitcoin) Guesmi, Saadi, Abid & Ftiti (2019) show that hedging strategies involving Bitcoin reduce considerably portfolio's risk. Figure 8, shows the location of the five proxy cryptocurrencies earlier examined. In addition, the plot illustrates in this mean-variance framework four portfolios strategies including all these five cryptocurrencies. In specific, (a) minVarinace was constructed by optimizing (minimizing) portfolio's variance, (b) MarketcapIndex computes weights based on each cryptocurrency market cap, (c) VolumeIndex follows the same logic, though taking into account volume and (d) stands for a naïve-portfolio (1/N) where N=5 the number of assets. Efficient frontier features the combination of the optimal portfolio assuming short-selling and a mix of Bitcoin and the stablecoin. In appendix 5, table 8 presents the relevant calculations. The plot visualized the realization of investment strategies across cryptocurrencies.

In the next plots, portfolio diversification possibilities are pointed out in combinations of the market leader (Bitcoin) with the three proxies taken above

Figure 9. Mean-variance portfolio including equity and cryptocurrency
Source: Authors, 2019

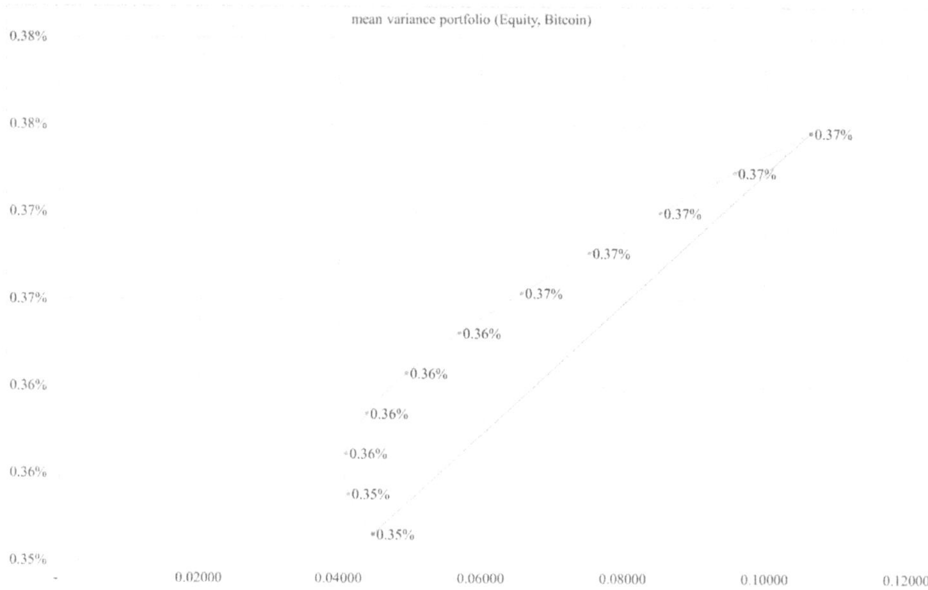

with regards to the three traditional and alternative investment classes i.e. equity (Western Union), FOREX market (Danish Korona) and commodity (Gold). Figure 9, 10 and 11 depict the diversification result.

Pricing Cryptocurrencies

Standardized valuation models have generated debate, such as over how best to price cryptocurrencies. It is most certain that the lack of widely acceptable valuation methodologies has been a reason why investment interest in cryptocurrencies remains in the sidelines with no room for adoption from professionals in the asset management industry. Is it a currency, commodity, security, derivative or combination?

Cryptocurrencies operate outside conventional concepts of both traditional and alternative investment assets. It is self-evident that cryptocurrencies and commodities are not alike since the former have no alternative use, thus have no intrinsic value. Moreover, cryptocurrencies and equity securities are not alike since the former do not formally enter into the equity structure of the firm.

Similarly, cryptocurrencies and sovereign currencies are not alike since the former are not associated (a) with legal tender, neither (b) with term structure of interest rates nor (c) with national trade imbalances, thus have no fundamentals. On account of that, traditional valuation models fall short.

Figure 10. Mean-variance portfolio including commodity and cryptocurrency
Source: Authors, 2019

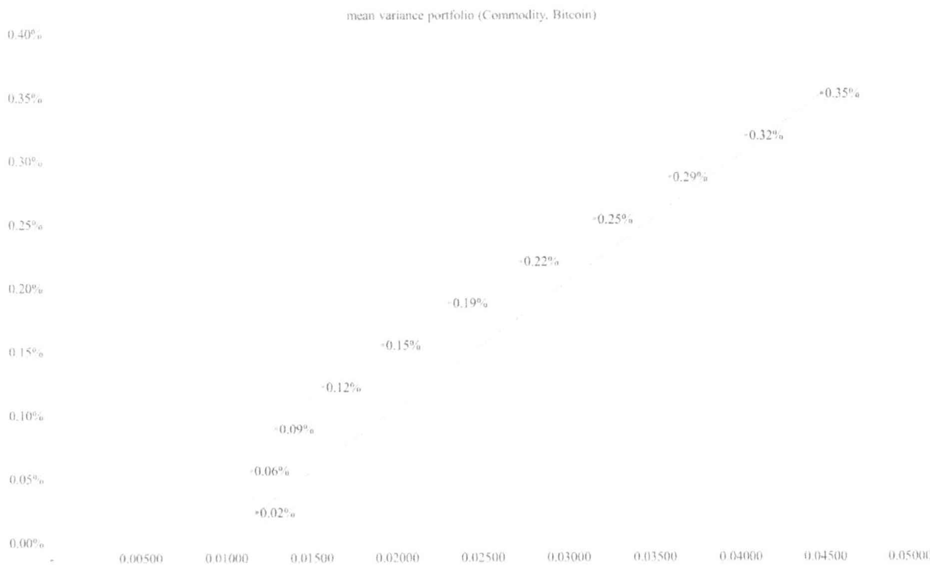

Figure 11. Mean-variance portfolio including FOREX and cryptocurrency
Source: Authors, 2019

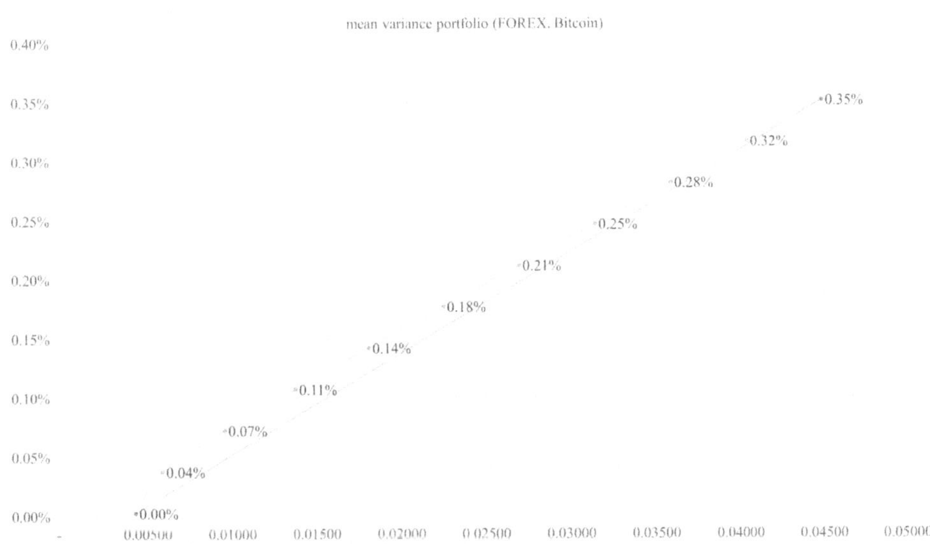

In the empirical price formulation literature on cryptocurrencies, until now studies have mostly expressed interest in Bitcoin. Methodology and findings can be grouped in three categories. First, (a) market forces of demand and supply (Kristoufek, 2013; Ciaian et al., 2014; de Roure & Tasca, 2014) where currency models are mostly applied to reject the hypothesis of medium of exchange motive. Second, implied motives (Brito and Castillo, 2013; Yermack 2013; Bouoiyour et al., 2014; Kristoufek, 2014; Glaser et al., 2014; Garcia et al., 2014; Bystrom & Krygier, 2018) which rely on revealed preferences drawn from search queries, social media big data, public information, attention of news that conclude in support of the speculation motive. Third, (c) macro-finance global financial markets (van Wijk, 2013; Ciaian et al., 2014; Sovbetov, 2018) which relate prices with indices, commodities, currency exchange rates, economic indicators and other cryptocurrencies etc.), yet inferences are inconclusive.

In conclusion, theory and practice have examined the following pricing methodologies:

- **Fundamental Analysis:** This refers to approaches to identify and model fundamental factors, if any of cryptocurrencies within traditional finance valuation literature (Zhang, Wang, Li & Shen, 2018).
    - **Currency Models**: Initially, Bitcoin was deemed as a currency, thus the initial belief was that it cannot be valued but rather "priced" by the interaction of supply/demand. Models that have been employed in literature include Quantity Theory of Money, Gold Standard, Purchasing Power Parity and neoclassical models with money in the utility function. All studies have strongly rejected the transaction motive hypothesis.
    - **Commodity Models**: Then, Bitcoin's high volatility was thought to resemble a commodity than a typical currency. Again, this has been proven problematic for that there is no actual alternative use of this asset like commodities that possess an intrinsic value. Though, in some cases the return may be perceived as a convenience yield.
    - **Securities Models**: Later on, the equity side of these asset was suggested. Opponents argued that they are not securities for that they do not generate money flows. It is true that, cryptocurrencies seem to trade more like perpetual bonds than stocks. As said, Steem Power cryptocurrencies have some features of equity.

An interesting argument is that as cryptocurrencies' markets lack efficiency and prices cannot be easily attributed to fundamentals, in contrast technical strategies may become more effective (El Alaoui, Bouri & Roubaud, 2018).

- **Technical Analysis:** This type of valuation analysis focus on past trading activity.
    - Algorithmic trading and strategies based on past statistical performance have been openly regarded as profitable for that they identify and restore trading opportunities. Cryptocurrencies like Bitcoin that are characterized by absence of "news" from the supply-side since they follow a pre-determined path may identify repeatable patterns of price movements and signals. This is because all these are exclusively attributed to demand factors like sentiment and arguably past behavior.
    - Relative valuation analysis based on trading metrics as earlier explained. Comparing these metrics for one cryptocurrency against a similar cryptocurrency of other asset traded in the real economy produces relative measures to identify possible misvaluations.

LIMITATIONS, OPPORTUNITIES & CHALLENGES

Limitations comprise the lack of the following structures divided into endogenous and exogenous factors. The former are limitations identified within these p2p systems while the latter are ones stemming from the society and economy as a whole. The endogenous factors include:

- **Barbaric Relic:** This refers to wasteful competition in the mining sector due to winners-takes-it-all mechanism in mineable cryptocurrencies like Bitcoin as all consume energy but only one miner receives the reward. By analogy with precious metals like gold which Keynes called an "barbaric relic" for using large amounts of labor and machinery, the usage of scarce energy resources questions the cost-effectiveness rationale.
- **Increasing Replenishment Cost:** This relates to the maintenance of the system in the mining sector as traction soars. So, when miners' reward will end or further reduced (less new bitcoins coming out of the system) or become unprofitable (due to high energy cost for mining), then there would be no incentive to mine and the continuity of the network would be at risk.
- **Unstable / Deflationary Economy:** If Bitcoin used as medium of exchange due to inflexible supply curve as the growth level of economic activity outpaces the growth level of currency creation. Capitalism is driven by entrepreneurs who assume business risks. A Bitcoin economic environment with declining prices will lead producers to delay investments.

- **No Lender of Last Resort:** In today's world banks lend funds and a central bank plays the role of Lender of Last Resort. In a fully cryptocurrency economy, can the protocol guarantee the appropriate policy reaction in the event of liquidity crises?
- **Total pure Decentralization is Utopia:** Possible concentration in the (a) exchanges sector due to need for liquidity and in the (b) mining sector due to formation of partnerships (and consequently distribution of profits) is already present.
- **Dishonest Behavior:** As Nakamoto, 2008 points out about her offspring, the Bitcoin: "*The system is secure as long as honest nodes collectively control more CPU power than any cooperating group of attacker nodes.*" cryptocurrencies are honest participation driven networks whereas central authorities trust driven.

On the other hand, the exogenous factors include:

- **Technological and Financial Literacy:** Cryptocurrencies require an electronic device (computer, mobile phone etc.) and internet access. Not all places and people in the world have access to digital infrastructure. In addition, their operation may confuse people who are not in the possession of the set of skills and knowledge that allow to make informed decisions.
- **Criminal Activity:** Cryptocurrencies have been openly condemned for easing illicit trade as criminals take advantage of the alleged complete anonymity of the system.
- **Awareness and Adoption:** Cryptocurrencies require an electronic device (computer, mobile phone etc.) and internet access. Not all places and people in the world have access to electronic and digital infrastructure.

Opportunities and challenges that may strive future success of cryptocurrencies and act as recommendation to tackle the above limitations may include:

- **Merchants Catalogues:** Now, goods are hardly expressed in cryptocurrency price on account of high volatility. Stable coins may offer new perspectives.
- **Asset Management Practices Embrace Cryptocurrencies:** From the investment perspective, cryptocurrencies will gain wider acceptance as reliable investment vehicles when institutional investors start to incorporate them in investment strategies. A way forward may be the recent developments in the United States (USA) where derivatives exchanges offered Bitcoin futures trading and waiting approvals for Exchange-Traded-Funds backed by Bitcoin.

- **Firms Raising Capital in Cryptocurrencies:** Capital raise comes in the form of equity and debt. Cryptocurrencies if wanted to be seen as long-term investments, need to establish themselves as an alternative non-conventional form of equity capital that offers specific corporate/community benefits. IOU cryptocurrencies issued by private entities may offer new perspectives.
- **Deposits and Income Denominated in Cryptocurrencies:** This implies that the general public removes deposits from banks and accept income (wages) in cryptocurrencies. Wider adoption and trust on stable and IOU cryptocurrencies is required in this field.
- **Critical Technological Factors of Success**: would be lowering transaction fees and blockchain's size that full-nodes need to download.

FUTURE RESEARCH DIRECTIONS

Indeed, this research topic is multidisciplinary and an exceptional paradigm for cooperative collaboration among dissimilar theoretical traditions and diverse applied disciplines. While the interest in risk-return relationship of cryptocurrencies based on their trading history will continue, new approaches to research will allow to study implications that influence cryptocurrencies behavior as alternative investment placements. These include the following.

Monetary Implications: Very little has been written on cryptocurrencies utility as money. Broader adoption of cryptocurrencies may take the form of various arrangements namely (i) adoption of decentralized crypto-currencies as store of value assets and (ii) sovereign-currencies in circulation competing with centralized (IOU) crypto-currencies both as store of value and means of payment. All these and others could be assessed in cooperation with institutions to compare the efficiency of the influence in each case and result in the submission of policy reforms. As a matter of fact, regulators are exploring digital currencies landscape, within the blockchain technology and whether it would be beneficial for their economies to issue their own central bank digital currency commonly called CBDC following the first work of Barrdear, J., & Kumhof, M. (2016).

Institutional Implications: It is worth studying the institutional perspective of such pure decentralized networks and what are the implications for current democratic systems of governance and political representation. More specifically, regulation of such decentralized clearing houses and risk management have not been properly studied in order to present recommendations. It goes without saying, that the benefits of centralization like highly-regulated stock-exchanges that scrutinize any capital raise project in order to protect investors, thus the general public and interest will be always impeccable. So, decentralization should be institutionally approached so that cryptocurrencies are not seen as part of a closed inefficient community prevailed by anarchism rather an open-innovation project of a digital ecosystem that will benefit the society in the real economy as a whole.

CONCLUSION

This chapter delved in to the newly emerged cryptocurrency market. By now, the reader should be familiar with the next two points:

- **Blockchain:** It is a peer-to-peer, thus without any middleman involved payment system.
- **Cryptocurrency:** It is a digital unique asset of known levels of supply which is (a) issued (a1) as a new asset like Bitcoin or (a2) has an underlying asset like a sovereign-currency (US Dollar, Euro) or good in the real economy and (b) is circulated in a transparent and irreversible manner within a blockchain either in-built or surrogate (called dApps).

This chapter aimed at bringing to the limelight this new class of assets arguably already part of alternative finance and investments. By now, the reader should have understood that cryptocurrencies arrive in different structures some of which resemble to even traditional investments in cash (stable coins) and others to alternative investments of highly sophisticated contracts and assets like derivatives (utility coins) and others to commodities such as the "Bing-Bang" asset that spurred this continuously expanding ecosystem, the 12-year old now infamous Bitcoin created by the pseudonymous Satoshi Nakamoto in 2008. This chapter underlined the importance of cryptocurrency asset class categorization. Investors in cryptocurrencies tend to follow the leader in each category as reinforcement effects become fiercer and substitution effects to raise only when a new kind of cryptocurrency emerge and attract investment interest for each innovative character. Innovation is a critical factor in this full of sentiment market. This research received no specific grant from any funding agency in the public, commercial, or not-for-profit sectors.

REFERENCES

Ankenbrand, T., & Bieri, D. (2018). Assessment of cryptocurrencies as an asset class by their characteristics. *Investment Management & Financial Innovations*, *15*(3), 169–181. doi:10.21511/imfi.15(3).2018.14

Barber, S., Boyen, X., Shi, E., & Uzun, E. (2012, February). Bitter to better—how to make bitcoin a better currency. In International Conference on Financial Cryptography and Data Security (pp. 399-414). Berlin, Germany: Springer. 10.1007/978-3-642-32946-3_29

Barrdear, J., & Kumhof, M. (2016). The macroeconomics of central bank issued digital currencies.

Baumöhl, E. (2019). Are cryptocurrencies connected to forex? A quantile cross-spectral approach. *Finance Research Letters*, *29*, 363–372. doi:10.1016/j.frl.2018.09.002

Boreiko, D., & Sahdev, N. K. (2018). To ico or not to ico–empirical analysis of initial coin offerings and token sales. *Available at SSRN 3209180.*

Brauneis, A., & Mestel, R. (2019). Cryptocurrency-portfolios in a mean-variance framework. *Finance Research Letters*, *28*, 259–264. doi:10.1016/j.frl.2018.05.008

Buchholz, M., Delaney, J., Warren, J., & Parker, J. (2012). Bits and bets, information, price volatility, and demand for Bitcoin. *Economics*, *312*, 2–48.

Bystrom, H., & Krygier, D., Corbet, S., Meegan, A., Larkin, C., Lucey, B., & Yarovaya, L. (2018). What Drives Bitcoin Volatility? Exploring the dynamic relationships between cryptocurrencies and other financial assets. *Economics Letters*, *165*, 28–34. doi:10.1016/j.econlet.2018.01.004

de Roure, C., & Tasca, P. (2014). Bitcoin and the PPP Puzzle.

Dyhrberg, A. H. (2016). Bitcoin, gold and the dollar–A GARCH volatility analysis. *Finance Research Letters*, *16*, 85–92. doi:10.1016/j.frl.2015.10.008

El Alaoui, M., Bouri, E., & Roubaud, D. (2018). Bitcoin price–volume: A multifractal cross-correlation approach. *Finance Research Letters.*

Gandal, N., & Halaburda, H. (2016). Can we predict the winner in a market with network effects? Competition in cryptocurrency market. *Games*, *7*(3), 16. doi:10.3390/g7030016

Glaser, F., Zimmermann, K., Haferkorn, M., Weber, M. C., & Siering, M. (2014). *Bitcoin-asset or currency? revealing users' hidden intentions. Revealing Users' Hidden Intentions (April 15, 2014)*. ECIS.

Griffin, J. M., & Shams, A. (2018). Is bitcoin really un-tethered?. Available at SSRN 3195066.

Grinberg, R. (2012). Bitcoin: An innovative alternative digital currency. *Hastings Sci. & Tech. LJ*, *4*, 159.

Guesmi, K., Saadi, S., Abid, I., & Ftiti, Z. (2019). Portfolio diversification with virtual currency: Evidence from bitcoin. *International Review of Financial Analysis*, *63*, 431–437. doi:10.1016/j.irfa.2018.03.004

Hileman, G., & Rauchs, M. (2017). Global cryptocurrency benchmarking study. Cambridge Centre for Alternative Finance, 33.

Kajtazi, A., & Moro, A. (2019). The role of bitcoin in well diversified portfolios: A comparative global study. *International Review of Financial Analysis*, *61*, 143–157. doi:10.1016/j.irfa.2018.10.003

Kurka, J. (2019). Do cryptocurrencies and traditional asset classes influence each other? *Finance Research Letters*, *31*, 38–46. doi:10.1016/j.frl.2019.04.018

Liu, W. (2019). Portfolio diversification across cryptocurrencies. *Finance Research Letters*, *29*, 200–205. doi:10.1016/j.frl.2018.07.010

Nakamoto, S. (2008). Bitcoin: A peer-to-peer electronic cash system.

Schilling, L., & Uhlig, H. (2019). Some simple bitcoin economics. *Journal of Monetary Economics*, *106*, 16–26. doi:10.1016/j.jmoneco.2019.07.002

Sovbetov, Y. (2018). Factors influencing cryptocurrency prices: Evidence from bitcoin, ethereum, dash, litcoin, and monero. *Journal of Economics and Financial Analysis*, *2*(2), 1–27.

Tapscott, D., & Tapscott, A. (2016). *Blockchain revolution: how the technology behind bitcoin is changing money, business, and the world*. Penguin.

Yermack, D. (2015). Is Bitcoin a real currency? An economic appraisal. In *Handbook of digital currency* (pp. 31–43). Academic Press. doi:10.1016/B978-0-12-802117-0.00002-3

Zhang, W., Wang, P., Li, X., & Shen, D. (2018). Some stylized facts of the cryptocurrency market. *Applied Economics*, *50*(55), 5950–5965. doi:10.1080/00036846.2018.1488076

ADDITIONAL READING

Antonopoulos, A. M. (2014). *Mastering Bitcoin: unlocking digital cryptocurrencies*. O'Reilly Media, Inc.

Arslanian, H., & Fischer, F. (2019). The Crypto-asset Ecosystem. In *The Future of Finance* (pp. 157–163). Cham: Palgrave Macmillan. doi:10.1007/978-3-030-14533-0_13

Böhme, R., Christin, N., Edelman, B., & Moore, T. (2015). Bitcoin: Economics, technology, and governance. *The Journal of Economic Perspectives*, *29*(2), 213–238. doi:10.1257/jep.29.2.213

Gomber, P., Koch, J. A., & Siering, M. (2017). Digital Finance and FinTech: Current research and future research directions. *Journal of Business Economics*, *87*(5), 537–580. doi:10.100711573-017-0852-x

Houben, R., & Snyers, A. (2018). Cryptocurrencies and blockchain: Legal context and implications for financial crime, money laundering and tax evasion.

Koning, J. P. (2016). Fedcoin: a central bank-issued cryptocurrency. R3 Report, 15.

Liew, J., Li, R. Z., Budavári, T., & Sharma, A. (2019). Cryptocurrency Investing Examined. The Journal of The British Blockchain Association, 8720.

Liu, Y., & Tsyvinski, A. (2018). *Risks and returns of cryptocurrency (No. w24877)*. National Bureau of Economic Research. doi:10.3386/w24877

KEY TERMS AND DEFINITIONS

Blockchain: A shared database between the nodes of a distributed ledger network where all past transactions are recorded in a chronological order.

Consensus Algorithm: A mechanism that enables the distributed network to reach an agreement over the true state of the Blockchain, thus which transactions are valid.

Cryptocurrency: An asset of digital nature that is recorded and transferred on a Blockchain. Cryptocurrency is a monetary application of Distributed Ledgers and part of crypto-assets which may also by non-monetary such as votes and real assets.

Crypto-exchanges: Market makers that emerged to facilitate trade between cryptocurrencies.

Distributed Ledgers: A software that includes a shared database (the Blockchain) and a digital asset (the Cryptocurrency). The latter is optional.

Fork: A fork is a disagreement between nodes. In case disagreement are significant (over the protocol and the algorithm) this is called hard-fork. If not that significant, this is called soft-fork.

Full-node: They form the backbone of the network for that they fully verify the rules enacted by the algorithm and the protocol of the distributed ledger. The requirement and downside is that the entire shared database need to be downloaded and continuously updated.

Hard-Fork: In a hard-fork the Blockchain results to a permanent divergence from the previous version of the Blockchain, though the latter still operates along the old path. This essentially creates two Blockchain, and the nodes who endorse the disagreement can upgrade to the new version while the others can continue to follow the old one.

Lightweight-node: She does need to download the shared database (Blockchain). Instead, can join the network and effectively rely upon full-nodes operations. The downside is that it is less secure compared to being a full-node.

Mining: A fork is a disagreement between nodes. In case disagreement are significant (over the protocol and the algorithm) this is called hard-fork. If not that significant, this is called soft-fork.

Node: Any electronic devise that connects to the distributed ledger network whereby contribute and use resources. There are two types of nodes i.e. the full-node and the lightweight-node. Wallets are operating through nodes.

Protocol: The protocol describes the rules within the distributed ledger network. By way of example the determination of the supply schedule of cryptocurrencies (frequency, new units etc.) is written in the protocol.

Satoshi Nakamoto: The alias used by the unidentified person or group of persons who published a paper with the title "Bitcoin: A peer-to-peer electronic cash system" in 2008 upon which Bitcoin as open-source software as developed.

ENDNOTES

1 In 2018, the word cryptocurrency was added to the Merriam-Webster Dictionary.

2 Thus far, there have been released almost 50 update versions of the Bitcoin software. Since 19/3/2014 has been renamed Bitcoin Core (available at www.bitcoin.org) and is the reference implementation (client) of Bitcoin nodes, which form the Bitcoin network. Changes (updates) are subject to voting. The way wherein the nodes that have downloaded the software exercise this voting right is by following, or ignoring the recommended change by the community. If the former is the case, then this results to what is called "forks".

3 A term coined by European Banking Association (2015)

4 The statement can be found here: https://www.basis.io

5 ECB: 'Virtual currency schemes'. Available on ecb.europa.eu/pub/pdf/other/virtualcurrencyschemes201210en.pdf

6 Bank of England. Quarterly Bulletin 2014 Q3. The economics of digital currencies (2014)

7 See, Judgement in Case C-264/14. Skatteverket v David Hedqvist". Press Release No 128/15, Luxembourg, 22 October 2015

8 See, article on Business Insider (2014). Available on http://www.businessinsider.com/the-future-of-the-payments-industry-2014-slide-deck-2014-7?op=1

Appendix 1

Table 4. Risk return (2017-2019)

	Daily average return	Risk (standard deviation)	Sharpe ratio (risk free assumed zero)
BITCOIN	0.287%	0.0453	0.0632
Ethereum	0.131%	0.0539	0.0244
RIPPLE	0.333%	0.0754	0.0442
Bitcoin cash	0.306%	0.0893	0.0342
Litecoin	0.293%	0.0645	0.0454
Binance coin	1.039%	0.0927	0.1121
Tether	0.019%	0.0072	0.0260
EOS	0.423%	0.0795	0.0532
Bitcoin SV	0.835%	0.1193	0.0700
MONERO	0.282%	0.0648	0.0435
STELLAR	0.490%	0.0851	0.0576
TRON	0.921%	0.1216	0.0758
CARDANO	0.578%	0.1017	0.0568
LEO	0.386%	0.0440	0.0876
Dash	0.103%	0.0622	0.0166

(Data Source: coinmarketcap, 2017-2019)

Appendix 2

Table 5. Correlation matrix by asset class market leaders

	BTC/USD	LTC/USD	ETH/USD	BNB/USD	USDT/USD
BTC/USD	1,00				
LTC/USD	0,85	1,00			
ETH/USD	0,71	0,90	1,00		
BNB/USD	0,54	0,37	0,00	1,00	
USDT/USD	-0,43	-0,34	-0,49	0,19	1,00

Source: (Authors, 2019)

Appendix 3

Table 6. Competition between cryptocurrencies against the US Dollar

	29-Jul-17	31-Oct-17	31-Jan-18	30-Apr-18	31-Jul-18	31-Oct-18	31-Jan-19	30-Apr-19	27-Jul-19
BTC/USD	1,00	2,37	1,58	0,90	0,84	0,81	0,55	1,55	1,77
LTC/USD	1,00	1,36	2,93	0,91	0,54	0,62	0,64	2,35	1,20
ETH/USD	1,00	1,49	3,66	0,60	0,65	0,45	0,54	1,51	1,28
BNB/USD	1,00	12,15	8,51	1,28	0,96	0,68	0,67	3,53	1,26
USDT/USD	1,00	1,00	0,99	1,01	1,00	0,99	1,02	1,00	0,99

(Data Source: coinmarketcap, 2017-2019)

Appendix 4

Table 7. Competition between cryptocurrencies in relation with Bitcoin

	29-Jul-17	31-Oct-17	31-Jan-18	30-Apr-18	31-Jul-18	31-Oct-18	31-Jan-19	30-Apr-19	27-Jul-19
BTC/USD	1,00	2,37	1,58	0,90	0,84	0,81	0,55	1,55	1,77
BTC/LTC	1,00	1,75	0,54	0,99	1,57	1,31	0,85	0,66	1,48
BTC/ETH	1,00	1,60	0,43	1,51	1,30	1,78	1,01	1,02	1,38
BTC/BNB	1,00	0,20	0,19	0,70	0,87	1,20	0,82	0,44	1,41
BTC/USDT	1,00	2,36	1,60	0,90	0,84	0,82	0,54	1,55	1,79

(Data Source: coinmarketcap, 2017-2019)

Appendix 5

Table 8. Construction of mean-variance cryptocurrency portfolios

	Weight Bitcoin	Weight Litecoin	Weight Ethereum	Weight Binance	Weight USDTether	mean	variance	std deviation
naïve (1/N) portfolio	20%	20%	20%	20%	20%	0.37%	0.18%	0.04189
market cap index portfolio	73%	3%	22%	1%	1%	0.26%	0.19%	0.04401
volume index portfolio	45%	6%	18%	1%	31%	0.18%	0.10%	0.03145
min variance portfolio	26%	0%	27%	0%	48%	0.11%	0.06%	0.02456
BTC	100%	0%	0%	0%	0%	0.28%	0.21%	0.04534
LTC	0%	100%	0%	0%	0%	0.30%	0.42%	0.06451
ETH	0%	0%	100%	0%	0%	0.15%	0.29%	0.05398
BNB	0%	0%	0%	100%	0%	1.14%	0.86%	0.09253
USDT	0%	0%	0%	0%	100%	0.00%	0.00%	0.00704
Efficient 1	55%	38%	-108%	111%	4%	1.37%	1.11%	0.10519
Efficient 2	50%	0%	0%	0%	50%	0.14%	0.05%	0.02335

Source: (Authors, 2019)

Chapter 11
Crowdfunding:
An Innovative Instrument for Development Finance and Financial Inclusion

Louka T. Katseli
National and Kapodistrian University of Athens, Greece

Paraskevi Boufounou
National and Kapodistrian University of Athens, Greece

ABSTRACT

Crowdfunding is an innovative fin-tech mechanism for financing sustainable development. As this chapter demonstrates, crowdfunding can prove to be a powerful tool for financial inclusion, as it opens up funding possibilities for stakeholders, activities, and projects which would not be able to tap funding through the banking system or traditional credit and/or equity providers. This chapter provides a review of the most important recent European crowdfunding initiatives and critically evaluates the present Greek crowdfunding mechanism and its extension into a loan-based and equity-based funding system. By identifying the institutional and functional factors that constrain its use, it provides recommendations for their alleviation. The development of a grant-based crowdfunding platform in Greece has proven to be a powerful innovative tool to meet urgent financial needs in the course of the recent crisis as well as a tool for financial inclusion.

DOI: 10.4018/978-1-7998-2436-7.ch011

INTRODUCTION

The expansion of international trade and investment activities as well as the need to address sustainability challenges through the implementation of Sustainable Development Goals (SDGs) have increased demand for effective development finance. As traditional forms of development finance have not produced the desired results (ERD 2015), increased attention is being paid to identifying Innovative Financing for Development Instruments (IFDIs). The main definitions of IFDIs are presented in Table 3 (in the Appendices).

According to the World Bank (2012, p.1) an Innovative Financing for Development Instrument can be defined as any financing approach that helps to:

- Generate **additional** development funds by tapping new funding sources and looking beyond conventional mechanisms -such as budget outlays from established donors and bonds from traditional international financial institutions- or by engaging new partners including emerging donors and actors in the private sector.
- Enhance the **efficiency** of financial flows, by reducing delivery time and/or costs, especially for emergency needs and in crisis situations.
- Make financial flows more **results-oriented**, by explicitly linking funding flows to measurable performance on the ground.

Most IFDIs involve combining available financial instruments into a new package or using them in a new context or setting, such as a new sector, country, or region. In some cases, the driving force behind the new financial mechanism is two-fold: to raise new resources and to make the use of those resources more effective.

IFDIs are sorted into four categories, based on the source of contribution (private or public sector) and on the range of their scale (international or national). As argued in ERD (2015), although public domestic mechanisms comprise the largest share of all IFDIs, the use of international private mechanisms has proliferated especially in emerging economies and developing countries. They have attracted significant attention as they have permitted direct access to development-related support by bypassing bureaucracy that has often hampered the flow of traditional forms of development assistance. International private IFDIs include crowdfunding platforms that provide donations, micro loans (e.g. KIVA) and/or equity investment (e.g. Symbid and Crowdcube).

Development finance has been evolving in a rapid pace. In both developed and developing economies, entrepreneurs and NGOs combine traditional debt and equity start-up finance such as personal support systems, angel investors, and venture capitalists with microfinance (Khavul, 2010), peer-to-peer lending, crowdfunding (Schwienbacher, Belleflamme & Lambert, 2013), as well as other financial innovations.

Crowdfunding is an Innovative Financing Development Instrument, whereby a large and otherwise unrelated number of people contribute mainly small financial donations for varied kinds of rewards (financial or not). It is usually conducted via Internet-based platforms that act as the bridge between fundraisers and funders. Crowdfunding usually attracts small contributions, usually from members of the public not familiar with the business world. It bears the risks that are associated with the internet's virtual nature. The aforementioned elements of crowdfunding distinguish it from traditional financing methods.

In very recent years, the position of crowdfunding in the alternative finance landscape has progressively shifted from being just a marginal option to becoming a well-established and mature funding mechanism. Having started from a limited pool of innovators, crowdfunding has become widespread among investors and supporters in both project and campaign-financing (ECN 2018).

In addition to being considered as an alternative finance option, crowdfunding has also earned a primary reputation as a means to "democratize finance". This is due not only to the mobilization of a large crowd of individuals, but also to the virtuous processes of co-decision, co-creation, engagement and ownership by all parties involved.

The present paper is organized as follows:

Following a review of the literature pertaining to crowdfunding, its potential for credit provision to SMEs as opposed to traditional financing mechanisms is discussed and its implications for social ventures and financial inclusion are highlighted. Act4Greece, the first crowdfunding platform established in Greece in 2015, in the midst of the economic crisis, is presented as a case study that illustrates the potential impact of crowdfunding on development and social inclusion.

CROWDFUNDING: DEFINITION AND MODELS

Crowdfunding is considered close to micro-finance (Morduch, 1999) and crowdsourcing (Poetz & Schreier, 2012). More specifically:

- Crowdfunding is close to the concept and practice of microfinance.

Muhammad Yunus, founded the Grameen Bank in 1976 in Bangladesh,his home country, providing small loans that were guaranteed by the borrower's community (Yunus, 1999). Later, microfinancing evolved into a form of crowdfunding when websites (e.g Kiva.org) developed the concept of lending money in developing countries to the crowd through an Internet website. Microfinance has in many occasions proven to help poverty and supply access to financial instruments that would not have been available to impoverished people (Mutengezanwa et al., 2011). Donations to the most vulnerable tend to come from "backers" who are culturally related and geographically close. Financial mediators underpin this process by providing trust mechanisms (Burtch et al., 2014). Crowdfunders tend to be motivated by a will to contribute. Empirical evidence suggests that successful campaigns appeal to crowdfunders' desire to support a project unlike campaigns whose end goal is to profit from business opportunities (Allison et al., 2014).

Crowdsourcing was coined by Howe and Robinson (2006). Kleemann et al. (2008, p.8) define it as follows: "Crowdsourcing takes place when a profit oriented firm outsources specific tasks essential for the making or sale of its product to the general public (the crowd) in the form of an open call over the Internet, with the intention of animating individuals to make a [voluntary] contribution to the firm's production process for free or for significantly less than what that contribution is worth to the firm." In other words, profit making companies create value by asking consumers to be volunteers and essentially a free workforce. Kleemann et al. (2008) illustrate seven different crowdsourcing modes:

- Participation of consumers in product development and configuration.
- Product design.
- Competitive bids on specifically designed tasks or problems.
- Permanent open calls.
- Community reporting.
- Product rating by consumers and consumer profiling.
- Customer-to-customer support.

Crowdfunding is not included distinctively in this classification, though it can be viewed broadly as part of consumers' support. Crowdfunding can be viewed as an aspect or form of crowdsourcing, one that caters to one or multiple crowdsourcing modes. Extending Kleemann's et al. (2008) discussion on crowdsourcing, crowdfunding projects have intrinsic value as utility is generated with task accomplishment comparable to monetary or career-related rewards .

According to Mollick (2014, p.2) "crowdfunding refers to the efforts by entrepreneurial individuals and groups – cultural, social, and for-profit – to fund their ventures by drawing on relatively small contributions from a relatively large number of individuals using the internet, without standard financial intermediaries". The main definitions of crowdfunding prevailing in contemporary literature are summarized in Table 4 (in the Appendices).

According to Kirby and Worner (2014) there exist four different models of crowdfunding, depending on the individual goals of the funders:

1. **Donation Model:** Funders acting as philanthropists do not expect any rewards for their donations.
2. **Reward Model:** Funders receive a small reward for backing a project such as being credited in a movie, or being treated as an "early customer" who receives "pre-selling" benefits to the products of the funded projects, including purchase on earlier date, better price, or with some other special benefit.
3. **Debt Model:** Funders extend a loan, with the expectation of some rate of return on capital invested, depending on the platform (Outlaw, 2013). This model, according to Alison et al. (2013), Meyskens and Bird (2014), and Moss et al (2014) "fills the gap where traditional financial institutions do not operate and offers alternative financial aid rather than serves a direct way to raise capital." When it comes to microfinance loans, funders tend to focus on philanthropic projects rather than focusing on the return per se. In this way, they adopt patronage model elements. Havrylchyk (2018) provides a synopsis of the latest developments on regulation and platform- operation for debt crowdfunding.
4. **Equity Model:** Funders are investors, receiving equity stakes in return for their funding. As Meyskens and Bird (2014) state, crowdfunding "is similar to the principles of Microfinance and the Rotating Savings and Credit Association (ROSCA), where, all members in a group contribute to a pot of money and can contribute and borrow from this combined financing (Armendáriz and Morduch 2010)". This model is predominantly suitable for projects which may not have access to traditional finance.

In recent years, new crowdfunding models have emerged that apply to specific needs, like Hybrid Crowdfunding (that combine features from the abovementioned models), Invoice-Trading Crowdfunding, etc.

The importance of crowdfunding is growing. Evaluating the use of financial instruments, OECD (2018) concludes that "online alternative finance" has strong growth potential, and can bridge the financing gap for SMEs, especially high credit risk young firms, which do not have easy access to affordable finance. OECD's report adds that "although in many countries crowdfunding and related online alternative finance activities are still in their infancy, activities are growing rapidly, doubling in volumes every year between 2013 and 2016 in a number of countries; large regional differences in the take-up of online alternative finance persist, with markets in the United Kingdom, United States and especially China vastly out-measuring those in continental Europe".

Table 1. Major drivers and constrains for crowdfunding uptake

Drivers	Constraints
Argawal et al. (2010) *Social Networks Coverage:* of particular importance **Collins, Swart and Zhang (2013)** • *The Economic Crisis:* the financial crisis was one of the main contributors to the expansion of crowdfunding • *E-commerce and Online Payment Systems:* Internet-based payment technologies foster crowdfunding as an attractive practice for entrepreneurs. **OECD (2014)** *Increased Regulations on bank LENDING:* Basel III has contributed to a decline in the supply of finance for SMEs and entrepreneurs. **Robano (2018)** *Low Interest Rates for Deposits*: investors are seeking higher returns.	**Bradford (2012)** *Cultural and Geopolitical Issues:* in Muslim countries a different instrument is used to interest-bearing loans to comply with Islamic law so the founder pays a service fee to the intermediary instead of interest. **Beualieu et al. (2014)** *Lack of Technological Means:* crowdfunding relies heavily on technology e.g. hosting websites and technologies supplying social media connections are needed to raise awareness about a project. **Robano (2018)** *Business Culture:* crowdfunding may fail to expand in countries with a stigma related to business failure.

Crowdfunding volumes, although small when compared to other IFDMs, have grown at rates above 100% per annum, similar to no other financial instrument. According to data from Massolution (2015) and Wardropetal (2015), worldwide crowdfunding platform transactions in 2014 increased by 167% to $ 16.2bn, while in 2015 they increased further by 120% to $ 34, 4 billion. In 2014, in Europe, transactions increased by 144% compared to 2014 to $ 3 billion and in 2015 by 115% compared to 2014 to about 6.5 billion, while authorized crowdfunding platforms more than doubled in the 2014-2016 period (from 44 in 2014 to 99 in 2016). Trading in North and South America increased by 145% and 167% to $ 9.5bn and $ 5.7m respectively in 2014, while trading in Africa rose more than 100% to $ 12m. Impressive rates of growth are also recorded in Asia (320% in 2013-2014 to $3.4bn and 210% in 2014-2015 to $10.5bn). This increase is mainly due to strong growth in India (where Fintech projects grow at a rate of 1000% per year) and China, which is estimated to invest $ 50 billion annually up to 2025. Internationally, the largest crowdfunding transactions for 2014 were geared to lending ($ 11.1bn, up 223% from 2014), followed by donations ($ 1.9bn, up 45%) and rewards ($ 1.33bn, up 84%) and equity ($ 1.1bn up by 182%).

The rapid growth of crowdfunding is mainly attributed to the growing use of the Internet and the ease of finding funding to promote innovative social ideas. Table 1 summarizes the main drivers and constraints of crowdfunding, according to the most recent bibliography:

In addition, EU (2017) identified potential barriers to cross-border transactions that prevent security-based and lending-based crowdfunding from scaling up across Europe and triggering appropriate regulatory changes.

According to Massolution (2015), the major trends that will affect the development of the crowdfunding market include inter alia changes in the composition of the crowd, the emergence of vertical platforms, the emergence of investor driven platforms, the entrance of major enterprises in the market as operators or service providers and growth in cross border deals. Massolution (2015) also expects a proliferation of regulatory reforms due to specific risks associated with the operation of crowdfunding platforms, such as counterparty (or credit) risk, risk of fraud, operational risks, liquidity risks, legal risks and money laundering.

CROWDFUNDING VS BUSINESS ANGELS AND VENTURE CAPITALS FOR SMES/STARTUPS

The diversification of financial instruments that are available and accessible to SMEs is a key enabler for securing their growth, profitability and sustainability. It enables them to reduce their overdependence on traditional financial instruments, improve their capital structure and upgrade their investment potential (Robano, 2015).

Financing sources are broadly separated into two main categories: equity and debt. Capital or equity investment result in money going directly to the company's capital against which investors receive shares. Consequently, investors attain some control over the company but also risk. On the other hand, those who provide debt financing remain affiliated with the company through a comprehensive contractual arrangement. At the same time, they bear lower risk due to the provision of collateral and the priority of their claims over equity. Startup companies may not be able to access debt finance, due to the fact that many of them do not have the collateral or stable cash flows needed to ensure regular interest costs (Berger & Udell, 1998).

Common equity financing sources include the entrepreneur himself and his team members, friends & family, Business Angels, Venture Capital and IPO to the Stock Markets (de Buysere et al., 2012) .Debt financing is usually sourced from banks, leasing companies, government agencies (different types of subsidies), trade financing (customers/suppliers) and bootstrapping.[1] (Schwienbacher & Larralde, 2010).

Schwienbacher and Larralde (2010) found that funding was not easily obtainable for small businesses. This was due to their small size and information asymmetry for investors due to little or no availability of historical data. Traditional financing methods such as VCs or business angels are unobtainable for small companies and bootstrapping hinders businesses' growth. This is due to the bootstrapping focus on cash generation which may deprioritize maximizing value creation. Crowdfunding thus becomes a feasible fundraising method especially for small entrepreneurial companies and/or project-based initiatives.

Crowdfunding is a preferred method for seeking finance, especially in the start-up stage of an entrepreneurial venture. According to Assenova et al. (2016), crowdfunding is both complementing and competing with venture capital. Successful crowdfunding campaigns can institute the traction and interest of the public ahead of venture capitalists. This way, such campaigns can help venture capitalists discover investment opportunities at a lower search cost. However, crowdfunding may end up becoming a threat to professional investment firms, thanks to its unregulated nature.

The main factors that influence the use of crowdfunding by SMEs against other financial instruments, according to the recent bibliography, can be summarized in Table 2 as follows:

As Dos Santos et al. (2011) note, competition for VCs is so intense that less than one in one hundred to one in one thousand business plans presented to a VC get funded. Meanwhile, crowdfunding is an innovative financial mechanism that considerably changes the institutionalized procedure of raising capital. Crowdfunding has been dubbed as "the democratization of entrepreneurial funding".

Rigby et al. (2002) argue that if demand for a product is strong, new entrants will not reduce the market share of existing firms but broaden the market; therefore crowdfunding may displace traditional stakeholders, but they may also embrace it.

According to Levin et al. (2013), Macht & Weatherston (2014), Manchanda & Muralidharan (2014), many projects are not appropriate for funding through traditional funding mechanisms due to an unproven track record, lack of growth potential, different commercial focus, or stage of the business circle that VCs/ and business angels look after. These traditional financing mechanisms were never an option for such projects and as a result crowdfunding has enlarged the market. As Beaulieu (2014) points out, traditional financing mechanisms may turn to crowdfunding as a value-added step through which a potential new market can be tapped: a VC may be more willing to participate in a company if a valuable market for it has been successfully identified through crowdfunding.

Robano (2015) and Paschen (2017) identify specific Crowdfunding models suitable for SMEs and startups depending on their business-cycle stage as follows:

1. **Donation Model:** Pre-startup stage (Idea/Inception and Prototype).
2. **Reward Model:** Pre-startup stage (Idea/Inception and Prototype).
3. **Debt Model:** Startup stage.
4. **Equity Model:** Early Growth stage.

Robano (2015) also notes that more traditional types of financing (Business Angels, Venture Capital, Private Equity) are likely to finance SMEs during their expansion stage, followed and/or coupled later by traditional funding through the banking system and potentially IPOs.[2]

Table 2. Factors affecting the use of crowdfunding, business angels and VCs

Factor	Bibliography Synopsis
Lack of Pre-existing Resources	Botazzi and Da Rin (2001), Keuschnigg (2004): Pioneering companies that benefit from VC funds' external support achieve more than the average company and have higher growth rates. Collateral is often essential for obtaining debt funding. Ueda (2004): Entrepreneurs with little collateral are more likely to obtain financing from VC funds than from banks.
Risk, Moral Hazard and Information Asymmetry	Short (1994): Managers take risks; shareholders are those who carry out the risks. This affects entrepreneurs' choices in financing. Bergemann and Hege (1998): A prominent way how equity investors deal with moral hazard is by staging their investments in several rounds, enabling investors to make decisions based on milestone achievement and on new information about the technological and market risks of a project. Myers and Majluf (1984), Narayanan (1998): Information asymmetry is an issue in financing entrepreneurial initiatives in which different parties engaged in a deal do not have access to information of equal importance. Ueda (2004): Entrepreneurs who choose VCs are more likely to have secured their ideas through intellectual property rights, showcasing that the entrepreneur's legal environment has direct influence on their choice.
Organizational Form (For-Profit or Non-Profit)	Glaeser and Shleifer (2001): Not-for-profit organizations focus less on their profit making and therefore focus more on quality, which may be a significant element in attracting donations. Lambert and Schwienbacher (2010): Not-for-profit organizations tend to be more successful in achieving their fundraising targets compared to for-profit organizations and project-based initiatives. This is due to the fact that not-for-profit organizations may be more inclined to commit to high quality products or services if quality comes at the expense of quantity.
Control Preferences	Berglöf (1994): Cash flow and control rights may shift hands over time, depending on pre-specified contingencies, which can be achieved with convertible preferred shares similar to how it is done by venture capitalists. Short (1994): Performance is affected by ownership structure due to its direct effects on a company's strategy. Berger and Udell (1998): Owner-managers seek to be their own boss and as a result they focus less on growth. Hellman (1998): Ownership and control are separate in VC contracts Czarnitzki and Kraft (2002): Owners tend to focus on maximizing profit in order to get the most out of dividends, while managers might have more value creation or prestige-related goals, such as focus on innovation.
Amounts Required	Bhidé (1992): 1. Financiers all have different pre-defined amounts that they are willing to invest. 2. VCs tend to have high minimum investments that prove to be not suited to the needs of small ventures. Berger and Udell (1998): Small business finance is disproportionally affected by macroeconomic conditions. The stock market's implementation cost is excessive and demands from companies to have reached a definite scale and have reduced the risk factor. Black and Gilson (1998): VC financing is affected by market conditions, since their entry is conditioned by their exit strategy in accordance to stock market's health. Botazzi and Da Rin (2001): For IPOs there is a legal minimal threshold to be placed on the stock market, which as a result prevents small companies from using it. Schwienbacher (2007): The above may lead to a decisive trade-off about the time of starting entrepreneurial activities, considering that smaller amounts need to be financed by other investor types (eg business angels).
Legal Issues About Equity Issuance	Sannajust, Roux & Chaibi (2014): Regulating equity issuance for private companies could hinder crowdfunding's financing abilities and the capacity of firms to seek public funding. Some countries impose a limit on the permitted number of shareholders that some forms of business organizations.
Efficiency And Decreased Risk	Sannajust, Roux & Chaibi (2014): In order to run a company or evaluate product value, entrepreneur rs may require external support. Crowdfunders may not have specialized knowledge about the industry, unlike business angels and venture capital funds. Therefore, a crowd could solve corporate issues better than individuals or teams, making crowdfunders as a crowd more efficient than a limited number of equity investors.

CROWDFUNDING FOR SOCIAL VENTURES

Most funders from the crowd are not too sophisticated and avoid evaluating business plans, cash-flow liquidity and collaterals (Ridley-Duff, 2009).

Crowdfunders' social projects are mostly driven by their purpose and their value creation goals. The different investment behavior characteristics of social investors in the UK are presented by Nicholls (2010). Social ventures face difficulties in attracting funding due either to liabilities of newness and smallness (Aldrich 1999) or to their focus on creating social value as opposed to long-term financial returns (Ridley-Duff 2009). Before the emergence of crowdfunding as an alternative means of finance (Lehner 2013), social ventures used to seek financing from a variety of sources including friends, donations, grants, social investors, earned income and bootstrapping (Lyons 2010; Meyskens & Carsrud 2013; Scarlata & Alemany 2013). Massolution (2015, p.103) points out that the Generations Xers and the Millennials show an increasing interest "in social impact investing, whereby a financial return is blended with a societal benefit. And in overall participation, it appears that these generations are the most active investors or patrons to crowdfunding campaigns".

Social ventures create economic value both directly and indirectly (Whitman 2009).There are many different types of economic and social values created from social ventures (Mairand 2006; Meyskens et al., 2011) They are associated with the provision of public goods and social benefits (e.g. education, health, freedom or helping the disadvantaged etc as argued by Whitman (2009)) or environmental protection (e.g. Green activities, recycling or alternative energy etc as argued by Meyskens and Carsrud (2013)). Myeskens and Bird (2014) propose a theoretical framework that compares social against economic value creation across the four aforementioned crowdfunding models, as follows:

- **Donation Model**:Low Economic Value - High Social Value.
- **Reward Model**: Low Economic Value - Low Social Value.
- **Debt Model**: High Economic Value - High Social Value.
- **Equity Model**: High Economic Value - Low Social Value.

CROWDFUNDING AND FINANCIAL INCLUSION

Crowdfunding is considered a potent supplementary funding mechanism that supports financial inclusion. This is due to the fact that it is both accessible to the public, hence to a wide range of investors and at the same time provides easy access to funding for a number of micro and small firms or entities which did not have access to credit before. The World Bank (2013, p.10) estimates that "there is an opportunity for up to 344 million people to participate in crowdfunding".

GPFI (2016, p.xix) points out that crowdfunding may support financial inclusion as it "can be a quick way to raise funds with potentially few regulatory requirements; it can be cost-efficient and can produce a good return for the lender; and its potential market reach is limited only by access barriers to the platform and regulatory restrictions where applicable". Jenik et al. (2017) argue that crowdfunding can assist financial inclusion by:

- Improving access to finance to excluded individuals and SMEs.
- Allowing for innovations of the existing financial model to serve "base of pyramid" customers through microfinance and mobile financial services as well as to promote government schemes and effectively channel remittances and investment flows.
- Opening access to more complex investment products for resilience and asset building. Cash & Gray's (2016) "theory of change of the microfinance industry" suggests that the use of financial services by poor households helps them anticipate, adapt to and/or recover from the effects of shocks in a manner that protects their livelihoods, reduces chronic vulnerability and facilitates growth.

Jenik et al. (2017) also estimate that due to the fact that crowdfunding platforms require some minimal infrastructure for their operation, crowdfunding might benefit different customer segments and in particular the "base of pyramid" customers, namely those excluded from traditional financial products. In addition, they note that crowdfunding development might also deepen the existing financial sector, whose maturity is limited especially in low-income countries. Furthermore, they argue that, from a development point of view, crowdfunding's success lies in its ability to promote and support financial inclusion and economic growth rather than to generate funds rapidly and cheaply or to finance risky and unsustainable investment projects. There are risks however that need to be taken into account such as:

- Inadequate legal and regulatory frameworks, (e.g. Mekar).
- Untested credit scoring models.
- Limited access to technology.
- Lack of awareness and trust.

Noppen (2018) argues that crowdfunding for inclusive finance was at first a non-profit activity, which later evolved into a highly regulated for-profit one. It was initially limited to donations to microfinance institutions. Thus, several non-profit organizations (e.g Kiva) would offer loans to microfinance institutions with no interest. Soon, other organizations (like Babyloan) imitated this model. By now, crowdfunders are supervised and many of them are for-profit, like Lendahand and Plumseeds which also operate as investment companies. Lendahand deals with retail customers, while Plumseeds caters to professional institutions. At first, many of these platforms were founded in developed markets. Soon however, crowdfunding platforms appeared in emerging markets (like Milaap in India and Mekar in Indonesia). These platforms mainly focus on microfinance and SME finance, but more and more platforms have integrated other key services (e.g renewable energy, education).

As Massolution (2015, p.20) specifically points out, "crowdfunding is quickly becoming a global methodology" and "many countries which understand the economic importance of SME finance for their local economies, have moved ahead swiftly from a legal and securities perspective to enable crowdfunding indigenously".

CROWDFUNDING IN GREECE

During periods of economic crises, the need to ensure "trust" when launching new financial instruments becomes crucial. UNDP (2012, p.32) notes that for all IFDMs, the delivering mechanism plays a key role for guaranteeing efficient structure, transparent implementation and sustainability stating that "it is about the 'capable institution' that is better to achieve the mandate". As Massolution (2015, p.19) points out, major development banks, NGOs, and similar institutions are seeking to leverage crowdfunding for sustainable development due to crowdfunding's social and environmental impact and its strong connection to micro-finance and the mitigation of wealth disparity. "Trust" in institutions serving as delivering mechanisms is considered a key enabler for crowdfunding success. As crowdfunding is vulnerable to the safety of online business transactions, banks increasingly participate in the crowdfunding market by running their own platforms or participating as strategic partners. Katseli & Boufounou (2017) have argued that during the recent financial crisis, European Banks (ABN AMRO, Societe Generale, BNP Paribas, Royal Bank of Scotland, Santader, Nordea, KBC, Basellandschaftliche Kantonalbank) have increased their engagement in crowdfunding activity.

It is thus no coincidence that in January 2016, the first Greek crowdfunding platform, named "Act4Greece", was established by the National Bank of Greece (NBG), the oldest Bank of the country founded in 1841. This was a response to the growing need for social projects as a consequence of the economic crisis that hit Greece in 2010, followed by the imposition of capital controls in 2015 and large refugee inflows during the same year. The lack of resources to finance needed projects prompted NBG to launch its donation and reward crowdfunding platform on February 1, 2016.

NBG's involvement underpinned "trust" in the operation of the platform by ensuring full transparency, accountability, compliance and supervision of the use of funds as well as professional, transparent and risk- free management of funds. Trust was further enhanced by the strategic partnership forged between NBG, the operator of the platform and major Greek non-profit organizations of high recognition, namely the Onassis Foundation, the Latsis Foundation, the Bodosakis Foundation, the Greek Commission of UNESCO and the CSR Hellas [3] which assist NBG in project selection.

As discussed in Boufounou (2018), "Act4Greece" promotes the following seven key social and development goals in line with the SDGs:

1. **Welfare, Health and Solidarity – *SGD3***: Good Health and Well-Being.
2. **Research, Education and Training - *SDG5***: Gender Equality.
3. **Culture and Cultural Entrepreneurship – *SDG4***: Quality Education, ***SDG5***: Gender Equality, ***SDG8***: Decent Work and Economic Growth.
4. **Social Economy and Entrepreneurship - *SDG5***: Gender Equality, ***SDG8***: Decent Work and Economic Growth.
5. **Environment and Sustainability – *SDG12***: Responsible Consumption and Production, ***SDG13***: Climate Action.
6. **Youth and Innovative Entrepreneurship – *SDG5***: Gender Equality, ***SDG8***: Decent Work and Economic Growth, ***SDG9***: Industry Innovation and Infrastructure.
7. **Sport Activities – *SDG11***: Sustainable Cities and Communities.

Act4Greece has succeeded in financially supporting and promoting a wide range of initiatives and projects in the area of sustainable banking. It has channeled funds to NGOs and legal entities to implement viable projects with positive social and environmental impact. More specifically it has not only ensured regular and consistent flow of funds to innovative projects/ventures but has also mobilized a number of loyal and committed crowdfunders and the Greek diaspora.

During the first 2 years of its operation, it managed to raise 1.8 mil Euros and to support 22 projects/ventures from 7,700 crowdfunders, deriving funds from individuals, businesses and institutions from Greece and abroad. Furthermore, the "Act4Greece" platform broadened public awareness in support of collective sustainable development initiatives (e.g. mobilizing funds to face the Syrian refugee crisis, etc) and entrepreneurship and highlighted the value of solidarity and social engagement in facing common challenges.

As discussed by Boufounou et al. (2019), the success of "Act4Greece" has been widely recognized as evidenced by the awards & prizes received during its first three years of operation both in Greece and internationally. More specifically, it was included as a "success story" in the "UNESCO Annual Report 2016" and in the "Crowdfunding4Culture" Report of the European Crowdfunding Network (ECN). It was also awarded the following distinctions:

- "1st prize in Communicating Efficiency" in the thematic section "Cause Related marketing Communications" in Marketing Excellence Awards 2017.
- "Bravo in Action Award" in the thematic section "Collaboration" in the Bravo Sustainability Awards 2017.
- "CSR Award" in the 18th InfoCom World Conference 2016.
- "Silver Award" in the thematic section "CSR Strategy Support" in the Bite Awards 2016.
- Furthermore, the non-profit organization "HOPEgenesis", whose project/action "Hope for more births" was uploaded in the "Act4Greece" platform, was awarded the "European Citizens Prize 2018" by the European Parliament.

According to the President of the Board of the Greek CSR network, "the Act4Greece program is a collective, pioneering effort in the case of Greece; for the first time new tools are provided that combine financing and social voluntary contributions; it reaches out to the public and legal entities and offers the same opportunity to people and agencies in Greece and abroad to collaborate on generating solutions and interventions that seek not only to heal the wounds created by the prolonged crisis, but also to provide remedies and ways to solve some of the problems, including the strengthening of the social economy and sustainable business plans."

Given Greece's severe credit crunch during the crisis, the need to develop innovative financing instruments for SMEs is vital for the resumption of growth in the Greek economy. The "Act4Greece" crowdfunding platform can be considered a potent pro-growth instrument, with a significant positive contribution to the country's efforts to overcome a deep social and economic crisis" (Katseli & Boufounou, 2017, p.198). Boufounou et al. (2017) undertook a SWOT Analysis of the equity crowdfunding potential in Greece arguing that it could indeed serve as an effective tool to broaden SMEs' financing and enhance financial inclusion. Equity crowdfunding has been regulated in Greece since September 2016; however, no such platform has been established as yet. Indicatively, the "Act4Greece" platform could easily expand to serve equity financing providing needed project finance to SMEs and startups that have been supported in the past by other programs such as the "NBG Seeds" program.

CONCLUSIONS

Financial innovations and IDFIs are increasingly being used by developed and developing countries alike to combat financial exclusion and costly access to finance. (Freedman, 2000; World Bank, 2013). Platform-mediated approaches are being used by new financial alternatives in order to cumulate many small individual transactions.

As demonstrated in the present paper, crowdfunding is an innovative fin-tech mechanism for financing sustainable development. While similar to conventional funding (both debt and equity), it is a valuable instrument especially for traditionally credit-constrained SMEs, startups and new ventures that promote social inclusion. Former President Barack Obama, remarked in 2012, upon signing the JOBS Act to legalize equity crowdfunding that "for start-ups and small businesses, this bill is a potential game changer". Massolution (2015, p.9) points out that "impact crowdfunding continues to develop, both at the micro and (importantly) at the macro levels, as part of government policy. In other words, crowdfunding is being embraced by nations around the world to frame economic development programs".

Crowdfunding started out as a way of making opportunities more equal and giving individual investors a chance to gather small amounts of money so they can meet the requirements needed for them to fund new or expanding ventures. Via the operation of social networks, many debt and equity peer-to-peer networks have made fund transfers more efficient and effective. The creation of new financial instruments, in particular crowdfunding, has provided valuable access to financial services for a number of entrepreneurs (Breedon, 2012) and has contributed to the development of a social community (Sannajust et al., 2014).

According to Massolution (2015), the main trends in crowdfunding finance include changes in the composition of the crowdfunders (credited and uncredited investors), the emergence of vertical platforms with offerings from different industries, mixed genres and varied interests, increasing investor interest towards P2P and SME lending, the adoption of crowdfunding by large organizations like Coca Cola, Nike, etc ("corporate crowdfunding") and the entrance of major enterprises as operators or service providers (e.g. the European Banks mentioned above). Continuous investment in crowdfunding platforms by VCs and strategic investors and the proliferation of crowdfunding platforms is expected to lead to market consolidation underpinned by advances in infrastructure models through an increasing number of providers and services offered (e.g. data analytics, etc). Network effects evidenced in an increasing number of markets, like North America and changes in the regulatory process are expected to expand the global reach and impact of crowdfunding. Last but not least, crowdfunding platforms are expected to be used increasingly to support the promotion of the Sustainable Development Goals through the implementation of sustainable projects by business, communities and financial institutions.

The lessons that can be drawn from the operation of the Greek crowdfunding platform "Act4Greece", presented in this paper as an interesting case study, can be summarized as follows:

- "Trust" to the delivering mechanism is a key precondition for mobilizing people and resources.

- Sponsorships and corporate social responsibility programs launched by organizations, institutions and businesses from all over the world can help alleviate financial and social crises and have enabled Greece to regain forward momentum.
- Crowdfunding is a catalyst for the development of social and green banking and can underpin sustainable development efforts.
- Equity crowdfunding could substantially improve SME financing and strengthen financial inclusion.

REFERENCES

Agrawal, A., Catalini, C., & Goldfarb, A. (2010). Friends, Family, and the Flat World: The Geography of Crowdfunding. *NBER Working paper*, 10-08, University of Toronto.

Agrawal, A., Catalini, C., & Goldfarb, A. (2015). Crowdfunding: Geography, Social Networks, and the Timing of Investment Decisions. *Journal of Economics & Management Strategy*, *24*(2), 253–274. doi:10.1111/jems.12093

Ahlers, G. K. C., Cumming, D., Günther, C., & Schweizer, D. (2015). Signaling in Equity Crowdfunding. *Entrepreneurship Theory and Practice*, *39*(4), 955–980. doi:10.1111/etap.12157

Aldrich, H. (1999). *Organizations Evolving*. Thousand Oaks, CA: Sage.

Allison, T. H., Davis, B. C., Short, J. C., & Webb, J. W. (2015). Crowdfunding in a Prosocial Microlending Environment: Examining the Role of Intrinsic Versus Extrinsic Cues'. *Entrepreneurship Theory and Practice*, *39*(1), 53–73. doi:10.1111/etap.12108

Allison, T. H., McKenny, A. F., & Short, J. C. (2013). The Effect of Entrepreneurial Rhetoricon Microlending Investment: An Examination of the Warm-Glow Effect. *Journal of Business Venturing*, *28*(6), 690–707. doi:10.1016/j.jbusvent.2013.01.003

Armendáriz, B., & Morduch, J. (2010). *The Economics of Microfinance*. Cambridge, MA: MIT Press.

Assenova, V. A., Best, J., Cagney, M., Ellenoff, D., Karas, K., Moon, J., ... Sorenson, O. (2016). The Present and the Future of Crowdfunding. *California Management Review*, *58*(2), 125–135. doi:10.1525/cmr.2016.58.2.125

Audretsch, D. B., Keilbach, M. C., & Lehmann, E. E. (2006). *Entrepreneurship and Economic Growth*. Oxford: Oxford University Press. doi:10.1093/acprof:oso/9780195183511.001.0001

Audretsch, D. B., & Thurik, A. R. (2001). What's New about the New Economy? Sources of Growth in the Managed and Entrepreneurial Economies. *Industrial and Corporate Change*, *10*(1), 267–315. doi:10.1093/icc/10.1.267

Beaulieu, T., Sarker, S., & Sarker, S. (2015). A Conceptual Framework for Understanding Crowdfunding, CAIS, 37(1) doi:10.17705/1CAIS.03701

Bechter, C., Jentzsch, S., & Frey, M. (2011). From wisdom of the crowd to crowdfunding. *Journal of Communication and Computer*, *8*, 951–957.

Bergemann, D., & Hege, U. (1998). Venture Capital Financing, Moral Hazard, and Learning. *Journal of Banking & Finance*, *22*(6-8), 703–735. doi:10.1016/S0378-4266(98)00017-X

Berger, A. N., & Udell, G. F. (1998). The Economics of Small Business Finance, the Roles of Private Equity and Debt Markets in the Financial Growth Cycle. *Journal of Banking & Finance*, *22*(6-8), 613–673. doi:10.1016/S0378-4266(98)00038-7

Berglöf, E. (1994). A Control Theory of Venture Capital Finance. *Journal of Law Economics and Organization*, *10*(2), 247–267.

Bessiere, V., Stephany, E., & Wirtz, P. (2018). Crowdfunding, Business Angels and Venture Capital: New Funding Trajectories for Start-Ups?, In *2nd Emerging trends in Entrepreneurial Finance Conference* 10.2139srn.3137095

Bhidé, A. (1992). Bootstrap Finance: The Art of Start-Ups. *Harvard Business Review*, *70*(6), 109–117. PMID:10122688

Black, B., & Gilson, R. (1998). Venture Capital and the Structure of Capital Markets: Banks versus Stock Markets. *Journal of Financial Economics*, *47*(3), 243–277. doi:10.1016/S0304-405X(97)00045-7

Botazzi, L., & Da Rin, M. (2001). Venture Capital in Europe and the Financing of Innovative Companies. *Economic Policy*, *34*, 231–269.

Boufounou, B., Triantafyllopoulou, D., & Mastrodemos, G. (2019). Indicators Predicting Donation-Crowdfunding Success in Greece, In *Proceedings of the 5th International Conference on Business and Economics HOU*, February 22-23, Athens. Academic Press.

Boufounou, B., & Tsaimou, T. (2017). Equity Crowdfunding - An Innovative Instrument for SME Financing: Challenges and Prospects, In *Proceedings 3rd International Conference on Business and Economics HOU*, April 21-22, Athens. Academic Press.

Boufounou, P. (2018). Crowdfunding in the Greek Economic Crisis: Lessons Learned, *In Proceedings of the 4th International Conference on Business and Economics HOU*, May 11-12, Athens. Academic Press.

Breedon, T. (2012). *Boosting Finance Options for Business*. London, UK: Department for Business Innovation and Skills.

Bruton, G., Khavul, S., Siegel, D., & Wright, M. (2015). New Financial alternatives in Seeding Entrepreneurship: Microfinance, Crowdfunding and Peer-to Peer Innovations. *Entrepreneurship Theory and Practice*, *39*(1), 9–26. doi:10.1111/etap.12143

Burtch, G., Ghose, A., & Wattal, S. (2013). An Empirical Examination of the Antecedents and Consequences of Contribution Patterns in Crowdfunded Markets'. *Information Systems Research*, *24*(3), 499–519. doi:10.1287/isre.1120.0468

Buttice, V., Colombo, M., Massimo, G., & Wright, M. (2017). Serial Crowdfunding, Social Capital and Project Success. *Entrepreneurship Theory and Practice*, *41*(2), 183–207. doi:10.1111/etap.12271

Buttice, V., & Franzoni, C., Rossi-Lamastra, C., & Rovelli, P. (2018). The Road to Crowdfunding Success: A Review of Extant Literature, Oxford University Press.

Buysere (de), K., Kleverlaan, R., & Maron, D. (2012). *A Framework for European Crowdfunding*, Impressum.

Colgren, D. (2014). The Rise of Crowdfunding: Social Media, Big Data, Cloud Technologies. *Strategic Finance*, *96*(4), 56–67.

Collins, L., Swart, R., & Zhang, B. (2013). *The Rise of Future Finance: The UK Alternative Finance Benchmarking Report.*

Czarnitzki, D., & Kraft, K. (2004). Firm Leadership and Innovative Performance Evidence from Seven EU Countries. *Small Business Economics*, *22*(5), 325–332. doi:10.1023/B:SBEJ.0000022209.72378.fe

Dos Santos, B. L., Patel, P. C., & D'Souza, R. R. (2011). Venture Capital Funding for Information Technology Businesses'. *Journal of the Association for Information Systems*, *12*(1), 57–87. doi:10.17705/1jais.00253

ERD. (2015). *European Report on Development 2015: Combining Finance and Policies to Implement a Transformative Post-2015 Development Agenda*, EU.

EU. (2017). *Identifying Market and Regulatory Obstacles to Cross-Border Development of Crowdfunding in the EU.*

Freedman, M. P. (2000). Challenges to Launching Grassroots Microlending Programs: A Case Study. *Journal of Developmental Entrepreneurship*, *5*(3), 235–248.

Gash, M., & Gray, B. (2016). *The Role of Financial Services in Building Household Resilience*. Washington, D.C.: CGAP.

Glaeser, E. L., & Shleifer, A. (2001). Not-for-Profit Entrepreneurs. *Journal of Public Economics*, *81*(1), 99–115. doi:10.1016/S0047-2727(00)00130-4

GPFI (Global Partnership for Financial Inclusion). (2016). *Global Standard-Setting Bodies and Financial Inclusion: The Evolving Landscape.*

Hart, O., & Moore, J. (1988). Incomplete Contracts and Renegotiation. *Econometrica*, *56*(4), 755–785. doi:10.2307/1912698

Havrylchyk, O. (2018). Regulatory Framework for the Loan-Based Crowdfunding Platforms, *OECD Economics Department Working Papers*, No. 1513, OECD Publishing, Paris.

Hellmann, T. (1998). The Allocation of Control Rights in Venture Capital Contracts. *The Rand Journal of Economics*, *29*(1), 57–76. doi:10.2307/2555816

Herciu, M. (2017). Financing Small Businesses: From Venture Capital to Crowdfunding. *Studies in Business and Economics*, *12*(2), 63–69. doi:10.1515be-2017-0022

Jenik, I., Lyman, T., & Nava, A. (2017). Crowdfunding and Financial Inclusion, CGAP (Consultative Group to Assist the Poor) *Working Paper*.

Katseli, L., & Boufounou, P. (2017). Crowdfunding and Social Banking for Cultural Heritage Projects: A Greek Case-study. In G. Mergos, & N. Patsiavos (Eds.), *Cultural Heritage as Economic Value for Sustainable Development: Economic Benefits*. Social Opportunities and Challenges of Cultural Heritage.

Keuschnigg, C. (2004). Venture Capital Backed Growth. *Journal of Economic Growth*, *9*(2), 239–261. doi:10.1023/B:JOEG.0000031428.35711.fc

Khavul, S. (2010). Microfinance: Creating Opportunities for the Poor? *The Academy of Management Perspectives*, *24*(3), 57–71. doi:10.5465/amp.24.3.58

Kirby, E., & Worner, S. (2014). *Crowdfunding: An Infant Industry Growing Fast.* Madrid, Spain: IOSCO.

Kleemann, F., Voss, G. G., & Rieder, K. (2008). Un(der)paid Innovators: The Commercial Utilization of Consumer Work through Crowdsourcing. *Science, Technology, & Innovation Studies*, *4*(1), 5–26.

Lambert, T., & Schwienbacher, A. (2010). An Empirical Analysis of Crowdfunding. *Social Science Research Network*, 1–23.

Lavinsky, D. (2011). *Funding Fathers*. Smart Business.

Leading Group on Innovative Financing for Development. (2010). *Innovative Financing to Fund Development: 2+3=8 Innovating in Financing Education*, Report 2010.

Lehner, O. M. (2013). Crowdfunding Social Ventures: A Model and Research Agenda. *Venture Capital*, *15*(4), 289–311. doi:10.1080/13691066.2013.782624

Lehner, O. M., & Nichols, A. (2014). Social Finance and Crowdfunding for Social Enterprises: A Public-Private Case Study Providing Legitimacy and Leverage. *Venture Capital*, *16*(3), 271–286. doi:10.1080/13691066.2014.925305

Levin, R. B., Nowakowski, J., & O'Brien, A. A. (2013). The JOBS Act--Implications for Raising Capital and for Financial Intermediaries. *Journal of Taxation & Regulation of Financial Institutions*, *26*(5), 21–29.

Ley, A., & Weaven, S. (2011). Exploring Agency Dynamics of Crowdfunding in Start-Up Capital Financing. *Academy of Entrepreneurship Journal*, *17*(1), 85–110.

Loher, J. (2016). The Interaction of Equity Crowdfunding Platforms and Ventures: An Analysis of the Preselection Process. *Venture Capital*, *19*(1-2), 51–74. doi:10.1080/13691066.2016.1252510

Lynn, D. M. (2012). The Crowdfunding Provisions of the JOBS Act, *Financial Executive*, May, 42-43.

Lyons, T. (2010). Social Entrepreneurship: How Businesses Can Transform Society. In *Approaches to Financing Social Entrepreneurship*. Santa Barbara, CA: Praeger.

Macht, S. A., & Weatherston, J. (2014). The Benefits of Online Crowdfunding for Fund-seeking Business. *Strategic Change*, *23*(1-2), 1–14. doi:10.1002/jsc.1955

Mair, J., & Marti, I. (2006). Social Entrepreneurship Research: A Source of Explanation, Prediction and Delight. *Journal of World Business*, *41*(1), 36–44. doi:10.1016/j.jwb.2005.09.002

Manchanda, K., & Muralidharan, P. (2014). Crowdfunding: A New Paradigm in Startup Financing, *Global Conference on Business & Finance Proceedings*, 9(1), 369-374. Institute for Business & Finance Research.

Massolution. (2015). *2015CF: The Crowdfunding Industry Report.*

Meyskens, M., Allen, I. E., & Brush, C. G. (2011). Human Capital and Hybrid Ventures. *Advances in Entrepreneurship, Firm, Emergence, and Growth*, *13*, 51–72. doi:10.1108/S1074-7540(2011)0000013007

Meyskens, M., & Bird, L. (2014). Crowdfunding and Value Creation. *Entrepreneurial Resource Journal*, *5*(2), 155–166.

Meyskens, M., & Carsrud, A. (2013). Nascent Green-Technology Ventures: An Exploratory Study Assessing the Role of Partnership Diversity in Firm Success. *Small Business Economics*, *40*(3), 739–759. doi:10.100711187-011-9400-1

Milana, C., & Ashta, A. (2012). Developing Microfinance: A Survey of the Literature. *Strategic Change*, *21*(7-8), 299–330. doi:10.1002/jsc.1911

Mitra, D. (2012). The Role of Crowdfunding in Entrepreneurial Finance. *Delhi Business Review*, *13*(2), 67–72.

Mollick, E. (2014). The Dynamics of Crowdfunding: An Exploratory Study. *Journal of Business Venturing*, *29*(1), 1–16. doi:10.1016/j.jbusvent.2013.06.005

Morduch, J. (1999). The Microfinance Promise'. *Journal of Economic Literature*, *37*(4), 1569–1614. doi:10.1257/jel.37.4.1569

Moritz, A., & Block, J. H. (2016). Crowdfunding: A Literature Review and Research Directions, In D. Bruntje, & O. Gajda (Eds.), Crowdfunding in Europe: State of the Art in Theory and Practice, FGF Studies in Small Business and Entrepreneurship, Springer, 25-54. doi:10.1007/978-3-319-18017-5_3

Moss, T., Neubaum, D., & Meyskens, M. (2014). The Effect of Virtuous and Entrepreneurial Orientations on Microfinance Lending and Repayment: A Signaling Theory Perspective. *Entrepreneurship Theory and Practice*, *39*(1), 27–52. doi:10.1111/etap.12110

Mutengezanwa, M., Gombarume, F. B., Njanike, K., & Charikinya, A. (2011). The Impact of Microfinance Institutions on the Socioeconomic Lives of People in Zimbabwe. *Annals of the University of Petrosani. Economics*, *11*, 161–170.

Myers, S., & Majluf, N. (1984). Corporate Financing and Investment Decisions When Firms have Information Investors do not Have. *Journal of Financial Economics, 13*(2), 187–221. doi:10.1016/0304-405X(84)90023-0

Nicholls, A. (2010). The Institutionalization of Social Investment: The Interplay of Investment Logics and Investor Rationalities. *Journal of Social Entrepreneurship, 1*(1), 70–100. doi:10.1080/19420671003701257

Noppen, M. (2018). What is Crowdfunding and How Could it Help Financial Inclusion?, Interview in preparation of the European Microfinance Week, Nov. 2018.

OECD. (2009). *Innovative Funding to Finance Development: Progress and Prospects', DCD, Issues Brief, November*. Paris, France: OECD Publishing.

OECD. (2009b). *The Impact of the Global Crisis on SME and Entrepreneurship Financing and Policy Responses*. France: OECD Publishing.

OECD. (2014). *The Role of Public Financial Institutions in Fostering SME Access to Finance*. OECD Publishing.

OECD. (2018). *Financing SMEs and Entrepreneurs 2018: An OECD Scoreboard*. OECD Publishing.

Paschen, J. (2017). Chose Wisely: Crowdfunding through the Stages of the Startup Life Cycle. *Business Horizons, 60*(2), 179–188. doi:10.1016/j.bushor.2016.11.003

Poetz, M. K., & Schreier, M. (2012). The Value of Crowdsourcing: Can Users Really Compete with Professionals in Generating New Product Ideas? *Journal of Product Innovation Management, 29*(2), 245–256. doi:10.1111/j.1540-5885.2011.00893.x

Powers, T. V. (2012). SEC Regulation of Crowdfunding Intermediaries under Title III of the JOBS Act. *Banking & Financial Services Policy Report, 10*(31), 1–7.

Ramsey, Y. A. (2012). What the Heck is Crowdfunding? *Business People*, November, 54-57.

Ridley-Duff, R. (2009). Co-Operative Social Enterprises: Company Rules, Access to Finance and Management Practice. *Social Enterprise Journal, 5*(1), 50–68. doi:10.1108/17508610910956408

Rigby, D. K., Christensen, C. M., & Johnson, M. W. (2002). Foundations for Growth: How to identify and Build Disruptive New Businesses. *MIT Sloan Management Review, 43*(3), 22.

Robano, V. (2018). Case Study on Crowdfunding. In *OECD SME and Entrepreneurship Papers, No. 4*. Paris, France: OECD Publishing.

Sannajust, A., Roux, F., & Chaibi, A. (2014). Crowdfunding In France: A New Revolution? *Journal of Applied Business Research*, *30*(6), 1919–1928. doi:10.19030/jabr.v30i6.8947

Scarlata, M., & Alemany, L. (2013). Philanthropic Venture Capitalists' Post-Investment Involvement with Portfolio Social Enterprises: What Do They Actually Do?, Entrepreneurship, Finance, Governance and Ethics, 75-85, Springer, Dordrecht.

Schwienbacher, A. (2007). A Theoretical Analysis of Optimal Financing Strategies for Different Types of Capital-Constrained Entrepreneurs. *Journal of Business Venturing*, *22*(6), 753–781. doi:10.1016/j.jbusvent.2006.07.003

Schwienbacher, A., Belleflamme, P., & Lambert, T. (2013). Crowdfunding: Tapping the Right Crowd. *Journal of Business Venturing*, *29*(4), 585–609.

Schwienbacher, A., & Larralde, B. (2010). Crowdfunding of Small Entrepreneurial Ventures. In *Handbook of Entreprenurial Finance*. Oxford University Press. doi:10.2139srn.1699183

Short, H. (1994). Ownership, Control, Financial Structure and the Performance of Firms. *Journal of Economic Surveys*, *8*(3), 203–249. doi:10.1111/j.1467-6419.1994.tb00102.x

Short, J. C., Ketchen, D. T., McKenny, A. F., Allison, T. H., & Ireland, R. D. (2017). "Research on Crowdfunding: Reviewing the (Very Recent) Past and Celebrating the Present", *Entrepreneurship Theory and Practice Special issue on Crowdfunding*, *41*(2), 149-10.

Sigar, K. (2012). Fret no More: Inapplicability of Crowdfunding Concerns in the Internet Age and the JOBS Act's Safeguards. *Administrative Law Review*, *2*(64), 474–505.

Stinchcombe, A. L. (1965). Social Structure and Organizations. In *J. G. March, Handbook of Organizations*. Chicago, IL: Rand McNally.

Ueda, M. (2004). Banks versus Venture Capital Project Evaluation, Screening, and Expropriation. *The Journal of Finance*, *59*(2), 601–621. doi:10.1111/j.1540-6261.2004.00643.x

UNDESA. (2012). World Economic and Social Survey 2012. In *Search of New Development Finance*. New York: United Nations Department of Economic and Social Affairs.

UNDP. (2012). *Innovative Financing for Development: A New Model for Development Finance?* New York: Bureau for Development Policy.

Valanciene, L., & Jegeleviciute, S. (2013). Valuation of Crowdfunding: Benefits and Drawbacks. *Economics and Management, 18*(1), 39–48.

Viotto, J. (2015). Competition and Regulation of Crowdfunding Platforms: A Two-Sided Market Approach. *Communications & Stratégies, 99*(3), 33–50.

Vismara, S. (2016). Equity Retention and Social Network Theory in Equity Crowdfunding. *Small Business Economics, 46*(4), 579–590. doi:10.100711187-016-9710-4

Wardrop, R., Zhang, B., Rau, R., & Gray, M. (2015). *Moving Mainstream. The European Alternative Finance Benchmarking Report,* 15-16.

Wheat, R. E., Wang, Y., Byrnes, J. E., & Ranganathan, J. (2012). Raising Money for Scientific Research through Crowdfunding. *Trends in Ecology & Evolution, 2*(28), 71–72. PMID:23219380

Whitman, J. R. (2009). Measuring Social Values in Philanthropic Foundations. *Nonprofit Management & Leadership, 19*(3), 305–325. doi:10.1002/nml.221

Wong, A., Bhatia, M., & Freeman, Z. (2009). Angel Finance: The Other Venture Capital. *Strategic Change, 18*(7-8), 221–230. doi:10.1002/jsc.849

World Bank. (2009). *Innovating Development Finance: From Financing Sources to Financial Solutions.*

World Bank. (2012). *Innovative Finance for Development Solutions: Initiatives of the World Bank Group.*

World Bank. (2013). *Crowdfunding's Potential for the Developing World.* Washington, DC: World Bank.

Yunus, M. (1999). *Banker to the Poor: Microlending and the Battle against World Poverty.* New York: Public Affairs.

ADDITIONAL READING

Baeck, P., Collins, L., & Zhang, B. (2014). *Understanding Alternative Finance - the UK Alternative Finance Industry Report 2014,* (November), 95

Cusmano, L (2015), 'New approaches to SME and Entrepreneurial Financing: Broadening the Range of Instruments'. *OECD Analytical Report*, 1 – 109.

Drover, W., Busenitz, L., Matusik, S., Townsend, D., Anglin, A., & Dushnitsky, G. (2017). A Review and Road Map of Entrepreneurial Equity Financing Research. *Journal of Management*, *43*(6), 1820–1853. doi:10.1177/0149206317690584

Ernst & Young. (2015). *Crowdfunding: Mapping EU Markets and Events Study*. Brussels: European Commission.

European Commission. (2016). *Crowdfunding in the EU Capital Markets Union*. Brussels: European Commission.

Golić, Z. (2014), "Advantages of Crowdfunding as an Alternative Source of Financing of Small and Medium-sized Entrerprises, *Proceedings of the Faculty of Economics in East Sarajevo*, (8), 39–48.

Place, C. (2013), "Sustainable Finance for Impact Social Innovation: A Mutual Trust", *Haute Ecole de Gestion de Geneve, Centre De Recherche Appliquee en Gestion, Cahier de Recherch*e no HES-SO/HEG-GE/C—13/3/1/--CH

Vulkan, N., Astebro, T. and A.F. Sierra (2015), "Equity Crowdfunding: A New Phenomena", *Said Business School Research Papers*, November

Wilson, K. E., & Testoni, M. (2014). *Improving the Role of Equity Crowdfunding in Europe's Capital Markets, Bruegel Policy contribution, No 2014/09*. Brussels: Bruegel.

ENDNOTES

11 Bootstrapping a company occurs when a business owner starts a company with little to no assets. This is in contrast to starting a company by first raising capital through angel investors or venture capital firms. Instead, bootstrapped founders rely on personal savings, sweat equity, lean operations, quick inventory turnover, and a cash runway to become successful. For example, a bootstrapped company may take preorders for its product, thereby using the funds generated from the orders actually to build and deliver the product itself (Investopedia)

22 There exists a series of recent studies that summarize the key factors that influence crowdfunding performance (Beualieu et al 2014, Robano 2015, Short et al 2017 and Buttice (2017, 2018), Bruton et al (2015) and provide a comparative analysis of microfinance, crowdfunding and peer-to-peer lending.

3 CSR Hellas is a network of the major companies in Greece pursuing CSR activities and applying CSR standards

APPENDICES - KEY TERMS AND DEFINITIONS

The main definitions of IFDIs are presented in Table 3 that follows:

Table 3. Innovative financing for development instruments

Author	Definition
WORLD BANK (2009)	Mechanisms that depart from traditional approaches to mobilizing development finance that is, through budget outlays from established sovereign donors or bonds issued by multilateral and national development banks exclusively to achieve funding objectives. Therefore they involve non-traditional applications of solidarity, PPP and catalytic mechanisms that i) support fundraising by tapping new sources and engaging investors beyond the financial dimension of transactions, as partners and stakeholders in development ii) deliver financial solutions to development problems on the ground
OECD (2009)	Mechanisms of fund raising stimulating actions in support of international development that go beyond traditional spending approaches, by either official or private sectors, such as: i) new approaches for pooling private and public revenue streams to scale up or develop activities for the benefit of partner countries ii) new revenue streams (e.g. a new tax, charge, fee, bond raising, sale proceed or voluntary contribution scheme) earmarked to developmental activities on a multi-year basis iii) new incentives (financial guarantees, corporate social responsibility or other rewards or recognition) to address market failure or scale up ongoing developmental activities
LEADING GROUP ON INNOVATIVE FINANCING FOR DEVELOPMENT (2010)	Mechanisms possessing the following features: 1. linked to global public goods such as eliminating diseases or reducing climate change which require a global intervention; 2. complementary and additional to traditional ODA. It may help to improve the quality of existing aid but innovative financing can never replace the quantity; 3. more stable and predictable than ODA
UNDESA (2012)	Mechanisms that have the following characteristics: i) official sector involvement, including the use of public resources, as well as arrangements in which official ??plays a catalytic role in leveraging private sector and/ or philanthropic resources ii) international cooperation and cross-border transfer of resources to developing countries iii) innovation in the sense that mechanisms are used in a new context or incorporate innovative features with respect to the type of resources, or in they are collected, or their governance structures. An additional desirable characteristic of the mechanisms considered is the capacity to generate additional development financing over and above existing ODA
WORLD BANK (2012)	Any financing approach that helps to: • generate additional development funds by tapping new funding sources (that is, by looking beyond conventional mechanisms such as budget outlays from established donors and bonds from traditional international financial institutions) or by engaging new partners (such as emerging donors and actors in the private sector). • enhance the efficiency of financial flows, by reducing delivery time and/or costs, especially for emergency needs and in crisis situations. • make financial flows more results-oriented, by explicitly linking funding flows to measurable performance on the ground.

The main definitions of crowdfunding prevailing in contemporary literature are summarized in Table 4 that follows:

Table 4. Crowdfunding definitions

Author	Definition
Lambert and Schwienbacher (2010)	An open call, essentially through the Internet, for the provision of financial resources either in form of donation or in exchange for some form of reward and/or voting rights in order to support initiatives for specific purposes
Bechter et al (2011)	An approach to raising capital required for a project or enterprise by appealing to large numbers of ordinary people for small contributions
Lynn (2012)	A relatively new outgrowth of social media that provides funding for a variety of ventures
Powers (2012)	A financial mechanism that allows startup companies to solicit funds from the general public through website intermediaries
Ramsey (2012)	The process of raising money to help turn promising ideas into business realities by connecting investees with potential supporters
Sigar (2012)	A capital formation strategy that raises small amounts of funds from a large group of people through online means
Lehner (2013)	Crowdfunding means tapping a large dispersed audience, dubbed as "the crowd" for small sums of money to fund a project or venture
Colgren (2014)	Crowdfunding is the convergence of social media, Big Data and cloud technologies to significantly revolutionize the means by which small and mid-sized entities (SMEs) and startups can access capital in a cost-effective manner.
Mollick (2014)	Crowdfunding refers to the efforts by entrepreneurial individuals and groups – cultural, social, and for-profit – to fund their ventures by drawing on relatively small contributions from a relatively large number of individuals using the internet, without standard financial intermediaries
Sannajust et al (2014)	It is a method for funding a variety of new ventures, allowing individual founders of for-profit, cultural or social projects to request funding from many individuals via internet
Ahlers et al (2015)	An umbrella term used to describe an increasingly widespread form of fundraising, typically via the internet, whereby groups of people pool money, usually (very) small individual contributions, to support a particular goal
Belleflamme et al (2015)	Crowdfunding can be seen as an open call to provide financial resources. Crowdfunding mostly takes place on crowdfunding platforms (CFPs) i.e. internet-based platforms that link fundraisers to funders with the aim of funding a particular campaign by typically many finders
Robano (2018)	Crowdfunding is a finance technique that uses the Internet to match investors and borrowers for projects of common interest. The matching is usually done through dedicated operating systems (platforms) and enables participants to invest in one or several projects, pooling resources to support projects initiated by borrowers

Chapter 12
A Bibliometric Analysis of Ethical Investments (EI) Research:
Alternative Investments

Christos Lemonakis
https://orcid.org/0000-0002-9024-0969
Hellenic Mediterranean University, Greece

Marios Nikolaos Kouskoukis
https://orcid.org/0000-0001-5840-3927
European University Cyprus, Nicosia, Cyprus

Alexandros Garefalakis
https://orcid.org/0000-0001-7980-3743
Hellenic Mediterranean University, Greece

Constantin Zopounidis
Technical University of Crete, Greece & Audencia Business School, France

Marianna Eskantar
Technical University of Crete, Greece

ABSTRACT

This chapter presents the evolution of academic research in Ethical Investments (EI) research between 1990 and 2019. The chapter analyzes the most influential journals in EI research by searching for papers, which were published on the Scopus database. Results show a steadily increasing rate of EI research during the past 30 years. The chapter reports the top academic journals that permanently publish articles about

DOI: 10.4018/978-1-7998-2436-7.ch012

EI research. The main contribution of this work is to develop a general overview of the leading journals in EI research, which leads to the development of a future research agenda for bibliometric analysis. The survey covers all main areas of Social Sciences, Business, Management and Accounting, Economics, Econometrics, and Finance as well as Decision Sciences and its connections with other analytical fields.

INTRODUCTION

Socially Responsible Investing (SRI) or Ethical Investment (EI) is broadly defined as an investment process that integrates not only financial but also social, environmental, and ethical (SEE) considerations into investment decision making (Cabello et al., 2014). SRI has grown rapidly around the world in the last two decades and has emerged into an en vogue investment strategy or philosophy that combines profit maximization with social endeavors (Puaschunder, 2019). In general, SRI is reflecting investors' growing awareness of social, environmental, ethical and corporate governance issues (De Oliveira et al., 2017). Socially conscientious investors search for both economic and social value maximization by integrating social, environmental, and financial aspects in investments. The importance of communicating corporate social responsibility (CSR) not only to socially responsible investors, but also to the mainstream of the financial community is gaining importance in a more competitive capital market environment (Fieseler, 2011). The data suggest that social responsible issues are becoming more and more part of mainstream investment analysis.

According to (Chamorro-Mera & Palacios-González, 2019) SRI is a way of promoting the social responsibility of companies. Specifically, socially responsible screenings are bottom line analyses of corporate economic performance and social responsibility, in which socially conscientious investors integrate CSR in the financial decision making and allocate financial resources based on the societal impacts of the funded entities (Puaschunder, 2019). Moreover, ethical financial products can be considered as a tool that drives the financial institutions CSR and also companies indirectly try to acquire financial resources through them (Chamorro-Mera & Palacios-González, 2019). Due to the global increase of social conscientiousness, varied national legislations and regulations have led to different SRI practices, which are worldwide recognized by the United Nations (UN).

This book chapter is trying to find a practical way, in order to analyze SRI and EI research over a period of 30 years by using bibliometric indicators. Bibliometrics is the field that quantitatively studies bibliographic material (Broadus, 1987). Bibliometric studies are becoming more and more popular in the scientific literature and they are strongly encouraged by the access to bibliographic data. A substantial amount of bibliometric analysis have been developed in a wide range of areas by different authors, such as management (Podsakoff et al., 2008), economics (Coupé, 2003), accounting (Merig_o et al., 2016), entrepreneurship (Landström et al., 2012) and innovation (Merig_o et al., 2016).

The research field of SRI or EI has grown remarkably over the past 30 years compared to other disciplines. Having the access to the location of the most cited papers, the citation structure underlines the citation level that this field has reached till nowadays. Furthermore, it reflects the number of papers, which have lower levels of citations, including those that have not been cited yet. The book chapter also develops an analysis of journals, which identifies the top-tier ones in the field. In particular, this work points out journals that have high number of citations, despite that they publish a large number of articles in SRI or EI research, such as the Journal of Business Ethics, the Journal of Banking and Finance and the Journal of Economics Psychology. Moreover, this work highlights, which journals have been the most influential throughout the period 1900-2019.

Having these in mind, this book chapter provides sufficient background information and literature review regarding its topic. Specifically, the authors have analyzed and assessed the field of SRI or EI in depth, since the content of this research is complete and based scientifically on the worldwide data and methods.

The proposed approach of this chapter is based partially on Cancino et al. (2018) research work that analyzes the most influential journals in Venture Capital research literature. They put emphasis in presenting the evolution of the relevant academic research between the years 1990 and 2014, analyzing research papers which were published on the Web of Science database.

This book chapter consists of: Section 2, which develops the literature review regarding to SRI or EI research, Section 3, which describes the research methodology by describing the bibliometric study, Section 4, which presents the results of the bibliometric analysis and Section 5, which offers a discussion regarding to the conclusions.

LITERATURE REVIEW

The origins of the modern SRI movement were traced for the first time in 1960, when powerful social undercurrents including environmentalism and anti-war activism fuelled a rise. In 2009 as Park (2009) supports, nearly 1 out of every 9 US $ under professional management in the United States was invested using social investment strategies. Meanwhile, the European ethical investment market was estimated to be 1 trillion € or as much as 10–15% of the total funds under management.

As Leys et al. (2009) mention, from 2009 governments are giving SRI more attention and, in some countries, are discussing whether and how to regulate the SRI market. Faced with the demands of their investors, listed companies have started to adopt CSR strategies (Valor et al., 2009). Already from 2003, many of the funding institutions have ethical investment arms, even where these are not their mainstream activity (Ross & Skerratt, 2003).

In his article Knoll (2002) documents how SRI has grown from a fringe movement practiced by a relatively small number of isolated investors into a major investment phenomenon that has become part of the financial mainstream. It is also described, how the SRI community tried to support this growth by convincing investors that they can make a significant difference in the world by screening their investments, without financial sacrifice. The results of his study highlight that the managing money according to ethical criteria can be as profitable as investing for financial gain and that SRI can directly change the behavior of the firms by drawing funds away from disapproved activities toward approved activities.

SRI has shown a rapid expansion over the past years, because of the investors' interest for this kind of investments. The study of Dupré et al. (2009) shows that the emergence of a social rating makes the price of ethical stocks increase, and thus the cost of capital of these firms decrease. Having this in mind, enterprises can be encouraged to adapt an ethical behavior, if the decrease in their cost of capital is lower than the cost of becoming ethical.

The 2008 World Financial Crisis underlined the importance of social responsibility for the sustainable functioning of economic markets (Puaschunder, 2017). A new era of economic thinking, which will integrate social facets into mainstream economic models has arrived. In a long history of classic finance theory, which had blocked out moral and ethical criteria in investment decision making, the socio-economic motives for SRI or EI investment are now more than ever required.

In their investment decisions, investors in SRI funds may be more concerned with ethical or social issues than with fund performance (Renneboog et al., 2011). In particular, the study of Jansson and Biel (2011) compares motives to invest in accordance with socially responsible criteria among different groups of investors. The results indicate that SRI among private and institutional investors was guided by environmental and social values. However, fund managers working in investment institutions were not affected by these values. Specifically, fund managers in investment institutions and private investors were affected by beliefs about long-term returns of SRI, while institutional investors made an effort to reduce the financial risks.

Moreover, empirical studies that tried to analyze the performance of SRI funds relative to conventional funds, found contradictory results. The results of the Rathner (2013) meta- analysis suggest that the consideration of the survivorship bias in a study increases (decreases) the probability of a significant outperformance (underperformance) of SRI funds relative to conventional funds. In addition, the meta-analysis of Revelli and Viviani (2015) tested the relationship between SRI and financial performance to determine whether including CSR and ethical concerns in portfolio management is more profitable than conventional investment policies. The results indicate that the consideration of CSR factor in stock market portfolios is neither an advantage nor a disadvantage compared with conventional investments. Finally, the meta-analysis of Von Wallis and Klein (2015), which covers the period between 1986 and 2012, underlines that the SRI perform equal to conventional investments, but these findings are challenged by contradictory results from other studies. However, while a diverse set of models have been developed, in order to support investment decision-making based on financial criteria, models including also social responsibility criteria are rather scarce (Cabello et al., 2014).

The article of Dorfleitner and Nguyen (2017) introduced two approaches for modeling the dependency of the optimal portfolio choice on the available amount of investment volume from the perspective of socially responsible investors, who seek both financial and ethical benefits. The results highlight how the optimal investment choice can change depending on the initial wealth and the investor's concern of sustainable and responsible objectives.

In recent years, SRI has acquired greater weight, for both individual and institutional investors (Chamorro-Mera & Palacios-Gonzâlez, 2018). According to Hebb et al. (2014) there are many ways of looking at SRI. It can be viewed as a financial product, where the financial performance is the most important factor or it can be regarded as a force for change to promote and stimulate a more sustainable development. SRI can represent a powerful tool, in the case of failure or stagnation of economic and financial growth. The analysis of Herrera- Cano and Gonzalez-Perez (2016) proves that SRI can be an essential tool in times of global economic and political crisis.

RESEARCH METHODOLOGY

Bibliometric research is a field suitable for almost all disciplines and is used by a plethora of scientists to identify and update research in a multitude of thematic topics (Broadus, 1987) by using a wide range of science indicators.

There are different ways of using material in a bibliometric analysis. The most common approaches use both the total number of articles of a specific field and the number of articles citations, or indices such as Citations per document per Journal, or the use of h-index (Hirsch, 2005), that combines articles with citations indicating the number of studies X that have received X or more citations. In other words, the H index is the number of publications (h) attributed to the unit under analysis, during the time interval analyzed, which has at least H reports. In Elsevier's Scopus, the largest abstract and citation database of peer-reviewed literature, the user can find the h-index by conducting a search and selecting as a hyperlink the name of an author in the research section. The index has the same disadvantage as other key indicators, since it emulates by comparing the research work of various types, published at different times, in completely different subjects.

The index tends to become, somehow, biased in favor of old researchers with many articles (Egghe, 2006), since they had been mentioned for their previous works before. However, this bias is somewhat tempered by the fact that every new article of an author with a high *H index* should have a high reference level to raise the already high H-index.

Google Scholar has adopted the h-Index influence method for publications and h5 variation for five full calendar years. H-index of a publication is the largest h number taken, so there are at least *h* articles in this publication that were reported at least *h* times each. For example, a version with five articles listed respectively, 17, 9, 6, 3, and 2, has an H-index of 3. Since there are three articles with at least three references and not four articles with at least four references. Also, the *H-core* of a publication is a set of the most reported h *articles* from the publication. For example, the above publication has as *H-Core* the one based on *H* with number three, namely those that they are reported with 17, 9 and 6 reports.

To collect the bibliographic data taken for this study, we used Elsevier's Scopus, which pro-vides comprehensive coverage of journals, and other sources of research work and edited volumes from a plethora of publishers. In a second layer of work, we performed searches on Journals' websites, mainly for these ones with limited information from Scopus for the examine period of time.

The search was based on a combination of various relevant in investments and ethics terms, ranging from general ones (e.g. "Investment analysis") to ones involving specific Corporate Social Responsibility techniques and approaches (e.g., "Corporate Social Responsibility and Techniques", "Corporate Social Responsibility and Investment", "Corporate Governance and Investment,"etc.). After several attempts we figured out taken mainly from abstracts sections of the examine papers that the most appropriate search is the one that consists of the word "Ethical" and the word "Investment" to better describe the examine framework. So, we use the following filter in the Elsevier's Scopus base:

TITLE-ABS-EY (ethical AND investments) AND DOCTYPE (ar) AND PUBYEAR > 1989

AND (LIMIT-TO (PUBYEAR, 2019) OR LIMIT-TO (PUBYEAR, 2018) OR LIMIT-TO (PUBYEAR, 2017) OR LIMIT-TO (PUBYEAR, 2016) OR LIMIT-TO (PUBYEAR, 2015) OR LIMIT-TO (PUBYEAR, 2014) OR LIMIT-TO (PUBYEAR, 2013) OR LIMIT-TO (PUBYEAR, 2012) OR LIMIT-TO (PUBYEAR, 2011) OR

LIMIT-TO (PUBYEAR, 2010) OR LIMIT-TO (PUBYEAR, 2009) OR LIMIT-TO (PUBYEAR, 2008) OR LIMIT-TO (PUBYEAR, 2007) OR LIMIT-TO (PUBYEAR, 2006) OR LIMIT-TO (PUBYEAR, 2005) OR LIMIT-TO (PUBYEAR, 2004) OR LIMIT-TO (PUBYEAR, 2003) OR LIMIT-TO (PUBYEAR, 2002) OR LIMIT-TO (PUBYEAR, 2001) OR LIMIT-TO (PUBYEAR, 2000) OR LIMIT-TO (PUBYEAR, 1999) OR LIMIT-TO (PUBYEAR, 1998) OR LIMIT-TO (PUBYEAR, 1997) OR LIMIT-TO (PUBYEAR, 1996) OR LIMIT-TO (PUBYEAR, 1995) OR LIMIT-TO (PUBYEAR, 1994) OR LIMIT-TO (PUBYEAR, 1993) OR LIMIT-TO (PUBYEAR, 1992) OR LIMIT-TO (PUBYEAR, 1991) OR LIMIT-TO (PUBYEAR, 1990)) AND (LIMIT-TO (SUBJAREA, "SOCI") OR LIMIT-TO (SUBJAREA, "BUSI") OR LIMIT-TO (SUBJAREA, "ECON") OR LIMIT-TO (SUBJAREA, "DECI"))

To search for articles focused on Ethical investment (EI) research, the study uses the keywords "ethical" and "investment" in the title, abstract and keywords of any work available in Elsevier's Scopus. The search was developed in May 2019 and consists of the period between January 1990 and May 2019. The research was limited to the fields of Social Sciences, Business, Management and Accounting, Economics, Econometrics and Finance and Decision Sciences. This search finds some 718 articles by only considering International Journals' articles.

In this chapter we analyze the Ethical Investment research during that period. We seek to discuss the contributions of EI in different areas of scientific research, especially in Business, Accounting and Decision-Making disciplines and to identify established and emerging research topics, as well as future opportunities and challenges in this thematic area. Furthermore, the study analyzes the citation structure focusing on specific journal and papers' characteristics. Also, it is on our prior scope to analyze key journals in terms of influence in the EI field. The next subsection presents and analyzes the main findings.

RESULTS

Herein we present the results of the study. Evolution of publications in venture capital research over the past 29 years, accounts for some 718 articles that have been published in EI research, according to the criteria set for this study. Figure 1 presents the evolution of the number of papers published annually.

In general, the growth of EI research over the past 39 years seems to be in higher terms than the growth in other fields of science worldwide. This growth is usually between 15 and 20 per cent and achieved over 100 per cent in 1998 and 2000 while it records a steady pace from 2014 and onwards.

Figure 1. Number of research papers

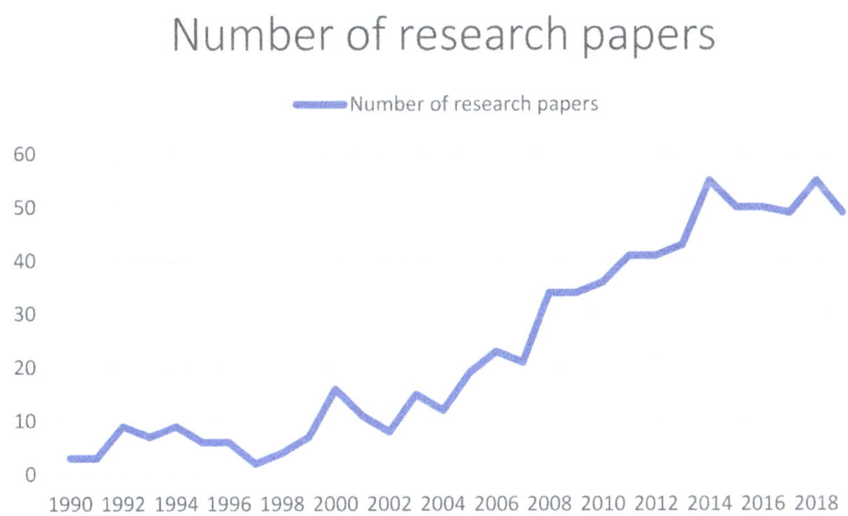

Research Citations in Ethical Investments (EI)

In Table 1 we present the number of citations for the whole sample of 718 Journals obtained by papers published during the examine period.

It is clear that most of the highly cited studies in EI were published in 2008 (i.e. 1,742 citations) and in years 2011 and 2012 with 847 and 843 citations respectively. It is obvious that there was a huge increase for the topic of EI because of the 2008 world financial crisis that set the function of US subprime market under serious questioning. Also, during the years 2011 and 2012, typically near the end term of the world crisis the number of articles published in EI increased and consistently so as the number of highly cited works also increased.

In general, only 14 out of 718 paper articles have received more than 100 citations (i.e. nearly 2% of the whole sample) and nearly 37 per cent of the articles received at least 10 citations.

In Table 2 we portray 25 scientific Journals with the greater number of research-works in the field of EI during the examine period 1990 to May of 2019. We consider nearly half of the year 2019 research activity in the relevant field in order to portray the trend in the area during the last available year. Also, in the same table we portray Journals with at least 4 papers in the field of EI during the examine period.

Table 1. Number of citations per year

Year of Publication	Number of Citations
1990	9
1991	103
1992	219
1993	163
1994	342
1995	221
1996	50
1997	64
1998	21
1999	151
2000	437
2001	655
2002	126
2003	475
2004	394
2005	728
2006	444
2007	456
2008	1,742
2009	595
2010	533
2011	847
2012	843
2013	602
2014	455
2015	417
2016	253
2017	114
2018	52
2019 (until May of 2019)	11
Total Sum	11,522

Table 2. Number of research papers in IE during the examine period (threshold with at least 4 papers in EI for each journal)

No	Journal	Number of Research Papers
1.	*Journal of Business Ethics*	94
2.	*Journal of Sustainable Finance and Investment*	11
3.	*Social Responsibility Journal*	10
4.	*Sustainability (Switzerland)*	9
5.	*Accounting, Auditing and Accountability Journal*	8
6.	*Business Ethics*	6
7.	*Journal of the International Academy for Case Studies*	6
8.	*Social Science and Medicine*	6
9.	*Business Ethics: A European Review*	5
10.	*Business Strategy and the Environment*	5
11.	*European Journal of Operational Research*	5
12.	*Journal of Banking and Finance*	5
13.	*Journal of Financial Regulation and Compliance*	5
14.	*Journal of Financial Services Marketing*	5
15.	*Business and Society*	4
16.	*Corporate Social Responsibility and Environmental Management*	4
17.	*Critical Studies on Corporate Responsibility, Governance and Sustainability*	4
18.	*International Journal of Social Economics*	4
19.	*Journal of Cleaner Production*	4
20.	*Journal of Economic Psychology*	4
21.	*Journal of Islamic Accounting and Business Research*	4
22.	*Managerial Finance*	4
23.	*Pacific Basin Finance Journal*	4
24.	*Public Integrity*	4
25.	*Research in International Business and Finance*	4
	Total number of research papers	**224**

Only 22.2 per cent of the work did not receive any citations until now (i.e. until May 2019). Among the most cited papers we pick up the articles with at least 90 citations in EI research during the examine period, accounting to the 27% of the citations of the whole sample of papers in the study (see Table 3).

Table 3. The most influential research works in EI (threshold of 90 citations per paper)

Authors	Title	Year	Source title- Journal	Cited by
Renneboog L., Ter Horst J., Zhang C.,	Socially responsible investments: Institutional aspects, performance, and investor behavior	2008	*Journal of Banking and Finance*	406
Bauer R., Koedijk K., Otten R.,	International evidence on ethical mutual fund performance and investment style	2005	*Journal of Banking and Finance*	376
Jamali D.,	A stakeholder approach to corporate social responsibility: A fresh perspective into theory and practice	2008	*Journal of Business Ethics*	355
Dasgupta P.,	Discounting climate change	2008	*Journal of Risk and Uncertainty*	238
Heinkel R., Kraus A., Zechner J.,	The effect of green investment on corporate behavior	2001	*Journal of Financial and Quantitative Analysis*	222
Renneboog L., Ter Horst J., Zhang C.,	The price of ethics and stakeholder governance: The performance of socially responsible mutual funds	2008	*Journal of Corporate Finance*	215
Guay T., Doh J.P., Sinclair G.,	Non-governmental organizations, shareholder activism, and socially responsible investments: Ethical, strategic, and governance implications	2004	*Journal of Business Ethics*	173
Bauer R., Derwall J., Otten R.,	The ethical mutual fund performance debate: New evidence from Canada	2007	*Journal of Business Ethics*	140
Alan Willis C.A.,	The Role of the Global Reporting Initiative's Sustainability Reporting Guidelines in the Social Screening of Investments	2003	*Journal of Business Ethics*	130
Friedman A.L., Miles S.,	Socially responsible investment and corporate social and environmental reporting in the UK: An exploratory study	2001	*British Accounting Review*	119
Wu M.-W., Shen C.-H.,	Corporate social responsibility in the banking industry: Motives and financial performance	2013	*Journal of Banking and Finance*	118
Klassen R.D.,	Plant-level environmental management orientation: The influence of management views and plant characteristics	2001	*Production and Operations Management*	116
Mallin C.A., Briston R.J.,	THE FINANCIAL PERFORMANCE OF ETHICAL INVESTMENT FUNDS	1995	*Journal of Business Finance & Accounting*	116
Hayat R., Kraeussl R.,	Risk and return characteristics of Islamic equity funds	2011	*Emerging Markets Review*	114
Bauer R., Otten R., Rad A.T.,	Ethical investing in Australia: Is there a financial penalty?	2006	*Pacific Basin Finance Journal*	95
Luther R.G., Matatko J., Corner D.C.,	The Investment Performance of UK "Ethical" Unit Trusts	1992	*Accounting, Auditing & Accountability Journal*	95
Cockburn I., Henderson R.,	Racing to Invest? The Dynamics of Competition in Ethical Drug Discovery	1994	*Journal of Economics and Management Strategy*	90

The most cited paper is the one of Renneboog et al. (2008), with 406 citations that provides a critical review of the literature on socially responsible investments (SRI), reviewing several questions on the causes and the shareholder-value impact of corporate social responsibility (CSR) and behavior of SRI investors.

Bouer et al. (2005) research is the next more citable work of the study with 376 citations. They use a database containing German, UK and US ethical mutual funds and they extend previous relevant research work. Their results suggest that ethical mutual funds tend to acquire nearly the same returns with the conventional mutual funds.

Jamali D. 2008 work, with 355 citations, present an overview of two traditional aspects of corporate social responsibility (CSR), providing further descriptions in the field. The work examines the CSR approach of a sample of firms with interest in CSR, while it tests and analyzes potential implications regarding this approach.

In a more recent work in EI, Dreyer et al. 2017 they present an alternative view on Responsible Innovation by a group of industry practitioners. The authors refer to the need for distinguishing between processes related to research and innovation practices and technics, and the enhanced role of contemporary business in society, including among others the solid frameworks of the CSR, the Corporate Shared Value (CSV), the Responsible Digital Innovation, etc.

In general, in a substantial number of research papers, the issue of ethical commitment to investments according to accepted global principles or best-practices in corporate governance technics is set. Also, there is a great deal of research regarding assurances that funding is not associated with companies and practices that pose a risk to global social and environmental justice.

Leading Journals in EI Research

As we've said earlier, the h-index is a measure of the quality of a journal. We use the h-index to compare herein journals of not that contradictory fields (i.e. Business, Accounting, Social Science and Decision making), because is the best measure one can use to compare journals within a field (Hodge & Lacasse 2011). In this study, we use the bibliometric indicators database of the SCImago Journal & Country Rank portal to take Journals' h-Index.

Also, there are quite many scientific journals in Elsevier's Scopus that publish material related to EI research. Table 4 presents a list of the journals in EI with their number of citations so far (May 2019) as well as their h-index taken from SCImago database. We set a threshold of h-index of 150 and upwards in EI research.

The top 3 Journals with the highest H-Index amongst the whole sample are the *Strategic Management Journal*, the *European Journal of Operational Research* and the *Journal of Financial Economics* with h-index of 253, 226 and 223 respectively.

Table 4. Top influential journals in EI according to their h-Index

No	Source title-Journal	Cited by	H-index
1.	Strategic Management Journal	33	253
2.	European Journal of Operational Research	125	226
3.	Journal of Financial Economics	49	223
4.	Social Science and Medicine	160 (*)	213
5.	Organization Science	15	211
6.	Ecological Economics	153 (*)	174
7.	Harvard business review	4	161
8.	Tourism Management	16	159
9.	Journal of Business Research	66	158
10.	Information Sciences	49	154
11.	Journal of Business Venturing	23	154
12.	Journal of Cleaner Production	77	150

(*) Top Journals in terms of h-index, cited at least by 150 scientific works in the field of EI.

However, these do not seem to have the highest numbers of citations. It is clear that scientific analysis on EI comes from many disciplines, and it is not possible to identify a specific group of journals leading the discipline. Herein the most influential in terms of numbers of citations is the Journal of Banking and Finance with h-index of 135.

We identify herein the group of the seventeen Journals with the most cited papers in EI according to Table 3: *Journal of Banking and Finance, Journal of Banking and Finance, Journal of Business Ethics, Journal of Risk and Uncertainty, Journal of Financial and Quantitative Analysis, Journal of Corporate Finance, Journal of Business Ethics, Journal of Business Ethics, Journal of Business Ethics, British Accounting Review, Journal of Banking and Finance, Production and Operations Management, Journal of Business Finance & Accounting, Emerging Markets Review, Pacific Basin Finance Journal, Accounting, Auditing & Accountability Journal* and *Journal of Economics and Management Strategy.*

Also, we find a group of the twelve Journals with the highest h-index amongst the whole sample of the study, with research papers in EI according to Table 4, that account for a 6.7 per cent of the overall number of citations of the sample (i.e. 11,522 citations in EI): *Strategic Management Journal, European Journal of Operational Research, Journal of Financial Economics, Social Science and Medicine, Organization Science, Ecological Economics, Harvard business review, Tourism Management, Journal of Business Research, Information Sciences, Journal of Business Venturing* and *Journal of Cleaner Production*. Among this group, two journals (*Social Science* and *Medicine and Ecological Economics*) present articles in EI cited at least by 150 scientific works in the field of EI.

We also discover that, several management journals are also very influential in the field of EI including the *European Journal of Operational Research* with 125 citations and the *Journal of Cleaner Production* with 77 citations.

Leading Journals in EI by Periods of Time

In this section, we focus on the evolution of top-12 and leading journals in ethical investment research throughout time, and more specifically during the years 1990 to 2019 (until May of 2019). In each period of time, the list with top-cited journals, i.e. the ones that have taken the greater numbers of citations in research studies regarding the ethical Investment is portrayed in Table 4. The list of examine Journal consist of the following: *Journal Accounting, Auditing & Accountability Journal, British Accounting Review, Emerging Markets Review, Journal of Banking and Finance, Journal of Business Ethics, Journal of Business Finance & Accounting, Journal of Corporate Finance, Journal of Financial and Quantitative Analysis, Journal of Risk and Uncertainty, Pacific Basin Finance Journal and Production* and *Operations Management.*

In Table 5 we portray the highest number of cited Journal throughout the examine period of nearly 30 years is the *Journal of Business Ethics (JBE)* with 2,713 citations during this period. Also, the same journal records a significant and yearly-distributed number of citations accounting for some 2,713 during the examine period. This Journal represents nearly the 23.5 per cent of the total number of citations in EI of our study. It clearly underscores the quite important scientific contribution of the *JBE* to the field, while it also expresses the most common in language title regarding the field of ethics in business and management in general.

The *Journal of Banking and Finance (JBF)* is the second Journal with the greatest overall number of citations in the relevant field during the 30 years of the research (i.e. with 917 citations).

It is outstanding that in 2015 it is recorded in the same Journal (JBF) a substantially increased number of citations in relevant scientific work made before the 2008 crisis period, which accounts for some 376 citations. It may show a signal in relevant research before the outbreak of crisis. On the other hand, Table 4 shows that overall research in EI, especially in the commence of the crisis period in year 2008, records the greatest number of citations in EI research for the examine period. It is clear that the consequences of the crisis period were amazingly affected the research activity in ethical investment literature and underscored the momentum of this scientific field during and right after the 2008 World financial crisis period.

Table 5. Top 12 cited Scientific journals in ethical Investment by periods of time (years 1990 to 2019)

Journals	90	91	92	93	94	95	96	97	98	99	00	01	02	03	04	05	06	07	08	09	10	11	12	13	14	15	16	17	18	19	Total sum
	Number of Citations in EI Per Year																														
Accounting, Auditing & Accountability Journal			95												65								12								172
British Accounting Review												119								23											142
Emerging Markets Review																						114	16								130
Journal of Banking and Finance																376			406					118	17						917
Journal of Business Ethics	*9*	*20*	*19*		*60*	*15*	*28*		*2*	*5*	*250*	*8*	*17*	*131*	*254*	*123*	*93*	*183*	*609*	*261*	*217*	*175*	*52*	*83*	*34*	*27*	*12*	*10*	*13*	*3*	*2,713*
Journal of Business Finance & Accounting						116																									116
Journal of Corporate Finance																			215												215
Journal of Financial and Quantitative Analysis												222																			222
Journal of Risk and Uncertainty																			238												238
Pacific Basin Finance Journal																	102										4				106
Production and Operations Management												116																			116
Total Sums	**9**	**20**	**114**	**0**	**60**	**131**	**28**	**0**	**2**	**5**	**250**	**465**	**17**	**131**	**319**	**499**	**195**	**183**	**1,468**	**284**	**217**	**289**	**80**	**201**	**51**	**27**	**16**	**10**	**13**	**3**	**5,087**

CONCLUSIONS

Socially Responsible Investing (SRI) is broadly used in scientific literature as the one that cares about the social and economic activity of a region. It represents somehow the process that contributes to integrating not only financial but also social, environmental, and ethical (SEE) considerations into viable and sustainable investment decisions. However, while a quite impressive set of researches do exist regarding the field of investment decisions, there is a limited but substantial set of research work that enhances the framework of investment decision-making based not only on pure financial criteria but also on accounting, social and environmental aspects, including also social responsibility criteria.

The proposed approach is based partially on Cancino et al. (2018) research work that takes into consideration a bibliometric analysis of venture capital research in scientific literature.

At the same time, the 2008 World financial crisis triggered several ethical issues placing them at the forefront of global interest among decision and policy makers. Ethical Investment research work can contribute to this endeavor of understanding the real framework of economic activity with the use of a holistic view of worldwide economy, enabling the consideration of social and environmental factors as well, opening the floor for corporate governance and social responsibility issues.

The aim of this chapter is to present the contributions of EI in literature and identify established and emerging research Journal with more influence than others in the relevant research field.

This chapter presents a general overview of the leading journals in ethical investment research between the period 1990 and 2019 (until May 2019). We use bibliometric indicators database of the SCImago Journal & Country Rank portal to take Journals' h-Index in order to take a measure of Journals' quality characteristics.

The analysis made focused on top-cited studies with at least 90 citations during the examine period. We found that most research work focus on ethical investment and performance, as well as other relevant issues regarding the implementation of corporate social responsibility practices and uses in socially responsible investments (SRI). Also, the role of sustainable financial reporting was reviewed in the literature as a prerequisite of business success.

The *Journal of Banking and Finance (JBF)*, the *Journal of Business Ethics (JBE)*, the *Journal of Risk and Uncertainty (JRU)*, as well as the *Journal of Financial and Quantitative Analysis (JFQA)* are among others the most citable and influential journals of the research field. Furthermore, we make further analysis with the use of h- index taken from SCimago Database by setting a threshold of h-index of 150 and upwards for EI research. The ranking of 12 leading journals that present a greater h-index in the discipline is taken in order to record potential liaison between the number of citations and the h-index score of the examine journals. We find that Journals with the greater h-Index score don't necessarily record the greater number of cited research papers. That is because the aforementioned topic is close to the ethical behavior in investing activities, so it is not that important only for scientific Journal of pure finance or in accounting in discipline, but also in those focused mainly in Business ethics, Banking and Finance and Risk and Uncertainty. Also, we find that it is highly possible to observe research Journals who have a greater quantity of published work, which do not act as the most influential factors in the relevant research field. We find, among others, that a group of 12 Journals (i.e. 2.8 per cent of the number of Scientific Journals consisted for the sample) with the highest h-index amongst the whole sample (i.e. 426 Journals) of the study, account for a 6.7 per cent of the overall number of citations of the sample (i.e. 11,522 citations in EI). This result is in line with Cancino et al. 2018 research work which expresses the same statement out of their work.

By examining also leading journals in EI by periods of time, we find that only one case, namely the *Journal of Business Ethics (JBE)* records some 2,713 citations overall. Also, the same journal records a significant and a well formed yearly-distributed number of citations during the examine period. This Journal represents nearly the 23.5 per cent of the total number of citations in EI of our study. In other words, the JBE summarizes and encapsulated with the most feasible way the influence in the field, by taking the greatest number of citations from all the journals in our sample not only classified by their main subject area of interest in business ethics, but also in any other field undertaken in this study.

A limitation in our research is that we didn't include other main explanatory to ethical behavior disciplines such as psychology, as well as various social aspects and investment characteristics, terms of innovation and sociology, among others, with which a more in-depth analysis may have been taken.

Finally, it is worth exploring extensions and potential integration of ethical investment with other fields of study, taking into account different methodologies in liaison with big data analytics and machine learning techniques.

REFERENCES

Broadus, R. N. (1987). Toward a definition of bibliometrics. *Scientometrics, 12*(5-6), 373–379. doi:10.1007/BF02016680

Cabello, J. M., Ruiz, F., Pérez-Gladish, B., & Méndez-Rodríguez, P. (2014). Synthetic indicators of mutual funds' environmental responsibility: An application of the Reference Point Method. *European Journal of Operational Research, 236*(1), 313–325. doi:10.1016/j.ejor.2013.11.031

Cancino, C. A., Merigo, J. M., Torres, J. P., & Diaz, D. (2018). A bibliometric analysis of venture capital research. *Journal of Economics, Finance, and Administrative Science, 23*(45), 182–195. doi:10.1108/JEFAS-01-2018-0016

Coupé, T. (2003). Revealed performances: Worldwide rankings of economists and economics departments, 1990-2000. *Journal of the European Economic Association, 1*(6), 1309–1345. doi:10.1162/154247603322752557

De Oliveira, E. M., Cunha, F. A. F. S., Cyrino Oliveira, F. L., & Samanez, C. P. (2017). Dynamic relationships between crude oil prices and socially responsible investing in Brazil: Evidence for linear and non-linear causality. *Applied Economics, 49*(22), 2125–2140. doi:10.1080/00036846.2016.1234695

Dorfleitner, G., & Nguyen, M. (2017). A new approach for optimizing responsible investments dependently on the initial wealth. *Journal of Asset Management, 18*(2), 81–98. doi:10.105741260-016-0011-x

Dupré, D., Girerd-Potin, I., Jimenez-Garces, S., & Louvet, P. (2009). The impact of social rating on stock prices: A theoretical model. *Revue Economique, 60*(1), 5–31.

Egghe, L. (2006). Theory and practice of the g-index. *Scientometrics, 69*(1), 131–152. doi:10.100711192-006-0144-7

Fieseler, C. (2011). On the corporate social responsibility perceptions of equity analysts. *Business Ethics (Oxford, England), 20*(2), 131–147. doi:10.1111/j.1467-8608.2011.01616.x

Hebb, T., Louche, C., & Hachigian, H. (2014). Exploring the societal impacts of SRI. *Critical Studies on Corporate Responsibility, Governance and Sustainability, 7*, 3–20. doi:10.1108/S2043-905920140000007001

Herrera-Cano, C., & Gonzalez-Perez, M. A. (2016). Global Financial Crisis and the Emergence and Maturing of Socially Responsible Investments. *Advances in Sustainability and Environmental Justice, 18*, 189–202. doi:10.1108/S2051-503020160000018008

Hirsch, J. (2005). An index to quantify an individual's scientific research output. In *Proceedings of the National Academy of Sciences of the United States of America, 102*(46), 16569–16572. doi:10.1073/pnas.0507655102 PMID:16275915

Hodge, D., & Lacasse, J. R. (2011). Evaluating journal quality: Is the H-index a better measure than impact factors? *Research on Social Work Practice*, *21*(2), 222–230. doi:10.1177/1049731510369141

Jansson, M., & Biel, A. (2011). Motives to engage in sustainable investment: A comparison between institutional and private investors. *Sustainable Development*, *19*(2), 135–142. doi:10.1002d.512

Knoll, M. S. (2002). Ethical screening in modern financial markets: The conflicting claims underlying socially responsible investment. *Business Lawyer*, *57*(2), 681–726.

Landström, H., Harirchi, G., & Aström, F. (2012). Entrepreneurship: Exploring the knowledge base. *Research Policy*, *41*(7), 1154–1181. doi:10.1016/j.respol.2012.03.009

Leys, J., Vandekerckhove, W., & Van Liedekerke, L. (2009). A puzzle in SRI: The investor and the judge. *Journal of Business Ethics*, *84*(2), 221–235. doi:10.100710551-008-9705-4

Merig_o, J. M., & Yang, J. B. (2016). Accounting research: A bibliometric analysis. *Australian Accounting Review*. doi:10.1111/auar.12109

Merig_o, J. M., Cancino, C., Coronado, F., & Urbano, D. (2016). Academic research in innovation: a country analysis, *Scientometrics, 108*(2), pp. 559-593.

Palacios-González, M. M., & Chamorro-Mera, A. (2018). Analysis of the predictive variables of the intention to invest in a socially responsible manner. *Journal of Cleaner Production*, *196*, 469–477. doi:10.1016/j.jclepro.2018.06.066

Palacios-González, M. M., & Chamorro-Mera, A. (2019). Analysis of the intention to invest in a socially responsible manner: A segmentation of the Spanish investor. *Revista Española de Financiación y Contabilidad*, 1–16. doi:10.1080/02102412.2019.1598700

Palacios-González, M. M., & Chamorro-Mera, A. (2019). Socially responsible investment: An analysis of the structure of preferences of savers. *Corporate Social Responsibility and Environmental Management*. doi:10.1002/csr.1757

Park, J. (2009). Sustainable consumption and the financial sector: Analysing the markets for responsible investment in Hong Kong and Japan. *International Journal of Consumer Studies*, *33*(2), 206–214. doi:10.1111/j.1470-6431.2009.00757.x

Podsakoff, P. M., MacKenzie, S. B., Podsakoff, N. P., & Bachrach, D. G. (2008). Scholarly influence in the field of management: A bibliometric analysis of the determinants of university and author impact in the management literature in the past quarter century. *Journal of Management*, *34*(4), 641–720. doi:10.1177/0149206308319533

Puaschunder, J. M. (2017). Socio-psychological motives of socially responsible investors. *Advances in Financial Economics*, *19*, 209–247. doi:10.1108/S1569-373220160000019008

Puaschunder, J. M. (2019). The History of Ethical, Environmental, Social, and Governance-Oriented Investments as a Key to Sustainable Prosperity in the Finance World. *Public Integrity*, *21*(2), 161–181. doi:10.1080/10999922.2018.1439563

Rathner, S. (2013). The influence of primary study characteristics on the performance differential between socially responsible and conventional investment funds: A meta-analysis. *Journal of Business Ethics*, *118*(2), 349–363. doi:10.100710551-012-1584-z

Renneboog, L., Ter Horst, J., & Zhang, C. (2011). Is ethical money financially smart? Nonfinancial attributes and money flows of socially responsible investment funds. *Journal of Financial Intermediation*, *20*(4), 562–588. doi:10.1016/j.jfi.2010.12.003

Revelli, C., & Viviani, J.-L. (2015). Financial performance of socially responsible investing (SRI): What have we learned? A meta-analysis. *Business Ethics (Oxford, England)*, *24*(2), 158–185. doi:10.1111/beer.12076

Ross Jayne, M., & Skerratt, G. (2003). The requirements of ethical fund managers and property investment. *Property Management*, *21*(2), 136–152. doi:10.1108/02637470310478882

Valor, C., De La Cuesta, M., & Fernandez, B. (2009). Understanding demand for retail socially responsible investments: A survey of individual investors and financial consultants. *Corporate Social Responsibility and Environmental Management*, *16*(1), 1–14. doi:10.1002/csr.172

Von Wallis, M., & Klein, C. (2015). Ethical requirement and financial interest: A literature review on socially responsible investing. *Business Research*, *8*(1), 61–98. doi:10.100740685-014-0015-7

Chapter 13
Islamic Finance

Vasileios Pappas
https://orcid.org/0000-0003-1885-4832
University of Kent, UK

ABSTRACT

The Islamic finance industry is estimated around $1.7 trillion with substantial growth momentum in the past decades. It is now too important to be ignored, particularly in the Middle and Far East. This chapter reviews the most salient features of Islamic finance that distinguish it from the rest of the conventional financial universe. A significant volume of research focuses on the comparative performance of Islamic and conventional banks across a wide range of metrics, such as profitability, risk, and efficiency. Islamic stock and bonds markets are also an important segment of the related comparative literature and we reviews these studies, too. This chapter provides a comprehensive and up-to-date review of the extant literature, useful for academics and practitioners with little or significant experience in the Islamic finance sector.

INTRODUCTION

Islamic finance has established itself on the global financial system, with total assets under management around $1.7 trillion, while maintaining a double-digit annual growth rate even amidst financial crisis and political turmoil (EY, 2016). The fast growth of the sector and its differences from the conventional one have spurred interest from practitioners and academics alike.

Islamic finance refers to these financial institutions where practices emanating from the Islamic law (Shariah) are accommodated into the business model. The prohibition of interest and speculative activities, the shunning of investments in

DOI: 10.4018/978-1-7998-2436-7.ch013

industries that are considered unlawful - alcohol, gambling and tobacco to name but a few – as well as investments in complex derivative products, debt instruments and short-selling are some of the most commonly acknowledged restrictions. As a consequence, Islamic financial institutions use two types of financial products: equity/participation type and fee-based services. Mudarabah is a commonly used equity/participation type of contract where an investor (usually an Islamic bank) and an entrepreneur (individual or institutional) enter a joint venture with the bank providing the necessary funds, the entrepreneur the know-how, and they agree to share the profits on a pre-determined ratio. Fee-based services include the widely used contracts of Murabahah and Ijarah. Murabahah is in essence a cost-plus-profit sale. The bank arranges to sell a good to a customer at a premium which incorporates risks, costs and a profit margin. Ijarah is a lease contract where the bank leases an asset to an investor (or consumer) and the latter pays fees for utilizing the asset.

Despite their restrictions and unique model, Islamic banks are considered as more profitable (Bitar, Madiès, & Taramasco, 2017; Hasan & Dridi, 2011), featuring superior asset quality and capitalization (Beck, Demirgüç-Kunt, & Merrouche, 2013), of similar risk profile to their conventional counterparts (Abedifar, Molyneux, & Tarazi, 2013; Baele, Farooq, & Ongena, 2014; Čihák & Hesse, 2010; Pappas, Ongena, Izzeldin, & Fuertes, 2017), and of higher technical efficiency (Bitar, Hassan, & Walker, 2017; Johnes, Izzeldin, & Pappas, 2014).[1] Like conventional banks, Islamic banks are also affected by economic shocks albeit in a more muted manner (Di, Shaiban, & Shavkatovich Hasanov, 2017; Olson & Zoubi, 2017), a fact that regulators should be wary of. Contrary to the conventional perception that firms are more likely to connect to a bank that is close by, firms wishing to connect to an Islamic bank are willing to do some extra sacrifices in terms of distance (Beck, Ongena, & Şendeniz-Yüncü, 2019), which may have important implications for Islamic bank branching strategies.

The distinct profile of Islamic banks, and Islamic finance in general, is of particular relevance to investors, as it enhances their diversification opportunities particularly during financial crises, as documented in Akhter, Pappas and Khan (2017), Alexakis, Pappas and Tsikouras (2017), Sorwar, Pappas, Pereira and Nurullah (2016) among others. Yet these benefits may be limited in countries where Islamic stocks may be particularly responsive to economic shocks due to religious restrictions on conventional stock trading (Alhomaidi, Hassan, Hippler, & Mamun, 2019). It is also argued that the performance of Islamic and conventional stock returns can create segmented financial markets consistent with investor recognition effects that grant Islamic stocks higher liquidity, lower risk, better integration with macroeconomic factors and higher systematic turnover (Alhomaidi et al., 2019). The presence of Islamic banks has important implications for the financial development and economic welfare of, particularly low income, countries (Abedifar, Hasan, & Tarazi, 2016), a fact which may be in part explained to the higher liquidity creation of these banks (Berger, Boubakri, Guedhami, & Li, 2018).[2]

The unique model of Islamic banks has also implications for their corporate governance and vice versa. In particular, Islamic banks maintain a Shariah Supervisory Board (SSB) which works alongside the Board of Directors, but is considered the "Supra Authority" in an Islamic bank (Choudhury & Hoque, 2006). Related research has found that a large and independent SSB is positively related to the financial performance of Islamic banks and financial stability (Farag, Mallin, & Ow-Yong, 2018; Mollah & Zaman, 2015). In particular, the SSB operates as a protective cushion that allows Islamic banks to take higher risk and achieve better performance, while being more capitalized and exhibiting lower failure risk compared to conventional banks (Miah & Uddin, 2017; Mollah, Hassan, Al Farooque, & Mobarek, 2017; Pappas et al., 2017). Besides, a large and active SSB reduces Shariah non-compliance risk (Basiruddin & Ahmed, 2017). Islamic banks have higher board of directors' independence, which is documented to be positively linked to capitalization and to a prudent risk-taking behavior (Mollah et al., 2017; Vallascas, Mollah, & Keasey, 2017). Hayat and Kabir Hassan (2017) examine the link between higher capitalization and good governance (Jeitschko & Jeung, 2005), for Islamic and non-Islamic firms and find that the former score higher on well-reputed governance indicator scores.

The price that Islamic banks have to pay for this dual-board structure is reflected in their cost efficiency (Miah & Uddin, 2017), particularly through the increased number of board committees (Alexakis et al., 2018). At the same time, there is an increasing need for a bank to operate at full efficiency commensurate with the increased competition in the financial services industry (Fiordelisi, Marques-Ibanez, & Molyneux, 2011; Schaeck & Cihak, 2014). Even though Islamic banks operating in dual-banking countries appear to be unaffected by competition from conventional banks with respect to deposit rate setting (Meslier, Risfandy, & Tarazi, 2017), it is unknown if this extends to other financial aspects, including profitability and financial stability, or depends on the Islamicity of the country's population (Rehman & Askari, 2010), or is related to how particular aspects of Islamic banking, such as Zakat, are implemented across countries. For example, in Pakistan and although the Zakat levy is managed by the government, there is uncertainty as to the timing and exact level of payment, both of which could pose a significant withdrawal risk to Islamic banks (Choudhary & Limodio, 2017).

Islamic finance is itself a topic of great ambiguity. Proponents of Islamic finance argue that certain unique features, such as the shunning of interest, debt instruments and complex derivatives as well as the use of risk-sharing and equity participation to mobilize investments from fund surplus to fund deficit units, create a new financial paradigm and enhance ethical investing. Critics of Islamic finance argue that the differences between the theoretically envisaged Islamic financial model and what is observed in reality are substantial, and that Islamic finance is simply conventional finance with Arabic names (Khan, 2010; Trad, Trabelsi, & Goux, 2017). To their defense they posit that the cornerstone of Islamic finance is equity participation, with profits and losses shared between the contracted parties according to some pre-determined ratio (Usmani, 2002). Yet equity financing constitutes a small percentage of a typical Islamic financial institution's asset portfolio (El-Gamal, 2006; Khan, 2010). Instead, fee-based financial products are the norm, where an "implicit" interest rate is charged that is often highly correlated with the "explicit" interest rate observed in the conventional banking sector.

ISLAMIC FINANCE BACKGROUND

Historical Overview

The prohibition of interest that is central to the Islamic finance paradigm is not a unique feature of the Islamic religion. Historically the term "usury" was used to describe the situation where money owed can attract a fee, and this practice is more than four thousand years old (Z. Iqbal & Mirakhor, 2011). Across time, this practice has been condemned by the most well-known religions (e.g. Christianity, Judaism, Hinduism and Islam) and philosophers (e.g. Plato, Aristotle and Cicero) on moral, ethical and social injustice grounds. Hence, *usury* was prohibited in ancient Rome circa 340 BC – but *interest* was still allowed under some restrictive covenants. A ceiling on interest rate was placed in Julius Caesar time of around 12%, which would fluctuate across time, and anything above this limit would constitute usury, which was illegal until early 12th century (Birnie, 1958). Within the Muslim religion, and Islamic finance in particular, the term "Riba" attracts a special meaning. The prohibition of Riba that is apparent in all Islamic religious writings typically refers to the "doubling and redoubling" of what is owned, and as such it is closer to usury than interest rate (A. Saeed, 1996). Still one needs to consider the fact that the majority of the assets and commodities of primary concern in these ages would face difficulties in measurement if modern interest rates (often much below 5% per annum) were to be applied. Additionally, some of these assets (e.g. cattle) would not be easily divisible.

The first religion to challenge the perception of interest and usury was Protestantism and the capitalism movement that emerged. Interest rate ceilings were raised, penalties were lowered, and a new rationale would be provided for the necessity of an interest rate system, centered on the concepts of efficient production, capital accumulation, time value of money and liquidity preference (Fisher, 1836; Keynes, 1936; Senior, 1836; Smith, 1776). The ethical and moral considerations that had been fostered into the religious teachings up to that point in time would be given less consideration from now on. Notable exceptions would be Hayek (1939) who would view the money supply mechanism, and such use of the interest rate, as a potentially destabilizing factor to the economy. The need to ensure that sufficient capital can be channeled to socially beneficial ventures was also highlighted (Jadlow, 1977; Levy, 1987). During this time most of the countries where the Islam was the dominant religion had been under occupation by the Western powers. As such, a clash between the centuries-long embedded perception of interest/usury and the new economic paradigm viewing interest as an important mechanism for economic growth imposed by the colonists would materialize. It is only after these Muslim countries gained their independence during the second half of the 20th century that a revival of interest in developing a modern version of the historic Islamic financial system has had the chance to re-emerge. Contrary to the Western systems, the Islamic financial system had not been based on interest for mobilizing resources. Instead it operated on the basis of partnership contracts that effectively allowed two (or more) parties to share the business risks and the associated rewards. These would constitute the profit and loss sharing (PLS) contracts. Besides the PLS contracts, the Islamic financial system would rely on trade (or fee-based) transactions that are also independent from interest rates.

The Re-Emergence of Islamic Finance

The Mit-Ghamr in Egypt during the mid-1960s is often regarded as the first Islamic financial institution in the post-colonial era. Despite its limited operations, only offering small saving accounts to the rural sector, it operated on Islamic finance principles. In particular, it did not offer any interest to account holders, while the investments were mobilized on the basis of profit and loss sharing contracts. The first time a government provided backing for a financial institution operating under Islamic finance principles was in the case of Nasser Social Bank, in Egypt in 1971. Although its operations were limited (e.g. micro-credit, interest-free loans to those in need), it provided the necessary spark to the upcoming appearance of private initiatives on Islamic financial institutions. The Dubai Islamic Bank, established in 1975 in the UAE, is until today one of the most prominent Islamic financial institutions offering a full spectrum of financial services. Catalytic to the development of Islamic financial institutions has been the establishment of the Islamic Development Bank (IDB) in 1975, whose key objectives were to promote and support economic and social development in the Muslim world in line with the Islamic Law (Shariah). Islamic finance expanded on capital markets with the first launch of an Islamic bond in 1978 followed by Islamic equity funds and Islamic insurance (Takaful) during the 1990s. Towards the late 1990s, Islamic equity indices are introduced, such as

Table 1. Islamic and conventional equity indices

Index Name	Stocks	Type	5-year Performance
DJ Islamic Market (DJIM)	2,639	Islamic	7.7%
DJ Global	6,909	Conventional	6.3%
DJIM Developed Markets	1,636	Islamic	8.1%
DJ Developed Markets	4,348	Conventional	6.7%
DJIM Emerging Markets	1,003	Islamic	3.6%
DJ Emerging Markets	2,561	Conventional	3.2%
DJIM Asia-Pacific	1,487	Islamic	6.2%
DJ Asia-Pacific	3,926	Conventional	4.4%
DJIM Europe	331	Islamic	4.2%
DJ Europe	869	Conventional	1.7%
DJIM GCC	107	Islamic	-0.3%
DJ GCC	189	Conventional	1.8%
Source: Dow Jones			

the Dow Jones Islamic Markets (DJIM) and the Financial Times Stock Exchange (FTSE) Shariah to name but a few (see Table 1).

The first Islamic products were largely developed to cater for government and corporate funding requirements. But the growth in size and wealth of the Muslim population fed the appetite for retail financial products that would be Shariah-compliant. Response at the government level included the introduction of a dedicated Islamic banking system in Iran, Sudan and Pakistan. Today only Iran maintains this system, while the rest of the countries operate a dual-banking system where conventional and Islamic banks operate alongside. At the corporate level the challenge has been to introduce financial products in accordance with Shariah that would cover the same needs as the conventional ones, while at the same time offering similar rates of return. Through the subsequent evolutionary process Islamic credit cards and mortgages have been made available to the investors in the recent years. Pressure on Islamic banks to continue to innovate is provided by the increasing appeal of the traditional values of Islamic finance to Western investors who were disappointed with the conventional banking practices in light of the 2007 global financial crisis (AT Kearney, 2012).

Interestingly, several multinational banks started offering Islamic financial products through dedicated subsidiaries (e.g. HSBC Amanah). The International Monetary Fund and the World Bank also recognized Islamic financial products as alternative means of financial intermediation (Bank, 2017). This constituted a clear recognition of the market potential. Appetite for Islamic finance is further enhanced by the academic and practitioner research that documents important implications to the investors, policy makers and the society. We review some of the most important studies in a next section of this chapter.

ISLAMIC FINANCIAL INSTRUMENTS

In this section we present the Islamic financial instruments typically available and discuss the most prominent ones in greater detail (see Figure 1). Islamic financial institutions apply Islamic finance practices in both sides of the balance sheet. Hence, an Islamic bank would attract deposits using two financial instruments. The first is a safekeeping account that offers no remuneration (Al-Wadiah). Under this deposit scheme the money is fully guaranteed on the spot. The bank can use it to make any profits that will not be distributed to the depositors. Nevertheless, the bank may offer a gift (Hibah) that is however not stipulated contractually. Banks offer it to signal that businesses are going well and to attract customers, especially if the country operates a dual-banking system.

The second is an equity partnership type of deposit (Mudarabah). Under this contract the depositor will give his/her money to the bank, which will, after collecting a sufficient amount of money, invest it to a particular project. Two forms of Mudarabah exist. In the unrestricted form the bank is allowed to invest the funds entirely up to its discretion whereas under the restricted form the depositor chooses the sectors he wants his funds to be invested into (Archer, Karim, & Al-Deehani, 1998). A profit share ratio is used to determine in what proportion the profits will be split between the bank and the depositors. Out of the profits, the bank will keep its share that compensates for its effort and business risk with the rest given to the depositors. For instance, a 70%-30% ratio means that 70% of the profits will be attributed to the investors whereas the 30% will be withheld by the bank.

At this point we would like to emphasize two points. First, because the future is unknown, it would be against the Shariah to stipulate the returns that an investor will have *ex ante*. The only thing that the profit-share ratio guarantees is that the investor will receive a fixed percentage of something uncertain at the time that the contract is signed. This is a key differentiating factor to the conventional interest rate that, whether fixed or variable, is known with certainty. Secondly, due to the uncertainty that surrounds every economic venture, profits are not guaranteed. Therefore, it might be the case that losses are made, in which case the depositors would bear the losses too. Consequently, the deposited capital is not at all guaranteed and the true rate of return can only be determined *ex post*. By contrast, in conventional settings deposit accounts offer capital protection, whether they are current or saving/time

Figure 1. Islamic financial instruments
Source: Z. Iqbal and Mirakhor (2011)

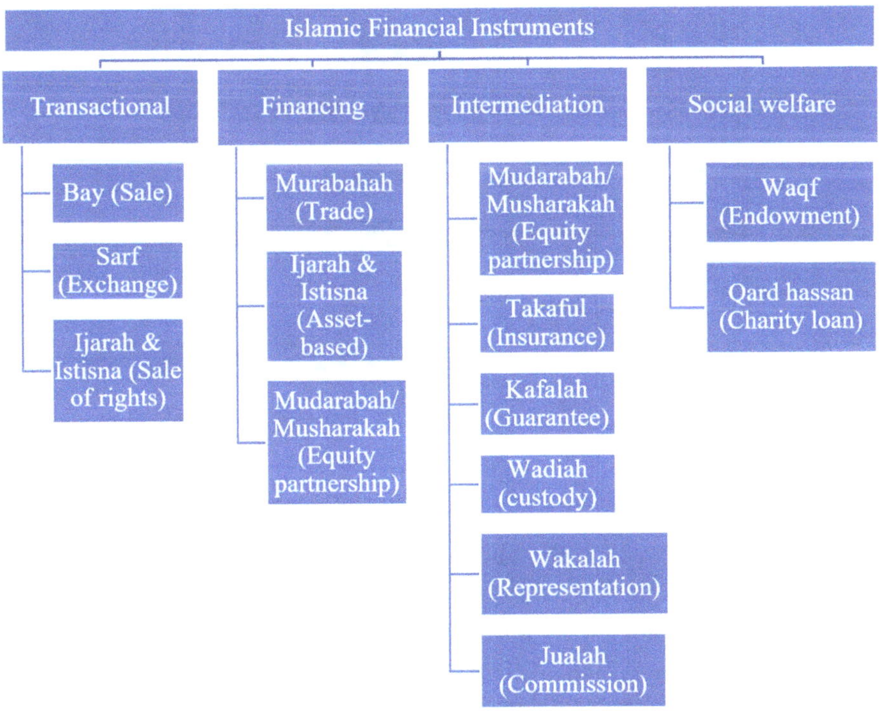

deposits. At this point is clear that Islamic banks' depositors are treated as investment account holders or preferred stockholders with a residual claim to profits but without explicit capital protection; hence, they share the risks of the banks' investments. Hence, they are often referred to as depositors/investors.

However, as Islamic financial institutions operate alongside conventional banks in countries where deposit protection schemes exist (or are gradually phased in), a competitive pressure exists for similar facilities (see Figure 2). The range of protection varies from no coverage of deposits and investments to full protection (with partial protection in some jurisdictions). Certain countries offer a single deposit protection scheme for both Islamic and conventional banks (e.g. Bahrain, Indonesia, Kenya, Lebanon, Luxemburg, Tunisia, Turkey, the U.K., and Yemen). Other countries operate separate deposit protection schemes for Islamic and/or conventional banks (e.g. Iraq, Malaysia, Sudan, Jordan, and Kazakhstan). In addition, Islamic banks maintain a profit equalization reserve (PER) and/or an investment risk reserve (IRR). These are necessary to alleviate competitive pressure on profitability mainly from the conventional banks that may affect withdrawal rates in an Islamic bank as

Figure 2. Deposit protection schemes
Source: Song and Oosthuizen (2014)

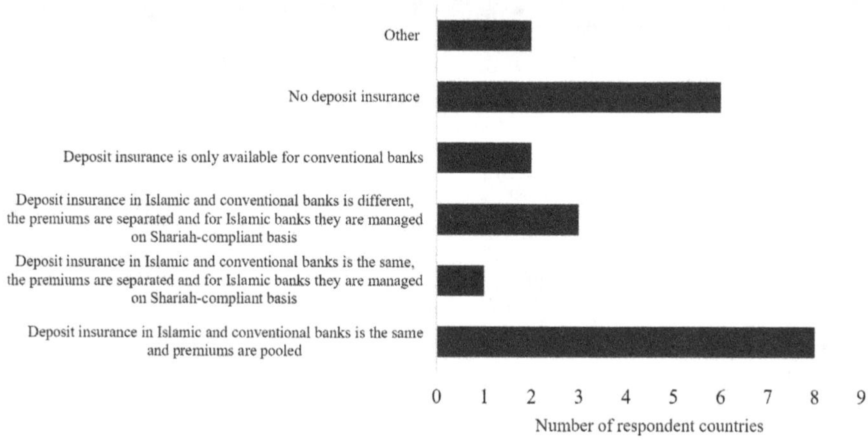

depositors/investors may look elsewhere for higher (or less volatile) returns. These reserves allow the Islamic bank to forgo some of its profit share when this is deemed necessary due to the commercial pressure (Alzahrani & Megginson, 2017; Mejia, Aljabrin, Awad, Norat, & Song, 2014).

On the asset side of the bank's balance sheet some of the most commonly used contracts used are: i) Ijarah; ii) Istisna; iii) Murabahah; iv) Mudarabah; v) Musharakah. The first three are fee-based contracts; the latter two belong to the participation/equity-based ones. We describe the key details of these next.

Ijarah

The contract of Ijarah is used to sell the right of usage of a material object to another party. The right of ownership remains with the lessor who has responsibility for the maintenance and the insurance of the asset. Compensation from the lessee can only be asked if the damages occurred due to his negligence. A variation of the contract (Ijarah wa Iqtina) gives the right to the lessee to buy the asset at the end of the originally agreed leasing period at an ex ante stipulated price. The leasing agreements that exist in the conventional world are similar to the Ijarah contract.

Istisna

The contract of Istisna is used in the case when the two parties agree for the asset to be manufactured and also on the payment scheme they will be employed for its sale. Unlike typical sale contracts (Bay') the payments need not be at the beginning and need not be in the form of a lump-sum amount. Moreover, the time and place of delivery can be altered and even cancelled as long as the construction of the asset has not started. Nowadays such a contract is applicable in house construction, ship building or large infrastructure projects. Common practices in the housing industry are that the contractor does not have all the necessary funds to build a block of flats and then sell it; rather he sells it either before the start of the construction or at the early stages of the construction, thus collecting money which will allow him to complete the structure. The construction of aircrafts, yachts, tankers or heavy machinery usually implements such contracts. By contrast, conventional practices do not require a different contract. The same contract of sale applies but usually a percentage of the total value of the good needs to be paid up front.

Murabahah

The rationale behind Murabahah is selling an asset with a mark-up. Party A purchases an asset at a price X and sells it to party B at a price $X+e$ where e is the profit that party A will make. This is acceptable under the Shariah as party A has made some valuable contribution, and has taken the necessary business risks for this transaction to take place. The benefit for party B is the credit character of the contract, which allows him to delay payments for an agreed time period, or to pay using instalments, or a combination of both. The Murabahah contracts can be used for low value commodities like a TV set or a computer, but also for high value assets like property or machinery. The value of the asset determines whether the Murabahah will be short-term or long-term. In case that party B defaults on some payments a penalty cannot be imposed as it is commonly done in conventional practices. However Shariah recognizes that party A can request the payment of some expenses that arose due to the default.

The first criticism of Murabahah is about its resemblance to a conventional loan. The difference is that Murabahah is used to purchase an asset and no money is lent, which is the case in a conventional loan. Furthermore, a close relationship has been observed between the mark-up price charged by an Islamic bank and a widespread interest rate indicator, such as LIBOR. While this relationship might be coincidental, Islamic banks argue that their techniques for determining the mark-up price are influenced by the prevailing interest rates, since no Islamic benchmark exists to provide an indication of the prevailing market return (Z. Iqbal & Mirakhor, 2011). The second criticism regards the practices used by banks that have adopted Murabahah as the contract in its pure form allows the final buyer, which is party B, to refuse to buy the asset he asked from party A. Hence, party A is facing the risk that the buyer will not keep his side of the deal. To deal with this problem Islamic banks have combined the original contract of Murabahah with the one of the pledge (Rahn), both of which are permitted by the Shariah. The combined product however reduces some of the rights Shariah gives to the final buyer, and may as such be deemed controversial. Empirical support exists for the fact that Islamic banks increasingly rely on fee-based income. For example, a study using data from 20 countries over the 2000-2015 period suggests that the bank fee is an important determinant of the profitability of an Islamic bank (Azad, Azmat, & Hayat, 2019).

Mudarabah

The contract of Mudarabah requires two parties, an investor who provides the capital, and an entrepreneur who provides the knowhow, to work together in some business venture. The profit made is split according to an *ex ante* profit sharing ratio, which is a known percentage of an unknown value. The investor does not intervene in the management of the project; quite the opposite the entrepreneur is the sole responsible. However, in case of losses the investor bears all the financial losses and the entrepreneur loses time, effort and a chance for making profit. If the losses however are due to the negligence of the entrepreneur then he absorbs the full loss and he will be liable with all his property (Rosli, 2005). The investor is usually an Islamic bank.

It has been argued that Muslims are generally trustworthy, which emanates from the belief that all their life must be in accordance with the Shariah otherwise they give up their spiritual benefits in the afterlife (Rosli, 2005). Consequently, Mudarabah may be a good way to decrease agency costs since the entrepreneur receives no high salaries like the entrepreneurs in western countries; on the contrary his salary will be paid out of the profits for which he is responsible. So it is arguable that an Islamic bank mostly dealing with Muslim investors will probably be facing fewer problems arising from asymmetric information than its conventional counterparts.

On the other hand, the worldwide spread of Islamic banks implies that more non-Muslim investors are attracted by this new form of banking, which may give rise to asymmetric information problems. In particular, Islamic banks may not be willing to use Mudarabah financing as problems like misreporting and uncertainty in profits are likely to appear. In particular, it is shown that such profit and loss sharing structures are in reality characterized by moral hazard behavior and excessive risk taking (Hamza, 2016). Islamic banks use screening and monitoring techniques to alleviate themselves from problems like the aforementioned but these represent considerable expenses. More specifically factors like reputation, qualification and experience of the entrepreneur as well as the amount of risk encompassed in the project would determine if the bank chooses to invest in such a way (Rickwood, Khalil, & Murinde, 2000). The same survey finds evidence that the investor intervenes in the decision-making process, which is contrary to the theory of the Mudarabah contract. The intervention includes restrictions on the assets, additional financing requirements and heavily influences production and investment decisions. The way of intervention is mainly through reports on the performance of the project as well as through decisions on project management (Rickwood et al., 2000). Costs incurred from all this monitoring process are not always bearable, while their effectiveness is questioned (Z. Iqbal & Sadr, 2001). The conventional way of ensuring that profits are not misreported employs a system of auditing. In case of faulty reporting by the entrepreneur a penalty may be imposed. However a penalty cannot be justified easily under Islamic Banking, in the same sense that when a borrower defaults on a payment on his loan, or repays a loan before the due date, he does not have to pay a penalty (besides a small amount relating to the bureaucratic and mailing expenses).

Another reason for the low use of Mudarabah contracts is that there is no capital protection for the investor, so capital is at risk if the venture goes wrong. Capital protection is common in conventional banks but it is contrary to the Shariah since it removes the exposure of the investor to the market risk, which is necessary to make the profits lawful. It is argued that the lack of capital protection schemes acts in favor of the large companies, which are the most financially secure. Instead, if collateral and other guarantees were allowed then financing of small and medium sized enterprises would be enhanced, which constitutes one of the reasons behind the adoption of deposit protection mechanisms and profit equalization reserves in Islamic banks.

Musharakah

Musharakah is similar to Mudarabah but there are more than two parties that contribute either capital or knowhow and share the profits according to a pre-determined ratio. In this case each party's profits will be determined according to the proportion of his invested capital, or if otherwise agreed, and each member has the same rights and obligations. In case of losses investors are liable according to their invested capital; consequently if the contribution of a member to the partnership is only effort, time and knowhow then his losses are limited to these (Z. Iqbal & Mirakhor, 2011). A slightly different version of Musharakah, known as diminishing partnership (Musharakah mutanaqisah), is used as a form of sale contract akin to the conventional mortgage deal. A typical application of this contract is when a house is sold. The bank and the buyer start co owning the house with the bank having a large percentage. As payments are met by the buyer, the percentage of bank's ownership diminishes while the buyer's percentage increases. At the end the buyer is the sole owner of the house.

Takaful

Islamic insurance (Takaful) is becoming increasingly popular as an alternative to conventional insurance services. Islamic insurance relies on the concepts of co-operation, solidarity and shared responsibility and can offer protection against business related and personal risks. As such, Islamic insurance works like a mutual fund where contributions are made to support a party that is in need. The insured pays a premium to the insurer with the latter being contractually obliged to offer financial protection against unexpected loss over a specified period of time. In a case of no claim by the insured over the specified period, the insured is entitled to ask for the whole amount of paid-premiums as well as a share of possible profits realized. The realized profits are made on the basis of Mudarabah, which is the principle used by the insurer to invest the pool of funds. The investment of the funds is made in accordance with Shariah principles. It is also possible for a participant to contribute funds to the pool for the purposes of investment and not insurance protection. Often the pool of funds may be separated into sub-pools some of which may be invested, with others being kept as a buffer to cover for unexpected losses.

ISLAMIC BANKING AND RELATED ISSUES

In this section we present and discuss empirical studies that compare Islamic and conventional banks with respect to two major issues in banking, namely financial risk and efficiency. Besides the plethora of studies in this field on these two topics, risk and efficiency have important connections within banking, see for example Altunbas, Carbo, Gardener and Molyneux (2007), Fiordelisi et al. (2011), Schaeck and Cihak (2014) and references therein.

Financial Risk

A number of papers examine risk in Islamic banking. Most of them find that the risk of Islamic banks is lower than that of conventional banks. That is not to say that Islamic banks are not subjected to economic shocks, but the claim is that these are more muted (Di et al., 2017; Olson & Zoubi, 2017). In particular, Čihák and Hesse (2010) find that small Islamic banks are more stable than equivalent sized conventional banks, although the opposite conclusion is reached for large financial institutions. Masood, Niazi and Ahmad (2011) also verified that small Islamic banks are more resilient to large banks. Abedifar et al. (2013) find that Islamic banks have lower credit risk than conventional banks. The results are stronger for small, leveraged banks as well as for those operating in countries with a Muslim population higher than 90%. They also find that the insolvency risk of small Islamic banks is lower than that of small conventional banks, as the former are more capitalized. A beneficial impact on the credit and the liquidity risk is evidenced for those conventional banks that have Islamic banking windows in Malaysia (How, Karim, & Verhoeven, 2005). Relatedly, Baele et al. (2014) document that the default rate of Islamic loans is less than half than that of conventional loans. In line with the view that the clients of Islamic banks have relatively low risk of default. Ongena and Sendeniz-Yüncü (2011) find that Islamic banks mainly have corporate clients that are young, transparent, industry-focused, and have multiple-bank relationships. Using market-based indicators of risk, Sorwar et al. (2016) document a lower risk for Islamic banks, in particular during the financial crisis. Based on the results of a survival analysis, Pappas et al. (2017) find that Islamic banks are more stable than conventional banks. Safiullah and Shamsuddin (2018) suggest that the lower credit and insolvency risk of Islamic banks compared to their conventional counterparts is partly attributed to their dual-board structure and the monitoring role of the Shariah supervisory board. Indeed the beneficial role of the Shariah supervisory board has been highlighted in various financial aspects of Islamic banks including risk and performance (Mollah et al., 2017; Mollah & Zaman, 2015). Islamic banks are also less exposed to political risk, while bearing similar levels of operational risk compared to their conventional counterparts (Belkhir, Grira, Hassan, & Soumaré, 2018; Safiullah & Shamsuddin, 2018).

Conversely, the analysis in Bourkhis and Nabi (2013) finds no difference in financial soundness between the two bank types during the global financial crisis. Ismail and Sulaiman (2008) find that Islamic banks are willing to take on more risk in their portfolio. However, this is mainly for those few Islamic banks that engage in profit and loss sharing contracts. Relatedly, an analysis comparing Islamic banks that engage/do not engage in profit and loss sharing contracts provided in K. Hassan and Grassa (2012) finds the former to exhibit higher risk and lower financial stability than the latter. Kabir, Worthington and Gupta (2015) find that based on accounting risk measures, Islamic banks exhibit higher risk than their conventional counterparts. Within the GCC, Islamic banks are found to exhibit higher hazard rates compared to the conventional ones, see for example the study of Alqahtani, Mayes and Brown (2017). In Malaysia Islamic banks are more susceptible towards credit and insolvency risk compared to their conventional counterparts, which may be justified by the market segmentation and the limited investment opportunities in the Malaysian banking system (Lassoued, 2018).

Efficiency

Efficiency can be measured either by using traditional financial ratio analysis (FRA) or by frontier estimation methods. A drawback of financial ratios is that they do not take into consideration the input prices and the output mix (Berger & Humphrey, 1991) and weights of the ratios are selected subjectively. Within frontier estimation methods a bank's observed production point is compared with a production frontier that denotes best practice, with data envelopment analysis (DEA) and stochastic frontier analysis (SFA) being the two principal methods used to estimate the production frontier. Contrary to FRA, the frontier techniques produce an objectively determined efficiency score and accommodate multiple inputs/outputs; thus being better suited to capture the activities of a complex financial institution (Thanassoulis, Boussofiane, & Dyson, 1996). Technical efficiency is associated with the bank's ability to obtain maximum output with a given set of inputs, allocative efficiency is associated with the bank's ability to use the optimal inputs mix given their prices, whereas cost efficiency is the product of technical and allocative efficiency.

Direct comparisons across studies are subject to a large degree of variation due to the array of parameters that can change (e.g. estimation method, sampled countries, time period, choice of inputs/outputs for the production function, the type of efficiency under investigation, outlier treatment techniques, use of consolidated/ unconsolidated accounts, balanced/unbalanced panels to name but a few); hence require careful interpretation. The literature that compares Islamic with conventional banks has typically focused on technical (Al-Muharrami, 2008; Alexakis, Izzeldin, Johnes, & Pappas, 2019; Belanès, Ftiti, & Regaïeg, 2015; Grigorian & Manole, 2005; Johnes et al., 2014; Mokhtar, Abdullah, & AlHabshi, 2007; Mokhtar, Abdullah, & Alhabshi, 2008; Rosman, Abd, & Zainol, 2014; Zuhroh, Ismail, & Maskie, 2015) and cost efficiency – often in the same study for completeness. We discuss each of these in turn.

With regards to technical efficiency, some studies find that Islamic banks are significantly less efficient than conventional ones (Kamarudin, Nordin, Muhammad, & Hamid, 2014; Mobarek & Kalonov, 2014; Mokhtar et al., 2007; Shawtari, Ariff, & Abdul Razak, 2015; Srairi, 2010), while other studies suggest that Islamic banks are significantly more efficient than conventional banks (Al-Jarrah & Molyneux, 2006; Al-Muharrami, 2008; Olson & Zoubi, 2008). The vast majority of frontier studies, however, find no significant difference between the two bank types (El-Gamal & Inanoglu, 2005; Grigorian & Manole, 2005; T. Hassan, Mohamad, & Bader, 2009; Mohamad, Hassan, & Bader, 2008; Mokhtar et al., 2007), or else the significance of the difference between the two bank systems is not tested (Ahmad & Luo, 2010; Al-Jarrah & Molyneux, 2005; Said, 2012). The analysis in Belanès et al. (2015) suggests that Islamic banks were more efficient than their conventional counterparts before and up to the first stages of the global financial crisis only. In addition, the starkest drop in efficiency of Islamic banks due to the global financial crisis was recorded with a two-year delay based on data from the GCC region (Belanès et al., 2015).

However, caution is needed regarding some studies where either the sample size - particularly the number of Islamic banks - is small or a variety of countries with markedly economies has been utilized; thus, making the isolation of an "Islamic banking" effect difficult. In methodological terms many of the studies investigating efficiency differences assume that the two bank types share a common production function, which might lead to biased conclusions. More recent work, however, recognizes this drawback and opts for a dual production function setup, often termed as meta-frontier[3], see for example (Abdul-Majid, Saal, & Battisti, 2008, 2010, 2011a, 2011b; Alexakis et al., 2019; Johnes et al., 2014).[4] The main advantage of the meta-frontier analysis is its ability to disentangle inefficiencies arising from managerial incompetency (e.g. net efficiency) and those pertaining to the business model itself (e.g. type efficiency). Efficiency meta-frontier studies conclude that managerial efficiency is not inferior in Islamic banks; it is rather the Islamic banking model *per se* that is inferior in efficiency terms to the conventional one, which may not be surprising given its business and financial restrictions (Abdul-Majid et al., 2008, 2010, 2011a, 2011b; Alexakis et al., 2019; Johnes et al., 2014). However, if a meta-frontier framework is not used, then the conclusion is markedly different. In that case the overall efficiency score cannot differentiate between managerial and business type practices; hence the Islamic banking sector would falsely appear as of lower efficiency and attributed to the lower quality of managerial personnel. Economic implications of such conclusion would be completely different.

The efficiency of the Islamic banking model per se also depends on the country particulars (e.g. supervisor quality, Islamic banking implementation), and it is found that within the GCC the efficiency of the Islamic banking model is higher than the conventional one (Alexakis et al., 2019). The higher efficiency of Islamic banks in the wider Middle Eastern region is also shown in the study of Rosman et al. (2014).

These studies illustrate the difficulties in this field of research where, in an attempt to boost the sample size of the limited number of Islamic banks, data from different countries are pooled together. While some of the cross-country heterogeneity may be controlled for in econometric analysis, Islamic banking model peculiarities may not be adequately controlled. An alternative may be to have country case-studies such as in the studies of El-Gamal and Inanoglu (2005) for Turkey, Abdul-Majid et al. (2008) for Malaysia, Matthews (2014), Rashid and Jabeen (2016) for Pakistan, and Asmild, Kronborg, Mahbub and Matthews (2018) and Miah and Sharmeen (2015) for Bangladesh.

Cost efficiency differentials between Islamic and conventional banks have been extensively studied too (Al-Jarrah & Molyneux, 2006; Alqahtani et al., 2017; Bader,

Mohamad, Mohamed, & Hassan, 2008; El-Gamal & Inanoglu, 2005; Kamarudin et al., 2014; Mobarek & Kalonov, 2014; Mokhtar et al., 2007; M. Saeed & Izzeldin, 2016; Srairi, 2010; Zuhroh et al., 2015). With regards to the technique followed, DEA is the preferred estimation approach in certain studies (Kamarudin et al., 2014; Mobarek & Kalonov, 2014; Mohamad et al., 2008), while others (Al-Jarrah & Molyneux, 2006; El-Gamal & Inanoglu, 2005; Mokhtar et al., 2007; M. Saeed & Izzeldin, 2016; Srairi, 2010; Zuhroh et al., 2015) use SFA, with some using both approaches (Alqahtani et al., 2017). Most of the studies feature are cross-country samples, such as M. Saeed and Izzeldin (2016) with a global coverage of listed banks, while other studies focus on the Gulf Cooperation Council countries that have a dominant presence of Islamic banks (Alqahtani et al., 2017; Srairi, 2010). Single-country studies focusing on Bangladesh (Miah & Sharmeen, 2015), Indonesia (Zuhroh et al., 2015), Malaysia (Mokhtar et al., 2007) and Turkey (El-Gamal & Inanoglu, 2005) are also typical.

When specifying the output distance function, data availability issues generally force the use of two outputs – one referring to the "interest revenue" and another to the "fee-generated income" of a bank.[5] For Islamic banks that neither issue loans nor have any interest revenue, these are substituted with the size and/or income stemming from the equity-type of contracts, where a profit-share ratio is applied. Perhaps as expected from this wide variation across the studies on the bank cost efficiency topic, there is little consensus on cost efficiency patterns between the two bank types. Most studies find Islamic banks to be of no higher cost efficiency than their conventional counterparts (Bader et al., 2008; El-Gamal & Inanoglu, 2005; Kamarudin et al., 2014; Miah & Sharmeen, 2015; Mobarek & Kalonov, 2014; Mokhtar et al., 2007; M. Saeed & Izzeldin, 2016; Srairi, 2010; Wanke, Azad, & Barros, 2016; Zuhroh et al., 2015), although only a subset is reporting proper statistical tests. The gist of the lower cost efficiency of Islamic banks is their more convoluted governance structure with the dual board structure and their lack of standardization in financial products, some of which need to be customized to the client/project at hand and obtain certification from the Shariah supervisory board.[6] The higher costs that Islamic banks face is also acknowledged in studies that utilize financial ratio analysis – most notably cost to income – such as Beck et al. (2013), Hasan and Dridi (2011), Olson and Zoubi (2017; 2008), Wanke, Azad, Barros and Hassan (2016) among others. The efficiency of Islamic financial institutions is also linked to market structure attributes, notably their relative market share (Abedifar et al., 2016; Meslier et al., 2017). We are only aware of a handful of studies that find Islamic banks to exhibit higher cost efficiency than conventional banks (Al-Jarrah & Molyneux, 2006; Safiullah & Shamsuddin, 2018).

Conclusion and directions for future research

In this chapter we have provided a review of the salient differences entailed in the Islamic finance profession with respect to the financial instruments and the rationale behind them. Following from that a large part of the extant literature compares Islamic and conventional banks with respect to different measures and metrics, including but not limited to credit risk, market risk, insolvency risk, liquidity risk, efficiency and financial performance. Although there are differences between the theoretically envisaged model of Islamic finance and what is practiced in reality, it may be arguable that certain deviations might have been unavoidable. Even so, statistically and often economically significant differences are found between the currently practiced Islamic finance paradigm and the conventional one across a wide variety of metrics, as outlined in a previous section.

However, as Islamic banking is not practiced in a fully standardized and homogenous way particularly across countries, care in the construction of the research design must be given (Beck et al., 2013; Hasan & Dridi, 2011; Pappas et al., 2017; Song & Oosthuizen, 2014). Early studies have relied on constructing pooled samples of Islamic banks from across the globe, and relied on a regression model with an Islamic banking dummy to justify distinctions (or lack of) between the two systems. More elaborate designs have used interactions of Islamic banking dummy to control variables, used latent factor models to identify similarity in the Islamic banking practices before constructing the final sample and/or used some of the increasingly available data on supervisor/regulatory quality, market structure data, Doing Business indicators from the World Bank, or hand-collected data on numerous metrics to better control for the cross-country or even cross-bank heterogeneity. Finally, as our focus has been mostly on empirical applications, we have left largely uncovered two important strands of literature within the Islamic finance; one dealing with theoretical models see for example the work of Ebrahim, Jaafar, Omar and Osman (2016); another that critiques the theoretical underpinnings of Islamic finance *per se*, see for example Ebrahim and Sheikh (2016; 2018) and references therein.

While for several years empirical research in this field has faced serious data limitations, over time the importance of this has diminished with several databases good cross-sectional and time coverage of Islamic banks and offering specific filters (e.g. FitchConnect). Future research should focus on other under-research areas where Islamic finance may have a chance to maximize its impacts on society – microfinance. Within the conventional financial research a lot of attention has been drawn upon two research strands, namely systemic market risk and liquidity risk, both of which have received much attention in light of the global financial crisis and Basel III accord (Adrian & Brunnermeier, 2016; DeYoung & Jang, 2016). However, the systemic risk that Islamic financial institutions may pose either to the global economic system, or more likely, to the countries in which they operate is open to future research. In addition, liquidity risk management in conventional financial institutions is moving towards bespoke ratios, such as the Liquidity Coverage Ratio (LCR) and the Net Stable Funding Ratio (NSFR), albeit the applicability and the challenges for these ratios within Islamic financial institutions are still unexplored.

ACKNOWLEDGEMENTS

I would like to thank GOLCER and its Director Professor Marwan Izzeldin that have been catalytic in defining this part of my research, and for which I am grateful. I would also like to thank Athina Petropoulou for her continued and wholehearted support.

REFERENCES

Abdul-Majid, M., Saal, D. S., & Battisti, G. (2008). The efficiency and productivity of Malaysian banks: An output distance function approach. *SSRN Working Paper Series*.

Abdul-Majid, M., Saal, D. S., & Battisti, G. (2010). Efficiency in Islamic and conventional banking: An international comparison. *Journal of Productivity Analysis*, *34*(1), 25–43. doi:10.100711123-009-0165-3

Abdul-Majid, M., Saal, D. S., & Battisti, G. (2011a). Efficiency and total factor productivity change of Malaysian commercial banks. *Service Industries Journal*, *31*(13), 2117–2143. doi:10.1080/02642069.2010.503882

Abdul-Majid, M., Saal, D. S., & Battisti, G. (2011b). The impact of Islamic banking on the cost efficiency and productivity change of Malaysian commercial banks. *Applied Economics*, *43*(16), 2033–2054. doi:10.1080/00036840902984381

Abedifar, P., Ebrahim, S. M., Molyneux, P., & Tarazi, A. (2015). Islamic Banking and Finance: Recent empirical literature and directions for future research. *Journal of Economic Surveys*, *29*(4), 637–670. doi:10.1111/joes.12113

Abedifar, P., Hasan, I., & Tarazi, A. (2016). Finance-growth nexus and dual-banking systems: Relative importance of Islamic banks. *Journal of Economic Behavior & Organization*, *132*, 198–215. doi:10.1016/j.jebo.2016.03.005

Abedifar, P., Molyneux, P., & Tarazi, A. (2013). Risk in Islamic banking. *Review of Finance*, *17*(6), 2035–2096. doi:10.1093/rof/rfs041

Adrian, T., & Brunnermeier, M. K. (2016). CoVaR. *The American Economic Review*, *106*(7), 1705–1741. doi:10.1257/aer.20120555

Ahmad, W., & Luo, R. H. (2010). Comparison of banking efficiency in Europe: Islamic versus conventional banks. In International Banking in the New Era: Post-Crisis Challenges and Opportunities (pp. 361–389). Emerald Group.

Akhter, W., Pappas, V., & Khan, S. U. (2017). A comparison of Islamic and conventional insurance demand: Worldwide evidence during the Global Financial Crisis. *Research in International Business and Finance*, *42*, 1401–1412. doi:10.1016/j.ribaf.2017.07.079

Al-Jarrah, I., & Molyneux, P. (2005). Efficiency in Arabian Banking. In M. Iqbal, & R. Wilson (Eds.), *Islamic Perspectives on Wealth Creation* (pp. 97–117). Edinburgh University Press. doi:10.3366/edinburgh/9780748621002.003.0007

Al-Jarrah, I., & Molyneux, P. (2006). Cost Efficiency, Scale Elasticity and Scale Economies in Arab Banking. *Banks and Bank Systems*, *1*(3), 60–89.

Al-Muharrami, S. (2008). An examination of technical, pure technical and scale efficiencies in GCC banking. *American Journal of Finance and Accounting*, *1*(2), 152–166. doi:10.1504/AJFA.2008.019950

Alexakis, C., Al-Yahyaee, K., Mamatzakis, E., Mobarek, A., Mollah, S., & Pappas, V. (2018). *Does Corporate Governance add value to Islamic banks? A quantitative analysis of cost efficiency and financial stability*. Retrieved from https://ideas.repec.org/p/rim/rimwps/18-40.html

Alexakis, C., Izzeldin, M., Johnes, J., & Pappas, V. (2019). Performance and productivity in Islamic and conventional banks: Evidence from the global financial crisis. *Economic Modelling*, *79*, 1–14. doi:10.1016/j.econmod.2018.09.030

Alexakis, C., Pappas, V., & Tsikouras, A. (2017). Hidden cointegration reveals hidden values in Islamic investments. *Journal of International Financial Markets, Institutions and Money*, *46*, 70–83. doi:10.1016/j.intfin.2016.08.006

Alhomaidi, A., Hassan, M. K., Hippler, W. J., & Mamun, A. (2019). The impact of religious certification on market segmentation and investor recognition. *Journal of Corporate Finance*, *55*, 28–48. doi:10.1016/j.jcorpfin.2018.08.012

Alqahtani, F., Mayes, D. G., & Brown, K. (2017). Islamic bank efficiency compared to conventional banks during the global crisis in the GCC region. *Journal of International Financial Markets, Institutions, and Money*, *51*, 58–74. doi:10.1016/j.intfin.2017.08.010

Altunbas, Y., Carbo, S., Gardener, E. P. M., & Molyneux, P. (2007). Examining the Relationships between Capital, Risk and Efficiency in European Banking. *European Financial Management*, *13*(1), 49–70. doi:10.1111/j.1468-036X.2006.00285.x

Alzahrani, M., & Megginson, W. L. (2017). Finance as Worship: A Survey of Islamic Finance Research. *SSRN Electronic Journal*, 1–89. doi:10.2139srn.2967619

Archer, S., Karim, R. A. A., & Al-Deehani, T. (1998). Financial contracting, governance structures and the accounting regulation of Islamic banks: An analysis in terms of agency theory and transaction cost economics. *The Journal of Management and Governance*, *2*(2), 149–170. doi:10.1023/A:1009985419353

Asmild, M., Kronborg, D., Mahbub, T., & Matthews, K. (2018). The efficiency patterns of Islamic banks during the global financial crisis: The case of Bangladesh. *The Quarterly Review of Economics and Finance*.

Azad, A. S. M. S., Azmat, S., & Hayat, A. (2019). What determines the profitability of Islamic banks: Lending or fee? *International Review of Economics & Finance*. doi:10.1016/j.iref.2019.05.015

Bader, M. K. I., Mohamad, S., Mohamed, A., & Hassan, T. (2008). Cost, Revenue, and Profit Efficiency of Islamic Versus Conventional Banks: International Evidence Using Data Envelopment Analysis. *Islamic Economic Studies*, *15*(2).

Baele, L., Farooq, M., & Ongena, S. (2014). Of religion and redemption: Evidence from default on Islamic loans. *Journal of Banking & Finance*, *44*, 141–159. doi:10.1016/j.jbankfin.2014.03.005

Bank, W. (2017). Global Report on IslamicFinance: A Catalyst for Shared Prosperity? *The World Bank. World Bank & IDBG.*

Basiruddin, R., & Ahmed, H. (2017). The role of corporate governance on Shariah non-compliant risk: Evidence from Southeast Asia. In *KFUPM Islamic Banking and Finance Research Conference 2017.*

Beck, T., Demirgüç-Kunt, A., & Merrouche, O. (2013). Islamic vs. conventional banking: Business model, efficiency and stability. *Journal of Banking & Finance*, *37*(2), 433–447. doi:10.1016/j.jbankfin.2012.09.016

Beck, T., Ongena, S., & Şendeniz-Yüncü, İ. (2019). Keep walking? Geographical proximity, religion, and relationship banking. *Journal of Corporate Finance, 55*(August 2018), 49–68. doi:10.1016/j.jcorpfin.2018.07.005

Belanès, A., Ftiti, Z., & Regaïeg, R. (2015). What can we learn about Islamic banks efficiency under the subprime crisis? Evidence from GCC Region. *Pacific-Basin Finance Journal, 33*, 81–92. doi:10.1016/j.pacfin.2015.02.012

Belkhir, M., Grira, J., Hassan, M. K., & Soumaré, I. (2018). Islamic banks and political risk: International evidence. *The Quarterly Review of Economics and Finance.*

Berger, A. N., Boubakri, N., Guedhami, O., & Li, X. (2018). Liquidity Creation Performance and Financial Stability Consequences of Islamic Banking: Evidence from a Multinational Study. *Available at SSRN 3278032.*

Berger, A. N., & Bouwman, C. H. S. (2017). Bank liquidity creation, monetary policy, and financial crises. *Journal of Financial Stability, 30*, 139–155. doi:10.1016/j.jfs.2017.05.001

Berger, A. N., & Humphrey, D. B. (1991). The dominance of inefficiencies over scale and product mix economies in banking. *Journal of Monetary Economics, 28*(1), 117–148. doi:10.1016/0304-3932(91)90027-L

Berger, A. N., & Sedunov, J. (2017). Bank liquidity creation and real economic output. *Journal of Banking & Finance, 81*(Supplement C), 1–19. doi:10.1016/j.jbankfin.2017.04.005

Birnie, A. (1958). *The History and Ethics of Interest*. London, UK: William Hodge.

Bitar, M., Hassan, M. K., & Walker, T. (2017). Political systems and the financial soundness of Islamic banks. *Journal of Financial Stability, 31*, 18–44. doi:10.1016/j.jfs.2017.06.002

Bitar, M., Madiès, P., & Taramasco, O. (2017). What makes Islamic banks different? A multivariate approach. *Economic Systems, 41*(2), 215–235. doi:10.1016/j.ecosys.2016.06.003

Bourkhis, K., & Nabi, M. S. (2013). Islamic and conventional banks' soundness during the 2007-2008 financial crisis. *Review of Financial Economics, 22*(2), 68–77. doi:10.1016/j.rfe.2013.01.001

Charnes, A., Cooper, W. W., & Rhodes, E. (1981). Evaluating program and managerial efficiency: An application of data envelopment analysis to program follow through. *Management Science, 27*(6), 668–697. doi:10.1287/mnsc.27.6.668

Choudhary, M. A., & Limodio, N. (2017). *Deposit Volatility, Liquidity and Long-Term Investment: Evidence from a Natural Experiment in Pakistan.*

Choudhury, M. A., & Hoque, M. Z. (2006). Corporate governance in Islamic perspective. *Corporate Governance: The International Journal of Business in Society*, *6*(2), 116–128. doi:10.1108/14720700610655132

Čihák, M., & Hesse, H. (2010). Islamic Banks and Financial Stability: An Empirical Analysis. *Journal of Financial Services Research*, *38*(2–3), 95–113. doi:10.100710693-010-0089-0

DeYoung, R., & Jang, K. Y. (2016). Do banks actively manage their liquidity? *Journal of Banking & Finance*, *66*, 143–161. doi:10.1016/j.jbankfin.2015.11.013

Di, L., Shaiban, M. S., & Shavkatovich Hasanov, A. (2017). Contagion effect from US banking to conventional and Islamic banking in dual-banking system during financial crisis. In *KFUPM Islamic Banking and Finance Research Conference 2017*.

Ebrahim, M. S., Jaafar, A., Omar, F. A., & Osman, M. (2016). Can Islamic injunctions indemnify the structural flaws of securitized debt? *Journal of Corporate Finance*, *37*, 271–286. doi:10.1016/j.jcorpfin.2016.01.002

Ebrahim, M. S., & Sheikh, M. (2016). Debt Instruments in Islamic Finance: A Critique. *Arab Law Quarterly*, *30*(2), 185–198. doi:10.1163/15730255-12341317

Ebrahim, M. S., & Sheikh, M. (2018). The Political Economy and Underdevelopment of the Muslim World: A Juridico-Philosophical Perspective. *Arab Law Quarterly*, *32*(4), 385–412. doi:10.1163/15730255-12324051

El-Gamal, M. A. (2006). *Islamic Finance: Law, Economics, and Practice*. Cambridge University Press. doi:10.1017/CBO9780511753756

El-Gamal, M. A., & Inanoglu, H. (2005). Inefficiency and heterogeneity in Turkish banking: 1990-2000. *Journal of Applied Econometrics*, *20*(5), 641–664. doi:10.1002/jae.835

EY. (2016). *World Islamic Banking Competitiveness Report 2016*. Retrieved from http://www.ey.com/Publication/vwLUAssets/EY-world-islamic-banking-competitiveness-report-2014-15/$FILE/EY-world-islamic-banking-competitiveness-report-2014-15.pdf

Farag, H., Mallin, C., & Ow-Yong, K. (2018). Corporate governance in Islamic banks: New insights for dual board structure and agency relationships. *Journal of International Financial Markets, Institutions and Money*, *54*, 59–77. doi:10.1016/j.intfin.2017.08.002

Fiordelisi, F., Marques-Ibanez, D., & Molyneux, P. (2011). Efficiency and risk in European banking. *Journal of Banking & Finance*, *35*(5), 1315–1326. doi:10.1016/j.jbankfin.2010.10.005

Fisher, I. (1836). *The Theory of Interest*. London, UK: Macmillan and Co.

Grigorian, D., & Manole, V. (2005). A Cross-Country Nonparametric Analysis of Bahrain's Banking System. *International Monetary Fund Working Paper, WP 05/117*.

Hamza, H. (2016). Does investment deposit return in Islamic banks reflect PLS principle? *Borsa Istanbul Review*, *16*(1), 32–42. doi:10.1016/j.bir.2015.12.001

Hasan, M., & Dridi, J. (2011). The effects of the global crisis on Islamic and conventional banks: A comparative study. *Journal of International Commerce Economic Policy*, *2*(2), 163–200.

Hassan, K., & Aliyu, S. (2018). A contemporary survey of Islamic banking literature. *Journal of Financial Stability*, *34*, 12–43. doi:10.1016/j.jfs.2017.11.006

Hassan, K., & Grassa, R. (2012). *Islamic banks' income structure and risk: Evidence from GCC countries*. Accounting Research Journal.

Hassan, T., Mohamad, S., & Bader, M. K. I. (2009). Efficiency of conventional versus Islamic banks: Evidence from the Middle East. *International Journal of Islamic and Middle Eastern Finance and Management*, *2*(1), 46–65. doi:10.1108/17538390910946267

Hayami, Y. (1969). Sources of agricultural productivity gap among selected countries. *American Journal of Agricultural Economics*, *51*(3), 564–575. doi:10.2307/1237909

Hayami, Y., & Ruttan, V. W. (1970). Agricultural productivity differences among countries. *The American Economic Review*, *60*(5), 895–911.

Hayat, R., & Kabir Hassan, M. (2017). Does an Islamic label indicate good corporate governance? *Journal of Corporate Finance*, *43*, 159–174. doi:10.1016/j.jcorpfin.2016.12.012

How, J. C. Y., Karim, M. A., & Verhoeven, P. (2005). Islamic financing and bank risks: The case of Malaysia. *Thunderbird International Business Review*, *47*(1), 75–94. doi:10.1002/tie.20041

Iqbal, Z., & Mirakhor, A. (2011). An introduction to Islamic finance. *Theory into Practice*, *687*. John Wiley & Sons.

Iqbal, Z., & Sadr, K. (2001). *Choice between Debt and Equity contracts and Asymmetrical Information: Some Empirical Evidence*. Edward Elgar Publishing.

Ismail, A. G., & Sulaiman, A. A. (2008). Whether Islamic Banks Chose to Adjust their Assets Due to Capital Adequacy Requirements. *Journal of Islamic Economics, Banking, and Finance*, *4*(1), 27–37.

Jadlow, J. M. (1977). Adam Smith on usury laws. *The Journal of Finance*, *32*(4), 1195–1200. doi:10.1111/j.1540-6261.1977.tb03319.x

Jeitschko, T. D., & Jeung, S. D. (2005). Incentives for risk-taking in banking - A unified approach. *Journal of Banking & Finance*, *29*(3), 759–777. doi:10.1016/S0378-4266(04)00057-3

Johnes, J., Izzeldin, M., & Pappas, V. (2014). A comparison of performance of Islamic and conventional banks 2004-2009. *Journal of Economic Behavior & Organization*, *103*, 1–45. doi:10.1016/j.jebo.2013.07.016

Kabir, N., Worthington, A., & Gupta, R. (2015). Comparative credit risk in Islamic and conventional bank. *Pacific-Basin Finance Journal*, *34*, 327–353. doi:10.1016/j.pacfin.2015.06.001

Kamarudin, F., Nordin, B. A. A., Muhammad, J., & Hamid, M. A. A. (2014). Cost, Revenue and Profit Efficiency of Islamic and Conventional Banking Sector: Empirical Evidence from Gulf Cooperative Council Countries. *Global Business Review*, *15*(1), 1–24. doi:10.1177/0972150913515579

AT Kearney. (2012). *The Future of Islamic Banking*. doi:10.1177/0967010693024004005

Keynes, J. M. (1936). *The General Theory of Employment, Interest, and Money*. Palgrave Macmillan.

Khan, F. (2010). How 'Islamic' is Islamic Banking? *Journal of Economic Behavior & Organization*, *76*(3), 805–820. doi:10.1016/j.jebo.2010.09.015

Khuram, S. B., Hayat, A., & Faareha, A. (2013). An evaluation of corporate governance practices of Islamic banks versus Islamic bank windows of conventional banks: A case of Pakistan. *Management Research Review*, *36*(4), 400–416. doi:10.1108/01409171311315003

Kumbhakar, S. C., Parmeter, C. F., & Tsionas, E. G. (2013). A zero inefficiency stochastic frontier model. *Journal of Econometrics*, *172*(1), 66–76. doi:10.1016/j.jeconom.2012.08.021

Lassoued, M. (2018). Comparative study on credit risk in Islamic banking institutions: The case of Malaysia. *The Quarterly Review of Economics and Finance*, *70*, 267–278. doi:10.1016/j.qref.2018.05.009

Levy, D. M. (1987). Adam Smith's Case for Usury Laws. *History of Political Economy*, *19*(3), 387–400. doi:10.1215/00182702-19-3-387

Masood, O., Niazi, G. S., & Ahmad, N. (2011). An analysis of the growth and rise of smaller Islamic banks in last decade. *Qualitative Research in Financial Markets*, *3*(2), 105–116. doi:10.1108/17554171111155348

Matthews, K. (2014). Cost inefficiency in the Pakistan banking sector 2002-2009. *SBP Research Bulletin*, *10*, 1–20.

Mejia, A. L., Aljabrin, S., Awad, R., Norat, M., & Song, I. (2014). *Regulation and supervision of Islamic banks*. International Monetary Fund. doi:10.5089/9781498361590.001

Meslier, C., Risfandy, T., & Tarazi, A. (2017). Dual market competition and deposit rate setting in Islamic and conventional banks. *Economic Modelling*, *63*(Supplement C), 318–333. doi:10.1016/j.econmod.2017.02.013

Miah, M. D., & Sharmeen, K. (2015). Relationship between capital, risk and efficiency: A comparative study between Islamic and conventional banks of Bangladesh. *International Journal of Islamic and Middle Eastern Finance and Management*, *8*(2), 203–221. doi:10.1108/IMEFM-03-2014-0027

Miah, M. D., & Uddin, H. (2017). Efficiency and stability: A comparative study between Islamic and conventional banks in GCC countries. *Future Business Journal*, *3*(2), 172–185. doi:10.1016/j.fbj.2017.11.001

Mobarek, A., & Kalonov, A. (2014). Comparative performance analysis between conventional and Islamic banks: Empirical evidence from OIC countries. *Applied Economics*, *46*(3), 253–270. doi:10.1080/00036846.2013.839863

Mohamad, S., Hassan, T., & Bader, M. K. I. (2008). Efficiency of conventional versus Islamic Banks: International evidence using the Stochastic Frontier Approach (SFA). *Journal of Islamic Economics, Banking, and Finance*, *4*(2), 107–130.

Mokhtar, H., Abdullah, N., & AlHabshi, M. (2007). Technical and cost efficiency of Islamic banking in Malaysia. *Review of Islamic Economics*, *11*(1), 5–40.

Mokhtar, H., Abdullah, N., & Alhabshi, S. (2008). Efficiency and competition of Islamic banking in Malaysia. *Humanomics*, *24*(1), 28–48. doi:10.1108/08288660810851450

Mollah, S., Hassan, M. K., Al Farooque, O., & Mobarek, A. (2017). The governance, risk-taking, and performance of Islamic banks. *Journal of Financial Services Research*, *51*(2), 195–219. doi:10.100710693-016-0245-2

Mollah, S., & Zaman, M. (2015). Shari'ah supervision, corporate governance and performance: Conventional vs. Islamic banks. *Journal of Banking & Finance*, *58*, 418–435. doi:10.1016/j.jbankfin.2015.04.030

Olson, D., & Zoubi, T. (2017). Convergence in bank performance for commercial and Islamic banks during and after the Global Financial Crisis. *The Quarterly Review of Economics and Finance*, *65*, 71–87. doi:10.1016/j.qref.2016.06.013

Olson, D., & Zoubi, T. A. (2008). Using accounting ratios to distinguish between Islamic and conventional banks in the GCC region. *The International Journal of Accounting*, *43*(1), 45–65. doi:10.1016/j.intacc.2008.01.003

Ongena, S., & Sendeniz-Yüncü, I. (2011). Which firms engage small, foreign, or state banks? And who goes Islamic? Evidence from Turkey. *Journal of Banking & Finance*, *35*(12), 3213–3224. doi:10.1016/j.jbankfin.2011.05.001

Pappas, V., Ongena, S., Izzeldin, M., & Fuertes, A. M. (2017). A Survival Analysis of Islamic and Conventional Banks. *Journal of Financial Services Research*, *51*(2), 1–36. doi:10.100710693-016-0239-0

Rashid, A., & Jabeen, S. (2016). Analyzing performance determinants: Conventional versus Islamic Banks in Pakistan. *Borsa Istanbul Review*, *16*(2), 92–107. doi:10.1016/j.bir.2016.03.002

Rehman, S. S., & Askari, H. (2010). How Islamic are Islamic Countries? *Global Economy Journal, 10*(2).

Rickwood, C., Khalil, A. F. A. A., & Murinde, V. (2000). *Evidence on agency-contractual problems in mudarabah financing operations by Islamic banks*. Edward Elgar Publishing.

Rosli, S. A. (2005). *Critical Issues on Islamic Banking and Financial Markets*. Malaysia: Dinamos Publishing.

Rosman, R., Abd, N., & Zainol, Z. (2014). Efficiency of Islamic banks during the financial crisis : An analysis of Middle Eastern and Asian countries. *Pacific-Basin Finance Journal*, *28*, 76–90. doi:10.1016/j.pacfin.2013.11.001

Saeed, A. (1996). *Islamic Banking and Interest: A Study of the Prohibition of Riba and Its Contemporary Interpretation*. The Netherlands: Brill.

Saeed, M., & Izzeldin, M. (2016). Examining the relationship between default risk and efficiency in Islamic and conventional banks. *Journal of Economic Behavior & Organization*, *132*, 127–154. doi:10.1016/j.jebo.2014.02.014

Safiullah, M., & Shamsuddin, A. (2018). Risk in Islamic banking and corporate governance. *Pacific-Basin Finance Journal, 47*, 129–149. doi:10.1016/j.pacfin.2017.12.008

Said, A. (2012). Comparing the change in efficiency of the Western and Islamic banking systems. *Journal of Money, Investment, and Banking, 23*(1), 149–180.

Schaeck, K., & Cihak, M. (2014). Competition, Efficiency, and Stability. *Financial Management, 43*(1), 215–241. doi:10.1111/fima.12010

Senior, N. W. (1836). *An Outline of the Science of Political Economy*. University Press of the Pacific.

Shawtari, F. A., Ariff, M., & Abdul Razak, S. H. (2015). Efficiency assessment of banking sector in Yemen using data envelopment window analysis: A comparative analysis of Islamic and conventional banks. *Benchmarking: An International Journal, 22*(6), 1115–1140. doi:10.1108/BIJ-10-2014-0097

Smith, A. (1776). *The Wealth of Nations*. New York: Modern Library.

Song, I., & Oosthuizen, C. (2014). *Islamic banking regulation and supervision: Survey results and challenges*. International Monetary Fund.

Sorwar, G., Pappas, V., Pereira, J., & Nurullah, M. (2016). To debt or not to debt: Are Islamic banks less risky than conventional banks? *Journal of Economic Behavior & Organization, 132*, 113–126. doi:10.1016/j.jebo.2016.10.012

Srairi, S. A. (2010). Cost and profit efficiency of conventional and Islamic banks in GCC countries. *Journal of Productivity Analysis, 34*(1), 45–62. doi:10.100711123-009-0161-7

Thanassoulis, E., Boussofiane, A., & Dyson, R. G. (1996). A comparison of data envelopment analysis and ratio analysis as tools for performance assessment. *Omega, 24*(3), 229–244. doi:10.1016/0305-0483(95)00060-7

Trad, N., Trabelsi, M. A., & Goux, J. F. (2017). Risk and profitability of Islamic banks: A religious deception or an alternative solution? *European Research on Management and Business Economics, 23*(1), 40–45. doi:10.1016/j.iedeen.2016.09.001

Usmani, M. I. A. (2002). *Meezanbank's Guide to Islamic Banking*. Pakistan: Darul-Ishaat Karachi.

Vallascas, F., Mollah, S., & Keasey, K. (2017). Does the impact of board independence on large bank risks change after the global financial crisis? *Journal of Corporate Finance, 44*(June 2014), 149–166. doi:10.1016/j.jcorpfin.2017.03.011

von Hayek, F. A. (1939). *Profit, Interest, and Investment*. Clifton, NJ: Augustus M. Kelley.

Wanke, P., Azad, M. A. K., & Barros, C. P. (2016). Financial distress and the Malaysian dual baking system: A dynamic slacks approach. *Journal of Banking & Finance*, *66*, 1–18. doi:10.1016/j.jbankfin.2016.01.006

Wanke, P., Azad, M. A. K., Barros, C. P., & Hassan, M. K. (2016). Predicting efficiency in Islamic banks: An integrated multicriteria decision making (MCDM) approach. *Journal of International Financial Markets, Institutions, and Money*, *45*, 126–141. doi:10.1016/j.intfin.2016.07.004

Zuhroh, I., Ismail, M., & Maskie, G. (2015). Cost Efficiency of Islamic Banks in Indonesia – A Stochastic Frontier Analysis. *Procedia: Social and Behavioral Sciences*, *211*, 1122–1131. doi:10.1016/j.sbspro.2015.11.150

ENDNOTES

1 We direct you to Abedifar, Ebrahim, Molyneux and Tarazi (2015), Alzahrani and Megginson (2017) and K. Hassan & Aliyu (2018).

2 More research is required in the link between liquidity creation and real economic activity as highlighted in (Berger & Bouwman, 2017) and the limited evidence suggest a positive link between liquidity creation and GDP/capita (Berger & Sedunov, 2017).

3 The incomparability of performance in different groups, which leads to the introduction of the meta-frontier concept dates back to Hayami (1969) and Hayami and Ruttan (1970). The meta-frontier in an efficiency context stems from the work of Charnes, Cooper and Rhodes (1981).

4 These are a mix of single and multiple country studies, which give a reassurance over our previous criticism, particularly to the methodological nature of the issue we subsequently describe.

5 By contrast, studies using US data can have as many as five outputs, see for example Kumbhakar, Parmeter and Tsionas (2013).

6 Khuram, Hayat and Faareha (2013) highlight the costs in time (2-3 months) and in money required for a product to be certified as in line with the Sharia law.

Compilation of References

Abdul-Majid, M., Saal, D. S., & Battisti, G. (2008). The efficiency and productivity of Malaysian banks: An output distance function approach. *SSRN Working Paper Series*.

Abdul-Majid, M., Saal, D. S., & Battisti, G. (2010). Efficiency in Islamic and conventional banking: An international comparison. *Journal of Productivity Analysis*, *34*(1), 25–43. doi:10.100711123-009-0165-3

Abdul-Majid, M., Saal, D. S., & Battisti, G. (2011a). Efficiency and total factor productivity change of Malaysian commercial banks. *Service Industries Journal*, *31*(13), 2117–2143. doi:10.1080/02642069.2010.503882

Abdul-Majid, M., Saal, D. S., & Battisti, G. (2011b). The impact of Islamic banking on the cost efficiency and productivity change of Malaysian commercial banks. *Applied Economics*, *43*(16), 2033–2054. doi:10.1080/00036840902984381

Abedifar, P., Ebrahim, S. M., Molyneux, P., & Tarazi, A. (2015). Islamic Banking and Finance: Recent empirical literature and directions for future research. *Journal of Economic Surveys*, *29*(4), 637–670. doi:10.1111/joes.12113

Abedifar, P., Hasan, I., & Tarazi, A. (2016). Finance-growth nexus and dual-banking systems: Relative importance of Islamic banks. *Journal of Economic Behavior & Organization*, *132*, 198–215. doi:10.1016/j.jebo.2016.03.005

Abedifar, P., Molyneux, P., & Tarazi, A. (2013). Risk in Islamic banking. *Review of Finance*, *17*(6), 2035–2096. doi:10.1093/rof/rfs041

Aboura, S., & Chevallier, J. (2014). Cross – market spillovers with "volatility surprise". *Review of Financial Economics*, *23*(4), 194–207. doi:10.1016/j.rfe.2014.08.002

Adams, Z., & Gluck, Z. (2015). Financialization in commodity markets: A passing trend or the new normal? *Journal of Banking & Finance*, *60*, 93–111. doi:10.1016/j.jbankfin.2015.07.008

Adrian, T., & Brunnermeier, M. K. (2016). CoVaR. *The American Economic Review*, *106*(7), 1705–1741. doi:10.1257/aer.20120555

Afonso, A., Argyrou, M., Gadea, M. D., & Kontonikas, A. (2018). "Whatever it takes" to resolve the European sovereign debt crisis? Bond pricing regime switches and monetary policy effects. *Journal of International Money and Finance*, *86*, 1–30. doi:10.1016/j.jimonfin.2018.04.005

Agrawal, A., Catalini, C., & Goldfarb, A. (2010). Friends, Family, and the Flat World: The Geography of Crowdfunding. *NBER Working paper*, 10-08, University of Toronto.

Agrawal, A., Catalini, C., & Goldfarb, A. (2015). Crowdfunding: Geography, Social Networks, and the Timing of Investment Decisions. *Journal of Economics & Management Strategy*, *24*(2), 253–274. doi:10.1111/jems.12093

Ahlers, G. K. C., Cumming, D., Günther, C., & Schweizer, D. (2015). Signaling in Equity Crowdfunding. *Entrepreneurship Theory and Practice*, *39*(4), 955–980. doi:10.1111/etap.12157

Ahmad, W., & Luo, R. H. (2010). Comparison of banking efficiency in Europe: Islamic versus conventional banks. In International Banking in the New Era: Post-Crisis Challenges and Opportunities (pp. 361–389). Emerald Group.

Akaike, H. (1973). Information Theory and an Extension of the Maximum Likelihood Principle. In B. N. Petrov, & F. Csaki (Eds.), *Proceedings of the 2nd International Symposium on Information Theory*, Budapest: Akademiai Kiado, pp. 267-281.

Akhter, W., Pappas, V., & Khan, S. U. (2017). A comparison of Islamic and conventional insurance demand: Worldwide evidence during the Global Financial Crisis. *Research in International Business and Finance*, *42*, 1401–1412. doi:10.1016/j.ribaf.2017.07.079

Aldrich, H. (1999). *Organizations Evolving*. Thousand Oaks, CA: Sage.

Alexakis, C., Al-Yahyaee, K., Mamatzakis, E., Mobarek, A., Mollah, S., & Pappas, V. (2018). *Does Corporate Governance add value to Islamic banks? A quantitative analysis of cost efficiency and financial stability*. Retrieved from https://ideas.repec.org/p/rim/rimwps/18-40.html

Alexakis, C., Izzeldin, M., Johnes, J., & Pappas, V. (2019). Performance and productivity in Islamic and conventional banks: Evidence from the global financial crisis. *Economic Modelling*, *79*, 1–14. doi:10.1016/j.econmod.2018.09.030

Alexakis, C., Pappas, V., & Tsikouras, A. (2017). Hidden cointegration reveals hidden values in Islamic investments. *Journal of International Financial Markets, Institutions and Money*, *46*, 70–83. doi:10.1016/j.intfin.2016.08.006

Alexakis, P., Kenourgios, D., & Dimitriou, D. (2016). On emerging stock market contagion: The Baltic region. *Research in International Business and Finance*, *36*, 312–321. doi:10.1016/j.ribaf.2015.09.035

Alhomaidi, A., Hassan, M. K., Hippler, W. J., & Mamun, A. (2019). The impact of religious certification on market segmentation and investor recognition. *Journal of Corporate Finance*, *55*, 28–48. doi:10.1016/j.jcorpfin.2018.08.012

Al-Jarrah, I., & Molyneux, P. (2005). Efficiency in Arabian Banking. In M. Iqbal, & R. Wilson (Eds.), *Islamic Perspectives on Wealth Creation* (pp. 97–117). Edinburgh University Press. doi:10.3366/edinburgh/9780748621002.003.0007

Al-Jarrah, I., & Molyneux, P. (2006). Cost Efficiency, Scale Elasticity and Scale Economies in Arab Banking. *Banks and Bank Systems*, *1*(3), 60–89.

Allison, T. H., Davis, B. C., Short, J. C., & Webb, J. W. (2015). Crowdfunding in a Prosocial Microlending Environment: Examining the Role of Intrinsic Versus Extrinsic Cues'. *Entrepreneurship Theory and Practice*, *39*(1), 53–73. doi:10.1111/etap.12108

Allison, T. H., McKenny, A. F., & Short, J. C. (2013). The Effect of Entrepreneurial Rhetoricon Microlending Investment: An Examination of the Warm-Glow Effect. *Journal of Business Venturing*, *28*(6), 690–707. doi:10.1016/j.jbusvent.2013.01.003

Al-Muharrami, S. (2008). An examination of technical, pure technical and scale efficiencies in GCC banking. *American Journal of Finance and Accounting*, *1*(2), 152–166. doi:10.1504/AJFA.2008.019950

Aloui, R., Ben Aossa, M. S., & Nguyen, D. K. (2011). Global financial crisis, extreme interdependences, and contagion effects: The role of economic structure? *Journal of Banking & Finance*, *35*(1), 130–141. doi:10.1016/j.jbankfin.2010.07.021

Alqahtani, F., Mayes, D. G., & Brown, K. (2017). Islamic bank efficiency compared to conventional banks during the global crisis in the GCC region. *Journal of International Financial Markets, Institutions, and Money*, *51*, 58–74. doi:10.1016/j.intfin.2017.08.010

Alquist, R., Bhattarai, S., & Coibion, O. (2019). Commodity-price comovement and global economic activity. Forthcoming at *Journal of Monetary Economics.*

Altunbas, Y., Carbo, S., Gardener, E. P. M., & Molyneux, P. (2007). Examining the Relationships between Capital, Risk and Efficiency in European Banking. *European Financial Management*, *13*(1), 49–70. doi:10.1111/j.1468-036X.2006.00285.x

Alzahrani, M., & Megginson, W. L. (2017). Finance as Worship: A Survey of Islamic Finance Research. *SSRN Electronic Journal*, 1–89. doi:10.2139srn.2967619

Ambler, S., & Rumler, F. (2019). The effectiveness of unconventional monetary policy announcements in the euro area: An event and econometric study. *Journal of International Money and Finance*, *94*, 48–61. doi:10.1016/j.jimonfin.2019.02.007

Ankenbrand, T., & Bieri, D. (2018). Assessment of cryptocurrencies as an asset class by their characteristics. *Investment Management & Financial Innovations*, *15*(3), 169–181. doi:10.21511/imfi.15(3).2018.14

Antonakakis, N., Chatziantoniou, I., & Filis, G. (2013). Dynamic co-movements of stock-market returns, implied volatility and policy uncertainty. *Economics Letters*, *120*(1), 87–92. doi:10.1016/j.econlet.2013.04.004

Anzuini, A., Lombardi, M. J., & Pagano, P. (2013). The Impact of Monetary Policy Shocks on Commodity Prices. *International Journal of Central Banking*, *9*(3), 125–150.

Apergis, N., Christou, C., & Kynigakis, I. (2019). Contagion across US and European financial markets: Evidence from the CDS markets. *Journal of International Money and Finance*, *96*, 1–12. doi:10.1016/j.jimonfin.2019.04.006

Apergis, N., Christou, C., & Payne, J. (2014). Precious metal markets, stock markets and the macroeconomic environment: A FAVAR model approach. *Applied Financial Economics*, *24*(10), 691–703. doi:10.1080/09603107.2014.899668

Apostolou, A., & Beirne, J. (2018). Volatility spillovers of unconventional monetary policy to emerging market economies. *Economic Modelling*, *79*(c), 118–129.

Archer, S., Karim, R. A. A., & Al-Deehani, T. (1998). Financial contracting, governance structures and the accounting regulation of Islamic banks: An analysis in terms of agency theory and transaction cost economics. *The Journal of Management and Governance*, *2*(2), 149–170. doi:10.1023/A:1009985419353

Arghyrou, M. G., & Kontonikas, A. (2012). The EMU sovereign-debt crisis: Fundamentals, expectations and contagion. *Journal of International Financial Markets, Institutions and Money*, *22*(4), 658–677. doi:10.1016/j.intfin.2012.03.003

Armendáriz, B., & Morduch, J. (2010). *The Economics of Microfinance*. Cambridge, MA: MIT Press.

Asmild, M., Kronborg, D., Mahbub, T., & Matthews, K. (2018). The efficiency patterns of Islamic banks during the global financial crisis: The case of Bangladesh. *The Quarterly Review of Economics and Finance*.

Assenova, V. A., Best, J., Cagney, M., Ellenoff, D., Karas, K., Moon, J., ... Sorenson, O. (2016). The Present and the Future of Crowdfunding. *California Management Review*, *58*(2), 125–135. doi:10.1525/cmr.2016.58.2.125

AT Kearney. (2012). *The Future of Islamic Banking*. doi:10.1177/0967010693024004005

Audretsch, D. B., Keilbach, M. C., & Lehmann, E. E. (2006). *Entrepreneurship and Economic Growth*. Oxford: Oxford University Press. doi:10.1093/acprof:oso/9780195183511.001.0001

Audretsch, D. B., & Thurik, A. R. (2001). What's New about the New Economy? Sources of Growth in the Managed and Entrepreneurial Economies. *Industrial and Corporate Change*, *10*(1), 267–315. doi:10.1093/icc/10.1.267

Azad, A. S. M. S., Azmat, S., & Hayat, A. (2019). What determines the profitability of Islamic banks: Lending or fee? *International Review of Economics & Finance*. doi:10.1016/j.iref.2019.05.015

Bader, M. K. I., Mohamad, S., Mohamed, A., & Hassan, T. (2008). Cost, Revenue, and Profit Efficiency of Islamic Versus Conventional Banks: International Evidence Using Data Envelopment Analysis. *Islamic Economic Studies*, *15*(2).

Baele, L., Farooq, M., & Ongena, S. (2014). Of religion and redemption: Evidence from default on Islamic loans. *Journal of Banking & Finance*, *44*, 141–159. doi:10.1016/j.jbankfin.2014.03.005

Bakas, D., & Triantafyllou, A. (2018). The impact of uncertainty shocks on the volatility of commodity prices. *Journal of International Money and Finance*, *87*, 96–111. doi:10.1016/j.jimonfin.2018.06.001

Baker, S. R., Bloom, N., & Davis, S. J. (2016). Measuring Economic Policy Uncertainty. *The Quarterly Journal of Economics*, *131*(4), 1593–1636. doi:10.1093/qje/qjw024

Bams, D., Blanchard, G., Honarvar, I., & Lehnert, T. (2017). Does oil and gold price uncertainty matter for the stock market? *Journal of Empirical Evidence*, *44*, 270–285. doi:10.1016/j.jempfin.2017.07.003

Bank for International Settlements (BIS). (2009). The international financial crisis: timeline, impact and policy responses in Asia and the Pacific. Bank for International Settlements (August).

Bank, W. (2017). Global Report on IslamicFinance: A Catalyst for Shared Prosperity? *The World Bank. World Bank & IDBG.*

Barber, S., Boyen, X., Shi, E., & Uzun, E. (2012, February). Bitter to better—how to make bitcoin a better currency. In International Conference on Financial Cryptography and Data Security (pp. 399-414). Berlin, Germany: Springer. 10.1007/978-3-642-32946-3_29

Barrdear, J., & Kumhof, M. (2016). The macroeconomics of central bank issued digital currencies.

Basak, S., & Pavlova, A. (2016). A Model of Financialization of Commodities. *The Journal of Finance*, *71*(4), 1511–1556. doi:10.1111/jofi.12408

Basiruddin, R., & Ahmed, H. (2017). The role of corporate governance on Shariah non-compliant risk: Evidence from Southeast Asia. In *KFUPM Islamic Banking and Finance Research Conference 2017.*

Batten, J. A., Ciner, C., & Lucey, B. M. (2010). The macroeconomic determinants of volatility in precious metals markets. *Resources Policy*, *35*(2), 65–71. doi:10.1016/j.resourpol.2009.12.002

Bauer, M. D., & Neely, C. J. (2013). International channels of the Fed's unconventional monetary policy. *Federal Reserve Bank of San Francisco, Working Paper Series*, 1-32.

Baumöhl, E. (2019). Are cryptocurrencies connected to forex? A quantile cross-spectral approach. *Finance Research Letters*, *29*, 363–372. doi:10.1016/j.frl.2018.09.002

Baur, D. G. (2012). Financial contagion and the real economy. *Journal of Banking & Finance*, *36*(10), 2680–2692. doi:10.1016/j.jbankfin.2011.05.019

Baur, D. G., & Lucey, B. M. (2010). Is Gold a Hedge or a Safe Haven? An Analysis of Stocks, Bonds and Gold. *Financial Review*, *45*(2), 217–229. doi:10.1111/j.1540-6288.2010.00244.x

Baur, D. G., & McDermott, T. K. (2010). Is gold a safe haven? International evidence. *Journal of Banking & Finance*, *34*(8), 1886–1898. doi:10.1016/j.jbankfin.2009.12.008

Beaulieu, T., Sarker, S., & Sarker, S. (2015). A Conceptual Framework for Understanding Crowdfunding, CAIS, 37(1) doi:10.17705/1CAIS.03701

Bechter, C., Jentzsch, S., & Frey, M. (2011). From wisdom of the crowd to crowdfunding. *Journal of Communication and Computer*, *8*, 951–957.

Beck, T., Ongena, S., & Şendeniz-Yüncü, İ. (2019). Keep walking? Geographical proximity, religion, and relationship banking. *Journal of Corporate Finance, 55*(August 2018), 49–68. doi:10.1016/j.jcorpfin.2018.07.005

Beck, T., Demirgüç-Kunt, A., & Merrouche, O. (2013). Islamic vs. conventional banking: Business model, efficiency and stability. *Journal of Banking & Finance*, *37*(2), 433–447. doi:10.1016/j.jbankfin.2012.09.016

Beebower, G., & Priest, W. (1980). The tricks of the trade. *Journal of Portfolio Management*, *6*(2), 36–42. doi:10.3905/jpm.1980.408739

Bekaert, G., Ehrmann, M., Fratzscher, M., & Mehl, A. (2014). Global crises and equity market contagion. *The Journal of Finance*, *69*(6), 2597–2649. doi:10.1111/jofi.12203

Bekaert, G., Harvey, C., & Ng, A. (2005). Market integration and contagion. *The Journal of Business*, *78*(1), 39–70. doi:10.1086/426519

Bekaert, G., Hoerova, M., & Lo Duca, M. (2013). Risk, Uncertainty and Monetary Policy. *Journal of Monetary Economics*, *60*(7), 771–788. doi:10.1016/j.jmoneco.2013.06.003

Belanès, A., Ftiti, Z., & Regaïeg, R. (2015). What can we learn about Islamic banks efficiency under the subprime crisis? Evidence from GCC Region. *Pacific-Basin Finance Journal*, *33*, 81–92. doi:10.1016/j.pacfin.2015.02.012

Belkhir, M., Grira, J., Hassan, M. K., & Soumaré, I. (2018). Islamic banks and political risk: International evidence. *The Quarterly Review of Economics and Finance*.

BenMim, I., & BenSaida, A. (2019). Financial contagion across major stock markets: A study during crisis episodes. *The North American Journal of Economics and Finance*, *48*, 187–201. doi:10.1016/j.najef.2019.02.005

Bergemann, D., & Hege, U. (1998). Venture Capital Financing, Moral Hazard, and Learning. *Journal of Banking & Finance*, *22*(6-8), 703–735. doi:10.1016/S0378-4266(98)00017-X

Berger, A. N., Boubakri, N., Guedhami, O., & Li, X. (2018). Liquidity Creation Performance and Financial Stability Consequences of Islamic Banking: Evidence from a Multinational Study. *Available at SSRN 3278032*.

Berger, A. N., & Bouwman, C. H. S. (2017). Bank liquidity creation, monetary policy, and financial crises. *Journal of Financial Stability*, *30*, 139–155. doi:10.1016/j.jfs.2017.05.001

Berger, A. N., & Humphrey, D. B. (1991). The dominance of inefficiencies over scale and product mix economies in banking. *Journal of Monetary Economics*, *28*(1), 117–148. doi:10.1016/0304-3932(91)90027-L

Berger, A. N., & Sedunov, J. (2017). Bank liquidity creation and real economic output. *Journal of Banking & Finance*, *81*(Supplement C), 1–19. doi:10.1016/j.jbankfin.2017.04.005

Berger, A. N., & Udell, G. F. (1998). The Economics of Small Business Finance, the Roles of Private Equity and Debt Markets in the Financial Growth Cycle. *Journal of Banking & Finance*, *22*(6-8), 613–673. doi:10.1016/S0378-4266(98)00038-7

Berglöf, E. (1994). A Control Theory of Venture Capital Finance. *Journal of Law Economics and Organization*, *10*(2), 247–267.

Berkowitz, S. A., Logue, D. E., & Noser, E. A. Jr. (1988). The total costs of transacting on the NYSE. *The Journal of Finance*, *43*(1), 97–112. doi:10.1111/j.1540-6261.1988.tb02591.x

Bernanke, B. S. (2010). What the Fed did and why: supporting the recovery and sustaining price stability. *The Washington Post,* November 4.

Bernanke, B. S. (2012). Monetary policy since the onset of the crisis. Federal Reserve Bank of Kansas City Economic Symposium, Jackson Hole, Wyoming.

Bernanke, B. S. (2012a). Monetary policy since the onset of the crisis. *Speech at the Federal Reserve Bank of Kansas city economic symposium*, Jackson Hole, 31 August.

Bernhard, S., & Ebner, T. (2017). Cross-border spillover effects of *unconventional monetary policies* on Swiss asset prices. *Journal of International Money and Finance*, *75*, 109–127. doi:10.1016/j.jimonfin.2017.04.001

Bessiere, V., Stephany, E., & Wirtz, P. (2018). Crowdfunding, Business Angels and Venture Capital: New Funding Trajectories for Start-Ups?, In *2nd Emerging trends in Entrepreneurial Finance Conference* 10.2139srn.3137095

Bewley, R. A. (1979). The Direct Estimation of the Equilibrium Response in a Linear Model. *Economics Letters*, *3*(4), 357–361. doi:10.1016/0165-1765(79)90011-9

Bhidé, A. (1992). Bootstrap Finance: The Art of Start-Ups. *Harvard Business Review*, *70*(6), 109–117. PMID:10122688

Bikker, J. A., Spierdijk, L., & van der Sluis, P. J. (2007). Market Impact Costs of Institutional Equity Trades. *Journal of International Money and Finance*, *26*(6), 974–1000. doi:10.1016/j.jimonfin.2007.01.007

Birnie, A. (1958). *The History and Ethics of Interest*. London, UK: William Hodge.

BIS. (2009). *The international financial crisis: Timeline, impact and policy responses in Asia and the Pacific*. Bank for International Settlements.

Bitar, M., Hassan, M. K., & Walker, T. (2017). Political systems and the financial soundness of Islamic banks. *Journal of Financial Stability*, *31*, 18–44. doi:10.1016/j.jfs.2017.06.002

Bitar, M., Madiès, P., & Taramasco, O. (2017). What makes Islamic banks different? A multivariate approach. *Economic Systems*, *41*(2), 215–235. doi:10.1016/j.ecosys.2016.06.003

Black, B., & Gilson, R. (1998). Venture Capital and the Structure of Capital Markets: Banks versus Stock Markets. *Journal of Financial Economics*, *47*(3), 243–277. doi:10.1016/S0304-405X(97)00045-7

Bloom, N. (2009). The impact of uncertainty shocks. *Econometrica*, *77*(3), 623–685. doi:10.3982/ECTA6248

Boako, G., Tiwari, A. K., Ibrahim, M., & Qiang, J. (2018). (in press). Analysing dynamic dependence between gold and stock returns: Evidence using stochastic and full-range tail dependence copula models. *Finance Research Letters*.

Bodie, Z., Kane, A., & Marcus, A. (2014). *Investments*. New York: McGraw-Hill Education.

Bollerslev, T. (1986). Generalized autoregressive conditional heteroskedasticity. *Journal of Econometrics*, *31*(3), 307–327. doi:10.1016/0304-4076(86)90063-1

Boreiko, D., & Sahdev, N. K. (2018). To ico or not to ico–empirical analysis of initial coin offerings and token sales. *Available at SSRN 3209180*.

Borrallo Egea, F., & Hierro, L. A. (2019). Transmission of Monetary Policy in the US and EU in times of expansion and crisis. *Journal of Policy Modeling*, *41*(4), 763–783. doi:10.1016/j.jpolmod.2019.02.012

Botazzi, L., & Da Rin, M. (2001). Venture Capital in Europe and the Financing of Innovative Companies. *Economic Policy*, *34*, 231–269.

Bouaziz, M., Selmi, N., & Boujelbene, Y. (2012). Contagion effect of the subprime financial crisis: Evidence of DCC multivariate GARCH models. *European Journal of Economics, Finance, and Administrative Sciences*, *44*, 66–76.

Boufounou, B., Triantafyllopoulou, D., & Mastrodemos, G. (2019). Indicators Predicting Donation-Crowdfunding Success in Greece, In *Proceedings of the 5th International Conference on Business and Economics HOU*, February 22-23, Athens. Academic Press.

Boufounou, B., & Tsaimou, T. (2017). Equity Crowdfunding - An Innovative Instrument for SME Financing: Challenges and Prospects, In *Proceedings 3rd International Conference on Business and Economics HOU*, April 21-22, Athens. Academic Press.

Boufounou, P. (2018). Crowdfunding in the Greek Economic Crisis: Lessons Learned, *In Proceedings of the 4th International Conference on Business and Economics HOU*, May 11-12, Athens. Academic Press.

Bouri, E., Roubaud, D., Jammazi, R., & Assaf, A. (2017). Uncovering frequency domain causality between gold and the stock markets of China and India: Evidence from implied volatility indices. *Finance Research Letters*, *23*, 23–30. doi:10.1016/j.frl.2017.06.010

Bourkhis, K., & Nabi, M. S. (2013). Islamic and conventional banks' soundness during the 2007-2008 financial crisis. *Review of Financial Economics*, *22*(2), 68–77. doi:10.1016/j.rfe.2013.01.001

Bowman, D., Londono, J. M., & Sapriza, H. (2015). U.S. unconventional monetary policy and transmission to emerging market economies. *Journal of International Money and Finance*, *55*, 27–59. doi:10.1016/j.jimonfin.2015.02.016

Boyer, B. H., Kumagai, T., & Yuan, K. (2006). How do crises spread? Evidence from accessible and inaccessible stock indices. *The Journal of Finance*, *61*(2), 957–1003. doi:10.1111/j.1540-6261.2006.00860.x

Brauneis, A., & Mestel, R. (2019). Cryptocurrency-portfolios in a mean-variance framework. *Finance Research Letters*, *28*, 259–264. doi:10.1016/j.frl.2018.05.008

Bredin, D., Conlon, T., & Potì, V. (2017). The price of shelter - Downside risk reduction with precious metals. *International Review of Financial Analysis*, *49*, 48–58. doi:10.1016/j.irfa.2016.12.005

Breedon, T. (2012). *Boosting Finance Options for Business*. London, UK: Department for Business Innovation and Skills.

Brière, M. A. C., & Szafarz, A. (2012). No contagion, only globalization and flight to quality. *Journal of International Money and Finance*, *31*(6), 1729–1744. doi:10.1016/j.jimonfin.2012.03.010

Broadus, R. N. (1987). Toward a definition of bibliometrics. *Scientometrics*, *12*(5-6), 373–379. doi:10.1007/BF02016680

Broman, M. (2012). Commonality in ETF Mispricing and Contagion. Available at https://www.semanticscholar.org/paper/Commonality-in-ETF-Mispricing-and-Contagion-Broman/a5716a1b908f2e626cccb86723a673803eb46867

Brooks, C. (2008). *Introductory Econometrics for Finance* (2nd ed.). Cambridge University Press. doi:10.1017/CBO9780511841644

Brunnermeier, K. (2009). Deciphering the liquidity and credit crunch 2007-2008. *The Journal of Economic Perspectives*, *23*(1), 77–100. doi:10.1257/jep.23.1.77 PMID:20052301

Bruton, G., Khavul, S., Siegel, D., & Wright, M. (2015). New Financial alternatives in Seeding Entrepreneurship: Microfinance, Crowdfunding and Peer-to Peer Innovations. *Entrepreneurship Theory and Practice*, *39*(1), 9–26. doi:10.1111/etap.12143

Buch, C. M., Bussiere, M., Goldberg, L., & Hills, R. (2019). The International Transmission of Monetary Policy. *Journal of International Money and Finance*, *91*, 29–48. doi:10.1016/j.jimonfin.2018.08.005

Buchholz, M., Delaney, J., Warren, J., & Parker, J. (2012). Bits and bets, information, price volatility, and demand for Bitcoin. *Economics*, *312*, 2–48.

Burke, G. (1994). A Sharper Sharpe Ratio. *Futures*, 56–57.

Burriel, P., & Galesi, A. (2018). Uncovering the heterogeneous effects of ECB unconventional monetary policies across euro area countries. *European Economic Review*, *101*, 210–229. doi:10.1016/j.euroecorev.2017.10.007

Burtch, G., Ghose, A., & Wattal, S. (2013). An Empirical Examination of the Antecedents and Consequences of Contribution Patterns in Crowdfunded Markets'. *Information Systems Research*, *24*(3), 499–519. doi:10.1287/isre.1120.0468

Buttice, V., & Franzoni, C., Rossi-Lamastra, C., & Rovelli, P. (2018). The Road to Crowdfunding Success: A Review of Extant Literature, Oxford University Press.

Buttice, V., Colombo, M., Massimo, G., & Wright, M. (2017). Serial Crowdfunding, Social Capital and Project Success. *Entrepreneurship Theory and Practice*, *41*(2), 183–207. doi:10.1111/etap.12271

Buysere (de), K., Kleverlaan, R., & Maron, D. (2012). *A Framework for European Crowdfunding*, Impressum.

Buyuksahin, B., & Robe, M. A. (2014). Speculators, commodities and cross-market linkages. *Journal of International Money and Finance*, *42*, 38–70. doi:10.1016/j.jimonfin.2013.08.004

Byrne, J. P., Fazio, G., & Fiess, N. (2013). Primary commodity prices: Co-movements, common factors and fundamentals. *Journal of Development Economics*, *101*, 16–26. doi:10.1016/j.jdeveco.2012.09.002

Bystrom, H., & Krygier, D., Corbet, S., Meegan, A., Larkin, C., Lucey, B., & Yarovaya, L. (2018). What Drives Bitcoin Volatility? Exploring the dynamic relationships between cryptocurrencies and other financial assets. *Economics Letters*, *165*, 28–34. doi:10.1016/j.econlet.2018.01.004

Cabello, J. M., Ruiz, F., Pérez-Gladish, B., & Méndez-Rodríguez, P. (2014). Synthetic indicators of mutual funds' environmental responsibility: An application of the Reference Point Method. *European Journal of Operational Research*, *236*(1), 313–325. doi:10.1016/j.ejor.2013.11.031

Calvo, S., & Mendoza, E. (2000). Rational contagion and the globalization of securities markets. *Journal of International Economics*, *51*(1), 79–113. doi:10.1016/S0022-1996(99)00038-0

Cancino, C. A., Merigo, J. M., Torres, J. P., & Diaz, D. (2018). A bibliometric analysis of venture capital research. *Journal of Economics, Finance, and Administrative Science*, *23*(45), 182–195. doi:10.1108/JEFAS-01-2018-0016

Caporin, M., Ranaldo, A., & Santucci de Magistris, P. (2013). On the predictability of stock prices: A case for high and low prices. *Journal of Banking & Finance*, *37*(12), 5132–5146. doi:10.1016/j.jbankfin.2013.05.024

Cerjan, M., Petricic, A., Delimer, M. (2019). HIRA model for short – term electricity price forecasting.

Chang, C., Hsieh, T., & McAleer, M. (2017). Connecting VIX and Stock Index ETF. *Tinbergen Institute Discussion Paper.*

Chan, L. K. C., & Lakonishok, J. (1993). Institutional Trades and Intraday Stock Price Behavior. *Journal of Financial Economics*, *33*(2), 173–199. doi:10.1016/0304-405X(93)90003-T

Charnes, A., Cooper, W. W., & Rhodes, E. (1981). Evaluating program and managerial efficiency: An application of data envelopment analysis to program follow through. *Management Science*, *27*(6), 668–697. doi:10.1287/mnsc.27.6.668

Chen, Q., Filardo, A., He, D., & Zhu, F. (2015). Financial crisis, US unconventional monetary policy and international spillovers. *IMF, Working Paper*, 1-31.

Chen, A. S., & Lin, J. W. (2014). The relation between gold and stocks: An analysis of severe bear markets. *Applied Economics Letters*, *21*(3), 158–170. doi:10.1080/13504851.2013.844321

Cheng, I.-H., & Xiong, W. (2013). The Financialization of Commodity Markets. NBER Working Paper No.19642

Chen, Q., Filardo, A., He, D., & Zhu, F. (2015). Financial crisis, US unconventional monetary policy and international spillovers. *Journal of International Money and Finance*, *67*, 62–81. doi:10.1016/j.jimonfin.2015.06.011

Chen, Y. C., Rogoff, K. S., & Rossi, B. (2010). Can exchange rates forecast commodity prices? *The Quarterly Journal of Economics*, *125*(3), 1145–1194. doi:10.1162/qjec.2010.125.3.1145

Chiang, T. C., Jeon, B. N., & Li, H. (2007). Dynamic correlation analysis of financial contagion: Evidence from Asian markets. *Journal of International Money and Finance*, *26*(7), 1206–1228. doi:10.1016/j.jimonfin.2007.06.005

Chiyachantana, C. N., Jain, P. K., Jiang, C., & Wood, R. A. (2004). International evidence on institutional trading behavior and price impact. *The Journal of Finance*, *59*(2), 869–898. doi:10.1111/j.1540-6261.2004.00651.x

Cho, J. W., Choi, J. H., Kim, T., & Kim, W. (2016). Flight-to-quality and correlation between currency and stock returns. *Journal of Banking & Finance*, *62*, 191–212. doi:10.1016/j.jbankfin.2014.09.003

Choudhary, M. A., & Limodio, N. (2017). *Deposit Volatility, Liquidity and Long-Term Investment: Evidence from a Natural Experiment in Pakistan.*

Choudhury, M. A., & Hoque, M. Z. (2006). Corporate governance in Islamic perspective. *Corporate Governance: The International Journal of Business in Society*, *6*(2), 116–128. doi:10.1108/14720700610655132

Christensen, J. H. E., & Gillan, J. M. (2018). Does quantitative easing affect market liquidity? *Federal Reserve Bank of San Francisco, Working Paper Series*, 1-35.

Christou, G. K. (2008). *Introduction in Econometrics*. Gutenberg Publications.

Churm, R., Joyce, M., Kapetanios, G., & Theodoridis, K. (in press). Unconventional monetary policies and the macroeconomy: The impact of the UK's QE2 and funding for lending scheme. *The Quarterly Review of Economics and Finance*.

Čihák, M., & Hesse, H. (2010). Islamic Banks and Financial Stability: An Empirical Analysis. *Journal of Financial Services Research*, *38*(2–3), 95–113. doi:10.100710693-010-0089-0

Colgren, D. (2014). The Rise of Crowdfunding: Social Media, Big Data, Cloud Technologies. *Strategic Finance*, *96*(4), 56–67.

Collin – Dufresne, P., & Goldstein, R. S. (2002). Do bonds span the fixed income markets? Theory and Evidence for Unspanned Stochastic Volatility. *The Journal of Finance*, *LVII*(4).

Collins, L., Swart, R., & Zhang, B. (2013). *The Rise of Future Finance: The UK Alternative Finance Benchmarking Report.*

Collins, B. M., & Fabozzi, F. J. (1991). A Methodology for Measuring Transaction Costs. *Financial Analysts Journal*, *47*(2), 27–36. doi:10.2469/faj.v47.n2.27

Conlon, T., Lucey, B. M., & Uddin, G. S. (2018). Is gold a hedge against inflation? A wavelet time-scale perspective. *Review of Quantitative Finance and Accounting*, *51*(2), 317–345. doi:10.100711156-017-0672-7

Conrad, J. S., Johnson, K. M., & Wahal, S. (2001). Institutional trading and soft dollars. *The Journal of Finance*, *56*(1), 397–416. doi:10.1111/0022-1082.00331

Conrad, J. S., Johnson, K. M., & Wahal, S. (2003). Institutional trading and alternative trading systems. *Journal of Financial Economics*, *70*(1), 99–134. doi:10.1016/S0304-405X(03)00143-0

Corgel, J., McIntosh, W., & Ott, S. (1995). Real estate investment trusts: A review of the financial economics literature. *Journal of Real Estate Literature*, *3*, 13–43.

Coskun, Y., Selcuk-Kestel, A. S., & Yilmaz, B. (2017). Diversification benefit and return performance of REITs using CAPM and FAMA – French: Evidence from Turkey. *Borsa Istanbul Review*, *17*(4), 199–215. doi:10.1016/j.bir.2017.08.003

Coupé, T. (2003). Revealed performances: Worldwide rankings of economists and economics departments, 1990-2000. *Journal of the European Economic Association*, *1*(6), 1309–1345. doi:10.1162/154247603322752557

Czarnitzki, D., & Kraft, K. (2004). Firm Leadership and Innovative Performance Evidence from Seven EU Countries. *Small Business Economics*, *22*(5), 325–332. doi:10.1023/B:SBEJ.0000022209.72378.fe

Daskalaki, C., Kostakis, A., & Skiadopoulos, G. (2014). Are there common factors in individual commodity futures returns? *Journal of Banking & Finance*, *40*, 346–363. doi:10.1016/j.jbankfin.2013.11.034

De Oliveira, E. M., Cunha, F. A. F. S., Cyrino Oliveira, F. L., & Samanez, C. P. (2017). Dynamic relationships between crude oil prices and socially responsible investing in Brazil: Evidence for linear and non-linear causality. *Applied Economics*, *49*(22), 2125–2140. doi:10.1080/00036846.2016.1234695

de Roure, C., & Tasca, P. (2014). Bitcoin and the PPP Puzzle.

Delle Chiaie, S., Ferrara, L., & Giannone, D. (2017). Common factors of commodity prices. Bank of France Working Paper

DeYoung, R., & Jang, K. Y. (2016). Do banks actively manage their liquidity? *Journal of Banking & Finance*, *66*, 143–161. doi:10.1016/j.jbankfin.2015.11.013

Dickey, D. A., & Fuller, W. A. (1979). Distribution of the Estimators for Autoregressive Time Series with a Unit Root. *Journal of the American Statistical Association*, *74*, 427–431.

Di, L., Shaiban, M. S., & Shavkatovich Hasanov, A. (2017). Contagion effect from US banking to conventional and Islamic banking in dual-banking system during financial crisis. In *KFUPM Islamic Banking and Finance Research Conference 2017*.

Dimitriou, D., & Kenourgios, D. (2013). Financial crises and dynamic linkages among international currencies. *Journal of International Financial Markets, Institutions and Money*, *26*, 319–332. doi:10.1016/j.intfin.2013.07.008

Dimitriou, D., Kenourgios, D., & Simos, T. (2013). Global financial crisis and emerging stock market contagion: A multivariate FIAPARCH-DCC approach. *International Review of Financial Analysis*, *30*, 46–56. doi:10.1016/j.irfa.2013.05.008

Dimitriou, D., Kenourgios, D., & Simos, T. (2017). Financial crises, exchange rate linkages and uncovered interest parity: Evidence from G7 markets. *Economic Modelling*, *66*, 112–120. doi:10.1016/j.econmod.2017.06.003

Dimitriou, D., & Simos, T. (2013). Contagion channels of the U.S. subprime crisis: Empirical evidence from USA, EMU, China and Japan equity markets. *Journal of Financial Economic Policy*, *5*(1), 61–71. doi:10.1108/17576381311317781

Dimitriou, D., & Simos, T. (2014). Contagion effects on stock and FX markets A DCC analysis among USA and EMU. *Studies in Economics and Finance*, *31*, 246–254. doi:10.1108/SEF-07-2012-0075

Domowitz, I., Glen, J., & Madhavan, A. (1999). *International Equity Trading Costs: A Cross-Sectional and Time-Series Analysis. Technical Report*. Pennsylvania State University, International Finance Corp., University of Southern California.

Domowitz, I., Glen, J., & Madhavan, A. (2001). Liquidity, volatility and equity trading costs across countries and over time. *International Finance*, *4*(2), 221–255. doi:10.1111/1468-2362.00072

Dorfleitner, G., & Nguyen, M. (2017). A new approach for optimizing responsible investments dependently on the initial wealth. *Journal of Asset Management*, *18*(2), 81–98. doi:10.105741260-016-0011-x

Dos Santos, B. L., Patel, P. C., & D'Souza, R. R. (2011). Venture Capital Funding for Information Technology Businesses'. *Journal of the Association for Information Systems*, *12*(1), 57–87. doi:10.17705/1jais.00253

Duffie, D., Garleanu, N., & Pedersen, L. H. (2007). Valuation in over-the counter markets. *Review of Financial Studies*, *20*(5), 1865–1900. doi:10.1093/rfs/hhm037

Dungey, M., Fry, R., González-Hermosillo, B., & Martin, V. (2006). Contagion in international bond markets during the Russian and LTCM crises. *Journal of Financial Stability*, *2*(1), 1–27. doi:10.1016/j.jfs.2005.01.001

Dupré, D., Girerd-Potin, I., Jimenez-Garces, S., & Louvet, P. (2009). The impact of social rating on stock prices: A theoretical model. *Revue Economique*, *60*(1), 5–31.

Dyhrberg, A. H. (2016). Bitcoin, gold and the dollar–A GARCH volatility analysis. *Finance Research Letters*, *16*, 85–92. doi:10.1016/j.frl.2015.10.008

Ebrahim, M. S., Jaafar, A., Omar, F. A., & Osman, M. (2016). Can Islamic injunctions indemnify the structural flaws of securitized debt? *Journal of Corporate Finance*, *37*, 271–286. doi:10.1016/j.jcorpfin.2016.01.002

Ebrahim, M. S., & Sheikh, M. (2016). Debt Instruments in Islamic Finance: A Critique. *Arab Law Quarterly*, *30*(2), 185–198. doi:10.1163/15730255-12341317

Ebrahim, M. S., & Sheikh, M. (2018). The Political Economy and Underdevelopment of the Muslim World: A Juridico-Philosophical Perspective. *Arab Law Quarterly*, *32*(4), 385–412. doi:10.1163/15730255-12324051

Efimova, O., & Serletis, A. (2014). Energy markets volatility modelling using GARCH. *Energy Economics*, *43*, 264–273. doi:10.1016/j.eneco.2014.02.018

Egghe, L. (2006). Theory and practice of the g-index. *Scientometrics*, *69*(1), 131–152. doi:10.100711192-006-0144-7

El Alaoui, M., Bouri, E., & Roubaud, D. (2018). Bitcoin price–volume: A multifractal cross-correlation approach. *Finance Research Letters*.

El-Gamal, M. A. (2006). *Islamic Finance: Law, Economics, and Practice*. Cambridge University Press. doi:10.1017/CBO9780511753756

El-Gamal, M. A., & Inanoglu, H. (2005). Inefficiency and heterogeneity in Turkish banking: 1990-2000. *Journal of Applied Econometrics*, *20*(5), 641–664. doi:10.1002/jae.835

Engle, F., & Granger, C. W. J. (1987). Co-Integration and Error Correction: Representation, Estimation, and Testing. *Econometrica*, *55*(2), 251–276. doi:10.2307/1913236

Engle, R. (2002). Dynamic conditional correlation: A simple class of multivariate generalized autoregressive conditional heteroskedasticity models. *Journal of Business & Economic Statistics*, *20*(3), 339–350. doi:10.1198/073500102288618487

ERD. (2015). *European Report on Development 2015: Combining Finance and Policies to Implement a Transformative Post-2015 Development Agenda*, EU.

Ernest & Young. (2018). *Global Perspectives: 2018 REIT report,* EY.

EU. (2017). *Identifying Market and Regulatory Obstacles to Cross-Border Development of Crowdfunding in the EU.*

European Public Real Estate Association. (2018). *Global REIT Survey 2018*. ERPA.

EY. (2016). *World Islamic Banking Competitiveness Report 2016*. Retrieved from http://www.ey.com/Publication/vwLUAssets/EY-world-islamic-banking-competitiveness-report-2014-15/$FILE/EY-world-islamic-banking-competitiveness-report-2014-15.pdf

Fabozzi, F. J., Focardi, S. M., & Kolm, P. N. (2010). *Quantitative Equity Investing: Techniques and Strategies*. Hoboken, NJ: John Wiley & Sons.

Fabozzi, F. J., & Markowitz, H. M. (2011). *The Theory and Practice of Investment Management*. Hoboken, NJ: John Wiley & Sons. doi:10.1002/9781118267028

Falagiarda, M., McQuade, P., & Tirpák, M. (2015). *Spillovers from the ECB's non-standard monetary policies on non-euro area EU countries: evidence from an event-study analysis*. European Central Bank.

Farag, H., Mallin, C., & Ow-Yong, K. (2018). Corporate governance in Islamic banks: New insights for dual board structure and agency relationships. *Journal of International Financial Markets, Institutions and Money*, *54*, 59–77. doi:10.1016/j.intfin.2017.08.002

FED. (2009). The financial crisis: A timeline of events and policy actions.

Feng, Z., Price, S., & Sirmans, C. (2011). An overview of equity REITs: 1993 - 2009. *Journal of Real Estate Literature*, *19*, 307–334.

Ferderer, J. P. (1996). Oil price volatility and the macroeconomy. *Journal of Macroeconomics*, *18*(1), 1–26. doi:10.1016/S0164-0704(96)80001-2

Fieseler, C. (2011). On the corporate social responsibility perceptions of equity analysts. *Business Ethics (Oxford, England)*, *20*(2), 131–147. doi:10.1111/j.1467-8608.2011.01616.x

Figuerola-Ferretti, I., & Gonzalo, J. (2010). Modelling and measuring price discovery in commodity markets. *Journal of Econometrics*, *158*(1), 95–107. doi:10.1016/j.jeconom.2010.03.013

Fiordelisi, F., Marques-Ibanez, D., & Molyneux, P. (2011). Efficiency and risk in European banking. *Journal of Banking & Finance*, *35*(5), 1315–1326. doi:10.1016/j.jbankfin.2010.10.005

Fisher, I. (1836). *The Theory of Interest*. London, UK: Macmillan and Co.

Flavin, T., & Panopoulou, E. (2010). Detecting shift and pure contagion in East Asian equity markets: A Unified Approach. *Pacific Economic Review*, *15*(3), 401–421. doi:10.1111/j.1468-0106.2010.00510.x

Flavin, T., Panopoulou, E., & Unalmis, D. (2008). On the stability of domestic financial market linkages in the presence of time-varying volatility. *Emerging Markets Review*, *9*(4), 280–301. doi:10.1016/j.ememar.2008.10.002

Forbes, K., & Rigobon, R. (2002). No contagion, only interdependence: Measuring stock market co-movements. *The Journal of Finance*, *57*(5), 2223–2261. doi:10.1111/0022-1082.00494

Frankel, J. A. (2013). *Effects of Speculation and Interest Rates in a 'Carry Trade' Model of Commodity Prices.* Written for Understanding International Commodity Price Fluctuations, an International Conference organized by the IMF and Oxford University 10.3386/w19463

Frankel, J. A. (1984). Commodity prices and money: Lessons from international finance. *American Journal of Agricultural Economics*, *66*(5), 560–566. doi:10.2307/1240954

Frankel, J. A. (2008). *The Effect of Monetary Policy on Real Commodity Prices. In J. Y. Campbell: Asset Prices and Monetary Policy* (pp. 291–333). University of Chicago Press.

Frankel, J. A., & Hardouvelis, G. A. (1985). Commodity Prices, Money Surprises and Fed Credibility. *Journal of Money, Credit, and Banking*, *17*(4), 425–438. doi:10.2307/1992439

Frankel, J. A., & Rose, A. K. (2010). Determinants of Agricultural and Mineral Commodity Prices. In *Inflation in an era of Relative Price Shocks*. Reserve Bank of Australia.

Fratzscher, M., Lo Duca, M., & Straub, R. (2013). On the international spillovers of US quantitative easing, *DIW Discussion Papers, no. 1304*.

Fratzscher, M., Lo Duca, M., & Straub, R. (2016). ECB Unconventional Monetary Policy: Market Impact and International Spillovers. *IMF Economic Review*, *64*(1), 36–74. doi:10.1057/imfer.2016.5

Freedman, M. P. (2000). Challenges to Launching Grassroots Microlending Programs: A Case Study. *Journal of Developmental Entrepreneurship*, *5*(3), 235–248.

Gandal, N., & Halaburda, H. (2016). Can we predict the winner in a market with network effects? Competition in cryptocurrency market. *Games*, *7*(3), 16. doi:10.3390/g7030016

Gang, H. (2009). Measures of Implicit Trading Costs and Buy-Sell Asymmetry. *Journal of Financial Markets*, *12*(3), 418–437. doi:10.1016/j.finmar.2009.03.002

Garcia, C. R., Contreras, J., Akkeren, M., & Garcia, J. B. C. (2005). A GARCH forecasting model to predict day – ahead electricity prices. *IEEE Transactions on Power Systems*, *20*(2), 867–874. doi:10.1109/TPWRS.2005.846044

García-Martos, C., Rodríguez, J., & Sánchez, M. J. (2011). Forecasting electricity prices and their volatility using Unobserved Components. *Energy Economics*, *33*(6), 1227–1239. doi:10.1016/j.eneco.2011.07.005

Gash, M., & Gray, B. (2016). *The Role of Financial Services in Building Household Resilience*. Washington, D.C.: CGAP.

Geman, H., & Roncoroni, A. (2006). Understanding the fine structure of electricity prices. *The Journal of Business*, *79*(3), 1225–1261. doi:10.1086/500675

Gilbert, C. L. (1989). The impact of exchange rates and developing country debt on commodity prices. *Economic Journal (London)*, *99*(397), 773–784. doi:10.2307/2233770

Gilbert, C. L. (2010). How to Understand High Food Prices. *Journal of Agricultural Economics*, *61*(2), 398–425. doi:10.1111/j.1477-9552.2010.00248.x

Glaeser, E. L., & Shleifer, A. (2001). Not-for-Profit Entrepreneurs. *Journal of Public Economics*, *81*(1), 99–115. doi:10.1016/S0047-2727(00)00130-4

Glaser, F., Zimmermann, K., Haferkorn, M., Weber, M. C., & Siering, M. (2014). *Bitcoin-asset or currency? revealing users' hidden intentions. Revealing Users' Hidden Intentions (April 15, 2014)*. ECIS.

Gordon, G., & Rouwenhorst, K. G. (2006). Facts and Fantasies about Commodity Futures. *Financial Analysts Journal*, *62*(2), 47–68. doi:10.2469/faj.v62.n2.4083

Gorton, G. B., Hayashi, F., & Rouwenhorst, K. G. (2012). The fundamentals of commodity futures returns. *Review of Finance*, *17*(1), 35–105. doi:10.1093/rof/rfs019

Gospodinov, N., & Jamali, I. (2012). The Effects of Federal Funds Rate Surprises on S&P 500 Volatility and Volatility Risk Premium. *Journal of Empirical Finance*, *19*(4), 497–510. doi:10.1016/j.jempfin.2012.04.009

Gospodinov, N., & Ng, S. (2013). Commodity Prices, Convenience Yields and Inflation. *The Review of Economics and Statistics*, *95*(1), 206–219. doi:10.1162/REST_a_00242

Government of Hong Kong. (2014). *Future fuel mix for electricity generation*. Environmental Bureau.

GPFI (Global Partnership for Financial Inclusion). (2016). *Global Standard-Setting Bodies and Financial Inclusion: The Evolving Landscape*.

Granger, C. W. J. (1969). Investigating causal relations by econometric models and cross - spectral methods. *Econometrica*, *3*(3), 424–438. doi:10.2307/1912791

Granger, C. W. J. (1986). Developments in the study of cointegrated economic variables. *Oxford Bulletin of Economics and Statistics*, *48*(3), 213–228. doi:10.1111/j.1468-0084.1986.mp48003002.x

Griffin, J. M., & Shams, A. (2018). Is bitcoin really un-tethered?. Available at SSRN 3195066.

Grigorian, D., & Manole, V. (2005). A Cross-Country Nonparametric Analysis of Bahrain's Banking System. *International Monetary Fund Working Paper, WP 05/117.*

Grinberg, R. (2012). Bitcoin: An innovative alternative digital currency. *Hastings Sci. & Tech. LJ*, *4*, 159.

Gubler, M., & Hertweck, M. S. (2013). Commodity price shocks and the business cycle: Structural evidence from the US. *Journal of International Money and Finance*, *37*, 324–352. doi:10.1016/j.jimonfin.2013.06.012

Guesmi, K., Saadi, S., Abid, I., & Ftiti, Z. (2019). Portfolio diversification with virtual currency: Evidence from bitcoin. *International Review of Financial Analysis*, *63*, 431–437. doi:10.1016/j.irfa.2018.03.004

Gujarati, D. N., & Porter, D. C. (2009). *Basic Econometrics*. Irwin, NY: McGraw-Hill.

Hair, J. F., Andersen, R. E., Tatham, R. L., & Black, W. C. (1995). *Multivariate data analysis* (4th ed.). Englewood Cliffs, NJ: Prentice Hall.

Hammoudeh, S., Nguyen, D. K., & Sousa, R. M. (2015). US Monetary Policy and Sectoral Commodity Prices. *Journal of International Money and Finance*, *57*, 61–85. doi:10.1016/j.jimonfin.2015.06.003

Hamza, H. (2016). Does investment deposit return in Islamic banks reflect PLS principle? *Borsa Istanbul Review*, *16*(1), 32–42. doi:10.1016/j.bir.2015.12.001

Harris, L. (2015). *Trading and Electronic Markets: What Investment Professionals Need to Know*. CFA Institute Research Foundation Publications.

Hart, O., & Moore, J. (1988). Incomplete Contracts and Renegotiation. *Econometrica*, *56*(4), 755–785. doi:10.2307/1912698

Hasan, M., & Dridi, J. (2011). The effects of the global crisis on Islamic and conventional banks: A comparative study. *Journal of International Commerce Economic Policy*, *2*(2), 163–200.

Hassan, K., & Aliyu, S. (2018). A contemporary survey of Islamic banking literature. *Journal of Financial Stability*, *34*, 12–43. doi:10.1016/j.jfs.2017.11.006

Hassan, K., & Grassa, R. (2012). *Islamic banks' income structure and risk: Evidence from GCC countries*. Accounting Research Journal.

Hassan, T., Mohamad, S., & Bader, M. K. I. (2009). Efficiency of conventional versus Islamic banks: Evidence from the Middle East. *International Journal of Islamic and Middle Eastern Finance and Management*, *2*(1), 46–65. doi:10.1108/17538390910946267

Havrylchyk, O. (2018). Regulatory Framework for the Loan-Based Crowdfunding Platforms, *OECD Economics Department Working Papers*, No. 1513, OECD Publishing, Paris.

Hayami, Y. (1969). Sources of agricultural productivity gap among selected countries. *American Journal of Agricultural Economics*, *51*(3), 564–575. doi:10.2307/1237909

Hayami, Y., & Ruttan, V. W. (1970). Agricultural productivity differences among countries. *The American Economic Review*, *60*(5), 895–911.

Hayat, R., & Kabir Hassan, M. (2017). Does an Islamic label indicate good corporate governance? *Journal of Corporate Finance*, *43*, 159–174. doi:10.1016/j.jcorpfin.2016.12.012

Hebb, T., Louche, C., & Hachigian, H. (2014). Exploring the societal impacts of SRI. *Critical Studies on Corporate Responsibility, Governance and Sustainability*, *7*, 3–20. doi:10.1108/S2043-905920140000007001

Hellmann, T. (1998). The Allocation of Control Rights in Venture Capital Contracts. *The Rand Journal of Economics*, *29*(1), 57–76. doi:10.2307/2555816

Herciu, M. (2017). Financing Small Businesses: From Venture Capital to Crowdfunding. *Studies in Business and Economics*, *12*(2), 63–69. doi:10.1515be-2017-0022

Herrera-Cano, C., & Gonzalez-Perez, M. A. (2016). Global Financial Crisis and the Emergence and Maturing of Socially Responsible Investments. *Advances in Sustainability and Environmental Justice*, *18*, 189–202. doi:10.1108/S2051-503020160000018008

Hileman, G., & Rauchs, M. (2017). Global cryptocurrency benchmarking study. Cambridge Centre for Alternative Finance, 33.

Hirsch, J. (2005). An index to quantify an individual's scientific research output. In *Proceedings of the National Academy of Sciences of the United States of America*, *102*(46), 16569–16572. doi:10.1073/pnas.0507655102 PMID:16275915

Hodge, D., & Lacasse, J. R. (2011). Evaluating journal quality: Is the H-index a better measure than impact factors? *Research on Social Work Practice*, *21*(2), 222–230. doi:10.1177/1049731510369141

Hohberger, S., Priftis, R., & Vogel, L. (in press). The distributional effects of conventional monetary policy and quantitative easing: Evidence from an estimated DSGE model. *Journal of Banking & Finance*.

Horta, P., Mendes, C., & Vieira, I. (2010). Contagion effects of the subprime crisis in the European NYSE Euronext markets. *Portuguese Economic Journal*, *9*(2), 115–140. doi:10.100710258-010-0056-6

How, J. C. Y., Karim, M. A., & Verhoeven, P. (2005). Islamic financing and bank risks: The case of Malaysia. *Thunderbird International Business Review*, *47*(1), 75–94. doi:10.1002/tie.20041

Huang, D., & Kilic, M. (2018). (in press). Gold, platinum, and expected stock returns. *Journal of Financial Economics*.

Huisman, R., & Mahieu, R. (2003). Regime jumps in electricity prices. *Energy Economics*, *25*(5), 425–434. doi:10.1016/S0140-9883(03)00041-0

Inoue, A., & Rossi, B. (2019). The effects of conventional and unconventional monetary policy on exchange rates. *Journal of International Economics*, *118*, 419–447. doi:10.1016/j.jinteco.2019.01.015

International Monetary Fund. (2018). A Decade after the Global Financial Crisis: Are We Safer?. *Global Financial Stability Report*, 1-99.

Iqbal, Z., & Mirakhor, A. (2011). An introduction to Islamic finance. *Theory into Practice*, *687*. John Wiley & Sons.

Iqbal, Z., & Sadr, K. (2001). *Choice between Debt and Equity contracts and Asymmetrical Information: Some Empirical Evidence*. Edward Elgar Publishing.

Irandoust, M. (2017). Metal prices and stock market performance: Is there an empirical link? *Resources Policy*, *52*, 389–392. doi:10.1016/j.resourpol.2017.05.001

Irwin, S. H., & Sanders, D. R. (2012). Financialization and Structural Change in Commodity Futures Markets. *Journal of Agricultural and Applied Economics*, *44*(3), 371–396. doi:10.1017/S1074070800000481

Ismail, A. G., & Sulaiman, A. A. (2008). Whether Islamic Banks Chose to Adjust their Assets Due to Capital Adequacy Requirements. *Journal of Islamic Economics, Banking, and Finance*, *4*(1), 27–37.

Israelsen, C. (2005). A Refinement to the Sharpe Ratio and Information Ratio. *Journal of Asset Management*, *5*(6), 423–427. doi:10.1057/palgrave.jam.2240158

Itzhak, B., Franzoni, A., & Moussawi, R. (2017). Exchange Traded Funds (ETFs). *Annual Review of Financial Economics*, *9*(1), 169–189. doi:10.1146/annurev-financial-110716-032538

Jadlow, J. M. (1977). Adam Smith on usury laws. *The Journal of Finance*, *32*(4), 1195–1200. doi:10.1111/j.1540-6261.1977.tb03319.x

Jansson, M., & Biel, A. (2011). Motives to engage in sustainable investment: A comparison between institutional and private investors. *Sustainable Development*, *19*(2), 135–142. doi:10.1002d.512

Jeitschko, T. D., & Jeung, S. D. (2005). Incentives for risk-taking in banking - A unified approach. *Journal of Banking & Finance*, *29*(3), 759–777. doi:10.1016/S0378-4266(04)00057-3

Jenik, I., Lyman, T., & Nava, A. (2017). Crowdfunding and Financial Inclusion, CGAP (Consultative Group to Assist the Poor) *Working Paper*.

Jensen, M. C. (1968). The Performance of Mutual Funds in the period 1945 –1964. *The Journal of Finance*, *23*(2), 389–416. doi:10.1111/j.1540-6261.1968.tb00815.x

Johansen, S. (1988). Statistical analysis of cointegration vectors. *Journal of Economic Dynamics & Control*, *12*(2-3), 231–254. doi:10.1016/0165-1889(88)90041-3

Johansen, S. (1991). Estimation and hypothesis testing of cointegrating vectors in Gaussian vector autoregressive models. *Econometrica*, *59*(6), 1551–1580. doi:10.2307/2938278

Johansen, S. (1995). *Likelihood-Based Inference in Cointegrated Vector Autoregressive Models*. New York: Oxford University Press. doi:10.1093/0198774508.001.0001

Johansen, S. (2008). A representation theory for a class of vector autoregressive models for fractional processes. *Econometric Theory, 24*(3), 651–676. doi:10.1017/S0266466608080274

Johansen, S., & Nielsen, M. O. (2010). Likelihood inference for a nonstationary fractional autoregressive model. *Journal of Econometrics, 158*(1), 51–66. doi:10.1016/j.jeconom.2010.03.006

Johansen, S., & Nielsen, M. O. (2012). Likelihood inference for a fractionally cointegrated vector autoregressive model. *Econometrica, 80*(6), 2667–2732. doi:10.3982/ECTA9299

Johansen, S., & Nielsen, M. O. (2016). The role of initial values in conditional sum-of-squares estimation of nonstationary fractional time series models. *Econometric Theory, 32*(5), 1095–1139. doi:10.1017/S0266466615000110

Johnes, J., Izzeldin, M., & Pappas, V. (2014). A comparison of performance of Islamic and conventional banks 2004-2009. *Journal of Economic Behavior & Organization, 103*, 1–45. doi:10.1016/j.jebo.2013.07.016

Jorion, P., & Zhang, G. (2007). Good and bad credit contagion: Evidence from credit default swap. *Journal of Financial Economics, 84*(3), 860–883. doi:10.1016/j.jfineco.2006.06.001

Joyce, M., Miles, D., Scott, A., & Vayanos, D. (2012). Quantitative easing and unconventional monetary policy – an introduction. *Economic Journal (London), 122*(564), F271–F288. doi:10.1111/j.1468-0297.2012.02551.x

Joy, M. (2011). Gold and the US dollar: Hedge or haven? *Finance Research Letters, 8*(3), 120–131. doi:10.1016/j.frl.2011.01.001

Junttila, J., Pesonen, J., & Raatikainen, J. (2018). Commodity market-based hedging against stock market risk in times of financial crisis: The case of crude oil and gold. *Journal of International Financial Markets, Institutions and Money, 56*, 255–280. doi:10.1016/j.intfin.2018.01.002

Jurado, K., Ludvigson, S. C., & Ng, S. (2015). Measuring Uncertainty. *The American Economic Review, 105*(3), 1177–1216. doi:10.1257/aer.20131193

Kabir, N., Worthington, A., & Gupta, R. (2015). Comparative credit risk in Islamic and conventional bank. *Pacific-Basin Finance Journal, 34*, 327–353. doi:10.1016/j.pacfin.2015.06.001

Kajtazi, A., & Moro, A. (2019). The role of bitcoin in well diversified portfolios: A comparative global study. *International Review of Financial Analysis, 61*, 143–157. doi:10.1016/j.irfa.2018.10.003

Kalbaska, A., & Gatkowski, M. (2012). Eurozone sovereign contagion. Evidence from the CDS market (2005-2010). *Journal of Economic Behavior & Organization, 83*(3), 657–673. doi:10.1016/j.jebo.2012.05.010

Kamarudin, F., Nordin, B. A. A., Muhammad, J., & Hamid, M. A. A. (2014). Cost, Revenue and Profit Efficiency of Islamic and Conventional Banking Sector: Empirical Evidence from Gulf Cooperative Council Countries. *Global Business Review*, *15*(1), 1–24. doi:10.1177/0972150913515579

Kaminsky, G. L., Reinhart, C. M., & Vegh, C. A. (2003). The Unholy Trinity of Financial Contagion. *The Journal of Economic Perspectives*, *17*(4), 51–74. doi:10.1257/089533003772034899

Karali, B., & Power, G. J. (2013). Short-and long-run determinants of commodity price volatility. *American Journal of Agricultural Economics*, *95*(3), 724–738. doi:10.1093/ajae/aas122

Katseli, L., & Boufounou, P. (2017). Crowdfunding and Social Banking for Cultural Heritage Projects: A Greek Case-study. In G. Mergos, & N. Patsiavos (Eds.), *Cultural Heritage as Economic Value for Sustainable Development: Economic Benefits*. Social Opportunities and Challenges of Cultural Heritage.

Keim, D. B. (2003). *The cost of trend chasing and the illusion of momentum profits*. Unpublished Working Paper, University of Pennsylvania.

Keim, D. B., & Madhavan, A. (1995). Anatomy of the trading process: Empirical evidence on the behavior of institutional traders. *Journal of Financial Economics*, *37*(3), 371–398. doi:10.1016/0304-405X(94)00799-7

Keim, D. B., & Madhavan, A. (1996). The upstairs market for large-block transactions: Analysis and measurement of price effects. *Review of Financial Studies*, *9*(1), 1–36. doi:10.1093/rfs/9.1.1

Keim, D. B., & Madhavan, A. (1997). Transaction costs and investment style: An inter-exchange analysis of institutional equity trades. *Journal of Financial Economics*, *46*(3), 265–292. doi:10.1016/S0304-405X(97)00031-7

Keim, D. B., & Madhavan, A. (1998). The Cost of Institutional Equity Trades. *Financial Analysts Journal*, *54*(4), 50–69. doi:10.2469/faj.v54.n4.2198

Kelly, B., Pastor, L., & Veronesi, P. (2016). The Price of Political Uncertainty: Theory and Evidence from the Option Market. *The Journal of Finance*, *71*(5), 2417–2480. doi:10.1111/jofi.12406

Kenourgios, D. (2014). On financial contagion and implied market volatility. *International Review of Financial Analysis*, *34*, 21–30. doi:10.1016/j.irfa.2014.05.001

Kenourgios, D., & Dimitriou, D. (2015). Contagion of the Global Financial Crisis and the real economy: A regional analysis. *Economic Modelling*, *44*, 283–293. doi:10.1016/j.econmod.2014.10.048

Kenourgios, D., Drakonaki, E., & Dimitriou, D. (2019a). ECB's unconventional monetary policy and cross-financial-market correlation dynamics. *The North American Journal of Economics and Finance*, *50*, 101045. doi:10.1016/j.najef.2019.101045

Kenourgios, D., Kagiana, N., & Katevatis, A. (2019b). ECB's unconventional monetary policy and European bank stock returns. *International Journal of Financial Engineering and Risk Management*, *3*(2), 180–199. doi:10.1504/IJFERM.2019.101301

Kenourgios, D., Nader, N., & Dimitriou, D. (2016). Islamic financial markets and global crises: Contagion or decoupling? *Economic Modelling*, *57*, 36–46. doi:10.1016/j.econmod.2016.04.014

Kenourgios, D., & Padhi, P. (2012). Emerging markets and financial crises: Regional, global or isolated shocks? *Journal of Multinational Financial Management*, *22*(1-2), 24–38. doi:10.1016/j.mulfin.2012.01.002

Kenourgios, D., Papadamou, S., & Dimitriou, D. (2015a). Intraday Exchange Rate Volatility Transmissions Across QE Announcements. *Finance Research Letters*, *14*, 128–134. doi:10.1016/j.frl.2015.05.007

Kenourgios, D., Papadamou, S., & Dimitriou, D. (2015b). On Quantitative Easing and High Frequency Exchange Rate Dynamics. *Research in International Business and Finance*, *34*, 110–125. doi:10.1016/j.ribaf.2015.01.003

Kenourgios, D., Samitas, A., & Paltalidis, N. (2011). Financial crises and stock market contagion in a multivariate time-varying asymmetric framework. *Journal of International Financial Markets, Institutions and Money*, *21*(1), 92–106. doi:10.1016/j.intfin.2010.08.005

Keuschnigg, C. (2004). Venture Capital Backed Growth. *Journal of Economic Growth*, *9*(2), 239–261. doi:10.1023/B:JOEG.0000031428.35711.fc

Keynes, J. M. (1936). *The General Theory of Employment, Interest, and Money*. Palgrave Macmillan.

Khan, F. (2010). How 'Islamic' is Islamic Banking? *Journal of Economic Behavior & Organization*, *76*(3), 805–820. doi:10.1016/j.jebo.2010.09.015

Khavul, S. (2010). Microfinance: Creating Opportunities for the Poor? *The Academy of Management Perspectives*, *24*(3), 57–71. doi:10.5465/amp.24.3.58

Khuram, S. B., Hayat, A., & Faareha, A. (2013). An evaluation of corporate governance practices of Islamic banks versus Islamic bank windows of conventional banks: A case of Pakistan. *Management Research Review*, *36*(4), 400–416. doi:10.1108/01409171311315003

Kim, B. S. (2009). The impact of the Global Financial Crisis on Asia – Pacific real estate markets: Evidence from Korea, Japan, Australia and US REITs. *Pacific Rim Property Research Journal*, *15*(4), 398–416. doi:10.1080/14445921.2009.11104288

Kirby, E., & Worner, S. (2014). *Crowdfunding: An Infant Industry Growing Fast*. Madrid, Spain: IOSCO.

Kirschen, D. S., Strbac, G., Cumperayot, P., & Mendes, D. (2000). Factoring the elasticity of demand in electricity prices. *IEEE Transactions on Power Systems*, *15*(2), 612–617. doi:10.1109/59.867149

Kissell, R. (2014). *The Science of Algorithmic Trading*. USA: Elsevier.

Kleemann, F., Voss, G. G., & Rieder, K. (2008). Un(der)paid Innovators: The Commercial Utilization of Consumer Work through Crowdsourcing. *Science, Technology, & Innovation Studies*, *4*(1), 5–26.

Knoll, M. S. (2002). Ethical screening in modern financial markets: The conflicting claims underlying socially responsible investment. *Business Lawyer*, *57*(2), 681–726.

Koekebakker, S., & Ollmar, F. 2005. Forward curve dynamics in the Nordic electricity market. Managerial Finance, 31(6), 73-94. doi:10.1108/03074350510769703

Köne, A. C., & Büke, T. (2007). An Analytical Network Process (ANP) evaluation of alternative fuels for electricity generation in Turkey. *Energy Policy*, *35*(10), 5220–5228. doi:10.1016/j.enpol.2007.05.014

Koutsokostas, D., & Papathanasiou, S. (2017). Mutual funds in Greece: Case study of domestic equity mutual funds during a financial crisis. *Managerial Finance*, *43*(7), 812–827. doi:10.1108/MF-10-2016-0293

Koutsokostas, D., Papathanasiou, S., & Balios, D. (2019). Adjusting for risk factors in mutual fund performance and performance persistence: Evidence from the Greek market during the debt crisis. *The Journal of Risk Finance*, *20*(4), 352–369. doi:10.1108/JRF-07-2018-0108

Koutsokostas, D., Papathanasiou, S., & Eriotis, N. (2018). Can mutual fund managers predict security prices to beat the market? The case of Greece during the debt crisis. *The Journal of Prediction Markets*, *12*(3), 40–62.

Kumbhakar, S. C., Parmeter, C. F., & Tsionas, E. G. (2013). A zero inefficiency stochastic frontier model. *Journal of Econometrics*, *172*(1), 66–76. doi:10.1016/j.jeconom.2012.08.021

Kurka, J. (2019). Do cryptocurrencies and traditional asset classes influence each other? *Finance Research Letters*, *31*, 38–46. doi:10.1016/j.frl.2019.04.018

Lago, J., Ridder, F. D., Vrancx, P., & Schutter, B. D. (2018). Forecasting day – ahead electricity prices in Europe: The importance of considering market integration. *Applied Energy*, *211*, 890–903. doi:10.1016/j.apenergy.2017.11.098

Lambert, T., & Schwienbacher, A. (2010). An Empirical Analysis of Crowdfunding. *Social Science Research Network*, 1–23.

Landström, H., Harirchi, G., & Aström, F. (2012). Entrepreneurship: Exploring the knowledge base. *Research Policy*, *41*(7), 1154–1181. doi:10.1016/j.respol.2012.03.009

Lassoued, M. (2018). Comparative study on credit risk in Islamic banking institutions: The case of Malaysia. *The Quarterly Review of Economics and Finance*, *70*, 267–278. doi:10.1016/j.qref.2018.05.009

Lavinsky, D. (2011). *Funding Fathers*. Smart Business.

Le Sourd, V. (2007). *Performance Measurement for Traditional Investment*. EDHEC Risk and Asset Management Research Centre.

Leading Group on Innovative Financing for Development. (2010). *Innovative Financing to Fund Development: 2+3=8 Innovating in Financing Education*, Report 2010.

Lehner, O. M. (2013). Crowdfunding Social Ventures: A Model and Research Agenda. *Venture Capital*, *15*(4), 289–311. doi:10.1080/13691066.2013.782624

Lehner, O. M., & Nichols, A. (2014). Social Finance and Crowdfunding for Social Enterprises: A Public-Private Case Study Providing Legitimacy and Leverage. *Venture Capital*, *16*(3), 271–286. doi:10.1080/13691066.2014.925305

Levin, R. B., Nowakowski, J., & O'Brien, A. A. (2013). The JOBS Act--Implications for Raising Capital and for Financial Intermediaries. *Journal of Taxation & Regulation of Financial Institutions*, *26*(5), 21–29.

Levy, D. M. (1987). Adam Smith's Case for Usury Laws. *History of Political Economy*, *19*(3), 387–400. doi:10.1215/00182702-19-3-387

Ley, A., & Weaven, S. (2011). Exploring Agency Dynamics of Crowdfunding in Start-Up Capital Financing. *Academy of Entrepreneurship Journal*, *17*(1), 85–110.

Leys, J., Vandekerckhove, W., & Van Liedekerke, L. (2009). A puzzle in SRI: The investor and the judge. *Journal of Business Ethics*, *84*(2), 221–235. doi:10.100710551-008-9705-4

Lie, H., & Shi, J. (2013). Applying ARMA – GARCH approaches to forecasting short – term electricity prices. *Energy Economics*, *37*, 152–166. doi:10.1016/j.eneco.2013.02.006

Lin, C. Y. (2018). *The Significance of Residential REITs in Japan as an Institutionalised property sector*. Department of Economic Finance and Property, Western Sydney University.

Liu, L., & Zhang, T. (2015). Economic policy uncertainty and stock market volatility. *Finance Research Letters*, *15*, 99–105. doi:10.1016/j.frl.2015.08.009

Liu, W. (2019). Portfolio diversification across cryptocurrencies. *Finance Research Letters*, *29*, 200–205. doi:10.1016/j.frl.2018.07.010

Loher, J. (2016). The Interaction of Equity Crowdfunding Platforms and Ventures: An Analysis of the Preselection Process. *Venture Capital*, *19*(1-2), 51–74. doi:10.1080/13691066.2016.1252510

Loo, W. K., Anuar, M. A., & Ramakrishnan, S. (2015). The dynamic linkage among the Asian REITS market. *Pacific Rim Property Research Journal*, *21*(2), 115–126. doi:10.1080/14445921.2015.1058036

Luchtenberg, K. F., & Vu, Q. V. (2015). The 2008 financial crisis: Stock market contagion and its determinants. *Research in International Business and Finance*, *33*, 178–203. doi:10.1016/j.ribaf.2014.09.007

Lucia, J. J., & Schwartz, E. S. (2002). Electricity prices and power derivatives: Evidence from Nordic Power Exchange. *Review of Derivatives Research*, *5*(1), 5 50. doi:10.1023/A:1013846631785

Lynn, D. M. (2012). The Crowdfunding Provisions of the JOBS Act, *Financial Executive*, May, 42-43.

Lyonnet, V., & Werner, R. (2012). Lessons from the Bank of England on "Quantitative Easing" and Other "Unconventional" Monetary Policies. *International Review of Financial Analysis, 25*, 94–105. doi:10.1016/j.irfa.2012.08.001

Lyons, T. (2010). Social Entrepreneurship: How Businesses Can Transform Society. In *Approaches to Financing Social Entrepreneurship*. Santa Barbara, CA: Praeger.

MacDonald, M. (2017). International capital market frictions and spillovers from quantitative easing. *Journal of International Money and Finance*, *70*, 135–156. doi:10.1016/j.jimonfin.2016.08.003

Macht, S. A., & Weatherston, J. (2014). The Benefits of Online Crowdfunding for Fund-seeking Business. *Strategic Change*, *23*(1-2), 1–14. doi:10.1002/jsc.1955

Maggio, M., Kermani, A., & Palmer, C. (2016). How quantitative easing works: Evidence on the refinancing channel, Working Paper 22638, National Bureau of Economic Research.

Maghyereh, A. (2004). Oil price shocks and emerging stock markets. *International Journal of Applied Econometrics and Quantitative Studies*, *1-2*, 27–40.

Mair, J., & Marti, I. (2006). Social Entrepreneurship Research: A Source of Explanation, Prediction and Delight. *Journal of World Business*, *41*(1), 36–44. doi:10.1016/j.jwb.2005.09.002

Mamatzakis, E., & Bermpei, T. (2016). What is the effect of unconventional monetary policy on bank performance? *Journal of International Money and Finance*, *67*, 239–263. doi:10.1016/j.jimonfin.2016.05.005

Mamaysky, H. (2018). The time horizon of price responses to quantitative easing. *Journal of Banking & Finance*, *90*, 32–49. doi:10.1016/j.jbankfin.2018.02.016

Manchanda, K., & Muralidharan, P. (2014). Crowdfunding: A New Paradigm in Startup Financing, *Global Conference on Business & Finance Proceedings*, 9(1), 369-374. Institute for Business & Finance Research.

Mari, C. (2014). Hedging electricity price volatility using nuclear power. *Applied Energy*, *113*, 615–621. doi:10.1016/j.apenergy.2013.08.016

Markowitz, H. (1952). Portfolio Selection. *The Journal of Finance*, *7*, 77–91.

Marzuki, M., & Newell, G. (2018). The emergence of Spanish REITs. *Journal of Property Investment & Finance*, *36*(5), 495–508. doi:10.1108/JPIF-05-2018-0032

Masood, O., Niazi, G. S., & Ahmad, N. (2011). An analysis of the growth and rise of smaller Islamic banks in last decade. *Qualitative Research in Financial Markets*, *3*(2), 105–116. doi:10.1108/17554171111155348

Massolution. (2015). *2015CF: The Crowdfunding Industry Report.*

Matousek, R., Papadamou, S., Sevic, A., & Tzeremes, N. (In press). The effectiveness of quantitative easing: Evidence from Japan. *Journal of International Money and Finance, 99*

Matthews, K. (2014). Cost inefficiency in the Pakistan banking sector 2002-2009. *SBP Research Bulletin, 10*, 1–20.

Meinusch, A., & Tillmann, P. (2016). The macroeconomic impact of unconventional monetary policy shocks. *Journal of Macroeconomics, 47*, 58–67. doi:10.1016/j.jmacro.2015.11.002

Mejia, A. L., Aljabrin, S., Awad, R., Norat, M., & Song, I. (2014). *Regulation and supervision of Islamic banks*. International Monetary Fund. doi:10.5089/9781498361590.001

Merig_o, J. M., & Yang, J. B. (2016). Accounting research: A bibliometric analysis. *Australian Accounting Review*. doi:10.1111/auar.12109

Merig_o, J. M., Cancino, C., Coronado, F., & Urbano, D. (2016). Academic research in innovation: a country analysis, *Scientometrics, 108*(2), pp. 559-593.

Meslier, C., Risfandy, T., & Tarazi, A. (2017). Dual market competition and deposit rate setting in Islamic and conventional banks. *Economic Modelling, 63*(Supplement C), 318–333. doi:10.1016/j.econmod.2017.02.013

Meyskens, M., Allen, I. E., & Brush, C. G. (2011). Human Capital and Hybrid Ventures. *Advances in Entrepreneurship, Firm, Emergence, and Growth, 13*, 51–72. doi:10.1108/S1074-7540(2011)0000013007

Meyskens, M., & Bird, L. (2014). Crowdfunding and Value Creation. *Entrepreneurial Resource Journal, 5*(2), 155–166.

Meyskens, M., & Carsrud, A. (2013). Nascent Green-Technology Ventures: An Exploratory Study Assessing the Role of Partnership Diversity in Firm Success. *Small Business Economics, 40*(3), 739–759. doi:10.100711187-011-9400-1

Miah, M. D., & Sharmeen, K. (2015). Relationship between capital, risk and efficiency: A comparative study between Islamic and conventional banks of Bangladesh. *International Journal of Islamic and Middle Eastern Finance and Management, 8*(2), 203–221. doi:10.1108/IMEFM-03-2014-0027

Miah, M. D., & Uddin, H. (2017). Efficiency and stability: A comparative study between Islamic and conventional banks in GCC countries. *Future Business Journal, 3*(2), 172–185. doi:10.1016/j.fbj.2017.11.001

Milana, C., & Ashta, A. (2012). Developing Microfinance: A Survey of the Literature. *Strategic Change, 21*(7-8), 299–330. doi:10.1002/jsc.1911

Mitra, D. (2012). The Role of Crowdfunding in Entrepreneurial Finance. *Delhi Business Review, 13*(2), 67–72.

Mobarek, A., & Kalonov, A. (2014). Comparative performance analysis between conventional and Islamic banks: Empirical evidence from OIC countries. *Applied Economics, 46*(3), 253–270. doi:10.1080/00036846.2013.839863

Modigliani, F., & Modigliani, L. (1997). Risk-Adjusted Performance. *Journal of Portfolio Management, 23*(2), 45–54. doi:10.3905/jpm.23.2.45

Mohamad, S., Hassan, T., & Bader, M. K. I. (2008). Efficiency of conventional versus Islamic Banks: International evidence using the Stochastic Frontier Approach (SFA). *Journal of Islamic Economics, Banking, and Finance, 4*(2), 107–130.

Mokhtar, H., Abdullah, N., & AlHabshi, M. (2007). Technical and cost efficiency of Islamic banking in Malaysia. *Review of Islamic Economics, 11*(1), 5–40.

Mokhtar, H., Abdullah, N., & Alhabshi, S. (2008). Efficiency and competition of Islamic banking in Malaysia. *Humanomics, 24*(1), 28–48. doi:10.1108/08288660810851450

Mollah, S., Hassan, M. K., Al Farooque, O., & Mobarek, A. (2017). The governance, risk-taking, and performance of Islamic banks. *Journal of Financial Services Research, 51*(2), 195–219. doi:10.100710693-016-0245-2

Mollah, S., & Zaman, M. (2015). Shari'ah supervision, corporate governance and performance: Conventional vs. Islamic banks. *Journal of Banking & Finance, 58*, 418–435. doi:10.1016/j.jbankfin.2015.04.030

Mollick, E. (2014). The Dynamics of Crowdfunding: An Exploratory Study. *Journal of Business Venturing, 29*(1), 1–16. doi:10.1016/j.jbusvent.2013.06.005

Moore, J., Nam, S., Suh, M., & Tepper, A. (2013). Estimating the impacts of US LSAPs on emerging market economies' local currency bond markets. *Federal Reserve Bank of New York, Staff Reports,* 1-43.

Morduch, J. (1999). The Microfinance Promise'. *Journal of Economic Literature, 37*(4), 1569–1614. doi:10.1257/jel.37.4.1569

Moritz, A., & Block, J. H. (2016). Crowdfunding: A Literature Review and Research Directions, In D. Bruntje, & O. Gajda (Eds.), Crowdfunding in Europe: State of the Art in Theory and Practice, FGF Studies in Small Business and Entrepreneurship, Springer, 25-54. doi:10.1007/978-3-319-18017-5_3

Moss, T., Neubaum, D., & Meyskens, M. (2014). The Effect of Virtuous and Entrepreneurial Orientations on Microfinance Lending and Repayment: A Signaling Theory Perspective. *Entrepreneurship Theory and Practice, 39*(1), 27–52. doi:10.1111/etap.12110

Mutengezanwa, M., Gombarume, F. B., Njanike, K., & Charikinya, A. (2011). The Impact of Microfinance Institutions on the Socioeconomic Lives of People in Zimbabwe. *Annals of the University of Petrosani. Economics, 11*, 161–170.

Myers, S., & Majluf, N. (1984). Corporate Financing and Investment Decisions When Firms have Information Investors do not Have. *Journal of Financial Economics, 13*(2), 187–221. doi:10.1016/0304-405X(84)90023-0

Nakamoto, S. (2008). Bitcoin: A peer-to-peer electronic cash system.

Neely, C. J. (2011). The large-scale asset purchases had large international effects. *Federal Reserve Bank of St. Louis, Working Paper Series*, 1-43.

Neely, C. J. (2015). Unconventional Monetary Policy Had Large International Effects. *Journal of Banking & Finance*, *52*, 101–111. doi:10.1016/j.jbankfin.2014.11.019

Newell, G., Adair, A., & Nguyen, K. (2013). The significance and performance of French REITs (SIICs) in a mixed-asset portfolio. *Journal of Property Investment & Finance*, *31*(6), 575–588. doi:10.1108/JPIF-01-2011-0004

Newell, G., & Marzuki, M. (2016). The significance and performance of UK - REITs in a mixed-asset portfolio. *Journal of European Real Estate Research*, *9*(2), 171–182. doi:10.1108/JERER-08-2015-0032

Newell, G., & Marzuki, M. (2018). The emergence and performance of German REITs. *Journal of Property Investment & Finance*, *36*(1), 91–103. doi:10.1108/JPIF-01-2017-0001

Newell, G., & Osmadi, A. (2009). The development and preliminary performance analysis of Islamic REITs in Malaysia. *Journal of Property Research*, *26*(4), 329–247. doi:10.1080/09599916.2009.485417

Newell, G., & Peng, H. W. (2009). The impact of the global financial crisis on A - REIT risk. *Pacific Rim Property Research Journal*, *15*(4), 453–470. doi:10.1080/14445921.2009.11104291

Newell, G., & Peng, H. W. (2012). The significance and performance of Japan REITs in a mixed-asset portfolio. *Pacific Rim Property Research Journal*, *18*(1), 21–34. doi:10.1080/14445921.2012.11104348

Newell, G., Pham, A. K., & Ooi, J. (2015). The significance and performance of Singapore REITs in a mixed-asset portfolio. *Journal of Property Investment & Finance*, *33*(1), 45–65. doi:10.1108/JPIF-12-2010-0027

Newell, G., Wu, Y., Chau, K. W., & Wong, S. K. (2010). The development and performance of REITs in Hong Kong. *Pacific Rim Property Research Journal*, *16*(2), 190–206. doi:10.1080/14445921.2010.11104301

Newey, W. K., & West, K. D. (1987). A simple, positive semi-definite, heteroskedasticity and autocorrelation consistent covariance matrix. *Econometrica*, *55*(3), 703–708. doi:10.2307/1913610

Newey, W. K., & West, K. D. (1987). Hypothesis Testing with Efficient Method of Moments Estimation. *International Economic Review*, *28*(3), 777–787. doi:10.2307/2526578

Ng, S., & Perron, P. (2001). Lag-length selection and the construction of unit root tests with good size and power. *Econometrica*, *69*(6), 1519–1554. doi:10.1111/1468-0262.00256

Nguyen, C., Bhatti, M. I., Komornikova, M., & Komornik, J. (2016). Gold price and stock markets nexus under mixed-copulas. *Economic Modelling*, *58*, 283–292. doi:10.1016/j.econmod.2016.05.024

Ng, V. K., & Pirrong, S. C. (1994). Fundamentals and Volatility: Storage, Spreads and the Dynamics of Metals Prices. *The Journal of Business*, *67*(2), 203–230. doi:10.1086/296630

Nicholls, A. (2010). The Institutionalization of Social Investment: The Interplay of Investment Logics and Investor Rationalities. *Journal of Social Entrepreneurship*, *1*(1), 70–100. doi:10.1080/19420671003701257

Nogales, F. J., Contreras, J., Conejo, A. J., & Espinola, R. (2002). Forecasting next – day electricity prices by time series models. *IEEE Transactions on Power Systems*, *17*(2), 342–348. doi:10.1109/TPWRS.2002.1007902

Noppen, M. (2018). What is Crowdfunding and How Could it Help Financial Inclusion?, Interview in preparation of the European Microfinance Week, Nov. 2018.

OECD. (2009). *Innovative Funding to Finance Development: Progress and Prospects', DCD, Issues Brief, November*. Paris, France: OECD Publishing.

OECD. (2009b). *The Impact of the Global Crisis on SME and Entrepreneurship Financing and Policy Responses*. France: OECD Publishing.

OECD. (2014). *The Role of Public Financial Institutions in Fostering SME Access to Finance*. OECD Publishing.

OECD. (2018). *Financing SMEs and Entrepreneurs 2018: An OECD Scoreboard*. OECD Publishing.

Olson, D., & Zoubi, T. (2017). Convergence in bank performance for commercial and Islamic banks during and after the Global Financial Crisis. *The Quarterly Review of Economics and Finance*, *65*, 71–87. doi:10.1016/j.qref.2016.06.013

Olson, D., & Zoubi, T. A. (2008). Using accounting ratios to distinguish between Islamic and conventional banks in the GCC region. *The International Journal of Accounting*, *43*(1), 45–65. doi:10.1016/j.intacc.2008.01.003

Ongena, S., & Sendeniz-Yüncü, I. (2011). Which firms engage small, foreign, or state banks? And who goes Islamic? Evidence from Turkey. *Journal of Banking & Finance*, *35*(12), 3213–3224. doi:10.1016/j.jbankfin.2011.05.001

Orden, D., & Fackler, P. L. (1989). Identifying monetary impacts on agricultural prices in VAR models. *American Journal of Agricultural Economics*, *71*(2), 495–502. doi:10.2307/1241620

Palacios-González, M. M., & Chamorro-Mera, A. (2018). Analysis of the predictive variables of the intention to invest in a socially responsible manner. *Journal of Cleaner Production*, *196*, 469–477. doi:10.1016/j.jclepro.2018.06.066

Palacios-González, M. M., & Chamorro-Mera, A. (2019). Analysis of the intention to invest in a socially responsible manner: A segmentation of the Spanish investor. *Revista Española de Financiación y Contabilidad*, 1–16. doi:10.1080/02102412.2019.1598700

Palacios-González, M. M., & Chamorro-Mera, A. (2019). Socially responsible investment: An analysis of the structure of preferences of savers. *Corporate Social Responsibility and Environmental Management*. doi:10.1002/csr.1757

Papathanasiou, S., Koutsokostas, D., Balios, D., & Eriotis, N. (2019a). Winemaking sector in Greece. An accounting-based approach. *International Journal of Corporate Finance and Accounting*, *6*(2), 1–17. doi:10.4018/IJCFA.2019070101

Papathanasiou, S., Papamatthaiou, N., & Balios, D. (2019b). Bitcoin as an alternative digital currency. Exploring the publics' perception vs experts. *International Journal of Financial Engineering and Risk Management*, *3*(2), 146–171. doi:10.1504/IJFERM.2019.101296

Pappas, V., Ongena, S., Izzeldin, M., & Fuertes, A. M. (2017). A Survival Analysis of Islamic and Conventional Banks. *Journal of Financial Services Research*, *51*(2), 1–36. doi:10.100710693-016-0239-0

Park, J. (2009). Sustainable consumption and the financial sector: Analysing the markets for responsible investment in Hong Kong and Japan. *International Journal of Consumer Studies*, *33*(2), 206–214. doi:10.1111/j.1470-6431.2009.00757.x

Paschen, J. (2017). Chose Wisely: Crowdfunding through the Stages of the Startup Life Cycle. *Business Horizons*, *60*(2), 179–188. doi:10.1016/j.bushor.2016.11.003

Pelizzon, L., Subrahmanyam, G. M., Tomio, D., & Uno, J. (2016). Sovereign credit risk, liquidity, and European central bank intervention: Deus ex machina? *Journal of Financial Economics*, *122*(1), 86–115. doi:10.1016/j.jfineco.2016.06.001

Peng, H. W., & Newell, G. (2012). The role of Taiwan REITs in investment Portfolios. *Pacific Rim Property Research Journal*, *18*(1), 67–80. doi:10.1080/14445921.2012.11104351

Pericoli, M., & Sbracia, M. (2003). A primer on financial contagion. *Journal of Economic Surveys*, *17*(4), 571–608. doi:10.1111/1467-6419.00205

Perold, A. F. (1988). The implementation shortfall: Paper versus reality. *Journal of Portfolio Management*, *14*(3), 4–9. doi:10.3905/jpm.1988.409150

Pesaran, M. H., & Pick, A. (2007). Econometric issues in the analysis of contagion. *Journal of Economic Dynamics & Control*, *31*(4), 1245–1277. doi:10.1016/j.jedc.2006.03.008

Pezier, J., & White, A. (2008). The relative Merits of Alternative Investments in Passive Portfolios. *Journal of Alternative Investments*, *10*(4), 37–49. doi:10.3905/jai.2008.705531

Pham, A. K. (2011). The performance of Thai-REITs in a mixed-asset portfolio. *Pacific Rim Property Research Journal*, *17*(2), 197–214. doi:10.1080/14445921.2011.11104324

Pham, A. K. (2011). The significance and performance of South Korean REITs in a mixed-asset portfolio. *Journal of Real Estate Literature*, *19*, 373–390.

Philippas, D., & Siriopoulos, C. (2013). Putting the "C" into crisis: Contagion, correlations and copulas on EMU bond markets. *Journal of International Financial Markets, Institutions and Money*, *27*, 161–176. doi:10.1016/j.intfin.2013.09.008

Phillips, P. C. B. (1988). *Spectral Regression for Cointegrated Time Series, Cowles Foundation Discussion papers 872, Cowles Foundation for Research in Economics*. Yale University.

Phylaktis, K., & Xia, L. (2009). Equity Market Comovement and Contagion: A Sectoral Perspective. *Financial Management*, *38*(2), 381–409. doi:10.1111/j.1755-053X.2009.01040.x

Pindyck, R. S., & Rotemberg, J. J. (1990). Excess co-movement of commodity prices. *Economic Journal (London)*, *100*(403), 1173–1189. doi:10.2307/2233966

Podsakoff, P. M., MacKenzie, S. B., Podsakoff, N. P., & Bachrach, D. G. (2008). Scholarly influence in the field of management: A bibliometric analysis of the determinants of university and author impact in the management literature in the past quarter century. *Journal of Management*, *34*(4), 641–720. doi:10.1177/0149206308319533

Poetz, M. K., & Schreier, M. (2012). The Value of Crowdsourcing: Can Users Really Compete with Professionals in Generating New Product Ideas? *Journal of Product Innovation Management*, *29*(2), 245–256. doi:10.1111/j.1540-5885.2011.00893.x

Powers, T. V. (2012). SEC Regulation of Crowdfunding Intermediaries under Title III of the JOBS Act. *Banking & Financial Services Policy Report*, *10*(31), 1–7.

Prokopczuk, M., Stancu, A., & Symeonidis, L. (2019). The economic drivers of commodity market volatility. *Journal of International Money and Finance*, *98*, 102063. doi:10.1016/j.jimonfin.2019.102063

Puaschunder, J. M. (2017). Socio-psychological motives of socially responsible investors. *Advances in Financial Economics*, *19*, 209–247. doi:10.1108/S1569-373220160000019008

Puaschunder, J. M. (2019). The History of Ethical, Environmental, Social, and Governance-Oriented Investments as a Key to Sustainable Prosperity in the Finance World. *Public Integrity*, *21*(2), 161–181. doi:10.1080/10999922.2018.1439563

Rachev, S. T., Mittnik, S., Fabozzi, F. J., Focardi, S. M., & Jašić, T. (2007). *Financial Econometrics: From Basics to Advanced Modeling Techniques*. Hoboken, NJ: John Wiley & Sons.

Ramsey, Y. A. (2012). What the Heck is Crowdfunding? *Business People*, November, 54-57.

Rashid, A., & Jabeen, S. (2016). Analyzing performance determinants: Conventional versus Islamic Banks in Pakistan. *Borsa Istanbul Review*, *16*(2), 92–107. doi:10.1016/j.bir.2016.03.002

Rathner, S. (2013). The influence of primary study characteristics on the performance differential between socially responsible and conventional investment funds: A meta-analysis. *Journal of Business Ethics*, *118*(2), 349–363. doi:10.100710551-012-1584-z

Rehman, S. S., & Askari, H. (2010). How Islamic are Islamic Countries? *Global Economy Journal, 10*(2).

Renneboog, L., Ter Horst, J., & Zhang, C. (2011). Is ethical money financially smart? Nonfinancial attributes and money flows of socially responsible investment funds. *Journal of Financial Intermediation, 20*(4), 562–588. doi:10.1016/j.jfi.2010.12.003

Revelli, C., & Viviani, J.-L. (2015). Financial performance of socially responsible investing (SRI): What have we learned? A meta-analysis. *Business Ethics (Oxford, England), 24*(2), 158–185. doi:10.1111/beer.12076

Rickwood, C., Khalil, A. F. A. A., & Murinde, V. (2000). *Evidence on agency-contractual problems in mudarabah financing operations by Islamic banks*. Edward Elgar Publishing.

Ridley-Duff, R. (2009). Co-Operative Social Enterprises: Company Rules, Access to Finance and Management Practice. *Social Enterprise Journal, 5*(1), 50–68. doi:10.1108/17508610910956408

Rigby, D. K., Christensen, C. M., & Johnson, M. W. (2002). Foundations for Growth: How to identify and Build Disruptive New Businesses. *MIT Sloan Management Review, 43*(3), 22.

Robano, V. (2018). Case Study on Crowdfunding. In *OECD SME and Entrepreneurship Papers, No. 4*. Paris, France: OECD Publishing.

Rodriquez, J. (2007). Measuring financial contagion: A copula approach. *Journal of Empirical Finance, 14*(3), 401–423. doi:10.1016/j.jempfin.2006.07.002

Roques, F. A., Newbery, D. M., & Nuttell, W. J. (2008). Fuel mix diversification incentives in liberalized electricity markets: A mean – variance portfolio theory approach. *Energy Economics, 30*(4), 1831–1849. doi:10.1016/j.eneco.2007.11.008

Rosa, C. (2011). The High-Frequency Response of Exchange Rates to Monetary Policy Actions and Statements. *Journal of Banking & Finance, 35*(2), 478–489. doi:10.1016/j.jbankfin.2010.09.008

Rosli, S. A. (2005). *Critical Issues on Islamic Banking and Financial Markets*. Malaysia: Dinamos Publishing.

Rosman, R., Abd, N., & Zainol, Z. (2014). Efficiency of Islamic banks during the financial crisis : An analysis of Middle Eastern and Asian countries. *Pacific-Basin Finance Journal, 28*, 76–90. doi:10.1016/j.pacfin.2013.11.001

Ross Jayne, M., & Skerratt, G. (2003). The requirements of ethical fund managers and property investment. *Property Management, 21*(2), 136–152. doi:10.1108/02637470310478882

Saeed, A. (1996). *Islamic Banking and Interest: A Study of the Prohibition of Riba and Its Contemporary Interpretation*. The Netherlands: Brill.

Saeed, M., & Izzeldin, M. (2016). Examining the relationship between default risk and efficiency in Islamic and conventional banks. *Journal of Economic Behavior & Organization, 132*, 127–154. doi:10.1016/j.jebo.2014.02.014

Safiullah, M., & Shamsuddin, A. (2018). Risk in Islamic banking and corporate governance. *Pacific-Basin Finance Journal*, *47*, 129–149. doi:10.1016/j.pacfin.2017.12.008

Said, A. (2012). Comparing the change in efficiency of the Western and Islamic banking systems. *Journal of Money, Investment, and Banking*, *23*(1), 149–180.

Samitas, A., & Tsakalos, I. (2013). How can a small country affect the European economy? the Greek contagion phenomenon. *Journal of International Financial Markets, Institutions and Money*, *25*, 18–32. doi:10.1016/j.intfin.2013.01.005

Sannajust, A., Roux, F., & Chaibi, A. (2014). Crowdfunding In France: A New Revolution? *Journal of Applied Business Research*, *30*(6), 1919–1928. doi:10.19030/jabr.v30i6.8947

Scarlata, M., & Alemany, L. (2013). Philanthropic Venture Capitalists' Post-Investment Involvement with Portfolio Social Enterprises: What Do They Actually Do?, Entrepreneurship, Finance, Governance and Ethics, 75-85, Springer, Dordrecht.

Schaeck, K., & Cihak, M. (2014). Competition, Efficiency, and Stability. *Financial Management*, *43*(1), 215–241. doi:10.1111/fima.12010

Schilling, L., & Uhlig, H. (2019). Some simple bitcoin economics. *Journal of Monetary Economics*, *106*, 16–26. doi:10.1016/j.jmoneco.2019.07.002

Scholtz, H., & Wilkens, M. (2005). A Jigsaw Puzzle of Basic Risk-adjusted Performance Measures. *Journal of Performance Measurement*, 57–64.

Schwienbacher, A. (2007). A Theoretical Analysis of Optimal Financing Strategies for Different Types of Capital-Constrained Entrepreneurs. *Journal of Business Venturing*, *22*(6), 753–781. doi:10.1016/j.jbusvent.2006.07.003

Schwienbacher, A., Belleflamme, P., & Lambert, T. (2013). Crowdfunding: Tapping the Right Crowd. *Journal of Business Venturing*, *29*(4), 585–609.

Schwienbacher, A., & Larralde, B. (2010). Crowdfunding of Small Entrepreneurial Ventures. In *Handbook of Entreprenurial Finance*. Oxford University Press. doi:10.2139srn.1699183

Senior, N. W. (1836). *An Outline of the Science of Political Economy*. University Press of the Pacific.

Serati, M., & Venegoni, A. (2019). The cross-country impact of ECB *policies*: Asymmetries in – Asymmetries out? *Journal of International Money and Finance*, *90*, 118–141. doi:10.1016/j.jimonfin.2018.09.008

Shadwick, W., & Keating, C. (2002). A universal performance measure. *Journal of Performance Measurement*, 55–84.

Shang, H., Yuan, P., & Huang, L. (2016). Macroeconomic factors and the cross-section of commodity futures returns. *International Review of Economics & Finance*, *45*, 316–332. doi:10.1016/j.iref.2016.06.008

Sharpe, W. F. (1966). Mutual Fund Performance. *The Journal of Business*, *39*(S1), 119–138. doi:10.1086/294846

Shawtari, F. A., Ariff, M., & Abdul Razak, S. H. (2015). Efficiency assessment of banking sector in Yemen using data envelopment window analysis: A comparative analysis of Islamic and conventional banks. *Benchmarking: An International Journal*, *22*(6), 1115–1140. doi:10.1108/BIJ-10-2014-0097

Sheedy, K. (2017). Conventional and unconventional monetary policy rules. *Journal of Macroeconomics 54*(A), 127-147.

Shikimi, M., & Yamada, K. (2019). Trade and financial channels as the transmission mechanism of the financial crisis. *International Review of Economics & Finance*, *63*, 364–381. doi:10.1016/j.iref.2019.04.008

Shogbuyi, A., & Steeley, J. M. (2017). The effect of quantitative easing on the variance and covariance of the UK and US equity markets. *International Review of Financial Analysis*, *52*, 281–291. doi:10.1016/j.irfa.2017.07.009

Short, J. C., Ketchen, D. T., McKenny, A. F., Allison, T. H., & Ireland, R. D. (2017). "Research on Crowdfunding: Reviewing the (Very Recent) Past and Celebrating the Present", *Entrepreneurship Theory and Practice Special issue on Crowdfunding, 41*(2), 149-10.

Short, H. (1994). Ownership, Control, Financial Structure and the Performance of Firms. *Journal of Economic Surveys*, *8*(3), 203–249. doi:10.1111/j.1467-6419.1994.tb00102.x

Sigar, K. (2012). Fret no More: Inapplicability of Crowdfunding Concerns in the Internet Age and the JOBS Act's Safeguards. *Administrative Law Review*, *2*(64), 474–505.

Silvennoinen, A., & Thorp, S. (2015). Financialization, crisis and commodity correlation dynamics. *Journal of International Financial Markets, Institutions and Money*, *24*, 42–65. doi:10.1016/j.intfin.2012.11.007

Singhal, S., Choudhary, S., & Biswal, P. C. (2019). Return and volatility linkages among International crude oil price, gold price, exchange rate and stock markets: Evidence from Mexico. *Resources Policy*, *60*, 255–261. doi:10.1016/j.resourpol.2019.01.004

Smith, A. (1776). *An inquiry into the nature and causes of the wealth of nations*. London, UK: W. Straham and T. Cadell.

Smith, A. (1776). *The Wealth of Nations*. New York: Modern Library.

Song, I., & Oosthuizen, C. (2014). *Islamic banking regulation and supervision: Survey results and challenges*. International Monetary Fund.

Song, Z., & Zhu, H. (2018). Quantitative easing auctions of Treasury bonds. *Journal of Financial Economics*, *128*(1), 103–124. doi:10.1016/j.jfineco.2018.02.004

Sortino, F. A., & Van der Meer, R. (1991). Downside Risk. *Journal of Portfolio Management, 17*(4), 27–32. doi:10.3905/jpm.1991.409343

Sortino, F. A., Van der Meer, R., & Plantinga, A. (1999). The Dutch Triangle. *Journal of Portfolio Management, 26*(1), 50–59. doi:10.3905/jpm.1999.319775

Sorwar, G., Pappas, V., Pereira, J., & Nurullah, M. (2016). To debt or not to debt: Are Islamic banks less risky than conventional banks? *Journal of Economic Behavior & Organization, 132*, 113–126. doi:10.1016/j.jebo.2016.10.012

Sovbetov, Y. (2018). Factors influencing cryptocurrency prices: Evidence from bitcoin, ethereum, dash, litcoin, and monero. *Journal of Economics and Financial Analysis, 2*(2), 1–27.

Srairi, S. A. (2010). Cost and profit efficiency of conventional and Islamic banks in GCC countries. *Journal of Productivity Analysis, 34*(1), 45–62. doi:10.100711123-009-0161-7

Stinchcombe, A. L. (1965). Social Structure and Organizations. In *J. G. March, Handbook of Organizations*. Chicago, IL: Rand McNally.

Syriopoulos, K., & Filippas, D. T. (2010). *Econometric Models and Applications in EViews*. Anikoula Publications.

Tang, K., & Xiong, W. (2012). Index investment and the financialization of commodities. *Financial Analysts Journal, 68*(5), 54–74. doi:10.2469/faj.v68.n6.5

Tapscott, D., & Tapscott, A. (2016). *Blockchain revolution: how the technology behind bitcoin is changing money, business, and the world*. Penguin.

Thanassoulis, E., Boussofiane, A., & Dyson, R. G. (1996). A comparison of data envelopment analysis and ratio analysis as tools for performance assessment. *Omega, 24*(3), 229–244. doi:10.1016/0305-0483(95)00060-7

Thorton, J., & Di Tomasso, C. (2018). Unconventional monetary policy and the 'currency wars'. *Finance Research Letters, 26*, 250–254. doi:10.1016/j.frl.2018.02.010

Tillmann, P. (2016). Unconventional monetary policy and the spillovers to emerging markets. *Journal of International Money and Finance, 66*, 136–156. doi:10.1016/j.jimonfin.2015.12.010

Timmer, Y. (2018). Emerging market corporate bond yields and monetary policy. *Emerging Markets Review, 36*, 130–143. doi:10.1016/j.ememar.2018.04.001

Todorov, K. (2019). (accepted for publication). Quantify the quantitative easing: Impact on bonds and corporate debt issuance. *Journal of Financial Economics*. doi:10.1016/j.jfineco.2019.08.003

Torre, N. G., Mark, J., & Ferrari, M. J. (1999). *The Market Impact Model*. Barra Research Insights.

Trad, N., Trabelsi, M. A., & Goux, J. F. (2017). Risk and profitability of Islamic banks: A religious deception or an alternative solution? *European Research on Management and Business Economics, 23*(1), 40–45. doi:10.1016/j.iedeen.2016.09.001

Treynor, J. (1965). How to Rate Management of Mutual Funds. *Harvard Business Review*, *8*, 63–75.

Treynor, J., & Black, F. (1973). How to Use Security Analysis to Improve Portfolio Selection. *The Journal of Business*, 61–86.

Treynor, J., & Mazuy, K. (1966). Can Mutual Funds Outguess the Market? *Harvard Business Review*, 131–136.

Triantafyllou, A., & Dotsis, G. (2017). Option-implied expectations in commodity markets and monetary policy. *Journal of International Money and Finance*, *77*, 1–17. doi:10.1016/j.jimonfin.2017.06.002

Ueda, M. (2004). Banks versus Venture Capital Project Evaluation, Screening, and Expropriation. *The Journal of Finance*, *59*(2), 601–621. doi:10.1111/j.1540-6261.2004.00643.x

UNDESA. (2012). World Economic and Social Survey 2012. In *Search of New Development Finance*. New York: United Nations Department of Economic and Social Affairs.

UNDP. (2012). *Innovative Financing for Development: A New Model for Development Finance?* New York: Bureau for Development Policy.

Usmani, M. I. A. (2002). *Meezanbank's Guide to Islamic Banking*. Pakistan: Darul-Ishaat Karachi.

Valanciene, L., & Jegeleviciute, S. (2013). Valuation of Crowdfunding: Benefits and Drawbacks. *Economics and Management*, *18*(1), 39–48.

Vallascas, F., Mollah, S., & Keasey, K. (2017). Does the impact of board independence on large bank risks change after the global financial crisis? *Journal of Corporate Finance*, *44*(June 2014), 149–166. doi:10.1016/j.jcorpfin.2017.03.011

Valor, C., De La Cuesta, M., & Fernandez, B. (2009). Understanding demand for retail socially responsible investments: A survey of individual investors and financial consultants. *Corporate Social Responsibility and Environmental Management*, *16*(1), 1–14. doi:10.1002/csr.172

Van Robays, I. (2016). Macroeconomic uncertainty and oil price volatility. *Oxford Bulletin of Economics and Statistics*, *78*(5), 671–693. doi:10.1111/obes.12124

Varghese, R., & Zhang, Y. S. (2018). A new wave of ECB's unconventional monetary policies: domestic impact and spillovers. *IMF Working Paper, WP/18/11*.

Viotto, J. (2015). Competition and Regulation of Crowdfunding Platforms: A Two-Sided Market Approach. *Communications & Stratégies*, *99*(3), 33–50.

Vismara, S. (2016). Equity Retention and Social Network Theory in Equity Crowdfunding. *Small Business Economics*, *46*(4), 579–590. doi:10.100711187-016-9710-4

von Hayek, F. A. (1939). *Profit, Interest, and Investment*. Clifton, NJ: Augustus M. Kelley.

Von Wallis, M., & Klein, C. (2015). Ethical requirement and financial interest: A literature review on socially responsible investing. *Business Research*, *8*(1), 61–98. doi:10.100740685-014-0015-7

Wang, X., Liu, H., Huang, S., & Lucey, B. (2019). Identifying the multiscale financial contagion in precious metal markets. *International Review of Financial Analysis*, *63*, 209–219. doi:10.1016/j.irfa.2019.04.003

Wang, Z., Fausti, S. W., & Qasmi, B. A. (2012). Variance risk premiums and predictive power of alternative forward variances in the corn market. *Journal of Futures Markets*, *32*(6), 587–608. doi:10.1002/fut.20527

Wanke, P., Azad, M. A. K., & Barros, C. P. (2016). Financial distress and the Malaysian dual baking system: A dynamic slacks approach. *Journal of Banking & Finance*, *66*, 1–18. doi:10.1016/j.jbankfin.2016.01.006

Wanke, P., Azad, M. A. K., Barros, C. P., & Hassan, M. K. (2016). Predicting efficiency in Islamic banks: An integrated multicriteria decision making (MCDM) approach. *Journal of International Financial Markets, Institutions, and Money*, *45*, 126–141. doi:10.1016/j.intfin.2016.07.004

Wardrop, R., Zhang, B., Rau, R., & Gray, M. (2015). *Moving Mainstream. The European Alternative Finance Benchmarking Report,* 15-16.

Wheat, R. E., Wang, Y., Byrnes, J. E., & Ranganathan, J. (2012). Raising Money for Scientific Research through Crowdfunding. *Trends in Ecology & Evolution*, *2*(28), 71–72. PMID:23219380

Whitman, J. R. (2009). Measuring Social Values in Philanthropic Foundations. *Nonprofit Management & Leadership*, *19*(3), 305–325. doi:10.1002/nml.221

Wong, A., Bhatia, M., & Freeman, Z. (2009). Angel Finance: The Other Venture Capital. *Strategic Change*, *18*(7-8), 221–230. doi:10.1002/jsc.849

World Bank. (2009). *Innovating Development Finance: From Financing Sources to Financial Solutions.*

World Bank. (2012). *Innovative Finance for Development Solutions: Initiatives of the World Bank Group.*

World Bank. (2013). *Crowdfunding's Potential for the Developing World.* Washington, DC: World Bank.

Yermack, D. (2015). Is Bitcoin a real currency? An economic appraisal. In *Handbook of digital currency* (pp. 31–43). Academic Press. doi:10.1016/B978-0-12-802117-0.00002-3

Ye, W., Liu, X., & Miao, M. (2012). Measuring the subprime crisis contagion: Evidence of change point analysis of copula functions. *European Journal of Operational Research*, *222*(1), 96–103. doi:10.1016/j.ejor.2012.04.004

Young, T. W. (1991). Calmar Ratio: A Smoother Tool, Futures magazine, pp. 40.

Yunus, M. (1999). *Banker to the Poor: Microlending and the Battle against World Poverty*. New York: Public Affairs.

Zhang, W., Wang, P., Li, X., & Shen, D. (2018). Some stylized facts of the cryptocurrency market. *Applied Economics*, *50*(55), 5950–5965. doi:10.1080/00036846.2018.1488076

Zietz, E., Sirmans, S., & Friday, S. (2003). The environment and performance of Real Estate Investment Trusts. *Journal of Real Estate Portfolio Management*, *9*, 127–165.

Zuhroh, I., Ismail, M., & Maskie, G. (2015). Cost Efficiency of Islamic Banks in Indonesia – A Stochastic Frontier Analysis. *Procedia: Social and Behavioral Sciences*, *211*, 1122–1131. doi:10.1016/j.sbspro.2015.11.150

About the Contributors

Dimitris Kenourgios is currently Associate Professor of Finance at the National and Kapodistrian University of Athens (NKUA), Department of Economics. He received a BSc in Economics from the NKUA, an MSc in Money, Banking and Finance from the University of Birmingham (UK), and a PhD in Finance from the NKUA. He has taught at the Athens University of Economics and Business, the University of Piraeus, the University of Thessaly, the Hellenic Open University and the Open University of Cyprus. He has published more than 50 academic research papers in peer-reviewed scientific journals. His research interests are in the areas of financial contagion, financial integration, emerging capital markets, quantitative easing, European banking union, financial modelling and risk management. He has an extensive experience in consulting, executive training and e-learning services in the areas of financial analysis, investments, and capital markets.

* * *

Panayotis Alexakis is a Professor of Business Economics and Markets at the Department of Business Administration of the National and Kapodistrian University of Athens. He has been a scholar of the "Alexander S. Onassis" Public Benefit Foundation. He has also taught at the Department of Business Administration of the University of the Aegean, at the Hellenic and Cypriot Open University, in postgraduate business programs and in business seminars. During his career he has also dealt with issues relating to the cooperation between universities and enterprises. He has worked at the Ministry of Finance, the Bank of Greece, enterprises and organizations as a consultant or executive and has held various management posts in the financial and non-financial sector. He has been chairman and CEO at the Athens Derivatives Exchange 1998-2004 and the Athens Stock Exchange 2000-2004. He has participated in scientific conferences with papers and has published articles in scientific journals. His scientific work is recognized worldwide. He is a member of scientific associations,

Dimitrios Antonopoulos holds a Master's Degree in Accounting and Finance with specialization in Banking and Risk Management from the Athens University of Economics and Business and has obtained his Bachelor's Degree in Business Administration from the University of Patras.

Paraskevi Boufounou is Asst. Professor of Development Finance at the Department of Economics, Nationtal and Kapodistrian University of Athens and Coordinator of the "MBA in Strategic Management and Competitiveness" degree. Dr. Boufounou holds an Honours First Class Bachelor Degree in Economics from the National & Kapodistrian Univ of Athens (scholarship during studies), a Master of Philosophy (M.Phil) in Economics from the Univ of Dundee (UK) and a Ph.D in Economics with High Distinction from the National & Kapodistrian Univ of Athens (teaching assistant scholarship during Ph. D. studies). She has a wide range of Academic experience in teaching at the Undergraduate and Postgraduate level in various Greek and Foreign Universities, and research experience in cooperation with Greek and International public and private research Institutions and Universities. She has numerous publications and her recent research interests are focused on the fields of development finance with specialization to innovative instruments for financing development (crowdfunding, green bonds, etc), financial systems for optimizing managerial efficiency, improving investment environment and investment implementation, cost-benefit analysis for socio-economic evaluation of investment decisions and policy measures. Furthermore, she has a long standing career (more than 30 years) in the Banking/Financial Sector, during which she was appointed top executive managerial positions, both in private and public sector, embracing the full spectrum of financial services, indicatively including: President of "Invest in Greece" (the official agency of the Greek state, under the auspices of the Ministry of Economy and Development, to promote investment in Greece, to attract FDIs and make Greece more attractive as an international business partner), Senior Economic Advisor to the Chair of the Board of National Bank of Greece and to the Chair of the Hellenic Bank Association, Special Economic Advisor to Greek Ministers, General Manager of Commercial Leasing (subsidiary of Commercial Bank of Greece), Director of Commercial Securities (subsidiary of Commercial Bank of Greece), senior executive of the Strategic Planning Department of the Commercial Bank of Greece.

George Chalamandaris is currently Assistant Professor in Finance at the Athens University of Economics and Business at the Department of Accounting and Finance. He graduated from the National Technical University of Athens and continued his studies at Imperial College in London where he also completed his PhD in Quantitative Finance. He has worked in Natwest Markets and Royal Bank of Scotland in London as well as in Emporiki Investment Bank and EFG Eurobank in Athens, holding senior positions in the areas of risk management, financial engineering, structuring and alternative investments. His main research interests are focused in the field of derivatives, credit risk and asset pricing involving dynamic trading strategies. He has published in highly acclaimed academic journals in the area of finance such as Journal of Banking and Finance, Journal of Empirical Finance, Journal of International Money and Finance, among other.

Dimitrios Dimitriou holds a BSc degree in Economics and a MSc degree in Applied Economics and Finance from National and Kapodistrian University of Athens. He also holds a PhD degree in Finance from the University of Ioannina (with distinction). He has taught at the University of Ioannina for 3 years. Now, he is visiting lecturer (based on P.D. 407/1980) at AUEB. He served at Ministry of Finance (MoF) for over 5 years in executive departments. Currently, he is member of the Specialized Scientific Staff at the Hellenic Fiscal Council (HFC). Additionally, he has published widely in journals such as: International Review of Financial Analysis, Journal of International Financial Markets, Institutions and Money, Economic Modelling, Research in International Business and Finance, etc.

Marianna Eskantar in a postgraduate student in the Department of Production Engineering and Management at Technical University of Crete and member of the Financial Engineering Laboratory, School of Production Engineering and Management, Technical University of Crete.

Alexandros Garefalakis is a Chartered Accountant (Fellow of CPA), Management Accountant (CMA Diploma) and Business Consultant in numerous companies and organizations. Also, he is an Assistant Professor at the Dept. of Business Administration and Tourism, Hellenic Mediterranean University (HMU). He holds a degree in Financial Applications, a Master degree in Accounting and Finance from the University of Southampton and a PhD in Accounting from the Hellenic Open University. He has co-authored 2 books on Audit Accounting and Management Accounting issues. He has more than 60 publications in peer-reviewed journals and participation in more than 21 national and international conferences. His areas of research interest include the quality of Narrative information of Financial Reports.

Constantinos Kakouris is a physicist and economist. After secondary education, he succeeded the PanHellenic exams in order to study economics at University of Macedonia, Thessaloniki, and he continued his studies at Science School of Aristotle University of Thessaloniki where he passed the entrance exams of physics department and successfully completed his studies. He also holds a master's degree in Energy and Environmental Management. During his dissertation, he focused in electricity markets. He worked as an economic and physics tutor in secondary education's private sector for two years in Thessaloniki, Greece. He was one of the invited speakers giving presentations concerning sustainable development and renewable energy in 2016 and 2018. As a volunteer, he guided groups in Optics Laboratory of Physics department in University's open day and he currently works an article, in collaboration with magazine's editors, concerning physics and economics in order to be published in physics department's scientific magazine called "Phenomenon".

Louka T. Katseli is Professor of International Economics and Development at the Department of Economics of the National Kapodistrian University of Athens (1987 -) and Chair of the Board of Directors of the National Bank of Greece in Cyprus, (11/2015 -). She is also Vice-Chair of the Executive Board and Chair of the Finance & Human Resources Committee of the African Capacity Building Foundation (ACBF), and Co-chair (with Poul N. Rasmussen) of the Independent Commission for Sustainable Equality, Progressive Alliance of Socialists and Democrats - S&D, (Progressive Society). She has served as Chair of the Board of Directors of the National Bank of Greece (3/15 – 11/16) and Chair of the Hellenic Banking Association (4/15 – 11/16). She was Greece's Minister of Labor and Social Security (2010 - 2011), Minister of Economy, Competitiveness and Shipping (2009-2010) and a member of the Hellenic Parliament (2007-2012). Prof. Katseli has also served as Director of the OECD Development Centre in Paris (2003-2007), Director General of the Center of Planning and Economic Research (KEPE) (1982-1986), Economic Advisor to the Greek Prime Minister (1993-1996) and member of the UN Committee of Development Policy (1996 - 2003), the European Commission's Economic and Monetary Policy Committees and the "Comité des Sages" on the Reform of the European Social Charter (1995-1997) et al. Prof. Katseli holds a Ph.D. (1978) in International and Development Economics from Princeton University (Distinguished Dissertation in Economics), an MPA in Public Affairs(1974) from the Woodrow Wilson School for Public and International Affairs, an MA in Economics (1975) from Princeton University and a BA in Economics (1972, cum laude and Phi Beta Kappa) from Smith College. She has served as Assistant and Associate Professor of Economics at Yale University's Department of Economics and the School of Organization and Management (1977-1985). She is the recipient of numerous distinctions and fellowships, including that of the Best Young Professor at Yale (1980). She has published extensively in the areas of development and international economics, migration management and institutional economics.

Apostolos Kiohos is an Assistant Professor in Financial Risk Management (Financial markets, Insurance, Forex) in the Department of International and European Studies, at the University of Macedonia. He holds a PhD in Financial Institutions

Risk Management from the Department of Economics, University of Thessaly, Greece. Also, he holds Masters degree in Insurance and Risk Management from Cass Business School of London. RESEARCH AREAS • Risk Management • International Financial Markets • International Monetary Relations • Insurance • Quantitative Methods for Management

Marios-Nikolaos Kouskoukis is a Visiting Lecturer at the Department of Management and Marketing of European University of Cyprus. Dr. Kouskoukis holds a Bachelor Degree in Economics from Democritus University of Thrace, a Master of Business Administration (M.B.A.) Degree in Total Quality Management from University of Piraeus and a Ph.D. in Economics with high distinction from Panteion University of Social and Political Sciences (teaching assistant during Ph. D. studies). He has been academic staff in the past in different Departments of different Universities. Particularly, he has taught in the Department of Economics and Business of Neapolis University of Pafos the courses «Business Administration», «Marketing», «Business Communication» and «Business Operations Management», as well as «Regional Economic Development» and «Regulatory Framework of Regional Development» in the Department of Economics and Regional Development of Panteion University of Social and Political Sciences. In addition, he has supervised and evaluated undergraduate essays at the Panteion University of Social and Political Sciences, as well as postgraduate assignments at the University of Piraeus in the courses «Business Administration» and «Marketing» and at the Neapolis University of Pafos. He has working experience, both in public and private sectors, specifically in the fields of Consulting, Education, Health and Finance. His published work includes articles, papers and book chapters in the research fields of Investment, Regional Economic Development and Economic Evaluation of Renewable Energy Sources.

Drosos Koutsokostas is a researcher and a scientific associate. He studied economics at the Aristotle University of Thessaloniki (BSc,2002) and Banking and Finance at the Hellenic Open University (MSc,2016). He has been teaching economics in state secondary schools of the Greek ministry of education for over a decade. He has also worked as an accountant in various companies of the private sector. He has published articles in scientific journals, including Managerial Finance, the Journal of Prediction Markets, the Journal of Risk Finance and International Journal of Corporate Finance and Accounting. His currrent research concern portfolio evaluation and market efficiency.

Dimitrios Koutsoupakis is a PhD candidate in Economics at the University of Athens. His research study is on the economic nature of distributed ledgers and cryptocurrencies. He holds bachelor degree in Economics from University of Athens, MSc in Public Management from Bocconi University and MPhil in Economics from University of Athens. He was offered a scholarship from London School of Economics & Political Science to spend the academic year 2016-2017 as Visiting Research Student. His teaching interest include money, banking, finance, accounting and history of economic thought. Professionally, he is an experienced accountant and financial analyst having worked in Luxembourg, Milan and Athens. Since 2017, he has been serving as Finance Director for a holding company based in Greece.

Christos Lemonakis is an Assistant Professor of Business Administration on SMEs Management at the Hellenic Mediterranean University, Department of Management Science and Technology (Agios Nikolaos). His research interests are SMEs Entrepreneurship, Auditing and Management Accounting.

Andreas Papanastasopoulos is a Civil Engineer (Department of Civil Engineering, School of engineering, University of Patras) with postgraduate degrees (MSc.) in Earthquake Engineering and Seismic Design of Structures at the Hellenic Open University and MSc in Finance and Banking, Applied Economics and Finance, Department of Economics, National and Kapodistrian University of Athens.

Spyros Papathanasiou is assistant professor at the National and Kapodistrian University of Athens. He studied economics at the University of Athens (BSc, 1995) and Banking at the Hellenic Open University (MSc, 2003). He also holds a Ph.D. in Finance from the Hellenic Open University (2009). Dr. Papathanasiou possesses an extensive academic and professional experience. He has worked at Solidus Securities, Prelium Securities, Value Capital Securities and ICAP Hellas S.A. Finally, he is certified Analyst and Portfolio Manager from Hellenic Capital Market Commission. His main research interests are in the areas of finance, financial markets, and alternative investments.

Vasileios Pappas is currently an Associate Professor in Finance at the University of Kent, UK. He holds a BSc in Economics (University of Piraeus, Greece), an MSc in Money, Banking & Finance (Lancaster University, UK) and a PhD in Economics (Lancaster University, UK). He has worked as a Senior Research Associate and member of the GOLCER research centre in Lancaster University and as a Lecturer in Finance at the University of Bath. His core research interests lie in the areas of banking with a focus on studies related to banking risk, efficiency and productivity analysis across banking systems (e.g. Islamic, community and commercial banks). Other research interests include financial contagion, efficiency modelling and financial econometrics, with a focus on realised volatility modelling and forecasting.

Panagiotis Petris graduated from the Civil and Environmental Engineering Department of Imperial College London. He holds a Master's Degree in Risk Management from Cass Business School – City University of London and a Ph.D. in Finance from the Department of Economics of the National and Kapodistrian University of Athens. His research interests are in the area of real estate finance. Panagiotis has taught, Financial Derivatives, Applications of Quantitative Analysis at the Department of Economics of the National and Kapodistrian University of Athens (NKUA). He also teaches Real Estate Finance and Investments at the executive post-graduate programs of the NKUA. His papers have been presented in domestic and international scientific conferences.

Dimitris Psychoyios is a Senior Lecturer in Finance & Investment at the University of Piraeus. He has graduated from the Department of Mathematics of the National and Kapodistrian University of Athens, and he obtained an MBA and his Ph.D. in Finance from the Athens University of Economics and Business (AUEB). His first placement was at Manchester Business School as a Lecturer in Finance. Dimitris' current research interests lie in corporate finance, environmental finance, energy finance, asset pricing, and risk management. Part of his research has been published in international scientific journals and it has been cited by more than 800 authors. He has taught in MBA programs in Greece, Europe, and the USA and did research, consulting and participated in executive education projects for Greek and European companies.

Efthimios Roumpis is a Financial Modeling Consultant of Deloitte's Financial Services practice in Greece. His fields of expertise include market risk modeling, financial analysis, valuation of financial instruments and management of large databases. He has gained experience in banking sector by participating in many assignments of the Financial Services Industry consulting team. Before joining Deloitte, Efthymios worked as advisor to Tufton Oceanic hedge fund. He had a key role in the development and maintenance of market risk models and financial models for shipping and energy sectors. Efthymios combines robust and advanced technical skills and he is an expert in programming languages (MatLab, VBA, Python, SQL). He hold a PhD on the subject of "Evaluation of Investment Strategies for the Formation of Dynamic Hedge Fund Portfolios".

Theodore Simos worked as researcher at the Centre of Planning and Economic Research, at the Directorate of Planning and Economic Studies of the National Bank of Greece at the Research Centre CORE, Universite Catholique de Louvain, Belgium, ICMM University of Strathclyde, ESRC – UK and at the Center for Labour Economics, LSE, UK. He has taught at the University of Crete, University of Aegean and the Athens University of Economics and Business. Currently he is Professor of Financial Econometrics at the Department of Economics - University of Ioannina.

Nikolaos Stoupos is an Adjunct Senior Lecturer at Department of Economics, University of Patras(based on Presidential Decree 407/80) and is currently teaching courses in Finance and Economics. Also, he is a Post-Doc Research Fellow at the University of Macedonia, Greece. He holds a Ph.D. in International and European Studies (2019) from the University of Macedonia, Greece. In 2010, he successfully completed his postgraduate studies with Merit, at the University of Portsmouth, UK by obtaining a M.Sc. in Business Economics, Finance and Banking. Also, he holds a Hons B.Sc. in Accounting and Finance from the University of Macedonia, Greece. He has participated in research projects of the EU. He has several publications in international academic journals, such as Research in International Business and Finance (2*), Quarterly Review of Economics and Finance (2*), International Review of Applied Economics (1*), International Economic Journal (1*) and Acta Oeconomica (1*). His research interests are related to European Finance, Exchange Rates Regimes, Euro Area, Energy Economics and Financial Econometrics.

Alexia Thomaidou is currently working as a custom clearer assistant and business consultant in SMEs. Her research interests include financial contagion, Exchange Traded Funds, Mutual Funds, market analysis, and applied corporate finance.

Athanasios Triantafyllou joined Essex Business School in October 2017 as Lecturer in Finance. He is currently a visiting lecturer at the department of Applied Mathematical and Physical Sciences, NTUA and a visiting scholar at SC Johnson College of Business, Cornell university. Athanasios holds a PhD in Finance and an MPhil in Economics from University of Athens, an MSc in Accounting and Finance from AUEB and a BSc in Mathematics from University of Athens. Prior to joining EBS, he was working as consultant in Quantitative Risk Management in Ernst & Young and he has participated in projects for large US investment banks (as part of the Ernst & Young US Quant Hub) dealing with market risk management and the pricing of complex derivative products. He has also worked as researcher in general equilibrium modeling at the E3Mlab of NTUA focusing on the modeling and the respective impact of macroeconomic and energy policy scenarios on EU-28 economies.

Ioannis Tsakalos is an adjunct researcher at the National and Kapodistrian University of Athens (Department of Economic Studies), the Hellenic Open University (School of Social Sciences, MSc in Banking) and the University of the Aegean (Business School). He graduated in Business Administration (2003) from the University of the Aegean, earned an MSc in Shipping, Trade and Transport (2004), an MBA (2005) and a PhD in Finance (2012) from the University of the Aegean (Business School). His teaching portfolio ranges among finance, banking and risk management, while his research interest focuses in risk management, energy, shipping finance and monetary policy. Also, he has extensive professional experience in Energy and Shipping sectors, focusing in risk management and also in credit analysis. Furthermore, he has presented his research projects in international conferences and he has published his research studies in international scientific journals. He is also member in different scientific associations and reviewer in scientific journals.

Index

R

S

T

U

V

www.ingramcontent.com/pod-product-compliance
Lightning Source LLC
LaVergne TN
LVHW080907300926
849162LV00003B/584
* 9 7 8 1 7 9 9 8 2 4 3 6 7 *